D1688930

Ihr Zugang zum E-Book auf www.scook.de:

wqyqr-a7h8j — Ihr Lizenzcode

Der Code beinhaltet nach Erstaktivierung eine 5-jährige Lizenz zur Nutzung des E-Books auf scook. Für die Nutzung ist die Zustimmung zu den AGB auf scook.de erforderlich.

9783060313570_EG 21 A4 geb

English G 21

A4
für Gymnasien

Cornelsen

English G 21 • Band A 4

Im Auftrag des Verlages herausgegeben von
Prof. Hellmut Schwarz, Mannheim

Erarbeitet von
Laurence Harger, Wellington, Neuseeland
David Christie, Banbury, Großbritannien
Barbara Derkow Disselbeck, Köln
Allen J. Woppert, Berlin
sowie Susan Abbey, Nenagh, Irland

unter Mitarbeit von
Wolfgang Biederstädt, Köln
Joachim Blombach, Herford
Helmut Dengler, Limbach
Dr. Annette Leithner-Brauns, Dresden
Jörg Rademacher, Ilvesheim
Jennifer Seidl, München
Sabine Tudan, Erfurt
sowie Ulrike Flach, Köln; Silke Lehmacher, Monheim

in Zusammenarbeit mit der Englischredaktion
Dr. Christiane Kallenbach (Projektleitung);
Dr. Christian v. Raumer (verantwortlicher Redakteur);
Susanne Bennetreu (Bildredaktion); Britta Bensmann;
Christiane Bonk; Dr. Philip Devlin; Gareth Evans;
Bonnie S. Glänzer; Mara Leibowitz; Uwe Tröger;
Klaus G. Unger *sowie* Nathalie Schwering

Beratende Mitwirkung
Peter Brünker, Bad Kreuznach; Helga Estor, Darmstadt;
Katja Fabel, Freiburg; Anette Fritsch, Dillenburg;
Patrick Handschuh, Köln; Ulrich Imig, Wildeshausen;
Dr. Ursula Mulla, Germering; Thomas Neidhardt,
Bielefeld; Wolfgang Neudecker, Mannheim; Birgit
Ohmsieder, Berlin; Albert Rau, Brühl; Angela Ringel-
Eichinger, Bietigheim-Bissingen; Dr. Jana Schubert, Genf/
Leipzig; Sieglinde Spranger, Chemnitz; Harald Weißling,
Mannheim; Monika Wilkening, Wehretal

Illustrationen
Silke Bachmann, Hamburg; Roland Beier, Berlin;
Stéphane Gamain/NB Illustration, London;
Michale Teßmer, Hamburg

Layoutkonzept und technische Umsetzung
Aksinia Raphael; Korinna Wilkes

Technische Umsetzung
Aksinia Raphael; Korinna Wilkes;
Stephan Hilleckenbach; Rainer Bachmaier

Umschlaggestaltung
Klein & Halm Grafikdesign, Berlin

www.cornelsen.de
www.EnglishG.de

Die Links zu externen Webseiten Dritter, die in diesem Lehrwerk angegeben sind, wurden vor Drucklegung sorgfältig auf ihre Aktualität geprüft. Der Verlag übernimmt keine Gewähr für die Aktualität und den Inhalt dieser Seiten oder solcher, die mit ihnen verlinkt sind.

Dieses Werk berücksichtigt die Regeln der reformierten Rechtschreibung und Zeichensetzung.

1. Auflage, 5. Druck 2013

Alle Drucke dieser Auflage sind inhaltlich unverändert und können im Unterricht nebeneinander verwendet werden.

© 2009 Cornelsen Verlag, Berlin
© 2013 Cornelsen Schulverlage GmbH, Berlin

Das Werk und seine Teile sind urheberrechtlich geschützt. Jede Nutzung in anderen als den gesetzlich zugelassenen Fällen bedarf der vorherigen schriftlichen Einwilligung des Verlages. Hinweis zu den §§ 46, 52a UrhG: Weder das Werk noch seine Teile dürfen ohne eine solche Einwilligung eingescannt und in ein Netzwerk eingestellt oder sonst öffentlich zugänglich gemacht werden. Dies gilt auch für Intranets von Schulen und sonstigen Bildungseinrichtungen.

Druck: Stürtz GmbH, Würzburg

ISBN 978-3-06-031307-5 – broschiert
ISBN 978-3-06-031357-0 – gebunden

Inhalt gedruckt auf säurefreiem Papier aus nachhaltiger Forstwirtschaft.

Dein Englischbuch enthält folgende Teile:

Introduction	Hier lernst du die jungen Leute von Band 4 kennen.
Units	die fünf Kapitel des Buches
Getting ready for a test	Hier kannst du dich gezielt auf einen Test vorbereiten.
EXTRA: Text File	viele interessante Texte zum Lesen (passend zu den Units)
Skills File (SF)	Beschreibung wichtiger Lern- und Arbeitstechniken
Grammar File (GF)	Zusammenfassung der Grammatik jeder Unit
Vocabulary	Wörterverzeichnis zum Lernen der neuen Wörter jeder Unit
Dictionary	alphabetische Wörterverzeichnisse zum Nachschlagen

Die Units bestehen aus diesen Teilen:

Lead-in	Einstieg in das neue Thema
A-Section	neuer Lernstoff mit vielen Aktivitäten und **Background File**
Practice	Übungen
Text	eine spannende oder lustige Geschichte
How am I doing?	Hier kannst du dein Wissen und Können überprüfen.

In den Units findest du diese Überschriften und Symbole:

Looking at language	Hier sammelst du Beispiele und entdeckst Regeln.
STUDY SKILLS	Einführung in Lern- und Arbeitstechniken
Dossier	Schöne und wichtige Arbeiten kannst du in einer Mappe sammeln.
All about ...	Hier lernst und übst du Wortschatz zum Thema der Unit.
READING COURSE	Lesekurs in fünf Kapiteln mit Hilfen zum Lesen von Texten
EVERYDAY ENGLISH	Übungen zum Bewältigen wichtiger Alltagssituationen
MEDIATION	Hier vermittelst du zwischen zwei Sprachen.
LISTENING	Aufgaben zu Hörtexten auf der CD
Now you	Hier sprichst und schreibst du über dich selbst.
REVISION	Übungen zur Wiederholung
WORDS	Übungen zu Wortfamilien, Wortfeldern und Wortverbindungen
Extra	zusätzliche Aktivitäten und Übungen
👥 👥👥	Partnerarbeit/Gruppenarbeit
🎧 🎧	nur auf CD / auf CD und im Schülerbuch
>	Textaufgaben

Contents

Die folgenden Angebote sind nicht obligatorisch abzuarbeiten. Die Auswahl der Übungen und Übungsteile richtet sich nach den Schwerpunkten des schulinternen Curriculums.

	Unit	Contents	Language: • grammatical structures • word fields	Study Skills, Reading Course, Everyday English, Background File
6	**Introduction** Welcome to the USA	Caitlin, Gracie, Luis, Jake and Madison are from different cities in the USA. They all spend their holidays at the Grand Canyon.		
14	**Unit 1** New York, New York	Caitlin's cousin Ryan from Ireland visits her in New York. Together they explore the city. • New York sights • Understanding directions and signs • NYC firefighters • The Empire State Building • A NYC deli • Ellis Island and immigrants **Text**: The writer and the firefighter	• REVISION adverbial clauses • gerunds • sights • BE and AE • collocations • jobs • directions	**STUDY SKILLS** Check yourself **READING COURSE (1)** Fire safety (Working out the meaning of words) **EVERYDAY ENGLISH** Making plans together **BACKGROUND FILE** All strangers
32	**Extra** Revision – Getting ready for a test 1			
36	**Unit 2** Both sides of the story	Gracie finds out more about the European settlement of Massachusetts and the history of her ancestors, the Wampanoag people. • Patuxet and Plimoth • Talking about history • Thanksgiving • A visit to Plimoth Plantation • The American Revolution • Massachusetts **Text**: I'm going to save my brother	• REVISION gerunds • REVISION conditional sentences 1 and 2 • REVISION past perfect • REVISION indirect speech: statements • conditional sentences 3 • indirect speech: questions with question words • indirect speech: yes/no questions, commands • daily routines • history	**STUDY SKILLS** Presentations: Handouts **READING COURSE (2)** National Day of what? (Skimming and scanning) **EVERYDAY ENGLISH** Visiting tourist sights **BACKGROUND FILE** Massachusetts
56	**Unit 3** California, land of dreams	Luis belongs to an immigrant family and lives in San Clemente, California. • Sights • National Parks • Mexican immigrants • Immigrant labour • Business • Growing up in two cultures • A conservation programme **Text**: The circuit	• REVISION passive: simple past • REVISION active and passive • personal passive • passive: modals and will-future, present perfect • participle clauses to replace relative clauses • infinitive constructions • business • minorities and ethnic groups • synonyms • word building (-ful, -less)	**STUDY SKILLS** Outlining **READING COURSE (3)** Soft drinks, hard facts (Finding the main ideas of a text) **EVERYDAY ENGLISH** Theme parks **BACKGROUND FILE** Welcome to California!

	Unit	Contents	Language: • grammatical structures • word fields	Study Skills, Reading Course, Everyday English, Background File
76	**Unit 4** **Hermann says 'Willkommen'**	The Schmidt family from Germany emigrates to Hermann, Missouri, and are welcomed by Jake Kruger and his family. • Hermann – a small town in the USA • German immigrants • Keeping traditions alive • American schools • Extracurriculars **Text**: Angus Bethune's moment	• REVISION infinitive constructions • countable/uncountable nouns • definite article • school (BE/AE) • word building (nouns from verbs and adjectives)	**STUDY SKILLS** Summary writing **READING COURSE (4)** Students between paid work and schoolwork (Careful reading) **EVERYDAY ENGLISH** Helping a tourist at the station **BACKGROUND FILE** Going west
94	**Extra** Revision – Getting ready for a test 2			
98	**Unit 5** **Atlanta rising**	Madison visits her father at work and finds out more about the fight for civil rights. • Atlanta timeline • US media • Take Your Child to Work Day • Martin Luther King, Jr **Text**: Melba's story	• REVISION defining relative clauses • REVISION nouns with or without a definite article • relative clauses with *which* to refer to a whole clause • non-defining relative clauses • opposites • the media • words that are both verbs and nouns	**STUDY SKILLS** Research; Using an English–English dictionary * **READING COURSE (5)** Fire (Text types: fiction and non-fiction) **EVERYDAY ENGLISH** Talking about films or TV shows **BACKGROUND FILE** The South
116	**Unit 6** **Extra** **Famous**	Excerpt from Mark Ravenhill's play *Totally over you*		**STUDY SKILLS** Using an English–English dictionary

128 Partner B

132 Key to How am I doing?

134 **Extra** Text File

    134 TF 1 The President and Mr Muir
    136 TF 2 A New York anthology
    138 TF 3 "How about them Yankees?"
    140 TF 4 "That's why you talk so funny"
    143 TF 5 In Room 56
    146 TF 6 **Bilingual module** Child labour on the US-Mexican border
    148 TF 7 Building the Gateway Arch
    150 TF 8 **Bilingual module** The American Civil War (1861–1865)
    152 TF 9 Barack Obama, the first African-American president
    153 TF 10 Black music

155 Skills File

172 Grammar File
187 Grammatical terms

190 Vocabulary

222 Dictionary (English–German)

259 Dictionary (German–English)
290 English sounds / The English alphabet
291 Classroom English
292 Irregular verbs
294 List of names
296 Countries and continents
297 Acknowledgments
300 The United States of America

* in Nordrhein-Westfalen verpflichtend

Introduction

Welcome to the United States of America

1 Imagine
Take a few minutes and imagine how the woman on the right is feeling and what she might be thinking about.

2 USA places
Do you know the place in the photo?
What other places in the USA do you know – cities, national parks, buildings, …? Find them on the map on the back inside cover. Tell the class what you know about them.

3 Extra USA poster
Make a poster about the USA. Look for photos of places, people, sports, activities, films, music events … Write your own short captions for the photos. Present your poster to the class. Explain why you chose your pictures.

▶ WB 1 (p. 2) • SF Describing pictures (p. 157)

7

1 Grand Canyon National Park

Grand Canyon National Park

For the last 6 million years, the Colorado River has been forming a gorge through colorful rocks in what is now the US state of Arizona. That gorge is known as the Grand Canyon.

The Grand Canyon is 277 miles (446 kilometers) long, from 4 to 18 miles (6.4 to 29 km) wide, and more than a mile (1.6 km) deep.

It was made a national park in 1919 and that year it received 44,000 visitors. Now, about 5 million people visit the Grand Canyon every year.

Park activities

Ranger programs
There are many ranger programs all year on the South Rim and from May to October on the North Rim. All are free and open to the public. Program information is listed in the park's newspaper, The Guide.

Mule trips
Overnight rides: Stay the night at Phantom Ranch, deep in the Canyon near the Colorado River. Includes accommodation, breakfast, lunch and steak dinner.

Down the Colorado
For many people, rafting down the Colorado River through the Grand Canyon is the ultimate adventure. Most trips take 7–18 days.

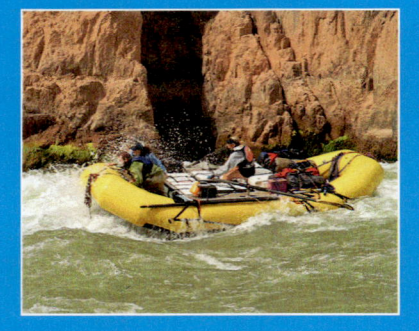

2 Now you
What would you most like to do at the Grand Canyon? Explain why. Now read the following pages and find out what five American kids did at the Grand Canyon.

▶ Text File 1 (pp. 134–135)

3 A blog

Caitlin's blog

About me

Name	Caitlin
Age	13
Birthday	July 9
Hometown	New York, New York

August 26

Hi, folks – I'm back from my summer vacation, so you can look forward to more of my daily blogs from New York. Like every year, my mom and dad packed me, my little brother and lots of camping gear into our car and drove … and drove and drove. We always go to a National Park, and this year it was the Grand Canyon.
It's 2,500 miles away from NYC. We crossed three time zones! It took us three and a half days.
The Grand Canyon is awesome! If you haven't been there, go! We camped at two different places on the rim and took trips in the car or hiked from there. My dad and I went on a two-day hike into the Canyon. It was very hard, and my whole body hurt for three days!

> How far is the Grand Canyon from Caitlin's home – in kilometres?
What time is it in the Canyon when it's 12 noon in New York?
The map on the back inside cover will help you.

4 Caitlin at the Grand Canyon

a) Look at the pictures in Caitlin's blog. Then add two more sentences to her blog about the campground and her hike into the Canyon.

b) **Extra** Where would you be if you travelled as far as Caitlin did when she went to the Grand Canyon?

5 A postcard

Wampanoag Tribal Identification Card
Name: Grace Smiling Sun James

Tusayan Ruin, Grand Canyon NP

Dear Grandpa,

We've been at the Grand Canyon for a couple of days now. Tomorrow we're going to the Havasupai Reservation. But it's not like our two-hour car-and-ferry trip from Mashpee to visit you on the reservation on Martha's Vineyard. It's a 100-mile drive and then a six-hour hike! (I'm glad we're coming back by horse.) Of course, Mom and Dad can't wait. Especially Dad. He's not just married to a Wampanoag, he thinks he *is* one. Yesterday we went on a walk with a ranger to an old Native American ruin. She told us about how they lived here 800 years ago.

That was cool.

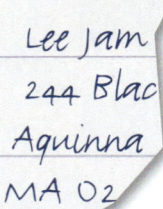

XOXO
Gracie

Lee Jam...
244 Blac...
Aquinna...
MA 02...

> What does Gracie like or dislike about her trip to the Grand Canyon? What do we find out about her family from the card?

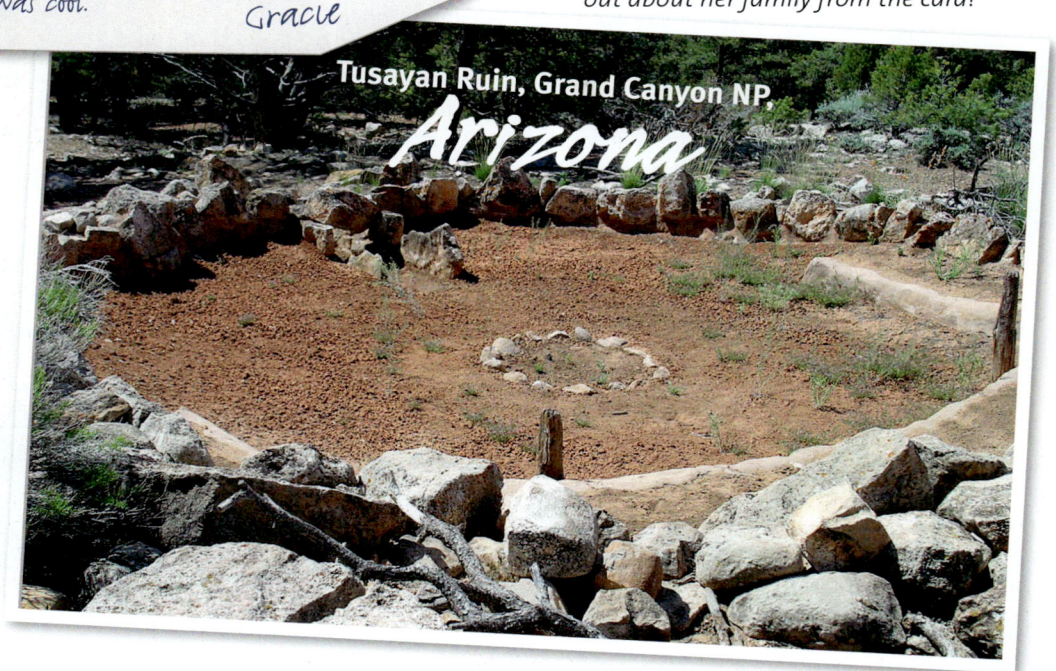

Tusayan Ruin, Grand Canyon NP, Arizona

6 Extra Now you

Describe what you can see in the photo of Tusayan Ruin. What do you think people did there 800 years ago?

7 A school essay

Shorecliffs Middle School
San Clemente, California

Student's name: Luis Morales
Grade: 8
Date: September 3

My summer vacation

This summer I was very lucky. I was able to go to Grand Canyon National Park with the youth group at my church. For months we were busy with fund-raising: We washed people's cars, cut their grass, cleaned their pools and had a bake sale to make money. (My mom's empanadas were sold out in two hours!)

We were all very excited when the bus came to pick us up. I'm 14 years old, and I'd never been so far from home – or from my mom.

The ride took about nine hours with a one-hour lunch break. We sang songs in Spanish and English the whole time – till the driver said we had to stop.

We stayed at the Canyon for three days. We went on long hikes around and into the Canyon. The colors were so beautiful. At night we slept in tents – it was my first time in a tent. We cooked our own meals too. But I prefer my mom's cooking!

The park rangers were very nice and told us a lot about the Canyon. One day they showed us how to use binoculars and other ranger tools in a discovery pack and then we were allowed to use them on our own for the rest of the day. We all got a patch at the end. My mom is going to sew mine onto my jacket when she has time.

> How was Luis able to pay for the trip?
Why do you think the group sang songs in English and Spanish?
What do you find out here and on page 10 about the work of park rangers? Do you know more about them?

8 Extra Now you

How do people raise money at your school, or how could you do that?
What would you like to spend it on?
If you spent it on a class trip, where would you go?

9 A summer vacation diary

Hermann High School, Hermann, Missouri

Name: Jake Kruger, 14
Grade: 9

August 7 Said goodbye to Mom at the farm and began our trip along Route 66 to the Grand Canyon. We traveled west – into Kansas and then Oklahoma. Dad has dreamed about this journey since he first saw the old TV series "Route 66" when he was a kid. And he just loves that song and sings it all the time. We stopped at every gas station and café and bought souvenirs for him. It's Day 1 and already we have a license plate for the car and a key ring! Tonight we're at a motel just outside Tulsa.

August 8 Early start. We crossed the Oklahoma state border into Texas. Stopped in Amarillo. Today was cattle market day – cattle all over! Then we drove on and on till we crossed into New Mexico. We're staying the night here in Tucumcari. Dad has added a cap to his souvenirs.

August 9 Dad let me see the awesome dinosaur collection before we got back on the road to Santa Rosa and the Route 66 Auto Museum. It was already dark when we crossed into Arizona, so we stopped at a motel in Holbrook.

August 10 Well, today we finally arrived at the Grand Canyon – and wow, IT IS GRAND! We left the car at our motel in the woods, then went straight to the rim of the Canyon. It stretches for hundreds of miles – layers and layers of multi-colored rock, really awesome. Later, when it got cooler, we walked down part of the Kaibab Trail into the Canyon. We saw a condor! What a bird – 9 feet from the tip of one wing to the other. Now I forgive Dad for all the hours in the car and all the "Route 66" stops and stories: today was a day I will never forget.

ROUTE 66

Well if you ever plan to motor west,
Just take my way, that's the highway that's the best
Get your kicks on Route 66
Well it winds from Chicago to L.A.
More than 2.000 miles all the way
Get your kicks on Route 66

by Bobby Troup

> Talk about Mr Kruger and Jake's trip. Explain
- what they did and saw,
- how far and through how many states they travelled,
- where they spent the night.

10 Now you
On the internet, find out two more interesting facts about Route 66. Tell the class.

Introduction   13

11 A computer presentation

My summer vacation

This presentation is by:
Madison Young (14),
Grade 9,
Martin Luther King High School,
Atlanta, Georgia

The journey
Atlanta – Las Vegas = 2,000 miles
Flight time = 4.5 hours
Drive Vegas – Canyon = 3.5 hours

Grand Canyon Skywalk

Inside the casino

Our mule train on the Black Bridge

The Excalibur from the Strip

12 Madison's trip

a) Look at the photos. What do you think Madison did in her summer holidays?

b) Listen to the CD. Point at the right photos while Madison is talking about them.

c) Read the questions below. Then listen again, take notes and answer the questions. What else can you say about the places and activities?
1 How long was Madison's trip? Why?
2 Did Madison think Las Vegas or the Grand Canyon was more exciting?
3 What was 'the big adventure'?

13 Extra Now you

Write about a special day in your summer holiday. Or choose a place in the USA you would like to visit and write about it.
Use one of the text types from pages 9–13. Brainstorm your ideas and look for useful phrases before you start. Add pictures or maps. Display your text in the classroom. Then put it in your DOSSIER.

▶ WB 2–7 (pp. 3–5)

Unit 1

New York, New York

1 **You and New York**

Do you know any of the places or sights in these photos? Have you ever been to New York City?
Get together in a group of 3 or 4. For a few minutes, discuss quietly what you know about New York. Then report back to the class.

2 New York sights 🎧

*Ryan from Ireland is visiting his cousin Caitlin in New York.
With her friend Ruth, they go on a bike tour of the Big Apple.*

a) Here is the list of the sights Ryan would like to see. Listen to the CD and say which ones he saw on the bike tour.

- ✗ the Brooklyn Bridge
- • Central Park
- ✗ Chinatown
- ✗ Ellis Island Immigration Station
- • the Empire State Building
- • Fifth Avenue
- ✗ Ground Zero
- ✗ the Statue of Liberty
- ✗ Times Square

b) 👥 Listen again and take notes on the sights from Ryan's list. Check your information with a partner.

c) Find out two or three more facts about the sights from the bike tour, or about any of the other sights on Ryan's list. Report back to the class.

▶ P 1 (p. 22) • SF Listening (p. 161) • WB 1–2 (p. 6)

1 A-Section

All about ... getting around an American city

1 Understanding directions

Look at what the woman tells the tourist. Would you know which way you had to go?
Match the words to their definitions:

- block
- a downtown bus
- 34th and Broadway
- subway

— an underground railway
— a bus towards the city centre (in Manhattan: a bus going south)
— the distance from one street to the next
— the corner of 34th Street and Broadway

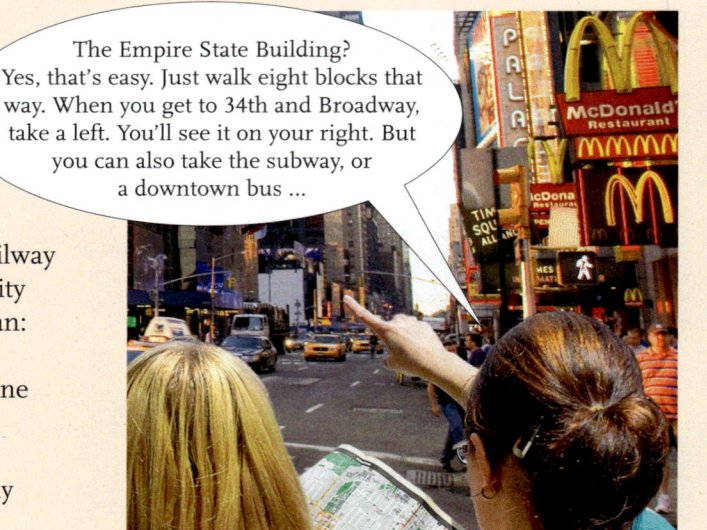

> The Empire State Building? Yes, that's easy. Just walk eight blocks that way. When you get to 34th and Broadway, take a left. You'll see it on your right. But you can also take the subway, or a downtown bus ...

2 Understanding American signs

a) Look at these signs and write down what you think they mean. Discuss with a partner. Then check the meanings in an English–German dictionary.

1. USE CROSSWALK
2. Line starts here
3. HOSTESS WILL SEAT You
4. SIDEWALK CLOSED PLEASE USE OTHER SIDE
5. Do Not Litter $250 FINE
6. DONT WALK

b) Where do you think you would find the signs? On the street, at a restaurant, ...

3 American and British English

a) Copy and complete the chart below. You can use a dictionary. (Tip: Look up the AE words to find the German, then look up the German to find the British expressions.)

American English (AE)	German	British English (BE)
subway	U-Bahn	...
downtown	(Stadt-)Zentrum	...
sidewalk		
line		

b) Extra Find the words below in a German–English dictionary. How do people usually say them in the USA? And in Britain? Add them to your chart.

Autobahn • Fahrstuhl • Kofferraum • Kreisverkehr • Lastwagen

▶ SF Using a bilingual dictionary (p. 156) • P 2 (p. 22) • WB 3–5 (pp. 7–8)

4 At the fire station 🎧

When the bike tour finished, Caitlin, Ruth and Ryan went back to the apartment where Caitlin lived with her parents. Ryan was very tired. He had only arrived from Ireland two days ago and he still had jet lag. 'Don't go to bed now,' Caitlin said. 'Otherwise you'll wake up in the middle of the night. Let's walk over to the fire station and say hi to Dad.'

'OK,' said Ryan. Visiting his uncle sounded like a good idea to him because he wanted to know all about life as a New York firefighter.

At the fire station, Mr O'Malley talked about his job.

'My dad and my grandpa were both firefighters, Ryan, and I always knew that I'd be a firefighter too. I still remember getting ready for the test when I was 17. Getting into the fire department was really important to me!

It's not an easy job. But I like being a firefighter. Sure, it's hard work. And nobody likes getting up in the middle of the night to fight a fire. But it feels good when you put out the fire and maybe save another person's life.

Working 15-hour shifts isn't easy either, but we spend a lot of time at the fire station. The men and women on my shift are like family: we don't just work together – we live together.

And some of the guys are great cooks. Ricardo was one. He made the best chili con carne. He always sang while he cooked and I enjoyed listening to him. Good old Ricardo. He's not with us any more – he died on 9/11.'

▶ Why was Ryan more tired than Caitlin and Ruth after the bike tour? What are the good and bad things about a firefighter's job?

Americana ★ ★ ★

9/11 and Ground Zero
On September 11th (9/11), 2001, 19 hijackers took over four US planes. They flew two of them into the Twin Towers of the World Trade Center, New York's highest buildings, in the south of the island of Manhattan. Both skyscrapers burned and collapsed. About 2,750 people died. The place where the Towers stood is now called 'Ground Zero'. Every year on 9/11 the 'Tribute in Light' helps New Yorkers remember the people who died in the two buildings.

Looking at language

a) Copy the table and write down all the sentences with -ing forms in **4**. Underline the -ing form.

-ing form before verb	-ing form after verb
Getting into the fire department was	I like being a ... ...

b) These -ing forms are called gerunds. In which sentences are the gerunds the subject of the sentence? In which the object?

▶ GF 1a–b: Gerund (p. 173) • P 3–6 (pp. 22–24) • WB 6–8 (pp. 9–10)

5 On top of the world 🎧

The next day, Caitlin wanted to show 'the best view in the world' to her Irish cousin Ryan, so they went to the Empire State Building.

'It's a perfect day for it', Caitlin said as she showed him the sign in the lobby: 'Visibility 45 miles'. 'This way, Ryan,' she went on. 'The ticket office is just one floor up.'

'But the sign says it's on the second floor,' said Ryan.

'That's right,' said Caitlin. 'This is the first floor, the next one up is two.'

After buying the tickets, the two cousins waited in the queue for the lifts. When they finally got in, the lift took them to the 86th floor in 50 seconds. Ryan went up without looking. When the doors opened he didn't move. His eyes were still closed and he was sweating.

'Come on, Ryan,' Caitlin said. 'We're there.'

'Thank God,' he said and explained his problem to her. 'I'm scared of going in lifts.'

Ryan loved it at the top, but after a while he had had enough of the view.

'Yes, I'm tired of all this sightseeing myself,' Caitlin said. 'I'll send Ruth a text and we'll meet her for lunch.'

> Why was it a good day to visit the ESB?
> Why do you think Ryan was confused about where the 'second floor' was?
> Do more people work in your town or the ESB?

▶ GF 1c: Gerund after prepositions (p. 174) • P 7–8 (pp. 24–25) • WB 9–11 (pp. 10–11)

6 Extra ESB quiz

a) Use the information on this page and write a five-question quiz about the Empire State Building.

b) 👥 Make groups of four. Choose the ten best questions you have to make your group quiz.

c) 👥 Swap your quiz with another group. Close your books. Who can finish the other group's quiz fastest and get all the answers right?

Empire State Building

The ESB in the movies

The Empire State Building has appeared in more than 90 movies. The most famous is **King Kong**.

It's the classic story of the huge gorilla Kong, who is taken from the jungle to New York, escapes, and, after finding the blonde woman he loves, climbs to the top of the ESB. There he is attacked by planes and falls to his death on the street below.

But whatever the movie, the ESB itself is the star.

ESB facts and fun

Building: The ESB was opened on May 1st, 1931. It is 1,454 feet (443.2 meters) high from top to bottom, has 103 floors and was the tallest building in the world from 1931 until 1972.

People: 15,000 people work in the ESB and another 10–20,000 people enter the building every day.

The 86th-floor **Observatory** is reached by high-speed elevators. It offers spectacular views to visitors from an inside area and outside areas on all four sides of the building.

Static: There is so much static electricity on top of the ESB that sometimes, if you stick your hand through the fence, St. Elmo's fire will come from your fingers. When people kiss, electric sparks sometimes come from their lips.

7 At the deli 🎧

Caitlin and Ryan met Ruth near her apartment, walked a couple of blocks and went into a crowded restaurant.

'Two onion bagels and cream cheese, one plain bagel and lox – hi there, Ruthy! – and two coffees to go,' shouted a young guy behind the counter.

'They know you here, Ruth?' asked Ryan.

'Oh sure, the local deli always knows everybody in the area. Say, how about you two grabbing that table there while I order? What do you want?'

'Ryan must have a bagel,' Caitlin said.

'Right,' Ruth agreed. 'I can't imagine you leaving New York before you've tasted our bagels. How about a bagel and lox?'

Ryan wasn't sure. 'Er, I've never had a bagel and I don't even know what lox is.'

'Salmon – in Yiddish!' explained Ruth.

'I don't like salmon. Maybe we could …'

'That's OK,' Ruth told him. 'They have plenty of other things with bagels. Come up to the counter with me. Then you can choose what you want.'

Twenty minutes later, when Ryan had finished his everything bagel with pastrami, he gave a big smile: 'Mmm, this is a great place. If I lived in New York, I'd come here every day!'

> What kind of a place does the deli seem to be? What does Ryan think about bagels at first? And afterwards?

▸ GF 1d: Gerund with 'its own subject' (p. 175)

Americana ★ ★ ★

Delis and bagels

Bagels are one of the New Yorkers' favourite breakfasts. On their way to work, they run into a deli (the name comes from the German *Delikatessen*) and grab a bagel and coffee to go.
Jewish immigrants from Europe brought the bagel – a sort of roll with a hole in it – with them in the 19th century. You make the dough and boil it in water and then put the bagel in the oven to get brown.
Bagels come with all sorts of fillings.

8 SONG A heart in New York 🎧

New York
To that tall skyline I come
flying in from London
To your door

New York
Looking down on Central Park
Where they say you should not wander
After dark

New York
Like a scene from all those movies
But you're real enough to me
But there's a heart
A heart that lives in New York

by Benny Gallagher and Graham Lyle

a) Which of the photos in the unit go with the song? Why?

b) Extra What do the lyrics tell you about New York? Give some examples.

▸ P 9–12 (pp. 25–27) • WB 12–16 (pp. 11–14) •
Text File 2–3 (pp. 136–139)

Extra | **Background File** | **ALL STRANGERS**

'I'd never seen such a big building. Compared with the size of the houses I left in my town, this was like a whole city in one. I almost felt smaller than I was. It looked beautiful.'
Celia Adler
12 when she arrived from Russia, 1914

'This is the only country where you're not a stranger, because we are all strangers.'
Lazarus Salamon
16 when he arrived from Hungary, 1920

'The steamer 'Florida', 14 days out of Naples, filled with 1600 Italians, had come through one of the worst storms the Captain could remember. We were glad, both children and grown-ups, to leave the open seas and come at last into the bay of New York. My family looked with wonder on this miraculous land of our dreams.'
Edward Corsi
10 when he arrived from Italy, 1907

'Our first home in America was a tenement flat near the East River at 112th Street ... the sunlight and fresh air of our mountain home in Lucania were replaced with four walls and people over and under and on all sides of us.'
Leonard Covello
9 when he arrived from Italy, 1896

'Going to America then was almost like going to the moon ... We were all bound for places about which we knew nothing at all and for a country that was totally strange to us.'
Golda Meir
8 when she arrived from Russia, 1906

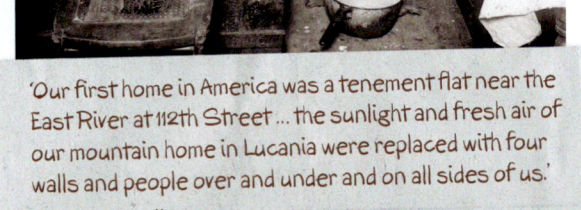

1 Immigrants

a) Look at the photos and statements. What do you find out about the lives of these children before they came to the USA? How did they feel after they arrived?

b) Choose one of the photos and imagine you are one of the children in it. Write part of a letter to your family in Europe about what you can hear and see, and what you are thinking and feeling.

▶ SF Describing pictures (p. 157)

The USA is a country of immigrants.

In a population of 300 million, only 4 million are Native Americans – all the rest have their roots in other countries around the world.

In the past many immigrants came to America because in their own countries they were not allowed to practise their religion or politics. But most came because at home they were poor and hungry.

Until the middle of the 20th century the main gateway to America was the port of New York. In 1892 the city opened the Ellis Island Immigration Station within sight of the Statue of Liberty and Manhattan Island. It was here that – between 1892 and 1924 – more than 12 million immigrants entered the USA.

Today Ellis Island is a National Monument and Museum. At its website you can trace immigrants to the US: www.ellisisland.org

New York is still a city of immigrants today.

> Look at the charts. Which continents did the immigrants who lived in the USA in 1900 mainly come from? And the immigrants who lived there in 2000? Why do you think the change happened?

In 1900 13.6 % of the US population was born outside the US. The three biggest groups were from:

Germany 2.66 million
Ireland 1.62 million
Canada 1.18 million

In 2000 10.8 % of the US population was born outside the US. The three biggest groups were from:

Mexico 9.18 million
China 1.52 million
The Philippines 1.37 million

(U.S. Census Bureau)

2 Immigration and you

Do either a) or b).

a) Has anybody from your family or from a family you know ever gone to live in the US? Check with your parents or grandparents. If yes, try and trace the person. Find out why they went.

b) Have you or anybody in your family or anybody you know immigrated into Germany? Check with your parents. Do you know when, where from and why? Write a short text.

▶ WB 17 (p. 15)

1 Practice

1 The five boroughs of New York

When people talk of New York, they usually mean Manhattan, where you can find most of the famous sights. But Manhattan is only one of five New York boroughs.

a) Partner B: Go to p. 128.
Partner A: Read out the texts below. Your partner must decide which boroughs you're describing.
– This is the biggest of New York's five boroughs. If you fly to Kennedy Airport, this is where you'll land. On the map it's east of Brooklyn.[1]
– A famous bridge over the East River links this borough to the island of Manhattan. A German, John Roebling, designed it.[2]

b) Now listen to your partner.
Which boroughs is he/she describing?

[1] *The correct answer is 'Queens'.* [2] *The correct answer is 'Brooklyn'.*

2 WORDS Verbs and nouns

a) You can use one verb with all the words in these groups. Find the verbs.
1 … a bus, a photo, the subway   *take*
2 … a train, a mouse, a thief
3 … a museum, a city, an aunt
4 … a bike, a horse, a mule

b) Find at least three words that go with each of these verbs.
1 arrive at   *a station, a hotel, …*
2 eat at   *a restaurant, …*
3 look up   *train times, …*
4 look at   *the sights, …*

c) Compare with a partner.

3 WORDS Jobs

a) Write down the words for the people who do these jobs:
1 a person who puts fires out
2 a person who catches thieves
3 a person who helps you in a shop
4 a person who plays the music at the disco

b) Paraphrase these jobs:
5 a paramedic
6 a doctor
7 a ranger
8 a hairdresser
9 a street cleaner

c) Describe two more jobs. Can your partner guess them?

4 REVISION Ryan in New York (Adverbial clauses)

Use the conjunctions from the box and make sentences with clauses from the left and the right.

Be careful where you put the conjunctions – they can go at the beginning or in the middle.

although • because • before • so that • when • where

1 Ryan flew to New York
2 he arrived at the airport
3 they were all very happy
4 the next day he walked around the area of Manhattan
5 Caitlin was only 14
6 he was really tired
7 they visited Caitlin's dad at the fire station
8 Ryan was glad
9 he went to bed at 9.30
10 he and Caitlin got up at 7

4 a) Caitlin and her family lived
5 b) he decided to go on a bike tour with her
7 c) he had never been in a fire station before
3 d) they hadn't seen each other for years
  e) he wanted to visit his family there
9 f) he was still tired in the morning
2 g) his cousin's parents were waiting for him
6 h) Ryan went to bed
8 i) the bike tour finished
10 j) they could get to the Empire State Building early

1 Ryan flew to New York because he wanted to visit his family there.
2 …

5 Visiting New York is great (Gerund as subject)

a) Partner B: Go to p. 128.
Partner A: Ask your partner the following questions:
1 What's a good way to see the sights of New York quickly?
2 How can you find out about immigrants and New York?
3 What will make you happy if you enjoy Chinese food?
4 What's a good way of getting a great view over the city on a clear day?
5 What's a good way of getting a good view of the Statue of Liberty?

b) Choose one of the phrases below to answer your partner's questions. First, make a gerund from the verb in brackets.
– (ride a bike) across Brooklyn Bridge
– (go to Union Square) on the last Friday of the month
– (visit) Washington Square
– (walk) up and down Wall Street
– (stand) in front of Ground Zero

1 Practice

6 What does Caitlin like doing? (Gerund as object)

a) Make gerunds from six of the verbs in the box and complete these sentences.

> answer • cycle • meet • read • travel •
> take • visit • work • write

1 Caitlin enjoys ... *visiting* her dad at the fire station.
2 When she goes out, she likes ... *reading / traveling* on the subway.
3 But she prefers ... *cycling*
4 In the evenings she loves ... *reading* her blog.
5 But she hates ... *writing* rude e-mails about her blog.
6 She imagines ... *working* as a journalist when she's older.

b) What about you? Write similar sentences about yourself.
I enjoy visiting my grandma.
When I go out I like *cycling or hiking*.
But I prefer traveling by train.
In the evenings I love reading or watching TV.
But I hate doing homework after dinner.
I imagine being an ac... whe... I'm olde...

7 LISTENING Different words 🎧

a) Look at the photos. Write down the British English (BE) word for the numbered things.
1 rubber
2 ...

b) Listen to the CD. You will hear two dialogues. Listen for the American English (AE) words in the box.

> cellphone • ⁺cookie • ⁺eraser •
> ⁺French fries • ⁺garbage • ⁺pants •
> ⁺potato chips • ⁺schedule • sidewalk •
> subway

c) Listen again and write down the correct AE words next to the BE words in your list from a).

Practice **1** 25

8 Clara is good at … (Gerund after prepositions)

a) Complete this text about Clara. Use words and phrases from the red box (these are in the right order) and the gerunds of the correct verbs in the blue box.

good at • dreams of • chance of • idea of • ask about • interested in • thinking of

become • go • join • see • speak • work • write

Clara is *good at speaking* English. So she … in New York. She's a big hip-hop fan and thinks she'll have a better … hip hop musicians there. She likes the … to concerts in Central Park. She'll … a dance class when she gets there. She's very … poems and she's … a rapper!

b) Choose eight phrases from the green box and, on a piece of paper, write sentences with gerunds about yourself.

Before eating my breakfast I always clean my teeth.

after • angry about • before • believe in • dream of • famous for • feel like • good at • interested in • look forward to • tired of • without • worried about

c) Put the pieces of paper in a box. Take turns to read one out to the class and guess who wrote it.

9 WRITING Taking a break in Central Park (Writing a text for a blog)

Look at this photo of Central Park. Imagine you are one of the people on the grass. Write about 150 words for a blog on your visit to New York City.

Use the 5 Ws and 'How?'
– Who was in the park with you? Who else was there? Why were you there?
– What did you see and do while you were there? What could you hear? What was the weather like?
– Where did you sit? Where did you come from? Where did you go afterwards?
– When did you arrive? When did you leave?
– How did you like it there? How did you get there? How did you feel? How long did you stay?

Remember

Remember these tips for better writing:
– Collect your ideas (mind map, list, 5 Ws).
– Make it interesting (adjectives, adverbs, linking words, good beginning and ending).
– Read and revise the first draft of your blog.

▶ SF Writing course (pp. 168–169)

10 MEDIATION On the bike tour (Mediating spoken information) 🎧

a) *Imagine you are on a bike tour of New York. A German man on the tour is finding it difficult to understand the guide. Try to help him.*

Tour guide	OK, there they are, folks, the Statue of Liberty and Ellis Island. Now, of course we can't go over there on our bikes. You have to get a ferry.
German man	Was sagt sie? Fahren wir jetzt dahin?
You	Nein, sie sagt, wir können nicht … Man muss …
Tour guide	The ferries leave from Battery Park every 25 minutes. But just remember the lines for tickets are very long at this time of year, so you need quite a bit of time if you want to go.
German man	Was, 25 Minuten dauert die Überfahrt?
You	…

b) *Listen to the rest of the conversation. Listen again and mediate.*

11 EVERYDAY ENGLISH SPEAKING Making plans together

Partner B: Look at p. 129.
Partner A: You and your partner are on holiday in New York. It's your last day.
You each have different information and interests, but you want to spend the day together.

a) You have chosen the activities below for your last day. Tell your partner
– about the activities you would like to do,
– where they are, what they cost, when the place is open,
– why you would like to do them.

The world's largest store!
Macy's – New York's most famous department store. With 10 floors and half a million things for sale – you'll need lots of time!
Open 9 to 9!
In Herald Square, on West 34th Street at Broadway

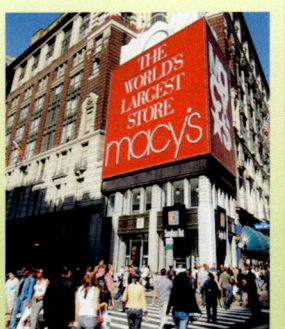

The Bronx Zoo
The Bronx Zoo is one of the largest zoos in the United States with over 4000 animals.
The Zoo is open 365 days a year!
10:00 a.m. – 5:00 p.m.
Admission: Adult $ 14.00
Child (ages 3–12) $ 10.00

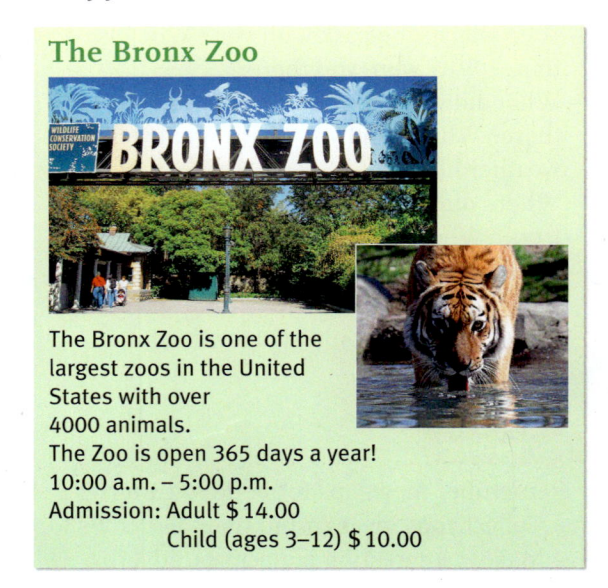

American Museum of Natural History
The home of the largest and maybe one of the most fantastic dinosaur collections in the world. 
At Central Park West and 79th Street in New York City.
Open daily,
10:00 a.m. – 5:45 p.m.
Adults: $ 14.00
Children (2–12): $ 8.00

b) *Listen to your partner's activities and take notes.*

c) *Now talk to her/him and choose the activities you'd like to do together – one for the morning, one for the afternoon. You each have $ 20 left. Check the prices and opening hours.*

12 READING Fire safety (Working out the meaning of words)

a) Read these fire safety instructions from a hotel room. You probably don't know all the highlighted words. The questions on the left and right will help you to understand them.

You know 'high', and you're in New York. What could a 'high-rise' building be?

'Smoke' comes from a fire – so what can it be?

You know 'stairs', you know 'way' – 'stairway' is easy! And what do you hold when you walk down stairs? What's 'railing'?

Fire safety in high-rise buildings

If the fire is IN your room

- If there is a fire, stay calm and think about what to do. Act quickly because every second counts.
- Get everyone out. Smoke from a fire rises. Stay close to the floor, where the air is better.
- Use your safest and nearest exit.
- CLOSE ALL DOORS as you leave.
- Alert others by knocking on their doors on your way out.
- DO NOT USE THE ELEVATOR.
- Go down the nearest STAIRWAY, holding the railing.
- To report a fire, dial 911 when you reach a safe location.

You know 'calm down'. What could 'calm' mean?

Does smoke from a fire go up or down? So what do you think 'rises' means?

You saw this sign on your way in. What could 'exit' mean?

FIRE EXIT →

'Report a fire' + a number – what could 'dial' mean?

These things can help you to understand words you don't know:
1. Headings, titles, pictures
2. Words like words from French, Latin, ...
3. Words that look like German words or other English words you know
4. Prefixes (**un**important) and suffixes (fight**er**)
5. Context: the words around the word you don't know
6. What you already know about the topic

▶ SF Reading Course (p. 163)

b) Try the techniques with these other words from the fire safety instructions above: alert, act, location.

c) Which techniques help you understand the highlighted words in the safety instructions below?

Fire safety in high-rise buildings

If the fire is NOT in your room

- Stay in your room. Do not enter smoke-filled hallways. Keep the door closed.
- If you are unable to leave your room, place a wet cloth over your mouth and nose to make breathing easier.
- Seal the door with clothes or wet towels from the guest bathroom.
- Turn off air conditioners.
- Fill your bathtub with water. If your door gets hot, wet it down.
- If no flames or smoke are coming from below, open your windows a few inches at the top or bottom.
- Dial 911 with a description of the conditions in your room.
- If you feel you are in grave danger, open a window and wave a bed sheet for rescuers to spot you.

The writer and the firefighter (abridged and adapted from *The Guys* by Anne Nelson)

Look at page 17 and read about 9/11 again. Or find out more about 9/11 on the internet. In this play, Joan, a writer, meets a firefighter a short time after 9/11. Imagine what the reason for their meeting could be.

A woman stands at center stage and addresses the audience directly.

Joan 'Where were you September eleventh?' Question of the year. I was at home. The phone rings and it's my father, 'Is your TV on?'

Now she acts as if she is talking to her father.

'No,' I say. 'Why?' 'A plane crashed into the World Trade Center. Must have been one of those little planes, pilot had a heart attack.' 'Dad,' I said. 'Maybe it's terrorism.' 'Why would someone do that?'

Long beat.

The week after the attack, I visited my sister. The phone rang; my sister answered. It was her friend the masseuse. The friend was giving emergency massages to rescue workers. Look, she said. I've been working on this guy. He's a fire captain, and he just lost most of his men. He's got to give the eulogies. The first one is on Thursday. He – can't write them. He needs a writer. The firefighter needs a writer.

I called him. Come now, I said. I have a few hours.

A knock. The lights come up on a living room. Joan walks stage right to meet Nick. He has ordinary clothes on. He holds a folder in his hand. He looks around, then offers his hand. They shake.

Nick Joan?
Joan Hi.
Nick Hi.
Joan I ... I'm really sorry about ... what happened.
Nick Oh. Yeah. Look, I feel really bad about this. It's a beautiful afternoon. It's the weekend. You should be with your kids.
Joan My kids have play dates. It's fine. Hey, do you want some coffee?
Nick Yeah, sure, if you've got some.
Joan Milk? Sugar?
Nick Just black.

See, I just don't know what to do. These guys ... the call came, and they went off, and ... they haven't found them yet but ... some of the families, they want to have the service now so they can try to move on ... I have to get up and talk in church ... I've been sitting in front of a piece of paper all day, and I haven't been able to write one sentence. Not a thing. I'm no writer anyway. What can I tell the families? What am I going to say?

Joan Hey, it's okay. Maybe I can help. I ... I've never written a eulogy before, but I've written some speeches. It's okay. Now, how many men did you say there were?

Nick *(He sighs)* Eight.
Joan Eight.
Nick Eight men. I lost eight men.
Joan So ... eight eulogies. *(She stares at the paper in front of her)* Well, we'll just take it a step at a time, do what we can. You say that one of the services is next week?
Nick Yeah, Thursday.
Joan So we'll do that one first. Thursday? *(She sits with her pen above her notepad)*
Nick Thursday. Yeah. Bill Dougherty. The families want me to say something. I'm the captain. What can I say to them? How can I explain it?
Joan Hey, it's okay ... *(Softly)* I mean ... You're doing this for the families. You'll comfort them. It's for them. It won't be about what happened that day. We'll talk about who they were, make it about them. That's what you can give the families.
Nick I hear all these speeches from the politicians on TV. The pictures in the papers. Hero this, hero that. I don't even recognize them.
Joan So that's why it's good you're doing this. You can give their families and friends something they can recognize. You can do that. So, hey, tell me about Bill.
Nick *(He takes a deep breath)* Bill. Yeah, Bill. Well, see, that's the problem. There's just not much to say. This hero stuff, like they

were some guys in a movie. But Bill – he wasn't like that. He was just an ordinary guy. If Bill walked into a room, nobody would even notice. *(Looks up at her helplessly)* You can't say that in a eulogy.

Joan Hey, it's okay. Don't worry. We'll do this. I mean, people who are ordinary ... in a ... an extraordinary situation. That's what this is about. Now tell me about him. What did he look like?

Nick Look like? Not a big guy. Reddish hair. Mid-forties. But he was the senior man. All the junior men depended on him. They had their eyes on him to know what to do. 'My men,' he called them.

Joan When you close your eyes, where do you see him? What's he doing?

Nick *(Thinks)* In the kitchen.

Joan The kitchen?

Nick The guys spend a lot of time in the kitchen. Bill's there. He was real good with the younger guys. He was always showing them things.

Joan *(She is writing it down)* Yeah?

Nick See, someone like Bill – he's real senior; he's been there sixteen years. There are always new guys. They're a little nervous, and they don't know where things are. A guy like Bill was always looking out for them. Here's the gear, here's the tools, here's how you do this, no, not like that, like this ...

Joan *(Writing)* Was he a family man? Religious?

Nick Oh, Bill was quiet. Never talked about himself. Half the company didn't even know he was married. I know he went to mass. He was proud of being Irish. You know, I think that's why he was a fireman – it's thick in the Irish blood.

Pause.

He loved New York. You know, these guys see the city from the outside and the inside, underground and in all the hidden places. Bill wanted to know the history of everything. You want to have a guy like that around, especially downtown, with all these crazy streets. Nowadays, you get a computer map when you get a call. But somebody can still call in and give you bad directions, or a building name with no address ...

On that day ... I still don't know what happened. I can't find anyone who saw the company. They told the driver, 'We're going to Tower One.' They're running down West Street about the time the second plane hit. And maybe they changed plans and went to Tower Two. But we don't know where to look for them. *(Stops, choked)*

Joan *(After a moment)* What else did Bill love? Any sports? Music? You said he hung out in the kitchen – did he like to cook?

Nick Oh, Bill wasn't exactly a cook. The guys take turns to cook. Sometimes it's okay, but it can get pretty bad. Bill tried the food and came up with some real crazy names for it.

Joan So he was more of a critic.

Nick Yeah, yeah! – he was the firehouse food critic. And he could zap 'em good. But not mean. He was never mean.

Joan Okay, okay. Yeah, this is good. This works. 'Cause you know, Nick, you want to give people someone they recognize. Not a saint. This is good. Wait a minute. *(She writes, crosses out, draws some arrows on the page)*

> What kind of man was Bill Dougherty? Read the play to this point again and take notes on him.
>
> **Extra** 👥 Use your notes to write a short description of Bill. Swap with a partner. Read and correct his/her text. Compare your texts and revise them.

Nick *(Watching her)* I'm really sorry. I'm not giving you anything to work with here.

Joan *(Still looking at the paper, shaking her head)* No, no, just wait. *(She tears off a sheet, copies from one sheet to another, then quickly numbers paragraphs)* Here. *(She hands pages to Nick)* Try this. Start here, and it jumps to there. And ... if you could read it out loud so I can hear it?

Nick (*Reads slowly*) 'I'm Nick Flanagan, captain of Ladder Company 60. I've worked with Bill Dougherty for a long time. I want to give my condolences to all of Bill's family here with us today.'
(*Nods*) Okay.
(*He goes on reading*) 'We've been hearing a lot about heroes, and Bill was one of them. He gave his life for others, and that is a noble thing. But Bill was a quiet hero. He never showed off. He was a firefighter for sixteen years, and he was a good one. He had the most important quality for a firefighter. He was absolutely dependable.'
(*He looks up and smiles at her*) Yeah. That's right. Dependable.
(*He continues reading*) 'Over time, we realized how important he was for the newer guys at the firehouse. Bill was always looking out for the new guys, showing them the ropes. And he did it in that quiet way of his, never made them feel small. "My men," he called them. "My men."'
(*Looks at her*) Yeah. You got it. You got it. That's him.

Joan They're your words. I just put them in order.

Nick No. You've got the skill. You know how to put it.
(*He reads on*) 'He was like an older brother to them. You have to have guys like Bill to build a strong team. They may not say much, but they hold things together. If Bill hadn't been a fireman, he could have been a food critic. Bill spent a lot of time in the kitchen. He spoke to the guys and tried what they cooked. When Bill tried a bad dish, he came up with some real crazy names for it. The restaurants of New York are lucky he went into another line of work.'
Yeah. The guys will like that. (*He goes on*) 'What did Bill love? He loved his family, and he loved this city. On September eleventh, he was the senior man. The younger men could look up to someone they could depend on and who was professional, to show the way. We know that Bill and the other firefighters of New York saved thousands of lives that day. That means that there are thousands of people and their family members who are able to go on because of them. We can only thank them and ask for God's blessing on those they have left behind.'

Joan (*She looks at him anxiously*) So it works?

Nick You got it. I can do this.

Joan (*She takes a breath, closes her eyes and sits back in her chair*)

Nick You okay?

Working with the text

1   Understanding the play

a) Were your ideas about why the writer and the firefighter meet correct?

b) Describe in two or three sentences what the play is about.

c) `Extra` Compare your text about Bill with the eulogy Joan wrote for Nick.

2   The characters

Try to imagine how Joan and Nick feel. Look at the stage directions for help.

3   Heroes

a) Scan the play for the word 'hero'. Describe what makes Bill Dougherty a hero.

b) Think of one of your heroes. What makes them a hero for you? Compare them with Bill. What is the most important quality a hero should have?

c) `Extra` Listen to Bruce Springsteen's song 'Into the fire' and explain what connects it to the play.

▶ WB 18 (p. 16) • **Checkpoint 1** WB (p. 17)

How am I doing?

Remember

1. Remember: Stop – Check – Go! Check yourself after every unit. Find out where your problems are. Make plans to improve your English in these areas. 'How am I doing?' will help you to do that.
2. Swap with a partner and check each other's work (grammar, spelling, vocabulary, …).

a) Fill in or choose the correct answers.

New York

1. The city of New York has five …
   A areas   B parts   C boroughs   D sections
2. Most of the sights and important places in New York are in …
   A Staten Island   B Queens   C Brooklyn   D the Bronx   E Manhattan
3. Downtown Manhattan is in the … of the island.
   A north   B south   C east   D west
4. When Americans speak of 9/11, they mean the date when planes flew into
   A the World Trade Center
   B the Empire State Building
   C Ground Zero   D Times Square
5. The place in New York where, for many years, immigrants entered the USA is called
   A the Statue of Liberty   B Ellis Island
   C Liberty Island   D the Brooklyn Bridge

American English

6. What are these British English (BE) words in American English (AE)?
   pavement • mobile phone • trousers • chips
7. What are these AE words in BE?
   elevator • line (Warteschlange) • subway • vacation

Words

8. Which word does not mean 'very good'?
   A awesome   B awful   C great   D fantastic
9. The job of a firefighter is to … fires.
   A put on   B put off   C put out   D put up
10. The library is three … west of here.
    A streets   B blocks   C corners   D sidewalks
11. Where can you not sleep?
    A motel   B tent   C hotel   D deli

Grammar

12. … in the Grand Canyon is very exciting.
    A Walk   B The walking   C Walking   D Walks
13. Ruth's hobby is … the guitar.
    A playing   B to play   C the play of   D play
14. Complete the sentences. Use gerunds:
    a) Ryan is scared of … on lifts.
    b) Caitlin feels like … her dad at the fire station.
    c) You can't leave New York without … down Fifth Avenue.
    d) Ruth's favourite deli is famous for … wonderful bagels.

b) Check your answers on p. 132 and add up your points.

c) If you had 19 or more points, well done! Maybe you can help students who had fewer points. If you had 18 points or fewer, it's a good idea to do some more work before you go on to the next unit. Where did you make mistakes? The chart below will tell you what you can do to improve your English.

No.	Area	Find out more	Exercise(s)
1–6	New York	Unit 1 (pp. 14–21, 28–30), P1 (p. 22)	WB 1, 2, 16 (pp. 6, 14)
7–8	American English	Unit 1 (p. 16)	P 7 (p. 24), WB 5, 9 (pp. 8, 10)
9–12	Words	Unit vocabulary (pp. 187–193)	WB 4, 6, 13 (pp. 7, 9, 12)
13–15	The gerund	GF 1–3 (pp. 167–169)	P 5, 6, 8 (pp. 23–25), WB 7, 8, 10 (pp. 9–11)

Getting ready for a test 1 Revision Extra

1 WORDS In a city

Look at this picture of an American city. Write down words for as many things or people as you can.

2 WORDS Describing towns and cities

a) Complete the sentences with words that mean the opposite.
1. A town can be large or *small*.
2. It can be in the east or the … of a country.
3. It can be exciting or …
4. It can be noisy or …
5. The buildings can be old or …
6. The streets can be clean or …
7. It can be a safe or a … town.
8. Life there can be quiet or …

b) Write a short text about the picture in 1.
– Is the city old, clean, …?
– What things could you do in the city?
– Would you like to live there? Give a reason for your answer.

3 You aren't allowed to park here! (Modal verbs)

Complete each sentence with an expression from the box.
1. Look at that NO PARKING sign! … park here!
2. … drive on the right in the US.
3. But … drive on the right in England!
4. Can you play football in the park? – Sure, and … skateboard there too.
5. … to take the subway to get to Central Park. It's only two blocks away.
6. If you want to visit the museum, … buy a ticket.
7. The sightseeing buses are great. … get on and off as often as you like.
8. Hey! … do that! It's forbidden.

> you don't have to • you have to •
> you're allowed to • you aren't allowed to

Extra Revision Getting ready for a test 1

4 What did you do last weekend? (Simple past and past perfect)

Rachel is telling her friend what she did last Saturday morning. Finish the sentences for her with the correct forms of the verbs – simple past or past perfect.

1. On Saturday morning I … (get up) at 9 o'clock.
   On Saturday morning I got up at 9 o'clock.
2. After I … (have) my breakfast, I … (watch) TV for a while.
3. Then I … (take) the bus into town.
4. First, I … (go) to 'Jeans World'.
5. I … (want) to buy some jeans but I … left my money at home! Arrrgh!
6. Outside in the street, I … (meet) Karen and Amy from our class.
7. They … (buy) some magazines so we … (look at) those and … (chat).
8. Suddenly I … (notice) the time! I … (be) in town for nearly three hours.
9. I … (run) to the bus stop.
10. When I … (get) home, my parents … (eat) lunch already. My mum … (not/be) happy!

5 STUDY SKILLS Writing better sentences (Linking words)

In a test, you might have to write an e-mail or letter. Remember that linking words can make them more interesting. Join the pairs of sentences with these words.

> although • and • because • ~~but~~ • or • so that • that • who

1. I like my town. It's big and exciting.
   I like my town because it's big and exciting.
2. I often look at expensive clothes. I never buy them!
3. I often eat fries. I know they're bad for me!
4. We could go to the cinema. We could watch a DVD at home.
5. Yesterday we saw a guy. He sells fun T-shirts.
6. Aaron's is a deli. It sells great bagels.
7. My mum often gives me money. I can go out with my friends.
8. My favourite place in town is the park. It's quiet and really pretty.
9. The film was long. It was boring too.

▶ SF Writing Course (p. 168)

6 What do you like doing? (Gerunds)

a) Work with a partner. Brainstorm ideas about things you enjoy/love/like doing (use gerunds). Make a network.

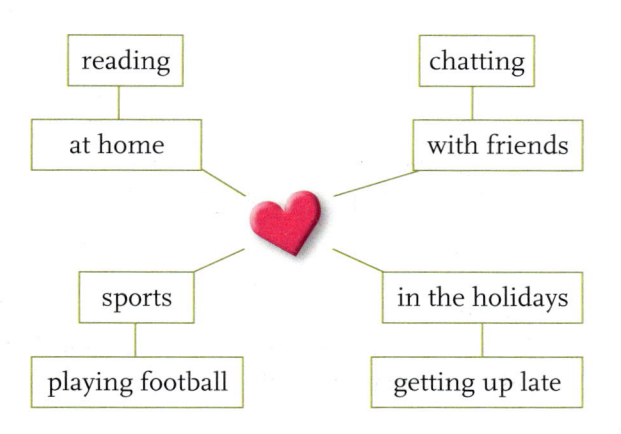

- reading
- at home
- sports
- playing football
- chatting
- with friends
- in the holidays
- getting up late

b) Make sentences that are true for you with words and phrases from your network.

*When I'm at home/with friends …
I (really) like/(absolutely) love …
I'm (very) interested in …
My hobby/favourite activity is …*

> **STUDY SKILLS** How to do well in a test
>
> If you have to do a test, you should
> – start revising at least a week before the test (texts, words, grammar),
> – during the test, read the instructions carefully,
> – pay attention to multiple-choice questions.

▶ WB 1–5 (pp. 18–19) • SF How to do well in a test (pp. 170–171)

34 ✓ Getting ready for a test 1 **Practice test** Extra

1 Reading

Greg Zimmermann is a teenager from New York. Read his blog this week and do the tasks below.

New York's yellow taxis are going green!
Hi! What do you think of when you hear the words New York? Skyscrapers? Delis? Central Park? The Statue of Liberty? I love all those things and places too, but for me, there's another thing that is so typical of the city. Taxis. The famous yellow New York taxicabs.
Taxicabs are everywhere in New York. In fact, there are 13,000 of them. Over half of all the cars you see in Manhattan are taxis. That's great if you need a cab. You can usually get one easily on the street. But there is a problem. They use a lot of gas – around a gallon every hour (that's 3.8 liters for you guys in Europe!). And all that gas makes the air in New York dirty. Very dirty!
But now something interesting is happening. The cabs are going green. No, I don't mean that people are painting them a different color. The cabs will still be yellow just like always. But they'll be 'environmentally friendly[1]'. The old cabs will slowly go, and there'll be new ones.
The new cabs (there are nearly 400 of them in the city already), will be 'hybrid cabs'. What does that mean? A normal cab uses gas all the time. A hybrid cab uses gas and electricity. It has a normal gas motor, and then it also has a battery[2] and an electric motor. It uses the electric motor when it's going slowly – and when it's stopped at a traffic light. And it uses the gas motor when it travels more quickly. Result: cleaner air! Cool.
Everybody is excited about the new cabs. The mayor[3] was on TV yesterday. His idea is that New York's image is really important. When tourists come here, they don't want to visit a dirty city. They want to find a place that's modern and that cares about the environment.
And what do the cab drivers think? Our neighbor, Mr Janjma, drives one of the new cabs, so I asked him. "Cab drivers have to buy their cabs," he said, "and the new ones cost more than the old ones. But they don't use so much gas. I save about 30 dollars a day now. I'm really happy!"
Until next week! Stay safe! Greg.

a) *Choose the right answers:*
1 New York taxicabs …
   A aren't typical of the city.   B don't use much gas.   (C) make the city's air dirty.   D aren't a problem.
2 In the future, New York's taxicabs will …
   A change colour.   B be environmentally friendly.   C travel slowly.   D all be old.
3 A hybrid taxi …
   (A) has two motors.   B doesn't stop at traffic lights.   C uses only gas.   D uses only electricity.
4 The mayor of New York says that the city should be … for tourists.
   A dirty   B famous   C on TV   (D) clean
5 Mr Janjma … his taxi.
   (A) pays $30 a day for   B likes   C never drives   D wants to buy

b) *Finish the sentences with information from the text.*
1 There are ... 13,000 taxis in New York and they all use about ... 3.8 litres of petrol every hour.
2 There are already nearly ... 400 hybrid cabs.
3 A hybrid cab only uses petrol when it ... drives fast
4 Millions of people visit New York every year so it's important that ... it is clean
5 Mr Janjma saves money now because ... he doesn't have to buy so much gas.

▶ SF Marking up a text (p. 162)

---
[1] environmentally friendly [ɪnˌvaɪrənˈmentəli ˈfrendli] *umweltfreundlich*   [2] battery [ˈbætri] *Akku, Batterie*   [3] mayor [meə] *Bürgermeister/in*

2 Reading

Here are some signs that you could see in town. Write a sentence for six of the signs. Use the phrases from the box.
Sign 1: This sign ...

- You aren't allowed to ... where you see this sign.
- You're allowed to ... here.
- Sorry, you can't ... here.
- It's OK to ... when you see this sign.
- You have to ... when you see this sign.

Signs

1. (No parking sign)
2. (No bicycles sign)
3. (No mobile phones sign)
4. STOP
5. DRUG-FREE SCHOOL ZONE
6. (Roller-skating sign)
7. SLOW CHILDREN AT PLAY
8. DRIVE ON LEFT IN AUSTRALIA
9. (Litter bin sign)

3 Writing

Choose one of the tasks below. Write an e-mail of 100–120 words. Begin and end your e-mail with suitable phrases. Count your words at the end.

a) Chloe is your new American penfriend. Tell her about the village or about the part of town where you live. Include the following things.

- Where in Germany?
- What can you do there?
- shops and buildings
- Is it old? Famous?
- Do you like it? Why (not)?

b) Your British penfriend Robert wants to know what you did last weekend. Tell him
– what you did on Saturday/on Sunday,
– who you did it with,
– if it was fun/boring/...

4 Speaking

You're starting an internet project with a school in Boston in the USA. Your class are making audio files about yourselves. Talk for about one minute about 'What I like doing'.

Unit 2

Both sides of the story

1 Two villages

a) Describe the pictures on page 37. In which of the two villages do you think the two young people below live? Imagine a day in the life of Tapenum or Sarah Morton. What do they do during the day? What are their interests and hobbies? Who are their friends? What do they like to do, eat and drink?

Tapenum

Sarah Morton

Massachusetts

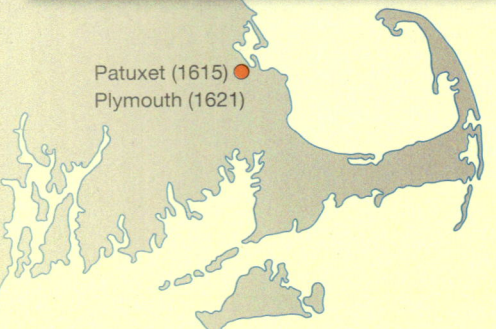

Patuxet (1615)
Plymouth (1621)

b) The map on the right shows that the two villages were in the same place at different times. What do you think happened between 1615 and 1621?

2 A day in the life of …

a) Listen to the CD. Explain where Sarah and Tapenum live and what they are talking about.

b) Listen again. Take notes and make two lists of what Tapenum and Sarah do during the day.

Tapenum	Sarah
– prepares for hunting (quietly)	– puts on clothes
– …	– …

c) 👥 Compare your notes, revise and expand them. Then write a paragraph about how the two young people's lives are similar and different.

3 Patuxet and Plymouth

Now answer question 1b again.

▶ P 1 (p. 45) • WB 1 (p.20)

bow and arrow

turkey

smoke

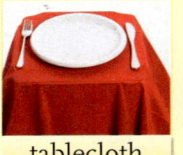

tablecloth

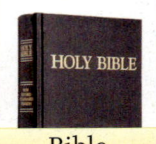

Bible

spring

candle

goat

doll

1615

Wampanoag Indians working in a field of corn, squash and beans in the village of Patuxet, population about 2,000

1621

Colonists in the English colony of Plymouth, population 52

All about ... history

1 Dates on a timeline

When you talk about history, you often need to use dates. To make dates clearer, in the Western world we use these abbreviations:
BC = before Christ
AD = Anno Domini (Latin for *in the year of the Lord* = after the birth of Christ)

A timeline is a list of dates with short texts or key words about important events in history.
Match the right events to the dates on this mixed-up timeline of Native American history in New England.

13,000 BC	Agriculture spreads to present-day New England; corn, beans and squash are grown.
9,200 BC	John Cabot from Bristol sails along the New England coast.
1000 AD	The Pilgrims and Wampanoag celebrate the Pilgrims' first harvest together.
1498 AD	Humans live in all of North and South America.
1620 AD	The first humans come to America from Asia.
1621 AD	The Pilgrims arrive on the *Mayflower* and found Plymouth Colony.

2 Causes and effects

Dates aren't the only important facts in history. You also need to explain *why* things happened – to talk about causes and effects.
Look at the three diagrams below and at the box. Which words from the box go with which parts of the diagram?

> as a result • led to • resulted in • so • that's the reason why

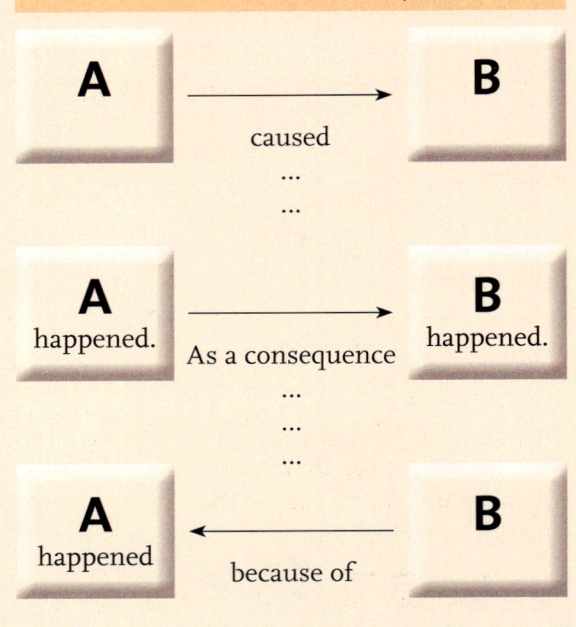

A → B
caused
...
...

A happened. → B happened.
As a consequence
...
...
...

A happened ← B
because of

▶ P 2 (p. 45) • WB 2–3 (p. 21)

Americana ★ ★ ★

Thanksgiving Day
is a national holiday in the USA on the fourth Thursday in November. On this day Americans remember the first harvest of the Pilgrim settlers in Plymouth Colony in 1621. Thanksgiving is usually celebrated with a turkey dinner. It is a time for family and friends to come together and give thanks for the good things in their lives. Thanksgiving Day parades and football games have become important traditions as well.

3 An argument in class 🎧

The week before Thanksgiving, Gracie's Social Studies class was talking about that holiday instead of studying the American Revolution, their topic for that semester.

'I'd go to Plymouth for the big parade if I could,' said Mike Lowe. 'It must be fabulous. Plymouth is where Thanksgiving began …'

Gracie couldn't stop herself. 'No, it didn't!' she interrupted.

'Of course it did,' Mike said. 'The first Thanksgiving was in 1621 when …'

'What do you know?' Gracie said in a loud voice. 'There were Thanksgivings before that.'

Mike shook his head. 'How, Gracie? The Pilgrims only came on the Mayflower in 1620, right? So there couldn't …'

'Yeah,' Gracie interrupted again. She felt angrier and angrier. 'But there were other people here before that.'

'Right,' Mike said, 'Indians like you. But they were friendlier then. That's the reason why the Pilgrims invited them …'

'That's crap, Mike! They …'

This time Mrs Tripp, the teacher, interrupted. 'OK, Gracie, I don't want to hear language like that in my classroom. Now, you both have different opinions on this. If you want to share them with us, we'll all be interested to hear more. So, Mike, Gracie – how about giving us a short presentation on the subject before we start our next period? OK?'

▶ *Why do you think that Gracie gets so angry? Explain why the teacher interrupts and what she tells Gracie and Mike to do.*

▸ GF 2a–b: Conditional sentences 1 and 2 (p. 175) • P 3–4 (pp. 45–46) • WB 4–5 (p. 22)

4 If you hadn't been so rude … 🎧

That evening at dinner, Gracie told her parents what had happened in her Social Studies class. 'I don't know enough about the history of that time for a presentation.'

'Well, Gracie,' her mother said, 'it's your own fault. <u>If you hadn't been so rude, Mrs Tripp wouldn't have given you this extra work.</u>'

'I don't think I was rude,' Gracie said. '<u>If Mike Lowe hadn't told that stupid old story, I wouldn't have interrupted him.</u>'

'And if you had just kept quiet,' her mother added, '<u>you'd have been free all weekend instead of researching on the internet.</u> Oh, Gracie, you're hopeless!'

'I've got a better idea than researching on the internet,' Gracie's dad said. 'Let's drive up to Plimoth Plantation on the weekend. That's the place to find out about Wampanoag history and Thanksgiving. What do you say?'

Gracie stood up and went round the table to give her dad a big hug. 'Oh, thanks, Dad. Yes!'

▶ *What could Gracie write about her day in her diary?*

Looking at language

a) Complete the table with the verbs from the *if*-sentences in **4**:

if-clause	main clause
If you hadn't been …	…

b) What tense is used in the *if*-clause, what verb form in the main clause?

c) Explain the difference in meaning between these two sentences:
If the weather was nice, I would go out.
If the weather had been nice, I would have gone out.

▸ GF 2c: Conditional sentences 3 (p. 176) • P 5–8 (pp. 46–48) • WB 6–10 (pp. 22–24)

5 At Plimoth Plantation 🎧

In the car on Saturday, Gracie and her dad talked about Plimoth Plantation. He told her that it was a living-history museum with a Wampanoag village and an English colonists' village from the 1620s. 'Native Americans work there and tell visitors about Wampanoag life then and now.' He added that in the English village, the staff dressed and acted as if they really were 17th-century colonists.

At the Wampanoag village at Plimoth Plantation Gracie asked a member of staff lots of questions.

Gracie Are these Wampanoag houses the village of Patuxet?
Staff No, no. Everyone in Patuxet died or went away before the English came. This was just one family's home.
Gracie So why did this family live next to the English colonists?
Staff They were keeping an eye on them. The Wampanoag chief Massasoit wanted to know what the English were doing.
Gracie Oh, right. So, did the English invite this Wampanoag family to the First Thanksgiving?
Staff The First Thanksgiving? You mean the harvest celebration in 1621?
Gracie Yes, right. I have to give a presentation on it at school.
Staff Maybe they did invite them. Maybe they didn't. If you're interested in that first harvest celebration, go back to the visitor center. There's an exhibition on it there. Don't miss the movie. It shows what really happened.
Gracie That sounds great. Thanks!

But first Gracie went to the English village.

Gracie Are you one of the Pilgrims?
Staff Pilgrims? We call ourselves Saints and our church the Church of Saints – though not everyone here in Plymouth is a member of our church.
Gracie Yes, OK, but did you come here on the *Mayflower*?
Staff Indeed, I came on that brave ship.
Gracie Why did you build your village here? This belonged to the Wampanoag.
Staff We found no Indians here and this was a most hopeful place for our plantation. It has fish, good water and soil. Walk around and you will see we use the land better than the Indians.

▶ Who answers Gracie's questions as a modern person? Who answers as someone from the 1620s? How can you tell?

6 Extra Now you

What do you know about the historical heritage of your area? Where did you find out about it? How and where could you find out more?

▶ P 9 (p. 48) • WB 11 (p. 25)

7 I can do it now 🎧

Back home in Mashpee on Saturday evening, Gracie's mother wanted to know all about Plimoth Plantation. 'I haven't gone there for a very long time.'

'It's a cool place, Mom,' said Gracie.

'So what did you find out?' Mrs James asked.

'Well, I asked a lot of questions …' Gracie began.

'Like what?'

'Like, I asked one guide whether the Wampanoag houses were the village of Patuxet. But she said they had just been one family's home.'

'Yes, that's right,' her mother said.

'So I asked her why this family had lived next to the English colonists. You know why?' Mrs James shook her head.

'They were keeping an eye on the English for the Wampanoag in the area. You know, finding out what the English were doing. Anyway, then I started thinking about my presentation. So I wanted to know if the English had invited those Wampanoag to the First Thanksgiving. You know, the harvest celebration the Pilgrims had. She was really helpful and that was when she gave me the best tip.'

'Which was?'

'She told me to go back to the visitor center.'

'And?'

'They have a whole exhibition on the first Thanksgiving there. She told me not to miss the movie. She was right. It was really interesting. And I got this booklet too. So maybe I can give the presentation now.'

▶ What does Gracie's mother find out from her daughter?

Looking at language

a) Look at these questions from **5** on page 40 and at how Gracie reports them in **7**.
– Are these Wampanoag houses the village of Patuxet?
– Why did this family live next to the English colonists?
– Did the English invite this Wampanoag family to the First Thanksgiving?

Write her indirect questions down in a table next to the direct questions. What changes do you notice?

Direct questions	Indirect questions
Are these Wampanoag … ?	I asked one guide whether …

b) Look at these two sentences from **5** on page 40. How does Gracie report them in **7**?
Go back to the visitor center.
Don't miss the movie.

8 👥 Now you

a) Find the questions Gracie asks at the English village in **5** on p. 40 and report what she asked.
– Are you one of the Pilgrims?
– Gracie wanted to know if/whether he …
She asked …

b) Ask three students in your class one question each. Note down their answers.
Now students report what other students asked them and say how they answered.
A: What did you do at the weekend?
B: I played football.
B: A asked me what I had done at the weekend.
A: B said she had played football.

▶ GF 3: Indirect speech (pp. 177–179) • P 10–14 (pp. 48–50) • WB 12–16 (pp. 25–27)

2 A-Section

9 We're still here 🎧

a) Below is part of a handout Gracie gave to the students in her class before she did her presentation. Use it to follow her presentation while you listen. Then put these headings for parts of her presentation into the right order.

1 Description of the celebration
2 More Wampanoag or English colonists?
3 The idea of Thanksgiving in America
4 Were Native Americans invited?

Harvest celebration 1621
Gracie James, 25 November

The usual story	The whole story	Your notes
• 1621: the first Thanksgiving in America	• Much older Wampanoag tradition of giving thanks	
• Colonists invited Indians.	• Nobody knows if Wampanoag were invited.	
• Only a few Indians came.	• 90 Wampanoag, but only 50 colonists	
• Just one dinner together	• Wampanoag stayed for 3 days: meals/entertainment/politics.	

b) Listen a second time and find out
1 for what things the Wampanoag give thanks,
2 why people believe the Wampanoag were invited to the harvest celebration,
3 how we know that 90 Wampanoag came,
4 what food the Wampanoag brought,
5 where they stayed and what they did.

c) Read the Study Skills box on the right. Which type of handout does Gracie use?

d) What do you think of Gracie's handout? How can she make it even better?

e) `Extra` At the end of her presentation, Gracie makes another point that is not on her handout. Listen to it again, take notes. Then write it down as an extra point for Gracie's handout.

> **STUDY SKILLS** | **Handouts**
>
> **Why use a handout?**
> • A handout you give listeners **before** your presentation can help them follow it more easily. Use short notes and key words.
>
> • A handout you give listeners **after** your presentation will help them to remember it better. Use complete sentences.
>
> **How do you make a good handout?**
> • Give your handout a title.
> • Put your name and a date on it.
> • Give sources for material you use.

▶ SF Handouts (p. 160) • P 15–16 (pp. 50–51) •
Text File 4 (pp. 140–142) • WB 17–18 (pp. 27–28)

A-Section 2

Extra | **Background File** | **MASSACHUSETTS**

1 From British colony to independent state – important dates and events

1620 101 men, women and children arrive from Plymouth, England, on the *Mayflower* and found a colony at the empty Wampanoag village of Patuxet. They call their colony Plymouth.

1630 Puritans found the Massachusetts Bay Colony. It grows quickly, governs itself and is almost like an independent state.

1675/6 British settlers defeat the Wampanoag and other Native Americans in "Metacom's War". As a consequence, settlers begin to move into Native American lands.

1750 In the 17th and 18th centuries more and more settlers arrive. As a result, by 1750 there are 13 British colonies in North America.

1760s The British Parliament places new taxes on its colonies in America. The colonists react angrily, because they have no representatives in Parliament. 'No taxation without representation,' many say and refuse to buy British goods. Tax collectors are attacked.

1770 The Boston Massacre: British soldiers fire on a crowd of angry Bostonians and kill five people.

1773 The Boston Tea Party: as a protest against a British tax on tea, colonists throw 45 tons of tea into Boston Harbour. This leads to the occupation of the city by the British army.

1775 British soldiers march from Boston to Lexington to arrest American leaders. They are warned and escape. The first shots are fired in the American Revolutionary War.

1776 Declaration of Independence: representatives of the 13 British colonies declare their independence from Britain as the "United States of America".

1778 France joins the war on the American side.

1781 The Battle of Yorktown: the Americans win the last important battle of the American Revolutionary War.

The *Mayflower* in Plymouth Harbour

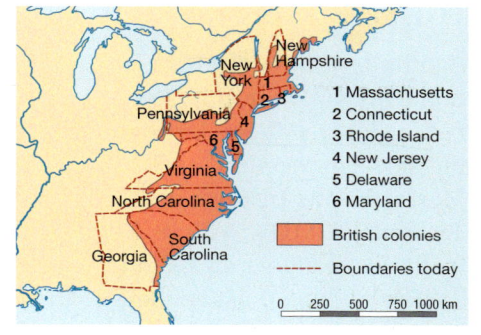

British colonies in America, 1750
1 Massachusetts
2 Connecticut
3 Rhode Island
4 New Jersey
5 Delaware
6 Maryland

The Boston Massacre

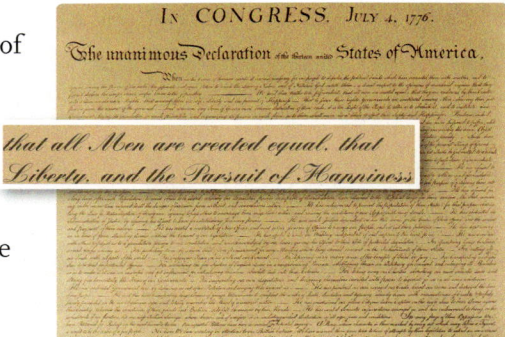

The Declaration of Independence

2 Massachusetts today

Size:	27,337 sq. km
Population:	6.4 million
Capital and largest city:	Boston 590,000
Highest mountain:	Mount Greylock 3,491 feet (1,064 m)
Economy:	important areas are higher education, biotechnology, finance, health care, tourism

THE BRAIN STATE

Cambridge, Massachusetts, is home of two of the USA's most famous universities: **Harvard**, the oldest in the USA, and the **Massachusetts Institute of Technology (MIT)**. With its 35 institutes of higher education, the Boston area must be the brainiest place in the USA.

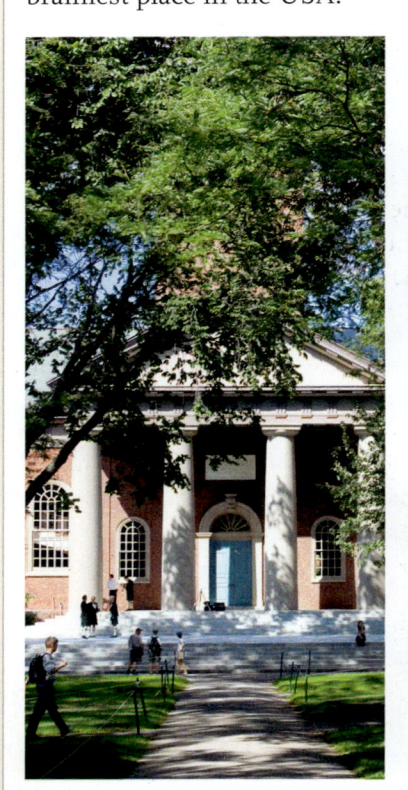

Harvard University

BOSTON SPORTS

Boston, the capital and largest city in Massachusetts, at the centre of a metropolitan area with a population of 4.4 million, is home to many professional sports teams:
the **Boston Bruins** (ice hockey),
the **Boston Celtics** (basketball),
the **Boston Red Sox** (baseball),
the **New England Revolution** (soccer) and the **New England Patriots** (American football)

Ice hockey

American football

CAPE COD

Only 230,000 people live on Cape Cod in the winter, but the population explodes in the summer, when millions of visitors come for the beaches, for fishing, whale watching and kayaking, for bike rides and beach walks, boating and golf.

Summer on a Cape Cod beach

👥 With a partner, choose an event, a date, a place, a picture, a text from page 43 or 44. Find out more about it and give a short presentation of about five minutes on it. Prepare a handout to go with your presentation. Decide whether to give out the handout before or after your presentation.

▶ WB 19 (p. 29)

1 WORDS Daily routines

a) Use the words and phrases and talk about Sarah and Tapenum's daily routines.

| Sarah Tapenum | cook
feed
⁺fetch
follow
go
have | hunt
learn
look after
make
⁺milk
play | prepare
put on
say
⁺shoot
tell | (a)
(her)
(herself)
(himself)
(his)
(the)
(their)
(…) | animals
bow and arrow
chickens
clothes
dinner
fish
fire
fishing
⁺for a run
hunting | goats
games
lessons
meal
⁺prayers
⁺secrets
to read
to write
⁺verse
water |

Sarah has her lessons in the evening.
Tapenum prepares for hunting.
…

b) What things from Sarah and Tapenum's daily routines do people still do today?

c) Extra Write five similar sentences about your daily routines.

2 WORDS History

a) 👥 On a piece of paper, make a timeline with five important dates from the history of your country/ your area/the world. Cut it into pieces and swap them with a partner. Can you put each other's timeline into the correct order? Check with your partner.

b) Complete the sentences with words or phrases from the box. Use the right form of the verbs.

> as a consequence/as a result • because of • cause • lead to/result in • the reason why

1. After Columbus reached America in 1492, European diseases … the deaths of millions of Native Americans.
2. The Pilgrims' first winter in America was very hard … the cold weather.
3. The Wampanoag showed the Pilgrims how to grow corn. That's … they had a very good harvest in 1621.
4. Stories about how rich America was … the arrival of many more European colonists.
5. …, Native Americans became very worried about all these new settlers.
6. This … war in the 1670s, when the native people thought that the Europeans were destroying their way of life.

3 REVISION I prefer … (Gerund)

a) Look at these pairs of activities. Which do you prefer? Write down five sentences. Think about your reasons.
1. give a presentation – have a class discussion
   I prefer giving a presentation to having …
2. celebrate my birthday with family – meet friends on my birthday
3. watch a DVD – go to the cinema
4. write an e-mail – send a text message
5. go to school by public transport – walk

b) Extra 👥 Make appointments with three partners. Compare your ideas and give reasons.
– I prefer doing a presentation to having a discussion because in a presentation, I know what to say.
– I don't agree. Doing a presentation is hard work. In a discussion the others talk a lot too.

2 Practice

4 REVISION What if …? (Conditional sentences 1 and 2)

a) Look at these two sentences. In which do they have a better chance of going hunting?
– If the weather is fine tomorrow, we'll go hunting.
– If the weather was fine tomorrow, we'd go hunting.

b) Complete the following sentences with the correct forms of the verb.
1 If Tapenum catches a lot of fish, his family … (have) enough food for a week.
   If Tapenum catches a lot of fish, his family will have enough food for a week.
2 He'd catch a turkey if he … (be) as strong as his father.
3 If Sarah learns to read and write, she … (be able to) read her mother's letters.
4 If people are rude in her classroom, Mrs Tripp … (get) angry.
5 If I lived in Plymouth, I … (go) to the Thanksgiving Parade.
6 If I ever go to the USA, I … (visit) Plymouth.
7 I … (be) very excited if I saw where the Pilgrims arrived.
8 If I met Gracie, I … (ask) her all about the Wampanoag.

c) **Extra** What would happen if you didn't do your homework today? Write three sentences. What would you do if your school was closed tomorrow? Write three sentences.

5 REVISION The empty village (Past perfect)

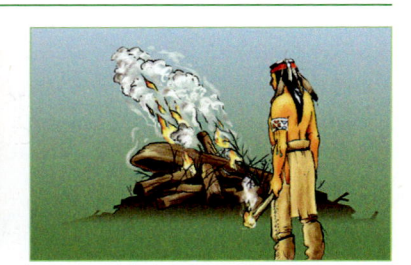

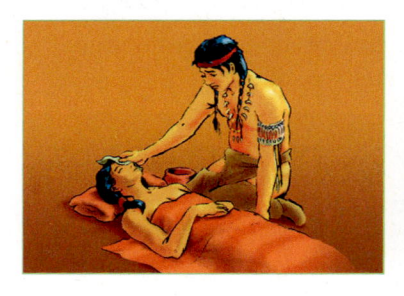

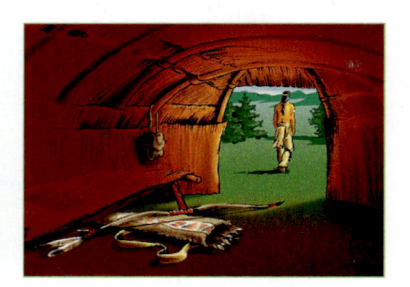

a) Imagine the Pilgrims have just arrived at Patuxet in 1620. The Wampanoag village is empty. Take turns and use the pictures to talk about what had happened before they arrived. Use the past perfect. These verbs will help:

destroy • die • disappear • hide • leave • look after

Before the Pilgrims arrived at Patuxet, …
1 … some of the Native Americans had …
2 …

b) **Extra** Think of one more thing that had happened before the Pilgrims arrived. Tell the class.

6 What would have been different? (Conditional sentences 3)

a) North America has changed a lot since European settlers came. Imagine what would have happened if they hadn't come. Complete the sentences. Use conditional sentences (type 3).
1. Christopher Columbus/not sail west – not find/a new continent
   If Christopher Columbus hadn't sailed west, he wouldn't have found a new continent.
2. Natives/not be/so friendly – they/kill/Columbus and his crew
3. Columbus/sail to North America – arrive/in New England
4. Columbus/arrive in New England – become/a Spanish colony
5. Europeans/not come to America – millions of Native Americans/not die/of European diseases
6. We/not know/corn and potatoes – Europeans/not find them/in America
7. Wampanoag/not show/Pilgrims/how to grow corn – they/all die/in their first winter
8. Patuxet/not be/empty – the Pilgrims/have to build/their village/somewhere else

b) Think about the history of where you live and of something important that happened there in the past. So what would have been different if …?
If Frederick II hadn't lived in Potsdam, he wouldn't have built Sanssouci there.

7 Game (Conditional sentences 3)

a) Choose one of the pictures and look at it for five minutes. Write down as many conditional sentences (type 3) as you can.
If the bag hadn't been so heavy, she wouldn't have fallen off her bike.

b) Now play in groups of 8–10. Divide each group into two teams (A and B). Choose one of the pictures to work with.
Team A begins. One student from team A makes a sentence with a conditional sentence (type 3). Then a student from team B must continue with a new conditional sentence. He or she must use the last part of team A's sentence. Teams get one point for each correct sentence with a conditional sentence.
– If the weather hadn't been nice, the two men wouldn't have driven into the mountains.
– If the two men hadn't driven into the mountains, …

8 REVISION WRITING I'm so ... (A personal e-mail)

When Gracie came home from school, she was still angry about the Social Studies lesson and wrote an e-mail to a friend. What did she write? Read page 39 again and write her e-mail. You might want to
– report what people said or did,
– give your opinions of what people said or did,
– describe your reactions.

Look at the box on the right for more help.

Hi ...,
I've just come home from school.
...
Gracie

> **Remember**
> **Tips for better writing:**
> • Brainstorm and structure your ideas.
> • Write a new paragraph for each new idea.
> • Make it interesting: use adjectives, adverbs, linking words, time phrases.
> • Check your e-mail and correct your mistakes.
> **Personal opinions and feelings:**
> In my opinion/view, ... • I think ... •
> The way I see it, ... • I still believe ... •
> I'm so ...

▶ SF Writing Course (pp. 168–169)

9 REVISION An English colonist (Indirect speech – statements)

a) On a trip to the USA you visit Plimoth Plantation. You meet Sarah, a young English colonist. She tells you about her life in 1620/21. Read what she says.
1 My parents and I came here because the people in England did not like our religion.
2 We lived in Holland before we came to New England.
3 We want to start a new life here.
4 The Indians here call themselves Wampanoag. I have met their chief, Massasoit.
5 The Wampanoag showed us how to catch fish.
6 I hope I can learn to read and write. Then I'll be able to send letters to my family in England.

b) After you return home, you tell a friend what Sarah told you. Use reporting verbs in the simple past, like *told me*, *said*, *explained*, ...
Sarah explained that her parents and she had come there ...

10 First days in a new country (Indirect speech – questions with question words)

At Plimoth Plantation, Gracie found out about the questions the English colonists had when they arrived in America. She reported them to her mother. How did she report them? Use reporting verbs in the simple past, like *asked*, *wanted to know*, ...
1 How can we survive here?
   The immigrants asked how they could survive here.
2 What vegetables grow here?
3 What is the weather like in winter?
4 Where can we build our first houses?
5 How can we keep in touch with our friends in England?
6 When will the next ship arrive?
7 How many Indians live near here?
8 What will we do if they attack us?

11 Other people's questions (Indirect speech – yes/no questions)

a) When Gracie was at Plimoth Plantation, other people asked questions too: her dad, other visitors, the staff. Read the questions and report them. Use reporting verbs in the simple past: **asked, wanted to know**. Remember the tense changes in indirect speech.

1 Gracie's dad asked whether Wampanoag houses …
2 Then he wanted to know if …
3 The other visitor …

b) Extra 👥 Think of three more yes/no-questions you could ask the staff at Plimoth Plantation. Swap with a partner and report your partner's questions to the class.
– Are you open on Thanksgiving Day?
– Thomas wanted to know if they were …

Gracie's dad:
- Are Wampanoag houses very warm in winter?
- Did you send my daughter to the Thanksgiving exhibition?

The other visitor:
- Do you still live in the traditional Wampanoag way?
- Is the Pilgrim village along this path?
- Could you tell us some more about Wampanoag history?
- Can we walk to the *Mayflower II*?

The staff member:
- Have you ever visited Plimoth Plantation before?
- Have you seen the Pilgrim village yet?
- Will you be in Plymouth for long?
- Do you want to learn how we make our canoes?
- Are you going to visit the *Mayflower II*?

12 It's a hard life (Indirect speech – commands and requests)

a) Young people have a hard time because everyone is always telling them what to do or what not to do. Report what the people told/asked/wanted this boy (not) to do.
1 **Teacher:** Don't forget your homework.
   His teacher told him not to …
2 **Mother:** Can you take out the rubbish before you go, please?
3 **Little sister:** Will you play with me now?
4 **Dad:** Don't sit in front of the computer for hours!
5 **Friends:** Come and play football with us.
6 **Girlfriend:** Don't spend all weekend with your friends.

b) What have people asked or told you to do this week? Report to the class.
– My brother asked me to give his e-mail address to a new girl in my class.

13 MEDIATION Wampanoag Immigration 🎧

As part of their visit to the Mayflower II at Plimoth Plantation, some German tourists have to go through 'Wampanoag Immigration'. Knut doesn't understand the immigration officer (IO). Marita helps him. What does she say? Listen to the CD and mediate for Knut.

IO   Where are you going to in Wampanoag Nation?
Knut   Was hat er gesagt?
Marita   Er will wissen, wohin du willst im Wampanoag-Gebiet.
Knut   Na ja, ich will nach Plymouth.
Marita   …

14 EVERYDAY ENGLISH SPEAKING Visiting tourist sights 🎧

a) How can you say it? Match the phrases on the left to the English questions on the right.
Du willst wissen,

1. wann eine Sehenswürdigkeit geöffnet ist;
2. ob sie jeden Tag offen ist;
3. wie man hinkommt;
4. ob man mit öffentlichen Verkehrsmitteln hinkommt;
5. wie viel der Eintritt kostet;
6. wie viel Zeit man normalerweise dort verbringt;
7. ob es Führungen gibt;
8. wie lange sie dauern.

A. Do they have guided tours? *no, but staff*
B. How long do people usually stay? *at least 3 h*
C. How long do the tours last? ✗ *4 h*
D. Are they open every day? ✓
E. How much are the tickets? *$20 $6 22 other*
F. What are the opening times? *9am–5pm*
G. Can you tell me how to get there, please? *Route 3, Exit 4, Signs*
H. Can we get there by public transport? ✓ *train, Taxi / Plymouth bus*

b) 👥 Listen to the CD and note down the information on Plimoth Plantation. Compare your answers with a partner.

c) 👥 Write a similar dialogue about a sight in your area. Act it out for the class.

15 STUDY SKILLS Making a handout 🎧

a) Listen to Mike's presentation on the First Thanksgiving and take notes.

b) 👥 Compare your notes with a partner's. Correct and expand them. Then listen again and revise your notes once more.

c) 👥 Produce a good handout to go with Mike's presentation.
– Look again at the Study Skills box on page 42 for ideas about good handouts.
– Decide whether you will make a handout for BEFORE or AFTER the presentation.
– Remember to give the handout a title, a date and to give your sources.
– Use the Skills File on page 160 for more ideas.

d) 👥👥 Get together with another pair and present your handout to them. Check the Skills File on page 160 and the Study Skills box on page 42 and give each other's handout points from 1 to 10 (1 = terrible, 10 = fantastic). Give reasons for your decision.

e) Extra 👥 Revise your handout with ideas from the other pair you worked with.

16 READING National Day of what? (Skimming and scanning)

Celebration and protest in America's hometown

Plymouth, Massachusetts calls itself 'America's Hometown' – after all, it's where Thanksgiving began. To celebrate, a Thanksgiving Parade is held there each year.

The Parade
The Thanksgiving Parade starts on Saturday morning and is greeted by thousands of "children of all ages" who line the streets and fill Cole's Hill. It aims to entertain but also to educate visitors about the story of the American Pilgrimage. Each float shows an event, a hero, a memory from America's history.
The parade and weekend of festivities has become a beloved holiday as well as an important link to our nation's history and heritage. Say some folks.

National Day of Mourning
Others haven't come to Plymouth to celebrate but to protest. Since 1970, they have held a National Day of Mourning there. How did it start?
In 1970, the Wampanoag leader Wamsutta Frank James was invited to give a speech at the Thanksgiving celebration in Plymouth. When the organizers saw his speech before the event, they did not like it at all. James was going to quote from a book one of the Pilgrims wrote. It described how the Pilgrims opened Indian graves, stole Indian food, sold Indians as slaves.

Protest
The organizers wanted to present a picture of friendship and respect between the Pilgrims and the Wampanoag. So they revised James's speech for him. James could not accept that, so he left with his supporters and went up to Cole's Hill. There, under the statue of Massasoit, the Wampanoag leader when the Pilgrims landed, he gave his original speech.

a) You have been looking for more information about Thanksgiving on the internet and have found this text. Skim it for 20 seconds. Does it help you? Say in no more than two sentences what it is about.

> **Remember**
>
> **Skimming** helps you find the main ideas of a text.
> • Read quickly – not word for word. Look at the first sentences of paragraphs and the last sentence of the text.
> • Look at titles, headings, words in **bold type**.

b) Now you know what the text is about and you want to look for more specific information. Scan the text – look for the key words from these questions. Is the information there?
1. Does it tell me anything about the **First Thanksgiving**?
2. How do they celebrate Thanksgiving in **Plymouth**?
3. What does the text tell me about the **parade**?
4. Why is there a **protest** in Plymouth on Thanksgiving Day?
5. Why is a **speech** important?
6. What else do I learn about the **history**?

> **Remember**
>
> **Scanning** helps you find specific information in a text.
> • Picture specific words and phrases in your mind.
> • Don't read. Move your eyes – over the page diagonally, across the page in an "S", up and down the page in a "U".

c) You cannot see the whole text here. From what you know about it so far – what do you think the rest of the text could be about?
For example, will it answer any unanswered questions from b)?

▶ SF Reading Course (p. 163)

I'm going to save my brother

(abridged/adapted from *My brother Sam is dead* by J L & C Collier)

Not all of the new words in this text are in the Dictionary at the back of this book. Use the techniques you have already learned to work out the meanings yourself. ▶ SF Reading Course (p. 163)

April, 1775, Redding, Connecticut

It was April, and outside in the dark the rain slammed against the windows of our tavern. We were having dinner, and everybody jumped when the door opened and hit the wall. My brother Sam was standing there, and he was wearing a uniform. Oh my, he looked proud.

'Sam,' my mother said. Sam was at college at Yale and we hadn't seen him since Christmas.

'Shut the door,' Father said, but Sam was too excited to listen.

'We've beaten the British in Massachusetts,' he shouted.

'Who has beaten the British?' Father said.

Sam shut the door. 'We have,' he said. 'The Minutemen. The damn Lobsterbacks—'

'By that I suppose you mean the soldiers of your King,' Father said.

Sam went red. 'All right, the British troops. From Boston. They marched up to Lexington. They were looking for Mr. Adams and the rest of our leaders, but they'd got away. Somebody signaled them from a church in Boston, so when the Lobst– British got to Lexington, there wasn't anybody there, only the Minutemen. Then the shooting started. Some men were killed, I don't know how many, and then the British went on up to some place called Concord. They didn't find very much and turned and started back to Boston. That was when the Minutemen really attacked them: they chased them all the way back home.'

After I went to bed that evening, I woke up in the middle of the night. Somebody was shouting downstairs. It was Sam.

'Sir, it's worth dying to be free.'

That made Father shout too. 'Free? Free to do what, Sam? Free to laugh at your King? To shoot your neighbor? Where have you been getting these ideas?'

'You don't understand, Father, you just don't understand. If they won't let us be free, we have to fight. Why should they get rich from our taxes back in England? They're 3,000 miles away, how can they make laws for us? They have no idea how things are here.'

'Sam, I will not have treason in my house. We are Englishmen, we are subjects of the King, this rebellion is the talk of madmen.'

'Father, I am not an Englishman, I am an American, and I am going to fight to keep my country free.'

'Oh God, Sam, fight? Is it worth war to save a few pence in taxes?'

'It's not the money, it's the principle.'

'Principle, Sam? You may know principle, Sam, but I know war. Have you ever seen a friend dead in the grass? I have, Sam, I have. I was at the Battle of Louisbourg against the French. Oh, it was a great victory. They celebrated it all over the colonies. And I carried my best friend's body back to his mother. Do you want to come home that way? Sam, it isn't worth it. Now take off that uniform and go back to college.'

'I won't, Father.'

They were silent. It was terrible.

'Go, Sam. Go. Get out of my sight. I can't look at you any more in that terrible costume. Get out. And don't come back until you are dressed as my son.'

'Father –'

'Go, Sam.'

Then the door slammed and I heard some funny sounds, sounds I'd never heard before. I went quietly downstairs. Father had his head down on the table, and he was crying. I'd never seen him cry before in my whole life; and I knew bad times were coming.

February, 1779, Redding, Connecticut

Four years later the war between the British and American armies has destroyed the country and left the people of Connecticut cold and hungry.

Mr Meeker, Tim and Sam's father, has died on a prison ship. Tim has had to grow up fast and now looks after the tavern with his mother. His brother, Sam, has returned to Redding with the American army for the winter. But Sam is in prison for stealing cattle from his family, a crime he did not commit. He has been sentenced to death.

Tim and his mother have tried to explain to General Putnam that Sam did not steal the cattle and asked the General to pardon him. But the general has said no. He needs the execution as an example to keep discipline among his troops.

We closed the tavern early that night. I pulled chairs up in front of the fire. 'We've got to think of something, Mother.'

'There's nothing,' she said. 'Let the dead bury the dead.'

'He isn't dead yet, Mother. He's still alive.'

'He's dead, Tim,' she said. 'He's dead as your father is.'

'No,' I said. I got up and took father's bayonet down from the wall.

Mother didn't lift her eyes from the fire. 'Going to get yourself killed, son?'

'I'm going to save my brother,' I said.

'No, you're not,' she said in a soft whisper. 'No, you're going to get yourself killed.'

I stared at her. Then I turned and went out the door.

The moonlight on the fields of snow was almost as bright as daylight. When I came to the line of trees above the camp, I dropped down and ran from tree to tree. At the last tree, I stopped and stared down. About a hundred yards below were the huts of the army camp.

The prison hut was right in front of me. I stared at it – the little hut just like the others was surrounded by a ten-foot-high fence. There was a guard at the corner of the fence.

I still hadn't made any plan, but about the only thing I could do was go down there from tree to tree, open the gate and let the prisoners out. And if the guard saw me first, I could throw the bayonet over the fence and hope that Sam could get away in the confusion. It wasn't a great plan, but it was the only one I could think of.

I began to go down the hill. I kept an eye on the guard. He didn't seem to be looking around. When the fence was only fifty feet away, I stared at him. He didn't move for several moments. He was leaning on his gun, with his head down, and I suddenly realized that he was asleep. I took the bayonet out and held it in my hand. My heart was pounding, I was breathing fast and my hand was shaking.

Then I stood up and charged into the moonlight. My feet went crunch, crunch in the snow. The guard moved a little. I ran faster. He lifted his head suddenly and stared at me, as if he was still half asleep. I ran on. 'Halt,' he shouted. He lifted his gun. I was twenty feet away.

I stopped. 'Sam,' I shouted, and 'Sam' again as loud as I could. The guard came towards me. I threw the bayonet into the air. It flashed in the moonlight and went over the fence. Then I turned and began running as fast as I could across the snow towards the safety of the trees on the hill. I had only gone three steps when the gun went off with a terrific roar. I felt something pull at my shoulder and I ran up the hill. I went from tree to tree. Behind me there was shouting and running. Another gun went off, and then another. Something hit a tree somewhere near me. When I reached the trees at the top, I threw myself down. They would never get me now. They couldn't come up here on horses, and I was too far away, they couldn't catch me on foot. I looked down. Men were running everywhere and people were shouting.

I stared into the prison. There was no action there, there were no people at all. Something shiny shone in the moonlight on the snow. And I knew it had all been a waste. The prisoners weren't in the prison any more. They had been moved. I held my shoulder where it was bleeding a little and ran all the way home.

Mother refused to go to the execution. I went. I knew that Sam would want somebody there, and somebody would have to take the body.

The execution was going to take place on a hill west of the camp. A crowd was already up there. I waited down the road until some soldiers came by. First came the drummers. Then the troops and then Sam in a cart. His hands were tied behind his back and there was a rope around his neck too that was tied to the cart. Behind him were more soldiers. 'Sam,' I shouted as he went by.

He looked around at me. His face was white but he gave me a smile – not much of one, but a smile.

I ran up to the crowd and began to push my way through. When people saw who it was they let me through. I pushed my way up near the front of the crowd.

They brought Sam out from somewhere in a group of soldiers. They pushed him into an empty space. He had a sack over his head. A minister said a prayer. I tried to pray myself, but my mouth was dry and I couldn't get the words out. Three soldiers stepped in front of Sam and raised their guns. I heard myself scream, 'Don't shoot him, don't shoot him.' I never heard the guns roar.

1826, Wilkes-Barre, Pennsylvania

I have written this story down in this year 1826, on our nation's fiftieth birthday, to remember the short life of my brother Samuel Meeker, who died 47 years ago in the service of his country.

It will be, I am sure, a great country. Free of the British, the nation has become rich and I with it. Father said, 'In war the dead pay the debts of the living' and they have paid us well. But even 50 years later, I keep thinking that there might have been another way, instead of war, to achieve the same end.

Working with the text

1 Understanding the story
Complete the sentences.

1775
1. Sam arrives home and describes …
2. Later, Sam and his father argue about … Sam thinks … His father thinks …

1779
3. Sam's brother Tim wants to …
4. His mother thinks …
5. Tim tries to … but he cannot because …
6. … goes to the execution, … does not …

1826
7. Tim has written the story because …
8. Since the war, the country …

▶ WB 20 (p. 30) • Checkpoint 2 WB (p. 31) • Selbsteinschätzung 1–2 WB (pp. 32–33)

2 Letters
Take notes and write one of these letters:
– Mr Meeker to his son Sam after their argument
– Sam to his family while he is in prison

3 Times of war
Sam did not steal his family's cattle but was sentenced to death for it. Explain what this tells you about this time of war.

4 Extra Another way
Read the last sentence of the story again. Think of 'another way, instead of war' the British and Americans could have solved their problem.

How am I doing?

a) *Fill in or choose the correct answers.*

American History

1. Explain what these are:
   a) the *Mayflower*   b) Patuxet
   c) Massasoit   d) the Wampanoag
2. The Pilgrims arrived in America in
   A 1776   B 1621   C 1620   D 1607
3. At the 'First Thanksgiving' they were celebrating
   A the Pilgrims' new village   B catching turkeys for dinner   C their first harvest
4. There were more Wampanoag than Pilgrims at the celebration. Right or wrong?

Words

5. At Thanksgiving, Americans often eat a ... dinner.
6. The Pilgrims learned how to grow ... from Native Americans.
   A bananas   B corn   C rice   D fruit
7. The people who work at a museum are
   A colonists   B natives   C staff   D visitors
8. I did it wrong, so it's my ...
9. If you watch somebody, you ... an eye on them.
   A have   B keep   C make   D put
10. The staff member answered lots of questions. She was really help...
11. We'll never get out of here. Our situation is hope...
12. Europeans brought their diseases with them to America. ... many Native Americans died.
    A As a result   B Because of

Grammar

13. If Gracie had kept quiet, she ... do a presentation.
    A had not to   B would not have to
    C would not have had to
14. If the Wampanoag ... them, the Pilgrims would not have survived their first winter.
    A did not help   B had not helped
    C would not help
15. Report Gracie's questions. Be careful with your tenses.
    a) 'Is this the Wampanoag village of Patuxet?' She wanted to know ... this ... the Wampanoag village of Patuxet.
    b) 'Did Massasoit live here?'
       She asked ... Massasoit ... there.
    c) 'How many natives came to the First Thanksgiving?'
       She asked ... natives ... to the First Thanksgiving.
    d) 'Why was Patuxet empty?'
       She wanted to know ... Patuxet ... empty.
16. Report what the staff member told Gracie.
    a) 'You should go and look at the Thanksgiving exhibition.'
       She told Gracie ... the Thanksgiving exhibition.
    b) 'Don't forget to watch the movie.'
       She told her ... the movie.

Skills

17. If you want people to remember it better, you give them a handout ... the presentation.
    A before   B after

b) *Check your answers on p. 132 and add up your points.*

c) *If you had 19 or more points, well done! Maybe you can help students who had fewer points. If you had 18 points or fewer, it's a good idea to do some more work before you go on to the next unit. Where did you make mistakes? The chart below will tell you what you can do to improve your English.*

No.	Area	Find out more	Exercise(s)
1– 4	American history	Unit 2	WB 1, 2, 18, 19 (pp. 20, 21, 28, 29)
5–12	Words	Unit vocabulary (pp. 201–207)	P 1–2 (p. 45), P 14 (p. 50), WB 3, 9 (pp. 21, 24)
13–16	Grammar	GF 2–3 (p. 175–179)	P 6–7 (p. 47), P 10–12 (pp. 48–49), WB 4–7, 11–14 (pp. 22–23, 25–26)
17	Skills	Unit 2 (p. 42), SF (p. 160)	P 15 (p. 50), WB 17 (p. 27)

Unit 3
California, land of dreams

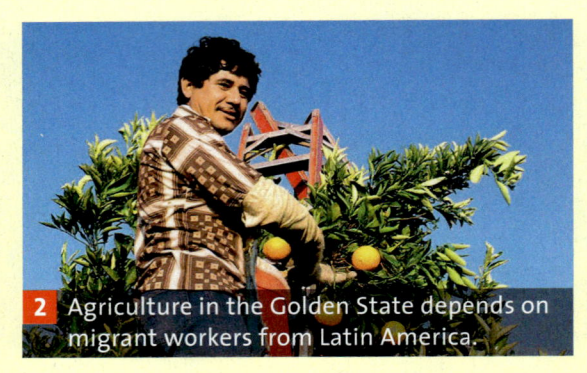

1 Arnold Schwarzenegger: Governor + Terminator = Governator

2 Agriculture in the Golden State depends on migrant workers from Latin America.

3 Some Californian cities have a huge homeless problem.

4 Asian culture is alive and kicking in California.

1 California and you
What do you think of when you hear the name 'California'? Brainstorm your ideas on the board.

2 Captions
a) Look at the photos. Which of your ideas from 1 are illustrated? Which are not?

b) With a partner, write captions for pictures 5–11. Don't write single words. The box below will help you.

> a big danger to • admire • centre • cliff • creative • expensive houses • forests • Hollywood Boulevard • homes • huge waterfall • innovation & technology • National Park • rich people • ride the waves • scenery • Silicon Valley • stars • surfing • walk along • wildfires • wildlife

c) **Extra** *Choose a photo and describe what it tells you about California. For photos with people in them, imagine what they are thinking and what California means to them.*

3 Extra Two songs 🎧
Read the lyrics below. Compare what they say about California. Explain how they are connected to the photos on these pages. Then listen to the songs.

Gone to California
Goin' to California, yes
To resurrect my soul
The sun is always shining
Or at least that's what I'm told
Goin' to California
There's a better life for me
Goin' to California
I'll write and tell you what I see
Goin' to California
Somebody say a prayer for me
by Alecia Moore and Linda Perry

Earthquakes and sharks
Earthquakes and sharks to start us off,
If Chupacabras ain't enough,
Black widow spiders and killer bees,
There ain't no shade, there ain't no trees.
Hot desert heat, polluted air,
And traffic jams beyond compare.
That's all I got to warn ya 'bout Mexico and California.
by Brandtson

▶ P 1 (p. 64) • WB 1–2 (p. 34)

3 A-Section

All about ... growing up in two cultures

1 Who lives in California and the USA?

Look at the two charts on the population of California and of the whole of the USA. What do you notice about them? Compare the two.

In the USA the majority of people are ...
In California ... not the majority.
The largest minority in the USA/California is ...
... % of the population of ... are ...
More/Fewer people in ... are ... than in ...

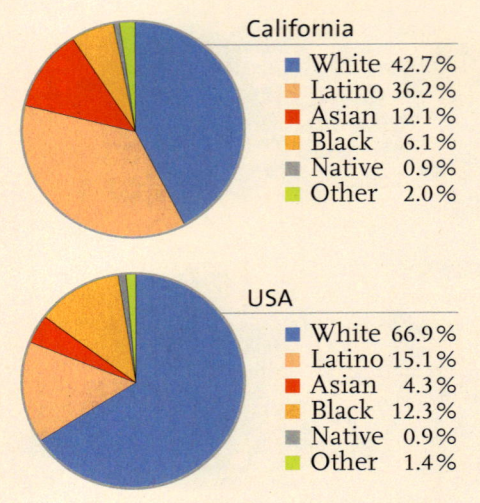

California
- White 42.7%
- Latino 36.2%
- Asian 12.1%
- Black 6.1%
- Native 0.9%
- Other 2.0%

USA
- White 66.9%
- Latino 15.1%
- Asian 4.3%
- Black 12.3%
- Native 0.9%
- Other 1.4%

(2007; U.S. Census Bureau estimate)

2 Online forum

A Californian website for teenagers has a forum about attitudes towards immigrants and minorities. Here are some of the comments on the forum.

Larry K., San Francisco
I'm Korean and we speak Korean at home. When I started school, I was useless at English. So I was teased a lot by the other kids. Asians believe in a good education so my parents told me to work hard in school. I did. Now I get good grades in English and most other subjects.

American Gal, Los Angeles
I'm not prejudiced against immigrants, and I would never discriminate against them. Larry, you got it right: if somebody wants to live in this country, they have to learn English, share our values, and act like real Americans!

Larry K., San Francisco
Hey American Gal, I guess you only speak English. Poor you! I'm growing up in two cultures and speak two languages. That's a big advantage I have over you and it will help me to be successful at what I do.

Luis M., San Clemente
I agree with Larry K. I'm proud to be a Latino. It's not a disadvantage. It means I'm bilingual like many people in California, so I can get along in the Latino and the Anglo worlds.

Hot Salsa, Fresno
Not all Latinos are bilingual, Luis. Round here lots of Mexican immigrants only speak Spanish, especially the "illegals". They get along because Spanish is spoken most places they go. But it's hard to find a good job if you only speak Spanish.

Luis M., San Clemente
Yeah, Salsa, I know that but I still feel very lucky to live in America – everybody can succeed here if they have the right attitude.

Hot Salsa, Fresno
Get real, Luis! Relations between Latinos and Anglos may be great in San Clemente, but not everywhere. There's lots of discrimination and prejudice in our country.

> Who is growing up in two cultures? Who isn't? Explain how you know. What do you think American Gal means by 'real Americans'? Name pros and cons of growing up in two cultures that are mentioned. Who is most/least positive about the good sides?

▶ GF 4a–b: Passive (p. 179) • P 2–6 (p. 64–66) • WB 3–7 (pp. 35–37)

3 Californian strawberries 🎧

After Luis Morales had put a second message on the forum website, he left the library and went home. He wanted to do a school assignment before his younger brother and sister, Diego and Maria, came home. So he took out his Geography book.

Geography Today 63

The strawberry industry

Like most food, strawberries are grown on large industrial farms. Over 85% of strawberries in the US come from California and they are one of the most important crops in the state. Read about how the plants are grown:
1 Before the strawberries can be grown, the fields must be prepared. They are sprayed with insecticide and covered with plastic.
2 After they have been planted, the strawberry plants will also be protected from insects by biological methods. Then less insecticide is necessary.
3 Strawberries are often picked by migrant workers from Mexico.

'Migrant workers from Mexico,' Luis thought. 'Just like Mamá and Papá when they first came to California. That farmer gave them their first jobs. What was his name?'

Luis couldn't remember. His parents were illegal immigrants then. They were given their first jobs by a fruit farmer. It was a hard life as migrant workers. They were paid very little and had to move from place to place for work.

Suddenly loud voices interrupted Luis's thoughts. Maria and Diego were home.

Maria wanted a soda and there weren't any more in the fridge. Diego had been given an English assignment and wanted some help. Luis closed his book. His assignment would have to wait.

> What do you find good/bad/surprising about how strawberries are grown in California? Are insecticides or biological methods used in Germany? Do migrant workers work on farms?

Looking at language

a) On the page from Luis's Geography book, find examples of passive sentences in the **present perfect** and **will-future** and with **can** and **must**.
After they have been planted, …
Explain how the passive is formed in these sentences.

b) Write down this active sentence from **3**:
That farmer gave them their first jobs.
Underline the subject and the two objects – the direct object and the indirect object.

c) Now look at this passive sentence:
They were given their first jobs by a fruit farmer.
What is the subject here? What has happened to the two objects of the active sentence?
Translate the sentence into German. What do you notice about the subject of the English and the subject of the German sentence?

d) Find more passive sentences like this one in the second part of **3**.

▶ GF 4: Passive (pp. 179–181) • P 7–11 (pp. 66–68) • WB 8–12 (pp. 37–39)

4 How was your day?

Mrs Morales had taken the bus from Avenida Pico in San Clemente to the wealthy suburb of Talega at 7 o'clock that morning. Now, after she had cleaned and cooked in two houses, she sat on the bus taking her back to San Clemente. It was six o'clock when she got off the bus at Bonita Park. She stopped at the supermarket on Calle Campo. She had to hurry: today was one of the three days a week when she had a third job in the evening – as a waitress.

She opened the front door and called out to the little girl and boy playing on the floor. 'Hi!'

Maria ran to her. 'Mamá! You're back!'

Mrs Morales carried her daughter over to the sofa. Diego followed. Luis looked over from the table covered with his books. 'Hey, Mom!' he said.

'Hola, hijo mío. How was your day?'

'Oh, OK, I guess,' Luis answered.

'I got an assignment from my English teacher, Mom,' Diego said. 'Luis said he'd help me when he's finished his homework.'

'Thank you, Luis. Oh, look at the time. I have to leave again soon. I must make your supper.'

'First a story, Mamá,' cried Maria. 'The story about you and Papá when you came across the border to California.'

'Yes,' Diego nodded, 'tell us that story, again, Mom. Please.'

'First supper,' said their mother. 'Then, if there's time, our story.'

> Describe Mrs Morales's day. Why do you think she has three jobs? What do you notice about the place and street names?

Americana ★ ★ ★

The border

The border between the USA and Mexico runs 2,100 miles from San Diego, California, in the west, to Brownsville, Texas, in the east. Along parts of the border the USA has built a high fence – with warning signs – to stop illegal immigrants. However, thousands of Mexican immigrants still cross the border illegally every year with hopes of a better life in the USA. Many are caught by the US Border Patrol; and many die when they try to cross, often from the heat or cold of the desert or by drowning in rivers and canals. Almost half of all Mexican immigrants, i.e. 3.8 million, live in California. Most legal and illegal Mexican immigrants work in agriculture and the manufacturing industry.

5 The story

a) What do you think might happen in Mrs Morales's story? Write down one or two ideas.

b) Make a table with the **5 Ws** and **how?**. Then listen to the story and take notes in the table.

c) Exchange information with your partner. Then listen again to check and maybe add missing information.

d) What information do you think Mrs Morales leaves out of her story? Explain why.

▶ GF 5: Participles (pp. 181–182) • P 12–14 (pp. 69–70) • **Text File 5** (pp. 143–145) • WB 13–14 (p. 40)

6 The San Clemente Clean Ocean Program

San Clemente, with its five miles of white sand beaches, is one of the best places to surf in California, so Luis's school offers surfing classes. During one class, Luis and the other kids noticed lots of rubbish on the water. After class, the coach told them to find out about the city's *Clean Ocean Program*. This flyer showed them how to help. Now they clean a local beach once a month and deliver flyers on the *Clean Ocean Program* to San Clemente homes.

San Clemente CLEAN OCEAN PROGRAM

Keeping Your Beaches and Ocean Clean

The San Clemente Clean Ocean Program is one of the best ways to stop storm drain pollution from flowing into the ocean. In the past four years, over 4,000 tons of garbage have been prevented from reaching the ocean. That would fill 230 giant dumpsters! Do you want to help? Well, we want you to help us. Check out www.sccleanocean.org or call us at (949) 361-6143 and we will tell you when, where and how to keep San Clemente's beaches and ocean clean.

16¢ a day from every homeowner helps San Clemente to:
- reduce bacteria on Poche and North Beaches
- repair the storm drain system
- collect 50 tons of garbage per month from the streets
- test water quality all over the city
- clean local beaches
- print environmental articles and ads in local papers

> Explain what the Clean Ocean Program is about and why and how Luis's class helps. Are there programmes like this in your area?

Looking at language

a) Look at these sentences from **6**:
Do you want to help?
Well, we want you to help us.
How is **want to** used differently in them?
Now find more examples of verb + object + infinitive with the verbs **tell** and **help**.

b) Look at this sentence from **6**:
This flyer showed them how to help.
Now find another example of an infinitive after a question word.
Look at the infinitive constructions again. How do you say them in German?

7 Now you

a) Ask for advice from your partner and give them advice.
A: I don't know what to do with my old computer.
B: You should take it to the recycling centre.

b) **Extra** How can you help to keep your city clean? Say what you would like people/the city/… to do.
I'd like everyone to pick up their own rubbish. I want our class to …

▶ GF 6: to-infinitive (pp. 182–183) • P 15–17 (pp. 70–71) • WB 15–18 (pp. 41–42)

Extra | **Background File** | **WELCOME TO CALIFORNIA!**

From 1769 to 1848 California was first a **Spanish colony** and then a **province of Mexico**. The USA won California from Mexico in the **Mexican-American War** (1846–48). The discovery of gold there in 1848 attracted hundreds of thousands of people from the East and all over the world to California in the **Gold Rush**. In 1850 California became the 31st state of the USA – the **Golden State**.

The 31st state is, in many ways, one of the first states. It is third in area (411,015 sq km), first in population (36.45 million in 2006), and first in wealth – if California was an independent country, it would have the seventh-largest economy in the world.

What makes it rich? Its wealth comes from
- its **natural resources** (oil, gas, sand, etc.),
- **agriculture** (fruit, vegetables, flowers, wine, dairy),
- **electronics** (computers, software),
- **entertainment** (films, TV),
- **tourism** (so let's go on a little tour now …).

Let's go to San Francisco …

… where you can see the Golden Gate Bridge, gateway to the Pacific Ocean, watch the sea lions at Fisherman's Wharf, take a ride on a cable car up the city's steep hills, visit the famous prison island of Alcatraz, or enjoy a stroll and some great food in one of the ethnic neighbourhoods, like Chinatown, Japantown or the Mission. Don't forget to visit the Haight-Ashbury district where 'Flower Power' and the hippies were born in 1967's 'Summer of Love'. A short drive south of the city takes you to Silicon Valley, not only the centre of the computer world, but also the major hub of high-tech innovation in America's economy.

… where the earth moves …

San Francisco and large parts of California can really shake you up sometimes – in an earthquake. In 1906 around 3,000 people were killed by the great earthquake, magnitude 7.8, and the fire that followed it. Almost three quarters of San Francisco's population became homeless. Fewer people (57) died in the 6.9-magnitude 1989 earthquake but the damage was about $6 billion.

Californians learn the code:
'Drop, cover and hold on!'
- drop down under a heavy table
- cover your eyes
- hold onto something

... or to the world-famous Sequoia National Park ...

... where the world's largest trees, the giant sequoias grow ... and grow ... and grow. The biggest of them is the General Sherman at 1,489 m³. There are many beautiful National Parks in California. You can go from the fierce summer heat of Death Valley NP to the majestic cliffs and waterfalls of Yosemite NP, or from the bird and sea life of Point Reyes National Seashore to the mud pots and boiling pools of Lassen Volcanic NP. And Sequoia NP proves that things in America are bigger than everywhere else!

General Sherman Tree

... and maybe end up in Los Angeles.

It's the largest city in California (second-largest in the US) and it has a very famous suburb: Hollywood, also known as 'The Dream Factory.' The first Hollywood movie was made in 1910. The sunshine and the wonderful locations (sea, mountains, desert) brought the movie makers and the stars to LA, and Hollywood has dominated the world of films and TV ever since.

Statements:
1. If I lived in California, I'd like to live in ... because ...
2. What surprises me most about California is ... because ...
3. The place I'd most like to visit in California is ... because ...
4. What I don't like about California is ... because ...

1 Four corners

a) Write each statement on the right on an A3 piece of paper. Hang one in each corner of your classroom.

b) Choose the two statements which interest you most. How could you finish them? Note down your ideas.

c) Go to one corner and exchange your ideas with at least three different partners. Take notes. Then go to your second corner and do the same.

d) Use your notes and write a short text about what you find most interesting. Put your text in your DOSSIER. ▶ WB 19 (p. 43)

3 Practice

1 WORDS Synonyms

a) Find a word or phrase in the second box that means the same as a word in the first box, e.g. *also – too*.

> afraid • also • awful • close • correct • difficult • film • great • kid • leave • loud • now • sad • start

> at the moment • begin • child • fantastic • go away • hard • movie • near • noisy • right • scared • terrible • too • unhappy

b) Choose five words from any of the boxes and make sentences with them.
e.g. *We had a great time in our summer holidays.*

c) 👥 Read your sentences to your partner. She/He replaces the word with its synonym.
A: We had a great time in our summer holidays.
B: We had a fantastic time in our summer holidays.

d) **Extra** Choose three words from each box and try to write one sentence that uses all of them and still makes sense.

2 WORDS Word building (-ful, -less)

> You can make new English adjectives if you add a suffix like -ful or -less to the end of a word:
> hope**ful** = full of hope
> hope**less** = without hope
> Be careful: some words can be used
> – with both suffixes (help, hope, pain, use)
> – only with -ful (beauty, hate, success),
> – only with -less (home, job, time).

a) Add suffixes to the nouns in brackets above. Think of as many nouns as you can that go with each new adjective and write them down.
helpful: a helpful friend, a helpful book
helpless: a helpless baby, helpless animals

b) Add the right suffix to these words. Be careful: check in a dictionary.

> age • bottom • end • event • forget • head • sleep

Then complete the sentences below.
1 I'm so tired – I've had a ... night.
2 Ben never stops talking. I hate his ... stories.
3 I must make a shopping list, I'm so ...
4 In the Harry Potter books I really like the ghost called Nearly ... Nick.
5 She is 60 but still looks so young. She seems ...
6 They fell down and down the ... hole.
7 So much happened yesterday. It was a very ... day.

3 WORDS Minorities and ethnic groups

Look back at A1 and A2 on p. 58 and find the right English expressions.

1 People who come to live in your country are ...
2 Find two collocations with *attitude*.
3 Find the opposite of *minority*.
4 Someone who can speak two languages is ...
5 Find the English for *in zwei Kulturen aufwachsen*.
6 If somebody is not allowed to be in a country but is there, they are called ...
7 Find a collocation with *discriminate*.
8 Which noun comes from *discriminate*?
9 Find an adjective that comes from *prejudice* and a collocation with that adjective.

4 WRITING More on 'Growing up in two cultures' (Writing a comment on a website)

a) Add your own comment to the forum on the website for Californian teenagers on page 58. Start with your internet name and where you come from. Explain what comment you are commenting on, what you agree or disagree with and why.

> Minorkid, Cologne, Germany
> I disagree with Larry K. I don't live in the United States, but I am a member of an ethnic minority too. He thinks working hard at school will make him successful. My brother did that, got good grades but cannot get a job because he's not white.

b) Proofread your comment and correct any mistakes you find. Then write out your comment on a transparency and ask your classmates to look for more mistakes.

c) Extra In a group, continue the forum. Read each other's comments from b) and write your own reactions to them. Then add your comments and reactions to your DOSSIER.

5 REVISION What came first? (Passive – simple past)

a) Partner B: Go to p. 130.
Partner A: Look at each pair of events. Think about which came first.
Then use the passive and tell your partner what you think:

1
- Eiffel Tower (build)
- first car (make)

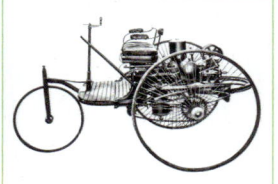

2
- America (discover) by Columbus
- China (visit) by Marco Polo

A: I think the Eiffel Tower was built before the first car was made.
B: That's right. / No, that's wrong. The first car was made in ..., and the Eiffel Tower was ...

3
- the Mona Lisa (paint)
- St. Paul's Cathedral (build)

4
- first plane (fly)
- first modern Olympic Games (hold)

b) Now listen to your partner's guesses and correct them if necessary. Use the dates below.
B: I think the planet Uranus was discovered before the first African slaves were taken to America.
A: That's right. / No, that's wrong. The planet Uranus was discovered in ..., and ...

1. planet Uranus (discover): 1781
   first slaves (bring) to America: 1502
2. Hollywood Sign (put up): 1923
   Empire State Building (build): 1930–1931
3. first tea bags (sell): 1904
   first helicopter (fly): 1907
4. John F. Kennedy (kill): 1963
   Berlin Wall (build): 1961

3 Practice

6 REVISION Thieves! (Active and passive)

A reporter spoke to the police about a crime in San Clemente. Read his notes and write his report. Be careful: some sentences will be in the passive.

```
- thieves entered shop through back window      - nothing very expensive kept there
- window opened with large knife                - shop assistant's MP3 player stolen
- glass not broken                              - left through front door
- thieves went to safe first, couldn't open it  - neighbors interviewed
- then went to front of shop                    - two men and woman seen when left shop
- broke open cupboards
```

1 The thieves entered the shop through the back window.
2 The window was opened with a large knife
3 ...

7 What has changed? (Passive – present perfect)

Look at the pictures and write down what has changed. Use the verbs in the box in the present perfect passive.

beat • eat • paint • pick • plant • present

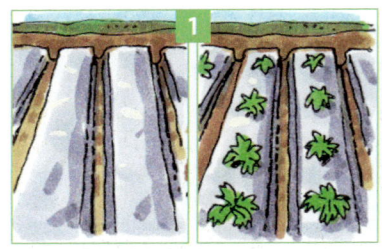

1 The strawberries have been ...   2 ...

8 Strawberry state (Passive – modals and will-future)

Use the verbs in the middle to complete the sentences.
1 Strawberries ... (can/grow) in California nearly all year round.
   Strawberries can be grown in California nearly all year round.
2 They ... (must/eat) soon because they go bad quite quickly.
3 Strawberries ... (have to/pick) when they're ripe.
4 If you want them to taste good, they ... (shouldn't/pick) when they're still green.
5 Strawberries ... (may/eat) with ice cream.
6 This year's Strawberry Festival ... (will/open) tomorrow.
7 This wonderful red fruit ... (will/celebrate) by thousands of visitors.

9 Sally was offered a job (Personal passive)

Partner B: Go to p. 131.

a) *Partner A: Read number 1 and put the sentence into the passive. Your partner will tell you if you have got it right. Then continue with 2, 3, 4.*
A: They offered Sally a job at the Bay Restaurant! Sally was offered a job …
B: Yes, that's right. / No, that's not right. It should be: Sally …

b) *Listen to B's sentences (5–8) in the passive and tell him or her if they are right or not.*

Your active sentences:	B's correct passive sentences:
1 They offered Sally a job at the Bay Restaurant!	5 On the train yesterday, I was given a free ticket for a movie.
2 They don't pay her very much.	6 Everyone on the train was given free tickets.
3 But a cook gave her an invitation to a rock concert last week.	7 But we're shown better films at school.
4 They sent her the ticket the next day by post.	8 Are you shown interesting films at your school?

10 Silicon Valley (Active and passive – mixed tenses)

a) *Complete the text with the verbs in the right tense in the active or passive.*

Silicon Valley … (not be) a valley at all but is (make up) of a number of cities in the southern part of the San Francisco Bay Area in Northern California. The largest … (be) San José. Other important ones … (be) Cupertino, Mountain View, Palo Alto, Santa Clara and Sunnyvale.

   Silicon Valley … (know) as the most important area of high-tech innovation in the world. The area … (give) the name Silicon Valley by a California businessman, Ralph Vaerst. The name … (first publish) in 1971 by Don Hoefler, a friend of Vaerst's, who … (work) as a reporter. He … (use) the name in some articles on the new computer industry.

   It … (first call) Silicon Valley because of the area's large number of companies that … (make) silicon chips for the computer industry. Nowadays it usually just … (mean) the high-tech industry in the region. And the high-tech companies which … (have) their head offices in Silicon Valley … (read) like an A–Z of the hardware and software industries: Adobe, Apple, Cisco, eBay, Google, Hewlett-Packard, Intel, Oracle, Sun Microsystems, Symantec and Yahoo!. All of them … (can/find) in Silicon Valley.

b) **Extra** *Think of five questions about Silicon Valley. Write them down and give them to your partner to answer.*

11 READING Soft drinks, hard facts (Finding the main ideas of a text)

What are the topic and the important ideas of a factual text? This is how you can find out quickly:

1 Topic
Every text is about something. This topic is often found in the title or first paragraph.

2 Important ideas
A text will often have several important ideas. They are sometimes found in the topic sentences of paragraphs.

3 Examples, reasons and explanations
The important ideas are usually illustrated by examples, reasons or explanations.

a) Skim the headline and the first paragraph of the article. What is its topic?

b) Now work with a copy of the text. Read the second paragraph carefully. Decide which sentences contain examples, reasons or explanations and highlight them.

c) Read paragraphs 3–5. Highlight a few other important ideas and the examples, reasons or explanations that support them.

d) Compare your results with another pair.

e) Extra 'German schools should not be allowed to sell soft drinks.' Write a short comment.

Soft drinks, hard facts

Drinking soda is one of the worst things you can do to your health. Experts agree that sugary soft drinks and fast food are the main reasons why so many American teenagers are obese. About 7 % of the calories in their diet come from soft drinks alone. That may not be a problem for teenagers now, but there could be heart and other health problems later.

The problem with soft drinks is that they do not still your hunger, says Wayne Campbell, a professor in the Department of Food and Nutrition at Purdue University. That's because your body doesn't notice all the calories that soft drinks contain – and they contain a lot. Drink a cola, for example, and you're getting 200 calories, but you still want a burger too.

American kids and teenagers are drinking more soft drinks than ever before, according to the U.S. Department of Agriculture. Soda has taken the place of other, healthier drinks. Thirty years ago, for example, boys drank more than twice as much milk as soft drinks.

So what can be done to change the way today's kids drink? In California, at least, children are no longer able to buy soda at schools. Schools aren't allowed to sell soft drinks any more, and other states may follow. The change isn't popular with students, and the food companies are against it, but teachers and doctors are happy.

What's the thinking behind the change? Studies have shown that having or not having soda machines in schools changes how much soda teenagers drink. If it's easy to buy soda, kids will drink more. If it's difficult, they won't. Experts hope that the new rules will help all children, not just those who are already obese.

▶ SF Reading Course (pp. 163–164)

12 Which one is Kim? (Participle clauses instead of relative clauses)

a) Luis wants to know which person is Kim. Ask his questions and answer them. Use these verbs:

> buy • carry • go into • listen • send • wait

1 girl – bus stop
A: *Is it the girl waiting at the bus stop?* –
B: *No, it isn't.*

2 boy – subway station
3 man – ice cream
4 boy – skateboard
5 girl – MP3 player
6 woman – text message

b) **Extra** Use a participle clause to describe someone in your classroom. Who can guess who it is first?
A: *My person is someone wearing red earrings.*
B: *Is it Jana?*

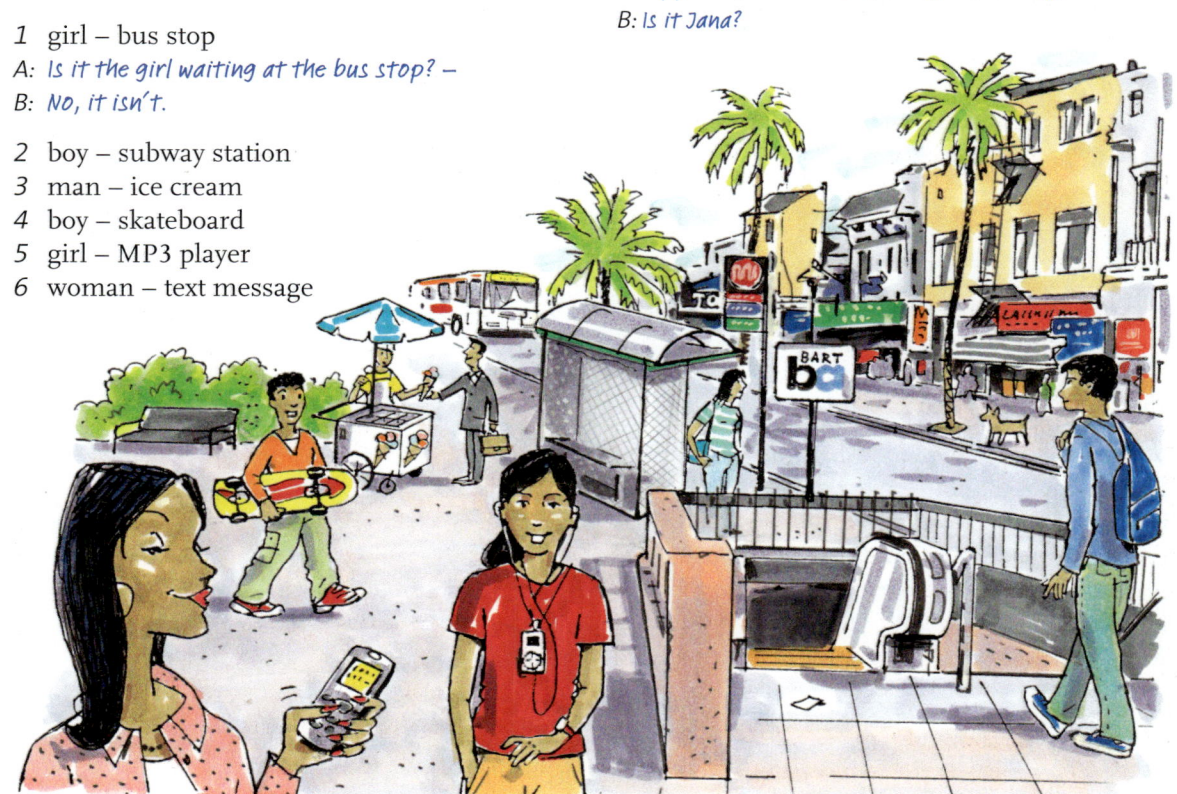

13 EVERYDAY ENGLISH   SPEAKING Theme parks (Discussing tourist activities)

a) Partner B: Go to p. 131.
Partner A: Read the information on this poster for the California Theme Park near San Clemente. Use the information to answer your partner's questions.

b) Your partner has information on Ocean Park. Ask him/her about the following:
1 exciting attractions for teenagers: Are there any …?
2 opening hours: What time …
3 ticket prices: How much …
4 any special tickets: …

c) Decide together which park you would like to go to. Tell the class your decision and give reasons.

The California Theme Park

The Big Thrill
Twist and turn upside down through the air! From 0 to 55 feet in less than ten seconds! Then fall 110 feet down!

Big Wave
Ride a wooden boat through the mountain. Fall over 50 feet down into a basin!

Wild Rat
Take a drive full of fun on this wild roller-coaster!

Special tickets Advance purchase family ticket $ 179.00

14 MEDIATION Best buy! (Understanding and explaining announcements) 🎧

The Walthers are shopping at a big supermarket during their holidays in California. They are listening to the announcements, but Mr Walther can't understand them. Listen to the announcements, take notes on what's important (prices, till when is the offer, what's special, ...), and explain to Mr Walther, in German, the important points in each.

1. Great summer fun sale
2. The latest men's running shoes
3. This week's deals!
4. Splash-resistant MP3 player

15 Save the world (Verb + object + to-infinitive)

a) Environmental organizations often advise people what to do to help the environment. Use the verbs in the boxes and complete the sentences with infinitive constructions.
1. They ... you ... money. They want you to give them money.
2. They ... people ... lights, TVs and computers.
3. They stand on the streets and ... shoppers ... their organization.
4. Of course, they also ... you ... the world's problems.
5. And they ... volunteers ... for charities all over the world.
6. So I always ... people ... to them carefully.
7. It's great that someone ... us all ... of the consequences of our actions.

> ask • help • prepare • tell • want
>
> give • join • listen • think • turn off • understand • work

b) Extra What are these organizations telling/asking people to do?
1. GREENPEACE: Save the whales! *Greenpeace wants people to save the whales.*
2. IPCC: Take climate change seriously.
3. EARTH FIRST: Stop killing seals in Canada.
4. FRIENDS OF THE EARTH: Put people's rights before big business.
5. WORLD WIDE FUND FOR NATURE: Save our one and only planet.

16 They can help (Question word + to-infinitive)

a) Use question words (how, when, where, ...) and infinitive constructions and say how these things help.
1. The San Clemente Clean Ocean Program – prevent ocean pollution
The San Clemente Clean Ocean Program tells people how to prevent ocean pollution.
2. A street map – find a sight
3. A timetable – arrive for your next lesson
4. A travel guide – see in a different country
5. My teacher – learn English

b) 👥 Complete these sentences with an infinitive construction. Compare your ideas and choose the best ones. Present them in class.
1. Thinking is the best way ...
2. There's only one way ...
3. The easiest way ... is ...
4. ... is the fastest way ...

17 STUDY SKILLS Outlining

a) An outline is a good way to organize your ideas before you write. Look at this student's outline and what he or she wrote. Check the Study Skills box below and the Skills File on page 159 and try to write the rest of the student's outline for the last paragraph of the text.

BUILDING GG BRIDGE

OUTLINE	NOTES
I. Location	
A. where it is	GG = SF Bay opening
B. how you got north of the city before	Marin County/Sausalito
1. by road	> 100 mile
2. by ferry	
II. History	
A. 1921: Joseph Strauss has idea for bridge	parents German immigrants / nobody liked design
B. 1933: team design	

STUDY SKILLS Outlining

A good way of organizing ideas before you write is to write an outline, e.g.:
Title
I. Main idea
   A. Important fact
      1. Example, reason, explanation, …
      2. Example, reason, explanation, …
   B. Important fact
…
II. Main idea
   …

Building the Golden Gate Bridge

The Golden Gate is where San Francisco Bay opens into the Pacific Ocean. Until 1937 if you wanted to go to Sausalito or to other places north of the city in Marin County, you had to drive for over a hundred miles round the bay or take a ferry.

  Joseph Strauss, the son of German immigrants, first had the idea for the bridge in 1921. But nobody liked his design, and it took another 12 years till work on the bridge began. The beautiful, world-famous bridge you can see today is really the result of a team design.

It took four years to build the bridge. It is 2.7 km long and cost over $27 million. The colour – International Orange – was chosen because it seemed right for the area and could also be seen in the famous San Francisco fogs. Tourists are often surprised that it can look orange, usually looks red, but never looks golden!

b) Do some more research on one of the topics you have learned about in this unit. There are some ideas below. Use the information you have collected to do an outline for a short text.

The US-Mexico Border

GROWING UP IN TWO CULTURES

San Clemente CLEAN OCEAN PROGRAM

CALIFORNIAN STRAWBERRIES

c) **Extra** Use your outline to write your text. Put it in your DOSSIER.

▶ SF Outlining (p. 159)

The circuit (by Francisco Jiménez, abridged and adapted) 🎧

Not all of the new words in this text are in the Dictionary at the back of this book. Use the techniques you have already learned to work out the meanings yourself.

▶ SF Using a bilingual dictionary (p. 156) •
SF Reading Course (pp.163–164)

Panchito's family are migrant workers from Mexico. They travel from place to place in California to pick strawberries, grapes, cotton and other crops. Imagine what life 'on the road' would be like for a child of your age.

It was that time of year again. Ito, the strawberry farmer, did not smile. It was natural. The best part of the strawberry season was over and the last few days the workers were not picking as many boxes as they had during the months of June and July.

When I opened the front door to our hut, I stopped. Everything we had was neatly packed in boxes. Suddenly I felt even more the weight of hours, days, weeks, and months of work. I sat down on a box. The thought of having to move to Fresno and of what I had to do there brought tears to my eyes.

That night I could not sleep. I lay in bed and thought about how much I hated moving.

A little before five o'clock in the morning, Papá woke everyone up. A few minutes later, the shouting of my little brothers and sister greeted the day – this was a great adventure for them.

While we packed the breakfast dishes, Papá went outside to start the *Carcachita*. That was the name Papá gave his old black Plymouth. He had bought it in Santa Rosa. Papá was very proud of this old car.

He left the car in front of the hut with the motor on. "*Listo*," he shouted. Without saying a word Roberto and I began to carry the boxes out to the car. Roberto carried the two big boxes and I carried the two smaller ones. Papá then tied the mattress on top of the car roof.

Everything was packed except Mamá's pot. I held the front door open as Mamá carefully carried out her pot, so that she did not spill the cooked beans. When she got to the car, Papá helped her with it. Roberto opened the back car door and Papá carefully put it on the floor behind the front seat. All of us then climbed in. Papá sighed, wiped the sweat from his forehead, and said tiredly: "*Es todo*."

As we drove away, I felt a lump in my throat. I turned around and looked at our little hut for the last time.

At sunset we drove into a work camp near Fresno. As Papá did not speak English, Mamá asked the camp foreman if he needed any more workers. "We don't need no more," said the foreman. "Ask Sullivan down the road. Can't miss him. He lives in a big white house with a fence around it."

When we got there, Mamá walked through a white gate, up the stairs to the house. She rang the doorbell. The light went on and a tall man came out. They exchanged a few words. After the man went in, Mamá hurried back to the car. "We have work! Mr. Sullivan said we can stay there the whole season," she said and pointed to an old garage.

The garage had no windows. The walls were eaten by termites, the roof full of holes, the dirt floor was covered in earthworms. It looked like a grey road map.

That night, by the light of a kerosene lamp, we unpacked and cleaned our new home. Roberto swept the dirt floor. Papá filled the holes in the walls with old newspapers. Mamá fed my little brothers and sister. Papá and Roberto then brought in the mattress and placed it in a corner of the garage. "Mamá, you and the little ones sleep on the mattress. Roberto, Panchito, and I will sleep outside under the trees," Papá said.

Early the next morning Mr. Sullivan showed us where his crop was, and after breakfast, Papá, Roberto, and I walked to the vineyard to pick.

Around nine o'clock the temperature had risen to almost one hundred degrees. I was completely covered in sweat and my mouth felt as dry as a handkerchief. I walked over to the end of the row, picked up the jug of water we had brought, and began drinking. "Don't drink too much: you'll get sick," Roberto shouted. As soon as he said that I felt sick. I dropped to my knees. I stayed still with my eyes on the hot sandy ground. All I could hear was the sound of insects. Slowly I began to recover. I poured water over my face and neck and watched the dirty water run down my arms to the ground.

I still felt sick when we had a break to eat lunch. It was past two o'clock and we sat under a large tree that was on the side of the road. While we ate, Papá wrote down the number of boxes we had picked. Suddenly I saw Papá's face go white as he looked down the road. "Here comes the school bus," he whispered loudly. Roberto and I ran and hid in the vineyards. We did not want to get in trouble for not going to school. The boys about my age got off. They carried books under their arms. After they crossed the street, the bus drove away. Roberto and I came out and joined Papá. "*Tienen que tener cuidado*," he warned us.

After lunch we went back to work. The sun beat down. With the insects, the wet sweat, and the hot dry dust, the afternoon seemed to last forever. Finally the mountains around the valley reached out and swallowed the sun. Less than an hour later it was too dark to continue. "*Vámonos*," said Papá. He took out a pencil and began to work out how much money we had made our first day. He wrote down the numbers, crossed some out, wrote down some more. "*Quince*," he said quietly.

When we arrived home, we had a cold shower under a water hose. We then sat down to eat dinner around some wooden boxes that were our table. Mamá had cooked a special meal for us. We had rice and tortillas with *carne con chile*, my favorite dish.

The next morning I couldn't move. My body hurt everywhere. This feeling went on every morning for days until my muscles finally got used to the work.

It was Monday, the first week of November. The grape season was over and I could now go to school. I woke up early that morning and lay in bed, looked at the stars and enjoyed the thought of not going to work and of starting school for the first time that year.

As I could not sleep, I decided to get up and join Papá and Roberto at breakfast. I sat at the table opposite Roberto, but I kept my head down. I did not want to look at him. I knew he was sad. He was not going to school today. He was not going tomorrow, or next week, or next month. He would not go until the cotton season was over, and that was sometime in February.

When Papá and Roberto left to go to work, I felt better. I walked up a small hill next to the hut and watched the *Carcachita* disappear in the distance in a cloud of dust.

Two hours later, around eight o'clock, I stood by the side of the road and waited for school bus number twenty. When it arrived I climbed in. Everybody was talking or shouting. I sat in an empty seat at the back.

When the bus stopped in front of the school, I felt very nervous. I looked out the bus window and saw boys and girls carrying books under their arms. I put my hands in my pockets and walked to the principal's office. When I entered I heard a woman's voice say: "May I help you?" I was surprised. I had not heard English for months. For a few seconds I said nothing. I looked at the lady who waited for an answer. My first instinct was to answer her in Spanish, but I stopped myself. Finally, I tried to tell her in English that I wanted to enroll. After answering many questions, I was led to the classroom.

Mr. Lema, the teacher, greeted me and gave

me a desk. He then introduced me to the class. I was so nervous and scared at that moment when everyone's eyes were looking at me that I wished I was with Papá and Roberto in the cotton field. Mr. Lema gave the class the assignment for the first hour. "The first thing we have to do this morning is finish reading the story we began yesterday," he said enthusiastically. He walked up to me, handed me an English book, and asked me to read. "We are on page 125," he said politely. I opened the book to page 125. My mouth was dry. My eyes began to water. I could not begin. "You can read later," Mr. Lema said understandingly.

During recess I went into the restroom and opened my English book to page 125. I began to read quietly, like I was in class. There were many words I did not know. I closed the book and went back to the classroom.

Mr. Lema was sitting at his desk and correcting papers. When I entered he looked up at me and smiled. I felt better. I walked up to him and asked if he could help me with the new words. "Gladly," he said.

The rest of the month I learned English in my lunch hours with Mr. Lema, my best friend at school.

One Friday during lunch hour Mr. Lema asked me to walk with him to the music room. "Do you like music?" he asked me as we entered the building. "Yes, I like *corridos*," I answered. He then picked up a trumpet, blew on it, and handed it to me. The sound gave me goose bumps. I knew that sound. I had heard it in many *corridos*. "How would you like to learn how to play it?" he asked. He must have read my face because before I could answer, he added: "I'll teach you how to play it during our lunch hours."

That day I could hardly wait to tell Papá and Mamá the great news. As I got off the bus, my little brothers and sister ran up to meet me. They were shouting. I thought they were happy to see me, but when I opened the door to our hut, I saw that everything we owned was neatly packed in boxes.

Working with the text

1 Understanding the story

a) Compare your ideas about life on the road from p. 72 with the real story.

b) Explain the title and say whether it fits the story or not.

c) Explain or describe
1 why Panchito's family moves to Fresno,
2 what their new home looks like,
3 what work they do there,
4 how you know it is hard work,
5 why the two brothers hide from the school bus,
6 how Panchito feels on his first school day,
7 what Mr Lema means to Panchito,
8 what the packed boxes mean.

d) Find the Spanish words in the text and try to explain what they mean from the context. Why do you think the author uses them?

2 Characters
Choose one of the characters below. Pick one scene and write down what the character might be thinking.
Panchito (the narrator) – Roberto – Panchito's father – Mr. Lema

3 What happens next?
Imagine what Panchito said to his parents when he came home. How did they reply? Write their conversation. Practise it and act it our for the class.

4 Children's lives, children's rights
Explain why Panchito has to go to work instead of school. What part of the story shows you that child labour is illegal? Do you think it is right or wrong that children have to work? Give reasons.

▶ **WB 20** (p. 44) • **Checkpoint 3** WB (p. 45) •
Text File 6 (pp. 146–147)

How am I doing?

a) *Fill in or choose the correct answers.*

California

1. California is sometimes called
   - A the Golden State B the Orange State
   - C the Sunny State D the Surfing State
2. California's centre of high-tech innovation is
   - A San Clemente B Yosemite
   - C Silicon Valley D San Diego
3. Because many of the people in California come from Mexico, they speak
   - A Mexican B English C French
   - D Spanish
4. People who cross the border from Mexico to the US without ID are called … immigrants.
   - A bad B illegal C bilingual
   - D border

Skills

5. You can use an outline to … your ideas.
   - A find out B organize C check
   - D research
6. You write an outline … you write your text.
   - A after B before C while

Words

7. It is illegal to … somebody because they belong to a different ethnic group.
   - A prejudice B prejudice against
   - C discriminate D discriminate against
8. I've got lots of Latino friends, but my parents don't like this because they're …
   - A prejudice B prejudiced
   - C discriminate D discriminated against
9. Which verb does *not* fit the sentence? 'Environmental groups want to … pollution.'
   - A prevent B reduce C repair
   - D fight against

Grammar

10. Which means the same as 'My camera was stolen'?
    - A I stole a camera. B A camera stole me. C Somebody stole my camera.
11. There are no more strawberries in the field. They … picked.
    - A are B have been C were
    - D will be
12. Now this is only grass, but strawberries … be grown there next year.
    - A are B must C will D have
13. Translate into German:
    a) He was sent to bed. Er wurde ins Bett gesch[ickt]
    b) He was sent a letter. Ihm wurde ein Brief geschi[ckt]
14. Which words can you leave out of this sentence without changing its meaning? 'I looked at the girl who was sitting on the wall.'
15. This map shows us … get there.
    - A how B how to C who D where to

b) *Check your answers on p. 132 and add up your points.*

c) *If you had 13 or more points, well done! Maybe you can help students who had fewer points. If you had 12 points or fewer, it's a good idea to do some more work before you go on to the next unit. Where did you make mistakes? The chart below will tell you what you can do to improve your English.*

No.	Area	Find out more	Exercise(s)
1– 4	California	Unit 3	WB 1, 17, 19, (pp. 34, 42, 43)
5– 6	Skills	P 17 (p. 71); SF (pp. 159, 163–164)	WB 18 (p. 42)
7– 8	Words: Minorities	Unit 3 (p. 58)	P 3 (p. 64); WB 3 (p. 35)
9	Words: environment	Unit 3 (p. 61)	P 15–16 (p. 70)
10–15	Grammar	Unit 3 (pp. 59, 61); GF 4–6 (pp. 179–183)	P 5–10 (pp. 65–67); P 12 (p. 69) P 15–16 (p. 70); WB 5–6, 9–11, 13, 15–16 (pp. 36–38, 40–41)

Hermann says 'Willkommen'

1 First impressions

a) Find Hermann on the map on the inside back cover. Find out more about where it's situated – the name of the river you can see in picture B, the nearest cities, …

b) Look at pictures A–E. Describe what you see. What are your first impressions of the town? Would you like to visit the town or even live there? Why or why not? What seems to be special about Hermann?

c) *Extra* From what you know about US immigration, what can you guess about Hermann's past?

2 The Krugers and the Schmidts

a) Look at photo F. Why do you think the Schmidts are in Hermann? Talk about your ideas with a partner.

b) Now listen and check. Note down as much information as you can about the two families, the Schmidts and the Krugers, then compare your notes with your partner's.

c) Listen again. True or false?
1. Anna is looking forward to making new friends.
2. Timo and Anna don't think that Hermann looks very German.
3. They think the town is really small.
4. Timo doesn't have a good first impression of the high school.
5. Anna thinks it will be easier in Hermann for her than for Timo.

d) *Extra* Mrs Schmidt wants Timo and Anna to write a diary in English to practise their language. Imagine you're either Timo or Anna and write your diary for today. Talk about what happened and describe your thoughts and feelings.

▶ P 1 (p. 84) • SF Listening (p. 161) • WB 1 (p. 46)

A Hermann's main industry is winemaking.

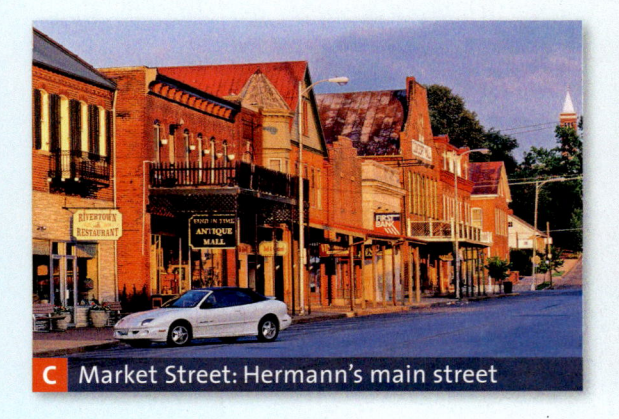

B The small town of Hermann (population 2,674) lies 15 miles south of Interstate 70, the main highway that runs east-west across the state of Missouri.

C Market Street: Hermann's main street

D Around 400 students go to Hermann High School.

E Hermann's "Festhalle"

F The Kruger family lives on a farm outside town. Today, they have visitors: the Schmidts from Germany.

All about ... American schools

1 The school system

High School	Grades 9–12	Ages 14–18
Middle School*	Grades 6–8	Ages 11–14
*sometimes called Junior High School		
Elementary School	Grades 1–5	Ages 6–11
Kindergarten		Ages 5–6

▷ Look at the diagram of the American school system (above) and at Jake Kruger's class schedule (right). Compare them with your system and your timetable. What's different, interesting, …?

2 A class schedule

Hermann High School — Jake Kruger — Grade: 9

Period	Time	Subject	Rm.
1	08:20–09:10	English 1	31
2	09:15–10:05	Science	36
	Recess		
3	10:10–11:00	Algebra 1	16
4	11:05–11:55	Health	28
5	Lunch/study hall		
6	01:15–02:05	American History and Government	21
7	02:10–03:00	Geography	54

3 From the school bulletin board

> Students who want to take part in extracurricular activities: please remember that you must not have any grades below a C.
> — Mrs. Kay

Student Dress Code
Student dress must be neat, clean and in good taste at all times. This means no clothing that is too small, too tight, see-through, or torn.

Students who break these rules will be sent home to change.

Copies of the complete dress code are available at the school office.

US school grades
A excellent   B good   C average
D below average   F failure

▷ Explain the two notices on the notice board. What do you think of them?
How would you explain the marks which are used in your school to an American student?

4 A chat about school 🎧
School starts for Timo at Hermann High next week. He has some last-minute questions for Jake. Listen as they talk and take notes on any new facts you find out about the school day, the school year, etc.

5 Talking about school
a) Collect all the information on this page about American schools into a mind map. Then use the mind map to give a short talk.

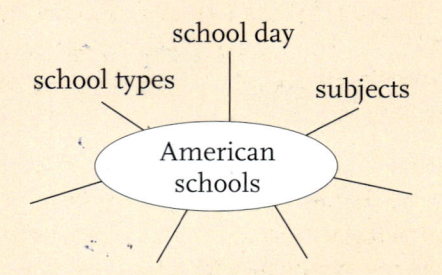

```
          school day
school types      subjects
      ( American
        schools )
```

b) **Extra** Some ninth-grade American high-school students are visiting your school next week. Your class has been asked to write a flyer for them about your school. Collect ideas on the board and write the flyer.

▶ P 2–3 (pp. 84–85) • WB 2–6 (pp. 47–49)

6 Future Farmers of America 🎧

It was Wednesday afternoon and Timo's second week at Hermann High. In the hallway he met Jake and his girlfriend Cindy. 'Hey, Timo,' said Jake. 'Are you coming to the FFA meeting? It starts in ten minutes.'

'FFA?' Timo asked. 'What's that?'

'Future Farmers of America,' Cindy explained. 'There'll be some important information about the County Fair on Saturday. Jake and I are both going to show hogs there.'

'Hogs?' Timo asked again.

'Pigs,' said Jake.

Timo found the whole thing strange. 'I've still got a little homework, if that's OK,' he said.

'School work is important,' Jake said. 'But you have to spend some time on other stuff too. Come on, the meeting will be interesting, you'll see.'

Timo expected to see very few students at the meeting, but the auditorium was full. He learned that a lot of students kept 'hogs'. They talked about how much money they had paid for them, how many hours a week they spent on them, and so on.

After the meeting Timo asked Jake: 'Are you going to be a farmer like your dad?'

'No,' answered Jake. 'I want to be a teacher. But FFA gives you a lot of good experience. And it'll look good when I apply for college or my first job.'

▶ *Compare how Timo and his new friends feel about school and extracurricular activities. How can doing extracurricular activities help people when they apply later for college or for their first job?*

Americana ★ ★ ★

Extracurricular activities

'Get involved!' That's what they say at American high schools, where sports and other extra-curricular activities are just as important as lessons. Students should be good at their school subjects, but also good at sports and interested in other things. FFA is only one of these activities – there are usually language clubs, dance groups, a school band, a drama group, cheerleaders and teams for every kind of sport from golf to football.

7 Now you

a) *Read the statement below and decide if you agree or disagree. Find as many reasons as you can for your opinion.*

'Having extracurricular activities at school is better than going to sports clubs and other kinds of clubs outside school.'

b) 👥 *Find somebody who disagrees with you about the statement. Try to persuade them that you are right.*

▶ GF 7: Countable and uncountable nouns (pp. 183–184) • P 4–7 (pp. 85–86) • WB 7–10 (pp. 49–51)

8 Keeping traditions alive

Hermann's festivals

Traditions are important everywhere in America. They remind us all of the countries and the cultures that our ancestors came from.

The traditions that we keep alive in Hermann are those of our old homeland: Germany. Here's a quick look at how Hermannites celebrate their German heritage.

HERMANN 'A little bit of Germany on the Missouri River'

There's something happening in Hermann all year round, but the most important events for us are our three big festivals. The first of these is **Wurstfest**. It takes place every March and lasts around a week. Good food is something we love here in Hermann. This festival highlights the food we're best known for: Wurst! And there's plenty of music and dancing at Wurstfest too.

Maifest is on the third weekend in May and it's another chance to enjoy the music and the dancing of our old homeland. The very first Maifest in Hermann took place in 1870.

And finally there's **Oktoberfest**. Wine is Hermann's most famous product. Visitors come from far and wide throughout October to taste the wine from our wineries – and generally to have a good time.

> What are Hermann's main festivals? When do they take place and why are they important for the people of Hermann?

Looking at language

a) Look at the word 'traditions' in these sentences:
1 Traditions are important everywhere in America.
2 The traditions that we keep alive in Hermann are those of our old homeland: Germany.

Which sentence gives you general information, which one gives specific information? What difference do you see?

b) Find these words in **8** with and without *the*. Explain how the meanings are different in the different sentences: food • music • dancing • wine

9 Now you

a) In groups of four, think of a festival in your town or village.

b) Write the name of the festival (it can be in German) in the centre of a piece of paper. Brainstorm ideas (when? what happens? ...?) and make a mind map about it.

c) Use the mind map to write a short text about your festival.

▶ GF 8: Definite article (p. 185) • P 8–9 (pp. 87–88) •
Text File 7 *(pp. 148–149)* • WB 11–13 *(pp. 51–52)*

10 From the local paper

Scrapbook — Hermann Advertiser-Courier — Wedn

New start in Hermann for German family

When Andreas Schmidt first visited Hermann 20 years ago, he never dreamed that one day he would return here to live. And his family had never planned to leave their home in Germany. But now here they are starting a new life in our town.

Andreas Schmidt was a member of the first group of high-school students that visited Hermann from our sister city of Bad Arolsen over 20 years ago. He stayed with the Kruger family, became friends with Chuck Kruger – who is his age – and has kept in touch ever since.

Now Chuck has helped Andreas to return to Hermann – this time to stay. He heard that the Hermannthal Winery needed extra staff and passed the information on to Andreas, an experienced winemaker.

"In the last two years in Germany, my wife and I often talked about moving and starting a new life," Schmidt says. "But we didn't know how to do it. Chuck's e-mail gave us the idea we needed."

So how has the family found the move? Schmidt again: "Leaving your country is a big step and I worried that it wouldn't work out. Actually, it's the best thing I've ever done."

Karla Schmidt is also happy about the move. "I see it as a big adventure," she says. "And now I have my own job here too. I work at the Hermann library, and it's a great way to meet people."

For son Timo (14), a student at Hermann High, the early days in Hermann were tough, he says. "Schools here are different from schools in Germany and I found things like FFA very strange. But it's all getting a lot better and I love baseball!"

Timo's sister Anna (12) is at Hermann Middle School. She also needed time to adjust. "I was really sad to leave my friends," she says. "I still miss them, but my new friends here are great too."

To Andreas, Karla, Timo and Anna: Hermann says "Willkommen".

▶ 'One small event can change a person's life.' Does this seem to be true for the Schmidt family? Explain your answer.
What do you think you would like or hate about moving to another country (language, friends, school, …)?

▸ P 10–11 (pp. 88–89) • WB 14–16 (pp. 53–54)

11 MEDIATION Calling Oma

Timo wants to call his grandmother to tell her about the newspaper article. Imagine you're Timo. Tell her in a few sentences what it says in the article.

4 A-Section

Extra | **Background File** | **GOING WEST**

1 READING Group puzzle (part 1)

Divide the class into four groups (A, B, C, D). Group A reads text A, Group B reads text B, etc. Take notes, then compare all your notes within your groups and agree on what you think are the most important points. Then go to 2 on p. 83.

A HERMANN

In the 18th and early 19th centuries, many Germans who had come to the New World were unhappy. English traditions and the English language dominated everyday life. The Germans were afraid that their children wouldn't learn their language and traditions. In 1836, they formed the 'Deutsche Ansiedlungs-gesellschaft zu Philadelphia'. The following year, this group bought land in Missouri and founded a colony there. And so the town of Hermann was born.

Hermann stayed very German until the First World War (1914–1918). The US was fighting the Germans in Europe, so many Americans worried about having Germans in the middle of their country. The school in Hermann was no longer allowed to teach in German. The proud Germans of Hermann stopped speaking their language and gave up their traditions for many years. Fortunately, those traditions are alive again today.

The first settlers in Hermann thought it looked like the Rhine Valley.

B THE ROLE OF MISSOURI

The first states in the United States of America were along the east coast, but as more and more Europeans arrived, the country grew towards the west. Missouri became a state in 1821, and by 1840 more than 380,000 people lived there – including the people who had founded Hermann. When gold was discovered in California in 1848, Missouri became the 'Gateway to the West', and the wagon trains to the west started there. But not everybody went west to look for gold. Thousands went to get free or cheap land where they could start a farm and a new life.

People who wanted to go to California, Oregon or other places in the American West travelled to St. Louis, where they bought everything they needed for the journey. Most then took a boat up the Missouri River to Independence, where they joined a wagon train. These 'trains' were the safest way to travel until a railway across the continent was finished in 1869.

Settlers got off the Missouri river boats and formed wagon trains for the journey to the West.

C THE TRAILS

The wagon trains followed one of many trails to the West. The Oregon Trail is the most famous. It was more than 2,000 miles long and the journey often took five months or more.

Many of the pioneers walked the whole way – their wagons were full of the things they needed for their new lives in the West. About ten per cent of the people died from accidents or illnesses. A few were killed in animal or Indian attacks.

Over the years more than half a million people went west this way. The journey was hard, so only those who were very strong were able to complete it. There are many stories about the brave men and women who made the journey, and Americans are still very proud of this 'pioneer spirit'. ■

D THE PLAINS INDIANS

When European settlers went west from Missouri, they entered the homelands of the Plains Indians – Native Americans like the Sioux and the Pawnee who lived on the great plains. Some of these Native Americans had met Europeans before, and although many had died from diseases brought by the first Europeans, they still accepted the new settlers and relations between the two groups were peaceful.

As more and more Europeans arrived and the United States grew bigger, however, the white settlers started pushing the Indians out of their traditional homes. The whites promised to leave the Indians alone if they agreed to move, and at first the Indians believed them. But most of these promises were broken, and relations between them and the settlers often became violent.

Before the first arrival of the Europeans, perhaps 4 million people lived in North America. In 1900, there were only about 250,000 Native Americans left. Today there are around 4 million Native Americans in the US, about 1.5% of the population. Even today, Native Americans earn far less money, and have poorer health and education than white Americans. ■

2 Group puzzle (part 2)

a) Give each person in your group a number (1, 2, 3, ...). Use the numbers to make new groups of four (A1 + B1 + C1 + D1; A2 + B2 + ...). Tell the others in your new group the important information from your text. Take notes on the other texts.

b) Go back to your first group (A, B, C, D) and compare your new information. Did you all understand the same things? If not, read the texts to check your facts.

▶ WB 17 (p. 55)

4 Practice

1 EVERYDAY ENGLISH MEDIATION Helping a tourist

a) At the train station in Bad Arolsen, on their way to Frankfurt Airport, the Schmidts met an American woman. Listen to the announcement and take Timo's role.

> Excuse me. What was that about?

> There's a problem with …

b) Now listen to the other train announcements on the CD. How would you help the tourists in these situations?

2 WORDS School

a) Copy and complete the chart.

AE	BE
grade (Schulnote)	mark/grade
grade (Jahrgangsstufe)	…
…	timetable
recess	…
…	notice board
(summer) vacation	(summer) …

b) 👥 Here are some more words that are used in American schools. Use them and the words from a) and make a quiz for your partner.

> extracurricular activities • school bus • study hall • library

A: You see it on a wall. Teachers and students put information on it.
B: Bulletin board. – It's something …
A: …

c) Read the sentences below. Then use the phrases in the box to write the sentences in a different way.

> break • change • get a good grade • join • schedule • take part in

1 Jake did well in his test.
   Jake got a good grade in his test.
2 Do you have to become a member of the drama club to act in the school play?
3 Billy's trousers were torn so he had to go home to get new clothes.
4 Two students from our year will be in tonight's discussion.
5 If you want to know where the lessons take place, look at your timetable.
6 You'll be in trouble if you don't obey the school rules.

3 WRITING A letter to a school magazine

a) *Read the student dress code on the right and the letter below from a ninth-grade student in a Missouri high school to her school magazine.*

> Dear Mag,
>
> In my opinion the dress code in school is stupid. As a ninth-grader I believe that I am now old enough to decide what I can wear. There are too many rules in school!
>
> Yours,
> Heidi Erl

STUDENT DRESS CODE

1. No hats or caps may be worn inside the school.
2. No clothes with holes should be worn.
3. Lycra or see-through clothes are not allowed.
4. All trousers or shorts must totally cover underwear, including boxer shorts.
5. All clothing, jewelry or tattoos must be free of violent images or gang-related symbols.
6. Safe footwear must be worn – no roller skates or bedroom slippers!
7. Sunglasses may only be worn inside if prescribed by a doctor.

b) *Talk in a group about student dress codes. Brainstorm ideas for and against.*

c) *Imagine that you are an exchange student at Heidi's school. Write a letter to the magazine, giving your ideas about a dress code. Say if you agree with Heidi. You can also talk about the situation in German schools.*

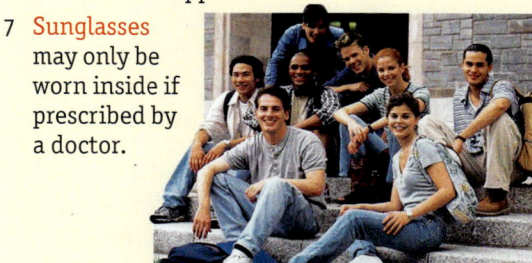

STUDY SKILLS Writing a letter to a magazine

When you write a letter to a magazine,
– begin your letter 'Dear Mag' or 'Dear + (name of the magazine)',
– give your opinion and also reasons for your opinion,
– end with 'Yours', 'Sincerely' or 'Yours sincerely' and your name.

▶ SF Writing course (pp. 168–169)

4 LISTENING School announcements and 'Thought for the day'

a) *Read the statements below. Write down the numbers 1–10. Then listen to the morning announcements at Hermann High School. Are the statements right (✓) or wrong (✗)?*

1. The win against Washington was a surprise.
2. The Hermann High School team is called the Bearcats.
3. Washington usually has a bad baseball team.
4. The school band will meet in the Music room this Saturday.
5. The band is going to play at Maifest.
6. The school play is called 'TV Hour'.
7. The play will be on Friday, Saturday and Sunday evenings.
8. Today's 'Thought for the day' says that when you give of yourself you truly give.
9. It also says that you shouldn't give food to poor people.

b) *Listen to the announcements again. Take notes, then correct the wrong statements.*

c) **Extra** *Write or choose a 'Thought for the day' for your class.*

5 One student – some time (Countable and uncountable nouns)

a) Copy the chart and write the nouns from the box in the correct columns.

Countable	Uncountable
student/students	homework
...	...

band • club • experience • homework • hour • information • lesson • money • music • student • team

b) *Much* or *many*? Complete the sentences.
1 Have you got … homework tonight?
2 How … lessons do you have each day?
3 Not … students came to the meeting.
4 I didn't find … information about this on the internet.
5 How … teams do you play in?
6 I'd like a new mobile phone but I haven't got … money.

c) 👥 Make sentences with *some* or *a lot of/lots of*, giving your personal opinion, then compare your answers with a partner's.
1 lessons/boring
   I think a lot of lessons …
2 music/rubbish
3 information on the internet/wrong
4 students in our class/very clever

6 What's your perfect sandwich? (Countable and uncountable nouns)

a) Some students are talking at lunchtime about their 'perfect sandwich'. Complete the sentences. Use *a few* with **countable** nouns, *a little* with **uncountable** nouns.
1 My perfect sandwich has a lot of cheese in it and … ketchup.
2 Mine has … cheese and a lot of ketchup!
3 I like to put … pieces of lettuce in mine.
4 Here's my perfect sandwich: … pieces of meat, … mustard, … pieces of tomato, and a lot of butter.
5 Too much butter isn't good for you! You should only put … butter on your sandwich.

b) Which words from the box can you use to complete sentences 1–6?

apples • bread • marmalade • milk • potatoes • sausages

1 How much … do we need?
2 How many … do we need?
3 We need ten …
4 We need some …
5 We need lots of …
6 We need a kilo of …

7 WORDS Word building (Nouns from verbs and adjectives)

a) 👥 Look at the nouns below. Which verb or adjective do they come from? Can you guess their meanings? Check your guesses with a dictionary.

cleverness • correction • friendliness • happiness • illness • imagination • possibility • reality • sadness

A: I think 'cleverness' comes from the word clever – *klug* or *schlau*. The German word is *Klugheit*.
B: I think that's right. My turn. 'Imagination' …

Tip
You can often understand nouns with the endings *-ation*, *-ion*, *-ity*, *-ness* because you know the verb or adjective they come from.

b) Write sentences with five of the nouns in a).

8 READING Students between paid work and schoolwork (Careful reading)

Texts can sometimes be complicated. You have to read them carefully before you can find and understand all the ideas and information.

1 Understanding the text:
First make sure that you understand all the main facts.

a) Read the text twice, then say if these sentences are true or false. Correct the false sentences.
1. Lots of students work because they want to buy nice things.
2. Half of the students at Watsonville High have a job.
3. All the students can work if they want to.
4. Some students have to work even if they don't want to.
5. A job can give you work experience – and that's good.
6. Students usually earn good money from their jobs.
7. Students often work 11 hours a week in their job.
8. A lot of students at Watsonville High suffer because they don't finish their education.

2 Information from different parts of the text:
You often have to link information from different paragraphs before you can understand the text fully.

b) Copy the table then complete it with ideas from the text.

Advantages	Disadvantages
You can earn money.	...
...	...

c) Does the writer think that paid work is a good or a bad thing? And what do you think?

▶ SF Reading Course (p. 164)

High school students between paid work and schoolwork

It's the same everywhere you look. Nike, Gap and J-Lo are all trying to sell you something. A lot of students don't want to miss out on the latest fashion and work after school so that they can buy clothing or fancy MP3 players – and they don't have to ask parents for money.

We talked to one hundred students from Watsonville High School in California and found that 30% of them work. Does their schoolwork suffer because they have a job?

"It really depends on the student," Ms. Viotti, a counselor at Watsonville High, said. "If students want to work, they have to have certain grades." That doesn't mean you have to be a top student. Average grades are enough to to be allowed to have a job.

"Working makes some students more disciplined about doing schoolwork," a chemistry teacher at Watsonville High said. "It teaches them to use their time better. It's a hard lesson to learn, but it's very useful." The problem for some students at the school is that they have to learn this lesson. They have no choice. A lot of parents in Watsonville are poor or don't have jobs. Their kids have to work so that they can help their families.

Learning how to organize your time is certainly one advantage of paid work. Another positive thing is that students get work experience. This can help them a lot in their future jobs. But having a job isn't always as great as it sounds. You have to do what other people tell you all day and you probably aren't paid very well.

Another thing is that students go to school for seven hours, and then often work another four hours a day. That's an 11-hour work day – without homework.

At Watsonville High the number of students who don't finish their education is very high. And because a good education is so important in today's world, their future can suffer a lot.

Millions of teens in the US work after school, and most of them don't know the price they might pay: their education and their future.

9 Do you like music? (The definite article)

a) Add *the* where you need it.
1 ... music is really important for me.
2 ... music I like best is hip hop.
3 ... people all over the USA like German sausage.
4 Yeah, and ... people of Hermann really love it.
5 ... life of a farmer must be very hard.
6 ... life is full of surprises!
7 Tickets for the Festhalle are free for ... students.
8 ... students who came to our school last week were from the USA.
9 At Wurstfest in Hermann there's a competition in the park for ... dogs.
10 All ... dogs you can see here are in the competition.
11 ... food we eat at home is usually Turkish and it's absolutely delicious.
12 Nobody can live without ... food.

b) Write sentence pairs with the words in the box. Write one sentence with *the* and one sentence without *the*. Write sentences that are true for you.

> clothes • hobbies • music • weather

Example: homework.
I don't like homework but it's important.
The homework we had yesterday was hard.

10 REVISION Everything's new (Infinitive constructions)

a) *Moving to a different country can be scary at first. Everything's new and you don't always know how to do things. Complete the sentences with the question words and the verbs in the boxes.*
1 When Timo arrived at his new school, he didn't know ... American football.
   When Timo arrived at his new school, he didn't know how to play American football.
2 Often, he didn't know ... for his next lesson.
3 Sometimes in lessons, he didn't know ... things in English.
4 And was lunch at 12.30 or 1.30? On his first day he wasn't sure ...
5 The dress code seemed strict. Were his old trainers OK at school? Timo wasn't always sure ... at first.
6 But Jake was a great friend. Timo always knew ... when he had a problem.

> who • what • where • when • how

> ask • eat • go • play • say • wear

b) Imagine that a new American student in your school asks you for advice about the things below. How would you answer? Write sentences and compare them with a partner's.
1 Meeting people and making friends
   I'd advise her/tell her to ...
2 Language problems in lessons
3 Things to do at the weekends
4 Travelling around in your city or area
5 Nice things to eat in Germany

11 STUDY SKILLS Summary writing

a) *Read this story about a rafting tour.*

A perfect day, by Carrie Langer
It all started at the Christmas Market. That's where I first got to know Jim Nielson. He's a student at Hermann High like me, but he's two grades above me. I say I 'got to know' him. Actually, we only chatted for a few seconds. But that was enough. I couldn't get him out of my mind.

Then in February, I saw the notice on the school bulletin board about the rafting tour in the spring vacation. Now, I hate water. But one of the tour guides was … Jim Nielson. I put my name on the list.

The first day of spring vacation came very slowly, but at last I was on a bus on the way to the Castor River, about three hours from Hermann. Jim was at the front of the bus with Nate, the other tour guide. At one point Jim walked down through the bus. I quickly got up and went toward the restroom.

"Hi," he said as we met. "Carrie, right?"
"Right," I said. "And you're – er, Jim?"
"Right. – Well, enjoy the tour."
"Thanks," I said. "I'm sure I will."

We arrived at the river, put on our gear, and got into the raft. At first the water was slow, and we just paddled along in the sunshine. But the Castor River can be very wild and after an hour the water got faster. Suddenly Jim turned and shouted, "Paddle left!" but it was too late – the raft hit a rock and I fell out. I panicked and went under the water. Then I felt a hand on my arm. It pulled me back onto the raft. When I looked up I saw Jim.

"Are you OK?" he asked. "Here, come and sit next to me." He smiled.

I smiled back. "Yes," I thought. "I'm just fine. It's a perfect day."

(312 words)

b) *In small groups, read the story again and try to write a first sentence for a summary. (Look at the box on the right for ideas). You could begin like this:*
The story is about Carrie, a student at Hermann High, who …

c) *Now find the most important events and ideas in the story. Note down key words. Try to use your own words, not words from the story. For example:*
Carrie – first meets – Jim – Christmas Market – can't forget him

d) *Use the key words and finish the summary in full sentences (about 100 words). Remember to use the simple present.*
Carrie first meets Jim at the Christmas Market and now she can't forget him. She finds out that …

STUDY SKILLS Summary writing

A summary is a shorter form of a text. It has all the important information from the original.
– In the first one or two sentences tell the reader what the story or text is about.
– In the main part describe the main events in the same order as in the original text.
– Write complete sentences.
– Use the simple present.
– Explain **who** does **what** in the story, **where**, **when** and **why**.
– Use your own words.
– Don't use examples or direct speech.

▶ SF Summary writing (p. 167)

Angus Bethune's moment (by Chris Crutcher, adapted)

In an American high school, being popular is everything. But even outsiders can dream of having their 'moment'. Outsiders like Angus Bethune.

> Look quickly at the pictures in this story and say what you think Angus Bethune's 'moment' is.

I'm a big kid.

And my parents named me Angus.

"Angus is a cow," I said to my mother. "You named me after a cow."

"Your father's uncle was named Angus," she said.

"So my father's uncle was named after a cow, too," I said. "What did he think of that?"

"Actually," Mom said, "I think he was kind of proud. Angus was a farmer, you know."

"Jesus help me," I said, and went to my room.

As Angus, the fat kid, I have my problems, although it isn't as bad as it sounds. I am incredibly quick for a fat kid, and I have great reflexes. When I play defense in football, nobody can get away from me. And I'm smart and get good grades. But I'd be happy to swap reflexes and being smart for a little beauty.

And that brings me to tonight. Tonight is a big night. See, I was elected Winter Ball King. That means I will be out on the dance floor of Lake Michigan High School with Melissa Lefevre, the girl of my dreams – and only my dreams. She was elected Winter Ball Queen. For a minute we'll be out there alone.

Alone with Melissa Lefevre.

Now I don't know how I was elected. I can't even imagine. I mean, it's a joke, I know that. And a good one. Somehow more than half the kids at my school voted for me and not for one of the many Adonises.

The problem is that, during those few seconds when Melissa and I are out there on the dance floor, everyone will see me dance. I can't dance.

I fell in love with Melissa in kindergarten. But I've never even talked to her. Until tonight. Tonight I'll have to talk to her.

All I want is my moment.

So here I sit. What can Melissa be thinking? She's probably telling herself that it's like a trip to the dentist. He's going to hurt you, but in an hour, you'll walk out of there. And you'll still be alive.

Of course, Melissa hasn't seen me dance.

So now I stand at the door to the gym. Melissa is inside.

Heads turn as I move through the door. I try to look cool and sit down at the nearest empty table. I see Melissa on the dance floor with her boyfriend – a real jerk, Rick Sanford – and I hear the announcement: the King and Queen have to be behind the stage in five minutes. I'm sweating. I want my moment.

I get up and start walking to the stage when I see Melissa on her boyfriend's arm. They're walking toward me through the crowd on the dance floor. As they get closer, I want to run. What am I doing here? What was I thinking?

They stand in front of me. "Angus, my man," Rick slurs, "I'm giving you this lovely thing for a few minutes. So she can compare."

Melissa drops his arm and smiles. "Don't listen to him. He's drunk. And rude."

Then she says, "Why don't we go?" and she takes my arm.

"Yeah," Rick says, "why don't you go, snowball king?"

Melissa drops my arm and grabs his. "Shut up," she whispers. "I'm warning you, Rick. Shut up."

"Have fun," Rick says to me. "Your election cost me a lot of money, probably about two dollars a pound." He looks at me from top to bottom. "And don't put your big fat hands on my girl," he says and starts to point at me. I look at his finger and he takes it back.

Melissa takes my arm and says, "Let's go."

At the side door to the stage I say, "By the way, there's something you should know."

She waits.

"I can't dance."

Melissa smiles. "Not everyone can," she says. "We'll survive."

I say, "I didn't say I can't dance well. I said I can't dance. Good people have been badly hurt when they tried to dance with me."

We're almost ready to start. "What did he mean, my election cost him a lot of money?" I whisper.

"Never mind."

I laugh and say, "I can take it."

"He's rich, and he's rude," she says. "I'm embarrassed I'm with him." She pauses and puts her arm in mine. "I'm not with him."

The curtains open and the trumpets play.

I look into the lights and smile. This would be silly even if they weren't crowning King Angus the Fat. Without moving her mouth, Melissa says, "I chose a slow song. We don't have to move much. Dance close to me. When you feel me move, you move. And don't listen to the music. It'll confuse you. Just follow."

She takes my arm and we go down the stairs to the dance floor. I remember to give her the red rose, and she takes it in her hand and smiles, then pulls me to her. She says, "Be my shadow."

A part of me goes to heaven. In my wildest dreams I never imagined that Melissa Lefevre would be nice to me in my moment. She whispers, "Relax," into my ear, and I follow her through a song I've never heard.

"Angus?"
"Yeah?"

"Do you ever get tired of who you are?"

I pull back a second, then pull close again. "Do you know who you're talking to?"

I feel her smile. "Yeah," she says, "I thought so. I know it's not the same, but it's not always so great to look like I do. I pay too."

She's right. I think it's not the same.

"I'm bulimic. Do you know what that is?"

"Yes, I know what that is. It means when you eat too much, you throw up so you don't look like me."

"Close enough. Don't worry, I'm in therapy for it," she says. "A lot of pretty girls are."

"Actually," I say, "I even tried it once, but when I put my finger down my throat, I was still hungry and I almost ate my arm."

Melissa laughs and holds me tighter. "You're the only person I've ever told. I just wanted you to know things aren't always as they appear. Would you do me a favor?"

"Yes."

"Would you leave with me?"

"You mean leave this dance? Leave this

140 dance with you?" I feel her nod.
　　The music ends; all dancers stop and clap politely. "I want to dance one more," Melissa says. "A fast one."
　　"I'll wait over by the table."
145 　"No. I want to dance it with you."
　　"You don't understand," I say. "When I dance rock and roll, people across the country feel earthquakes."
　　She takes my hand. "Listen. Do what you do
150 on the football field. Don't listen to the music; just follow me the way you follow the guy from the other team."
　　I try to protest, but then the band starts to play "Bad Moon Rising," and the dance floor is
155 full. Melissa pushes me back, and I watch her body the way I would watch an opponent on the football field. I'm like a mirror and move with her, from top to bottom. Soon lots of kids are watching us; I'm in a circle of kids, and 160 they're cheering. I'm Angus Bethune, the Fat Man, and I'm dancing with Melissa Lefevre.
　　When the band finishes, everyone is clapping, even Melissa. I tell God he can take me now. 165
　　"You bitch!" Rick shouts. "You practiced with this fatty. You've been dancing together. You bitch. You wanted to make me look stupid." He turns to me. "I'm gonna kill you, fat boy," he says. He's looking at my fist. 170
　　I say, "Don't even think it. After dancing, fighting is what I do best."

Working with the text

1 Understanding the story

a) Were you right about Angus's 'moment'?

b) Describe and explain:
– how Angus is an outsider,
– why Melissa is important in his life,
– how Angus's moment becomes possible,
– how things work out for Angus when his moment comes and why this happens.

c) Do you think Angus's life at Lake Michigan High has changed at the end of the story? Give reasons for your answer.

2 Extra What did they mean?

Who said these things and what did they mean?
1 "… the girl of my dreams – and only my dreams." (ll. 24–25)
2 "I'm giving you this lovely thing for a few minutes. So she can compare." (ll. 62–63)
3 "I just wanted you to know things aren't always as they appear." (ll. 134–136)
4 "I'm like a mirror …" (l. 157)

▶ WB 18 (p. 56) • **Checkpoint 4** WB (p. 57) • Selbsteinschätzung 3–4 (pp. 60–61)

3 Making a film of the story

In groups, plan a film version of the story.
a) Divide the story into scenes. Decide:
– who is in the scene (the characters),
– where it takes place (the setting),
– what are the most important events in the scene,
– what the scene must show (are the characters angry/nervous/…)?

b) Draw a box for each scene on a large piece of paper and add notes. You can add a diagram or pictures. For example:

> SCENE 1
> Angus's house
> Angus is angry with his mum about his name.
> They argue – he goes to his room.

c) Show and explain your plan to the class.

4 Life can be hard

'Life can be hard for teenagers.' Do you agree? What teenage problems does this story deal with? Do you think it's a good story about teenage problems?

How am I doing?

a) Fill in or choose the correct answers

American schools

1. The type of school that almost all 14–18-year-olds in the USA go to is called … high school
2. It starts with the 9th … grade
3. Sports and school clubs are known in the USA as … extracurricular
4. The rules that tell you what to wear in school are called a … dress code

Hermann and Missouri

5. Missouri is the name of a state and a …
   A national park   B forest   ~~C~~ river
   D big city
6. Hermann's main industry is …
   ~~A~~ winemaking   B sausage making
   C farming   D festivals
7. Hermann and other places in Missouri keep German … alive.
   A immigrants   B sausages
   C minorities   ~~D~~ traditions

Summary writing

8. Which statement is not true of a summary?
   A A summary should have all the important information from the original text.   B You should write a summary in your own words.   ~~C~~ A summary should have lots of details from the original text.
   D A summary should have complete sentences, not just key words.

Words

9. real – reality
   possible – ? possibility
10. present – presentation
    imagine – ? imagination
11. Hermann's … city in Germany is Bad Arolsen. sister
12. Wurstfest takes … every year in March. place
13. Mr Schmidt said that leaving your country was a big … step
14. When you leave school, you … for a job. apply
15. The best school … in the USA is 'A'. grade

Grammar

16. Choose the correct word or expression:
    a) I couldn't find *much*/*many* information.
    b) How *much*/*many* students play in the school band?
    c) Very *few*/*little* people came to the meeting.
    d) Could I have a *few*/*little* milk in my tea, please?
17. Add 'the' where necessary:
    a) … food is important at all of Hermann's festivals. The food they eat most often is traditionally German, like sausage.
    b) The students in Timo's class are crazy about football. Football is popular with … students all over the USA.
    c) I thought the people and the music in the school play yesterday were great.

b) Check your answers on p. 133 and add up your points.

c) If you had 18 or more points, well done! Maybe you can help students who had fewer points.
If you had 17 points or fewer, it's a good idea to do some more work before you go on to the next unit. Where did you make mistakes? The chart below will tell you what you can do to improve your English.

No.	Area	Find out more	Exercise(s)
1–4	American schools	Unit 4 (pp. 78–79)	P 2–4 (pp. 84–85), WB 2–4 (pp. 47–48)
5–7	Hermann and Missouri	Unit 4 (pp. 76–77; 80)	WB 1, 7, 16, 17 (pp. 46, 49, 54–55)
8	Summary writing	Unit 4, P 11 (p. 89), SF (p. 167)	P 11 (p. 89), WB 16 (p. 54)
9–10	Word building	Unit 4, P 7 (p. 86)	P 7 (p. 86), WB 10 (p. 51)
11–15	Words	Unit 4, A 1–6, 8 (pp. 78–80)	WB 1b, 11 (pp. 46, 51), 2–3 (p. 47)
16	(Un-)countable nouns	Unit 4, A 6 (p. 79), GF 7 (p. 183)	P 5–6 (p. 86), WB 8–9 (p. 50)
17	Definite article	Unit 4, Looking at Language (p. 80), GF 8 (p. 185)	P 9 (p. 88), WB 12 (p. 51)

Getting ready for a test 2 Revision Extra

1 WORDS Holidays

a) Collect ideas about holidays in four lists.

Getting there	Where to stay	Things to do	Describing things
fly/go by plane	stay with friends	see the sights	the main sights
go by ...	stay at a ...	relax on the beach	a beautiful/lonely/... beach
		visit a ...	an interesting ...

b) Write a short advertisement for an exciting holiday place. Use ideas from your lists.

> Come to ...!
> It's easy to get here. ...
> Stay at ...
> There's lots to do. You can ...

2 WORDS Numbers

Dates, times and prices are important on holidays.
a) Practise these numbers.

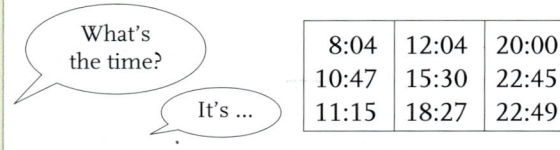

What's the time?
It's ...

8:04	12:04	20:00
10:47	15:30	22:45
11:15	18:27	22:49

18 April • 12 May • 1 July • 2 October
23/8 • 3/1 • 25/12 • 30/11 • 29/2 • 21/9

| $1.50 | $8.30 | $15 | $17.56 | $44.99 | $71.65 |

Tip

	You see	You say
Times	6:00	six o'clock/six am
	9:30	nine thirty/half past nine
	10:47	ten forty-seven
	17:00	five o'clock/five pm
	19:08	eight minutes past seven/ nineteen o eight
	22:15	quarter past ten/ten fifteen/ twenty-two fifteen
Dates	17 March	the seventeenth of March
	22/6	the twenty-second of June
Prices	$1	a/one dollar
	$1.20	a/one dollar twenty
	$5	five dollars
	$8.59	eight dollars fifty-nine

b) Write down ...
– the times of three things you're doing next week,
– three dates that are important to you,
– the prices of three things you bought last week.
Read everything to your partner. He/she writes it down. Then compare.

3 My school holidays start ... (Prepositions in time phrases)

Complete the sentences with *at*, *in* or *on*.
1 My school holidays start on Thursday.
2 I want to relax on the first day of the holidays.
3 Visit Las Vegas in May – it's too hot in July.
4 We often go to the beach in the summer.
5 Hurry! The train leaves at 8:04.
6 We arrived in London on Monday morning.
7 We arrived in London in the morning.
8 When's the concert? – It's on 10 June.
9 We spent two weeks in the US in 2006.
10 What do you want to do at the weekend?

Extra Revision Getting ready for a test 2 ✓ 95

4 SPEAKING Let's go to the park

a) It's the summer vacation.
Matt and Jon are talking about things to do today. Read their conversation with a partner.

Matt Let's go to the park. We can skate there.
Jon   No, I don't really want to do that again. We went to the park yesterday. We could go to the cinema today.
Matt I'm not sure if I like that idea. I don't have so much money. What about going back to my house? We could play a computer game.
Jon   That's a good idea. Let's do that.
Matt Cool. Come on then. Let's go.

Tip

When you talk about things to do, you usually make suggestions, disagree and agree.
Making suggestions
– Let's go/watch/…
– We could go/watch/…
– What about going/watching/…
Disagreeing
– I don't really want to do that.
– I'm not sure if I like that idea.
When you disagree, try and give a reason:
– We went there yesterday.
– I haven't got that much money.
Agreeing
– That's a good/great/… idea.
– Yes, let's do that.

b) Make a conversation like the one on the left. Here are some ideas for things to do.

go shopping/swimming/… • go on a trip to … • make a pizza • watch a film • play frisbee/… • visit the natural history museum/…

5 STUDY SKILLS Writing (Linking sentences)

A good text needs linking words and time phrases. Use these words and phrases to complete the text.

after breakfast • and • At about one o'clock • because • before they went to bed • but (2x) • Last year • later in the afternoon • 90 minutes later • One morning in July • On their third day • so • when • where (2x)

… (1) there was a competition in UK schools. It was organized by the German Tourist Office and the first prize was four days in Germany.
… (2) the 15 winners left London and just … (3) they arrived at Cologne Bonn Airport. They took a train into Cologne … (4) left their bags at their hotel.
… (5) the teenagers had lunch in town and … (6) they visited the cathedral and a sports museum. Supper was at a restaurant … (7) you could try traditional food, and … (8) they went for a short walk through the old town.
The next day … (9) they all went shopping. (They had to use their German … (10) not all the shop assistants spoke English!) Later they went on a boat trip on the Rhine and visited a chocolate museum.
… (11) they travelled to Bonn. There they saw the house … (12) Beethoven was born, … (13) there wasn't enough time to go to the city's other museums. In the evening they had tickets for a rock festival. It wasn't over until 1 am, … (14) they all went to bed really late.
Everyone was very tired … (15) they arrived back in London the next day, … (16) they had all had a fantastic time in Germany.

▶ WB 1–4 (pp. 58–59)

1 Listening 🎧

You will hear five travel announcements and mini-dialogues.
For each one choose the correct answer: A, B, or C. At the end you will hear the recordings again.

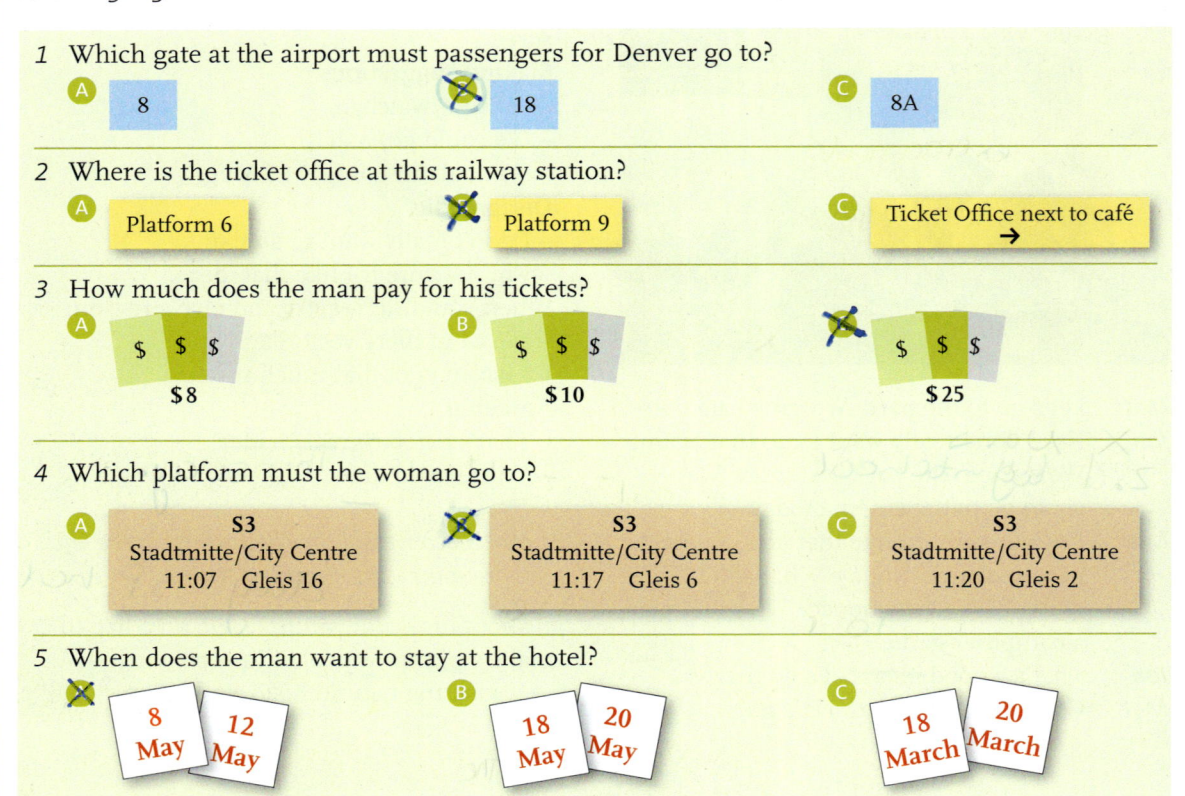

1 Which gate at the airport must passengers for Denver go to?
   A 8   ✗B 18   C 8A

2 Where is the ticket office at this railway station?
   A Platform 6   ✗B Platform 9   C Ticket Office next to café →

3 How much does the man pay for his tickets?
   A $8   B $10   ✗C $25

4 Which platform must the woman go to?
   A S3 Stadtmitte/City Centre 11:07 Gleis 16
   ✗B S3 Stadtmitte/City Centre 11:17 Gleis 6
   C S3 Stadtmitte/City Centre 11:20 Gleis 2

5 When does the man want to stay at the hotel?
   ✗A 8 May / 12 May
   B 18 May / 20 May
   C 18 March / 20 March

2 Listening 🎧

You will hear a radio programme from the USA. Read the questions below.
Then listen and choose the correct answer: A, B, or C. You will hear the programme twice.

1 You can hear the programme once a …
   A day   ✗B week   C month
2 Later in the show Annie will talk about …
   A school grades   B sport   ✗C fashion
3 Katie went on an interesting vacation last …
   ✗A summer   B winter   C autumn
4 She was a … for a week.
   A pop singer   B circus clown   ✗C cowgirl
5 She went with her …
   ✗A uncle and aunt   B parents   C sisters
6 During her vacation, Katie … every day.
   A swam   B ran 20 miles   ✗C rode horses
7 One day she helped Ben and Ted with a …
   A baby cow   ✗B baby horse   C baby lion
8 Once they had a … in the mountains.
   ✗A camp fire   B concert   C picnic
9 During her vacation, Katie slept in a …
   A hostel   B tent   ✗C cabin
10 Katie says the vacation would be great for …
   A everyone   ✗B some people   C kids only

3 Speaking

You're on holiday with your partner. You want to discuss things to do tomorrow.
– Look at the pictures below. Choose three things that you'd like to do.
– Tell your partner about your ideas. How many things can you find that you both want to do?

Give reasons why you want (or don't want) to do something.
Partner A: You begin. *Let's …*

4 Writing

Buddy is a magazine for teenagers. They want readers' letters about 'The best holiday I've ever had'. Write a short letter to the magazine. Say …
– when the holiday was,
– where,
– who you went with,
– some things you did,
– why you liked the holiday so much.

Begin:
Dear Buddy,
You wanted to know about the best holiday I've ever had. It was …

Unit 5

Atlanta rising

1 Atlanta today

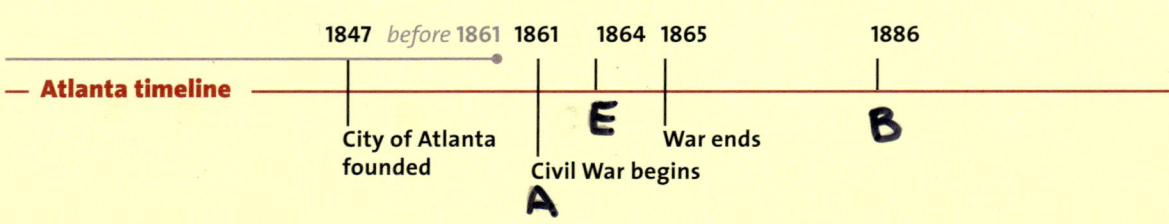

Look at the photo of the city and talk to your partner about what you discover.

Atlanta seems to be/looks like …
I imagine the city …
… is surrounded by …

downtown • freeways • green • grid • modern • skyscraper • stadium • …

Atlanta timeline

1847 — City of Atlanta founded
before 1861
1861 — Civil War begins (A)
1864 — (E)
1865 — War ends
1886 — (B)

A Black slaves work in terrible conditions on the cotton plantations and are often beaten.

B The world's most famous soft drink is born.

C President Clinton opens the 26th Olympic Games.

D Dr Martin Luther King, Jr. (born Atlanta, 1929), leader of the Civil Rights Movement, is murdered.

E Atlanta burns during the American Civil War.

F Shirley Franklin is elected first black woman mayor of Atlanta.

G Worldwide news network CNN founded in Atlanta

2 Atlanta's history 🎧

a) Look at the small pictures and captions. What can you learn from them about Atlanta's history? What happened there? What is it famous for?

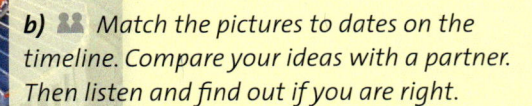

b) Match the pictures to dates on the timeline. Compare your ideas with a partner. Then listen and find out if you are right.

c) Choose the picture that interests you most. Listen again and take notes on your picture. Then get together with others who have chosen the same one and prepare a one-minute talk for the class.

d) Think about all you have found out about Atlanta and say what you think the title of the unit means.

1968	1980	1996	2002
D	G	C	F

▶ WB 1 (p. 62) • Text File 8 (pp. 150–151)

All about ... the media

1 Americans and the media

a) Read the following text and then take notes on when and why the Young family use the media.

> We Americans are spending more time using the media every year, says a new government report. TV, radio and the internet now take up 3500 hours a year, more time than most of us spend in bed. US teenagers and adults watch TV for an average of 70 days.
>
> (U.S. Census Bureau, 2008)

The Young family from Atlanta, Georgia use the media just like many other Americans. Mrs Young works for the TV news network *CNN*, so for her it's important to watch the other TV news stations. She also reads lots of newspapers and news agency reports online. Her daughter Madison, 14, spends a lot of time online, too, on social networking and video sharing websites, like *Facebook* and *YouTube*. Her favourite TV programmes are crime and drama series and reality shows. She doesn't listen to the radio very much but wakes up in the morning to Top-40 station 955 *The Beat*.

Mr Young gets his news from Atlanta's biggest daily newspaper, *The Atlanta Journal-Constitution,* and from the good programmes that *NPR* (National Public Radio) broadcasts. He's a big music fan and always has his car radio tuned to a jazz or blues station.

b) Compare your media use to Americans' in general and Madison's in particular. What's different? What's the same?

Madison likes crime and drama series but I prefer soaps. Unlike Madison, I've always got the radio on ...

2 Gallery walk: media words

a) Make a media network on a large piece of paper. Collect words and phrases from this page; add as many more words as you can remember.

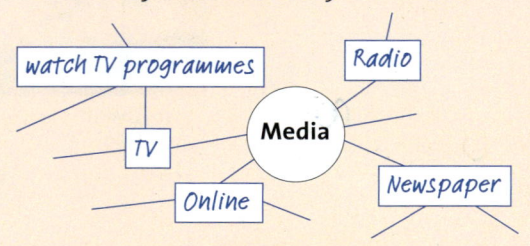

- watch TV programmes
- Radio
- TV
- Media
- Online
- Newspaper

b) Put all the networks on the floor outside the classroom. You have five minutes: walk past them, check the others and add to yours if you want to.

▶ P 1–3 (p. 106) • WB 2–4 (pp. 63–64)

3 Silent discussion: your class and the media

a) Agree on five questions for a survey of your class's media use.
Have you got a TV in your bedroom?
How much time do you ...

b) Pass a copy of your questions to the next group. Look at the other group's questions and add any new ones to your list. Go on like this until your own questions return to you.

c) Answer all the questions on your list. Compare your media use with the others in your group.

d) **Extra** Imagine you are alone on a desert island. You can only take one type of media with you (TV, internet, print, ...). Which would you choose? Explain why.

4 'Take Your Child to Work Day'

Mr Young and Madison had been sitting in the kitchen and having breakfast for half an hour when Mrs Young came down.

'Good morning,' she said. 'Are you ready to go to work with me, Madison?'

'You bet, Mom!' Madison said. 'I've told everybody at school about it too.'

Mr Young put down his paper. 'You know, Madison, we have Take Your Child to Work Day at the King Center too.'

'I know, Dad. But I promised Mom weeks ago. You should have asked me before. And besides, when I finish school I want to be a reporter, just like Mom.'

Later, in the car on the way to the CNN studios, Madison was checking the calendar on her phone. When she realized the car had been waiting in the traffic for a few minutes, she looked up and said, 'What's up, Mom? Why ...'

Just then Mrs Young's cellphone rang. She answered it. It was Dan, her boss at CNN.

'Josephine,' he said, 'I need you at the airport. There's a big fire there. The camera team is just leaving.'

'I'm on my way,' Mrs Young said.

'Cool,' said Madison after her mom told her about the call. 'My day at CNN is going to be very exciting!'

'No, sorry. Your day at CNN has just ended. I can't take you with me while we're shooting this story. You'd be in the way. I'll drop you off at Dad's office before I go to the airport.'

> Explain why Madison is going with her mother, not her father.
Imagine what Madison said to her mother on the way to her father's office.

▶ GF 9: Past perfect progressive (p. 186)

Americana ★ ★ ★

Take Your Child to Work Day
TYCTWD is a day when parents are allowed to take their children to their workplace. The kids can see what their mom or dad does there and it introduces them to the world of work. It takes place on the fourth Thursday in April.

Not all companies or schools participate in TYCTWD. But every year more than 25 million children visit their mother's or father's place of work on this special day.

▶ P 4–6 (pp. 107–108) • WB 5–8 (pp. 64–66)

5 Now you

Would you like to have TYCTWD in Germany too? Why? Why not? Describe your parents' jobs and workplaces.

Never make a doctor's appointment on Take Your Kids to Work Day.

6 At the King Center 🎧

When Madison arrived at the King Center, she couldn't find her dad. She knew the people who worked at the Center, so she was allowed to wait for him in his office. She went to the chair which was next to the window.

'Hey, Madison,' Mr Young said when he came back, 'I haven't seen you for at least …' – he looked at his watch – '… 45 minutes!'

'Not funny, Dad.'

'So, did you get bored with the TV studios?'

'We never got to the studios,' said Madison angrily. 'There's a fire at the airport and Mom had to go and report on it, which sounded pretty exciting to me. But she said I'd be in the way. So she dropped me off here.'

'Oh, too bad, honey. Well, I have to put away some of Dr King's letters, which won't take long,' said her dad. 'They've been on display since the anniversary of his death …'

'April 4, 1968,' Madison said.

'Hey, that's right.' Her dad was impressed. 'Which means you have learned something from me.'

'No,' Madison said. 'It means it says it here on your computer.'

'Oh, right. I was just looking at that. I have to prepare some material for school students.'

The King Center has a library and archives on Martin Luther King.

Looking at language

a) What does *which* refer to in this sentence from **6**?
She went to the chair which was next to the window.

b) What does *which* refer to in the following sentence?
There's a fire at the airport and Mom had to go and report on it, which sounded pretty exciting to me.
How could you translate which *into German?*

c) Find two more examples of this new type of relative clause in **6**.

▶ GF 10a–b: Relative clauses (p. 186) • P 7–8 (p. 109) • WB 9–10 (p. 67)

7 Martin Luther King

Here is some of the online information Mr Young was looking at.

Martin Luther King, Jr. (January 15, 1929–April 4, 1968):

King was a Baptist minister from Atlanta, who became a civil rights activist. He was one of the main leaders of the American civil rights movement, which successfully ended segregation in the USA. and won equal rights for blacks. King believed in non-violent protest and led the Montgomery Bus Boycott (1955–1956) and the 1963 protest, March on Washington. There, King made his famous "I Have a Dream" speech, which has been called one of the greatest speeches in American history.

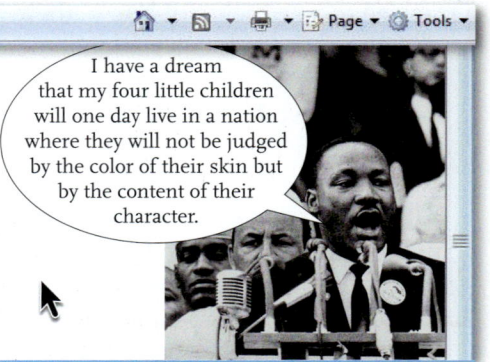

> I have a dream that my four little children will one day live in a nation where they will not be judged by the color of their skin but by the content of their character.

▶ *The information on Martin Luther King is taken from an online source. Why are some words underlined in blue?*

▶ GF 10c: Non-defining relative clauses (p. 187) • P 9–10 (p. 110) • WB 11–12 (p. 68)

8 Finding out more about MLK

a) Find out more about Martin Luther King. Research one of the topics underlined in blue in **7** on page 102, or another aspect of MLK's life (his early life, the awards he won, his death, …).

b) Produce a short text with illustrations about your topic. Hang up your text on the classroom wall. Read the other students' texts. Which topics from the article on page 102 would you still like to know more about?

STUDY SKILLS | Research

When you do research:
- Use more than one source. Make sure the sources are reliable.
- Try to use sources in English.
- Do not just copy from sources. Take notes in your own words.
- Use your notes to write your own texts for your essays, presentations, etc.
- Sort the information you use into facts and opinions.
- Explain difficult or unknown vocabulary or use a word list. (You may want to use an English–English dictionary for help.)
- Name your sources at the end of your work.
- Give addresses and dates with internet sources.
- Put exact quotations in quotation marks and give the source in brackets or a footnote.

THE MONTGOMERY BUS BOYCOTT

The Montgomery Bus Boycott was a protest against the system of segregation on the buses in the town of Montgomery, Alabama. It began on December 1st, 1955, when a bus driver asked the blacks on the bus to give up their seats to white people. One black

▶ SF Working with an English–English dictionary (p. 157) • SF Research (p. 158)

9 Breaking news 🎧

For the rest of the morning, Madison helped her dad at the King Center. Then she remembered her mum. She and her dad wondered what had been going on at the airport. He turned on the TV.

▶ Make a list of what is boring, interesting, exciting, … about Mr and Mrs Young's jobs. Which would you prefer to do?

A fire in one of the parking lots has delayed many flights this morning at the world's busiest passenger airport in Atlanta. The fire was started by a gas explosion at about 8.30 this morning. Firefighters were on the scene quickly and say they now have the fire under control. The good news is that no one has been hurt. This is Josephine Young for CNN in Atlanta – breaking news.

▶ P 11 (p. 110) • WB 13–16 (pp. 69–70) • **Text File 9** (p. 152)

THE SOUTH

Extra | **Background File**

The American South is a region with a culture and traditions in many ways distinct from the rest of the USA. In 1861, eleven states started the Civil War when they broke away from the United States to form their own country. Let's take a quick trip around some of these states, where the summers are long and hot. The composer George Gershwin caught the atmosphere of summer in the South in his great song "Summertime", from the opera *Porgy and Bess* (1935):

> Summertime,
> And the livin' is easy
> Fish are jumpin'
> And the cotton is high
> Your daddy's rich
> And your mamma's good lookin'
> So hush little baby
> Don't you cry
>
> by George Gershwin, Ira Gershwin and Heyward DuBose

Group puzzle

a) Divide the class into groups of seven (A, B, C, ...) and give everyone a number from 1 to 7. No. 1 from each group works on Tennessee, no. 2 on Louisiana, and so on.

b) Read about your state and research one or two more facts about it. Then join all the students from other groups who are working on your state, (e.g. A1, B1, C1, ...) and exchange information.

c) Report back to your original group (A, B, C, ...) and tell them what you have learned about your state.

1 Tennessee is home to the most popular National Park in the USA, Great Smoky Mountains NP. It is also world-famous for music. Nashville is the capital of country music. In Memphis you can visit *Graceland*, the home of the 'king of rock and roll', Elvis Presley. Another rock and roll singer, Chuck Berry, made the city famous with his hit "Memphis, Tennessee".

2 Louisiana is another state where music is king, from the jazz and blues mecca, New Orleans, to the bayou country with its Cajun music and Zydeco sounds. The French Quarter in New Orleans still draws thousands of tourists every day, even after large parts of the city were flooded and destroyed by Hurricane Katrina in 2005. More than 1800 people lost their lives in the disaster.

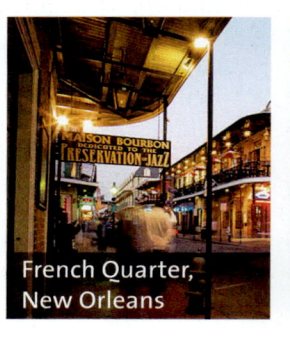

3 **Arkansas** played an important role in 20th-century American politics. When, in 1957, nine black kids were chosen to go to an all-white high school in Little Rock, it was the beginning of the end of segregation in American schools. 35 years later, a little-known governor of Arkansas surprised America by winning the election and becoming the 42nd president of the United States. Bill Clinton served two four-year terms as president (1993–2001).

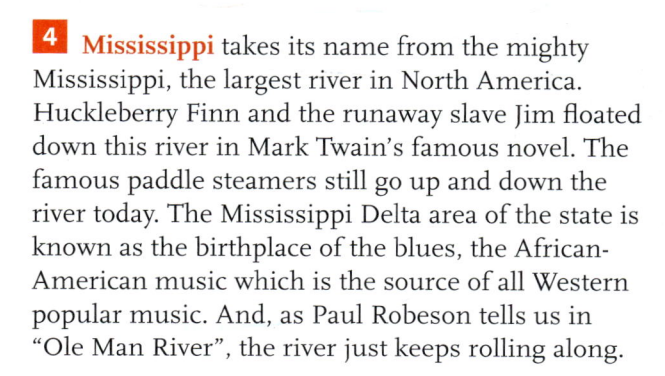

Former US president Bill Clinton

4 **Mississippi** takes its name from the mighty Mississippi, the largest river in North America. Huckleberry Finn and the runaway slave Jim floated down this river in Mark Twain's famous novel. The famous paddle steamers still go up and down the river today. The Mississippi Delta area of the state is known as the birthplace of the blues, the African-American music which is the source of all Western popular music. And, as Paul Robeson tells us in "Ole Man River", the river just keeps rolling along.

A paddle steamer on the Mississippi

5 **Virginia** was the first British colony in North America and is named after Queen Elizabeth I, who was known as the Virgin Queen because she never married. The colony was founded in 1607 at Jamestown and played a big role in the American Revolution. Three of the first four presidents of the United States were Virginians: George Washington, Thomas Jefferson and James Madison. Virginia was also at the centre of the American Civil War. Its capital, Richmond, was the capital of the Confederate States.

State Capitol, Richmond, Virginia

6 **Georgia** is the economic dynamo of the South and Atlanta is at the centre of it. World-famous companies Coca-Cola, UPS, Delta Airlines and many TV networks such as TBS and CNN – founded by Ted Turner – have their head offices in Georgia. Of course, we shouldn't forget the music industry in the state, with its famous bands like R.E.M. and the B-52s. Tourists come from all over the world to Athens, Georgia, where these two bands grew up. They want to see the tower of the church where R.E.M. lived, recorded and played, or the "Love Shack" the B-52s made famous in their song of the same name.

7 **Alabama** has seen some of the most important struggles by African-Americans for civil rights, including the Montgomery Bus Boycott, which started in 1954 when Rosa Parks refused to give up her seat on a bus to a white person. In the 1970s, those struggles even became a part of pop music when Neil Young criticized racism in Alabama in his song "Southern Man". The southern band Lynyrd Skynyrd replied with their song "Sweet Home Alabama", in which they told Young to mind his own business.

▶ WB 17 (p. 71) • **Text File 10** (pp. 153–154)

5 Practice

1 WORDS Opposites

a) Find the opposites in the two boxes and make a list.

b) Partner A: Close your book and don't look at your list from a). Partner B: Say a word from the list. Partner A: Try to remember its opposite. Swap after about ten words.
B: 'Last'.
A: That's easy. It's 'first'.

c) Choose 5–8 pairs from your list and make sentences with them:
I'm usually the first one in the pool, but it was so cold on Saturday that I was the last one.

against · arrival · background · cheap · clean · dead · early · easy · full · interesting · last · lose · married · modern · near · never · poor · quiet · remember · safe · slow · top · warm

alive · always · boring · bottom · cool · dangerous · ⁺departure · difficult · dirty · divorced · empty · expensive · far · fast · find · first · for · foreground · forget · late · loud · ⁺old-fashioned · rich

2 WORDS The media

Take it in turns: For each verb in the box on the left, find nouns from the box on the right that go with it. (You can also add nouns that aren't in the box.) Make lists.

A: What can you change?
B: You can change a CD, a station, …
A: And you can change money too.
B: Money isn't a media word, but OK, let's add that.

change · copy · download · listen to · play · read · record · send · surf · turn on/off · turn up/down · tune to · use · watch

books · CD · computer · DVD · DVD player · DVD recorder · film · internet · magazines · MP3 player · music · newspapers · programme · radio · text message · station · TV · video · video games · weather report

3 EVERYDAY ENGLISH · SPEAKING Talking about films or TV shows 🎧

a) Listen to Madison and Sally and try to complete their dialogue.
Sally   Hey Madison! What did you do last night?
Madison Oh, it was one of those evenings. I just … and …
Sally   Why do you do that? I … there's something on I want to see.
Madison Yeah, but you're weird. So, was there anything you wanted to see last night? Like the Simpsons?
Sally   No, I … the Simpsons. What …?
Madison Oh, Marge opened a fitness center.
Sally   And, …?
Madison It wasn't bad … was really funny.
Sally   I … on gorillas.
Madison Oh, yeah. You're really interested in … … that Brad Pitt movie tonight. Maybe we can …
Sally   You know, I don't often like those ….
Madison No, all you watch is documentaries.
Sally   So? And anyway, I don't. I love …
Madison Me too.

b) Compare your answers in class. If you have to, listen again.

c) Extra Make appointments with three partners. Ask them about how they watch TV.

4 READING Fire (Text types: fiction and non-fiction)

a) Skim the two texts below and decide which is a newspaper article and which is a short story. Then read the texts and, in one or two sentences, say what they are about.

■ MOTHER

Scarlett was out late that night. She waited in a dark alley and listened for signs of life. But all she heard was the traffic on New York's streets.

She stretched and turned to look back at her house across the street. The orange glow in the upstairs window told her that something was wrong. As she started to run back down the alley, one window broke and with a huge 'whoosh!', flames shot into the night sky.

'My babies!' Scarlett screamed silently. She dashed into the house through an open window. Smoke was beginning to fill the room and it was hard to see, but the sound of her babies' cries guided her.

She picked up the first baby, gently, ran back outside and laid it on the sidewalk. When she came back for her second child, the flames were already dancing down the stairs. She could feel their hot breath on her back as she escaped through the window with her second baby.

She returned three more times for the others. The fire was all around her now and it roared at her like a wild animal. It burned her ears and her eyelids and the skin on her legs. She could barely see. After she carried her last child out, the roof and walls fell, and Scarlett's home was no more.

When the fire was out, a firefighter walked over to the six cats on the sidewalk across the street – the mother and her five kittens. The mother was badly burned. He had seen how she had saved them, how she had gone into the burning house again and again and returned with a kitten in her mouth each time. 'Now,' he thought, 'it's my turn to save her.'

Fire Kills Woman, 2 Young Daughters

FRANKLIN, N.H. — A fire in a 19th-century garden house killed two sisters and their mother, who had run into the building to save them.

The Fire Department identified the victims of the fire early Sunday as Beth MacDonald and daughters Molly, 11, and Jenny, 9. The cause of the fire was still under investigation.

The girls had spent the night in the house, just yards from their home, after decorating it for Easter, the Fire Department said. The parents woke during the night to the smell of smoke. While the father, George, called 911, the mother ran into the building. The father later also tried to enter but was driven back by the flames.

The Fire Department said firefighters arrived in minutes, but it was too late.

b) Which of the texts above – the article or the short story – is fiction? Which is non-fiction? Now look at the text characteristics below and put them into three lists: Fiction – Non-fiction – Both

Text characteristics
The writer ...
1. has invented the story and characters.
2. informs the reader about something that has really happened.
3. tells a story that is sad, exciting, funny, scary, ...
4. wants the reader to think about the topic.
5. wants the reader to use their imagination.
6. deals with real facts, people and events.
7. wants to entertain the reader.
8. wants to give an opinion about something.

c) 👥 Compare your lists with a partner. Give reasons for your decisions. Then make changes to your lists if you need to. Add any other characteristics you can think of.

d) 👥👥 Discuss whether the following text types are fiction or non-fiction. Refer to your lists from c) and give reasons.

advert • biography • blog • diary • entry in an encyclopedia • flyer • novel • play • poem • report • speech

e) Extra Look through the book and find other examples of fiction and non-fiction.

▶ SF Reading Course (p. 16)

5 WRITING A story

a) Look at the photo and caption on the right. Can you write a fictional story about it? Remember what you have already learned about writing stories.

- Brainstorm your ideas, then organize them in an outline for your story. Make sure it has a beginning, middle and end.
- Who is the narrator of your story?
- How can you interest the reader at the beginning (funny/exciting/... start)?
- Think about your style: adjectives, relative clauses, linking words, time phrases, ...

b) When you are ready to start, write your story. Proofread your story when you have finished.

- Is the story clear and does it make sense?
- Is it interesting, exciting, funny, ...? Do you think people will want to read it?
- Have you checked the grammar and the spelling for your favourite mistakes?

c) Extra 👥 Swap stories with a partner. Read their story. Then listen to each other's comments and suggestions. Revise your story once more if you want to and put it in your DOSSIER.

Take Your Child To Work Day goes wrong.

It all began on the morning that my mother took me to work.

The boy had one thought in his head: 'This is going to be the last day of my life!'

'So you think you can be a stuntman just like me?' Red Johnson said to his son. 'OK – let's see.'

6 WORDS Verbs = nouns

a) In these sentences, some words are used as both a noun and a verb. Find them, then say which is the noun and which the verb. Write down their German translations.

1 Sometimes at night I dream I can fly. It's a crazy dream, but lots of fun.
1st 'dream' = verb (träumen); 2nd 'dream' = noun (Traum)
2 If you really need help, there will always be someone who can help you.
3 This test is difficult. Why do they test us on grammar, vocabulary *and* reading?
4 Our friends want to name their baby Elvis. Can you imagine a b with a name like that?
5 When we go to the dance at the community hall we always dance all evening.
6 We visited my grandma last week. It was a very short visit: ten minutes!

b) The words in the box can also be used as both a noun and a verb. Choose five of them and make sentences like the ones in a).

change • cost • cut • fight • hike • hope • hug • move • paint • programme • report • scream • smoke • support • surprise • sweat • talk • work

c) Extra 👥👥 Sit in groups of four and read your sentences to your partners. Can they work out which is the verb and which is the noun?

7 REVISION He was the minister who ... (Defining relative clauses)

Look at the names of people, places and organizations from this unit in box A.
Choose the correct information in boxes B, C and D to describe them.
Be careful with your tenses.
Martin Luther King Jr. was the minister who gave a famous speech in Washington, D.C.

A	B	C	D
Martin Luther King Jr.	city	broadcast	a famous speech in Washington, D. C.
CNN	minister	burn	Atlanta as its capital.
Atlanta	president	give	during the Civil War.
Bill Clinton	radio station	have	for CNN.
Georgia	reporter	open	funny videos.
Mrs Young	US state	play	good news programmes.
Madison	student	show	news 24 hours a day.
NPR	TV network	want	the Olympic Games in Atlanta.
YouTube	website	work	to go to work with her mum for a day.

8 What do you think? (Relative clauses with *which* to refer to a whole clause)

a) Add comments from the box on the right to these statements. Use a relative clause with *which*.
1 Schwarzenegger was born in Austria but still became governor of California →
Schwarzenegger was born in Austria but still became governor of California, which is pretty amazing.
2 When you're on the Skywalk you can see the Grand Canyon thousands of feet below you.
3 We got the boat to the Statue of Liberty.
4 The *Mayflower* was a very small ship and ran into a lot of big storms in the Atlantic.
5 The journey from St. Louis to California took months and went across unknown lands.
6 I'd like to spend a year at an American high school.

- I think it would be good for my English.
- It's so scary.
- It was the most exciting part of our trip.
- It was very dangerous.
- That must have been terrible.
- That's pretty amazing.

b) Comment on these statements yourself. Use a relative clause with *which*.
1 It's more than 40 years since men first stood on the moon, which ...
2 For many Americans, English is a second language, which ...
3 Martin Luther King was only 39 when he was killed, which ...
4 Native Americans make up only about 1% of the population of the USA, which ...
5 Almost all pop music in the West today comes from the music of black Americans, which ...

9 The death of MLK (Non-defining relative clauses)

a) Carefully read the text about Martin Luther King's death. Then decide where you could add the relative clauses with extra information and write this down, e.g. clause 1 after l. 3 ("... workers there").

In late March 1968, Martin Luther King went to Memphis, Tennessee, to support black workers there.¹ On April 3 he gave his "I've been to the mountaintop" speech.²

MLK (second from the right) on the balcony of the Lorraine Motel

King was staying in room 306 at the Lorraine Motel. He was shot on April 4 at 6:01 p.m. while he was standing on the second-floor balcony.
   According to the civil rights activist Jesse Jackson,³ King's last words were to the musician Ben Branch.⁴ King asked Branch to play "Take My Hand, Precious Lord".⁵

"Play it real pretty," he added.
   The death of the civil rights leader shocked the nation and the world.⁶ 300,000 people came to his funeral.⁷
   The Lorraine Motel is now home to the National Civil Rights Museum.⁸

Relative clauses with extra information
1 who had been on strike since March 12
2 which was to be the last speech of his life
3 who was with him on the balcony
4 who was going to play at an event for King that night
5 which was his favourite song
6 which led to riots in more than 60 cities
7 which took place five days later
8 which is in downtown Memphis near the Mississippi River

b) 👥 Now read your text with the extra information to each other. Take turns, sentence for sentence. Also read the punctuation (commas, full stop, ...).

10 REVISION The South (Nouns with or without definite article)

Complete the sentences with **the** where necessary.
1 ... life must have been very hard for slaves on the old cotton plantations.
2 The most interesting thing to learn about in Atlanta is ... life of Martin Luther King.
3 King was one of the greatest black leaders in ... history.
4 King played an important role in ... history of American blacks.
5 ... food is always very important for a region's identity.
6 ... food of the South is often called 'soul food'.

11 LISTENING An interview with Mayor Shirley Franklin 🎧

a) Listen to part 1 of the interview and try to complete the statements below.
1 'If you make me mayor, I'll ...'
2 'I still hear this slogan a lot when I'm out visiting ...'
3 'I've made people proud by being ...'
4 '... do my best every single day so that ...'

Remember: It doesn't matter if you don't understand everything.

b) 👥 Listen to part 2. Describe the three issues Franklin wants to address. Compare with a partner.

Melba's story

Background

Before you read 'Melba's story', look at this background information on segregation in the US in the 1950s.

Slavery ended in the US in 1865. But for almost a century after that, blacks in many states, especially in the South, did not have the same rights as whites and were segregated from them.

'Segregation' meant that laws kept African Americans and white Americans apart – on buses and trains, in restaurants and hostels. There were separate waiting rooms and drinking fountains for 'white' and for 'colored' people. There were schools for white children and schools for black children. And the schools for whites were almost always newer, bigger and better.

In 1954, the Supreme Court of the United States ended school segregation. All schools now had to open their doors not only to white, but also to black children. But some states did not obey the law. One of them was Arkansas.

In 1957, nine black students moved from the high school for black children in Little Rock, Arkansas, to the big high school for whites, Central High. Soon they would be known as the Little Rock Nine.

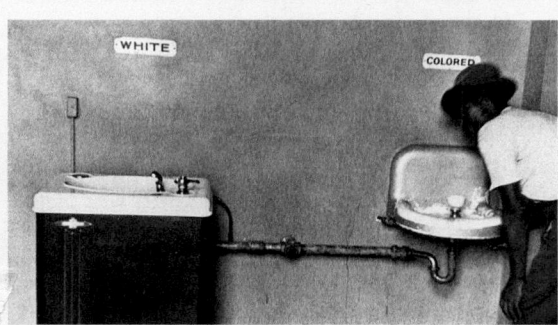

Classroom in a black school

Classroom in a white school

a) Look at the photos and describe what you see.

b) What do the photos tell you about the life of blacks under segregation?

c) With the help of the photos, explain what segregation means. Compare your definition with a partner's.

The story

One of the Little Rock Nine was Melba Pattillo, and this is her story.

Melba Pattillo was born in Little Rock, Arkansas, on 7th December 1941. Arkansas was a segregated state, so when Melba was little she only had contact with black people. Even at the 4th July picnics, the blacks were always in a separate part of the park.

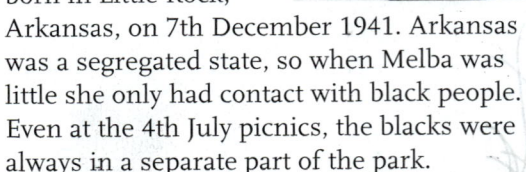

When Melba was five years old, she saved up five cents for 4th July: she wanted to ride one of the horses on the merry-go-round in the park that year. On 4th July the family packed their holiday picnic and went to the part of the park where the blacks were allowed to celebrate. Melba, with her five cents in her hand, ran off to the part of the park where the merry-go-round stood.

She put the money on the ticket man's counter and asked for a ticket. She wanted to ride the black and white horse and could see that it was empty.

'Could I have one ticket for the merry-go-round please, sir?' she asked.

'There's no place for you here,' the ticket man said.

When the little black girl pointed to the empty horse, he shouted:

'You don't belong here, you little nigger!'

In her autobiography *Warriors don't cry*, Melba wrote later: 'Angry faces looked at me as if I had done something very wrong. As I ran past the people who were waiting I was terrified. I didn't even pick up my money. At the age of five I learned that – even if all the horses on the merry-go-round were empty – there would be no place for me.'

In 1955, after the Supreme Court's decision against segregation in public schools, a teacher at Melba's all-black school asked for volunteers: two years from now some black students would be able to go to the big Central High School in Little Rock – until now there were only white students there. Melba immediately volunteered. She was only 13 years old.

In 1957, at the start of the school year on 3rd September, the time had come for nine black students to join the 2000 white students at Little Rock Central High School. But the governor of Arkansas supported the white people who didn't want blacks at their children's school. Crowds of angry white people came to the school. It was too dangerous for the nine black students: they had to stay at home.

The next day, the nine black students decided to meet and go into the school together. But the governor sent the National Guard to the school to stop them. Melba, aged 15, and her mother tried to get through the angry white crowd, to the steps of the school, but they couldn't.

They saw Melba's friend Elizabeth, all alone, trying to get through the National Guard line. But whenever she tried to walk past the guards, they moved closer and blocked her way. The white crowd shouted, 'Get her. Get the nigger out of there. Hang her.'

Elizabeth escaped to a bus stop where two white people protected her till the bus came and then took her home. Melba and her mother ran away from the angry white crowd and escaped in their car. That night Melba wrote in her diary:

'I was disappointed not to see what is inside Central High School. I don't understand why the governor sent soldiers to keep us out. I don't know if I should go back. But Grandma is right. If I don't go back they will think they have won.'

On 23rd September, the black students tried to get into the school again. This time they were smuggled in through a side door. All the white students were cruel to them – they called them names, kicked them and spat at them. In Melba's first class a boy shouted at the teacher: 'Are you going to let that nigger sit in our class?' The teacher did nothing.

Outside the crowd got angrier and angrier. In the end the police decided that they had to get the nine out or they might be killed. They escaped from an underground garage. That night Melba wrote in her diary:

'There seems to be no place for me at Central High. I don't want integration to be like the merry-go-round. Please, God, make a place for me.'

Two days later the US President sent in US Army soldiers to help the black students. The soldiers drove them to the school and protected them as they entered the school through the front door for the first time.

And each of the nine got a soldier as bodyguard for the school day. Melba's was a young soldier called Danny. That night she wrote:

'I feel specially cared about because the soldier is there. If he wasn't there I'd hear more of the voices of those people who say I'm a nigger ... that I'm not valuable, that I have no right to be alive. Thank you, Danny.'

But even Danny couldn't stop one attack on Melba. This is how she describes it in her autobiography.

'Near the end of the day I was walking down a dark hallway, Danny was following me, when I saw a boy coming directly towards me. The boy flashed a shiny black object in my face. The sudden pain in my eyes was so terrible I thought I would die. It was like nothing I had ever felt before. I couldn't hear or see or feel anything except the fire in my eyes. I heard myself cry out.

'Someone grabbed my ponytail and pulled me along very fast. Hands grabbed my wrists and forced me to take my hands from my eyes. Then cold, cold water was splashed in my eyes. The water felt so good.'

The hands were the hands of Danny, Melba's bodyguard. It was his fast action that saved her eyes: what the boy had thrown in them was acid.

Melba was one of the eight black students who got through a whole year at Central High. But the following year, because he didn't want the black kids to graduate with the white kids, the governor of Arkansas closed the school. Little Rock had become so dangerous for the black students at Central High that two of their families had moved away. People all over the country were asked to give them a safe place to live and help them finish their education. The McCabe family in California offered Melba a new home and the chance to finish her education. They were white.

Melba went on to university and became a journalist. Today she lives in San Francisco. Her autobiography makes clear that the work that the Little Rock Nine started is still not finished: 'Today, when I see how far we have come with school integration, in some areas I am pleased. In other areas I am very angry. Why have we not come up with a plan for solving this problem? We put a man on the moon because we gave it enough resources. Today, 36 years after the Central High crisis, school integration is still not a reality.'

Melba Pattillo Beals in 2007

Working with the text

1 Your reaction
a) For you, what is the most shocking sentence in Melba's story? Give reasons.

b) Which of the pictures from pages 111–114 would you put on the cover of Melba's autobiography? Explain why.

2 Headings for the story
Talk to a partner about the following parts of the story. Decide on good headings for them. In one or two sentence say what each part is about.
1 ll. 1–47
2 ll. 48–91
3 ll. 92–108
4 ll. 109–122
5 ll. 123–175

3 Feelings
What link can you see between the painting on the right and Melba's story? How does the artist show how the little girl is feeling?

▶ WB 18 (p. 72) • **Checkpoint 5** WB (p. 73)

4 Integration and segregation
List all the people who showed courage to support integration in schools. What did they do? Then list all those who supported segregation. What did they do?

5 Extra Courage
Melba Patillo had the courage to stand up for what she believed in. Do you know of anyone who has shown courage like this in your town/area/country? Or in another country? Research their story and write a report on them for your DOSSIER.

"The problem we all live with" by Norman Rockwell (1894–1978)

How am I doing?

a) *Fill in or choose the correct answers.*

Atlanta and its history

1. The US Civil War was fought between …
   A black slaves and white farmers
   B states in the north and states in the south
   C the USA and Britain
   D Native Americans and European settlers
2. Martin Luther King worked hard to stop …
   A the Civil Rights Movement
   B the selling of blacks as slaves
   C Shirley Franklin
   D discrimination against blacks
3. Which of these is not at home in Atlanta?
   A Google   B CNN   C Coca Cola
   D the King Center

TV and other media

4. Write down the words that match these definitions:
   a) a TV show that's on one or more times a week
   b) a show with real people, not actors, who do things naturally
   c) a website like *Facebook*
   d) Atlanta's biggest newspaper
   e) a film or TV show that tells you about things that really happened
5. Americans watch TV for an average of
   A 25   B 70   C 100   D 180
   days a year.
6. Mr Young reads a real newspaper in the mornings, but you can also read lots of newspapers …

Research

7. When you do research, always use …
   A Wikipedia   B one good source
   C more than one source
   D sources in your own language
8. The notes on your research should …
   A use your own words   B use the words of your sources as much as possible
   C never say where you got your information   D always use complete sentences
9. In your work, you should …
   A never name your sources
   B name only your most important sources
   C name all your sources

Reading

10. Which are fiction and which are non-fiction?
    a) a short story   b) a flyer
    c) an article   d) a novel

Grammar

11. Join the two sentences with a relative clause.
    The Little Rock Nine were trying to fight segregation in schools. That was a brave thing to do.
12. Complete each sentence with a different relative pronoun (who, which, that).
    a) I like birds … sing at night.
    b) So I'm the one … feeds them.
    c) Listening to birds singing at night is very relaxing, … is why I like it.

b) *Check your answers on p. 133 and add up your points.*

c) *If you had 17 or more points, well done! Maybe you can help students who had fewer points. If you had 16 points or fewer, it's a good idea to do some more work before you go on to the next unit. Where did you make mistakes? The chart below will tell you what you can do to improve your English.*

No.	Area	Find out more	Exercise(s)
1–3	Atlanta and its history	Unit 5 (pp. 98–99, 102–103)	P 7, 9, 10 (pp. 109–110); WB 1 (p. 62)
4–6	TV and other media	Unit 5 (p. 100)	WB 2–4 (pp. 63–64)
7–9	Research	Unit 5 (p. 103); SF (p.158)	WB 15 (p. 70)
10	Reading	P 4 (p. 107)	WB 6 (p. 65)
11–12	Grammar	Unit 5 (p. 102); GF 9–10 (pp. 186–187)	P 7–9 (pp. 109–110); WB 9–11 (pp. 67–68)

Unit 6

Extra **Famous** (abridged and adapted from *Totally over you* by Mark Ravenhill)

Before you read

What makes someone famous? Brainstorm a few ideas with a partner and write them down. When your teacher tells you, find a new partner, listen to what your teacher says and brainstorm some more. Now read the play.

CAST (all aged 14 to 16)

Kitty	Jake
Rochelle	Dan
Hannah	Tyson
Sinita	Framji
Letitia	Victor
Donna	Michael
Rachel	Rubin
Indu	

An empty stage.
Kitty and Jake enter. Kitty is carrying a bag.

Kitty Don't laugh, Jake, don't laugh at me.
Jake I'm sorry, Kit. But when you talk about celebrity, when you tell me that you and Roche and H and Sin are going to be famous ———
Kitty We are.
Jake – I have to laugh.
Kitty Because …?
Jake Because … In six months – six months when I thought we'd told each other all our secrets – six months and you've never told me that –
Kitty And when I do you laugh at me.
Jake I'm sorry, Kit.
Kitty I choose to share my dream with you and you laugh.
Jake I shouldn't but – I just never knew. Tell me. Tell me what you dream about.
Kitty You mustn't laugh.
Jake I won't.
Kitty Even a little laugh and I'll stop.
Jake I promise. I want to understand girls. I want to understand what goes on in their heads. I want to know what you talk about. You and Roche and H and Sin. Tell me. Tell me about your dream.
Kitty OK. We're going to be celebrities. Pretty soon, you're going to see us everywhere. Huge billboards[1] with our faces on. TV screens with us talking, moving, dancing, laughing. The front pages will tell you what we're up to[2] every day. If we choose the fish over the caviar in a restaurant they're going to talk about it live on CNN. You go to buy a can of coke – they'll have our faces on the side. Lots of Japanese kids are going to dress like us. Your screensaver, your desktop, your mobile's welcome screen – all of them will be me and Roche and H and Sin.

Pause. Then Jake laughs.

Kitty Oh piss off[3], Jake. Just piss off.
Jake I'm sorry, Kit. I just … You know.
Kitty What?
Jake Look at us. This town, this school. It just seems such a fantasy.
Kitty An ambition. That's the trouble with you, Jake. You don't want anything.
Jake I want ———
Kitty I am so fed up with you.
Jake I'm sorry, I'll ———
Kitty I don't want to see you any more.
Jake What, you're …?
Kitty I'm ending this relationship. Here. Now. Goodbye.
Jake No. Kit. Wait. You can't just walk away.
Kitty Why not?
Jake Because I love you.
Kitty That's nice.

---

[1] billboard ['bɪlbɔːd] *Reklametafel*   [2] (to) be up to *treiben, machen*   [3] Piss off. [ˌpɪs ˈɒf] *Hau ab.*

	Jake	And you love me.	
70	Kitty	Do I? Do I really, Jay? I don't think so. No. I think I used to. But I'm growing up fast. Six months ago I was a kid and now …	
	Jake	Now you're a celebrity.	
75	Kitty	Now I'm ready to be a celebrity. And I don't need you any more.	
	Jake	Kitty, please.	
	Kitty	You're a nice guy. You're quite good-looking. You have a sense of humour. Someone else will go out with you.	
80			
	Jake	No.	
	Kitty	Goodbye. I'm not you're girlfriend any more.	
85	Jake	I've still got the photo of you up beside my bed. The photo I put up the day I asked you out and you said yes.	
	Kitty	You have to go now. Rochelle's on her way here and we've got a lot to talk about.	
90			
	Jake	Plans for the future?	
	Kitty	Sort of.	
	Jake	So what now? Talk to your stylists? Talk to your PR people? Sort out a few photo-shoots[1]? A few interviews?	
95			
	Kitty	Piss off, Jake.	
	Jake	Or maybe you're just going to sit here with your magazines like *Heat* and *Hello* –––	
100			
	Kitty	No, actually, no.	
	Jake	––– sit here and waste your time with pointless[2], pointless dreams?	
	Rochelle enters.		
105	Rochelle	Hi, guys.	
	Jake	What are you going to be?	
	Kitty	How do you mean?	
	Jake	In five years, ten years, twenty years. What are you going to be?	
110	Kitty	I told you, Jacob. Celebrities.	
	Rochelle	That's right.	
	Jake	Are you going to be in a band?	
	Kitty	Maybe. I don't know.	
	Jake	Or act?	

Kitty	Yeah. Could do.		115
Jake	Or model or present on MTV or –?		
Kitty	Yeah, yeah, Jake –––		
Jake	Well – which one? What's going to make you famous?		
Kitty	I don't know. I don't care. It doesn't matter.		120
Jake	You've got to have a talent.		
Kitty	Of course, yeah.		
Jake	And I hate to tell you this, girls, but you can't sing, you can't act, you're OK-looking but you're not models –––		125
Kitty	We'll find a way.		
Jake	You're dreaming, the pair of you.		
Kitty	You think so?		
Jake	Yeah. Silly, silly girls.		130
Kitty	OK. You want to know? You want to know what's going to make us famous?		
Jake	Yes. I want to know what's going to make you famous.		135
Kitty	OK. We're going to date celebrities.		
Rochelle	That's right.		
Jake	Oh, really?		
Kitty	Not boys, not children, not the kids we have to hang around with here, but proper, A-list, friends-of-Elton-John celebrities.		140
Rochelle	That's right.		
Jake	Ridiculous.		
Kitty	To you. To you. You boy. You baby. But to us. Have you any idea how frustrating[3] it's been going out with you when you know you should be going out with a star?		145
Jake	Fantastic. Sleep your way to the top.		150
Kitty	No, Jake. Love my way to the top. And the top is going to love me. Now can you please go? Roche needs to talk to me, don't you, Roche?		
Rochelle	That's right.		155
Kitty	Roche is really upset, aren't you, Roche?		
Rochelle	That's right.		
Jake	And where are you going to meet him? Where are you going to meet your celebrity?		160

[1] photo-shoot *Fototermin, Fotoshooting*   [2] pointless ['pɔɪntləs] *sinnlos*   [3] frustrating [frʌ'streɪtɪŋ] *frustrierend, ärgerlich*

	Kitty	I don't know.	Rochelle	No, Kit. I didn't.
	Jake	Just going to bump into[1] him at the shop?	Kitty	You had to do it, Roche. Dan's a nice guy –
165	Kitty	Maybe.	Rochelle	He's a really nice guy.
	Jake	He spills his Fanta over you and the next week you're kissing on a beach on page four of *Heat*?	Kitty	– but can you imagine him with David Beckham or Sting or the Queen?
	Kitty	Possibly, yes, possibly.	Rochelle	No. No, I can't.
170	Jake	You're ridiculous, Kit.	Kitty	He'd say all the wrong things. And what about his skin?
	Kitty	I hate you, Jake. Freak off[2]. Go on. I don't want you here. It's going to happen. Today. By the end of the day I'm going to be dating a celeb.	Rochelle	It is a bit zitty[5].
			Kitty	Exactly. "Rochelle and her zitty boyf[6] welcome you into their new luxury home."
175	Rochelle	That's right.	Rochelle	Yuck. No way.
	Jake	By the end of the day? That's a promise?	Kitty	We're going to find you a nice Calvin Klein model.
	Kitty	That's a promise.	Rochelle	Oh, yeah. Skinny[7] but fit.
	Jake	Ha. Ha. Ha.	Kitty	With a tattoo like a barcode on his bum[8].
180	*Jake exits*[3].			
			Hannah enters.	
	Kitty	Loser. We'e going to show him.	Hannah	Oh God. I feel like such a bitch[9]. "Tyson, this is the end." He just kept on repeating in this really miserable voice: "Why? Why" Why?" Over and over again. "Why? Why? Why?" And now he wants back everything he ever gave me: CDs, videos, T-shirts. Everything. I'm going to miss them so much. This better be worth it, Kit.
	Rochelle	Maybe he's right, Kit. Maybe we're never going to make it.		
185	Kitty	No. You know what that horoscope said.		
	Rochelle	I know.		
	Kitty	"Finish old relationships and prepare to live your dreams." And that's exactly what we've got to do. Did you do it?		
190			Kitty	Worth it? H, what's Tyson when you are going to have your pick of film stars, singers, footballers, models? You want Brad Pitt?
	Rochelle	Yeah. I did it just like you said. Only …		
	Kitty	I need you with me, Rochelle. We've got to stick together[4]. Everybody else in this stupid school, this stupid town, is going to laugh at us, but you and me and H and Sin, we've got to be there for each other. OK?	Hannah	I'd love Brad Pitt but –––
195			Kitty	Then work it, girl. We're going to be so famous he won't resist.
			Hannah	But isn't he with –––?
	Rochelle	OK. Just …	Kitty	You'll be all over the papers for days. Your PR people will have to work so hard. "I'm sorry about all the hurt I've caused," you'll say. "But Brad and I are so happy together."
200	Kitty	Yeah?		
	Rochelle	Dan cried. When I said, "I don't want to be your girlfriend any more," he started to cry. With great big tears. And I wanted to say, "Dan, Dan. Stop. I didn't mean it. I still love you."		
205			Hannah	Yes. A quiet wedding. Brad. Our families. And a few friends.
	Kitty	But you didn't.		

[1] (to) bump into sb. [bʌmp] *jn. stoßen, jm. über den Weg laufen* [2] Freak off. [ˌfriːk ˈɒf] *Hau ab.* [3] (to) exit [ˈeksɪt] *abgehen (von Bühne)*
[4] (to) stick together *zusammenhalten* [5] zitty [ˈzɪti] *pickelig, voller Pickel* [6] boyf [bɔɪf] *(infml)* = boyfriend [7] skinny [ˈskɪni] *dünn* [8] bum [bʌm] *Hintern* [9] bitch [bɪtʃ] *Schlampe, Miststück*

	Kitty	That's it. And where's Tyson going to be? The supermarket? The call centre?
	Hannah	Car-park attendant maybe.
	Kitty	Let him read about it in the papers.
	Hannah	Brad and I are going to meditate together for an hour every morning.

Sinita enters, crying.

	Sinita	I hate you, Kitty. Why did you make me do that? I love Framji, I do. And now. I finished with him. *(She cries.)*
	Rochelle	Come on, babe.
	Sinita	He says he never wants to see me again. Or walk down the same street as me. Or take the same bus as me. Or use the same search engine as me. Totally – gone. Forever. And what am I going to do without him?
	Kitty	Do without him? Do without him? You know what you're going to do without him. Same as me without Jay, same as Roche without Dan, same as H without Ty. Be a celebrity.
	Sinita	And are you sure about that, Kit?
	Kitty	Yes of course. Totally sure. Aren't you?
	Sinita	Well …
	Kitty	Sin. You can't give up this easily. I know this is hard. But think of the reward[1]. Think of waking up in this totally fantastic house next to your totally fantastic boyfriend.
	Rochelle	And there's a TV crew already there as you open your eyes. They're making a documentary about you 24/7. There's a whole channel that shows it all totally live.
	Hannah	And then you exercise with your personal trainer.
	Kitty	Make some calls to Japan as you eat your breakfast – they're planning this Barbie-type doll of you for markets all around the world.
	Rochelle	The morning: photo-shoots – a calendar. Some measurements[2] for your wedding dress. *Hello* is sponsoring your wedding. Only fourteen months to go.
	Hannah	Lunch with Beyoncé and Madonna. Chatter, chatter. You debate: is hatha yoga now out? Then cameras: flash, flash, flash.
	Kitty	The afternoon: a massage and a meeting with a team from LA who want to turn you into a cartoon series for TV. You tell them: nice idea but you want to see what happens with the movie rights first.
	Rochelle	Then off to a gallery. You've done a painting for charity. Just a fun thing. "I'm no artist," you tell the reporters. "But I do care about sick children and I just wanted to do what I could to help."
	Hannah	And then up the red carpet at a film première. "Is it true that they're making you into a musical?" "No comment." Then party, party. "Hi, Nicole! Hi, Ewan! Hallo, Uma!"
	Kitty	And as you fall into your bed you say: "I did it. This is me. My dream, my hope, my destiny[3]. Celebrity." Today was hard. I know that, girls. "Finish old relationships"; that's hard. But now it's time, time to live your dreams. Are you going to do that, Sin?
	Sinita	Will I have a stalker[4]?
	Kitty	Maybe.
	Sinita	I'd like a stalker. Someone who fills their house with pictures of me. Goes through my bins. Names all their children after me. Who can't get me out of their head.
	Kitty	Of course you'll have a stalker.
	Sinita	And says he'll shoot himself if I don't return his calls.
	Kitty	Yes. Absolutely.
	Sinita	Oh wow.
	Kitty	Are we sticking together, girls? Are we sistas?

---

[1] reward [rɪˈwɔːd] *Belohnung*   [2] measurement [ˈmeʒəmənt] *Maßnehmen*   [3] destiny [ˈdestɪni] *Schicksal*   [4] stalker [ˈstɔːkə] *jd., der/die Prominente verfolgt und belästigt*

	Rochelle	
345	Hannah	*(together)* Yeah.
	Sinita	
	Kitty	Then come on. New *OK* out today. New *Sugar*. See what our horoscopes say today.

Kitty takes magazines from her bag and hands them round.

Kitty   OK. Horoscope time. Oh my God. Oh my God. Look at this. "A stranger will show you the way to future happiness today." What does that mean? Keep your eyes open for a stranger, girls.

Letitia, Donna, Rachel, Indu, Michael and Rubin enter.

Kitty   Ugh. Look.
Hannah   Do I see the most uncool people on the whole planet?
Sinita   The whole universe.
Rochelle   Oh no. The drama class.
Indu   Hey, girls, you missed a great drama class today.
Kitty   We've got no time to talk to you guys. We're waiting for a stranger.
Rachel   We had all these numbers and that was the status you were. Status is like a power, yeah, a sort of power, status sort of thing.
Sinita   Right.
Rubin   So – say you're a king. Then you're like a ten. Unless you're a low status, sort of nervous king. Then you're like a three or something.
Hannah   Wow. Sounds amazing.
Letitia   And I got a two. Which is really, really low. Like a really stupid, clumsy[1] sort of person.
Rochelle   Wow, Tish. That must have been hard.
Letitia   Yeah. That's what I thought at first. But then – when I got into it – wow – I was like this total two.
Kitty   Tish. You're sad.

Donna   Not as sad as you, bunking off[2] so you can ———
Sinita   Drama's for losers, Donna.
Michael   But if you want to be celebrities ———
Hannah   And what do they teach us? Improvization? Theatre games? Romeo and Juliet? No, thank you. That's not the stuff we need to know.
Rochelle   Yeah. We want to know how to make love to the camera.
Kitty   How to use a microphone. When to listen to your stylist and when to listen to your instincts.
Hannah   How to handle[3] the press. What dress to choose for a première.
Sinita   How to mime in videos, voice-over[4] for an ad.
Kitty   And who's the best agent if you're going to be a star. But do they teach us that? No.
Rochelle   This is the twenty-first century. Drama's for losers.
Letitia   But I just think it would be so great.
Sinita   What would?
Letitia   To lose yourself. Become another person.
Kitty   That's not the way it works any more, Tish. You're a brand[5]. You sell yourself. You don't become another person.
Letitia   But that's what I want to ———
Kitty   Then you keep going to drama classes. You keep wasting your time with silly games. But me and the girls aren't doing that. Are we, girls?

	Rochelle	
	Hannah	*(together)* No.
	Sinita	

Kitty   Come on, girls. Let's find a stranger to show us the way to future happiness. Enjoy the acting, Letitia.

Kitty, Rochelle, Hannah and Sinita exit.

Letitia   Status ten. Status ten. Status ten. Status one. Status one. Status one.

Letitia exits.

---

[1] clumsy ['klʌmzi] tollpatschig   [2] bunk off [bʌŋk] schwänzen   [3] handle ['hændl] steuern, managen   [4] voice-over ['vɔɪsˌəʊvə] Filmkommentar, Offstimme   [5] brand [brænd] Marke

Donna   Tish? Tisha? She is so upset.

Donna, Indu, Rachel, Michael and Rubin exit.
435 *Jake and Victor enter.*

Jake   Victor. Will you stop following me? I want to be alone.
Victor But we said we'd go to a movie.
Jake   Yeah. Well, I've changed my mind.
440 Victor There's a sci-fi thing. Which sounds good. Or an action thing. Which sounds OK. Or a comedy. Which sounds really funny. Which do you fancy[1]?
445 Jake   None of them.
Victor I've got some DVDs if you want to ---
Jake   No.
Victor Or games. My mum left pizza and some oven chips ---
450 Jake   Vic. I want to be by myself. Please.
Victor But – why?
Jake   Kit finished with me.
Victor No way.
Jake   Yeah. She chucked me. So ---
455 Victor I'm sorry.
Jake   And I just want to go into my room and be alone.
Victor But surely a movie would ---
Jake   No, Vic. I'm sorry.
460 Victor Or a pizza or just hanging out at Burger King.
Jake   Victor. No.
Victor OK. But maybe if we just talked ---
Jake   This isn't freaking[2] Oprah OK? It's
465   not: "Jake – My Girlfriend Just Chucked Me." Then talk, talk, talk and out she comes from behind a freaking screen[3]. And she talks and Oprah talks. And the crowd goes
470   "Ooo" and then we hug and I cry. And it's the end and Oprah says: "When you talk the hurt begins to heal[4]." OK?
Victor OK.
475 Jake   Why does everybody want to talk? Confess[5]? Kiss and tell? I hate this freaking world we live in.
Victor I know you do, Jay.

Jake   These freaking silly boybands and models and movie stars who confess   480
        everything just so they can fill up magazines. It's all shit.
Victor That's right, Jay.
Jake   Well, I'm not talking. Because no one understands what's happening   485
        inside me. No one knows and there's no way I can make them know. And I don't want to make them know.
Victor But I'm your friend.
Jake   I know and ---   490
Victor All the things we've done together. Things I've done for you.
Jake   But Vic – you're a dork[6]. You've never been out with a girl.
Victor I'd like to.   495
Jake   And I don't want to talk to someone who doesn't know anything about girls.
Victor You know Letitia?
Jake   If you haven't been out with a girl   500
        you're a child, Vic.
Victor She did the Nurse in that scene from Romeo and Juliet.
Jake   That's the difference between us, Vic.   505
Victor I like Letitia. I keep on having dreams about her. I want to ask her out.
Jake   You're a child and I'm a man.

Dan enters.   510

Dan   I don't believe it. I just don't believe it. Roche finished with me.
Jake   She chucked you?
Dan   Just sat down and said: "I don't want to see you any more. We're finished.   515
        Over." She wants to be a celebrity, Jay.
Jake   Oh my God.
Victor Do you want to see a movie?
Dan   Where do you get Prozac from? Do   520
        you have to go to a doctor?
Victor I think the action movie could be good.

---

[1] (to) fancy sth. ['fænsi] *auf etwas Lust haben*   [2] freaking ['fri:kɪŋ] *verdammt*   [3] screen [skri:n] *Trennwand*   [4] (to) heal [hi:l] *heilen*
[5] (to) confess [kən'fes] *beichten, gestehen*   [6] dork [dɔ:k] *Depp, Idiot*

525	Dan	Or can you just buy it? She's going to be famous and she doesn't want to be seen with a boy like me. Would you call me zitty?	Kitty	Come on, girls. They're not going to help us.

Tyson enters.

Kitty, Rochelle, Hannah and Sinita exit.

	Tyson	Bitch. Bitch. Bitch.	Framji	Did you see that? Didn't even look at me.
530	Jake	What's that, Ty?	Jake	We need to show them, guys.
	Tyson	Hannah. What a freaking bitch. Chucked me. I've never been chucked. Never.	Tyson	Yeah. We need to punish them.
			Dan	We need to hurt them.
			Framji	To teach them a lesson.
	Jake	Did she say she wanted to be ---?	Jake	To show them how stupid they are.
535	Tyson	A celebrity. Can you believe that? I told her: no freaking way, baby. And then she got mad at me and chucked me. I'm just so angry.	Dan	But how?
			Victor	Maybe if I ---?
			Dan	What's the best way to make them suffer?
			Victor	Can I ---? I've got an idea.
	Victor	Maybe going to a movie would help?	Tyson	Victor. You don't know anything about girls. You go off to the library and let us figure this thing out¹.
540	Tyson	What's he doing here? What are you doing here?		
	Victor	There's a sci-fi movie ---	Framji	They're coming back. They're coming this way.
	Tyson	Shut up, Victor, shut up.	Dan	Run.

Framji enters.

			Jake	Stay.
545	Framji	Guys. You'll never guess. Sin finished with me.	Tyson	Hide.
			Victor	Guys. I'm going to show you ... Can I show you? Guys.
	Jake	We know. Same for all of us, Fram. Me and Kit. Dan and Roche. H and Ty. You and Sin. We've all been chucked.		

Jack, Dan, Tyson and Framji hide.
Kitty, Rochelle, Hannah and Sinita enter.
Victor covers his face.

550			Victor	The future. The future. I see the future.
	Dan	On the same day.		
	Tyson	At the same time.	Rochelle	Ugh. Look. A loony².
	Framji	But – they must have planned this.	Sinita	A loony homeless person.
	Jake	That's right.	Hannah	Ugh. Gross³. They don't wash. And they really smell.
555	Framji	I don't believe it. What a bitch.		
	Tyson	Yeah. Total bitches. All of them.	Sinita	And they get really aggressive if you don't give them money.

Kitty, Rochelle, Hannah and Sinita enter.

			Rochelle	Well, I'm not giving him anything.
	Kitty	Oh, hi. We didn't know you were here.	Kitty	Girls. Listen for a moment. Just listen to what he's saying.
560	Jake	Yeah. That's right. We're here.		
	Hannah	We're looking for a stranger. To show the way to future happiness.	Victor	The mortal⁴ man walks backward His face toward what's gone The future is a mystery But still he travels on.
	Tyson	Right.		
	Rochelle	Like it says here. You seen a stranger?		
565			Sinita	It's like mad person's talk.
	Dan	No. Don't think so. No.	Kitty	No. It makes sense if you listen.

---

¹ (to) figure sth. out ['fɪgə] etwas begreifen, schlau werden aus etwas   ² loony ['luːni] verrückt   ³ gross [grəʊs] ekelhaft
⁴ mortal ['mɔːtl] sterblich

	Victor	But I am not as other men	
		Who only see what's done	
		My brain is burnt with future lives	
615		I see the world to come.	
		The future. The future. I see the future.	
	Kitty	Who are you?	
	Hannah	Kit, I think we ought to be going	
620		now.	
	Kitty	No, no. We've got to talk to him. Find out ---	
	Rochelle	He's really creepy[1], Kit.	
	Sinita	Yeah. I think he may be dangerous.	
625	Kitty	But girls – if he sees the future ---	
	Victor	I know you. I know you. I know you. I know you.	
	Sinita	Oh my God. He's going completely mental[2].	
630	Rochelle	I want another Diet Coke. Let's all go and buy another Diet Coke.	
	Sinita	Yeah, Roche. Good idea.	
	Kitty	Girls. We've got to ask him. We've got to make him tell us. What happens to us? How do we get to be celebrities?	
635			
	Hannah	There's no point asking him. He's a loony.	
	Kitty	Stick together, girls. We've got to stick together.	
640			
	Victor	I know you. I know you. I know you. I know you.	
	Kitty	Me?	
	Victor	Everybody knows you.	
645	Kitty	In the future.	
	Victor	You are famous in the future.	
	Kitty	Oh my God. That's amazing.	
	Victor	Your picture is everywhere in the future. A hotel in Bangkok, an IMAX in New Mexico, a hologram in Times Square – it's you.	
650			
	Kitty	I knew it. I knew I was right.	
	Victor	You are a line of clothes, a cola drink, a fitness video, a salad dressing, a doll, a video game, a mouse pad, a car sticker[3], a newspaper column, a talkshow, the most hits in a day on AOL, a remix, beauty tips, a diet plan, a chain of restaurants, a sex symbol, role-model superstar. You are live action, animation, computer-generated[4], holographic, CD ROM, exclusive pictures, pay-to-view[5]. All of them are you and you are all of them. Oh, yes, I know you. In the future I know you. In the future everybody knows you.	
655			
			660
			665
	Kitty	And Roche and H and Sin as well?	
	Victor	And Roche and H and Sin as well.	
	Rochelle	Oh, my God.	670
	Hannah	Oh, my God.	
	Sinita	Amazing.	
	Victor	The bedrooms that you live in now will be museums – a place for all your fans to come. Coaches will stop outside your school: "That's the place. That's where she studied."	675
	Rochelle	That is so cool.	
	Victor	Everybody who ever knew you will sell everything you gave them. "This item personally touched by Kitty." And everything bought – instantly.	680
	Sinita	What will we be famous for?	
	Victor	Do you know the band "Awesome"?	
	Sinita	No.	685
	Victor	Four boys. The finest voices, best dance routines. Best songs. The four most famous faces of the future.	
	Kitty	And we're …	
	Victor	You date them. And they bring you fame.	690
	Hannah	And when do we meet them? Where do we meet them?	
	Victor	You've already met them.	
	Kitty	We have?	695
	Victor	They are here in your town, your school right now. "Awesome" are amongst you. The four most famous faces of the future, the biggest celebrities the world has ever known are Jake and Dan and Ty and Framji.	700
	Sinita	But we just … Oh no …	
	Victor	Yes?	
	Rochelle	We just chucked them.	

[1] creepy ['kri:pi] *gruselig* [2] (to) go mental ['mentl] *verrückt werden, durchdrehen* [3] sticker *Aufkleber* [4] computer-generated ['dʒenəreɪtɪd] *mithilfe des Computers erzeugt* [5] pay-to-view *Pay-TV, „Bezahlfernsehen"*

705	Victor	You ...? Oh no. Then you must unchuck them fast. You can't meddle[1] with the future. You have to date them or the future's empty: blank[2] videos, blank ads, blank T-shirts, blank covers on the magazines. Without your faces, there is nothing. Quick, quick. Find your friends. Oh God. It's hurting. When time is bent[3] like this it hurts me. Ugh. Ugh. Put the future right. Go out with Jake and Dan and Ty and Fram. Date "Awesome"! Agh! Agh!
	Kitty	Oh my God!
	Victor	Before it's too late! Aaaaaaggh!

Kitty, Rochelle, Hannah, Sinita exit.

	Framji	Woah! Yes! Yes! Yes! Excellent, Victor!
	Tyson	Yeah! Fantastic! That was so cool.
	Jake	Brilliant! You are such a good actor.
725	Victor	Thank you.
	Dan	Yeah. You were totally convincing[4].
	Jake	And now. Now we can get our own back[5].
	Tyson	Yeah.
730	Jake	'Cos we know what it's like to want someone, need someone, love someone and be pushed aside. We know that feeling, don't we, guys?
	Dan	Oh, yeah.
735	Jake	Well, now it's their turn. They are going to beg us, guys. They are going to cry and do anything they can to get us back. But we are going to say: no way. Agreed?
740	Framji Tyson Dan	(*together*) Agreed.
	Jake	Come on then. Let the fun begin.

Jake, Framji, Tyson and Dan start to leave.

745	Victor	Listen, guys. I've got another idea. Make them look really stupid.
	Jake	What's that, Vic?
	Victor	Let's play with their minds. These girls want to meet celebrities. Then let's arrange for them to meet a few. Let's make them think they've made it. Then destroy them.
	Tyson	Yeah.
	Victor	You're going to see those girls looking so stupid. Follow me.

Letitia enters.

	Letitia	Hey. What you up to?
	Victor	We're sort of ... We're going to do some acting.
760	Letitia	Acting? I love acting.
	Victor	I saw you in that scene. The Nurse.
	Letitia	Oh yes. The Nurse. I wanted to be Juliet but ...
	Victor	You want to do some acting with us?
765	Tyson	Vic. This is a boy thing.
	Dan	Yeah, Victor. This is us against them.
	Letitia	Who against who?
	Jake	Sorry, Vic. But we don't want her in on it. No girls.

Jake, Dan, Tyson and Framji exit.

	Letitia	What do they mean, us against them?
	Victor	They just – they've sort of gone off[6] girls.
775	Letitia	And you? Are you off girls?
	Victor	Oh no. I'm on girls. I mean I like girls. I like a girl.
	Letitia	Yeah?
	Victor	Listen. If you want to do the acting with us ...
780	Letitia	OK.
	Victor	I'll try and persuade them. I'd like to give you a big part. And we'll need the drama class as well.
785	Letitia	Are we putting on a play?
	Victor	A sort of play. Well, more a sort of concert. A play-concert-media-event sort of ... You'll see.

---

[1] (to) meddle with sth. ['medl] *an etwas herumdoktern*   [2] blank [blæŋk] *leer*   [3] bent [bent] *verbogen, verzerrt*
[4] convincing [kən'vɪnsɪŋ] *überzeugend*   [5] (to) get one's own back *sich revanchieren, es (jm.) heimzahlen*
[6] (to) go off sb./sth. *jn./etwas nicht mehr mögen, das Interesse an jm./etwas verlieren*

Working with the text

1 Understanding the play

a) What is the play about? What is its message? Write down five ideas on five cards.

b) 👥 Compare your ideas in a group and choose the three best ones. Present your ideas to the class.

2 Understanding the details

a) Answer these questions:
1 What dream does Kitty share with Jake on page 116?
2 What reasons does Kitty give for finishing with Jake? Find as many reasons as you can.
3 How do Kitty and her friends plan to become celebrities?

b) Write five more questions about the play. Collect the ten best questions on the board and try to answer them in class.

3 What happens next?

a) 👥 Work in groups of four. What do you think Victor is planning? Brainstorm ideas about what will happen in the second half of the play.

b) Now work on your own. Choose your favourite ideas and write down the series of events (the 'plot') which form the second half of the play.

c) 👥 Read your plot ideas to each other and discuss them. Together, choose the best ideas and write a new plot. Then write a short scene (20–30 lines) from your plot. The scene should also be for four characters.

d) 👥 Practise reading your scene and then perform it for the class.

4 Your reactions to the play

Which of the adjectives below describe what you think of the play? Explain your reactions.

> annoying • boring • clever • funny •
> interesting • realistic • sad • silly •
> uninteresting • unrealistic

5 The characters

a) On a piece of A4 paper make a diagram like the one below for these four characters from the play.
How do the characters feel about each other? How do they behave towards each other? Make notes on your diagram.

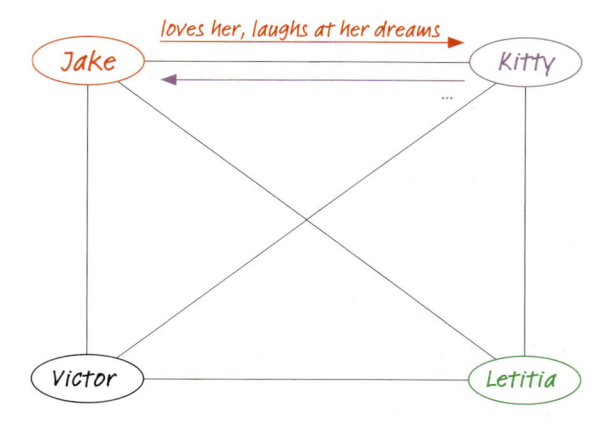

```
         loves her, laughs at her dreams
  Jake ──────────────────────────────▶ Kitty
    ◀─────────────────────────────
       ╲           ╱
        ╲         ╱
         ╲       ╱
          ╲   ╱
           ╳
          ╱   ╲
         ╱     ╲
        ╱       ╲
       ╱         ╲
  Victor ──────────────────────── Letitia
```

b) 👥 Discuss your diagrams. Then each choose a character. In front of the class, show what you think of the other characters, but don't use words. Just make a movement that expresses your feelings and then stand still like a statue.

c) Which character do you think is most interesting? Why?
I think … is most interesting because he/she …
… is the only one who …
… says what he/she is really thinking.
… tries very hard to help …
… is very funny/understanding/clever/…

d) Would you like the character you chose in c) as a friend in real life? Why?/Why not?
I'd like … as a friend because …
I wouldn't want … as a friend because …
… would make me angry / …
… would be a great/terrible friend because he/she …

6 　 Putting on the play

a) Divide the class into groups of students who would like to
- act (15 students),
- find props, make costumes and think of make-up (4–6),
- choose the music and do the lighting (2–4),
- design a programme (2–4).

b) Work in your groups as follows:

Actors

First go through the play and divide it into scenes (they should end/start where people exit or enter). Practise reading a few scenes. You might like to add to or change the stage directions.

> **Tip**
>
> **Stage directions**
> The stage directions sometimes tell you about the scenery and props, and sometimes about the actors, e.g. what they should do, how they should do it, how they speak or what their characters feel.
> The stage directions in this play are very simple. More detailed stage directions might help you for your own performance.

Discuss how the characters walk, move and speak.
- Tyson seems very aggressive, so I think he speaks loudly.
- Maybe that's true when he first comes on because he's angry about Hannah, but later I think …

> **Tip**
>
> **How do characters feel and speak?**
> If the stage directions don't help, you have to read the play closely to understand how characters feel or speak.
> Look at the following lines in the play and say how you think the characters are feeling. The words at the bottom might help.
> Jake: l. 138; Kitty: l. 145; Rochelle: ll. 182–183, l. 225; Hannah: ll. 258–259; Sinita: ll. 269–270
>
> angry • bitter • dreamy • enthusiastic • lonely • sarcastic • scared • unhappy • unsure • …

Work with a partner. Choose an adverb from below and ask your partner to say this line from the play in that way:
'What are you doing here?' (ll. 540–541)

> angrily • coldly • curiously • happily • in surprise • loudly • quietly • excitedly

Can the others guess how he/she was trying to say it?

In groups of five, decide how Victor and the girls should act lines 694–720 (including the stage direction). Then act the scene for the class.

Now decide who acts which role. Study and learn your roles and rehearse as often as you can.

Props, costume and make-up artists

Read through the play and decide what objects ('props') the actors need.
- Kitty needs a school bag for her magazines.
- Yes, and how does Victor know about all the films? Perhaps he's got …

Make a list of the characters and decide on what clothes they should wear and if make-up is necessary.
- I think the four girls' clothes should be really cool – you know, like real celebrities.
- Maybe the drama class could wear funny costumes to show that …

Music and lighting

Choose music and lighting that match the atmosphere in each scene.
- We need to decide whether this all happens outside or inside, maybe at school.
- Perhaps there should be some music every time somebody enters or exits. But what sort?

Programme designers

Design a programme for the audience.
Think of an illustration for the cover that will show people something about the play and make them want to see it.
Include a cast list and the names of the actors.
Write a short summary of the play (but don't give away too much).

Don't forget the time and place of the performance.
- We have to design a poster too because the cover of the programme should be the same as the poster.

c) Put on the play for other students in your year/for the school/for your parents/…

7 Understanding the English in the play

a) Use an English–English dictionary and find out:
1. two different meanings of **celebrity**,
2. what part of speech (verb, noun, adjective, etc.) **pretty** is in l. 33.
3. What are the **front pages** (l. 37)?
4. The word **chuck** is used a lot in the play – but with what meaning? Find another way of saying it in the play.
5. How else could you say **ridiculous** (l. 144)?

b) Look up any other interesting new words from the play in an English–English dictionary.
If you need a dictionary to do any of the other tasks on pp. 126–127, try to use an English–English dictionary first.

STUDY SKILLS Using an English–English dictionary

You use an **English–German** dictionary when you want to find out what English words mean.
You use a **German–English** dictionary when you want to find out how you can say or write something in English.
With an **English–English** dictionary, you can do both.
An **English–English** dictionary will also show you better how English words are used.

▶ SF Using an English–English dictionary (p. 157)

B Partner

Unit 1

1 The five boroughs of New York

a) Listen to your partner. Which of the five boroughs of New York is she/he describing?

b) Now read out the texts below. Your partner must decide which boroughs you're describing.
- A famous ferry goes between this borough – it's an island – and Manhattan. On the way it goes past the Statue of Liberty. It's south-west of Manhattan.[1]
- There's a river between this borough and the island of Manhattan. It's north of Manhattan. Lots of famous black singers and bands come from here.[2]

[1] The correct answer is 'Staten Island'. [2] The correct answer is 'The Bronx'.

5 Visiting New York is great (Gerund as subject)

a) Choose one of the phrases below to answer your partner's questions. First, make a gerund from the verb in brackets.
(visit) Ellis Island
(have) lunch in Chinatown
(go) on a bus tour
(take) the Staten Island Ferry
(look down) from the Empire State Building

b) Ask your partner the following questions.
1 How can you see thousands of people on their bikes?
2 What's a good way to get great views of Manhattan from the other side of the East River?
3 What makes most New Yorkers sad?
4 What's a good way of seeing the centre of the 'capital of money'?
5 What's one way of seeing a statue of the USA's first president?

Partner **B**   129

Unit 1

11 EVERYDAY ENGLISH SPEAKING Making plans together

Partner B: You and your partner are on holiday in New York. It's your last day. You each have different information and interests, but you want to spend the day together.

a) Listen to your partner's activities and take notes.

b) You have chosen the activities below for your last day. Tell your partner
– about the activities you would like to do,
– where they are, what they cost, when the place is open,
– why you would like to do them.

Welcome to the world-famous
APOLLO THEATER 
… where stars are born! Stevie Wonder, Lauryn Hill, Ella Fitzgerald, Marvin Gaye – they all started here at the Apollo!
253 W 125 St,
Harlem, NY 10027
History tours: Monday, Tuesday, Thursday, Friday 11 a.m., 1 p.m. & 3 p.m.
Admission: $16/person

SKYSCRAPER MUSEUM
Opened in 1997, the Skyscraper Museum – the only museum of its kind – explores the history of tall buildings.
It's located at 39 Battery Place at the south-western tip of Manhattan.
Museum hours are 12–6 p.m., Wednesday–Sunday.
Admission is $5, $2.50 for students and seniors.

BATTERY PARK
Watch the boats along the Hudson River and enjoy one of New York's best locations for ball games and frisbee. Or just sit on the grass and play board games you can borrow in the park.
Hudson River between Chambers Street and Battery Place
Open: 6 a.m.–1 a.m. daily
Admission: free

c) Now talk to your partner and choose the activities you'd like to do together – one for the morning, one for the afternoon. You each have $20 left. Check the prices and opening hours.

B Partner

Unit 3

5 REVISION What came first? (Passive – simple past)

a) Your partner is going to guess which of the two events in each pair came first.
Listen to his/her guesses and correct them if necessary. Use the dates below

1 Eiffel Tower (build): 1887 ◄► first car (make): 1885
A: I think the Eiffel Tower was built before the first car was made.
B: That's right. / No, that's wrong. The first car was made in ..., and the Eiffel Tower was ...

2 America (discover): 1492 ◄► China (visit) by Marco Polo: 1266
3 the Mona Lisa (paint): 1506–1519 ◄► St. Paul's Cathedral (build): 1675–1708
4 first plane (fly): 1903 ◄► first modern Olympic Games (hold): 1896

b) Look at each pair of events. Think about which came first.
Then use the passive and tell your partner what you think:

5
- planet Uranus (discover)
- first African slaves (take) to America

6
- Hollywood Sign (put up)
- Empire State Building (build)

B: I think the planet Uranus was discovered before the first African slaves were taken to America.
A: That's right. / No, that's wrong. The planet Uranus was discovered in ..., and ...

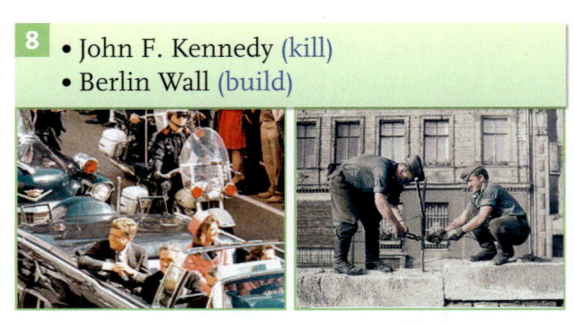

7
- first tea bags (sell)
- first helicopter (fly)

8
- John F. Kennedy (kill)
- Berlin Wall (build)

Unit 3

9 Sally was offered a job (Personal passive)

a) *Partner B: Listen to A's sentences (1–4) in the passive and tell him or her if they are right or not.*
A: They offered Sally a job at the Bay Restaurant!
   Sally was offered a job …
B: Yes, that's right. / No, that's not right. It should be: Sally …

b) *Read number 5 and put that sentence into the passive.*
Your partner will tell you if you have got it right. Then continue with 6, 7, 8.

A's correct passive sentences:	Your active sentences:
1 Sally was offered a job at the Bay Restaurant!	5 On the train yesterday, somebody gave me a free ticket for a movie.
2 She isn't paid very much.	6 They gave free tickets to everyone on the train.
3 But she was given an invitation to a rock concert last week, by a cook.	7 But they show us better films at school.
4 She was sent the ticket by post.	8 Do they show you interesting films at your school?

13 EVERYDAY ENGLISH SPEAKING Theme parks (Discussing tourist activities)

a) *Your partner has information on The California Theme Park. Ask him/her about the following:*
1 exciting attractions for teenagers:
   Are there any …?
2 opening hours:
   What time …
3 ticket prices:
   How much …
4 any special tickets:
   …

b) *Now read the information you have on this poster for Ocean Park near San Clemente. Use the information to answer your partner's questions.*

c) *Decide together which park you would like to go to. Tell the class your decision and give reasons.*

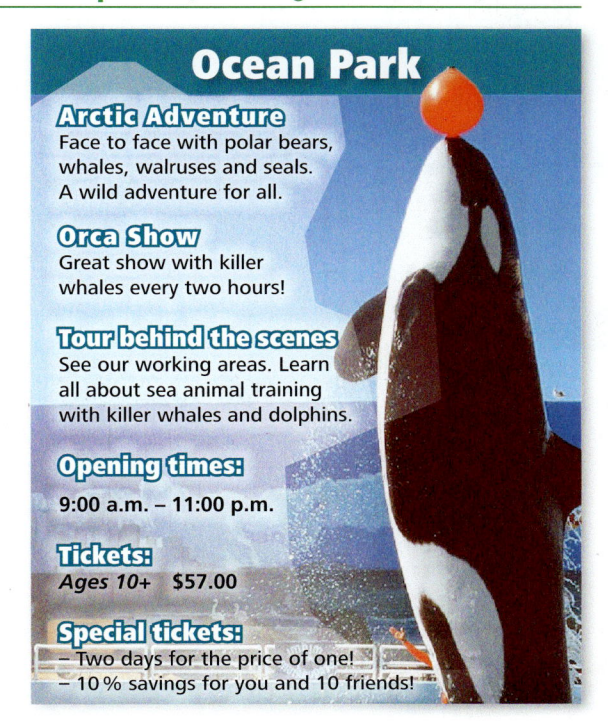

Ocean Park

Arctic Adventure
Face to face with polar bears, whales, walruses and seals. A wild adventure for all.

Orca Show
Great show with killer whales every two hours!

Tour behind the scenes
See our working areas. Learn all about sea animal training with killer whales and dolphins.

Opening times:
9:00 a.m. – 11:00 p.m.

Tickets:
Ages 10+ $57.00

Special tickets:
– Two days for the price of one!
– 10 % savings for you and 10 friends!

How am I doing?

Key to the self-assessment tests

Unit 1 ▶ p. 31

1. **C** boroughs
2. **E** Manhattan
3. **B** south
4. **A** the World Trade Center
5. **B** Ellis Island
6. sidewalk • cellphone • pants • French fries
7. lift • queue • underground • holiday(s)
8. **B** awful
9. **C** put out
10. **B** blocks
11. **D** deli
12. **C** Walking
13. **A** playing
14. Here any gerund answer that makes sense will count.
    a) riding/going/going up/...
    b) visiting/seeing/phoning/calling/...
    c) walking/driving/riding/cycling/...
    d) making/serving/having/...

Unit 2 ▶ p. 55

1. a) the ship the Pilgrims came on
   b) the Wampanoag village where the Pilgrims built their own village
   c) the Wampanoag sachem/leader in the 1620s
   d) the Native Americans that live where the Pilgrims landed
2. **C** 1620
3. **C** their first harvest
4. Right
5. turkey
6. **B** corn
7. **C** staff
8. fault
9. **B** keep
10. helpful
11. hopeless
12. **A** As a result
13. **C** would not have had to
14. **B** had not helped
15. a) if/whether – was
    b) if/whether – had lived
    c) how many – had come/came
    d) why – had been/was
16. a) to go and look at
    b) not to forget to watch
17. **B** after

Unit 3 ▶ p. 75

1. **A** the Golden State
2. **C** Silicon Valley
3. **D** Spanish
4. **B** illegal
5. **B** organize
6. **B** before
7. **D** discriminate against
8. **B** prejudiced
9. **C** repair
10. **C** Somebody stole my camera.
11. **B** have been
12. **C** will
13. a) Er wurde ins Bett geschickt.
    b) Ihm wurde ein Brief geschickt. / Er erhielt einen Brief.
14. who was
15. **B** how to

How am I doing?

Key to the self-assessment tests

Unit 4   ▶ p. 93

1 high school
2 grade
3 extracurricular activities (extracurriculars)
4 student dress code
5 **C** river
6 **A** winemaking
7 **D** traditions
8 Not true: **C**
9 possibility
10 imagination
11 sister
12 place
13 step
14 apply, look
15 grade
16 a) much   b) many   c) few   d) little
17 a) Food is important at all of Hermann's festivals. *The* food they eat most often is traditionally German – like sausage.
   b) *The* students in Timo's class are crazy about football. Football is popular with students all over the USA.
   c) I thought *the* people and *the* music in the school play yesterday were great.

Unit 5   ▶ p. 115

1 **B** states in the north and states in the south
2 **D** discrimination against blacks
3 **A** Google
4 a) series
   b) reality show
   c) a social network website
   d) Atlanta Journal-Constitution
   e) documentary
5 **B** 70
6 online
7 **C** more than one source
8 **A** use your own words
9 **C** name all your sources
10 a) fiction   b) non-fiction
   c) non-fiction   d) fiction
11 The Little Rock Nine were trying to fight segregation, which was a brave thing to do.
12 a) that   b) who   c) which

TF 1   The President and Mr Muir

Theodore Roosevelt (1858–1919)

Theodore Roosevelt at age 25

John Muir (1838–1914)

John Muir at age 23

Theodore Roosevelt grew up in a wealthy family in New York and became the 26th president of the United States in 1901, but as a boy he had poor eyes and asthma and was often ill. After he was bullied as a 13-year-old, he decided to take up[1] boxing.

Boxing and lots of physical exercise turned Theodore into a strong and fit young man. When he was at university, he not only boxed but also rowed[2] for the university team. Later he fought in the Spanish-American War of 1898 and led a charge[3] on Kettle Hill in Cuba. This made him famous in the USA and when he returned from the war he was seen as a hero by his countrymen.

Theodore not only loved sports – he loved the natural world too. When he was only seven, he started his own natural history museum, and at age nine he wrote about insects and later about birds.

Theodore Roosevelt's other great love was books: he sometimes read one a day and wrote 35 himself. His photographic memory helped him remember them. One day he discovered the books of John Muir.

John Muir was eleven years old when his family left Scotland to live in the US. The Muirs had a farm in the state of Wisconsin, and John later went to university in Madison, Wisconsin. It was there that he had his first botany lesson. After that he decided another university was better for him: the 'university of the wilderness'.

In those days, much of the eastern US was still wilderness and Muir walked from Indiana to Florida to enjoy it. His plan was to go from Florida to South America, but when he got malaria, he decided that California was a better idea.

When Muir arrived in San Francisco, he found the big city (149,000 people) terrible. He had read about a beautiful valley called Yosemite almost 300 km east of San Francisco – so he walked there.

Muir loved Yosemite. Over the following years he became America's most famous conservationist[4] and fought everybody – from the governor of California to big business – to protect the place. He wrote books, articles and letters and founded the Sierra Club to tell people that they must protect not only Yosemite, but wilderness areas everywhere.

▶ *Compare the two men. What did they have in common? How were they different? Later in life they met. What do you think they talked about?*

---

[1] (to) take up sth. [teik 'ʌp]   *mit etwas (z. B. einem Hobby) anfangen*   [2] (to) row [rəʊ]   *rudern*   [3] charge [tʃɑːdʒ]   *Angriff*
[4] conservationist [ˌkɒnsəˈveɪʃənɪst]   *Naturschützer/in*

A camping trip

When the people of Yosemite Valley heard that the president of the United States was coming, they were very excited. This was the most exciting thing that had ever happened in the valley!

They wanted to welcome the president with a bang: they bought $400 worth of fireworks – a lot of money in 1903! They set up special lights to light up the waterfalls of the Valley. They even borrowed a cook from a French restaurant in San Francisco.

But President Roosevelt had other plans. He had written to Mr Muir and suggested[1] that the two of them go camping. And that's what they did. President Theodore Roosevelt and Mr John Muir spent four days and three nights in Yosemite. Under the stars, without a tent.

Muir talked a lot while he was with the president. He talked about the importance of nature, and how important it was to protect it. And the president listened. When he got back to Washington, D.C., Roosevelt started the work that saved Yosemite, and later other natural places in the US.

Roosevelt was president until 1909. By the time he left the White House, there were 785,000 km² of national parks and preserves and 170,000 km² of national forests. He started the National Forest Service in 1905. (The National Park Service came later.)

Although there were national parks in the United States before the famous camping trip, Roosevelt and Muir did more to preserve wild areas in the US than anyone before – or since. That's why John Muir is often called the 'Father' of the American National Parks.

Yosemite Falls

Roosevelt and Muir in Yosemite

The 'California quarter', a 25-cent coin, commemorates[2] Muir.

1 The camping trip
Explain why the Roosevelt-Muir camping trip was important. Are the things they talked about still relevant today? Give examples.

2 Protecting the environment
Research an environmental organization like the Sierra Club and report on it to the class.

---

[1] (to) suggest sth. [səˈdʒest] *etwas vorschlagen*   [2] (to) commemorate sb./sth. [kəˈmeməreɪt] *an jn./etwas erinnern*

TF 2 A New York anthology

Read the poems, essay extracts and song about New York. When you have read each one, write down one word or phrase that comes to mind. Explain your choice.

The word that came to mind when I read "Skyscraper" was 'tickle'. I like the idea of a building that tickles the sky.

Three poems

Skyscraper
Skyscraper, skyscraper
Scrape me some sky:
Tickle the sun
While the stars go by.
Tickle the stars
While the sun's climbing high,
Then skyscraper, skyscraper
Scrape me some sky.

Dennis Lee

From "The New Yorkers"
In front of the bank building
after six o'clock the gathering[1]
of the bag people[2] begins
In cold weather they huddle[3]
around newspapers
when it is freezing they get
cardboard boxes
Someone said they are all rich eccentrics
Someone is   of course   crazy …

Nikki Giovanni

Subway rush hour[4]
Mingled[5]
breath and smell
so close
mingled
black and white
so near
no room for fear

Langston Hughes

---

[1] gathering ['gæðərɪŋ] *Versammlung*   [2] bag people ['bæg ˌpiːpl] *(infml) Obdachlose*   [3] (to) huddle ['hʌdl] *sich zusammendrängen*
[4] rush hour ['rʌʃ aʊə] *Hauptverkehrszeit, Stoßzeit*   [5] mingled ['mɪŋgld] *vermischt*

Extracts from an essay

To the visitor

Visitors force you to think. They arrive with that helpless do-with-me-what-you-will look and when you ask what they'd like to do or see they say, 'Oh, what's good?'

What's good? In New York?

You tell them – gently[1] – that this is New York where everything is good. Everything, baby.

A hot dog at Nathan's in Coney Island is good.

A westward walk on the Brooklyn Bridge when the sun is setting in New Jersey is good.

A ride on the Staten Island Ferry at sunset when the sky is a golden backdrop[2] to the Statue of Liberty and Ellis Island is very good.

Walk down Broadway. Watch people lining up for the ferry to Ellis Island and the Statue of Liberty. Just look at the people. Look. You're looking at the country's history. And listen to them in their various tongues. You're not eavesdropping[3]. You're listening to generations and yourself.

And all that is good.

Frank McCourt

A song

New York, New York

Start spreading the news, I'm leaving today
I want to be a part of it –
New York, New York

These vagabond[4] shoes
are longing to stray[5]
Right through the very heart of it –
New York, New York

I want to wake up in a city that doesn't sleep
And find I'm king of the hill – top of the heap

These little town blues are melting away
I'll make a brand new start of it –
in old New York
If I can make it[6] there, I'll make it anywhere
It's up to you – New York, New York

Fred Ebb

1 The poems
Learn your favourite poem and recite it to your partner as well as you can. Explain why you like it.

2 The essay
a) Which of the things Frank McCourt describes would/wouldn't you like to do? Explain why.

b) Write two or three similar things that are good about a town you know or like.

3 The song
Explain how you know where the singer comes from and why he wants to go to New York.

4 A word-picture of New York
What picture of New York have you now got in your mind? Try to describe that picture of the city in words.
Or bring pictures of New York to class. Swap with a partner and write about his/her pictures.

---

[1] gently ['dʒentli] *(adv.) sanft, vorsichtig*   [2] backdrop ['bækdrɒp] *Kulisse, Hintergrund*   [3] (to) eavesdrop ['iːvzdrɒp] *heimlich lauschen*
[4] vagabond ['vægəbɒnd] *Landstreicher/in*   [5] (to) stray [streɪ] *streunen*   [6] (to) make it *es schaffen*

TF 3 "How about them Yankees?" by Louie D'Agostino

> Look at the pictures. Do you know what sport this text is about?

"'How about them Yankees?' That's all you need."

"I don't understand," I said to my old English teacher, Signor Bertanelli. I had come to visit him before leaving our little town in Sicily to go to the US – I was emigrating[1].

"Of course you don't understand, Luigi," he said. "You never were very good at English. Just remember this: 'How about them Yankees?'" He repeated it slowly, as he would to any other stupid student. "Then you will be fine when you get to New York."

I had no idea what the old man was talking about, but he had always been kind[2] to me, although I was terrible at English. So I decided that I would remember the question: "How about them Yankees?" It didn't take long before I understood why it was a good sentence to know. And that was before I learned that the Yankees are a baseball team from the Bronx.

I made my way to Rome and the airport there, and soon I was sitting on a plane between two very large American men who said they were from Brooklyn. They asked me lots of easy questions, but after a few minutes, my English was no longer enough. I almost panicked, but then I thought of what Signor Bertanelli had told me.

"How about them Yankees?" I asked. And just as my old professor had promised, it was all I needed. The two men talked the rest of the way to New York – I didn't have to say anything. Yes, this one sentence was going to take me a long way.

When I got to New York, I used Signor Bertanelli's question with the Immigration man at JFK Airport. I used it to get a room, and it worked when I went to get my first job in America. For three months I washed dishes in a restaurant. (Now I own one.)

I'll never forget the night when I went to my first bar in America. I was talking to a group of guys. When I couldn't think of anything to say, I asked them, "So, how about them Yankees?" I became everybody's best friend! They bought me drinks. And they gave me my American name: Louie. As in "Hey, Joe. Meet Louie. Louie here's a big baseball fan." I had a great time, and I didn't have to pay for my beers: "Joe, Louie's drinks are on me[3]."

Soon after that I learned that the question usually doesn't work with women. (My wife was an exception.) And that there are men who don't like baseball. (Not many though.) And that you have to be careful: Queens has its own baseball team, the Mets, and Mets fans don't react well to the question. (This was especially true in 2000, when the Mets lost the all-important World Series to the Yankees.)

After a few months in the US, I was a big Yankees fan and a regular[4] at their home games at Yankee Stadium in the Bronx. I still am. And now I can talk with the best of them when somebody uses that great conversation opener, "How about them Yankees?"

Thank you, Signor Bertanelli.

Yankee stadium has room for about 53,000 fans.

---

[1] (to) emigrate ['emɪgreɪt] *auswandern*   [2] kind [kaɪnd] *nett*   [3] Drinks are on me. *Die Getränke spendiere ich.*   [4] regular ['regjələ] *Stammgast*

1 Understanding the story

a) Explain why it was helpful for Louie to know the question 'How about them Yankees?'.

b) Describe what Louie thinks of baseball now.

c) How do you know he has been successful in the US?

2 Conversation openers

a) With a partner, how many 'conversation openers' can you think of? Write them down.
Have you been here before?…

b) Imagine you're at a party and don't know anyone. Walk round your class and try out your conversation openers.

Baseball terms used in everyday English
If you want to understand American English, it's good to know a little bit about baseball.

■ **out of the ballpark**
As in: 'The batter hit the ball out of the ballpark.'
Common use: 'She wants $75 for her old MP3 player. That price is way out of the ballpark.'
Means: The price is much too high.

Parts of a baseball field
- outfield wall
- outfield
- 2nd base
- left foul line
- 3rd base
- 1st base
- right foul line
- infield
- home plate
- fair territory
- foul territory

■ **throw somebody a curveball**[1]
As in: 'Wilkins is usually a good hitter, but not if somebody throws him a curveball.'
Common use: 'I thought I was ready for the test, but the teacher really threw me a curveball.'
Means: The teacher asked questions that I wasn't expecting.

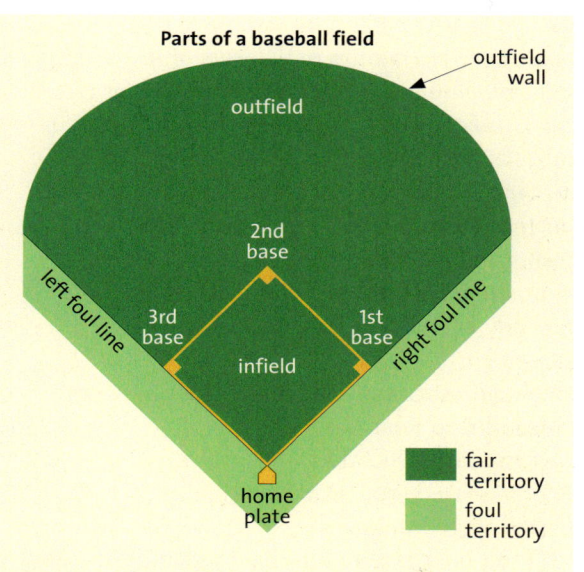

■ **get to first base**
As in: 'It wasn't a very good hit, but he got to first base with it.'
Common use: 'I tried to do the Math homework, but I couldn't even get to first base.'
Means: I couldn't even do a small part of it.

3 Sport expressions in German
Write down German sport expressions that are used in real life, like 'ein Eigentor schießen'. Explain what they mean in English.

---

[1] curveball ['kɜːvbɔːl] Ball, der so geworfen wurde, dass seine Flugbahn eine Kurve beschreibt und für den batter schwer zu treffen ist

TF 4 "That's why you talk so funny"
(abridged and adapted from *The absolutely true diary of a part-time Indian* by Sherman Alexie)

> How would you prepare for your first day at a new school? Imagine a situation in which somebody says, 'That's why you talk so funny'. Now read the story.

14-year-old Junior lives on the Spokane Indian Reservation in Washington State. When he decides he wants to be the first kid to go to school outside the reservation in the town of Reardan, most people on the reservation hate him for it – even his best friend Rowdy, who punches[1] him in the face. They think he is a traitor[2] and call him an 'apple' – because he is red on the outside, like an Indian, but white on the inside.
Junior thinks he has to get away from the reservation if he wants a better life. How will his first day at Reardan High School be?

The next morning, Dad drove me the twenty-two miles to Reardan.
"I'm scared," I said.
"I'm scared too," Dad said.
5 He hugged me close.
"You don't have to do this," he said. "You can always go back to the rez school."
"No," I said. "I have to do this."
Can you imagine what would have happened
10 to me if I'd turned around and gone back to the rez school?
I would have been beaten up.
You can't just be a traitor to your tribe and then change your mind ten minutes later.
15 I was on a one-way bridge. There was no way to turn around, even if I wanted to.
"Just remember this," my father said. "Those white people aren't better than you."
But he was so wrong. And he knew he was
20 wrong. He was the loser Indian father of a loser Indian son in a world built for winners.
But he loved me so much. He hugged me even closer.
"This is a great thing," he said. "You're so
25 brave. You're a warrior."
It was the best thing he could have said.
"Hey, here's some lunch money," he said and gave me a dollar.

We were poor enough to get free lunch, but I didn't want to be the only Indian *and* a sad
30 guy who needed a free lunch.
"Thanks, Dad," I said.
"I love you," he said.
"I love you too."
I felt stronger so I got out of the car and
35 walked to the front door. It was locked.
So I stood alone on the sidewalk and watched my father drive away. I hoped he'd drive right home and not stop in a bar and spend all his money.
40 I hoped he'd remember to come back and pick me up after school.
I stood alone at the front door for a few very long minutes.
It was still early and I had a black eye from
45 Rowdy's goodbye punch. No, I had a purple, blue, yellow, and black eye. It looked like modern art.
Then the white kids began arriving for school. Those white kids were so white I could
50 see the blue veins through their skin like rivers.
Most of the kids were my size or smaller, but there were ten or twelve monster dudes. Giant white guys. They looked like men, not boys.
55 Some of them looked like they had to shave[3] two or three times a day.
They stared at me, the Indian boy with the black eye, my going-away gift from Rowdy. Those white kids couldn't believe their eyes.
60 They stared at me like I was Bigfoot or a UFO. What was I doing at Reardan, whose mascot was an Indian? That made me the only *other* Indian in town.
So what was I doing in racist Reardan, where
65 more than half the students went to college after they graduated? Nobody in my family had ever gone near a college.

---

[1] (to) punch sb. [pʌntʃ] *jn. schlagen*   [2] traitor ['treɪtə] *Verräter/in*   [3] (to) shave [ʃeɪv] *sich rasieren*

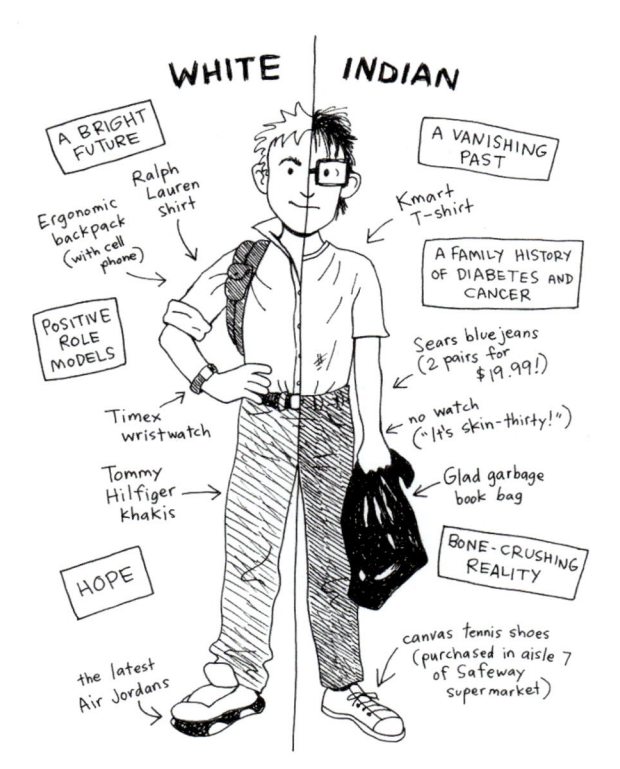

Reardan was the opposite of the rez. It was the opposite of my family. It was the opposite of me. I didn't deserve to be there. I knew it; all of those kids knew it. Indians don't deserve shit.

So, I felt worthless[1] and stupid and just waited. And pretty soon, a janitor[2] opened the front door and all of the other kids walked inside.

I stayed outside.

Maybe I could just drop out[3] of school completely. I could go live in the woods like a real Indian.

Of course, as I was allergic to almost every plant that grew on earth, I would have been a real Indian with a head full of snot[4].

"Okay," I said to myself. "Here I go."

I walked into the school, found the front office, and told them who I was.

"Oh, you're the one from the reservation," the secretary said.

"Yeah," I said.

I couldn't tell if she thought the reservation was a good or bad thing.

"My name is Melinda," she said. "Welcome to Reardan High School. Here's your schedule and a student ID. You're with Mr. Grant for homeroom. You better hurry on down there. You're late."

"Ah, where is that?" I asked.

"We've only got one hallway here," she said and smiled. She had red hair and green eyes and was kind of sexy for an old woman. "It's all the way down on the left."

I put everything in my backpack and hurried down to my homeroom.

I waited a second at the door and then walked inside.

Everybody, all of the students and the teacher, stopped to stare at me.

They stared hard.

Like I was bad weather.

"Take your seat," the teacher said. He was a strong guy. He had to be a football coach.

I went and sat in the back row and tried to ignore all the stares and whispers, until a blonde girl leaned over toward me.

Penelope!

Yes, there are still places in the world where people are named Penelope!

"What's your name?" Penelope asked.

"Junior," I said.

She laughed and told her girlfriend at the next desk that my name was Junior. They both laughed. Word spread around the room and pretty soon everybody was laughing.

They were laughing at *my name*.

I had no idea that Junior was a weird name.

---

[1] worthless ['wɜːθləs] *wertlos* [2] janitor ['dʒænɪtə] *Hausmeister/in* [3] (to) drop out [ˌdrɒp 'aʊt] *die Schule abbrechen* [4] snot [snɒt] *(infml) Nasenschleim, Rotz*

It's a common[1] name on the rez. You walk into any store on any rez in the United States and shout, "Hey, Junior!" and seventeen guys will turn around.

And three women.

But there were no other people named Junior in Reardan, so I was being laughed at because I was the only one who had that silly name.

And then I felt smaller because the teacher was taking attendance[2] and he called out my *name* name.

"Arnold Spirit," the teacher said.

No, he shouted it.

He was so big and strong that his whisper was probably a scream.

"Here," I said as quietly as possible. My whisper was only a whisper.

"Speak up," the teacher said.

"Here," I said.

"My name is Mr. Grant," he said.

"I'm here, Mr. Grant."

He moved on to other students, but Penelope leaned over toward me again, but she wasn't laughing at all. She was mad[3] now.

"I thought you said your name was Junior," Penelope said.

Well, okay, it wasn't completely my real name. My full name is Arnold Spirit Jr. But nobody calls me that. Everybody calls me Junior. Well, every other *Indian* calls me Junior.

"My name is Junior," I said. "And my name is Arnold. It's Junior and Arnold. I'm both."

I felt like two different people inside of one body.

No, I felt like a magician. I cut myself in half. Junior lived on the north side of the Spokane River and Arnold lived on the south.

"Where are you from?" she asked.

She was so pretty and her eyes were so blue.

I suddenly realized that she was the prettiest girl I had ever seen up close. She was movie star pretty.

"Hey," she said. "I asked you where you're from."

Wow, she was tough.

"Wellpinit," I said. "Up on the rez, I mean, the reservation."

"Oh," she said. "That's why you talk so funny."

And yes, I had that singsong reservation accent that made everything I said sound like a bad poem.

Man, I was freaked[4].

I didn't say another word for six days.

1 Junior, his dad and the Reardan kids

a) Find examples where Junior thinks he is not as good as the white students.

b) What does Junior think about his father? Find out in lines 17–42.

c) What do the reactions of the white children to Junior tell you about the town of Reardan?

2 Reardan and the rez

a) Look at the cartoon 'White – Indian' at the top left of p. 141. Explain how it illustrates lines 69–71.

b) Draw a cartoon like this one for yourself and a classmate of the opposite sex. Call it 'Girl – Boy' or 'Boy – Girl'.

3 Penelope

a) How do Junior and Penelope meet? What does Junior think of her?

b) When Penelope says 'That's why you talk so funny' (ll. 176–177), Junior doesn't speak for another six days. Explain why.

c) Work with a partner and decide how Junior could reply to what Penelope says.

4 New student

Work out a programme for welcoming a new student into your class. Present your ideas to the class.

---

[1] common ['kɒmən] *alltäglich, normal*   [2] (to) take attendance [əˈtendəns] *die Anwesenheit kontrollieren*   [3] mad *wütend*
[4] be freaked (infml.) *zutiefst verunsichert sein*

TF 5 In Room 56

1 Schedules and Shakespeare

a) Look at this timetable from an American school. What age do you think the students are?

b) Compare the timetable to your own. What subjects look interesting? What subjects do you have that the students here don't have? Say what surprises you about this timetable and what you like or dislike about it.

c) 👥 Look at what takes place at 3:00 pm. Who is Shakespeare? With a partner, write down what you know about him and collect the results for the whole class.

d) Read what some students say about their experiences and their teacher, Rafe Esquith. What does Rafe mean to them?

Daily Schedule	
6:30 A.M.	Doors open
7:00 A.M.	Problem Solving
8:00 A.M.	Written Language
8:30 A.M.	Mathematics
9:30 A.M.	Literature
10:30 A.M.	Science
11:00 A.M.	Classical Guitar Lessons
11:20 A.M.	United States History
12:00 P.M.	Geography/Economics
12:30 P.M.	Lunch/Rock 'n' Roll Guitar Lessons
1:20 P.M.	Fine Arts
2:20 P.M.	Physical Education
3:00 P.M.	Shakespeare
4:00 P.M.	Band Rehearsals
5:00 P.M.	Dismissal

> The play we did was *King Lear* and Rafe was talking to us and said, "This is the hardest play we're going to do – ever. It's going to be hard work. There will be no vacations. There will be no weekends. But it will be fun, I promise you." And man, was it fun. And man, was it worth it.

> It's been worth it because Rafe, he gives us a lot of advice on life.

> He's always with us, every step of the way. And when it's really hard for us, he always makes jokes, so it's not really that hard.

e) Now read about what goes on in Rafe Esquith's class.

In the audience tonight at a book store in Raleigh, North Carolina, there are old and young teachers, parents who care about education, and the simply curious.

A Shakespeare play is being performed here this evening, but from where I sit I see microphones and amplifiers, electric guitars and drums. Off to the side, a group of well-behaved elementary-school students – the stars of this evening's show – sits on the floor.

Kids, guitars, and Shakespeare? Yes. We're here tonight to meet a world-famous, inner-city teacher whose elementary-school students perform Shakespeare so well that it makes audiences cry. Rafe Esquith leads the Hobart Shakespeareans, a group of his fifth graders, on tour from Room 56 at Hobart Elementary School, Los Angeles. And by the time these little Shakespeareans are ready to perform and rock and roll, there is standing room only.

Between scenes from Shakespeare which they perform sensitively and with humour, the Hobart Shakespeareans play and sing versions of modern rock/pop songs by U2, R.E.M., Nirvana, Radiohead and the Beatles. The lyrics go well with the Shakespearean scenes, and dance completes the performance. People in the audience are visibly moved[1]. This is not your average kids' performance. This is extraordinary.

But maybe we shouldn't be so surprised. After all, Esquith isn't. He says, if they have the chance, all kids can be as sharp and good as his. And his students are from an area of Los Angeles where drugs and street violence are part of everyday life. For most of them, English is their second language and is not often spoken at home.

But there is more than Shakespeare and rock and roll to Room 56. Esquith's students experience learning, respect, and values, and are challenged to expect[2] more from themselves than they ever thought possible.

The classroom mottos are simple – "Be nice. Work hard. There are no shortcuts." – and they accurately describe what goes on in Room 56. His fifth-grade students get 80–90 percent at reading, while the school's fifth-graders overall get 42 percent. They read Dickens, Salinger and Steinbeck, but also do algebra and take long trips, sometimes even overseas. It all works, he said, because they are in class from 6:30 a.m. to 5 p.m., and because he does not take vacations (he uses the time to meet with students during the nine-week summer vacation).

At least 90 minutes a day, the class reads adult novels aloud. Weaker readers get shorter, easier assignments but have to do more as the year goes on.

The day starts with a grammar exercise. The students have to get 90 percent on it. If they don't, they do the exercise until they can correct their mistakes, and once a month, each student reads at least one book from a collection of youth literature in the classroom.

---

[1] visibly moved *sichtbar ergriffen* [2] (to) expect [ɪkˈspekt] *erwarten*

After regular classes end, Esquith offers an hour of Shakespeare. Students rehearse a single play all year and then perform it. And in case anyone thinks they're performing a kids' version – think again. Esquith's kids study hard until they understand every word. They perform full-length[1] versions of the plays. They have performed all over the USA and even at Shakespeare's own theater, the Globe in London.

Of course, it is hard work because Esquith believes it's wrong to think learning should always be fun or that hard lessons are bad for kids from poor homes. But all the hard work pays off[2]. The Hobart Shakespeareans regularly score in the top 5–10 percent of standard national tests and show that hard work and self-discipline can change lives for the better.

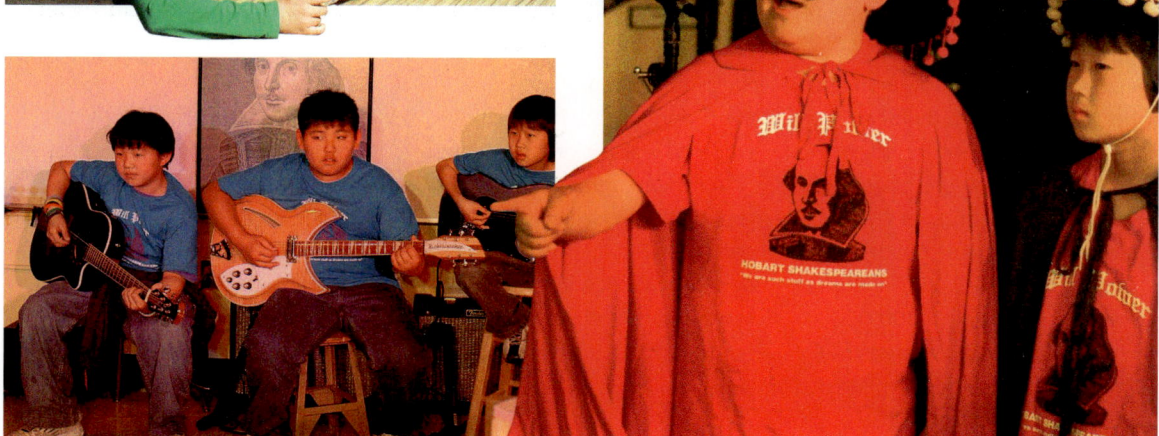

2 A great class?

a) Make a list of positive and negative things about the students and their daily life.

b) Compare your list with a partner's.

3 Learning and school

Rafe Esquith doesn't believe learning should always be fun and the article finishes like this: '... hard work and self-discipline can change lives for the better.' Would you like to be a student in Rafe Esquith's class? Why or why not? Use your answers from above to help you. Present your ideas to the class.

4 You and the Shakespeareans

a) Imagine you can interview a boy or a girl from Room 56 about their school life. Decide on six questions you would like to ask.

b) Swap questions with another group. Answer their questions as if you are a student in Room 56.

5 Shakespeare's plays

Shakespeare wrote at least 37 plays. Choose one, research the story of the play and present a simple summary to your class. Try to make it sound as interesting or exciting as you can.

---

[1] full-length [ˌfʊl ˈleŋθ] *vollständig, ungekürzt*   [2] (to) pay off [ˌpeɪ ˈɒf] *sich auszahlen*

TF 6 Child labour[1] on the US–Mexican border

by Chris Hawley, The Arizona Republic (adapted)

■ **SINALOA STATE, Mexico.**

For migrant farm workers, the work day often begins long before the sun rises. Today, Javier and a few other workers sit around a fire until the boss arrives and tells them to start working.

Javier (not his real name) is just 10 years old, but he has been in these fields since he was 7. He will pick chili peppers for the next eight hours and earn about seven US dollars.

When Javier finishes working, he will go to a school run[2] by the company that employ[3] him and his family. He'll study for only two or three hours and then return to camp to get together with his family and get some sleep before the next workday begins.

Every year, about 300,000 children between the ages of 6 and 14 move to northern Mexico with their parents to work in the fields. Migrant farm workers usually arrive in Sinaloa in September or October and work until early May.

It is not only in Mexico that children work on farms. 100,000 work in the United States. About two thirds of these children are immigrants, and 80 percent are from Mexico.

Working in the fields not only keeps these children from school but can also be terribly dangerous. In January, David Salgado Aranda, 9, was run over[4] and killed by a tractor while he was picking tomatoes.

A human rights organization reported that twelve migrant children died on farms in northern Mexico in 2006. 'The tomato that is sold in New York is the product of the blood of these children,' said Abel Barrera, the organization's director.

UNICEF Child Protection Officer Theresa Kilbane adds: 'The fact that they're migrants means that they move from place to place, and so nobody really protects their rights.'

UNICEF is working to improve these kids' education and gives them school kits, books and other materials. But many companies don't want to cooperate to improve the living conditions of the migrant workers. There is still a long way to go until children like Javier will be able to get a good education.

1 Children who have to work

Answer the following:
1 What kind of work has Javier got to do?
2 How do you know that some of the things these children pick are sent to the US?
3 What is the education of these children like?
4 What other problems do they face?
5 How does UNICEF try to help child workers?
6 Do these things help? Give examples.

2 What's the law?

Child labour laws in Mexico
- Children must be 14 before they can work on a farm.
- Children between 14 and 16 can work up to six hours a day if they have finished school and have a medical certificate[5] and permission from their parents.
- Children between 16 and 18 must have finished secondary school and need a medical certificate.

Compare these labour laws with the information from the newspaper article. What do you notice? What could be the reasons for this situation?

---

[1] labour ['leɪbə] *Arbeit*   [2] (to) run sth. (e.g. a business) *etwas (z.B. eine Firma) führen, etwas unterhalten*   [3] (to) employ sb. [ɪmˈplɔɪ] *jn. als Arbeitskraft beschäftigen*   [4] (to) run sb. over *jn. überfahren*   [5] medical certificate [səˈtɪfɪkət] *ärztliches Attest*

3 Child labour around the world

Describe what the map below shows. In which regions do many children have to work?

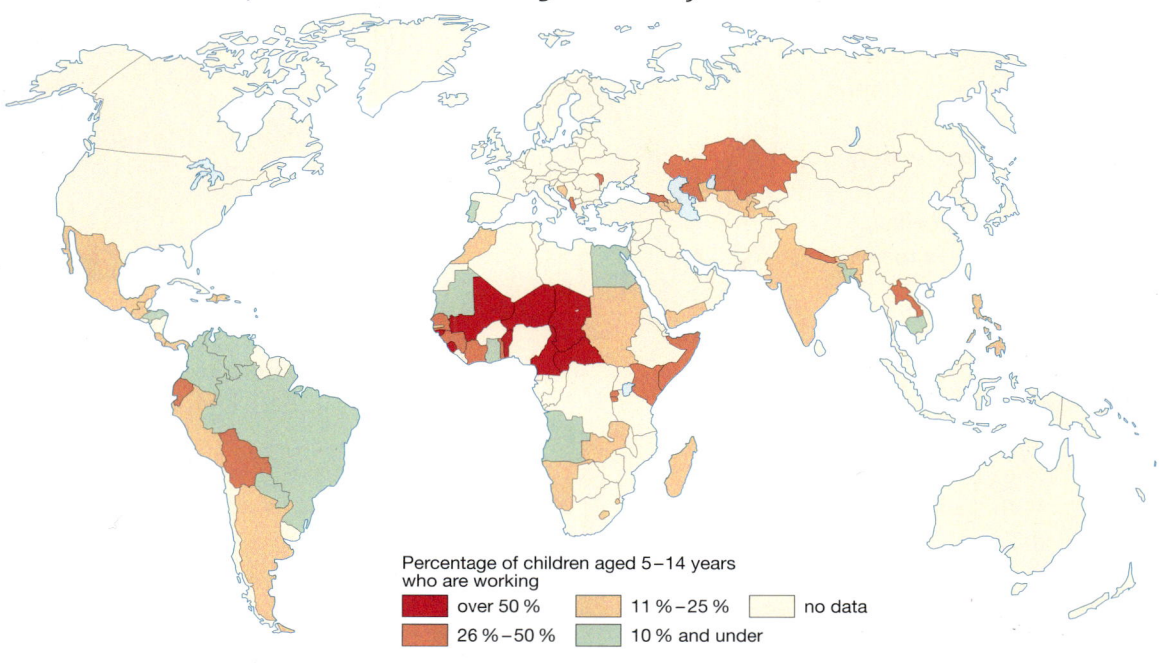

Percentage of children aged 5–14 years who are working
- over 50 %
- 26 % – 50 %
- 11 % – 25 %
- 10 % and under
- no data

Activate your English
– The map shows/gives information about …
– It shows the percentage[1] of children …
– You can see that the situation is …
– There is more child labour in … than in …
– Over/more than 20/30/50/… % of the children in Mexico/India/… work.

GEORAPHY SKILLS — Talking about maps

If you talk about maps,
- look at the title and the legend[2] and make sure you understand what the map is about,
- start with a general statement about the map,
- then talk about details.

4 How can you help?

a) Describe the poster on the right. What do you see?

b) What problem does the poster illustrate? How does the poster illustrate it?

c) What can you do to stop child labour? Think of organisations like UNICEF.

When can I play and go to school?

STOP CHILD LABOUR

---

[1] percentage [pə'sentɪdʒ] *Anteil, Prozentsatz*   [2] legend ['ledʒənd] *Legende (erläuternder Text zu einer Abbildung oder Landkarte)*

TF 7 Building the Gateway Arch

The Gateway Arch is a monument to the men, women and children who settled the western US and reflects the role of St. Louis, Missouri, in that process. The Arch was designed by the architect Eero Saarinen, but he needed a team of engineers to find a way to build it.

■ Climbing cranes
The first 72 feet of the Arch were made with cranes on the ground. After that, special cranes rode up the sides with their heavy loads[1].

■ Triangular sections
The sections were made in a factory far from the building.

■ Tracks[2]
Two steel tracks took the cranes up the sides. The tracks were taken away when work was finished.

■ Elevator
A special elevator carried construction workers up to their jobs.

■ South Entrance

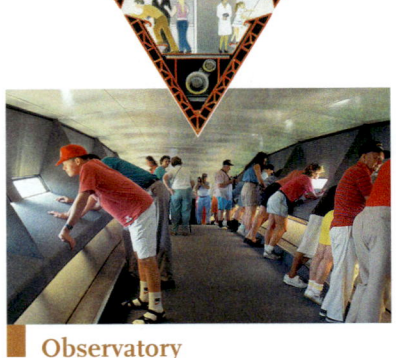

■ Observatory
The view from the windows 630 feet high stretches for miles east and west.

■ Passenger trams
Two trams, one in each leg, take visitors to the top of the Arch. The ride takes four minutes.

■ Jefferson National Expansion Memorial
The Arch is in this park in downtown St. Louis.

■ Museum of Westward Expansion
A place to learn about how the nation grew. You can see how the pioneers travelled and how they lived.

---

[1] load [ləʊd] *Last*   [2] track [træk] *Gleis*

Text File **4**   149

■ **The skin**
The architect wanted it to be timeless, so he chose stainless steel[1].

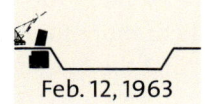

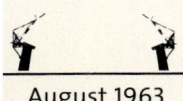

■ **Construction progress**

Feb. 12, 1963

August 1963

Sept. 1963

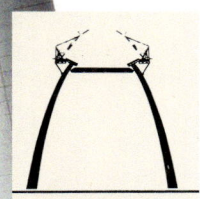

July 4, 1965

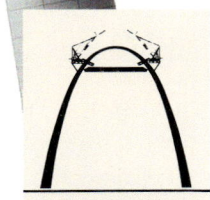

Oct. 28, 1965

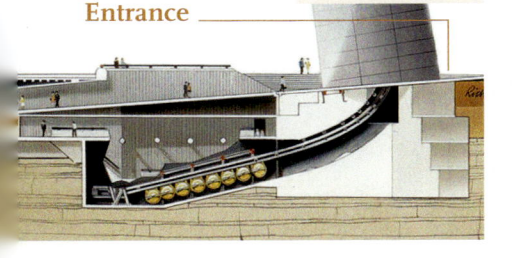

■ **North Entrance**

1 Tracks and climbing crane

2 A platform held the two legs during the last few months of construction.

3 A triangular section

4 The last piece of the Arch

1   Understanding the pictures and texts
Look carefully at the drawing, photos and texts and do the following:
1. Say how tall the Arch is in feet and in metres.
2. Describe how the work was done up to 72 feet and then above that. What do you think that meant for the construction progress?
3. Work out how long it took to build the Arch.
4. Say what you can see and do at the monument today.

2   Who is it for?
What is the idea behind the Gateway Arch? Why do you think it was given this name? Who might not agree that the idea behind the Arch is a good idea?

3   A different monument
Research when, where, how and why another monument in the US was built, e.g. the Lincoln Memorial, the Grand Canyon Skywalk, Mount Rushmore, …

[1] stainless steel [ˌsteɪnləs ˈstiːl] *Edelstahl*

TF 8 — The American Civil War (1861–1865)

1 The causes and course of the war.

From 1830 till 1860, tension[1] grew between the northern and the southern states of the US over the question of slavery. Agriculture was the most important part of the economy in the South, and the large plantations there depended on black slaves as cheap workers. The North, however, had become industrialized and did not really use slaves in its factories. So a lot of Northerners came to see slavery as inhumane[2] and called for its abolition[3].

In 1860 and 1861 eleven states in the South left the Union and formed the Confederate States of America. The North invaded the South to force the states back into the Union. For President Lincoln, getting the Union back together was even more important than quickly ending slavery all over the US. As a result, people in many of the border states were allowed to keep their slaves at first.

A civil war began, with many men fighting against their brothers, and fathers against their sons. At the end of the war, 620,000 soldiers had died: more than in all the other wars together that the US has fought since!

2 A timeline of the Civil War

1860	1861	1862	1863	1865
Abraham Lincoln from the anti-slavery Republican Party is elected president.	**13 February:** Southern states leave the Union. Confederate States of America formed. **March:** Lincoln rejects secession, tries diplomacy. **April:** Union fort in S. Carolina attacked. Civil War begins.	**17 July:** Militia Act allows blacks to join army or navy.	**1 January:** President Lincoln declares all slaves in the Confederate States free.	**9 April:** The Confederate general Robert E. Lee surrenders. **14 April:** President Lincoln is assassinated[4]. **18 December:** The 13th Amendment to the Constitution ends slavery in the US.

3 The United States – divided by war

a) Describe what the map shows.

Activate your English
– The map shows …
– Between 1861 and 1865 the US was divided into … main parts: …
– The areas marked in dark blue/light blue/grey …
– The blue and grey areas were part of the Union, but …

The United States of America 1861–1865

- Union states
- Union territories
- Confederate states
- Border states

b) Find the following states on the map: California, Missouri, New York, Georgia. Which side were they on in the Civil War?

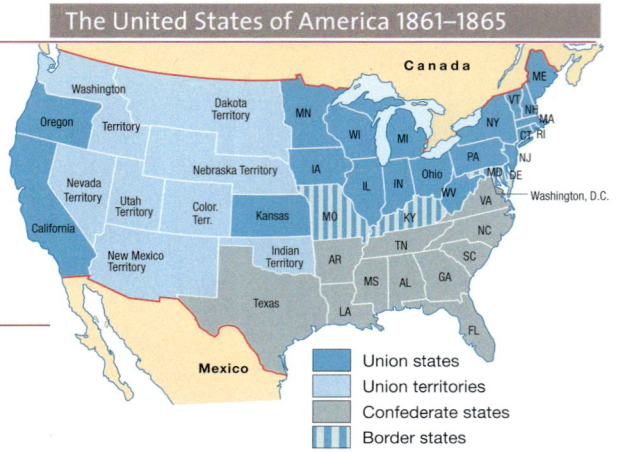

---

[1] tension ['tenʃn] *Spannung* [2] inhumane [ˌɪnhjuː'meɪn] *unmenschlich* [3] abolition [ˌæbə'lɪʃn] *Abschaffung* [5] (to) assassinate sb. [ə'sæsɪneɪt] *jn. (eine wichtige oder berühmte Person) ermorden*

4 Causes and effects

Copy and complete the diagram. Use the information from p. 150.

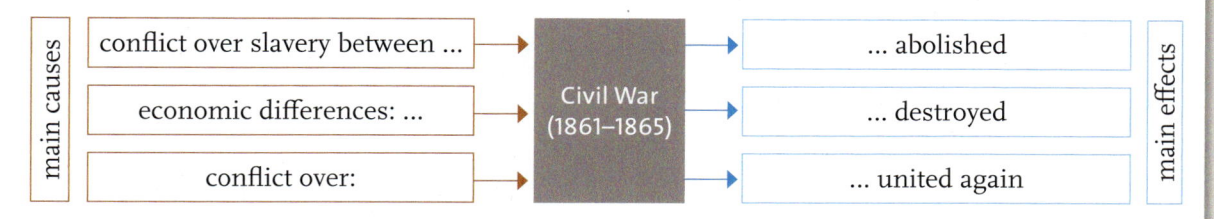

main causes:
- conflict over slavery between …
- economic differences: …
- conflict over:

→ Civil War (1861–1865) →

main effects:
- … abolished
- … destroyed
- … united again

5 Sullivan Ballou: extracts from a letter to his wife Sarah, 14th July, 1861

a) *Why do soldiers fight in wars? Make a list of reasons. Now read the text and the letter.*

Sullivan Ballou was a major and fought for the North in the Civil War. At the age of 32, he died in one of its first battles[1], the Battle of Bull Run, Virginia, in July 1861. Shortly before the battle, he wrote a letter to his wife and family.

> My very dear Sarah:
>
> I feel impelled[2] to write lines that may fall under your eye when I shall be no more. (…) If it is necessary that I should fall on the battlefield for my country, I am ready. (…) And I am willing – perfectly willing – to lay down all my joys in this life, to help maintain[3] this Government, and to pay that debt[4].

b) *Read about primary sources and then use the sentences to help you talk about Sullivan Ballou's letter.*
- The letter was written by …
- The letter was written in the year …
- At that time the writer was …
- In the letter we learn that …
- The writer also writes about …
- In the end he says that …
- He writes to … to tell him/her/them about …
- He wrote about his feelings when …
- The letter shows us that …

HISTORY SKILLS | Primary sources[5]

Primary sources are texts or materials that were produced at the time of a historical event. To understand a primary source, e. g. a letter, you have to know about its background:
– **When** and **where** was it written?
– **Why** was it written? **Who** wrote it?

c) *Are the reasons on your list in a) the same as Sullivan Ballou's?*

---

[1] battle ['bætl] *Schlacht*   [2] impelled [ɪm'peld] *gezwungen*   [3] (to) maintain sth. [meɪn'teɪn] *etwas aufrechterhalten*
[4] debt [det] *Schuld*   [5] primary source ['praɪməri ˌsɔːs] *Primärquelle*

TF 9 Barack Obama, the first African-American president

1 So we all can fly

Two million people came to Washington to see the inauguration[1] of the first African-American president on 20 January, 2009. The ceremony was watched live on TV by 38 million people in the US and many more millions around the world. After the ceremony, Barack Obama and his wife Michelle walked down Pennsylvania Avenue to their new home, the White House, which black slaves had helped to build a little more than 200 years before.

One of Barack Obama's heroes is **Abraham Lincoln**. He was president during the Civil War (1861–1865), and he ended slavery. After the war the slaves were free, but segregation continued for nearly a hundred years. One day in 1955, on a bus in Montgomery, Alabama, **Rosa Parks** (1913–2005) refused to give up her seat to a white man.

The movement that grew from the Montgomery Bus Boycott was led by **Martin Luther King** (1929–1968). In the 1960s new laws gave blacks equal rights and made segregation and discrimination illegal. This was another big step on the journey.

In the words of rapper Jay Z: 'Rosa Parks sat so Martin Luther King could walk. Martin Luther King walked so Obama could run[2]. Obama's running, so we all can fly.'

a) Explain the meaning of the sign held by the Obama supporter on the photograph below.

b) Find out more about one of the following:
- Barack Obama's life before he became president
- Abraham Lincoln
- Rosa Parks
- Martin Luther King.

Give a presentation.

2 Yes we can

'And tonight, I think about (...) the heartache[3] and the hope; the struggle and the progress; the times we were told that we can't, and the people who pressed on with that American creed[4]: Yes we can.'

The words "Yes we can" were Barack Obama's most popular slogan in his election campaign. Another expression he frequently used was "change we can believe in". Say which slogan you prefer and why.

3 Listening: We cannot walk alone 🎧

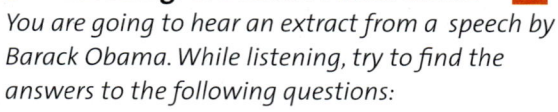

You are going to hear an extract from a speech by Barack Obama. While listening, try to find the answers to the following questions:

a) Which of the following words is important in the first part of the extract: problems – education – promise – tradition?

b) Which of the people mentioned in **1** does Obama refer to in the second part when he mentions a young preacher?

c) In the third part of the extract, which sentence could be used as a slogan?

---

[1] inauguration [ˌɪnɔːgjəˈreɪʃn] *Amtseinführung*   [2] run for sth. *für etwas (ein Amt) kandidieren*   [3] heartache [ˈhɑːteɪk] *große Sorge, Trauer*
[4] creed [kriːd] *Glaube, Überzeugung*

TF 10 Black music

1 A black music quiz

a) Look at the photos and read the texts. Then answer as many quiz questions as you can.

b) Listen to the radio quiz show. Check your answers and find the answers you haven't got.

1. What were the songs called that the slaves sang in the fields?
2. What were their religious songs called?
3. What's the name of the musical style that influenced rock musicians to this day?
4. The musical style 'rhythm and blues' is better known by a shorter name. What is it?
5. What sort of boy was 'Johnny B. Goode' in the first version of Chuck Berry's song?
6. What was the real name of 'the King'?
7. Name at least three 'Hitsville USA' stars.
8. What are the three elements of hip hop culture?

African-American slaves sang songs in the cotton fields with rhythms that helped them to do their work. They also sang songs called spirituals to keep up hope for a better life. In "Swing low, sweet chariot[1]", another famous song, the 'chariot' was going to take the slaves 'home' to freedom in heaven.
Elements of the spirituals survive in today's gospel songs, which are popular in the black churches of America – and with people all over the world.

Swing low, sweet chariot
Swing low, sweet chariot,
Comin' for to carry me home!
I looked over Jordan and what did I see,
Comin' for to carry me home!
A band of angels comin' after me,
Comin' for to carry me home!

◀ **Robert Johnson** (1911–1938) was one of the most famous musicians of the Mississippi delta. He sang the blues, a mix of the early slave work songs and spirituals. His musical style has influenced[2] rock musicians like Eric Clapton.
In the 1940s, blues musicians used elements of jazz and gospel: a new musical style was created, which was later called rhythm and blues.

---

[1] chariot ['tʃærɪət] *Triumphwagen*   [2] influence sb./sth. ['ɪnfluəns] *jn./etwas beeinflussen*

Johnny B. Goode

Deep down Louisiana close to New Orleans I Way back up in the woods among the evergreens[1] I There stood a log cabin[2] made of earth and wood I Where lived a country boy named Johnny B. Goode I Who never ever learned to read or write so well. I But he could play the guitar just like ringing a bell. I Go go I Go Johnny go

by Chuck Berry

The songs of the first rock 'n' roller, **Chuck Berry** (born in 1926) greatly influenced later generations of musicians.
His "Johnny B. Goode" was a favourite of the Beatles.

'**The King of Rock 'n' Roll**': He was born on January 8, 1935 and died on August 16, 1977. He sang rock 'n' roll songs and sounded like the best African-American singers. But his skin was white. He became one of the most famous American singer/musicians ever – simply 'The King'.

In a studio in this house called 'Hitsville, USA' a new style of black music was born in the 1960s. It was a mixture of rhythm and blues and gospel music – great on the car radio. Its stars were Stevie Wonder, Marvin Gaye, and Diana Ross & the Supremes, just to name a few.

In New York City in the late 1970s, DJs began to speak between songs, greeting people, telling jokes and stories, trying to keep the audience excited. A new musical style was born: **rap**. Although most rappers are male, female artists like Missy Elliot, Lauryn Hill or Lil' Kim have also been very successful.

2 Your black music

Present your favourite black music artist(s) to the class.

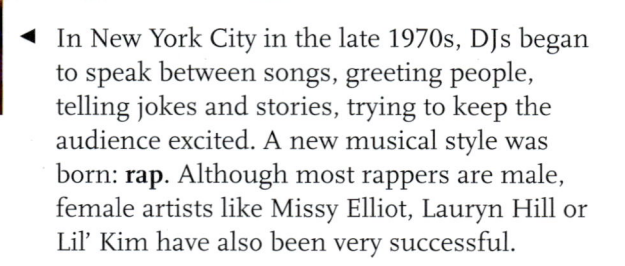

---

[1] among the evergreens *zwischen den immergrünen Bäumen*   [2] log cabin [ˌlɒg ˈkæbɪn] *Blockhütte*

Skills File – Inhalt

Seite

STUDY AND LANGUAGE SKILLS
REVISION	Learning words	155
REVISION	Using a bilingual dictionary	156
	Using an English-English dictionary	157
REVISION	Describing pictures	157
	Research	158
	Outlining	159
REVISION	Giving a presentation	160
	Handouts	160

LISTENING AND READING SKILLS
REVISION	Listening	161
REVISION	Taking notes	162
REVISION	Marking up a text	162
READING COURSE	Zusammenfassung	163–164

MEDIATION SKILLS
REVISION	Mediation	165

SPEAKING AND WRITING SKILLS
REVISION	Paraphrasing	166
REVISION	Brainstorming	166
	Summary writing	167
REVISION	Writing Course	168–169

EXAM SKILLS
How to do well in a test	170–171

> Im **Skills File** findest du Hinweise zu Arbeits- und Lerntechniken. Was du in den Skills-Kästen der Units gelernt hast, wird hier näher erläutert.
>
> Was du bereits aus Band 3 von English G 21 kennst, ist mit **REVISION** gekennzeichnet, z. B.
> – **REVISION** Describing pictures, Seite 157
> – **REVISION** Giving a presentation, Seite 160.
>
> Viele neue Hinweise helfen dir bei der Arbeit mit Hör- und Lesetexten, beim Sprechen, beim Schreiben von eigenen Texten, bei der Sprachmittlung, beim Lernen von Methoden und bei der Vorbereitung auf eine Klassenarbeit.
>
> Tipps und Aufgaben können dir zusätzlich helfen.

STUDY AND LANGUAGE SKILLS

SF REVISION Learning words

Worauf solltest du beim Lernen und Wiederholen von Vokabeln achten?

– Lerne neue und wiederhole alte Vokabeln regelmäßig – am besten jeden Tag 5–10 Minuten. Lerne immer 7–10 Vokabeln auf einmal.

– Lerne mit jemandem zusammen. Fragt euch gegenseitig ab.

– Schreib die neuen Wörter auch auf und überprüfe die Schreibweise mithilfe des *Dictionary* oder *Vocabulary*.

Wie kannst du Wörter besser behalten?

– Sammle **Gegensatzpaare**, z. B. alive – dead, majority – minority, find – lose.

– Sammle Wörter mit **gleicher Bedeutung**, z. B. (to) train – (to) practise.

– Sammle Wörter in **Wortfamilien**, z. B. (to) dance, dance, dancer, dancing lessons, shop, shopper, shopping, shopping list, shop assistant, …

– Sammle und ordne Wörter in **Wortnetzen** *(networks)*.

SF REVISION   Using a bilingual dictionary

Wann brauche ich ein zweisprachiges Wörterbuch?

Du verstehst einen Text nicht, weil er zu viele Wörter enthält, die dir unbekannt sind, und die Worterschließungstechniken (▶ *Working out the meaning of words, p. 163*) helfen dir nicht weiter?
Du sollst einen Text auf Englisch schreiben, und dir fehlt das eine oder andere Wort, um deine Ideen auszudrücken? Du willst z.B. über die Ankunft eines Einwanderers in einem neuen Land schreiben (vgl. S. 21) und kennst das Wort für „Grenze" nicht?
Dann hilft dir ein zweisprachiges Wörterbuch.

Wie benutze ich ein zweisprachiges Wörterbuch?

– Die **Leitwörter** *(running heads)* oben auf der Seite helfen dir, schneller zu finden, was du suchst. Auf der linken Seite steht das erste Stichwort, auf der rechten Seite das letzte Stichwort der Doppelseite.

– **Grenze** ist das **Stichwort** *(headword)*. Stichwörter sind alphabetisch geordnet: **g** vor **h**, **ga** vor **ge** und **gre** vor **gri** usw.

– Die *kursiv gedruckten* Hinweise helfen dir, die für deinen Text passende Bedeutung zu finden.

– Die **Ziffern** 1, 2 usw. zeigen, dass ein Stichwort mehrere ganz verschiedene Bedeutungen hat.

– **Beispielsätze** und **Redewendungen** sind dem Stichwort zugeordnet. In den Beispielsätzen und Redewendungen ersetzt eine **Tilde** (~) das Stichwort.

– Im englisch-deutschen Teil der meisten Wörterbücher findest du außerdem Hinweise auf **unregelmäßige Verbformen**, auf die **Steigerungsformen der Adjektive** und Ähnliches.

– Die **Lautschrift** gibt Auskunft darüber, wie das Wort ausgesprochen und betont wird.

– Bei kniffligen Wörtern gibt es in vielen Wörterbüchern **Info-Boxes**, in denen dir mehr Hilfen und Hinweise gegeben werden.

---

gottlos

 divinely
 gottlos godless, wicked
 gottverlassen *umg.* godforsaken
 Götze, **Götzenbild** idol ['aɪdl]

 Grazie grace
 graziös 1 *Adj* graceful (△ *nicht* gracious) 2 *Adv* gracefully; ~ **tanzen** dance gracefully
 greifen 1 *Verb mit Obj* seize, take* hold of 2 *Verb ohne Obj*; *übertragen*: *von Maßnahmen* take* effect; ~ **nach** reach *for*; *fest* grab *at*; **sie griff in ihre Handtasche** she reached into her handbag
 Greis old man
 greisenhaft senile (*auch* MED)
 Greisin old woman
 grell *Licht* glaring, harsh; *Farbe* garish; *Ton* shrill
 Grenze border; *Linie* boundary; *übertragen* limit; **es hält sich in Grenzen** it's not too bad
 grenzen. ~ **an** border on (*auch übertragen*)
 grenzenlos 1 *Adj* boundless 2 *Adv*; *sehr*

---

schwer krank

schwer

Das deutsche **schwer** hat drei Hauptbedeutungen:
1) *schwer von Gewicht*: **heavy**;
2) *schwerwiegend, ernst*: **serious**, **bad**;
3) *schwierig*: **difficult**, **hard**, **tough**.

Welche Entsprechung von „Grenze" brauchst du in diesen Sätzen?
1. Die Grenze zwischen den USA und Mexiko ist 3169 km lang.
2. Beim 15-Kilometer-Lauf kam ich gestern an meine Grenze.

Tipp

Lies immer erst den **gesamten Wörterbucheintrag**, bevor du dich für eine bestimmte Übersetzung entscheidest. Nimm nicht einfach die erste Übersetzung, die dir angeboten wird.

SF Using an English–English dictionary ▶ Unit 6 (p. 127)

Wenn du englische Texte liest oder selbst einen englischen Text schreibst, kannst du ein einsprachiges englisches Wörterbuch zur Hilfe nehmen. Hier findest du mehr über ein englisches Wort heraus als in einem zweisprachigen Wörterbuch:

– Das einsprachige Wörterbuch erklärt die **Bedeutung** eines englischen Wortes **auf Englisch**. Manche Wörter haben mehrere Bedeutungen. Lies alle Einträge und Beispielsätze genau und vergleiche sie mit deinem englischen Text, um die richtige Bedeutung herauszufinden.

– Das Wörterbuch hilft dir auch, die **passende Verbindung mit anderen Wörtern** zu finden, z. B. zu Verben, Präpositionen oder in bestimmten Wendungen. Das ist besonders nützlich, wenn du selbst einen englischen Text schreiben willst und nach den richtigen Wörtern suchst.

> **deadly** ['dedli] *adj*
> ▶ **1** *able or likely to kill people* {= lethal}: This is no longer a deadly disease.
> **deadly to** The HSN virus is deadly to chickens.
> **a deadly weapon** The new generation of biological weapons is more deadly than ever.
> ▶ **2** (*only before noun*) {= complete}:
> **deadly silence** There was deadly silence after his speech.
> ▶ **a deadly secret** Don't tell anyone – this is a deadly secret.
> **in deadly earnest** *completely serious*: Don't you laugh – I am in deadly earnest!
> ▶ **3** (*informal*) *very boring*: Many TV programmes are pretty deadly!
> ▶ **4** *always able to achieve something*: The new Chelsea striker is said to be a deadly goal scorer.

SF REVISION   Describing pictures

Wie kann ich Bilder beschreiben?

– Um zu sagen, wo genau auf dem Bild etwas Bestimmtes dargestellt ist, verwende
  at the top/bottom • **in the foreground/background** • **in the middle** • **on the left/right** • **behind** • **between** • **in front of** • **next to** • **under**

– Um zu beschreiben, was die Personen auf dem Bild tun, verwende das **present progressive**.
  The girl is looking down into the Grand Canyon.

at the top • *in the background* • *in the middle* • *on the left* • *on the right* • *in the foreground* • *at the bottom*

Wie kann ich beschreiben, was die abgebildeten Personen fühlen?

Oft sollst du dich in eine Person auf einem Foto hineinversetzen und beschreiben, was sie fühlt oder denkt. Schau dir das Foto genau an und nimm dir Zeit, dir die Situation vorzustellen. Beim Formulieren helfen dir *phrases* wie:
Maybe the woman/man in the photo feels … / is thinking about … •
I think he/she might want to …

SF Research ▸ Unit 5 (p. 103)

Material sammeln (recherchieren)

Wenn du über ein Thema etwas schreiben oder einen Vortrag halten sollst, suchst du zuerst Informationen in Büchern oder in Zeitschriften, im Internet und in anderen Quellen. Verwende möglichst englischsprachige Quellen.

Damit du die Übersicht behältst, solltest du das Gefundene in einem Ordner sammeln und von vornherein sortieren. Orientiere dich dafür an der Gliederung bzw. *outline*, die du für deinen Text oder deine Präsentation vorbereitet hast (▸ *Outlining, p. 159*). Du kannst deine Materialien auch danach ordnen, ob es sich um sachliche Informationen, also Tatsachen, oder um persönliche Meinungen handelt.

Wichtiges herausschreiben (exzerpieren)

Sichte das Material und entscheide, welche Informationen du tatsächlich verwenden möchtest. Du kannst die betreffenden Passagen markieren (▸ *Marking up a text, p. 162*), herausschreiben oder auch ausschneiden und in fortlaufender Reihenfolge auf DIN-A4-Blätter kleben. Vergiss die Quellenangabe nicht. Deine eigenen Gedanken fügst du in Stichpunkten an den entsprechenden Stellen hinzu. Wenn du eine Präsentation vorbereitest, kannst du am Rand notieren, welche Medien du jeweils einsetzen möchtest.

Aus Materialien, die du im Internet gefunden und in elektronischen Ordnern gesammelt hast, überträgst du die wichtigen Informationen mit „Kopieren" und „Einfügen" in ein neues Dokument, wo du sie dann bearbeiten (also kürzen, ergänzen, umschreiben usw.) kannst.

Zitieren, umschreiben, Quellen angeben

Formuliere deinen Text oder deine Präsentation mit deinen eigenen Worten – schreibe nicht einfach aus deinen Quellen ab. Wenn du deine Argumentation einmal mit einer Expertenaussage unterstützen oder deinen Text mit einem Auszug aus einem Buch, einem Interview o. Ä. interessanter und abwechslungsreicher gestalten möchtest, markiere solche Zitate durch Anführungszeichen und gib Autor und Quelle einschließlich Seitenzahl an (bei Internetquellen die Webadresse und das Datum des Aufrufs). Das gilt auch dann, wenn du eine fremde Aussage mit eigenen Worten umschreibst. Gib auch bei einer Abbildung den Fundort an.

Kündige in deiner mündlichen Präsentation deine Zitate an und erkläre schwierige Wörter. Schaffe logische Übergänge zu deinen eigenen Argumenten.

Aber denk daran: Lange Zitate können deine Leser oder Zuhörer auch ermüden und erwecken leicht den Eindruck, dass du selbst nur wenig zu sagen hast. In der Kürze liegt die Würze!

www.karenrinaldogallery.com

Skills File **159**

SF Outlining ▶ Unit 3, P 17 (p. 71)

Wenn du zu einem komplexen Thema einen Text schreiben oder eine Präsentation vorbereiten sollst, sammelst du zunächst Informationen und Unterlagen (▶ *Research, p. 158*). Eine zuvor erstellte Gliederung (*outline*) hilft dir dabei, denn so weißt du von vornherein genau, was du suchst. Und auch beim Ordnen deines Materials solltest du dich gleich an einer *outline* orientieren.

Outlines werden in Stichpunkten oder kurzen Sätzen verfasst. Schreibe dir zunächst deine Hauptpunkte auf. Bestimme dann Unterthemen und überlege dir, mit welchen Beispielen und Erläuterungen du deine Gedanken dazu unterstützen möchtest. Wenn du eine Mindmap erstellt hast, kannst du sie für deine Gliederung verwenden.

Achte auf eine logische Reihenfolge deiner Gedanken. Sie sollen sich in deiner *outline* widerspiegeln. Beim Gliedern kannst du verschiedene Möglichkeiten der Aufzählung (Zahlen, Groß- und Kleinbuchstaben, ...) nutzen. Mach dir einen Vermerk, z. B. am Rand des Blattes, welche Zitate, Statistiken, Bilder, Medienbeiträge usw. du an welcher Stelle einsetzen möchtest.

Die *outline* dient dir als Vorlage für deinen Text bzw. als Ausgangspunkt für deine Präsentation. Darüber hinaus kannst du sie dazu verwenden, deinen Lesern oder Zuhörern einen Überblick über dein Thema zu geben, indem du sie deinem Text oder deiner Präsentation voranstellst, z. B. bei einem mündlichen Vortrag auf einer Folie.

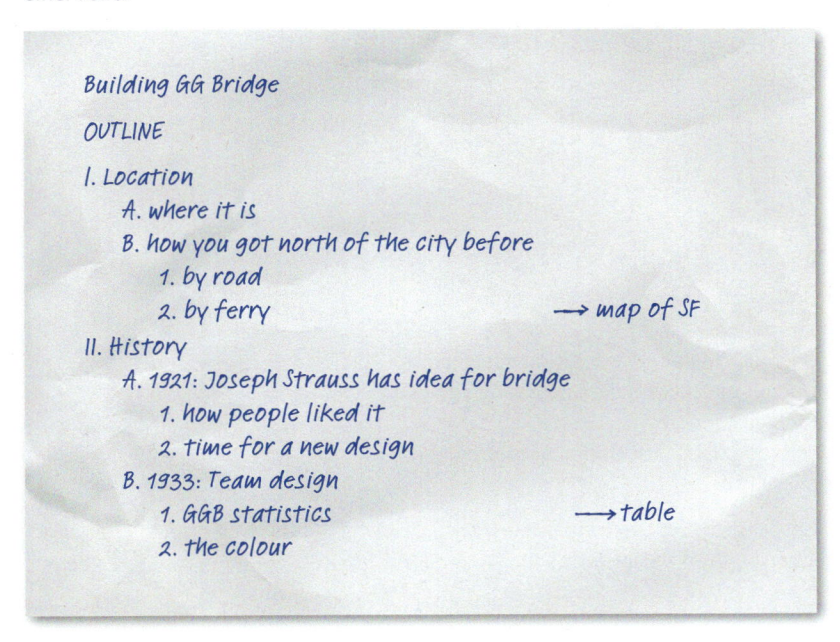

Building GG Bridge

OUTLINE

I. Location
    A. where it is
    B. how you got north of the city before
        1. by road
        2. by ferry   ⟶ map of SF
II. History
    A. 1921: Joseph Strauss has idea for bridge
        1. how people liked it
        2. time for a new design
    B. 1933: Team design
        1. GGB statistics   ⟶ table
        2. the colour

Tipp
- Eine Gliederung (*outline*) hilft dir beim Recherchieren und beim Ordnen deines Materials.
- Bestimme zuerst die Hauptpunkte, dann die Unterthemen.

SF REVISION Giving a presentation

Wie mache ich eine gute Präsentation?

Vorbereitung
- Ordne deine Gedanken und notiere sie, z.B. auf nummerierten Karteikarten oder als Mindmap.
- Bereite ein Poster, eine Folie oder ein Handout (▶ *Handouts, siehe unten*) vor. Schreib groß und für alle gut lesbar.
- Übe deine Präsentation zu Hause vor einem Spiegel. Sprich laut, deutlich und langsam, mach Pausen. Reicht die Zeit?

Durchführung
- Bevor du beginnst, bereite deine Medien vor und sortiere deine Vortragskarten.
- Warte, bis es ruhig ist. Schau die Zuhörer an.
- Erkläre zu Anfang, worüber du sprechen wirst.
- Lies nicht von deinen Karten ab, sondern sprich frei.
- Schreibe die Gliederung sowie unbekannten Wortschatz und Eigennamen an die Tafel.

Schluss
- Sag, dass du fertig bist.
- Frag die Zuhörer, ob sie Fragen haben.
- Bedanke dich fürs Zuhören.

> My presentation is about …
> First, I'd like to talk about …
> Second, …

> This picture/photo/ … shows …

> That's the end of my presentation. Thank you for listening. Have you got any questions?

SF Handouts   ▶ *Unit 2 (p. 42) • P 15 (p. 50)*

Ein Handout enthält die wichtigsten Informationen einer Präsentation. Manchmal bietet es auch zusätzliche Informationen an, z.B. in Form von Statistiken, Quellenangaben oder Illustrationen.
Ein Handout kannst du vor, während oder nach deiner Präsentation austeilen:
- vor oder während der Präsentation, damit die Zuhörer die Gliederung deines Vortrags verstehen und ihm besser folgen können;
- nach der Präsentation, damit die Zuhörer später noch einmal nachlesen und sich besser an die Präsentation erinnern können.

Strukturiere dein Handout klar und übersichtlich, z.B. durch eine Überschrift, deinen Namen, das Datum, durch Teilüberschriften, Beispiele, tabellarische oder grafische Übersichten.

Du kannst in ganzen Sätzen schreiben, z.B. bei einer Zusammenfassung, oder in Stichpunkten.

Wenn du Abbildungen verwendest, gib ihnen eine Bildunterschrift und vergiss nicht die Quellenangabe. Mit Symbolen kannst du dein Handout übersichtlicher gestalten und die wesentlichen Informationen hervorheben.

Lass ausreichend Platz für die Notizen der Zuhörer, z.B. durch einen breiten Rand an der Seite oder im unteren Teil des Blattes.

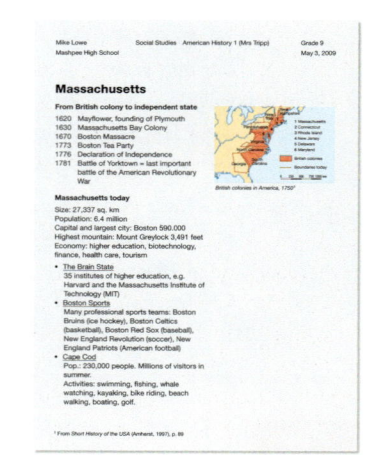

LISTENING AND READING SKILLS

REVISION   Listening

Vor dem Hören

- Frag dich, was du schon über das Thema weißt.
- Nutze Überschriften oder Bilder um zu erahnen, was dich z. B. bei einer Geschichte erwarten könnte.
- Lies dir die Aufgaben auf deinem Aufgabenblatt genau durch und überlege, auf welche Informationen du dich konzentrieren musst.
- Bereite dich darauf vor, Notizen zu machen. Leg z. B. eine Tabelle oder Liste an.

Während des Hörens

Listening for gist:
Konzentriere dich beim ersten Hören auf allgemeine Informationen, z. B. die Personen (unterschiedliche Stimmen), das Thema, die Umgebung (Geräusche), die Atmosphäre (die Sprechweise der Leute).

Listening for detail:
- Mach dir noch einmal bewusst, worauf du genau achten willst (Hörauftrag), besonders bei Durchsagen (*announcements*), die du vielleicht nur einmal hören kannst.
- Gerate nicht in Panik, wenn du meinst, du hättest gerade etwas Wichtiges verpasst. Konzentriere dich auf die nächste wichtige Information.
- Lass dich nicht von anderen Einzelheiten oder Geräuschen ablenken.
- Mach nur kurze Notizen, z. B. Anfangsbuchstaben, Symbole oder Stichworte.
- Manche Signalwörter machen es dir leichter, den Hörtext zu verstehen.
  Aufzählung: **and**, **another**, **too**
  Gegensatz: **although**, **but**
  Grund, Folge: **because**, **so**, **so that**
  Vergleich: **larger/older/… than**, **as … as**, **more**, **most**
  Reihenfolge: **before**, **after**, **then**, **next**, **later**, **when**, **at last**, **at the same time**
- Auch andere Details wie z. B. die Stimme, der Akzent oder der Tonfall des Sprechers oder der Sprecherin können dir helfen, Informationen über seine oder ihre Gefühle, Herkunft usw. zu bekommen.
- Unterteile Telefonnummern beim Aufschreiben: 0171 572 42 589.

Nach dem Hören

- Vervollständige deine Notizen sofort.
- Wenn du den Text ein zweites Mal hören kannst, konzentriere dich auf das, was du beim ersten Mal nicht genau verstanden hast.
- Schau dir noch einmal die Aufgabenstellung an. Sollst du die gehörten Informationen nutzen, um einen neuen Text zu schreiben? Dann achte auf die richtige Textform: Bericht, Beschreibung, …

SF REVISION Taking notes

Worum geht es beim Notizen machen?

Wenn du beim Lesen oder Zuhören Notizen machst, kannst du dich später besser daran erinnern, wenn du etwas vortragen, nacherzählen oder einen Bericht schreiben sollst.

Wie mache ich Notizen?

In Texten oder Gesprächen gibt es immer wichtige und unwichtige Wörter. Die wichtigen Wörter werden Schlüsselwörter **(key words)** genannt und nur die solltest du notieren. Meist sind das Substantive und Verben, manchmal auch Adjektive oder Zahlen.

> **Tipp**
> - Verwende Ziffern (z. B. „7" statt „seven").
> - Verwende Symbole und Abkürzungen, z. B. ✔ (für Ja) und + (für und) oder GB für Great Britain, K für Katrina.
>   Du kannst auch eigene Symbole erfinden.
> - Verwende **not** oder ✗ statt „doesn't" oder „don't".

Hmm, da hab ich wohl ein paar Symbole zu viel benutzt …

SF REVISION Marking up a text

Wann sollte ich einen Text markieren?

Du hast einen Text mit vielen Fakten vor dir liegen und sollst später über bestimmte Dinge berichten. Dann wird es dir helfen, die für dich wichtigen Informationen im Text zu markieren.

Wie gehe ich am besten vor?

Lies den Text und markiere nur die für dein Thema wichtigen Informationen. Nicht jeder Satz enthält Informationen, die für deine Aufgabe wichtig sind, und oft reicht es aus, nur ein oder zwei Wörter in einem Satz zu markieren.

- Du kannst wichtige Wörter einkreisen.
- Du kannst sie unterstreichen.
- Du kannst sie mit einem Textmarker hervorheben.

ABER:
Markiere nur auf Fotokopien von Texten oder in deinen eigenen Büchern.

American Museum of Natural History
In the American Museum of Natural History you'll find the largest and probably one of the most awesome (dinosaur collections) in the world.

American Museum of Natural History
In the American Museum of Natural History you'll find the largest and probably one of the most awesome dinosaur collections in the world.

American Museum of Natural History
In the American Museum of Natural History you'll find the largest and probably one of the most awesome dinosaur collections in the world.

READING COURSE – ZUSAMMENFASSUNG

REVISION Working out the meaning of words

Das Nachschlagen unbekannter Wörter im Wörterbuch kostet Zeit und nimmt auf Dauer den Spaß am Lesen. Oft geht es auch ohne Wörterbuch:

1. Bilder und Zeichen erklären und ergänzen oft Dinge aus dem Text. Schau sie dir deshalb vor und nach dem Lesen genau an.
2. Manche Wörter erklären sich aus dem Textzusammenhang, z.B. *When we reached the station, Judy bought our tickets.*
3. Zu manchen englischen Wörtern fallen dir vielleicht deutsche, französische oder lateinische Wörter ein, die ähnlich geschrieben oder ausgesprochen werden, z.B. **excellent, millionaire, nation, reality**.
4. Es gibt neue Wörter, in denen du bekannte Teile entdeckst, z.B. **friendliness, helpless, understandable, gardener, tea bag, waiting room**.

REVISION Skimming and Scanning   ▶ Unit 2, P 16 (p. 51)

Beim **Skimming** überfliegst du einen Text schnell, um dir einen **Überblick** zu verschaffen. Du willst dabei herausfinden, worum es in dem Text geht. Achte dabei auf
– die **Überschrift**,
– die **Zwischenüberschriften** und hervorgehobene Wörter oder Sätze,
– die **Bilder** und **Bildunterschriften**,
– den **ersten Satz** und den **letzten Satz** jedes Absatzes,
– **Grafiken**, **Statistiken** und die **Quelle** des Textes.

Beim **Scanning** suchst du nach **bestimmten Informationen**. Dazu suchst du den Text nach Schlüsselwörtern *(key words)* ab und liest nur dort genauer, wo du sie findest. Geh dabei so vor:

Schritt 1: Denk an die Schlüsselwörter und geh mit deinen Augen oder dem Finger schnell durch den Text, in breiten Schlingen wie bei einem „S" oder „Z" oder von oben nach unten wie bei einem „U". Die gesuchten Wörter werden dir sofort „ins Auge springen".

Schritt 2: Wenn das gesuchte Wort nicht im Text vorkommt, überlege dir andere, themenverwandte Wörter (z.B. **lesson** → **school, subject**) und suche nach diesen.

Finding the main ideas of a text   ▶ Unit 3, P 11 (p. 68)

Zeitungsartikel, Berichte oder Kommentare verstehst du besser, wenn du ihre wesentlichen Aussagen erkennst und dir klar machst, wie sie zusammenhängen. Die wichtigsten Aussagen findest du so:

1. Jeder Text hat ein Thema mit mindestens einer Hauptaussage, z.B.: *Drinking soda is one of the worst things you can do to your health.*
Diese Hauptaussage findest du oft im **ersten Absatz**.

▶▶

2. Die Hauptaussage wird in der Regel durch weitere Aussagen bzw. Gedanken unterstützt, z. B.: *Experts agree that sugary soft drinks and fast food are the main reasons why so many American teenagers are fat.*

3. Diese weiteren Aussagen bzw. Gedanken werden oft durch Beispiele und Begründungen ergänzt, z. B.: *About 7 % of the calories that they take in come from soft drinks alone.*

Careful reading ▶ Unit 4, P 8 (p. 87)

Schwierige Texte musst du besonders sorgfältig und konzentriert lesen, damit du alle darin enthaltenen Informationen und Gedanken verstehst.

1. Lies den Text genau. Welches sind seine wesentlichen Aussagen? (▶ *Finding the main ideas of a text, p. 163*)

2. Manchmal findest du die Antwort auf eine Frage nicht deutlich formuliert an einer Stelle im Text, sondern du musst dir diese Antwort aus einzelnen Informationen erschließen, die du an verschiedenen Stellen im Text findest. Nimm z. B. den Text auf Seite 87: Wirkt sich ein Job positiv oder negativ auf die schulischen Leistungen aus? Für die Antwort musst du mehrere Aussagen aus dem Text zusammentragen:

FACTS: students have an 11-hour work day; after work they're often too tired to do their homework = negative effects
working makes students more disciplined; they learn to organize their time = positive effects

CONCLUSION: for some students it's good, but for many it means worse grades

Text types: fiction and non-fiction ▶ Unit 5, P 8 (p. 107)

Wenn du einen Text liest, ist es sinnvoll sich klar zu machen, ob er von einer vom Autor erdachten Welt handelt (*fictional text*) oder sich mit der Wirklichkeit auseinandersetzt (*non-fictional text*).

Fiktionale Texte sind z. B. Kurzgeschichten und Romane. Der Autor wählt Figuren (*characters*) aus und erzählt von ihren Gefühlen und Handlungen, von deren Motiven und Hintergründen. Die Handlungen finden in einem oder mehreren Handlungsrahmen statt, z. B. an einem Ort, zu einer bestimmten Zeit und unter bestimmten Umständen (*setting*). Die Ereignisse können aus verschiedenen Perspektiven erzählt werden (*point of view*). Oft verwendet der Autor für seine Geschichte eine anschauliche Sprache, z. B. ausschmückende Adjektive, Metaphern, Vergleiche, direkte Rede oder er lässt den Leser an den Gedanken seiner Figuren oder des Erzählers teilhaben.

Nicht-fiktionale Texte sind z. B. Berichte in Zeitungen, wissenschaftliche Artikel, Aufsätze oder Kommentare. Hier informiert der Autor über ein Thema der realen Welt oder nimmt Stellung dazu.

Es gibt auch Texte, die ein **Mischform** aus beiden Textarten sind.

MEDIATION SKILLS

SF REVISION Mediation ▶ *Unit 1, P 10 (p. 26)*

REVISION Wann muss ich zwischen zwei Sprachen vermitteln?

Manchmal musst du zwischen zwei Sprachen vermitteln. Das nennt man **mediation**.

1. Du gibst englische Informationen auf Deutsch weiter:
   Du fährst z. B. mit deiner Familie in die USA und deine Eltern oder Geschwister wollen wissen, was jemand in einem Café gesagt hat oder was an einer Informationstafel steht.

2. Du gibst deutsche Informationen auf Englisch weiter:
   Vielleicht ist bei dir zu Hause eine Austauschschülerin aus den USA oder Dänemark zu Gast, die kein Deutsch spricht und Hilfe braucht.

3. In schriftlichen Prüfungen musst du manchmal in einem englischen Text gezielt nach Informationen suchen und diese auf Deutsch wiedergeben. Oder du sollst Informationen aus einem deutschen Text auf Englisch wiedergeben.

Worauf muss ich bei *mediation* achten?

– Übersetze nicht alles wörtlich, sondern gib den Sinn wieder.
– Gib nur das Wesentliche weiter, lass Unwichtiges weg.
– Verwende kurze und einfache Sätze.
– Wenn du ein Wort nicht kennst, umschreibe es oder ersetze es durch ein anderes Wort.

Was kann ich tun, wenn ich ein wichtiges Wort nicht kenne?

Vielleicht findest du es manchmal schwer, mündliche Aussagen oder schriftliche Textvorlagen in die andere Sprache zu übertragen, z. B. weil
– dein Wortschatz nicht ausreicht,
– dir bekannte Wörter „im Stress" nicht einfallen,
– spezielle Fachbegriffe auftauchen.

Manche Wörter kannst du umschreiben, z. B. mithilfe von Relativsätzen wie:
It's somebody/a person who ...
It's something that you use to ...
It's an animal that ...
It's a place that/where ...

▶ *Paraphrasing, p. 166*

Entschuldigung, kannst du mir vielleicht helfen? Mein Englisch ist nicht so gut.

You can go to Times Square by subway. It takes too long by bus and you have to change twice.

Wir können mit der U-Bahn zum Times Square fahren.

Was hältst du davon, wenn wir einen Hubschrauberrundflug machen würden? Frag doch mal, wo man so was machen kann.

Excuse me, we'd like to do a tour of New York with ... something that you can fly with.

... a helicopter ...

SPEAKING AND WRITING SKILLS

SF REVISION Paraphrasing

Worum geht es beim Paraphrasing?

„Paraphrasing" bedeutet, etwas mit anderen Worten zu erklären. Das ist hilfreich, wenn dir ein bestimmtes Wort nicht einfällt oder wenn dein Gegenüber dich nicht verstanden hat. Paraphrasing ist auch besonders nützlich für **mediation** (▶ *Mediation, p. 165*).

Wie gehe ich beim Paraphrasing vor?

– Man kann mit einem Ausdruck umschreiben, der dieselbe Bedeutung hat:
  'To wonder' is the same as 'to ask yourself'.
  Oder man sagt das Gegenteil:
  'Alive' is the opposite of 'dead'.
– Manchmal braucht man mehrere Wörter, z. B. wenn man etwas beschreibt oder erklären will, wie man etwas verwendet. Dabei verwendet man ein allgemeines Wort (**general word**) und nennt weitere Eigenschaften:
  A skyscraper is a very tall building.
– Oder du umschreibst das Wort mit **... is/are like ...**
  A lodge is like a small house or cabin. You find it in the country.
– Du kannst auch einen Relativsatz (**relative clause**) verwenden:
  She looks after small children. – Ah, she's a nanny!
  A ticket office is a shop where you can buy tickets for shows and concerts.

SF REVISION Brainstorming

Was ist Brainstorming und wofür ist es gut?

Bei vielen Aufgaben ist es nützlich, wenn du im ersten Schritt möglichst viele Ideen zum Thema sammelst. Beim Sammeln und beim Auswerten der Ideen helfen dir die folgenden Techniken.

Drei verschiedene Brainstorming-Techniken

Technik 1: Making a list
Schreib die Ideen so auf, wie sie dir einfallen, und zwar für jede Idee eine neue Zeile. Lies im zweiten Schritt alle deine Ideen durch. Überlege, welche Ideen davon für dein Thema sinnvoll sind und nummeriere sie nach Nützlichkeit.

Technik 2: Making a mind map
Leg eine Mindmap an. Überlege dafür, welche Oberbegriffe zu deinem Thema passen. Verwende unterschiedliche Farben für jeden Oberbegriff. Ergänze jede Idee, die zu einem Oberbegriff passt, auf einem Nebenast. Nimm dafür nur wichtige Schlüsselwörter. Du kannst statt Wörtern auch Symbole verwenden und Bilder ergänzen.

Technik 3: The 5 Ws
Schreib die Fragewörter **Who? What? When? Where? Why?** in eine Tabelle. Die Ideen, die dir zu der jeweiligen Frage kommen, werden darunter geschrieben.

6. watch DVDs
3. swimming pool
   no jobs for parents
   parents not at home
1. sleep late – every morning
   ~~hang out~~
2. no homework
5. disco/party with friends
   watch TV
4. see friends cinema

SF Summary writing ▶ Unit 4, P 16 (p. 89)

Wenn du einen Lese- oder Hörtext oder einen Filmausschnitt zusammenfassen möchtest, schreibst du eine *summary*. Dabei gehst du folgendermaßen vor:

1. Lies dir den Text noch mindestens einmal genau durch (bzw. hör ihn dir ein weiteres Mal an oder sieh dir den Filmausschnitt noch einmal an). Bei einem Lesetext markierst du wichtige Passagen oder machst am Rand des Textes kurze Anmerkungen. Auch bei Hörtexten und Filmausschnitten machst du dir Notizen (▶ *Listening, p. 161*).

2. Wenn es sich um einen geschriebenen Text handelt, lies ihn jetzt ein weiteres Mal, Satz für Satz. Wenn du mit einer Kopie arbeitest, unterstreiche die Passagen im Text, die dir Antwort auf die **5 Ws** geben:

   Who?   Who does … / Who is the … about?
   What?   What happens? / What does he/she do?
   When?   When does it take place?
   Where?   Where does it happen?
   Why?   Why does he/she act in this way?

   Zusätzlich zum Unterstreichen kannst du alle Sätze, Satzteile und Wortgruppen einklammern, die *nicht* zu den wesentlichen Gedanken des Autors gehören. Dazu gehören auch Beispiele, Vergleiche, symbolhafte Ausdrücke, Zitate, direkte Rede, ausschmückende Adjektive und andere Textteile, die der Beschreibung dienen.

3. Notiere dir alles, was du nicht eingeklammert hast, in Stichpunkten auf einem separaten Blatt Papier. Überprüfe noch einmal, ob du wirklich alle unnötigen Textstellen weggelassen hast.

4. Nun schreibe mit deinen eigenen Worten einen neuen Text im *simple present* (auch wenn du eine Geschichte zusammenfasst, die in der Vergangenheit spielt). Bringe die Informationen in eine logische Reihenfolge. So kannst du anfangen:
   The story is about … • The text describes … • The article shows … • In the story we get to know …
   Im Hauptteil solltest du die wichtigsten Ereignisse einer Geschichte oder die Hauptpunkte eines Artikels wiedergeben. Verwende dafür deine Notizen zu den 5 Ws. Schreib den Text nicht ab, sondern verwende deine eigenen Worte.

5. Überprüfe deinen Entwurf noch einmal. Enthält dein Text wirklich die wichtigsten Gedanken, Ereignisse, Ideen aus dem Original? Achte auch auf sprachliche Fehler, besonders auf

   – die Rechtschreibung,
   – die Verwendung des *simple present*,
   – die Wortstellung,
   – logische Übergänge zwischen den Sätzen durch *linking words* (*and, therefore, that's why, but, because* …).

6. Bringe den korrigierten Entwurf in eine Reinschrift.

REVISION Writing course – Zusammenfassung

The steps of writing

1. Brainstorming – Ideen sammeln und ordnen (▶ *Brainstorming, p. 166*)

2. Schreiben. Dabei achte darauf,
– deine Sätze zu verbinden und auszubauen *(Writing better sentences)*,
– deinen Text gut zu strukturieren *(Using paragraphs)*,
– bei einem Bericht die 5 Ws abzudecken *(Writing a report)*,
– bei einem Leserbrief an eine Zeitschrift eine höfliche Anrede und Schlussformel zu verwenden *(Writing a letter to a magazine)*.

3. Deinen Text inhaltlich und sprachlich überprüfen *(Correcting your text)*

Writing better sentences

Linking words verbinden Sätze und machen sie interessanter. Verwende z. B.
– **Time phrases** wie **at 7 o'clock**, **every morning**, **in the afternoons**, **a few minutes later**, **suddenly**, **then**, **next …**,
– **Konjunktionen** wie **although**, **and**, **because**, **but**, **so … that**, **that**, **when**, **while**,
– **Relativpronomen** wie **who**, **which** und **that**.

Auch mit **Adjektiven** und **Adverbien** kannst du deine Sätze verbessern.
– **Adjektive** bestimmen Personen, Orte, Gegenstände oder Erlebnisse genauer und machen sie ebenfalls interessanter:
The man looked into the room. → **The young man looked into the empty room.**
– Mit **Adverbien** kannst du beschreiben, wie jemand etwas macht:
The young man looked nervously into the empty room.

Using paragraphs

Structuring a text

Einen Text versteht man viel besser, wenn er in Absätze gegliedert ist:
– eine Einleitung (**beginning**) – hier schreibst du, worum es geht;
– einen Hauptteil (**middle**) – hier schreibst du mehr über dein Thema,
– einen Schluss (**end**) – hier bringst du den Text zu einem interessanten Ende.

Am Anfang eines Absatzes sind kurze, einleitende Sätze (**topic sentences**) gut, die den Lesern sofort sagen, worum es geht, z. B.
– Orte: **My trip to … was fantastic. / … is famous for … / … is a great place.**
– Personen: **… is great/funny/interesting/clever/…**
– Aktivitäten: **… is great fun. / Lots of people … every day.**

Wie kann ich meine Absätze interessant gestalten?

– Beginne mit einem interessanten Einstiegssatz:
Guess what happened to me today! / Did I tell you that …?
– Fang für jeden neuen Aspekt einen neuen Absatz an.
– Beende deinen Text mit einer Zusammenfassung oder etwas Persönlichem.

Writing a report – organizing ideas

Hierauf kommt es bei einem Bericht an:
- Gib dem Leser eine **schnelle Orientierung**, was passiert ist.
- Beginne mit **wichtigen Informationen** und gib erst dann Detailinformationen.
- Gib Antwort auf die **5 Ws**: **Who? What? When? Where? Why?** und manchmal auch auf **How?**
- Verwende das *simple past*.

Writing a letter to a magazine   ▶ *Unit 4 (p. 85)*

Wenn du auf einen Zeitschriftenartikel reagieren und einen Leserbrief schreiben möchtest,
- beginne deinen Brief mit **Dear + (Name der Zeitschrift/des Autors des Artikels)**,
- lege deine Meinung dar und begründe sie (**I would like to comment on …**, **I agree/disagree with …**, **I think …**, **That is why …**, **For example, …**),
- beende deinen Brief mit **Yours sincerely** oder **Yours**.

Correcting your text

Lies jeden Text, den du geschrieben hast, mehrmals durch
- um zu sehen, ob er vollständig und gut verständlich ist,
- um ihn auf Fehler zu überprüfen, z. B. **Rechtschreibfehler** *(spelling mistakes)* und **Grammatikfehler** *(grammar mistakes)*.

REVISION Spelling mistakes

Beachte folgende Regeln:
- Manche Wörter haben Buchstaben, die man nicht spricht, aber schreibt, z. B. **talk**, **climb**.
- Manchmal ändert sich die Schreibweise, wenn ein Wort eine Endung erhält, z. B. **take → taking**, **terrible → terribly**, **lucky → luckily**, **try → tries** (aber **stay → stays**), **run → running**, **drop → dropped**.
- Beim Plural tritt manchmal noch ein *-e* zum *-s*, z. B. **church → churches**.

REVISION Grammar mistakes

Diese Tipps helfen dir, typische Fehler zu vermeiden:
- Im **simple present** wird in der 3. Person Singular **-s** angehängt: **she knows**
- **Unregelmäßige Verben**: Manche Verben bilden die Formen des *simple past* und des Partizip Perfekt *(past participle)* unregelmäßig. Die unregelmäßigen Formen musst du lernen. Die Liste steht auf S. 292–293.
  go – went – gone; **buy – bought – bought**
- **Verneinung**: Im *simple present* werden Vollverben mit **don't/doesn't** verneint, im *simple past* mit **didn't**.
- **Satzstellung**: Im Englischen gilt immer (auch im Nebensatz):
a) subject – verb – object (SVO):   **… when I saw my brother.**
     … als ich meinen Bruder sah.
b) Orts- vor Zeitangabe: **I bought a nice book in the city yesterday**.

EXAM SKILLS

SF **How to do well in a test** ▶ *Getting ready for a test 1 (p. 32)*

Countdown zum Testerfolg

Ein Test ist angekündigt? Kein Grund zur Panik. Wichtig ist, dass du weißt, worauf du dich vorbereiten musst. Im Zweifelsfall frag deine Lehrerin oder deinen Lehrer. Der Countdown kann beginnen!

Eine Woche vor dem Test

1. Lies noch einmal die **Texte** der zuletzt durchgenommenen Unit (A-Section und Text, eventuell auch das Background File). Fasse mündlich oder schriftlich zusammen, worum es ging.

2. Wiederhole den **Wortschatz** der Unit mit Hilfe des *Vocabulary* oder des *Wordmaster*. Schreibe dir die Wörter und Wortverbindungen, die du immer wieder vergisst, auf ein Blatt Papier. Eine Mindmap oder ein Wortfeld helfen beim Behalten.

3. Geh auch noch mal die neue **Grammatik** durch. Aufgaben zur Selbstüberprüfung und zum Üben findest du im *Practice*-Teil, auf der Seite „How am I doing?", im *Grammar File* (S. 172–189), in deinem *Workbook* und im *e-Workbook*.

Zwei Tage vor dem Test

1. Wiederhole den **Wortschatz**. Manche Wörter sitzen noch nicht? Schreibe einen kurzen Text, in dem du sie verwendest.

2. Lies die **Texte** ein weiteres Mal.

3. Erkläre einem Freund oder einer Freundin die neue **Grammatik**. Das klappt nicht richtig? Dann lies nochmal im *Grammar File* nach.

Am Abend vor dem Test

1. Entspanne dich. Du kannst lesen, dich in die Badewanne legen, Musik hören, fernsehen, …

2. Geh zur gewohnten Zeit ins Bett.

Am Morgen des Tests

1. Steh rechtzeitig auf, damit du nicht hetzen musst.

2. Lies irgendetwas „zum Aufwärmen", aber schau nicht mehr in dein Schülerbuch.

Während des Tests

1. Denk daran: Du hast dich gut vorbereitet. Es gibt keinen Grund, nervös zu sein.

2. Konzentriere dich auf den Test, lass dich nicht ablenken.

3. Lies dir die Aufgaben genau durch. Dann löse zuerst die Aufgaben, die dir einfach scheinen. Wende dich erst danach den schwereren Aufgaben zu.

4. Aufgaben, die du bearbeitet hast, hakst du ab. So siehst du, wie du vorankommst, und behältst den Überblick.

5. Schau ab und zu auf die Uhr. Du solltest dir für den Schluss noch etwas Zeit einplanen, um deine Antworten noch einmal durchzulesen und wenn nötig zu korrigieren.

Aufgabenstellungen verstehen

Bevor du anfängst, die Aufgaben zu bearbeiten, vergewissere dich, dass du genau weißt, was du tun sollst. Lies die Aufgabe Wort für Wort langsam und gründlich und von Anfang bis Ende durch. Du kannst besonders wichtige Teile der Aufgabenstellung unterstreichen und die Aufgabe, wenn nötig, für dich in einzelne Schritte unterteilen.

Den folgenden Arbeitsanweisungen begegnest du häufig:

Add	Verbinde eine Information oder einen Sachverhalt mit einer/einem anderen auf die geforderte Art und Weise.
Choose	Wähle zwischen verschiedenen Möglichkeiten die passende Information aus.
Comment	Kommentiere einen Sachverhalt durch die Darstellung deiner eigenen Meinung dazu. Begründe und erläutere sie möglichst genau.
Compare	Vergleiche Dinge, Wörter oder Sachverhalte, indem du prüfst, ob und auf welche Weise sie gleiche oder verschiedene Eigenschaften, Aussehen, Bedeutungen oder Funktionen haben.
Complete	Ergänze eine Information, indem du sie an dem dafür vorgesehenen Platz einträgst und damit z. B. einen Satz sinnvoll beendest.
Describe	Beschreibe ein Objekt oder eine Person, d.h. stelle dar, wie sie aussehen, wie das Objekt funktioniert oder die Personen handeln. Vermeide eigene Wertungen wie z. B. „beautiful", „useful" oder „great".
Discuss	Diskutiere ein Thema, eine Behauptung oder eine Aussage. Untersuche möglichst viele Seiten davon, z. B. Vor- und Nachteile, und stelle diese geordnet dar.
Explain	Erkläre einen Sachverhalt, d. h. gib wesentliche Fakten über ihn und erläutere, wie sie logisch zusammenhängen.
Fill in	Trage die geforderten Informationen in den dafür vorgesehenen Platz ein, z. B. in eine Lücke oder eine Tabelle.
List	Schreibe einzelne oder mehrere Informationen übersichtlich und geordnet auf, z. B. in einer Reihe, Tabelle oder einem anderen Verzeichnis.
Listen	Höre dir einen Text, einzelne Informationen oder Sachverhalte an.
Match	Ordne die angegebenen Informationen einander zu, wie es die Aufgabe erfordert. Finde z. B. Satzanfänge und passende Satzenden und füge sie zusammen.
Use	Verwende eine Tatsache, ein Wort usw. so, wie es in der Aufgabe gefordert wird.
Write a …	Schreibe etwas in einem geforderten Textformat auf, z. B. deinen Kommentar zu etwas oder eine Geschichte.

Grammar File – Inhalt

				Seite
Unit 1	GF	1	**The gerund** Das Gerundium	**173**
Unit 2	GF	2	**Conditional sentences** Bedingungssätze	**175**
	GF	3	**Indirect speech** Die indirekte Rede	**177**
Unit 3	GF	4	**The passive** Das Passiv	**179**
	GF	5	**Participles** Partizipien	**181**
	GF	6	**The *to*-infinitive** Der Infinitiv mit *to*	**182**
Unit 4	GF	7	**Countable and uncountable nouns** Zählbare und nicht zählbare Nomen	**183**
	GF	8	**The definite article *the*** Der bestimmte Artikel *the*	**185**
Unit 5	GF	9	Additional information **The past perfect progressive** Die Verlaufsform des *past perfect*	**186**
	GF 10		**Relative clauses** Relativsätze	**186**

Grammatical terms (Grammatische Fachbegriffe) — **187**

Lösungen der Grammar-File-Aufgaben — **189**

Im **Grammar File** (S. 172–189) wird zusammengefasst, was du in diesem Band **über die englische Sprache** lernst.

In der **linken Spalte** findest du **Beispielsätze** und **Übersichten**.

Indirect speech (reporting verb: simple past)	Gracie's dad said (that) Plimoth Plantation was a living-history museum.

Reporting verb in the simple past ▸ backshift o...		
present	▸ past	will-future
past*	▸ past perfect	going to-fu...
present perfect	▸ past perfect	can, may

In English: ...
Diese Abschnitte enthalten kurze Zusammenfassungen der wichtigsten grammatischen Regeln auf Englisch.

Additional information
So gekennzeichnete Abschnitte enthalten Grammatik, die du nicht selbst zu verwenden brauchst.
Du solltest aber verstehen, was dort erklärt wird, damit du keine Schwierigkeiten mit Texten hast, in denen diese Grammatik vorkommt.

In der **rechten Spalte** stehen **Erklärungen** und nützliche **Hinweise**.

Das **rote Ausrufezeichen** (**!**) macht dich auf besondere Fehlerquellen aufmerksam.

Hinweise wie ▸ *Unit 1 (p. 17)* • *P 5–6 (pp. 23–24)* zeigen dir, zu welcher Unit und welcher Seite ein **Grammar-File**-Abschnitt gehört und welche Übungen du dazu im Practice-Teil findest.

Die **grammatischen Fachbegriffe** (*grammatical terms*) kannst du auf den Seiten 187–188 nachschlagen.

Am Ende der Abschnitte stehen wieder kleine Aufgaben zur Selbstkontrolle. Schreib die Lösungen in dein Heft. Überprüfe sie dann auf Seite 189.

Unit 1
GF 1 The gerund — Das Gerundium

a) Use and form

Flying is exciting.
Fliegen ist aufregend.

Travelling makes me tired.
Reisen macht mich müde.

Taking a taxi is quite expensive.
Mit dem Taxi zu fahren / Taxifahren ist ziemlich teuer.

Cycling in New York can be fun.
In New York Rad zu fahren / Radfahren in New York kann Spaß machen.

Gebrauch und Form

Wenn die *-ing*-Form eines Verbs im Satz die Funktion eines **Nomens** hat, wird sie **Gerundium** *(gerund)* genannt.
Die *-ing*-Form wird, wie du weißt, durch Anhängen von *-ing* an den Infinitiv gebildet: **fly → flying**.

Wie ein Verb kann das Gerundium erweitert werden, z. B. durch ein Objekt *(a taxi)* oder eine Orts- oder Zeitangabe *(in New York)*.

Im Deutschen wird das Gerundium oft durch einen Infinitiv mit „zu" oder durch ein Nomen wiedergegeben.

b) The gerund as subject and object

Cycling in a big city isn't very healthy.

But I like **riding my bike in Central Park**.

I **enjoy living** in a big city. I can't **imagine living** in the country.

Ich wohne gern in einer Großstadt. / Ich genieße es, in einer Großstadt zu wohnen. Ich kann mir nicht vorstellen, auf dem Land zu leben.

When I got to Times Square, it **started** **raining. / to rain.**

I **like/love** **riding / to ride** my bike in the rain.

I'd **like/love** to travel in a New York taxi too.
I **would hate** to live in the country.

▶ Unit 1 (p. 17) • P 5–6 (pp. 23–24)

Das Gerundium als Subjekt und als Objekt

Das Gerundium (und seine Erweiterung) kann wie ein Nomen **Subjekt** oder **Objekt** eines Satzes sein:

Subjekt
Flying is exciting.
Cycling in a big city isn't very healthy.

Objekt
My sister likes **skating**.
I like **riding my bike in Central Park**.

! Beachte:

◀ 1 Nach einigen Verben – z. B. **enjoy, finish, imagine, miss, practise** – muss ein weiteres Verb als Gerundium stehen:

   I **enjoy living** …, I can't **imagine living** …

   Anders als im Deutschen darf nach diesen Verben **kein Infinitiv** stehen!
   Also nicht: I ~~enjoy to live~~ …, I can't ~~imagine to live~~ …

◀ 2 Nach **begin/start, continue, hate, like, love, prefer** kann – bei gleicher Bedeutung – ein Gerundium oder ein *to*-Infinitiv stehen.

◀ 3 Nach **would like, would love, would hate** kann nur der *to*-Infinitiv stehen.

1 Grammar File

c) The gerund after prepositions

After so much **walking**, we were tired.
Nach all der Herumlauferei … /
Nachdem wir so viel herumgelaufen waren, …

Never cross a street **without looking**.
Überquere nie eine Straße, ohne zu schauen.

Ryan is **scared** of going in lifts.
Ryan hat Angst davor, mit dem Lift zu fahren.

Ryan had often **dreamed** of seeing New York from above.
… davon geträumt, New York von oben zu sehen.

Ryan is **interested** in learning about New York firefighters.
Ryan ist daran interessiert, etwas über … zu erfahren.
He's **excited** about meeting some of them.
Er freut sich sehr darauf, einige von ihnen zu treffen.

Ryan had the **chance** of going to New York.
Ryan hatte die Möglichkeit, nach New York zu fahren.
His **reason** for going there was to visit family.
Sein Grund, dort hinzufahren, war …

Caitlin **was** against visiting any more sights.
Caitlin war dagegen, noch weitere Sehenswürdigkeiten anzuschauen.
Caitlin **talked** about sending Ruth a text.
Caitlin sprach darüber, Ruth eine SMS zu schicken.

▶ Unit 1 (p. 18) • P 8 (p. 25)

Das Gerundium nach Präpositionen

Nach einer Präposition *(after, without, for, of, …)* muss ein Verb als Gerundium stehen.

Beachte die unterschiedlichen Entsprechungen im Deutschen:

englisch		deutsch
after walking	→	**Präposition + Nomen** („nach …") oder **Nebensatz** („nachdem …")
without looking	→	„ohne zu" + **Infinitiv**
scared of going	→	„zu" + **Infinitiv**

Nützliche Wendungen mit Präposition + Gerundium:

	interested in	
	excited about	
(to) be	afraid of	doing sth.
	good/bad at	
	tired of	

	chance of	
the	reason for	doing sth.
	idea of	
	danger of	

	be against	
(to)	talk about	doing sth.
	think of	
	worry about	

In English: The gerund

1 An *-ing* form which is used like a noun is called a **gerund**.
2 Gerunds can be – the <u>subject</u> of a sentence: *Flying / Making models is fun.*
                 – the <u>object</u> of a sentence: *I love skating / swimming in the sea.*
3 Verbs which follow a <u>preposition</u> take the form of a gerund: *He left the shop without paying.*

Stop hitting your brother! You really mustn't do that!

But Mum always says that giving is better than taking.

Grammar File 1–2

Vervollständige die Sätze in deinem Heft. Wähle ein Verb aus dem Kästchen. Achte auf die richtige Form.

1. … alone to New York was very exciting for Ryan.
2. He didn't enjoy … in the queues at the airport.
3. At first he was a bit afraid of … up the ESB in a fast lift.
4. He was very interested in … all the sights.
5. Later he talked for hours about … down from the ESB.

(to) fly • (to) go • (to) look • (to) see • (to) wait

Additional information

d) The gerund with 'its own subject'

1. **Ryan** can't **imagine moving** to New York.
   Ryan kann sich nicht vorstellen, nach New York zu ziehen.

2. Ryan can't **imagine his family moving** to New York.
   Ryan kann sich nicht vorstellen, dass seine Familie nach New York zieht.

▶ Unit 1 (p. 19)

Das Gerundium mit „eigenem Subjekt"

◀ Vergleiche die Sätze 1 und 2:
In Satz 1 bezieht sich *moving* auf *Ryan* – Ryan kann sich nicht vorstellen, dass er selbst nach New York zieht.

In Satz 2 hat das **Gerundium ein „eigenes Subjekt"**: *moving* bezieht sich auf *his family* – Ryan kann sich nicht vorstellen, dass seine Familie nach New York zieht.

Unit 2
GF 2 Conditional sentences — Bedingungssätze

a) REVISION Conditional sentences (type 1)

If Gracie **is** quiet, Mrs Tripp **won't give** her extra work.
Wenn Gracie still ist, gibt Mrs Tripp ihr keine zusätzlichen Aufgaben. /
Wenn Gracie still ist, wird Mrs Tripp ihr keine zusätzlichen Aufgaben geben.

▶ Unit 2 (p. 39) • P 4 (p. 46)

Bedingungssätze (Typ 1)

Bedingungssätze vom Typ 1 („**Was ist, wenn …**"-Sätze) beziehen sich auf die **Gegenwart** oder die **Zukunft**.

Sie sagen aus, was unter bestimmten Bedingungen **geschieht** oder **nicht geschieht**.

b) REVISION Conditional sentences (type 2)

If Gracie **was** quiet, Mrs Tripp **wouldn't give** her extra work.
Wenn Gracie still wäre, würde Mrs Tripp ihr keine zusätzlichen Aufgaben geben.

▶ Unit 2 (p. 39) • P 4 (p. 46)

Bedingungssätze (Typ 2)

Bedingungssätze vom Typ 2 („**Was wäre, wenn …**"-Sätze) beziehen sich auch auf die **Gegenwart** oder die **Zukunft**.

Sie drücken aus, was unter bestimmten Bedingungen **geschehen** oder **nicht geschehen würde**.

2 Grammar File

c) Conditional sentences (type 3)

Speech bubble: If I **had been** quiet, Mrs Tripp **wouldn't have given** me extra work.

Wenn ich still gewesen wäre, hätte Mrs Tripp mir keine zusätzlichen Aufgaben gegeben.

If Mike **hadn't told** that stupid story, …
… Gracie **wouldn't have interrupted** him.

Gracie If I**'d known** about the extra work,
I**'d have kept** quiet in class.

If I**'d known** … = If I **had known** …
I**'d have kept** … = I **would have kept** …

If Gracie hadn't got extra work,
she **could have been** free all weekend.
…, hätte sie das ganze Wochenende frei haben können.

If she hadn't said 'That's crap!',
Mrs Tripp **might not have been** angry.
…, wäre Mrs Tripp vielleicht nicht wütend gewesen.

▶ Unit 2 (p.39) • P 6–7 (p.47)

Bedingungssätze (Typ 3)

Bedingungssätze vom Typ 3 sind „**Was wäre gewesen, wenn …**"-**Sätze**. Sie beziehen sich auf die **Vergangenheit**.

Sie drücken aus, was **geschehen** oder **nicht geschehen wäre**, wenn eine Bedingung eingetreten wäre.

Der *if*-**Satz** nennt eine Bedingung, die nicht eingetreten ist: Gracie war nicht still.

Der **Hauptsatz** drückt aus, was geschehen oder nicht geschehen wäre, wenn die Bedingung eingetreten wäre: Wenn Gracie still gewesen wäre, dann hätte Mrs Tripp ihr keine zusätzlichen Aufgaben gegeben.

◂ Im *if*-**Satz** steht das **past perfect** (hadn't told).

◂ Im **Hauptsatz** steht
would(n't) + have + Partizip Perfekt
(wouldn't have interrupted).

! Beachte:
Die Kurzform **'d** steht im *if*-Satz für *had*, im Hauptsatz aber für *would*.

Im Hauptsatz können statt **would have + past participle** auch **could have + past participle** oder **might have + past participle** stehen.

In English: Conditional sentences (type 3)

– We use conditional sentences (type 3) to talk about something that did not happen.
– Conditional sentences (type 3) refer to a situation in the past that cannot be changed.
– In the *if*-clause: past perfect; in the main clause: would/could/might + have + past participle.

Vervollständige die Bedingungssätze (Typ 3) in deinem Heft. Achte auf die richtige Form der Verben.

1 If Gracie hadn't been rude to Mike, Mrs Tripp … (not interrupt) her.
2 If Mike … (not tell) a stupid old story, Gracie wouldn't have said 'That's crap!'
3 Mrs Tripp … (not give) Gracie a presentation to do if she … (keep) quiet in class.
4 Gracie … (find) lots of information for the presentation on the internet if she … (look).
5 What might you have done if you … (be) in the classroom with Gracie?

GF 3 Indirect speech   Die indirekte Rede

a) REVISION Direct and indirect speech — Direkte und indirekte Rede

Plimoth Plantation is a living-history museum.

Das, was jemand sagt (oder gesagt hat), kannst du <u>direkt</u> oder <u>indirekt</u> wiedergeben:

Direct speech Gracie's dad says, 'Plimoth Plantation is a living-history museum.'

◀ In der **direkten Rede** wird **wörtlich** wiedergegeben, was jemand sagt, schreibt oder denkt.

Indirect speech (reporting verb: <u>simple present</u>) Gracie's dad says (that) Plimoth Plantation is a living-history museum.

◀ In der **indirekten Rede** (*indirect* oder *reported speech*) wird berichtet, was jemand sagt, schreibt oder denkt. Häufig vorkommende einleitende Verben sind *say, tell sb., answer, explain, believe, think*.

Indirect speech (reporting verb: <u>simple past</u>) Gracie's dad said (that) Plimoth Plantation was a living-history museum.

◀ Wenn das **einleitende Verb im *simple past*** steht (*said, told sb., answered* usw.), dann werden die Zeitformen der direkten Rede meist verändert: Sie werden um eine Zeitstufe in die Vergangenheit „zurückverschoben" (*backshift of tenses*). Vergleiche:
Plimoth Plantation *is* …
He *said* that Plimoth Plantation *was* …

Reporting verb in the simple past ▶ backshift of tenses			
present	▶ past	will-future	▶ would + infinitive
past*	▶ past perfect	going to-future	▶ was/were going to + infinitive
present perfect	▶ past perfect	can, may	▶ could, might

* In der Umgangssprache bleiben *past*-Formen der direkten Rede manchmal unverändert, werden also nicht ins *past perfect* verändert.

▶ Unit 2 (p. 41) • P 9 (p. 48)

b) Questions in indirect speech — Fragen in der indirekten Rede

Direct question (yes/no question) Do tourists come to the plantation in winter too?

Indirect question Gracie asked if/whether tourists came to the plantation in winter too.

Auch bei Fragen in der indirekten Rede erfolgt der *backshift of tenses*, wenn das einleitende Verb im *simple past* steht.

Handelt es sich bei der direkten Frage um eine **Frage ohne Fragewort** (*yes/no question*), dann wird die indirekte Frage mit ***if*** oder ***whether*** („ob") eingeleitet.

Direct question (with question word) When did the museum open?

Indirect question She wanted to know when the museum had opened.

Wenn die direkte **Frage mit einem Fragewort** beginnt (*why, how, what, when, where* usw.), dann wird das Fragewort in der indirekten Frage beibehalten.

Word order in indirect questions: S – V – …

		S	V	
Statement		They	lived	next to the colonists.
Direct question	Why did	they	live	next to the colonists?
Indirect question	She asked when / why / whether/if	they	had lived	next to the colonists.

! Beachte:
Die Wortstellung in indirekten Fragen ist wie in Aussagesätzen:
S – V – …

Es gibt keine Umschreibung mit *do/does/did*.

▶ Unit 2 (p. 41) • P 10–11 (pp. 48–49)

Berichte, was Gracies Klassenkameraden fragten.

1 'Did Thanksgiving begin in Plymouth?' — Scott asked whether …
2 'When did the Pilgrims celebrate the first Thanksgiving?' — Sam asked …
3 'What do people really know about the first Thanksgiving?' — Jessie wanted to know …
4 'Did the Pilgrims really invite the Wampanoag?' — Andy wanted to know …

c) Commands and requests in indirect speech

Aufforderungssätze und Bitten in der indirekten Rede

Go back to the visitor center. And don't miss the movie.

The guide **told** Gracie **to go** back to the visitor center. And she **told her not to miss** the movie.
Die Fremdenführerin sagte Gracie, sie solle zum Besucherzentrum zurückgehen. Und sie riet ihr, den Film nicht zu verpassen.

Aufforderungssätze werden in der indirekten Rede meist mit **tell sb. to do sth.** (bzw. **tell sb. not to do sth.**) wiedergegeben.

Can you give me a booklet about the exhibition, please?

Gracie **asked someone** at the visitor center **to give** her a booklet about the exhibition.
Gracie bat jemanden im Besucherzentrum, ihr eine Broschüre über die Ausstellung zu geben.

Eine **Bitte** wird meist mit **ask sb. to do sth.** (bzw. **ask sb. not to do sth.**) wiedergegeben.

▶ Unit 2 (p. 41) • P 12 (p. 49)

Berichte, was gesagt wurde. Verwende told … *oder* asked …

1 'Gracie, please don't argue with Mike.' — Mrs Tripp asked Gracie not to …
2 'Mike and Gracie, discuss your opinions quietly.' — Mrs Tripp told …
3 'Gracie, don't use bad language in my classroom.' — Mrs Tripp …
4 'Gracie, could you say sorry to Mike, please?' — Mrs Tripp …
5 'Don't interrupt lessons again, Gracie.' — Gracie's mum …

In English: Indirect speech

1. If the reporting verb is in the past (*said, told sb.* etc.), there is usually a change of tenses ('backshift'):
   present ▸ past   past ▸ past perfect   present perfect ▸ past perfect
   will ▸ would   can ▸ could   may ▸ might.
   Gracie **said** that she **had to** give a presentation at school.
2. In indirect questions the word order is the same as in statements: **subject – verb** – ...
   Gracie wanted to know if **the English had invited** the Wampanoag family to the First Thanksgiving.
3. In indirect commands and requests the *to*-infinitive is used after *tell sb.* and *ask sb.*
   A visitor **asked Gracie to show** him where the booklets were.

Unit 3

GF 4 The passive   Das Passiv

a) REVISION Active and passive

Active: People **speak** Spanish in a lot of places in California.
In vielen Orten in Kalifornien sprechen die Menschen Spanisch.

Passive: Spanish **is spoken** in a lot of places in California.
In vielen Orten ... wird Spanisch gesprochen.

California's first church was built in 1769.
Gold was found in California in 1848.
Today California is called 'The Golden State'.

Aktiv und Passiv

Mit einem **Aktivsatz** drückst du aus, **wer oder was etwas tut**. Das Subjekt des Aktivsatzes führt die Handlung aus.

Mit einem **Passivsatz** drückst du aus, **mit wem oder womit etwas geschieht**. Das Objekt des Aktivsatzes *(Spanish)* ist Subjekt des Passivsatzes geworden.

Mit **Passivsätzen** kannst du Handlungen beschreiben, ohne zu sagen, wer die Handlung ausführt. (Oft ist gar nicht bekannt oder nicht wichtig, wer die Handlung ausführt.) Das Passiv wird daher oft verwendet in Zeitungsartikeln, in Berichten, in technischen Beschreibungen und auf Schildern.

b) Form

The passive	
Simple present	Spanish is spoken by a lot of people in California.
	... wird von vielen Menschen ... gesprochen
Simple past	In 1989, parts of San Francisco were destroyed by an earthquake.
	... wurden zerstört
Present perfect	Relations between Anglos and Latinos have been improved by new laws.
	... wurden verbessert/sind verbessert worden

Das Passiv bildest du mit einer **Form von *be*** und der 3. Form des Verbs (Partizip Perfekt, *past participle*).

▸ Unit 3 (p. 58–59) • P 5–7 (pp. 65–66)

c) The passive: *will*-future and modal auxiliaries

These strawberries will be planted tomorrow.
… werden morgen gepflanzt werden.

Strawberries can be grown all the year round.
… können das ganze Jahr über angebaut werden.

Strawberries must be picked by hand.
… müssen von Hand gepflückt werden.

▶ Unit 3 (p. 59) • P 8 (p. 66)

Das Passiv:
will-future und modale Hilfsverben

Passivsätze mit Hilfsverben *(will, can, could, …)* bildest du mit *be* + Partizip Perfekt:

will	be	planted
can	be	grown
could	be	done
must	be	picked
should	be	kept
may	be	harvested
might	be	used

d) The passive of verbs with two objects

	Indirect object	Direct object
Active: The teacher gave	Luis	an assignment.

Die Lehrerin gab Luis eine Hausarbeit auf.

Passive:

	Dativobjekt	Subjekt	
	Luis/Ihm	wurde **eine Hausarbeit**	aufgegeben.

	Subject		
1	Luis/He	was given	an assignment.

	Subject		
2	An assignment	was given	to Luis.

I was offered a holiday job in a music shop.
Mir wurde ein Ferienjob … angeboten. /
Man hat mir einen Ferienjob … angeboten.

Fruit pickers aren't paid very much.
Obstpflückern wird nicht viel gezahlt. /
Obstpflücker bekommen nicht viel Geld.

Luis has been sent a funny postcard.
Jemand hat Luis eine lustige Postkarte geschickt.

▶ Unit 3 (p. 59) • P 9–10 (p. 67)

Das Passiv von Verben mit zwei Objekten

Manche Verben haben zwei Objekte nach sich:
– ein **indirektes Objekt** (meist eine Person, daher auch: **Personenobjekt**) und ein
– **direktes Objekt** (meist eine Sache, daher auch: **Sachobjekt**).

◀ Im Deutschen kann nur das **direkte Objekt** (das Sachobjekt) zum **Subjekt des Passivsatzes** werden.

◀ Im Englischen kann
1 das **Personenobjekt** (hier: *Luis/He*) zum **Subjekt des Passivsatzes** werden. (Diese Art des Passivs nennt man *personal passive*, deutsch „persönliches Passiv".)
2 das **Sachobjekt** (hier: *an assignment*) zum **Subjekt des Passivsatzes** werden. (Beachte, dass das Personenobjekt in diesen Fällen mit *to* angehängt wird.)

◀ Meist wird im Englischen das **Personenobjekt zum Subjekt** des Passivsatzes (Beispiele siehe links). Im Deutschen steht oft ein Aktivsatz.

Häufig vorkommende Verben mit zwei Objekten sind *give, offer, pay, promise, send, show, tell*.

In English: The personal passive

The indirect object (the 'person object') of an active sentence can be the subject of a passive sentence:
Active: *A farmer gave **Luis's parents/them** (indirect object) their first jobs.*
Passive: ***Luis's parents/They** (subject) were given their first jobs (by a farmer).*

Grammar File **3**   **181**

Schreibe die Sätze ins personal passive *um.*

1 My parents gave **me** a new computer for my birthday.   I was ...
2 Someone has offered **my brother** a job at the supermarket.   My brother ...
3 The teacher showed **us** how to do the exercise.   We ...
4 Some friends sent **Luis** a really nice present when he was ill.   ...
5 My parents have promised **my sister** a new bike for Christmas.   ...

GF 5 Participles   Partizipien

a) REVISION Participle forms
Formen des Partizips

Present participle *(-ing)*:

| play | → | **play**ing | try | → | **try**ing |
| phon**e** | → | **phon**ing | plan | → | **plann**ing |

◀ Das **Partizip Präsens** *(present participle)* bildest du durch Anhängen von **-ing** an den Infinitiv.
Beachte die Besonderheiten bei der Schreibung.

Past participle, regular verbs *(-ed)*:

| play | → | **play**ed | try | → | **tri**ed |
| phon**e** | → | **phon**ed | plan | → | **plann**ed |

◀ Das **Partizip Perfekt** *(past participle)* eines regelmäßigen Verbs wird durch Anhängen von **-ed** an den Infinitiv gebildet. Beachte auch hier die Besonderheiten bei der Schreibung.

Past participle, irregular verbs:

go	→	**gone**	grow	→	**grown**
make	→	**made**	sit	→	**sat**
take	→	**taken**	write	→	**written**

Unregelmäßige Verben haben eigene 3. Formen, die du einzeln lernen musst.

b) Participle clauses instead of relative clauses
Partizipialsätze anstelle von Relativsätzen

Partizipialsätze können Relativsätze ersetzen.

1 Mrs Morales sat in the **bus taking** her back to San Clemente.
Mrs Morales saß im Bus, der sie ... zurückbrachte.

◀ Das **present participle** (Sätze **1** und **2**) entspricht einem Relativpronomen + Verb im **Aktiv**:
1 ... *taking* her back = ... **that was taking** her back

2 She spoke to the **children playing** on the floor.
... mit den Kindern, die auf dem Boden spielten.

2 ... *playing* on the floor = ... **who were playing** ...

3 Have you ever eaten **strawberries grown** in **California?**
..., die in Kalifornien angebaut wurden?

◀ Das **past participle** (Satz **3**) entspricht einem Relativpronomen + Verb im **Passiv**:
3 ... *grown* in California = ... **that were grown** ...

▶ Unit 3 (p. 60) • P 12 (p. 69)

In English: Participle clauses

Participle clauses can be used instead of relative clauses:
Participle clause: *Illegal immigrants **caught** by the US Border Patrol are sent back.*
Relative clause: *Illegal immigrants **that are caught** by the US Border Patrol are sent back.*

Kürze die Sätze: Benutze Partizipialsätze anstelle der Relativsätze.

1 The men who work on the strawberry farms are from Mexico. The men ...
2 Most of the strawberries that are produced in California are sold fresh. ...
3 Most tourists who visit California go to San Francisco. ...
4 The woman who is getting on the bus to San Clemente is Mrs Morales. ...

GF 6 The *to*-infinitive   Der Infinitiv mit *to*

a) Verb + object + *to*-infinitive

The Clean Ocean Program flyer **asks people not to leave** garbage on the beaches.

... bittet die Leute, keinen Müll an den Stränden liegen zu lassen.

Luis's coach **would like** the class to help with the Clean Ocean Program.
... möchte, dass die Klasse ... mithilft.

He **told** them to find out about the program.
... dass sie sich über das Programm informieren sollten.

The flyer says, 'We **want** you to help us.'
... „Wir wollen, dass du uns hilfst."

▶ Unit 3 (p. 61) • P 15 (p. 70)

Verb + Objekt + *to*-Infinitiv

Nach bestimmten Verben kann ein **Objekt + *to*-Infinitiv** stehen, z.B.
ask/help/invite/teach sb. (not) to do sth.
Im Deutschen steht meist ein Infinitiv mit „zu":
jn. bitten/jm. helfen/..., etwas (nicht) zu tun.

◀ Auch nach den Verben *cause, tell, want, would like* kann ein **Objekt + *to*-Infinitiv** stehen.

❗ Nach den entsprechenden deutschen Verben steht ein Nebensatz mit „dass", aber auf die englischen Verben darf kein *that*-Satz folgen:
Wir **wollen**, dass du uns hilfst. We **want** you to help us.
                                   Nicht: We want ~~that you help~~ us.

Vervollständige die Sätze in deinem Heft.

1 Luis's coach would like ... (his class – read about the Clean Ocean Program)
2 San Clemente wants ... (tourists – keep its beaches clean)
3 Environmental organizations ask ... (people – join them)
4 They want ... (we – understand environmental problems)

b) Question word + *to*-infinitive

Luis When we saw all the garbage, we wanted to help. But we didn't **know** what to do.
Als wir all den Müll sahen, wollten wir helfen. Aber wir wussten nicht, was wir tun sollten.

The flyer **showed** the students how to help.
... wie sie helfen könnten.

The Clean Ocean Program **tells** you when, where and how to keep our beaches clean.
... wann, wo und wie du ... sauber halten kannst.

▶ Unit 3 (p. 61) • P 16 (p. 70)

Fragewort + *to*-Infinitiv

Der *to*-Infinitiv steht oft nach einem **Fragewort** (*what, who, how, when, where* usw.). Er entspricht meist einem Nebensatz mit modalem Hilfsverb (*can, could, should, ...*). Vergleiche:
... *we didn't know what to do.*
... *we didn't know what we should do.*

Die Kombination aus Fragewort und *to*-Infinitiv steht oft nach den Verben *ask, explain, find out, know, show, tell, wonder.*

Vervollständige die Sätze in deinem Heft. Welches Fragewort passt?

1 I don't understand this exercise. Can you show me ... do it?
2 Can you tell us ... eat in San Francisco? We're looking for a cheap restaurant.
3 If you want to know ... see in San Francisco, read this guide book.
4 Can anyone help me with this project? I don't know ... ask.

In English: The *to*-infinitive

The *to*-infinitive is used
1 after *ask, cause, help, tell, want, would like, ...* + object:
   Mrs Tripp **wants her class to be** quiet.
2 after a question word, instead of a subordinate clause:
   I don't know **how to do it**. (= ... how I should do it.)

Unit 4
GF 7 Countable and uncountable nouns   Zählbare und nicht zählbare Nomen

a) Countable nouns   Zählbare Nomen

a friend	– two friends
a CD	– lots of CDs
one hour	– many hours

◀ Die meisten Nomen sind **zählbar** – sie bezeichnen etwas, das man zählen kann. Zählbare Nomen kommen im Singular und im Plural vor.

b) Uncountable nouns   Nicht zählbare Nomen

bread *Brot*	jewellery *Schmuck*
butter *Butter*	milk *Milch*
cheese *Käse*	money *Geld*
experience *Erfahrung(en)*	music *Musik*
furniture *Möbel*	mustard *Senf*
homework *Hausaufgabe(n)*	news *Nachricht(en)*
information *Information(en)*	traffic *Verkehr*

◀ **Nicht zählbare** Nomen dagegen bezeichnen etwas, das man nicht zählen kann. Dazu gehören viele Bezeichnungen für Lebensmittel und viele abstrakte Begriffe.

❗ Auch die Nomen **experience, furniture, homework, information** und **news** sind nicht zählbar – anders als ihre deutschen Entsprechungen.

not: ~~a bread; breads~~
~~an information; many informations~~
~~a homework; two homeworks~~

◀ Nicht zählbare Nomen haben **keinen Plural** und stehen nie mit *a/an* oder mit *one/two/three/...*

That's too much **homework**. I can't do **it**.
Das sind zu viele **Hausaufgaben**. Ich kann sie nicht machen.

◀ Auch die zugehörigen **Begleiter, Verben und Pronomen** stehen immer **im Singular**.

Where did you get **this information**?
Wo hast du **diese Information(en)** her?

Would you like **a glass of milk**.
Möchtest du **ein Glas Milch**?

◀ Wenn du **bestimmte Mengen** oder eine **bestimmte Anzahl** nennen willst, musst du passende Wendungen wie *a glass of ..., a kilo of ..., a piece of ...* verwenden.

That's **a** useful **piece of information**.
Das ist **eine** nützliche **Information**.

c) Quantifiers: *some, a lot of, many, much, a few, a little*

Countable nouns	Uncountable nouns
some students einige/ein paar …	some bread/information etwas Brot/einige Informationen
a lot of students viele …	a lot of bread/information viel Brot/viele Informationen
how many students? wie viele …?	how much bread/information? wie viel Brot? / wie viele Informationen?
a few students wenige/ein paar …	a little bread/information wenig/ein bisschen Brot / wenig(e) Informationen

▶ Unit 4 (p.79) • P 5–6 (p.86)

Mengenangaben: *some, a lot of, many, much, a few, a little*

Die Mengenangaben *some* und *a lot of* (oder *lots of*) verwendest du sowohl mit dem **Plural von zählbaren Nomen** als auch mit **nicht zählbaren Nomen**.

! – *many* („**viele**") steht nur mit dem **Plural** von zählbaren Nomen.
 much („**viel**") steht nur mit **nicht zählbaren Nomen**.
– *a few* („**wenige/ein paar**") steht nur mit dem **Plural** von zählbaren Nomen.
 a little („**wenig/ein bisschen**") steht nur mit **nicht zählbaren Nomen**.

In English: Countable and uncountable nouns

1 **Countable nouns** have a singular and a plural form. They can be used with *a/an* and with numbers.
 a boy – two boys, one girl – two girls
2 **Uncountable nouns** have no plural form. They cannot be used with *a/an* or with numbers, but you can use phrases like *a glass of, two kilos of, a piece of* with uncountable nouns.
 a glass of milk, two cups of tea, a piece of information
3 The quantifier **many** is used only with the plural of countable nouns: *how many oranges/potatoes?*
 The quantifier **much** is used only with uncountable nouns: *how much juice/bread?*
4 The quantifier **a few** is used only with the plural of countable nouns: *a few oranges/potatoes*
 The quantifier **a little** is used only with uncountable nouns: *a little juice/bread*

Sieh dir die Bilder an und vervollständige die Sätze mit a/an (2x), some (2x), many (1x), much (3x).

1 There's … milk but there isn't … bread.
2 Here's … information about the Grand Canyon. I'm doing … project on it.  
3 We haven't got … eggs, and we haven't got … butter.
4 I haven't got … homework, just … exercise for French.

GF 8 **The definite article** *the*   Der bestimmte Artikel *the*

Wenn ein Nomen **ganz allgemein** gebraucht wird, steht es **ohne** den bestimmten Artikel (auch, wenn ein Adjektiv davor steht).

Das gilt insbesondere für

1. For Timo and his family, life is exciting at the moment.
   … ist das Leben im Moment aufregend.

1. **abstrakte Begriffe** wie *life, history, health, quality*

2. Clean air is important to health.
   Saubere Luft ist wichtig für die Gesundheit.

2. **Stoffbezeichnungen** wie *air, oil, gold, wine*

3. American students do lots of extracurricular activities.

3. **Nomen im Plural** (hier: *students*).

1a. At the FFA meeting Timo learned a lot about the life of Missouri farmers.
   … über das Leben der Farmer in Missouri.

◂ Solche Nomen stehen jedoch **mit** bestimmtem Artikel, wenn sie **näher bestimmt** sind, z.B. durch eine *of*-Fügung (Satz 1a) oder einen Relativsatz (Satz 3a).

2a. The Schmidts are happy that the air in Hermann is clean.
   … die Luft in Hermann

Vergleiche die Sätze 1–3 mit den Sätzen 1a–3a.

3a. The students who went to the FFA meeting were very interested in hogs.

▸ Unit 4 (p. 80) • P 9 (p. 88)

In English: The definite article

- We do not use **the** with **abstract nouns** (*life, love, health, …*), **material nouns** (*air, gold, water, …*) and **plural nouns** (*students, children, …*) when they are used in a <u>general sense</u>.
  Life is too short. / Gold is expensive. / Children like chips.
- But we use **the** with these nouns when they are used in a <u>specific sense</u>, for example when they are followed by an *of*-phrase or a relative clause.
  the life of farmers in Missouri / the gold that was found in California / the children who live in my village

---

Mit oder ohne the? *Schreib die Sätze in dein Heft.*

1. We can learn a lot from … history.
2. What do you know about … history of England?
3. … tourists like to visit Hermann's Festhalle.
4. … tourists who asked us the way were from Germany.

Unit 5

Additional information

GF 9 The past perfect progressive — Die Verlaufsform des *past perfect*

Madison and her dad **had been sitting** in the kitchen for half an hour when Mrs Young **came down**.

... hatten schon eine halbe Stunde in der Küche gesessen, als Mrs Young herunterkam.

▶ Unit 5 (p. 101)

Auch das *past perfect* (Plusquamperfekt, Vorvergangenheit) hat eine *progressive form*: das *past perfect progressive*. Es wird gebildet mit *had been* + *-ing*-Form des Verbs.

Mit dem *past perfect progressive* drückt man aus, dass eine Handlung oder ein Vorgang in der Vergangenheit schon begonnen hatte (hier: *had been sitting*), bevor eine andere Handlung in der Vergangenheit einsetzte (hier: *came down*).

GF 10 Relative clauses — Relativsätze

a) REVISION Defining relative clauses

1. Madison knew the **people** who/that worked at the King Center.
2. She was interested in the **letters** which/that were on display in the Center.

▶ Unit 5 (p. 102) • P 7 (p. 109)

Bestimmende Relativsätze

Bestimmende Relativsätze kennst du bereits. Sie werden mit den Relativpronomen
– *who* oder *that* für Personen **(1)** und
– *which* oder *that* für Dinge **(2)**
eingeleitet.

Ein bestimmter Relativsatz gibt Informationen über ein Nomen, die **zum Verständnis des Satzes notwendig** sind:
Ohne die Relativsätze ... *people who worked ...* bzw. ... *letters which were on display ...* würde man gar nicht wissen, welche Leute bzw. welche Briefe gemeint sind.

❗ Beachte, dass ein bestimmender Relativsatz nicht durch Kommas abgetrennt wird.

b) Relative clauses with *which* to refer to a whole clause

Mom had to go to the airport to report on a big fire, which sounded pretty exciting to me.

..., was sich ziemlich aufregend anhörte.

On April 4, 1968, Martin Luther King was murdered, which shocked the whole nation.
..., was die ganze Nation schockierte.

▶ Unit 5 (p. 102) • P 8 (p. 109)

Satzbezogene Relativsätze mit *which*

Relativsätze mit *which* können sich auch auf einen ganzen Satz beziehen. Mit solchen Relativsätzen wird die Aussage im vorausgehenden Hauptsatz kommentiert.
◀ Im Beispiel links kommentiert Madison die Tatsache, dass ihre Mutter zum Flughafen musste, um über ein Feuer zu berichten: Sie sagt, dass sie das aufregend fand.

Im Deutschen werden solche Relativsätze mit „was" eingeleitet.

Additional information

c) Non-defining relative clauses

King was a Baptist minister from Atlanta, **who became a civil rights activist.**

He was one of the leaders of the civil rights movement, **which ended segregation in the USA.**

Madison, **whose father works at the King Center,** wanted to go to CNN with her mother.

▶ Unit 5 (p. 102) • P 9 (p. 110)

Nicht bestimmende Relativsätze

Nicht bestimmende Relativsätze kommen hauptsächlich in geschriebenem Englisch vor. Sie geben **Zusatzinformationen**, die zum Verständnis des Satzes nicht notwendig sind: Man versteht den Satz *King was a Baptist minister from Atlanta* auch ohne den Relativsatz *who became a civil rights activist*.

! In nicht bestimmenden Relativsätzen können die Relativpronomen *who*, *which* und *whose* verwendet werden, nicht aber *that*! Nicht bestimmende Relativsätze werden durch Kommas abgetrennt.

In English: Relative clauses

– A **defining** relative clause gives **necessary** information. It defines the noun that it refers to. We do not use commas: *Madison is the girl **who lives in Atlanta**.*
– Relative clauses with *which* can **refer to the whole main clause**. We use them to make a **comment** on the main clause: *Madison knew the anniversary of King's death**, which impressed her dad**.*
– A **non-defining** relative clause gives **extra** information about the noun that it refers to. The information is not necessary for the correct understanding of the sentence. Because it is extra, we use commas. *Madison, **who lives in Atlanta**, goes to Martin Luther King High School.*

Grammatical terms (Grammatische Fachbegriffe)

active ['æktɪv]	Aktiv	Beckham **scored** the final goal.
adjective ['ædʒɪktɪv]	Adjektiv	*good, red, new, boring*
adverb ['ædvɜːb]	Adverb	*always, badly, here, really, today*
adverb of frequency ['friːkwənsi]	Häufigkeitsadverb	*always, often, never*
adverb of indefinite time [ɪnˌdefɪnət 'taɪm]	Adverb der unbestimmten Zeit	*already, ever, just, never*
adverb of manner ['mænə]	Adverb der Art und Weise	*badly, happily, quietly, well*
adverbial clause [ædˌvɜːbiəl 'klɔːz]	adverbialer Nebensatz	*I went to bed **because I was tired**.*
article ['ɑːtɪkl]	Artikel	*the, a/an*
auxiliary [ɔːg'zɪliəri]	Hilfsverb	*be, have, do; will, can, must*
backshift of tenses ['bækʃɪft]	Verschiebung der Zeitformen (bei der indirekten Rede)	'**I'm** sorry.' ▶ Sam said he **was** sorry.
command [kə'mɑːnd]	Befehl, Aufforderungssatz	*Open your books. Don't talk.*
comparison [kəm'pærɪsn]	Steigerung	*old – older – oldest*
conditional sentence [kənˌdɪʃənl 'sentəns]	Bedingungssatz	*I'd call him if I knew his number.*
conjunction [kən'dʒʌŋkʃn]	Konjunktion	*and, or, but; because, before*
contact clause ['kɒntækt klɔːz]	Relativsatz ohne Relativpronomen	*She's the girl **I love**.*
countable noun ['kaʊntəbl]	zählbares Nomen	*girl – girls, pound – pounds*
defining relative clause [dɪ'faɪnɪŋ]	bestimmender Relativsatz	*There's the girl **who helped me**.*
definite article ['defɪnət]	bestimmter Artikel	*the*
direct speech [ˌdaɪrekt 'spiːtʃ]	direkte Rede, wörtliche Rede	'*I'm sorry*.'
gerund ['dʒerənd]	Gerundium	*I like **dancing**. **Dancing** is fun.*
***going to*-future**	Futur mit *going to*	*I'**m going to watch** TV tonight.*
***if*-clause** ['ɪf klɔːz]	*if*-Satz, Nebensatz mit *if*	*If I see Jack, I'll tell him.*
imperative [ɪm'perətɪv]	Imperativ (Befehlsform)	*Open your books. Don't talk.*
indirect speech [ˌɪndərekt 'spiːtʃ]	indirekte Rede	*Sam said **(that) he was sorry**.*
infinitive [ɪn'fɪnətɪv]	Infinitiv (Grundform des Verbs)	*(to) open, (to) see, (to) read*

Term	Pronunciation	German	Example
main clause		Hauptsatz	**I like Scruffy** because I like dogs.
modal, modal auxiliary	[ˌməʊdl_ɔːɡˈzɪliəri]	modales Hilfsverb, Modalverb	can, could, may, must
negative statement	[ˌneɡətɪv ˈsteɪtmənt]	verneinter Aussagesatz	I don't like bananas.
non-defining relative clause	[dɪˈfaɪnɪŋ]	nicht bestimmender Relativsatz	Madison, **who lives in Atlanta**, goes to M. L. King High School.
noun	[naʊn]	Nomen, Substantiv	Sophie, girl, brother, time
object	[ˈɒbdʒɪkt]	Objekt	My sister is writing **a letter**.
object form	[ˈɒbdʒɪkt fɔːm]	Objektform (der Personalpronomen)	me, you, him, her, it, us, them
participle	[ˈpɑːtɪsɪpl]	Partizip	planning, taking; planned, taken
participle clause	[ˌpɑːtɪsɪpl ˈklɔːz]	Partizipialsatz	I saw a boy **playing in the street**.
passive	[ˈpæsɪv]	Passiv	The goal **was scored** by Beckham.
past participle	[ˌpɑːst ˈpɑːtɪsɪpl]	Partizip Perfekt	cleaned, planned, gone, taken
past perfect	[ˌpɑːst ˈpɜːfɪkt]	Plusquamperfekt, Vorvergangenheit	He cried – he **had hurt** his knee.
past perfect progressive	[ˌpɑːst ˌpɜːfɪkt prəˈɡresɪv]	Verlaufsform des past perfect	She **had been working** in the garden since 12 o'clock.
past progressive	[ˌpɑːst prəˈɡresɪv]	Verlaufsform der Vergangenheit	At 7.30 I **was having** dinner.
personal passive	[ˌpɜːsənl ˈpæsɪv]	persönliches Passiv	I was offered a job.
personal pronoun	[ˌpɜːsənl ˈprəʊnaʊn]	Personalpronomen (persönliches Fürwort)	I, you, he, she, it, we, they; me, you, him, her, it, us, them
plural	[ˈplʊərəl]	Plural, Mehrzahl	
positive statement	[ˌpɒzətɪv ˈsteɪtmənt]	bejahter Aussagesatz	I like oranges.
possessive determiner	[pəˌzesɪv dɪˈtɜːmɪnə]	Possessivbegleiter (besitzanzeigender Begleiter)	my, your, his, her, its, our, their
possessive form	[pəˌzesɪv fɔːm]	s-Genitiv	Jo's brother; my sister's room
possessive pronoun	[pəˌzesɪv ˈprəʊnaʊn]	Possessivpronomen	mine, yours, his, hers, ours, theirs
preposition	[ˌprepəˈzɪʃn]	Präposition	after, at, in, next to, under
present participle	[ˌpreznt ˈpɑːtɪsɪpl]	Partizip Präsens	cleaning, planning, going, taking
present perfect	[ˌpreznt ˈpɜːfɪkt]	present perfect	We**'ve made** a cake for you.
present perfect progressive	[ˌpreznt ˌpɜːfɪkt prəˈɡresɪv]	Verlaufsform des present perfect	We**'ve been waiting** for an hour.
present progressive	[ˌpreznt prəˈɡresɪv]	Verlaufsform der Gegenwart	The Hansons **are having** lunch.
pronoun	[ˈprəʊnaʊn]	Pronomen, Fürwort	
quantifier	[ˈkwɒntɪfaɪə]	Mengenangabe	some, a lot of, many, much
question tag	[ˈkwestʃən tæɡ]	Frageanhängsel	This place is great, **isn't it?**
question word	[ˈkwestʃən wɜːd]	Fragewort	what?, when?, where?, how?
reflexive pronoun	[rɪˌfleksɪv ˈprəʊnaʊn]	Reflexivpronomen	myself, yourself, themselves
relative clause	[ˌrelətɪv ˈklɔːz]	Relativsatz	There's the girl **who helped me**.
relative pronoun	[ˌrelətɪv ˈprəʊnaʊn]	Relativpronomen	who, that, which, whose
reported speech	[rɪˌpɔːtɪd ˈspiːtʃ]	indirekte Rede	Sam said **(that) he was sorry**.
request	[rɪˈkwest]	Bitte	Can you help me with this?
short answer	[ˌʃɔːt ˈɑːnsə]	Kurzantwort	Yes, I am. / No, I don't.
simple past	[ˌsɪmpl ˈpɑːst]	einfache Form der Vergangenheit	Jo **wrote** two letters yesterday.
simple present	[ˌsɪmpl ˈpreznt]	einfache Form der Gegenwart	I always **go** to school by bike.
singular	[ˈsɪŋɡjələ]	Singular, Einzahl	
subject	[ˈsʌbdʒɪkt]	Subjekt	**My sister** is writing a letter.
subject form	[ˈsʌbdʒɪkt fɔːm]	Subjektform (der Personalpronomen)	I, you, he, she, it, we, they
subordinate clause	[səˌbɔːdɪnət ˈklɔːz]	Nebensatz	I like Scruffy **because I like dogs**.
uncountable noun	[ʌnˈkaʊntəbl]	nicht zählbares Nomen	bread, milk, money, news, work
verb	[vɜːb]	Verb	hear, open, help, go
will-future		Futur mit *will*	I think it **will be** cold tonight.
word order	[ˈwɜːd_ˌɔːdə]	Wortstellung	
yes/no question		Entscheidungsfrage	Are you 13? Do you like comics?

Lösungen der Grammar-File-Aufgaben

p.175
1. **Flying** alone to New York was very exciting for Ryan.
2. He didn't enjoy **waiting** in the queues at the airport.
3. At first he was a bit afraid of **going** up the ESB in a fast lift.
4. He was very interested in **seeing** all the sights.
5. Later he talked for hours about **looking** down from the ESB.

p.176
1. If Gracie hadn't been rude to Mike, Mrs Tripp **wouldn't have interrupted** her.
2. If Mike **hadn't told** a stupid old story, Gracie wouldn't have said 'That's crap!'
3. Mrs Tripp **wouldn't have given** Gracie a presentation to do if she **had kept** quiet in class.
4. Gracie **would have found** lots of information for the presentation on the internet if she **had looked**.
5. What might you have done if you **had been** in the classroom with Gracie.

p.178/1
1. Scott asked whether **Thanksgiving had begun** in Plymouth.
2. Sam asked **when the Pilgrims had celebrated the first Thanksgiving**.
3. Jessie wanted to know **what people really knew about the first Thanksgiving**.
4. Andy wanted to know **if/whether the Pilgrims had really invited the Wampanoag**.

p.178/2
1. Mrs Tripp asked Gracie not to **argue with Mike**.
2. Mrs Tripp told **Mike and Gracie to discuss their opinions quietly**.
3. Mrs Tripp **told Gracie not to use bad language in her classroom**.
4. Mrs Tripp **asked Gracie to say sorry to Mike**.
5. Gracie's mum **told Gracie not to interrupt lessons again**.

p.181
1. I was given a new computer for my birthday.
2. My brother has been offered a job at the supermarket.
3. We were shown how to do the exercise.
4. Luis was sent a really nice present when he was ill.
5. My sister has been promised a new bike for Christmas.

p.182/1
1. The men **working** on the strawberry farms are from Mexico.
2. Most of the strawberries **produced** in California are sold fresh.
3. Most tourists **visiting** California go to San Francisco.
4. The woman **getting** on the bus to San Clemente is Mrs Morales.

p.182/2
1. Luis's coach would like **his class to read** about the Clean Ocean Program.
2. San Clemente wants **tourists to keep** its beaches clean.
3. Environmental organizations ask **people to join them**.
4. They want **us to understand** environmental problems.

p.183
1. … Can you show me **how to** do it?
2. Can you tell us **where to** eat in San Francisco? …
3. If you want to know **what to** see in San Francisco, read this guide book.
4. … I don't know **who to** ask.

p.184
1. There's **some** milk but there isn't **much** bread.
2. Here's **some** information about the Grand Canyon. I'm doing **a** project on it.
3. We haven't got **many** eggs, and we haven't got **much** butter.
4. I haven't got **much** homework, just **an** exercise for French.

p.185
1. We can learn a lot from history.
2. What do you know about **the** history of England?
3. Tourists like to visit Hermann's Festhalle.
4. **The** tourists who asked us the way were from Germany.

Vocabulary

Diese Wörterverzeichnisse findest du in deinem Englischbuch:

- Das **Vocabulary** (Vokabelverzeichnis – S. 190–221) enthält alle Wörter und Wendungen, die du lernen musst. Sie stehen in der Reihenfolge, in der sie in den Units vorkommen.
- Das **Dictionary** besteht aus zwei alphabetischen Wörterlisten zum Nachschlagen:
  Englisch – Deutsch: S. 222–258
  Deutsch – Englisch: S. 259–290.

So ist das Vocabulary aufgebaut:

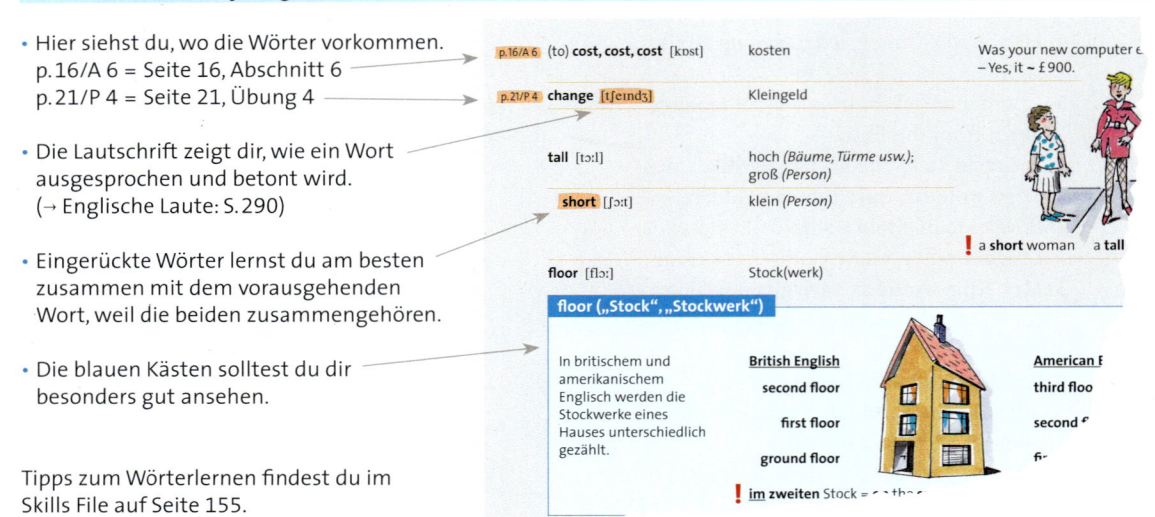

- Hier siehst du, wo die Wörter vorkommen.
  p. 16/A 6 = Seite 16, Abschnitt 6
  p. 21/P 4 = Seite 21, Übung 4

- Die Lautschrift zeigt dir, wie ein Wort ausgesprochen und betont wird.
  (→ Englische Laute: S. 290)

- Eingerückte Wörter lernst du am besten zusammen mit dem vorausgehenden Wort, weil die beiden zusammengehören.

- Die blauen Kästen solltest du dir besonders gut ansehen.

Tipps zum Wörterlernen findest du im Skills File auf Seite 155.

p. 16/A 6	(to) **cost, cost, cost** [kɒst]	kosten
p. 21/P 4	**change** [tʃeɪndʒ]	Kleingeld
	tall [tɔːl]	hoch *(Bäume, Türme usw.)*; groß *(Person)*
	short [ʃɔːt]	klein *(Person)*
	floor [flɔː]	Stock(werk)

floor ("Stock", "Stockwerk")

In britischem und amerikanischem Englisch werden die Stockwerke eines Hauses unterschiedlich gezählt.

British English	American English
second floor	third floor
first floor	second floor
ground floor	first floor

❗ **im zweiten** Stock = on the ...

❗ a **short** woman   a **tall** ...

Was your new computer e... – Yes, it ~ £900.

Abkürzungen:

n	= noun	v	= verb
adj	= adjective	adv	= adverb
prep	= preposition	conj	= conjunction
pl	= plural	no pl	= no plural
p.	= page	pp.	= pages
sb.	= somebody	sth.	= something
jn.	= jemanden	jm.	= jemandem
AE	= American English	BE	= British English
infml	= informal (umgangssprachlich, informell)		

Symbole:

❗ Hier stehen Hinweise auf Besonderheiten, bei denen man leicht Fehler machen kann.

◀▶ ist das „Gegenteil"-Zeichen: **alive** ◀▶ **dead** (**alive** ist das Gegenteil von **dead**)

~ Die **Tilde** in den Beispielsätzen steht für das neue Wort.

Ⓕ verwandtes Wort im Französischen
Ⓛ verwandtes Wort im Lateinischen

Introduction – Welcome to the United States of America

p. 8	(to) **form** [fɔːm]	bilden	How do you ~ the adjective from the noun 'danger'? – You add '-ous': 'dangerous'.
			Ⓕ former Ⓛ formare
	gorge [ɡɔːdʒ]	Schlucht	Ⓕ la gorge Ⓛ gurges
	colorful [ˈkʌləfl] *(AE)*, **colourful** [ˈkʌləfl] *(BE)*	bunt	
	kilometer *(AE)*	Kilometer	= *BE* **kilometre**. See box on page 194.
	deep [diːp]	tief	
	rim [rɪm]	Rand, Kante	rims

Tipps zum Wörterlernen → S. 155 · Englische Laute → S. 290 · Alphabetische Wörterverzeichnisse → S. 222–258 / S. 259–290

Vocabulary Introduction

the public [ˈpʌblɪk]		die Öffentlichkeit	The castle is open to **the ~** = Das Schloss ist öffentlich zugänglich.
public [ˈpʌblɪk]		öffentlich	(F) public, publique (L) publicus
(to) **raft** [rɑːft]		mit einem Schlauchboot/ Floß fahren	a **raft** — Rafting
ultimate [ˈʌltɪmət]		ultimativ, perfekt	
mule [mjuːl]		Maultier	a **mule** (F) le mulet (L) mulus
(to) **include** [ɪnˈkluːd]		einschließen	The team **~s** two women. (= Zum Team gehören zwei Frauen.) Does the trip ~ a tour of London? (L) includere
accommodation [əˌkɒməˈdeɪʃn]		Unterkunft	
p.9 (to) **look forward to** sb./sth. [ˈfɔːwəd]		sich auf jn./etwas freuen	I'm really **looking ~ to** the weekend. We're going to drive to the Grand Canyon.
daily [ˈdeɪli]		täglich, Tages-	noun: **day** – adjective/adverb: **daily**
three and a half days/weeks		dreieinhalb Tage/Wochen	❗ With '**and**': three <u>and</u> a half days
awesome [ˈɔːsəm] (AE, infml)		klasse, großartig	= very good, great
(to) **hike** [haɪk]		wandern	(to) go for long walks in the country
hike		Wanderung, Marsch	= a long walk in the country
p.10 **tribal** [ˈtraɪbl]		Stammes-	(F) tribal(e)
tribe [traɪb]		(Volks-)Stamm	(F) la tribu
identification, ID [aɪˌdentɪfɪˈkeɪʃn], [ˌaɪˈdiː]		Ausweis	The police told us that we couldn't go in without ~.
ruin [ˈruːɪn]		Ruine	(L) ruina
reservation [ˌrezəˈveɪʃn]		Reservat	
drive [draɪv]		(Auto-)Fahrt	verb: (to) **drive** – noun: **drive**
glad [glæd]		froh, dankbar	Tim is a good friend. I'm really ~ I met him.
especially [ɪˈspeʃəli]		besonders; vor allem	
Native American [ˌneɪtɪv əˈmerɪkən]		amerikanische(r) Ureinwohner/in, Indianer/in	

Classroom English → S.291 · Personen-, Orts- und Ländernamen → S.294–296 · Unregelmäßige Verben → S.292–293

Introduction Vocabulary

p.11	middle school	(USA) Schule für 11- bis 14-Jährige	
	grade [greɪd] (AE)	Jahrgangsstufe, Klasse	= BE year
	(to) raise money (for) [reɪz]	Geld sammeln (für)	
	(to) cut the grass [grɑːs]	Rasen mähen	
	grass	Gras; Rasen	She's **cutting the grass**.
	sale [seɪl]	(Aus-, Schluss-)Verkauf	
	tent [tent]	Zelt	F la tente
	(to) prefer sth. (to sth.) (-rr-) [prɪˈfɜː]	etwas (einer anderen Sache) vorziehen; etwas lieber tun (als etwas)	I ~ dogs **to** cats. (= I like dogs more than cats.) Do you ~ to watch football or play it? F préférer L praeferre
	how to do sth.	wie man etwas tut / tun kann / tun soll	

Question words + to-infinitive: how to … / what to … / where to … / …

Nach **Fragewörtern** kannst du einen **Infinitiv mit** *to* verwenden.
Er entspricht einem Nebensatz mit Modalverb („können", „sollen" usw.).

Can you tell me **how to get** to the station?	Können Sie mir sagen, wie ich zum Bahnhof komme / kommen kann?
I don't know **what to do**.	Ich weiß nicht, was ich tun soll.
He had no idea **where to go** or **who to ask**.	Er hatte keine Ahnung, wohin er gehen oder wen er fragen sollte.

	binoculars (pl) [bɪˈnɒkjuləz]	Fernglas	! My ~ **were** very expensive – don't lose **them**. Mein Fernglas **war** sehr teuer – verliere **es** nicht.
	tool [tuːl]	Werkzeug	
	on our/my/… own [əʊn]	allein, selbstständig (ohne Hilfe)	Did you go with Emma? – No, I went **on my ~**. His room looks great. Did he paint it **on his ~**?
	(to) sew (on) [səʊ], sewed [səʊd], sewn [səʊn]	(an)nähen	The doctors were able to ~ his finger back **on**. ! pronunciation: (to) sew [səʊ]
p.12	high school [ˈhaɪ skuːl]	(USA) Schule für 14- bis 18-Jährige	
	route [ruːt]	Strecke, Route	! In den USA werden wichtige Fernstraßen mit **Route** + **Nummer** bezeichnet.

Tipps zum Wörterlernen → S.155 · Englische Laute → S.290 · Alphabetische Wörterverzeichnisse → S.222–258 / S.259–290

Vocabulary 1

gas [gæs] *(AE)*, **petrol** ['petrəl] *(BE)*	Benzin	
gas station *(AE)*, **petrol station** *(BE)*	Tankstelle	
license plate ['laɪsns pleɪt] *(AE)*, **number plate** ['nʌmbə pleɪt] *(BE)*	Nummernschild	

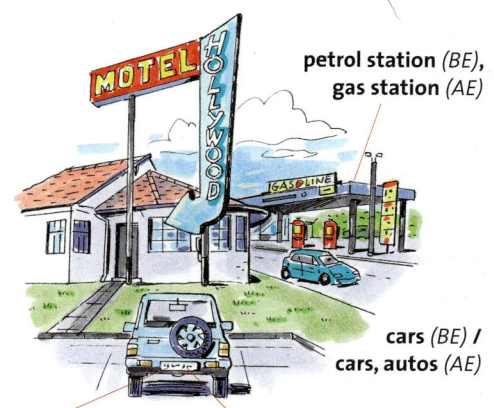

petrol station *(BE)*, **gas station** *(AE)*

cars *(BE)* / **cars, autos** *(AE)*

number plate *(BE)*, **license plate** *(AE)*

border ['bɔːdə]	Grenze	The US only has a ~ with Canada and Mexico.
cattle *(pl)* ['kætl]	Vieh, Rinder	
dinosaur ['daɪnəsɔː]	Dinosaurier	❗ stress: d**i**nosaur ['---]
collection [kə'lekʃn]	Sammlung	verb: (to) **collect** – noun: **collection**
finally *(adv)* ['faɪnəli]	endlich, schließlich	Ⓕ finalement
grand [grænd]	eindrucksvoll, beeindruckend	The hotel looked ~ from outside, but our room was small and dark.
straight [streɪt]	direkt	We drove ~ to Paris and didn't stop on the way.
(to) **stretch** [stretʃ]	sich (er)strecken	The history of London ~**es** over centuries. He woke up, ~**ed** and went to the bathroom.
layer ['leɪə]	Schicht	
multi- ['mʌlti]	viel-, mehr-; multi-, Multi-	**multi**-coloured; a **multi**-millionaire Ⓛ multus
trail [treɪl]	(Lehr-)Pfad	We learned a lot about trees on the forest ~.
foot [fʊt], *pl* **feet** [fiːt]	Fuß *(Längenmaß; ca. 30 cm)*	The cabin was quite small, only six **feet** high.
tip [tɪp]	Spitze	
wing [wɪŋ]	Flügel	

wings
tip

(to) **forgive** sb. **for** sth. [fə'gɪv], **forgave** [fə'geɪv], **forgiven** [fə'gɪvn]	jm. etwas vergeben, verzeihen	I know that she has hurt you, but try to ~ her. He **forgave** me **for** my rude words.
stop [stɒp]	Halt, Aufenthalt	After a short ~ we drove on.
highway ['haɪweɪ]	*(USA)* Fernstraße *(oft mit vier oder mehr Spuren)*	

Unit 1: New York, New York

p.15	**immigration** [ˌɪmɪ'greɪʃn]	Einwanderung	Ⓕ l'immigration *(f)*
	immigrant ['ɪmɪgrənt]	Einwanderer/Einwanderin	❗ stress: **i**mmigrant ['---]
	(to) **immigrate** ['ɪmɪgreɪt]	einwandern	Ⓕ immigrer Ⓛ immigrare
	avenue ['ævənjuː]	Allee, Boulevard	Ⓕ une avenue
	Ground Zero [ˌgraʊnd 'zɪərəʊ]	Bodennullpunkt *(Bezeichnung für das zerstörte World Trade Center in New York)*	

Classroom English → S.291 · Personen-, Orts- und Ländernamen → S.294–296 · Unregelmäßige Verben → S.292–293

1 Vocabulary

	liberty [ˈlɪbəti]	Freiheit	(F) la liberté (L) libertas
p.16/A 1	**block** [blɒk]	(Häuser-, Wohn-)Block	
	also [ˈɔːlsəʊ]	auch	Jack is nice and Ben is nice too. = Ben is ~ nice.
	downtown bus [ˌdaʊntaʊn ˈbʌs] *(AE)*	Bus in Richtung Stadtzentrum	! In New York, the south of Manhattan is called **downtown**.
	distance [ˈdɪstəns]	Entfernung	(F) la distance (L) distantia
p.16/A 2	**crosswalk** [ˈkrɒswɔːk] *(AE)*, **pedestrian crossing** [pəˌdestrɪən ˈkrɒsɪŋ] *(BE)*	Fußgängerüberweg	
	pedestrian [pəˈdestrɪən]	Fußgänger/in	(L) pedes
	line [laɪn] *(AE)*, **queue** [kjuː] *(BE)*	Schlange, Reihe *(wartender Menschen)*	a **queue** *(BE)*, a **line** *(AE)*
	hostess [ˈhəʊstəs]	Gastgeberin *(in USA auch: Frau, die im Restaurant die Gäste empfängt und an ihren Platz führt)*	
	host [həʊst]	Gastgeber	
	sidewalk [ˈsaɪdwɔːk] *(AE)*, **pavement** [ˈpeɪvmənt] *(BE)*	Gehweg, Bürgersteig	**pavement** *(BE)*, **sidewalk** *(AE)*

American English (I)

Different words

American English	British English	
apartment	flat	Wohnung
cellphone	mobile (phone)	Handy
downtown	city centre	Stadtzentrum, Innenstadt
elevator	lift	Fahrstuhl, Aufzug
gas	petrol	Benzin
grade	class, form	(Schul-)Klasse
line	queue	Schlange, Reihe
sidewalk	pavement	Gehweg, Bürgersteig
subway	underground	U-Bahn
vacation	holiday(s)	Ferien, Urlaub

Different spelling

American English: **-ter**	British English: **-tre**
cen**ter**	cen**tre**
me**ter**	me**tre**
thea**ter**	thea**tre**

American English: **-or**	British English: **-our**
col**or**	col**our**
fav**or**ite	fav**our**ite
harb**or**	harb**our**
neighb**or**	neighb**our**

American English:	British English:
traveled, traveling	travelled, travelling

	dollar ($) [ˈdɒlə]	Dollar	How much is £900 in ~s?
	fine [faɪn]	Geldstrafe	My mum got a ~ for speeding.
	(to) litter [ˈlɪtə]	Abfälle zurücklassen	
	litter	Abfall	
p.17/A 4	**fire station** [ˈfaɪə ˌsteɪʃn]	Feuerwache	**fire station**
	otherwise [ˈʌðəwaɪz]	sonst	Go to bed now. **Otherwise** you'll be tired tomorrow.
	firefighter [ˈfaɪəfaɪtə]	Feuerwehrmann, -frau	
	(to) put out a fire	ein Feuer löschen	

Tipps zum Wörterlernen → S.155 · Englische Laute → S.290 · Alphabetische Wörterverzeichnisse → S.222–258 / S.259–290

shift [ʃɪft]	Schicht *(bei der Arbeit)*		My dad works 8-hour **~s**. There are eight men and women on his **~**.
9/11 [ˌnaɪn_ɪˈlevn] *(AE)*	Nine Eleven *(der Terroranschlag am 11. September 2001)*	**!**	Dates are different in American English: *AE:* 11**/**25**/**2010 = *BE (and German):* 25.11.2010
hijacker [ˈhaɪdʒækə]	(Flugzeug-)Entführer/in		
(to) **take** sth. **over**	etwas übernehmen; etwas in seine Gewalt bringen		
skyscraper [ˈskaɪskreɪpə]	Wolkenkratzer		
(to) **burn** [bɜːn]	brennen; verbrennen		The light in the bedroom was still **~ing** at 4 am. Don't **~** those newspapers! Recycle them!
(to) **collapse** [kəˈlæps]	zusammenbrechen; einstürzen		
p.18/A 5 the **best** view **in** the world	die beste Aussicht der Welt	**!**	He's the **most intelligent** student **in** the class. *(nicht:* ~~of~~ *the class)*
perfect [ˈpɜːfɪkt]	perfekt; ideal; vollkommen	**!**	stress: **p**erfect [ˈ--]

Verbs with two objects

Im Englischen gibt es wie im Deutschen Verben, nach denen zwei Objekte stehen können:
– ein **indirektes Objekt** (meist eine Person – daher auch **Personenobjekt**)
– ein **direktes Objekt** (meist eine Sache – daher auch **Sachobjekt**).

Die normale Wortstellung ist wie im Deutschen: **Personenobjekt vor Sachobjekt** (wie im Alphabet: **P vor S**):
I'll send **Ruth a text**.   Ich werde Ruth eine SMS schicken.
Caitlin showed **Ryan the sign**.   Caitlin zeigte Ryan das Schild.

Die Wortstellung **Sachobjekt + *to* + Personenobjekt** wird verwendet, wenn
– das Sachobjekt ein Pronomen *(it, them)* ist:
  Caitlin wrote a text and sent **it *to*** Ruth.   Caitlin schrieb eine SMS und schickte sie Ruth.
– das Personenobjekt sehr lang ist:
  Caitlin showed the view ***to* her Irish cousin Ryan**.   Caitlin zeigte die Aussicht ihrem irischen Cousin Ryan.
– das Personenobjekt betont werden soll:
  Caitlin sent a text ***to* Ruth** (not to Sarah).   Caitlin schickte Ruth (nicht Sarah) eine SMS.

! Nach **describe**, **explain**, **present** und **report** wird ein Personenobjekt immer mit ***to*** angeschlossen:
Describe the picture ***to* your partner**.   Ryan **explained** his problem ***to* Caitlin**.
Present your poster ***to* the class**.   I **reported** the information ***to* my boss**.

lobby [ˈlɒbi]	Eingangshalle	
visibility [ˌvɪzəˈbɪləti]	Sicht(weite)	The fog was so bad that **~** was only 10 feet. *F* la visibilité
ticket office [ˈtɪkɪt_ˌɒfɪs]	Kasse *(für den Verkauf von Eintrittskarten)*; Fahrkartenschalter	

1 Vocabulary

floor [flɔː] — Stock(werk)

floor („Stock", „Stockwerk")

In britischem und amerikanischem Englisch werden die Stockwerke eines Gebäudes unterschiedlich gezählt.

British English	American English	
second floor	third floor	zweiter Stock
first floor	second floor	erster Stock
ground floor	first floor	Erdgeschoss

! **im zweiten** Stock = **on** the **second** floor (BE) / **on** the **third** floor (AE)

one floor **up** [ʌp]	ein Stockwerk höher	one floor **up** ◄► one floor **down**
(to) **sweat** [swet]	schwitzen	
Thank God.	Gott sei Dank.	
a while [waɪl]	eine Weile, einige Zeit	We waited a ~ and went on.
(to) **be tired of** sth.	genug von etwas haben, etwas satt haben	I'm really ~ of that CD. / I'm really ~ of listening to that CD. Can't you play something else?
myself [maɪˈself]	selbst	

German „selbst"

I did it all **myself**.	Ich habe es alles selbst gemacht.
This is good. Did you cook it **yourself**?	Das schmeckt gut. Hast du es selbst gekocht?
The president **herself** welcomed us.	Die Präsidentin selbst hieß uns willkommen.
The house **itself** is big, but the garden is very small.	Das Haus selbst ist groß, aber der Garten ist sehr klein.
We **ourselves** are the people who made the mistake.	Wir selbst sind die Leute, die den Fehler gemacht haben.
Yesterday we went to a Beatles concert. It wasn't the Beatles **themselves**, of course, just the music.	Gestern waren wir auf einem Beatles-Konzert. Es waren natürlich nicht die Beatles selbst, bloß die Musik.

movie [ˈmuːvi] (bes. AE)	Film	= BE **film** (to) go to the **movies** (AE) = (to) go to the **cinema** (BE)
jungle [ˈdʒʌŋgl]	Dschungel	(F) la jungle
(to) **escape from** sb./sth. [ɪˈskeɪp]	vor jm./aus etwas fliehen; entkommen	His father ~d from Germany before the war. They ~d from the police but were caught later.
death [deθ]	Tod	
whatever the movie [ˌwɒtˈevə]	egal, welcher Film	I just want to go to the cinema, ~ the **film**.

whatever, wherever, whenever, whoever

Wherever you go, I'll come with you.	Wo auch immer du hingehst, … / Egal wo du hingehst …
Visit me **whenever** you like.	…, wann immer du willst.
I won't open the door, **whoever** you are.	…, wer immer Sie auch sind.
Whoever told you that was wrong.	Wer immer dir das auch erzählt hat, hatte Unrecht.
I'll help you **whatever** happens.	…, was immer auch geschieht. / …, egal, was geschieht.

Tipps zum Wörterlernen → S.155 · Englische Laute → S.290 · Alphabetische Wörterverzeichnisse → S.222–258 / S.259–290

Vocabulary 1

tall [tɔːl]	*(Gebäude)* hoch		
(to) enter ['entə]	betreten; *(in ein Land)* einreisen	(F) entrer	(L) intrare
observatory [əb'zɜːvətri]	*hier:* Aussichtsplattform	(F) un observatoire	
(to) offer ['ɒfə]	(an)bieten	(F) offrir	(L) offerre
spectacular [spek'tækjələ]	spektakulär, atemberaubend		
static ['stætɪk], static electricity [ˌstætɪk_ɪˌlek'trɪsəti]	elektrische Aufladung		
fence [fens]	Zaun	a **fence**	
(to) kiss [kɪs]	(sich) küssen		
kiss [kɪs]	Kuss	He's **kissing** her.	
spark [spɑːk]	Funke		
lip [lɪp]	Lippe		
p.19/A 7 deli ['deli]	Deli *(Lebensmittelgeschäft mit Fastfoodrestaurant)*	If you're hungry, we can get some sandwiches at the ~ on the way home.	
bagel ['beɪgl]	Bagel *(ringförmiges Brötchen)*		
cream cheese [ˌkriːm 'tʃiːz]	Frischkäse		
cream [kriːm]	Sahne; Creme		
plain [pleɪn]	einfach, schlicht; *hier:* „natur", „ohne alles"	I want a ~ answer in ~ English: where were you last night?	
coffee ['kɒfi]	Kaffee		
counter ['kaʊntə]	Theke, Ladentisch		
(to) taste	probieren, kosten; schmecken	Have you ever ~d kangaroo? **Taste** this and tell me if it's too sweet. This ~s wonderful! Did you make it?	
taste [teɪst]	Geschmack	She doesn't like the ~ of whisky. He has terrible ~ in music.	
plenty of ['plenti_əv]	reichlich, viel(e)	We don't have to hurry: we've got ~ of time still. There are ~ of reasons to learn English.	
(to) give (sb.) a smile	(jn. an)lächeln	He **gave** her **a** big/shy/silly **smile**. = He smiled in a big/shy/silly way.	
Jewish ['dʒuːɪʃ]	jüdisch		
dough [dəʊ]	Teig		
(to) boil [bɔɪl]	kochen *(Flüssigkeit, Speise)*		(F) bouillir
oven ['ʌvn]	Ofen, Backofen	❗ pronunciation: **oven** ['ʌvn]	
filling ['fɪlɪŋ]	Füllung, (Brot-)Belag		
(to) fill sth. (with sth.)	etwas (mit etwas) (aus)füllen		
p.19/A 8 (to) wander ['wɒndə]	schlendern, herumirren		

Classroom English → S. 291 · Personen-, Orts- und Ländernamen → S. 294–296 · Unregelmäßige Verben → S. 292–293

1 Vocabulary

New York: the five boroughs

p.22/P 1

the Bronx	[brɒŋks]	der nördlichste Bezirk; liegt als einziger auf dem Festland
Manhattan	[mæn'hætn]	Insel zwischen dem Hudson und dem East River, berühmt für ihre Wolkenkratzer
Queens	[kwi:nz]	der größte Bezirk; im Südwesten der Insel Long Island gelegen; vor allem Wohngebiet
Brooklyn	['brʊklɪn]	wie Queens auf Long Island gelegen; die berühmte Brooklyn Bridge verbindet Brooklyn mit Manhattan
Staten Island !	[ˌstætn ˈaɪlənd]	Insel an der Einfahrt zum Hafen von New York, mit Manhattan durch Fährbetrieb verbunden

p.24/P 6 **journalist** ['dʒɜːnəlɪst]   Journalist/in

American English (II)

Different words

American English	British English	
cookie ['kʊki]	biscuit	Keks
eraser [ɪ'reɪsə(r)]	rubber	Radiergummi
French fries [fraɪz]	chips	Pommes frites
garbage ['gɑː(r)bɪdʒ]	rubbish	Müll, Abfall
pants [pænts]	trousers	Hose
potato chips	crisps	Kartoffelchips
schedule [AE: 'skedʒuːl, BE: 'ʃedjuːl]	timetable	Stundenplan; Fahrplan

Different pronunciation

	AE: [æ]	BE: [ɑː]
ask, last	[æsk], [læst]	[ɑːsk], [lɑːst]
	AE: [uː]	BE: [juː]
new, Tuesday	[nuː], ['tuːzdeɪ]	[njuː], ['tjuːzdeɪ]
	AE: [ɑː]	BE: [ɒ]
clock, hot	[klɑːk], [hɑːt]	[klɒk], [hɒt]

– In American English, you can usually hear the '**r**' in words like **here, more, shirt, farm**.
– The '**t**' in words like **city, better, writer** sounds more like a '**d**' in American English.

p.25/P 9

(to) **take a break**	eine Pause machen	We've worked long enough now. Let's **take a ~**.
(to) **revise** [rɪ'vaɪz]	überarbeiten; wiederholen	She had to ~ her work because there were lots of mistakes. (= überarbeiten) I've got a test tomorrow, so I must ~ tonight. (= (Lernstoff) wiederholen)
draft [drɑːft]	Entwurf	

p.27/P 12

safety ['seɪfti]	Sicherheit	
(to) **work** sth. **out** [ˌwɜːk ˈaʊt]	etwas herausfinden, -arbeiten	
heading ['hedɪŋ]	Überschrift	! **headline** = Schlagzeile; **heading** = Überschrift
suffix ['sʌfɪks]	Suffix, Nachsilbe	**suffix** ◄► **prefix**
context ['kɒntekst]	Zusammenhang, Kontext	What does 'get' mean? – It has lots of meanings. Show me the word in ~.
technique [tek'niːk]	(Arbeits-)Verfahren, Technik, Methode	How do you learn new words? Do you have a special ~? ! stress: **technique** [-'-]

Tipps zum Wörterlernen → S.155 · Englische Laute → S.290 · Alphabetische Wörterverzeichnisse → S.222–258 / S.259–290

The writer and the firefighter

p.28	**pilot** [ˈpaɪlət]	Pilot/in	❗	stress: **pi**lot [ˈ--]
	terrorism [ˈterərɪzm]	Terrorismus	❗	stress: **te**rrorism [ˈ----]
	emergency [ɪˈmɜːdʒənsi]	Notfall; Not-		In an ~ you must call the police.
	rescue [ˈreskjuː]	Rettung; Rettungsdienst		
	service [ˈsɜːvɪs]	Gottesdienst; *hier:* Trauerfeier		
	speech [spiːtʃ]	Rede		
	(to) **make/give** a speech	eine Rede halten		I'm nervous when I have to **make a speech** in front of a lot of people. He **gave a** lovely **speech** at the service.
	The families **want me to** say something.	Die Familien möchten, dass ich etwas sage.	❗	I **want you to** help your sister. = Ich möchte, dass du deiner Schwester hilfst. *not:* I want that you help your sister.
	(to) **comfort** [ˈkʌmfət]	trösten		
	politician [ˌpɒləˈtɪʃn]	Politiker/in		Ⓕ le politicien, la politicienne
	(to) **recognize** [ˈrekəgnaɪz]	erkennen		Oh, it's you. I didn't ~ you: have you been to the hairdresser's?
p.29	(to) **notice** [ˈnəʊtɪs]	(be)merken		I didn't ~ John because he was so quiet. I ~d that I had forgotten my money.
	extraordinary [ɪkˈstrɔːdnri]	außergewöhnlich		Ⓕ extraordinaire Ⓛ extraordinarius
	situation [ˌsɪtjuˈeɪʃn]	Situation	❗	stress: situ**a**tion [,--ˈ--]
	reddish [ˈredɪʃ]	rötlich		You can add the suffix **-ish** to many words to mean **more or less** *(mehr oder weniger, ungefähr)*: His hair isn't really red, but it's **reddish**. I don't know how old she is; I suppose **thirtyish**. See you **eightish**. (= Bis ungefähr um 8.)
	senior (to sb.) [ˈsiːniə]	(rang)höher (als jd.); leitende(r, s)		My mum has become my dad's boss, so now she's ~ **to** him. Mr Smith is a ~ manager in a big company.
	junior (to sb.) [ˈdʒuːniə]	(jm.) untergeordnet		junior ◀▶ senior
	(to) **depend on** sth./sb. [dɪˈpend]	sich auf etwas/jn. verlassen		Please don't forget. Can I ~ **on** you to remember?
	dependable [dɪˈpendəbl]	zuverlässig		a ~ person = you can **depend on** him or her
	a little [ˈlɪtl]	ein bisschen, ein wenig		
	religious [rɪˈlɪdʒəs]	gläubig, religiös	❗	stress: re**li**gious [-ˈ--]
	religion [rɪˈlɪdʒən]	Religion	❗	stress: re**li**gion [-ˈ--]
	mass [mæs]	Messe *(Gottesdienst)*		Bernadette goes to ~ every Sunday (besucht die Messe).
	nowadays [ˈnaʊədeɪz]	heutzutage		today, now, in our time

Classroom English → S.291 · Personen-, Orts- und Ländernamen → S.294–296 · Unregelmäßige Verben → S.292–293

1 Vocabulary

(to) **change** [tʃeɪndʒ]	(ver)ändern	

> **(to) change**
>
> | | |
> |---|---|
> | They **changed** their plans. | Sie **änderten** ihre Pläne. |
> | America has **changed** a lot since Columbus arrived. | Amerika hat **sich** sehr **verändert** … |
> | Your clothes are dirty. Please **change**. | Deine Kleider sind schmutzig. **Zieh dich um**, bitte. |
> | We **changed** our dollars into euros. | Wir **tauschten** unsere Dollar in Euro **um**. |
> | I don't like pop music. Can I **change** stations? | … Kann ich **umschalten**? |
> | British kids **change** rooms between lessons. | … **wechseln** das Klassenzimmer … |
> | We **changed** at Manchester. | Wir **stiegen** in Manchester **um**. |

(to) **take turns** (to do sth.) [tɜːnz]	sich abwechseln (etwas zu tun)	We both want to use the computer, so we'll have to **take** ~. You first or me first?
(to) **come up with** sth.	sich etwas ausdenken	I thought for a long time and finally **came** ~ ~ a really good idea.
critic [ˈkrɪtɪk]	Kritiker/in	(F) le/la critique
mean [miːn] (AE)	gemein	Don't be so ~ to your sister! It's not fair!
saint [seɪnt]	Heilige(r)	! In Namen wird **Saint** zu **St** abgekürzt, und die Aussprache ändert sich: **St Paul's** [sənt ˈpɔːlz]
p.30 **ladder** [ˈlædə]	Leiter	
noble [ˈnəʊbl]	ehrenhaft; adlig	(L) nobilis
(to) **show off** [ˌʃəʊ ˈɒf]	angeben, prahlen	Stop ~ing off! We know you're the best.
quality [ˈkwɒləti]	Eigenschaft; Qualität	What **qualities** does a good teacher need? The ~ of your work is very good.
absolutely [ˌæbsəˈluːtli]	absolut, völlig	(L) absolutus
(to) **put** sth. **in order**	etwas ordnen	
skill [skɪl]	Geschick, Fähigkeit	
You know how to **put** it.	Sie wissen, wie man es formuliert/ausdrückt.	How shall I ~ it? I don't know how to ~ it.
line of work [ˌlaɪn əv ˈwɜːk]	Beruf, berufliche Richtung	What ~ of ~ are you in? = Was machen Sie beruflich?
(to) **look up to** sb.	jn. respektieren, zu jm. aufsehen	
professional [prəˈfeʃnl]	professionell	! stress: **professional** [-ˈ---]
because of	wegen	(F) à cause de (L) causa (mit Gen.)

> **Giving reasons**
>
> | | |
> |---|---|
> | I'm not happy **because** my job is boring. | …, **weil** mein Job langweilig ist. |
> | I want to have an interesting job, **so** I'll have to move. | …, **daher/deshalb** muss ich umziehen. |
> | **That's why** I thought of the USA. | **Daher/Deshalb** dachte ich an die USA. |
> | I chose New York **for** lots of **reasons**. | … **aus** vielerlei **Gründen**. |
> | One **reason** (**why**) I chose NY was its skyline. | Ein **Grund** (**dafür, dass** …), war … ▶▶▶ |

Vocabulary 1–2

> **Giving reasons**
>
> Yes, I chose NY **because of** its skyscrapers. … **wegen** seiner Wolkenkratzer.
> I've written to my uncle in NY **to** ask him for help. …, **um** ihn um Hilfe **zu** bitten.
> Now I'm working hard **so (that)** I can buy the ticket. …, **damit** ich das Ticket kaufen kann.

blessing ['blesɪŋ]	Segen	
(to) **leave** sb. **behind** [bɪ'haɪnd], **left, left**	jn. zurücklassen	

Unit 2: Both sides of the story

p.36	**bow** [bəʊ]	Bogen	Violins are usually played with a ~.
	arrow ['ærəʊ]	Pfeil	bow and arrow = Pfeil und Bogen
	turkey ['tɜːki]	Pute, Truthahn	
	smoke [sməʊk]	Rauch	There's no **smoke** without fire. (= Wo Rauch ist, ist auch Feuer.)
	tablecloth ['teɪblklɒθ]	Tischdecke	
	Bible ['baɪbl]	Bibel	❗ The religious book is written with a capital **B**. This new biography is a **bible** for fans of U2.
	spring [sprɪŋ]	Quelle *(Wasserquelle)*	❗ **spring** = 1. Frühling; 2. Quelle
	candle ['kændl]	Kerze	Ⓛ candela
	goat [gəʊt]	Ziege	
	doll [dɒl]	Puppe	When I was little, I had a teddy bear and two ~s.
p.37	**Indian** ['ɪndiən]	Indianer/in	❗ • Der Begriff **Native American** wird heute von vielen dem älteren Begriff **Indian** vorgezogen. • **Indian** = *(auch)* Inder/in (Bürger/in Indiens)
	corn *(no pl)* [kɔːn] *(AE)* **maize** *(no pl)* [meɪz] *(BE)*	Mais	
	squash, *pl* **squash** [skwɒʃ]	Kürbis	
	bean [biːn]	Bohne	
	colonist ['kɒlənɪst]	Kolonist/in; Siedler/in	❗ stress: **co**lonist ['---]
	colony ['kɒləni]	Kolonie	❗ stress: **co**lony ['---] India was a British ~ until 1947. Ⓕ la colonie Ⓛ colonia
p.38/A1	**timeline** ['taɪmlaɪn]	Zeitstrahl	
	abbreviation [əˌbriːviˈeɪʃn]	Abkürzung	Ⓕ une abréviation
	BC [ˌbiː ˈsiː]	v. Chr.	70 **BC** = 70 years before Christ was born 70 **AD** or **AD** 70 = 70 years after Christ was born
	Christ [kraɪst]	Christus	
	Lord [lɔːd]	Herr(gott)	
	birth [bɜːθ]	Geburt	Please fill in your address, **date of** ~ (= Geburtsdatum) and **place of** ~ (= Geburtsort).
	agriculture ['ægrɪkʌltʃə]	Landwirtschaft	She's a farming expert. She knows a lot about ~. Ⓕ agriculture *(f)* Ⓛ (agri)cultura

Classroom English → S.291 · Personen-, Orts- und Ländernamen → S.294–296 · Unregelmäßige Verben → S.292–293

2 Vocabulary

(to) **spread** [spred], **spread, spread**	(sich) ausbreiten, (sich) verbreiten	The fire quickly ~ to all parts of the building. The bird ~ its wings and flew away.	
present-day [ˌpreznt 'deɪ]	heutige(r, s)	**Present-day** music is just electronic noise.	
(to) **grow** [grəʊ], **grew** [gruː], **grown** [grəʊn]	(Getreide usw.) anbauen, anpflanzen	We have a garden now and ~ our own vegetables.	
(to) **sail** [seɪl]	(mit dem Schiff) fahren; segeln	We're not flying to New York – we're ~ing! The *Titanic* ~ed from Southampton. My uncle Eddie once ~ed to America.	
pilgrim ['pɪlgrɪm]	Pilger/in	The *Pilgrims* (with a capital 'p') were the English colonists who arrived in America in 1620.	
(to) **celebrate** ['selɪbreɪt]	feiern	My great-grandmother ~d her 100th birthday last week. ⒡ célébrer ⓛ celebrare	
celebration [ˌseləˈbreɪʃn]	Feier	⒡ la célébration ⓛ celebratio	
harvest ['hɑːvɪst]	Ernte		
human ['hjuːmən]	Mensch, menschliches Wesen	a person, not an animal or a machine	
(to) **found** [faʊnd]	gründen	❗ (to) **found** – founded – founded = gründen (to) **find** – found – found = finden	
p.38/A 2 **cause** [kɔːz]	Ursache	⒡ la cause ⓛ causa	
(to) **cause** [kɔːz]	verursachen		
effect [ɪ'fekt]	Wirkung, Folge	⒡ un effet ⓛ effectus	
consequence ['kɒnsɪkwəns]	Folge, Konsequenz	❗ stress: **co**nsequence ['---] ⒡ la conséquence ⓛ consequentia	
(to) **lead (to** sth.**)** [liːd], **led, led** [led]	(zu etwas) führen	This road ~s to the next village. You ~ and we'll follow.	
settler ['setlə]	Siedler/in		
parade [pəˈreɪd]	Parade, Umzug		
p.39/A 3 **Social Studies** [ˌsəʊʃl 'stʌdiz]	Sozial-, Gemeinschaftskunde		
instead of [ɪn'sted_əv]	statt, anstelle von	Why can't you help me ~ of just sitting there?	
revolution [ˌrevə'luːʃn]	Revolution	❗ stress: **revo**lution [ˌ--'--]	
semester [sɪ'mestə]	Semester, Schulhalbjahr	❗ In Großbritannien ist das Schuljahr in drei **terms** unterteilt, in den USA in zwei **semesters**.	

Tipps zum Wörterlernen → S.155 · Englische Laute → S.290 · Alphabetische Wörterverzeichnisse → S.222–258 / S.259–290

Vocabulary 2

	(to) **interrupt** [ˌɪntəˈrʌpt]	unterbrechen	Please don't ~ me when I'm talking. Wait till I've finished. (F) interrompre (L) interrumpere
	opinion (on, of) [əˈpɪnjən]	Meinung (zu, von)	United were great. – Do you think so? **In my ~**, City played better. (= Meiner Meinung nach …) (F) une opinion (L) opinio
	(to) **share** sth. **with** sb. [ʃeə]	etwas mit jm. teilen; etwas mit jm. gemeinsam haben/nutzen; Meinungen (mit)teilen	He ~**d** the last piece of the cake **with** me. She still ~**s** a room **with** her brother. Please ~ (your opinion) **with** the class.
	period [ˈpɪəriəd] (bes. AE)	Unterrichtsstunde	
p.39/A 4	**fault** [fɔːlt]	Schuld, Fehler	You didn't wake me up this morning. It's your ~ that I'm late for school. (= du hast Schuld)
	(to) **keep quiet** [ˌkiːp ˈkwaɪət], **kept, kept** [kept]	still sein, leise sein	Please ~ **quiet** for a minute: I want to make a phone call.
	hopeless [ˈhəʊpləs]	hoffnungslos	You're **hopeless**. = Dir ist nicht zu helfen.
	(to) **give** sb. **a hug** [hʌg]	jn. umarmen	
	hug [hʌg]	Umarmung	When she arrived, she **gave** him **a** big ~.
p.40/A 5	**living-history museum**	Freilichtmuseum (mit kostümierten Fremdenführer/innen, historischen Aufführungen usw.)	
	staff [stɑːf]	Personal, Belegschaft; Lehrerkollegium	the people who work at a company/school
	staff member [ˌstɑːf ˈmembə] (AE) **member of staff** (BE)	Mitarbeiter/in	
	(to) **dress** [dres]	sich kleiden; sich anziehen	Emily has very nice clothes and always ~**es** well. ! The verb (to) **get dressed** is used more often than (to) **dress** to mean 'sich anziehen': After I got up, I **got dressed** and went to school.
	(to) **keep an eye on** sth./ sb.	auf etwas/jn. aufpassen	**Keep an ~ on** the milk while I answer the phone.
	chief [tʃiːf]	Häuptling	
	exhibition (on) [ˌeksəˈbɪʃn]	Ausstellung (über)	
	brave [breɪv]	tapfer, mutig	She was very ~: she jumped into the river and saved the child's life.
	soil [sɔɪl]	(Erdreich) Erde	You've got ~ on your shoes. – Yes, I was outside.
p.41/A 7	**guide** [gaɪd]	Fremdenführer/in, Reiseleiter/in	
	whether [ˈweðə]	ob	I don't know ~ I can come to your party or not. ! **whether** is a little more formal than **if**
	helpful [ˈhelpfəl]	hilfreich	
p.42/A 9	**usual** [ˈjuːʒuəl]	üblich	10 o'clock is my ~ time to go to bed.
	tradition [trəˈdɪʃn]	Tradition	It's a ~ to sing songs on someone's birthday.

Classroom English → S. 291 · Personen-, Orts- und Ländernamen → S. 294–296 · Unregelmäßige Verben → S. 292–293

	entertainment [ˌentəˈteɪnmənt]	Unterhaltung (Vergnügen)	For the passengers on the ship there was lots of ~: films, shows, concerts, competitions, etc. ! Unterhaltung (Gespräch) = **conversation** Unterhaltung (Vergnügen) = **entertainment**
	politics [ˈpɒlətɪks]	(die) Politik	! **Politics** ist Singular, trotz des **-s**: **Politics is** very interesting for some people and **it is** very boring for others.
	handout [ˈhændaʊt]	Arbeitsblatt, Informationsblatt, Handout	
	source [sɔːs]	Quelle (Informations-, Textquelle)	For research, a book is better than an online ~. ! Quelle (Wasser) = **spring** (Informationen) = **source** (F) la source
p.45/P 1	routine [ruːˈtiːn]	Routine	(F) la routine
	(to) fetch [fetʃ]	(ab)holen	I'll ~ you from the airport if you want. Can you ~ me some cola from the kitchen?
	(to) milk [mɪlk]	melken	noun: **milk** – verb: (to) **milk**
	(to) shoot [ʃuːt], shot, shot [ʃɒt]	(er)schießen	John Lennon was **shot** in 1980. She **shot** the thief in the leg.
	prayer [preə]	Gebet	(F) la prière
	(to) pray [preɪ]	beten	(F) prier
	secret (n) [ˈsiːkrət]	Geheimnis	I can't tell you. It's a ~. (F) le secret (L) secretum
	secret (adj) [ˈsiːkrət]	geheim	We made a ~ deal: we didn't tell anyone.
	verse [vɜːs]	Vers (in der Bibel); Strophe (eines Liedes)	The first words of the first ~ of the Bible are 'In the beginning …'. Some old folk songs have very, very many ~s.
p.45/P 2	disease [dɪˈziːz]	(ansteckende) Krankheit	! • Eine ansteckende oder ernsthafte Krankheit heißt **disease**: Thousands of trees died from **disease**. He has a blood **disease**. • Es gibt auch das allgemeinere Wort **illness**: After a week of **illness**, she went back to school.
p.50/P 13	guided tour [ˌgaɪdɪd ˈtʊə]	Führung	We went on a **guided** ~ of the castle.
p.51/P 16	sub-heading [ˈsʌbˌhedɪŋ]	Zwischenüberschrift	Long articles in newspapers are often broken up with ~-**headings**.
	protest [ˈprəʊtest]	Protest	! stress: **pr**o**test** [ˈ--]
	specific [spəˈsɪfɪk]	bestimmte(r, s), spezifische(r, s)	Let's meet between three and six. – No. Let's agree on a ~ time.

I'm going to save my brother

p.52	tavern [ˈtævən]	Schenke, Gastwirtschaft (bis ins 19. Jahrhundert)	(today) = **pub** (L) taberna
	Minuteman [ˈmɪnɪtmən], pl Minutemen [ˈmɪnɪtmen]	Angehöriger der amerikanischen Miliz (der innerhalb einer Minute gegen die Briten kampfbereit sein sollte)	

Vocabulary 2

damn [dæm] *(infml)*	verdammt	❗ spelling: **dam<u>n</u>**	
soldier ['səʊldʒə]	Soldat/in		
(to) chase sb. [tʃeɪs]	jn. jagen; jm. hinterherjagen		
it is worth doing sth. [wɜːθ]	es lohnt sich, etwas zu tun	❗ It's **worth it**. = Es lohnt sich. It isn't **worth it**. = Es lohnt sich nicht.	
law [lɔː]	Gesetz	In Britain, parliament makes the country's ~s. Ⓕ la loi	
treason ['triːzn]	Hochverrat	Ⓕ la trahison	
subject ['sʌbdʒɪkt]	Untertan/in; Staatsangehörige(r) *(in einer Monarchie)*	He was born in Germany but is now a British ~.	
rebellion [rɪ'beljən]	Aufstand	Ⓛ rebellio	
victory ['vɪktərɪ]	Sieg	❗ The noun **win** is more informal than **victory**. Chelsea's **win** over United Wellington's **victory** over Napoleon Ⓛ victoria	
Get out of my sight.	Geh mir aus den Augen.		
p.53 **prison** ['prɪzn]	Gefängnis	Three men escaped from ~ last night. The police are looking for them. Ⓕ la prison ❗ Er ist **wegen** Mordes **im** Gefängnis. = He is **in** prison **for** murder.	
prisoner ['prɪznə]	Gefangene(r)	Ⓕ le prisonier	
army ['ɑːmɪ]	Armee, Heer		
crime [kraɪm]	Verbrechen; Kriminalität	The worst ~ is murder. Ⓕ le crime Ⓛ crimen **Crime** is a big problem in most cities. ❗ German *Krimi* = **crime film, crime story**	
(to) commit (-tt-) [kə'mɪt]	begehen	People who ~ crimes are often sent to prison.	
(to) sentence sb. **(to** sth.**)** ['sentəns]	jn. verurteilen (zu etwas)	She was ~d to four years in prison.	
sentence	Urteil, Strafe	a **life** ~ (= eine lebenslängliche Haftstrafe), a **death** ~ (= eine Todesstrafe)	
(to) pardon ['pɑːdn]	begnadigen	She was ~ed after two years of her sentence. Ⓕ pardonner	
execution [ˌeksɪ'kjuːʃn]	Hinrichtung	Ⓕ une exécution	
among [ə'mʌŋ]	unter, zwischen *(mehreren Personen oder Dingen)*	**among** the boys **between** the boys	
(to) bury ['berɪ]	begraben, vergraben; beerdigen	He died on holiday in NY and was **buried** there.	
(to) be alive [ə'laɪv]	leben, am Leben sein	Is he dead? – No, he's ~. He's just asleep.	
(to) lift [lɪft]	(an-, hoch)heben		
yard [jɑːd]	Yard *(Maß, 0,91 m)*	There are 1,760 ~s in a mile. Three feet are a ~.	

Classroom English → S.291 · Personen-, Orts- und Ländernamen → S.294–296 · Unregelmäßige Verben → S.292–293

2 Vocabulary

hut [hʌt]	Hütte	They spent the night on the mountain in a mountain ~.
(to) **be surrounded** [sə'raʊndɪd]	umgeben sein	The lake **was** ~ by trees.
guard [gɑːd]	Wachposten	Ⓕ le gardien, le garde

a **guard**

confusion [kən'fjuːʒn]	Verwirrung	Ⓕ la confusion Ⓛ confusio
(to) **confuse** [kən'fjuːz]	verwirren	Ⓕ confondre Ⓛ confundere
several ['sevrəl]	mehrere, verschiedene	= some, but not very many My parents have got ~ books about the USA.
gun [gʌn]	Schusswaffe	
(to) **breathe** [briːð]	atmen	
(to) **shake** [ʃeɪk], **shook** [ʃʊk], **shaken** ['ʃeɪkn]	zittern; schütteln	Look, he's nervous: his hands are **shaking**. **Shaking** your head means 'no'.
(to) **charge (at** sb.**)** [tʃɑːdʒ]	stürmen; jn. angreifen	He ~**d** into my room and hit me. The British soldiers ~**d at** the Minutemen.
(to) **flash** [flæʃ]	aufblitzen; leuchten	
(to) **go off** [ˌgəʊ_'ɒf], **went, gone**	(Waffe) losgehen; (Bombe) explodieren	The gun **went** ~ by mistake (= aus Versehen). A **bomb** [bɒm] **has gone** ~ in central London.

not at all, no ... at all

p.54

There were **no** people **at all**. [ət_'ɔːl]	Es gab **überhaupt keine** Menschen.
I'm **not at all** rich. I have**n't** got any money **at all**.	Ich bin **überhaupt nicht** reich. Ich habe **gar kein** Geld.
I hate you. I do**n't** like you **at all**.	Ich hasse dich. Ich mag dich **überhaupt nicht**.
I saw **nothing at all**.	Ich sah **gar nichts**.
Do you like meat? – **Not at all**.	Magst du Fleisch? – **Ganz und gar nicht.** / **Überhaupt nicht.**

waste [weɪst]	Verschwendung	verb: (to) **waste** – noun: **waste**
(to) **bleed** [bliːd], **bled, bled** [bled]	bluten	noun: **blood** – verb: (to) **bleed**
cart [kɑːt]	Wagen, Karren	Ⓛ carrus
(to) **tie** [taɪ]	(fest)binden	She's **tying** her hair back. ❗ -ing form: **tying**
rope [rəʊp]	Seil	
neck [nek]	Hals	**neck** **throat**

Tipps zum Wörterlernen → S.155 · Englische Laute → S.290 · Alphabetische Wörterverzeichnisse → S.222–258 / S.259–290

minister ['mɪnɪstə]	Pfarrer/in, Pastor/in	❗ minister = 1. Minister – The British **prime minister** (Premierminister/in) lives at 10 Downing Street, London. 2. Pfarrer/in, Pastor/in (der protestantischen Kirche)	
(to) scream [skri:m]	schreien		
debts (pl) [dets]	Schulden	❗ Silent letter **b**: de**b**ts [dets]	Ⓛ debitum
(to) keep doing sth., kept, kept	etwas weiterhin tun; etwas ständig tun	I asked you to be quiet but you ~ talking! I ~ thinking I know her from somewhere.	
(to) achieve [ə'tʃi:v]	erreichen, erzielen, zustande bringen	I've been working all day, but I haven't ~d much. ❗ ein Ziel erreichen = (to) **achieve** an end einen Ort erreichen = (to) **reach** a place/ (to) **arrive at** a place	

⌜Unit 3: California, land of dreams

p.56	caption ['kæpʃn]	Bildunterschrift		
	governor ['gʌvənə]	Gouverneur/in	❗ stress: **g**overnor ['---]	Ⓕ le gouverneur
	migrant worker [ˌmaɪgrənt 'wɜ:kə]	Wanderarbeiter/in		
	homeless ['həʊmləs]	obdachlos	Last night I saw a ~ man asleep in the park.	
	(to) admire [əd'maɪə]	bewundern	I ~ Gandhi because he was a man of peace. We stopped at the lake to ~ the view.	Ⓕ admirer Ⓛ admirare
	creative [kri'eɪtɪv]	kreativ, einfallsreich		Ⓕ créatif,-ve
	innovation [ˌɪnə'veɪʃn]	Innovation, Neuerung	❗ stress: innov**a**tion [ˌ--'--]	
	wave [weɪv]	Welle		
	wildfire ['waɪldfaɪə]	Wald-, Buschbrand		
	wildlife ['waɪldlaɪf]	Tierwelt; frei lebende Tiere	Australia's ~ is very different from Europe's. The park is home to all kinds of ~.	
p.58/A 1	majority [mə'dʒɒrəti]	Mehrheit	There are 26 girls and three boys in my class. The girls are in the ~.	Ⓕ la majorité
	minority [maɪ'nɒrəti]	Minderheit	The boys are in the ~. **majority ◀▶ minority**	Ⓕ la minorité
	fewer ['fju:ə]	weniger	Only three boys? That's ~ than I expected.	
p.58/A 2	attitude to/towards ['ætɪtju:d]	Haltung gegenüber, Einstellung zu	What's your ~ to/towards clothes? Do you always buy the latest fashion?	Ⓕ une attitude
	comment ['kɒment]	Kommentar	No **comment**! Ⓕ le commentaire	
	useless ['ju:sləs]	nutzlos, unfähig	I'm ~ at PE. = Turnen liegt mir überhaupt nicht.	
	education [ˌedʒu'keɪʃn]	(Schul-, Aus-)Bildung; Erziehung	You need a good ~ if you want to get a good job. Ⓕ l'éducation (f) Ⓛ educatio	

3 Vocabulary

grade [greɪd] *(bes. AE)* (BE auch:) **mark** [mɑːk]	(Schul-)Note, Zensur	❗ **grade** = 1. *(AE)* Klasse, Jahrgangsstufe *(= BE* **year***)* 2. *(bes. AE)* Note, Zensur
(to) **be prejudiced (against)** [ˈpredʒədɪst]	voreingenommen sein, Vorurteile haben (gegenüber)	I can't understand why some people **are ~ against** minorities.
prejudice (against) [ˈpredʒudɪs]	Voreingenommenheit (gegen), Vorurteil (gegenüber)	I think Americans speak really awful English. – I'm sorry, but that's just a **~**. Ⓕ le préjugé
(to) **discriminate against** sb. [dɪˈskrɪmɪneɪt]	jn. diskriminieren, jn. benachteiligen	❗ jn. diskriminieren = (to) **discriminate against** sb. I think it's wrong to **~ against** minorities. Ⓕ discriminer
discrimination (against) [dɪˌskrɪmɪˈneɪʃn]	Diskriminierung (von), Benachteiligung (von)	Ⓕ la discrimination

they

Nach **everybody, someone, nobody** usw. kannst du **they/them/their** verwenden, um die schwer zu lesenden Ausdrücke *he or she / him or her / his or her* zu vermeiden.

Auch nach **person, friend, student** usw. kann **they/them/their** stehen, wenn es nicht wichtig oder nicht klar ist, ob ein Mann oder eine Frau gemeint ist.

Not **everybody** cares if **their** food is fresh. *(statt: … if his or her food …)*
Someone left **their** purse on the table. *(statt: … his or her purse …)*
Nobody likes it when **they** lose a game. *(statt: … he or she …)*

In this game, you think of a **person** and what clothes **they** might wear. *(statt: … he or she …)*
If you have a good **friend** and you ask **them** for help, **they** will help you.
Each **student** reads the sentence **they** wrote to **their** group.

value [ˈvæljuː]	Wert	The **~** of my car has gone down by £900 since I bought it. Ⓕ la valeur Do young people share older people's **~s**?
advantage (over sb./sth.**)** [ədˈvɑːntɪdʒ]	Vorteil (gegenüber jm./etwas)	**advantage ◂▸ disadvantage** Ⓕ un avantage Cats have an **~ over** dogs: they can climb trees.
disadvantage [ˌdɪsədˈvɑːntɪdʒ]	Nachteil	Not being able to drive can be a **~** when you're looking for a job. Ⓕ le désavantage
bilingual [ˌbaɪˈlɪŋgwəl]	zweisprachig	**Bilingual** people speak two languages really well (often because they learned them as children). Ⓕ bilingue
(to) **get along** [əˈlɒŋ]	zurechtkommen	How are you **~ting ~** with Latin? – I found it hard at first, but now it's OK.
illegal [ɪˈliːgl]	illegal, ungesetzlich	❗ stress: **illegal** [-ˈ--]
legal [ˈliːgl]	legal	❗ stress: **legal** [ˈ--]
(to) **succeed (in** sth.**)** [səkˈsiːd]	Erfolg haben, erfolgreich sein (mit etwas, bei etwas)	(to) **be successful (at** sth.**)** Ⓛ succedere
relations *(pl)* [rɪˈleɪʃnz]	Beziehungen	Germany has good **~** with all its neighbours. Ⓕ les relations *(f)*

Tipps zum Wörterlernen → S.155 · Englische Laute → S.290 · Alphabetische Wörterverzeichnisse → S.222–258 / S.259–290

Vocabulary **3**   209

p.59/A 3	**assignment** [əˈsaɪnmənt] *(AE)*	Hausaufgabe	= *BE* **homework**
	plant [plɑːnt]	Pflanze	⒡ la plante Ⓛ planta
	(to) **plant** [plɑːnt]	(ein-, aus-, be-)pflanzen	Our school green group **~ed** some trees. The farmer **~ed** two fields of potatoes. ⒡ planter
	(to) **spray** [spreɪ]	spritzen; (be)sprühen, sprayen	Have those apples been **~ed** with anything? Is that a new car? – No, it's only been **~ed**. **Spraying** graffiti is illegal. The walls were **~ed** with graffiti.
	(to) **cover** [ˈkʌvə]	zudecken; bedecken	It was cold so she **~ed** her baby with her jacket. You can't see Philip's desk because it's always **~ed** with books. ⒡ couvrir Ⓛ cooperire
	plastic [ˈplæstɪk]	Plastik, Kunststoff	
	(to) **protect** sb./sth. **(from** sb./sth.) [prəˈtekt]	jn./etwas (be)schützen (vor jm./etwas)	Wear a hat to **~** your head **from** the sun. Animals can get dangerous if they're **~ing** their babies. ⒡ protéger Ⓛ protegere
	insect [ˈɪnsekt]	Insekt	❗ stress: **insect** [ˈ--] ⒡ un insecte
	biological [ˌbaɪəˈlɒdʒɪkl]	biologisch	❗ stress: **biological** [--ˈ---] – **biology** [-ˈ---]
	method (of doing sth.) [ˈmeθəd]	Methode (etwas zu tun)	❗ stress: **method** [ˈ--] ⒡ la méthode Ⓛ methodus
	less [les]	weniger	I've got **~** money than you. = You've got more money than me.
	(to) **pick** fruit/flowers [pɪk]	Obst/Blumen pflücken	**Picking** fruit
	thought [θɔːt]	Gedanke	verb: (to) **think**, **thought**, **thought** – noun: **thought**
	soda [ˈsəʊdə] *(AE)*	Limonade	
p.60/A 4	**wealthy** [ˈwelθi]	reich	= **rich**
	wealth [welθ]	Reichtum	The **~** of Las Vegas comes from entertainment. This class shows a **~** of talent.
	supper [ˈsʌpə]	Abendessen, Abendbrot	❗ **supper**: an evening meal, hot or cold, at home **dinner**: more formal; hot; home or restaurant
	(to) **run (-nn-), ran, run**	verlaufen *(Straße; Grenze)*	The cycle path **~s** on both sides of the river.
	warning [ˈwɔːnɪŋ]	Warnung	
	(to) **warn** sb. **(of** sth.) [wɔːn]	jn. (vor etwas) warnen	❗ jn. davor warnen, etwas zu tun = (to) **warn** sb. **not** to do sth. My parents **~ed** me **not to** walk home alone.

Classroom English → S.291 · Personen-, Orts- und Ländernamen → S.294–296 · Unregelmäßige Verben → S.292–293

3 Vocabulary

	however [haʊ'evə]	jedoch; trotzdem	I can read French. **However**, I can't speak it. I was tired. **However**, I didn't want to go to bed.
	patrol [pə'trəʊl]	Streife, Patrouille	The thieves saw the police ~ and ran away.
p.61/A 6	**desert** ['dezət]	Wüste	
	(to) **drown** [draʊn]	ertrinken	I jumped into the river to save the man from ~ing.
	ocean ['əʊʃn]	Ozean	❗ The Americans often use the word **ocean** where the British just say **sea**: AE: We spent our **vacation** at the **ocean**. BE: We spent our **holiday** by the **sea**. Ⓕ un océan Ⓛ oceanus
	flyer ['flaɪə]	Flugblatt, Flyer	
	(to) **deliver** [dɪ'lɪvə]	(aus)liefern, austragen	They ~ed our new sofa last week.
	pollution [pə'lu:ʃn]	Verschmutzung	Ⓕ la pollution
	(to) **flow** [fləʊ]	fließen	After 500 km, the Hudson River ~s into New York Bay.
	(to) **prevent** sb./sth. **from** doing sth. [prɪ'vent]	jn./etwas daran hindern, etwas zu tun	The guard ~ed me **from** entering the castle.
	(to) **prevent** sth.	etwas verhindern	Will the new law help to ~ crime?
	giant ['dʒaɪənt]	riesige(r,s); Riesen-	He works for a ~ oil company. **Giant** tortoises can weigh over 300 kilograms.
	homeowner ['həʊm,əʊnə]	Eigenheimbesitzer/in	**owner** ['əʊnə] Besitzer/in, Eigentümer/in
	(to) **own** [əʊn]	besitzen	My dream is to ~ a very fast car. ❗ He **owns** (besitzt) his **own** (eigenes) home.
	(to) **reduce** sth. **(by)** [rɪ'dʒu:s]	etwas reduzieren (um)	The price was ~d by 50%. Ⓕ réduire
	bacteria (pl) [bæk'tɪərɪə]	Bakterien	
	system ['sɪstəm]	System	❗ stress: **system** ['--]
	environmental [ɪn,vaɪrən'mentl]	Umwelt-	**Environmental** groups work to protect the **environment**.
	environment [ɪn'vaɪrənmənt]	Umwelt	
p.64/P 1	**synonym** ['sɪnənɪm]	Synonym (Wort mit gleicher oder sehr ähnlicher Bedeutung)	Words with the same meaning (or almost the same meaning) are called ~s. **synonym** ◄► **antonym** ['æntənɪm]
p.64/P 2	**nearly** ['nɪəli]	fast, beinahe	= almost There were 997 in the audience: ~ a thousand.

p.64/P 3	**ethnic** [ˈeθnɪk]	ethnisch, Volks-	The Turks are the biggest ~ minority in Germany.
	collocation [ˌkɒləˈkeɪʃn]	Kollokation *(Wörter, die oft zusammen vorkommen)*	words that are used together, for example: **make the bed** (*not*: ~~do~~ the bed), **do homework** (*not*: ~~make~~ homework)
	opposite [ˈɒpəzɪt]	Gegenteil	❗ **opposite** (*preposition*) = gegenüber **opposite** (*noun*) = Gegenteil
p.66/P 8	**ripe** [raɪp]	reif	Don't pick those apples: they're not ~ yet.
p.66/P 11	**soft drink**	alkoholfreies Getränk	
	factual text [ˈfæktʃuəl]	Sachtext	
	(to) illustrate [ˈɪləstreɪt]	veranschaulichen, illustrieren	This example ~s the problem well. The book is ~d with photos and drawings.
p.70/P 15	**organization** [ˌɔːgənaɪˈzeɪʃn]	Organisation	
p.71/P 17	**outline** [ˈaʊtlaɪn]	Gliederung	

The circuit

p.72	**grape** [greɪp]	Weintraube	some **grapes**
	cotton [ˈkɒtn]	Baumwolle	**cotton** Ⓕ le coton
	weight [weɪt]	Gewicht	You must eat less if you want to lose ~. verb: **(to) weigh** – noun: **weight**
	(to) greet [griːt]	begrüßen	When I arrived I was ~ed by a large black dog.
	except [ɪkˈsept]	außer, bis auf	
	(to) spill [spɪl]	verschütten	Get a towel quickly. I've ~ed water on your book.
	seat [siːt]	Sitz, Platz	When you fly, you get the best views from a window ~.
	(to) wipe [waɪp]	(ab)wischen	The table is dirty. Could you ~ it please?
	sweat [swet]	Schweiß	noun: **sweat** – verb: **(to) sweat**
	forehead [ˈfɔːhed, ˈfɒrɪd]	Stirn	
	sunset [ˈsʌnset]	Sonnenuntergang	
	sunrise [ˈsʌnraɪz]	Sonnenaufgang	

Classroom English → S.291 · Personen-, Orts- und Ländernamen → S.294–296 · Unregelmäßige Verben → S.292–293

3 Vocabulary

	earthworm [ˈɜːθwɜːm]	Regenwurm	
	(to) sweep [swiːp], **swept**, **swept** [swept]	fegen, kehren	We **swept** the room and made it really clean.
	vineyard [ˈvɪnjəd]	Weinberg	Grapes grow in **~s**. Ⓛ vinea
	(to) rise [raɪz], **rose** [rəʊz], **risen** [ˈrɪzn]	(auf)steigen	Clouds of smoke **rose** from the factory. Prices **have risen** by 10 per cent since last year.
p.73	**handkerchief** [ˈhæŋkətʃiːf]	Taschentuch	He was crying so I gave him my **~**.
	row [rəʊ]	Reihe	We sat in the front **~** of the cinema.
	sick [sɪk]	krank	❗ In *AE*, **sick** is used more often than **ill**. After a verb you can use **sick** or **ill**: He's **sick/ill**. Before a noun you can only use **sick**: The **sick** boy. (Not: the ~~ill~~ boy.)
	I feel **sick**.	Mir ist schlecht.	
	still [stɪl]	still *(bewegungslos)*	Please be very **~**! Don't move at all!
	dust [dʌst]	Staub	I tied a handkerchief in front of my mouth to prevent me from breathing in the **~**.
	hose [həʊz]	Schlauch	

a garden **hose**

	(to) get used to sb./sth. [juːst]	sich an jn./etwas gewöhnen	When I moved to the UK, it was difficult to drive on the left, but I soon **got ~ to** it. ❗ pronunciation: **used** [s]
	(to) lie [laɪ], **lay** [leɪ], **lain** [leɪn]	liegen	❗ -ing form: **lying**
	principal *(bes. AE)* [ˈprɪnsəpl]	Schulleiter/in	*BE auch:* **head teacher**
	(to) enroll (for/in/on) sth. [ɪnˈrəʊl]	sich (für etwas) anmelden	I have **~ed for** a French course. It's starting next month.
p.74	**(to) introduce** sb. **(to** sb.**)** [ˌɪntrəˈdjuːs]	jn. (jm.) vorstellen	You don't know him? Let me **~** you **to** him.
	(to) hand sb. sth. [hænd]	jm. etwas reichen	= **(to) pass** sb. sth.
	polite [pəˈlaɪt]	höflich	Ⓕ poli,e Ⓛ politus
	understanding [ˌʌndəˈstændɪŋ]	verständnisvoll	
	recess [ˈriːses] *(AE)*	Pause *(zwischen Schulstunden)*	= *BE* **break**
	restroom [ˈrestˌruːm] *(AE)*	(öffentliche) Toilette	= *BE* **toilet**
	goose bumps *(pl)* [ˈguːs ˌbʌmps] *(AE)*	Gänsehaut	= *BE* **goose pimples** *(pl)*
	narrator [nəˈreɪtə]	Erzähler/in	Ⓕ le narrateur Ⓛ narrator

Unit 4: Hermann says 'Willkommen'

p.76	**winemaking** [ˈwaɪnmeɪkɪŋ]	Weinherstellung		
	wine [waɪn]	Wein		
p.78/A 1	**elementary school** [ˌelɪˈmentri skuːl]	*(USA)* Grundschule *(für 6-bis 11-Jährige)*	Ⓕ une école élémentaire	
	kindergarten [ˈkɪndəgɑːtn]	Kindergarten; *(USA)* Vorschule *(für 5-bis 6-Jährige)*		
p.78/A 2	**health** [helθ]	Gesundheit; Gesundheitslehre	noun: **health** – adjective: **healthy**	
	study hall [ˈstʌdi hɔːl]	Zeit zum selbstständigen Lernen in der Schule	At Hermann High, students have ~ **hall** every day after lunch.	
	government [ˈgʌvənmənt]	Regierung *(als Schulfach etwa: Staatskunde)*	Ⓕ le gouvernement	Ⓛ gubernatio
p.78/A 3	**bulletin board** [ˈbʊlətɪn bɔːd] *(AE)* **notice board** [ˈnəʊtɪs bɔːd] *(BE)*	schwarzes Brett, Anschlagtafel	a **bulletin board** *(AE)* / **notice board** *(BE)*	
	extracurricular activities *(or:* **extracurriculars***) (pl)* [ˌekstrəkəˈrɪkjələz]	schulische Angebote außerhalb des regulären Unterrichts, oft als Arbeitsgemeinschaften		
	clothing *(no pl)* [ˈkləʊðɪŋ]	Kleidung	❗ **Clothing** is more formal than **clothes**. To describe one thing that someone wears, you use **piece**: 'You're wearing a strange **piece of clothing**. What is it called?'	
	tight [taɪt]	eng; fest	Do the shoes fit? – No, they're too ~. He held her ~, kissed her and said, 'I love you'.	
	see-through [ˈsiːθruː]	durchsichtig		
	(to) **tear** [teə], **tore** [tɔː], **torn** [tɔːn]	(zer)reißen	My jeans **tore** as I climbed over the fence. I was so angry that I **tore** the letter into pieces.	
	(to) **break** a rule [breɪk], **broke** [brəʊk], **broken** [ˈbrəʊkən]	gegen eine Regel verstoßen	She was sent home because she **had broken** one of the school rules.	
	(to) **obey** [əˈbeɪ]	gehorchen; sich halten an	I'm so good: I always ~ my parents. If you don't ~ the rules, we won't play with you. Ⓛ oboedire	
	copy [ˈkɒpi]	Kopie, Abschrift	Don't write it all out – make a ~.	Ⓕ la copie
	available [əˈveɪləbl]	erhältlich; vorrätig	Tickets for the concert will be ~ next week.	

US school grades

+	A	**excellent** [ˈeksələnt]	ausgezeichnet, hervorragend
↑	B	**good**	gut
	C	**average** *(n; adj)* [ˈævərɪdʒ]	Durchschnitt; durchschnittlich
↓	D	**below average**	unter Durchschnitt; unterdurchschnittlich
−	F	**failure** *(n)* [ˈfeɪljə]	ungenügend

p.79/A 6	**hallway** [ˈhɔːlweɪ] *(AE)*	Korridor, Gang	
	meeting [ˈmiːtɪŋ]	Versammlung, Besprechung	The drama club **~s** take place every Monday.

Using the simple present to talk about the future

We can use the simple present for future events which are part of a timetable or a calendar.

The meeting **starts** in ten minutes.	Die Versammlung fängt in zehn Minuten an.
When **do** you **have** PE tomorrow?	Wann hast du morgen Sport?
The next train to London **leaves** at 8.45.	Der nächste Zug nach London fährt um 8.45 Uhr ab.

	little [ˈlɪtl]	wenig	❗ This plant needs very **~** water. (= nicht viel) This plant needs **a little** water. (= ein bisschen)
	(to) **expect** [ɪkˈspekt]	erwarten, annehmen, vermuten	How many guests are you **~ing**? Ⓛ exspectare Ann is late. I **~** she has missed the bus again.

little („wenig") – few („wenige")

- **little** + uncountable nouns: **a** <u>little</u> time, money, water, bread, …
 <u>wenig</u> + nicht zählbare Nomen: ein <u>wenig</u>/ein <u>bisschen</u> Zeit, Geld, Wasser, Brot, …
- **few** + plural of countable nouns: **a** <u>few</u> hours, dollars, bottles, sandwiches, …
 <u>wenige</u> + Plural von zählbaren Nomen: <u>wenige</u>/ein <u>paar</u> Stunden, Dollar, Flaschen, Sandwiches, …

Are you hungry? We've got **<u>a little</u>** bacon and **<u>a few</u>** eggs. … ein wenig/ein bisschen Schinken und ein paar Eier

Comparison (Steigerung):

little – less – (the) least

I've got so **little** hair. … so wenig Haare	I've got **less** hair. … weniger Haare	I've got **the least** hair. … die wenigsten Haare

	(to) **be a farmer, teacher, …**	Bauer/Bäuerin, Lehrer/in, … werden	❗ When you talk about lines of work, you usually use **be** for the German 'werden': What do you want to **be** when you're older? Are you going to **be** a farmer like your dad?
	experience [ɪkˈspɪəriəns]	Erfahrung; Erlebnis	He didn't get the job. He hasn't got enough **~**. How was your trip to Italy? – It was a great **~**. Ⓕ l'expérience *(f)* Ⓛ experientia
	experienced [ɪkˈspɪəriənst]	erfahren	I've worked for eight companies, so I'm very **~**.
	(to) **apply (for** sth.**)** [əˈplaɪ]	sich bewerben (um/für etwas); etwas beantragen	Did your sister **~ for** the job? – Yes, but she didn't get it.
	(to) **get involved (in)** [ɪnˈvɒlvd]	sich engagieren (für, bei); sich beteiligen (an)	Alex **got ~ in** the drama club soon after he started school.
	just as … as …	genauso … wie …	He plays football **~ as** beautifully **as** he sings.
p.80/A 8	**ancestor** [ˈænsestə]	Vorfahr/in	Caitlin's **~s** came to New York from Ireland.
	homeland [ˈhəʊmlænd]	Heimat(land)	He was born in London and lives in Germany, but still thinks England is his **~**.
	heritage [ˈherɪtɪdʒ]	(Kultur-, Natur-)Erbe	Ⓕ l'héritage *(m)* Ⓛ hereditas
	throughout October [θruːˈaʊt]	den ganzen Oktober hindurch	I didn't go away last summer. I stayed at home **~** the school holidays.

Vocabulary 4

p.81/A 10	**scrapbook** ['skræpbʊk]	Sammelalbum	
	sister city ['sɪstə ˌsɪti] *(AE)*	Partnerstadt	= *BE* **twin town**
	(to) **pass** sth. **on** [ˌpɑːs ˈɒn]	etwas weiterleiten, -geben	Please ~ **on** this e-mail to your friends. I'll read the book and ~ it **on** to my sister.
	move [muːv]	Umzug	Is your new flat ready? – Yes, the ~ is on Monday.
	(to) **work out** [ˌwɜːk ˈaʊt]	klappen, gutgehen	Gordon's job in London didn't ~ ~, so he moved back to Scotland.
			❗ (to) **work out** = klappen, gut verlaufen (to) **work** sth. **out** = etwas herausfinden

actually

The word **actually** is difficult to translate. Possible translations are *eigentlich*, *tatsächlich*, *übrigens* and *zwar*. Sometimes it cannot be translated at all.

You can use it to show a difference between how you expected something and how it is:
I worried that it wouldn't work out. **Actually**, it's the best thing I've ever done.
I didn't think I would enjoy the party, but it was **actually** fun.

You can use it to stress something:
Have you **actually** met the Queen? – Yes, I've **actually** talked to her. I went to her party last year.
I haven't **actually** finished the book, but I know you would like it.

You can use it to tell someone politely that they are wrong:
I'm not English, **actually**: I'm Scottish.
Oh no, you don't smoke, do you? – I do **actually**. Sorry.

You can use it to tell someone something that is embarrassing *(peinlich)*:
My favourite city in Spain is Madrid. – I've never **actually** been to Spain, so I can't say.
When are you going to give me my MP3 player back? – **Actually**, I can't. I've lost it.

	tough [tʌf]	schwierig, hart	Starting a new job is a ~ thing for many people. Cowboys are ~ men.
	(to) **adjust (to** sth.**)** [əˈdʒʌst]	sich (an etwas) gewöhnen	I needed three months to ~ **to** life in the city.
p.85/P 3	**Sincerely** [sɪnˈsɪəli] *(AE)*	Mit freundlichen Grüßen	

Beginning and ending letters

Writing ...	You start with:	You end with	and:
to good friends and family	Dear Mum / Uncle Tom / John	Love / Lots of love	your first name
to other friends	Dear Robert/Katrina	Best wishes / All the best	your first name
formal letters – if you know the person's name	Dear Ms Jones / Mr Smith / Dr Brown	Yours sincerely *(BE)* Sincerely *(AE)*	both names
formal letters – if you don't know the person's name	Dear Sir or Madam *(BE)* To whom [huːm] it may concern [kənˈsɜːn] *(AE)*	Yours faithfully [ˈfeɪθfəli] *(BE)* Sincerely / Sincerely yours / Yours truly [ˈtruːli] *(all AE)*	both names

Sometimes a comma is used after the beginning (Dear John**,**) or after the ending (Love**,** Ann).
When you write to friends and family, you can write kisses after your name: **xxx** *(BE)* and **xoxo** *(AE)*.

p.86/P 6	**mustard** [ˈmʌstəd]	Senf	Ⓕ la moutarde
	butter [ˈbʌtə]	Butter	
p.87/P 8	(to) **make sure** that ...	sich vergewissern, dass ...	Revise your work and **make** ~ that you haven't made any mistakes.

	(to) **suffer (from)** ['sʌfə]	leiden (an/unter)	I don't like to see animals ~**ing**. I sometimes ~ **from** bad earaches. (F) souffrir
p.89/P 11	**summary** ['sʌməri]	Zusammenfassung	What happens in the film? Give me a quick ~.
	original (n) [əˈrɪdʒənl]	Original	He understands English so well that he can read Shakespeare in the ~. **!** stress: **original** [-'---]; pronunciation: **original** [dʒ]
	original (adj) [əˈrɪdʒənl]	Original-, ursprünglich	a film in the **original version** ['vɜːʃn] = ein Film in der Originalfassung

Angus Bethune's moment

p.90	**fat** [fæt]	dick	

a fat cat

	incredible [ɪnˈkredɪbl]	unglaublich	This is ~! I don't believe it! (L) incredibilis
	reflex ['riːfleks]	Reflex	**!** stress: **reflex** ['--] (F) le réflexe
	smart [smɑːt] (bes. AE)	schlau	= **clever**
	(to) **elect** sb. sth. [ɪˈlekt]	jn. zu etwas wählen	They ~ed her leader of the youth club. = **!** … wählten sie **zur** Leiterin … (L) eligere
	election [ɪˈlekʃn]	Wahl (von Kandidaten bei einer Abstimmung)	(F) une élection
	somehow ['sʌmhaʊ]	irgendwie	I don't know how to do it, but I'll do it ~.
	(to) **vote for/against** sb./sth. [vəʊt]	für/gegen jn./etwas stimmen	I ~d **for** the man who lost the election. She ~d **against** building the new road.
	(to) **fall in love (with** sb.**)**	sich verlieben (in jn.)	My best friend has **fallen in** ~ **with** my sister.
	dentist ['dentɪst]	Zahnarzt, -ärztin	
	gym [dʒɪm]	Sport-/Turnhalle; Fitnessstudio	We have PE in the school ~. My dad goes to the ~ because he feels too fat. (F) le gymnase (L) gymnasium
p.91	**drunk** [drʌŋk]	betrunken	If you drink too much wine, you'll get ~.
	I can take it.	Ich halt's aus. / Ich kann's aushalten.	
	embarrassed [ɪmˈbærəst]	verlegen	I was the only student who got an 'F' in the test and felt very ~. (F) embarrassé,e
	embarrassing [ɪmˈbærəsɪŋ]	peinlich	It was very ~ for me and I went terribly red.
	heaven ['hevn]	Himmel (im religiösen Sinn)	**!** (clouds) in the **sky** = (Wolken) am Himmel (to) go to **heaven** = in den Himmel kommen
	(to) **throw up** [ˌθrəʊ ˈʌp], **threw up, thrown up** (infml)	sich übergeben	The man was so drunk that he **threw** ~ in the taxi.
	(to) **do** sb. **a favour** ['feɪvə]	jm. einen Gefallen tun	Could you **do** me a ~ and post this letter for me?
p.92	(to) **clap (-pp-)** [klæp]	(Beifall) klatschen	At the end, the audience ~**ped** for ten minutes.

Tipps zum Wörterlernen → S.155 · Englische Laute → S.290 · Alphabetische Wörterverzeichnisse → S.222–258 / S.259–290

earthquake [ˈɜːθkweɪk]	Erdbeben		
(to) **protest** (against/about) [prəˈtest]	protestieren (gegen)	noun: **protest** [ˈprəʊtest] = Protest – verb: (to) **protest** [prəˈtest] = protestieren	
opponent [əˈpəʊnənt]	Gegner/in	Germany's ~s in the final were Spain.	
fist [fɪst]	Faust	a fist	

Unit 5: Atlanta rising

p.98	civil war [ˌsɪvl ˈwɔː]	Bürgerkrieg	The English **Civil War** (1642–1649) was fought between the King and Parliament.
	freeway [ˈfriːweɪ] (AE) motorway [ˈməʊtəweɪ] (BE)	Autobahn	There are strict speed limits on American **freeways** and British **motorways**.
	grid [grɪd]	Gitter; Rechteckschema	The streets in lots of cities in the USA (and some in Europe) were built as a ~ system.
p.99	Olympic Games [əˌlɪmpɪk ˈgeɪmz]	Olympische Spiele	
	civil rights (pl) [ˌsɪvl ˈraɪts]	Bürgerrechte	
	right [raɪt]	Recht	! (to) **be right** = Recht haben, im Recht sein
	mayor [ˈmeə]	Bürgermeister/in	! pronunciation: **mayor** [meə] (F) le/la maire
	network [ˈnetwɜːk]	(Fernseh-/Radio-)Sender(netz)	
p.100/A 1	news agency [ˈnjuːz ˌeɪdʒənsi]	Nachrichtenagentur	
	programme [ˈprəʊgræm] (BE) program (AE)	(Fernseh-/Radio-)Sendung	! **programme** (BE) / **program** (AE) = 1. Programm – a research ~, a theatre ~ 2. Sendung – Did you watch the ~ about R.E.M. on MTV last night?
	drama [ˈdrɑːmə]	Fernsehspiel; Drama	
	(to) **broadcast, broadcast, broadcast** [ˈbrɔːdkɑːst]	senden; (eine Sendung) ausstrahlen	CNN started ~ing in 1980. 'Mr Bean' was first ~ in 1990.
	(to) **tune** a radio to a station [tjuːn]	ein Radio auf einen Sender einstellen	You're ~d to Radio Bristol. Here is the news. (Sie hören gerade …)
p.101/A 4	You bet! [bet] (infml)	Aber klar! / Und ob!	Did you enjoy your trip to Paris? – You ~!
	you **should have** asked	du hättest fragen sollen	I said yes but it was a mistake. I **should have** said no.
	besides [bɪˈsaɪdz]	außerdem	It's too late to go to the cinema. And ~, I've already seen the film.
	What's up? [ˌwɒts ˈʌp]	Was ist los?	= **What's the matter**?
	(to) **shoot** [ʃuːt], **shot, shot** [ʃɒt]	(Film) drehen; fotografieren	The new Bond film was **shot** in Panama. She was **shot** for the front page of Vogue.

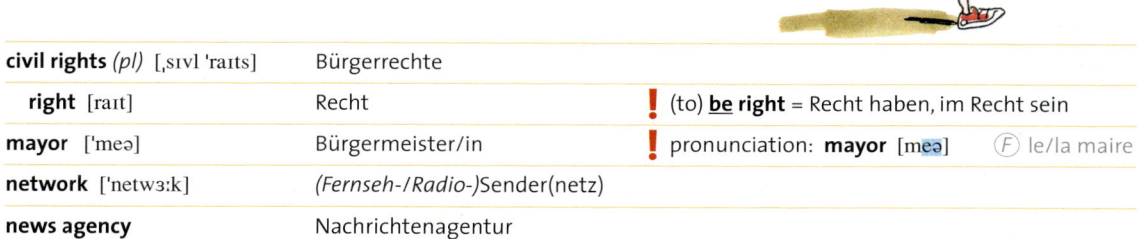

5 Vocabulary

	(to) **drop** sb. **off** (-pp-) [drɒp]	jn. absetzen *(aussteigen lassen)*	He **~ped** her **off** at the station.
	(to) **introduce** sb. **to** sth. [ˌɪntrəˈdjuːs]	jn. in etwas einführen	This book **~s** the reader **to** a difficult topic. noun: **introduction** – verb: (to) **introduce** ⒡ introduire ⓛ introducere
	(to) **participate** (**in**) [pɑːˈtɪsɪpeɪt]	teilnehmen (an)	= (to) **take part** (**in**) ⒡ participer (à) ⓛ participare
p.101/A 5	**bone** [bəʊn]	Knochen	There are over 200 **~s** in the human body.
p.102/A 6	(to) **be on display** [dɪsˈpleɪ]	ausgestellt sein	❗ stress: **display** [-ˈ-]
	anniversary [ˌænɪˈvɜːsəri]	Jahrestag	May 8th is the **anniversary** of John's death. (… Johns Todestag) ⒡ un anniversaire ⓛ anniversarium
	impressed [ɪmˈprest]	beeindruckt	Jo wrote a great essay. His teacher was really **~**. ⒡ impressionné/e
	archive [ˈɑːkaɪv]	Archiv	❗ stress: **archive** [ˈ--]; pronunciation: **archive** [k]
p.102/A 7	**segregation** [ˌsegrɪˈgeɪʃn]	(Rassen-)Trennung	**Segregation** in South Africa lasted for 40 years and was called 'Apartheid'.
	(to) **segregate** [ˈsegrɪgeɪt]	trennen *(nach Rasse, Religion, Geschlecht)*	Some people say that boys and girls learn better if they're **~d** at school. ⓛ segregare
	equal [ˈiːkwəl]	gleich	⒡ égal,e ⓛ aequalis
	non-violent [ˌnɒn ˈvaɪələnt]	gewaltlos, gewaltfrei	**non-violent** ◀▶ **violent**
	violent [ˈvaɪələnt]	gewalttätig; gewaltsam	⒡ violent,e ⓛ violentus
	violence [ˈvaɪələns]	Gewalt; Gewalttätigkeit	My dad says there's too much sex and **~** on TV.
	boycott [ˈbɔɪkɒt]	Boykott	We organized a **~** of the company because it supports violence in Africa. ❗ stress: **boycott** [ˈ--]
	march [mɑːtʃ]	Marsch, Demonstration	
	(to) **judge** sb. (**by**) [dʒʌdʒ]	jn. beurteilen, einschätzen (nach)	You shouldn't **~** people **by** their clothes.
	skin [skɪn]	Haut	I need some face cream. My **~** is very dry.
	but [bʌt]	sondern	He not only has two cars **but** also owns a boat. (nicht nur …, sondern auch …) ❗ **but** = 1. aber – I like apples **but** not bananas. 2. sondern – I'm not American **but** Canadian.

Tipps zum Wörterlernen → S.155 · Englische Laute → S.290 · Alphabetische Wörterverzeichnisse → S.222–258 / S.259–290

Vocabulary 5

	character ['kærəktə]	Charakter, Persönlichkeit	! stress: character ['---]	
p.103/A 8	reliable [rɪ'laɪəbl]	zuverlässig		
	(to) sort [sɔːt]	einteilen; sortieren	Please help me to ~ the clothes for the washing machine. Dark stuff on the left, please. We ~ed the ripe apples from the unripe ones.	
	bracket ['brækɪt]	Klammer (in Texten)	( ) = round brackets; [ ] = square brackets	
	footnote ['fʊtnəʊt]	Fußnote		
p.103/A 9	parking lot ['pɑːkɪŋ lɒt] (AE)	Parkplatz (für viele Autos)	= car park (BE)	(F) le parking
	(to) delay [dɪ'leɪ]	aufhalten	Sorry I'm late: I was ~ed at the office. Bad weather ~ed our plane for two hours.	
	delay [dɪ'leɪ]	Verspätung	We started after a ten-minute ~.	
	explosion [ɪk'spləʊʒn]	Explosion	! stress: explosion [-'--]	(F) une explosion
	on the scene [siːn]	vor Ort, zur Stelle	A doctor was called and he arrived on the ~ five minutes later.	
p.106/P 1	departure [dɪ'pɑːtʃə]	Abfahrt; Abflug	departure ◄► arrival	(F) le départ
	old-fashioned [ˌəʊld'fæʃnd]	altmodisch	old-fashioned ◄► trendy	
p.107/P 4	fiction ['fɪkʃn]	Prosaliteratur; Belletristik	Does he only read biographies and history books? – No, he likes ~ too, like *Animal Farm*.	
	non-fiction ['nɒnˌfɪkʃn]	Sachliteratur	Does she only read plays and poems? – No, she likes ~-~ too, like biographies.	
	characteristic [ˌkærəktə'rɪstɪk]	(charakteristisches) Merkmal	Friendliness is a very nice ~.	
	(to) inform sb. (about/ of sth.) [ɪn'fɔːm]	jn. (über etwas) informieren	verb: (to) inform – noun: information	
	(to) deal with sb./sth. [diːl], dealt, dealt [delt]	sich mit jm./etwas beschäftigen; handeln von etwas	The film ~s with the life of a very fat dog.	
	(to) entertain sb. [ˌentə'teɪn]	jn. unterhalten	noun: entertainment – verb: (to) entertain	
	novel ['nɒvl]	Roman	The *Harry Potter* books are a series of seven ~s.	
p.108/P 5	(to) interest sb. ['ɪntrəst]	jn. interessieren	! sich interessieren (für) = (to) be interested (in)	

Verbs and nouns with the same form

p.108/P 6	(to) cost cost	kosten Preis, Kosten	(to) protest [-'-] protest ['--]	protestieren Protest	
	(to) cut (-tt-) cut	schneiden Schnitt	(to) scream scream	schreien Schrei	
	(to) delay delay	aufhalten Verzögerung	(to) smoke smoke	rauchen Rauch	
	(to) fight fight	kämpfen Kampf	(to) sort sort	sortieren Sorte	
	(to) hug (-gg-) hug	umarmen Umarmung	(to) support support	unterstützen; Fan von ... sein Unterstützung	
	(to) paint paint	malen Farbe, Lack	(to) talk talk	reden Rede, Gespräch; Vortrag, Referat	
	(to) program(me) program(me)	programmieren; planen Programm; Sendung	(to) taste taste	schmecken; kosten, probieren Geschmack	

p.110/P 9	**funeral** ['fju:nərəl]	Trauerfeier	ⓛ funus (*Gen.* funeris)
	riot ['raɪət]	Aufruhr, Krawall	The high price of rice in India has led to ~s.
p.110/P 10	**identity** [aɪ'dentɪti]	Identität	Ⓕ l'identité (*f*)

Melba's story

p.111	**slavery** ['sleɪvəri]	Sklaverei	
	apart [ə'pɑ:t]	voneinander getrennt, auseinander	Keep your dog and my cat ~. They don't get along.
	separate ['seprət]	getrennt, separat, extra	The library has a ~ room for children's books. ❗ stress: **se**parate ['--] Ⓕ séparé/e
	court [kɔ:t]	Gericht(shof)	Do you have to appear in ~ if you break traffic rules? Ⓕ la cour
p.112	**contact** ['kɒntækt]	Kontakt	❗ stress: **con**tact ['--]
	merry-go-round ['merɪɡəʊ,raʊnd]	Karussell	a **merry-go-round**
	sir [sɜ:]	Sir (*höfliche Anrede, z.B. für Kunden/Vorgesetzte/Lehrer*)	Can I help you, ~? – No thanks, I'm just looking.
	as if [əz_'ɪf]	als ob	Those flowers look ~ ~ they need water.
	(to) **be terrified (of)** ['terɪfaɪd]	schreckliche Angst haben (vor)	Everyone was ~ when the bank robber pulled out a gun.
	immediately [ɪ'mi:dɪətli]	sofort	My dog usually comes ~ when I call her. Ⓕ immédiatement
	(to) **volunteer** [,vɒlən'tɪə]	sich freiwillig melden, sich bereit erklären	Hundreds of doctors ~ed to help the earthquake victims. ⓛ voluntarius
	step [step]	Stufe	step — stairs
p.113	(to) **block** [blɒk]	blockieren, (ver)sperren	A tree fell down in the storm and ~ed the road.
	(to) **hang** sb. [hæŋ]	jn. hängen	❗ (to) **hang** a picture – hung – hung (to) **hang** sb. – hanged – hanged
	disappointed (with sb./sth.**)** [,dɪsə'pɔɪntɪd]	enttäuscht (von jm./etwas)	I'm ~ **with** you. I know you can do better. She was ~ **with** the result of the game.
	(to) **disappoint** sb. [,dɪsə'pɔɪnt]	jn. enttäuschen	He didn't get the job and that ~ed all of us.
	(to) **smuggle** ['smʌɡl]	schmuggeln	He got a 10-year sentence for **smuggling** heroin.
	cruel ['kru:əl]	grausam	Don't you think it's ~ to keep animals in cages? Ⓕ cruel/le ⓛ crudelis
	(to) **kick** sb. [kɪk]	jn. treten	He ~ed his opponent instead of ~ing the ball and was given a yellow card.

Tipps zum Wörterlernen → S.155 · Englische Laute → S.290 · Alphabetische Wörterverzeichnisse → S.222–258 / S.259–290

(to) **spit** (at sb.) (-tt-) [spɪt], **spat, spat** [spæt]	(jn. an)spucken	
wrist [rɪst]	Handgelenk	I wear my watch on my right ~.
(to) **force** sb. **to do** sth. [fɔːs]	jn. dazu bringen / jn. zwingen, etwas zu tun	You can't ~ him **to** eat if he doesn't want to.
(to) **splash** [splæʃ]	spritzen	He's **~ing** water on his face.
acid ['æsɪd]	Säure	(F) l'acide (m)
p.114 (to) **graduate** (AE) ['grædʒueɪt]	den Schulabschluss machen	(to) **graduate** (BE) = den Hochschulabschluss machen
(to) **be pleased** [pliːzd]	sich freuen	I got good marks in Art. My parents **are** very ~.
(to) **solve** [sɒlv]	lösen	The problem was very difficult but in the end we **~d** it. (L) solvere
resources (pl) [rɪ'zɔːsɪz, rɪ'sɔːsɪz]	Mittel, Ressourcen	
crisis ['kraɪsɪs], pl **crises** ['kraɪsiːs]	Krise	(F) la crise (L) crisis
reaction (to) [riː'ækʃn]	Reaktion (auf)	Her quick **~s** saved the man's life. (F) la réaction

Dictionary (English – German)

Das Dictionary besteht aus zwei alphabetischen Wörterlisten:

Englisch – Deutsch (S. 222–258)
Deutsch – Englisch (S. 259–290).

Das **English – German Dictionary** enthält den Wortschatz der Bände 1 bis 4 von *English G 21*.
Wenn du wissen möchtest, was ein Wort bedeutet, wie man es ausspricht oder wie es genau geschrieben wird, kannst du hier nachschlagen.

Im **English – German Dictionary** werden folgende **Abkürzungen und Symbole** verwendet:

jm. = jemandem	sb. = somebody	pl = plural (Mehrzahl)	AE = American English
jn. = jemanden	sth. = something	no pl = no plural	infml = informal

° Mit diesem Kringel sind Wörter markiert, die nicht zum Lernwortschatz gehören.
▶ Der Pfeil verweist auf Kästchen im Vocabulary (S. 190–221), in denen du weitere Informationen zu diesem Wort findest.

Die **Fundstellenangaben** zeigen, wo ein Wort zum ersten Mal vorkommt.
Die Ziffern in Klammern bezeichnen Seitenzahlen:

I = Band A1 • II = Band A2 • III = Band A3 • IV = Band A4
IV Intro (9)   = Band 4, Introduction, Seite 9
IV Intro (11/195) = Band 4, Introduction, Seite 195 (im Vocabulary, zu Seite 11)
IV 1 (15)   = Band 4, Unit 1, Seite 15
IV 1 (29/200)   = Band 4, Unit 1, Seite 200 (im Vocabulary, zu Seite 29)

Tipps zur Arbeit mit dem **English – German Dictionary** findest du im Skills File auf Seite 156.

1

1950s [ˌnaɪntiːnˈfɪftiz] die Fünfzigerjahre (des 20. Jahrhunderts) III
9/11 [ˌnaɪn_ɪˈlevn] Nine Eleven (der Terroranschlag am 11. September 2001) IV 1 (17)

A

a [ə]
1. ein, eine I
2. **once/twice a week** einmal/zweimal pro Woche III • **a bit** ein bisschen, etwas II • **a few** ein paar, einige II • **a lot (of)** eine Menge, viel, viele II • **He likes her a lot.** Er mag sie sehr. I
abbey [ˈæbi] Abtei II
abbreviation [əˌbriːviˈeɪʃn] Abkürzung IV 2 (38)
able [ˈeɪbl]: **be able to do sth.** etwas tun können; fähig sein/in der Lage sein, etwas zu tun II
about [əˈbaʊt]
1. über I
2. ungefähr II
ask about sth. nach etwas fragen I • **know about sth.** von etwas wissen; über etwas Bescheid wissen II • **learn about sth.** etwas über etwas erfahren, etwas über etwas herausfinden II • **This is about Mr Green.** Es geht um Mr Green. I • **What about …? 1.** Was ist mit …? / Und …? I; **2.** Wie wär's mit …? I • **What are you talking about?** Wovon redest du? I • **What was the best thing about …?** Was war das Beste an …? II
above [əˈbʌv] über, oberhalb (von) III
°**abridge** [əˈbrɪdʒ] kürzen
abroad [əˈbrɔːd] im Ausland II
go abroad ins Ausland gehen/fahren II
absolutely [ˌæbsəˈluːt] absolut, völlig IV 1 (30)
accent [ˈæksənt] Akzent II
°**accept** [əkˈsept] akzeptieren
accident [ˈæksɪdənt] Unfall II
accommodation [əˌkɒməˈdeɪʃn] Unterkunft IV Intro (8)
accurate [ˈækjərət] genau, akkurat III
achieve [əˈtʃiːv] erreichen, erzielen, zustande bringen IV 2 (54)
achieve an end ein Ziel erreichen IV 2 (54)
acid [ˈæsɪd] Säure IV 5 (113)
acrobat [ˈækrəbæt] Akrobat/in III
across [əˈkrɒs]
1. (quer) über II
2. hinüber, herüber III
act [ækt] aufführen, spielen I
action [ˈækʃn] Action; Handlung, Tat III
active [ˈæktɪv] aktiv III
activist [ˈæktəvɪst] Aktivist/in IV 5 (102)
activity [ækˈtɪvəti] Aktivität, Tätigkeit I
actor [ˈæktə] Schauspieler/in II
actually [ˈæktʃuəli] eigentlich, tatsächlich, übrigens, zwar IV 4 (90)
▶ S. 215 actually
ad [æd] Anzeige, Inserat; (im Fernsehen) Werbespot IV 3 (61)
AD [ˌeɪ ˈdiː] (from Latin: Anno Domini) nach Christus III
°**adapt** [əˈdæpt] adaptieren
add (to) [æd] hinzufügen, ergänzen, addieren (zu) I
°**address** [əˈdres]: **address an issue** sich mit einer Frage/Aufgabe befassen
address [əˈdres] Anschrift, Adresse II
adjust (to sth.) [əˈdʒʌst] sich (an etwas) gewöhnen, sich (auf etwas) einstellen IV 4 (81)
admire [ədˈmaɪə] bewundern IV 3 (56)
°**admission** [ədˈmɪʃn] Eintritt
adult [ˈædʌlt] Erwachsene(r) III
adult life das Leben als Erwachsene/r III

°**advance purchase** [əd‚vɑ:ns 'pɜ:tʃɪs] Vorverkauf
advantage (over sb./sth.) [əd'vɑ:ntɪdʒ] Vorteil (gegenüber jm./etwas) IV 3 (58)
adventure [əd'ventʃə] Abenteuer II
advert ['ædvɜ:t] Anzeige, Inserat; *(im Fernsehen)* Werbespot II
°**advice** [əd'vaɪs] Rat
°**advise sb. to do sth.** [əd'vaɪz] jm. raten, etwas zu tun
afraid [ə'freɪd]
1. **be afraid (of)** Angst haben (vor) I
2. **I'm afraid** leider II
°**African-American** [‚æfrɪkən_ə'merɪkən] afro-amerikanisch
after ['ɑ:ftə] nach *(zeitlich)* I • **after that** danach I
after ['ɑ:ftə] nachdem II
afternoon [‚ɑ:ftə'nu:n] Nachmittag I • **in the afternoon** nachmittags, am Nachmittag I • **on Friday afternoon** freitagnachmittags, am Freitagnachmittag I
°**afterwards** ['ɑ:ftəwədz] danach
again [ə'gen] wieder; noch einmal I • **now and again** ab und zu, von Zeit zu Zeit III
against [ə'genst] gegen I
age [eɪdʒ] Alter III • **at (the age of) 16** mit 16; im Alter von 16 III
°**aged** [eɪdʒd] im Alter von
agency ['eɪdʒənsi]: **news agency** Nachrichtenagentur IV 5 (100)
ago [ə'gəʊ]: **a minute ago** vor einer Minute I
agree [ə'gri:]: **agree (on)** sich einigen (auf) I • **agree (with sb.)** (jm.) zustimmen I
°**agriculture** ['ægrɪkʌltʃə] Landwirtschaft IV 2 (38)
aim [eɪm] Ziel II
°**ain't** [eɪnt] *(infml)* = **isn't** • **there ain't no** *(infml)* = **there isn't any**
air [eə] Luft II
airport ['eəpɔ:t] Flughafen III
alarm clock [ə'lɑ:m klɒk] Wecker I
album ['ælbəm] Album II
alcohol ['ælkəhɒl] Alkohol III
°**algebra** ['ældʒɪbrə] Algebra
alive [ə'laɪv]: **be alive** leben, am Leben sein IV 2 (53) • °**alive and kicking** gesund und munter **keep sth. alive** etwas am Leben halten IV 2 (80)
all [ɔ:l] alle; alles I • **2 all** 2 beide (2:2 unentschieden) III • **all day** den ganzen Tag (lang) I • **all over the world** auf der ganzen Welt III • **all right** [ɔ:l 'raɪt] gut, in Ordnung II • **All the best** Viele Grüße

IV 4 (85/215) • **all the time** die ganze Zeit I • **all we have to do now ...** alles, was wir jetzt (noch) tun müssen, ... II • **from all over the world** aus der ganzen Welt II • **This is all wrong.** Das ist ganz falsch. I • **all year round** das ganze Jahr hindurch IV 4 (80)
▶ S.215 Beginning and ending letters
°**all-black/all-white school** Schule, die ausschließlich von Schwarzen/Weißen besucht wird
allergic (to sth.) [ə'lɜ:dʒɪk] allergisch (gegen etwas) III
allow [ə'laʊ] erlauben, zulassen II • **be allowed to do sth.** [ə'laʊd] etwas tun dürfen II
almost ['ɔ:lməʊst] fast, beinahe II
alone [ə'ləʊn] allein I • °**leave sb./sth. alone** jn. in Ruhe lassen; jn. allein lassen
along [ə'lɒŋ]: **along the road** entlang der Straße / die Straße entlang II • **get along** zurechtkommen IV 3 (58)
alphabet ['ælfəbet] Alphabet I
already [ɔ:l'redi] schon, bereits II
also ['ɔ:lsəʊ] auch IV 1 (16) • **not only ... but also ...** nicht nur ... sondern auch ... IV 5 (102/218)
although [ɔ:l'ðəʊ] obwohl III
always ['ɔ:lweɪz] immer I
am [‚eɪ_'em]: **7 am** 7 Uhr morgens/vormittags I
amazing [ə'meɪzɪŋ] erstaunlich, unglaublich II
ambulance ['æmbjələns] Krankenwagen III
°**Americana** [ə‚merɪ'kɑ:nə] *Sammelbegriff für alles, was als „typisch amerikanisch" empfunden wird*
American football [ə‚merɪkən 'fʊtbɔ:l] Football II
among [ə'mʌŋ] unter, zwischen (mehreren Personen oder Dingen) IV 2 (53)
an [ən] ein, eine I
ancestor ['ænsestə] Vorfahr/in IV 4 (80)
and [ənd, ænd] und I • **and now for** und jetzt ... (kündigt ein neues Thema an) III • **nice and cool/clean/...** schön kühl/sauber/... I
angel ['eɪndʒl] Engel II
°**Anglo** ['æŋgləʊ] *Person europäischer Abstammung*
angry (about sth./with sb.) ['æŋgri] wütend, böse (über etwas/auf jn.) II
animal ['ænɪml] Tier I
anniversary [‚ænɪ'vɜ:səri] Jahrestag IV 5 (102) • **anniversary of sb.'s death** Todestag IV 5 (102/218)

announce [ə'naʊns] bekanntgeben III
announcement [ə'naʊnsmənt] Bekanntgabe, Ankündigung; Durchsage; Ansage II
°**annoying** [ə'nɔɪɪŋ] ärgerlich
anorak ['ænəræk] Anorak, Windjacke III
another [ə'nʌðə] ein(e) andere(r, s); noch ein(e) I • **another 70 metres** weitere 70 Meter, noch 70 Meter II
answer ['ɑ:nsə] (be)antworten I • **answer (the phone)** rangehen (ans Telefon) IV 1 (28)
answer (to) ['ɑ:nsə] Antwort (auf) I
antonym ['æntənɪm] Antonym IV 3 (64/210)
any ['eni]: **any ...?** (irgend)welche ...? I • **not (...) any** kein(e) I • **not (...) any more** nicht mehr II
anybody ['enibɒdi]: **anybody?** (irgend)jemand? I • **not (...) anybody** niemand II
anyone ['eniwʌn]: **anyone?** (irgend) jemand? III • **not (...) anyone** niemand III
anything ['eniθɪŋ]: **anything?** (irgend)etwas? II • **Did you do anything special?** Habt ihr irgendetwas Besonderes gemacht? I • **not (...) anything** nichts II
anyway ['eniweɪ]
1. sowieso I
2. trotzdem II
anywhere ['eniweə]: **anywhere?** irgendwo(hin)? II • **not (...) anywhere** nirgendwo(hin) II
apart [ə'pɑ:t] voneinander getrennt, auseinander IV 5 (111)
apartment [ə'pɑ:tmənt] Wohnung IV 1 (17)
appear [ə'pɪə] erscheinen, auftauchen II
appetite ['æpɪtaɪt] Appetit III
apple ['æpl] Apfel I
apply for [ə'plaɪ] sich bewerben (um/für etwas); etwas beantragen IV 4 (79)
appointment [ə'pɔɪntmənt] Termin, Verabredung I
April ['eɪprəl] April I
architect ['ɑ:kɪtekt] Architekt/in III
archive ['ɑ:kaɪv] Archiv IV 5 (102)
°**Arctic** ['ɑ:ktɪk] arktisch
are [ɑ:] bist; sind; seid I • **How are you?** Wie geht es dir/Ihnen/euch? II • **The pencils are 35 p.** Die Bleistifte kosten 35 Pence. I
area ['eəriə] Gebiet, Gegend; Bereich III
argue ['ɑ:gju:] sich streiten, sich zanken I

argument [ˈɑːgjumənt] Streit, Auseinandersetzung II • **have an argument** eine Auseinandersetzung haben, sich streiten II
arm [ɑːm] Arm I
armchair [ˈɑːmtʃeə] Sessel I
army [ˈɑːmi] Armee, Heer IV 2 (53)
around [əˈraʊnd] in … umher, durch, um … (herum) III • **around six** um sechs Uhr herum, gegen sechs III • **around the lake** um den See (herum) III • **around the town** in der Stadt umher, durch die Stadt III • **look around** sich umsehen III • **turn around** sich umdrehen IV 2 (52) • **walk/run/jump around** herumgehen/-rennen/-springen, umhergehen/-rennen/-springen III
°**arrest** [əˈrest] verhaften
arrival [əˈraɪvl] Ankunft III
arrive [əˈraɪv] ankommen, eintreffen II
arrow [ˈærəʊ] Pfeil IV 2 (36) • **bow and arrow** Pfeil und Bogen IV 2 (36/201)
art [ɑːt] Kunst I
article [ˈɑːtɪkl] (Zeitungs-)Artikel I
artificial [ˌɑːtɪˈfɪʃl] künstlich, Kunst- III
°**artist** [ˈɑːtɪst]: **make-up artist** Maskenbildner/in
as [əz, æz]
1. als, während II
2. wie II • **as you know** wie du weißt II
3. **as nice/big/exciting as** so schön/groß/aufregend wie II • **just as … as** ebenso … wie IV 4 (79) • **as soon as** sobald, sowie II
as if [əzˈɪf] als ob IV 5 (112)
ask [ɑːsk] fragen I • **ask about sth.** nach etwas fragen I • **ask questions** Fragen stellen I • **ask sb. for sth.** jn. um etwas bitten II • **ask sb. the way** jn. nach dem Weg fragen II
asleep [əˈsliːp]: **be asleep** schlafen II
°**aspect** [ˈæspekt] Aspekt
assignment [əˈsaɪnmənt] *(AE)* Hausaufgabe IV 3 (59)
assistant [əˈsɪstənt] Verkäufer/in I
at [ət, æt]: **at 7 Hamilton Street** in der Hamiltonstraße 7 I • **at 8.45** um 8.45 I • **at (the age of) 16** mit 16; im Alter von 16 III • **at break** in der Pause *(zwischen Schulstunden)* II • **at home** zu Hause, daheim I • **at last** endlich, schließlich I • **at least** zumindest, wenigstens I • **at night** nachts,

in der Nacht I • **at school** in der Schule I • **at sea** auf See II • **at that table** an dem Tisch (dort) / an den Tisch (dort) I • **at the back (of the room)** hinten, im hinteren Teil (des Zimmers) II • **at the bottom (of)** unten, am unteren Ende (von) II • **at the chemist's/doctor's/hairdresser's** beim Apotheker/Arzt/Friseur III • **at the end (of)** am Ende (von) I • **at the moment** im Moment, gerade, zurzeit I • **at the Shaws' house** im Haus der Shaws, bei den Shaws zu Hause I • **at the station** am Bahnhof I • **at the top (of)** oben, am oberen Ende, an der Spitze (von) I • **at the weekend** am Wochenende I • **at work** bei der Arbeit / am Arbeitsplatz I
°**West 34th Street at Broadway** West-34.-Straße, Ecke Broadway
ate [et, eɪt] *siehe* **eat**
athletics [æθˈletɪks] Leichtathletik III
attack [əˈtæk] Angriff III • **heart attack** Herzinfarkt IV 1 (28)
attack [əˈtæk] angreifen III
attitude to/towards [ˈætɪtjuːd] Haltung gegenüber, Einstellung zu IV 3 (58)
°**attract** [əˈtrækt] locken
attraction [əˈtrækʃn] Attraktion IV 3 (69)
°**audience** [ˈɔːdɪəns] Publikum
°**auditorium** [ˌɔːdɪˈtɔːrɪəm] *(AE)* Hörsaal, Aula
August [ˈɔːgəst] August I
aunt [ɑːnt] Tante I • **auntie** [ˈɑːnti] Tante II
°**author** [ˈɔːθə] Autor/in
auto [ˈɔːtəʊ] *(AE)* Auto, PKW IV Intro (12)
autobiography [ˌɔːtəʊbaɪˈɒgrəfi] Autobiografie IV 5 (112)
autumn [ˈɔːtəm] Herbst I
available [əˈveɪləbl] erhältlich; vorrätig IV 4 (78)
avenue [ˈævənjuː] Allee, Boulevard IV 1 (15)
average [ˈævərɪdʒ] Durchschnitt; durchschnittlich IV 4 (78)
▶ S.213 US school grades
away [əˈweɪ] weg, fort I • **get away from sth./sb.** von etwas / jm. weggehen, sich entfernen III • **put sth. away** wegräumen IV 5 (102)
awesome [ˈɔːsəm] *(AE, infml)* klasse, großartig IV Intro (9)
awful [ˈɔːfl] furchtbar, schrecklich II

B

baby [ˈbeɪbi] Baby I • **have a baby** ein Baby/Kind bekommen II
back [bæk]: **at the back (of the room)** hinten, im hinteren Teil (des Zimmers) II • **back home** zurück zu Hause IV 2 (41)
back door [ˌbæk ˈdɔː] Hintertür II
background [ˈbækgraʊnd] Hintergrund II • **background file** *etwa:* Hintergrundinformation II
bacon [ˈbeɪkən] Schinkenspeck II
bacteria *(pl)* [bækˈtɪərɪə] Bakterien IV 3 (61)
bad [bæd] schlecht, schlimm I
bad timing schlechtes Timing, schlechte Wahl des Zeitpunkts III
°**badly hurt** schwer verletzt
badminton [ˈbædmɪntən] Badminton, Federball I • **badminton racket** Federballschläger III
bag [bæg] Tasche, Beutel, Tüte I; Handtasche III
bagel [ˈbeɪgl] Bagel *(ringförmiges Brötchen)* IV 1 (19)
°**bake sale** [ˈbeɪk seɪl] *Verkauf von Selbstgebackenem zum Zwecke der Geldbeschaffung*
°**balcony** [ˈbælkəni] Balkon
ball [bɔːl]
1. Ball *(zum Sport)* I
2. Ball *(Tanz)* I
balloon [bəˈluːn] Heißluftballon; Luftballon II
banana [bəˈnɑːnə] Banane I
band [bænd] Band, (Musik-)Gruppe I
banjo [ˈbændʒəʊ] Banjo III
bank [bæŋk] Bank, Sparkasse I
bank robber [ˈbæŋk ˌrɒbə] Bankräuber/in I
°**Baptist** [ˈbæptɪst] Baptist/in, baptistisch
bar [bɑː] Bar II
bark [bɑːk] bellen II
baseball [ˈbeɪsbɔːl] Baseball I
baseball cap Baseballmütze II
°**basin** [ˈbeɪsən] Becken
basket [ˈbɑːskɪt] Korb I • **a basket of apples** ein Korb Äpfel I
basketball [ˈbɑːskɪtbɔːl] Basketball I
bass [beɪs] Kontrabass; Bassgitarre III • **bass guitar** Bassgitarre III **double bass** Kontrabass III
bat [bæt]: **table tennis bat** Tischtennisschläger III
bath [bɑːθ] Bad, Badewanne II • **have a bath** baden, ein Bad nehmen II

bathroom ['bɑːθruːm; 'bɑːθrʊm] Badezimmer I
°**battle** ['bætl] Kampf, Schlacht
bay [beɪ] Bucht III
BC [ˌbiː 'siː] v. Chr. IV 2 (38)
be [biː], **was/were, been** sein I • **be into sth.** (infml) etwas mögen III • **be a farmer, a teacher, ...** Bauer/Bäuerin, Lehrer/in, ... werden IV 4 (79)
beach [biːtʃ] Strand II • **on the beach** [biːtʃ] am Strand II
bean [biːn] Bohne IV 2 (37)
bear [beə] Bär II • **teddy bear** Teddybär III
beat [biːt], **beat, beaten** schlagen; besiegen III • °**beat down** herunterbrennen (Sonne)
beaten ['biːtn] siehe **beat**
beautiful ['bjuːtɪfl] schön I
beauty ['bjuːti] Schönheit III
became [bɪ'keɪm] siehe **become**
because [bɪ'kɒz] weil I
because of [bɪ'kɒz_əv] wegen IV 1 (30)
▶ S.200–201 Giving reasons
become [bɪ'kʌm], **became, become** werden II
bed [bed] Bett I • **Bed and Breakfast (B&B)** [ˌbed_ən 'brekfəst] Frühstückspension I • **go to bed** ins Bett gehen I • **put sb. to bed** jn. ins Bett bringen III
bedroom ['bedruːm; 'bedrʊm] Schlafzimmer I • °**bedroom slipper** Hausschuh
°**bee** [biː]: **killer bee** „Killerbiene", Afrikanisierte Honigbiene
°**beef** [biːf] Rindfleisch IV 1 (19)
been [biːn] siehe **be**
before [bɪ'fɔː] vor (zeitlich) I • **the day before yesterday** vorgestern II
before [bɪ'fɔː] bevor II
before [bɪ'fɔː] (vorher) schon mal II
began [bɪ'gæn] siehe **begin**
begin (-nn-) [bɪ'gɪn], **began, begun** beginnen, anfangen (mit) I
beginning [bɪ'gɪnɪŋ] Anfang, Beginn III
begun [bɪ'gʌn] siehe **begin**
°**behave** [bɪ'heɪv] sich verhalten
behind [bɪ'haɪnd] hinter I • **leave behind** zurücklassen IV 1 (30) °**those they have left behind** die Hinterbliebenen
bell [bel] Klingel, Glocke I
believe [bɪ'liːv] glauben III • **believe in sth.** an etwas glauben IV 1 (25) • **She couldn't believe her eyes.** Sie traute ihren Augen kaum. III

belong (to) [bɪ'lɒŋ] gehören (zu) II
below [bɪ'ləʊ] unter, unterhalb (von) III
besides [bɪ'saɪdz] außerdem IV 5 (101)
best [best] am besten II • **All the best** Viele Grüße IV 4 (85/215) • **Best wishes** Viele Grüße IV 4 (85/215) • **the best** ... der/die/das beste ...; die besten ... I • **What was the best thing about ...?** Was war das Beste an ...? II
▶ S.215 Beginning and ending letters
bet (-tt-) [bet], **bet, bet** wetten III • **You bet!** (infml) Aber klar! / Und ob! IV 5 (101)
better ['betə] besser I • **like sth. better** etwas lieber mögen II
between [bɪ'twiːn] zwischen II
°**beyond compare** [bɪˌjɒnd kəm'peə] ohne Vergleich
Bible ['baɪbl] Bibel IV 2 (36)
big [bɪg] groß I • **big wheel** Riesenrad III
°**big business** [ˌbɪg 'bɪznəs] Großunternehmentum
bike [baɪk] Fahrrad I • **bike tour** Radtour II • **ride a bike** Rad fahren I
bilingual [ˌbaɪ'lɪŋgwəl] zweisprachig IV 3 (58)
°**billion** ['bɪljən] Milliarde(n)
bin [bɪn] Mülltonne II
binoculars (pl) [bɪ'nɒkjʊləz] Fernglas IV Intro (11)
biography [baɪ'ɒgrəfi] Biografie III
biological [ˌbaɪə'lɒdʒɪkl] biologisch IV 3 (59)
biology [baɪ'ɒlədʒi] Biologie I
°**biotechnology** [ˌbaɪəʊtek'nɒlədʒi] Biotechnologie
bird [bɜːd] Vogel I
birth [bɜːθ] Geburt IV 2 (38) • **date of birth** Geburtsdatum IV 2 (38)
birthday ['bɜːθdeɪ] Geburtstag I • **Happy birthday.** Herzlichen Glückwunsch zum Geburtstag. I • **My birthday is in May.** Ich habe im Mai Geburtstag. I • **My birthday is on 13th June.** Ich habe am 13. Juni Geburtstag. I • **When's your birthday?** Wann hast du Geburtstag? I • **for his birthday** zu seinem Geburtstag III
°**birthplace** ['bɜːθpleɪs] Geburtsort
biscuit ['bɪskɪt] Keks, Plätzchen I
bit [bɪt]: **a bit** ein bisschen, etwas II
°**bitch** [bɪtʃ] (infml) Schlampe, Miststück
°**bitter** ['bɪtə] bitter, verbittert
black [blæk] schwarz I

°**black widow spider** [ˌblæk ˌwɪdəʊ 'spaɪdə] Schwarze oder Echte Witwe (giftige Spinne)
blame sb. (for) [bleɪm] jm. die Schuld geben (an); jm. Vorwürfe machen (wegen) II
bled [bled] siehe **bleed**
bleed [bliːd], **bled, bled** bluten IV 2 (54)
bleep [bliːp] piepsen II
bleep [bliːp] Piepton II
blessing ['blesɪŋ] Segen IV 1 (30)
blew [bluː] siehe **blow**
blind [blaɪnd] blind III
block [blɒk] blockieren, (ver)sperren IV 5 (112)
block [blɒk] (Häuser-, Wohn-)Block IV 1 (16)
blog [blɒg] Blog (Weblog, digitales Tagebuch) IV Intro (9)
blond (bei Frauen oft: **blonde**) [blɒnd] blond IV 1 (18)
blood [blʌd] Blut III • °**It's thick in the Irish blood.** etwa: Es liegt den Iren im Blut.
blouse [blaʊz] Bluse II
blow [bləʊ], **blew, blown** pusten, blasen; wehen III
blown [bləʊn] siehe **blow**
blue [bluː] blau I
blues [bluːz] Blues III
board [bɔːd] (Wand-)Tafel I • **on the board** an der/die Tafel I
°**board game** ['bɔːd geɪm] Brettspiel
boat [bəʊt] Boot, Schiff I
body ['bɒdi] Körper I
bodyguard ['bɒdigɑːd] Bodyguard, Leibwächter/in, Leibwache IV 5 (113)
boil [bɔɪl] kochen (Flüssigkeit, Speise) IV 1 (19) • °**boiling pool** siedender Teich
°**bold type** [ˌbəʊld 'taɪp] Fettdruck
bone [bəʊn] Knochen IV 5 (101)
bomb [bɒm] Bombe IV 2 (53/206)
book [bʊk] Buch I
booklet ['bʊklət] Broschüre II
boot [buːt] Stiefel I
border ['bɔːdə] Grenze IV Intro (12)
bored [bɔːd]: **get bored** sich langweilen; gelangweilt sein IV 5 (102)
boring ['bɔːrɪŋ] langweilig I
born [bɔːn]: **be born** geboren sein/werden II
borough ['bʌrə, AE: 'bɜːrəʊ] (Stadt-)Bezirk II
borrow sth. ['bɒrəʊ] sich etwas (aus)leihen, etwas entleihen II
boss [bɒs] Boss, Chef/in I
both [bəʊθ] beide I
bottle ['bɒtl] Flasche I • **a bottle of milk** eine Flasche Milch I

bottom [ˈbɒtəm] unteres Ende II
  at the bottom (of) unten, am unteren Ende (von) II
bought [bɔːt] *siehe* **buy**
°**bound for** [ˈbaʊnd fə] unterwegs nach
bow [bəʊ] Bogen *(Waffe und zum Musizieren)* IV 2 (36) • **bow and arrow** Pfeil und Bogen IV 2 (36/201)
bowl [bəʊl] Schüssel I • **a bowl of cornflakes** eine Schale Cornflakes I
box [bɒks] Kasten, Kästchen, Kiste I
box office [ˈbɒks ˌɒfɪs] (Theater-, Kino-)Kasse III
°**boxer shorts** [ˈbɒksə ʃɔːts] Boxershorts
boy [bɔɪ] Junge I • **boy!** *(AE, infml)* Mann! Mensch! III
boycott [ˈbɔɪkɒt] Boykott IV 5 (102)
bracket [ˈbrækɪt] Klammer *(in Texten)* IV 5 (103) • **round brackets** runde Klammern IV 5 (103) • **square brackets** eckige Klammern IV 5 (103)
°**brain** [breɪn] Gehirn
brainstorm [ˈbreɪnstɔːm] brainstormen *(so viele Ideen wie möglich sammeln)* III
brave [breɪv] tapfer, mutig IV 2 (40)
bread *(no pl)* [bred] Brot I
break [breɪk], **broke, broken** (zer)brechen; kaputt machen; kaputt gehen II • **break a rule** gegen eine Regel verstoßen IV 4 (78) • °**break a promise** ein Versprechen nicht einhalten
break open aufbrechen IV 3 (66)
°**breaking news** Eilmeldung, aktuelle Nachricht
break [breɪk] Pause I • **at break** in der Pause *(zwischen Schulstunden)* II • **take a break** eine Pause machen IV 1 (25)
breakfast [ˈbrekfəst] Frühstück I
have breakfast frühstücken I
°**breath** [breθ]: **take a breath** Luft holen
breathe [briːð] atmen IV 2 (53)
bridge [brɪdʒ] Brücke I
bridle path [ˈbraɪdl ˌpɑːθ] Reitweg III
bright [braɪt] hell, leuchtend II
bring [brɪŋ], **brought, brought** (mit-, her)bringen I
British [ˈbrɪtɪʃ] britisch II
°**brittle** [ˈbrɪtl] brüchig
broadcast [ˈbrɔːdkɑːst], **broadcast broadcast** senden; *(eine Sendung)* ausstrahlen IV 5 (100)
broke [brəʊk] *siehe* **break**
broken [ˈbrəʊkən] *siehe* **break**

broken [ˈbrəʊkən] gebrochen; zerbrochen, kaputt II
brother [ˈbrʌðə] Bruder I
brought [brɔːt] *siehe* **bring**
brown [braʊn] braun I
°**bubble** [ˈbʌbl]: **thought bubble** Denkblase
budgie [ˈbʌdʒi] Wellensittich I
build [bɪld], **built, built** bauen II • **the ship was built in Bristol** das Schiff wurde in Bristol gebaut II
building [ˈbɪldɪŋ] Gebäude II
built [bɪlt] *siehe* **build**
°**bulimic** [buˈlɪmɪk] bulimisch
bulletin board [ˈbʊlɪtɪn bɔːd] schwarzes Brett, Anschlagtafel IV 4 (78)
bully [ˈbʊli] einschüchtern, tyrannisieren II
bully [ˈbʊli] (Schul-)Tyrann III
bummer [ˈbʌmə]: **What a bummer!** *(infml)* So ein Mist! Wie schade! III
bunk (bed) [bʌŋk] Etagenbett, Koje II
burn [bɜːn] brennen; verbrennen IV 1 (17)
bury [ˈberi] begraben, vergraben; beerdigen IV 2 (53)
bus [bʌs] Bus I
bus pass [ˈbʌs pɑːs] Bus-Monatskarte III
bus stop [ˈbʌs stɒp] Bushaltestelle III
business [ˈbɪznəs]: °**big business** Großunternehmentum • **Mind your own business.** Das geht dich nichts an! / Kümmere dich um deine eigenen Angelegenheiten! II
°**businessman** [ˈbɪznəsmən] Geschäftsmann
busy [ˈbɪzi]
1. beschäftigt I
2. belebt, verkehrsreich; hektisch III
but [bət, bʌt]
1. aber I
2. sondern IV 5 (102) • **not only ... but also ...** nicht nur ... sondern auch ... IV 5 (102/218)
butter [ˈbʌtə] Butter IV 4 (86)
button [ˈbʌtn] Knopf III
buy [baɪ], **bought, bought** kaufen I
by [baɪ]
1. von I
2. an; (nahe) bei II
by car/bike/... mit dem Auto/ Rad/... II • **by the end of the song** (spätestens) bis zum Ende des Lieds III • **by the way** übrigens; nebenbei (bemerkt) III
Bye. [baɪ] Tschüs! I

C

cabin [ˈkæbɪn] Hütte III
°**cable car** [ˈkeɪbl ˌkɑː] Kabelstraßenbahn
café [ˈkæfeɪ] *(kleines)* Restaurant, Imbissstube, Café I
cafeteria [ˌkæfəˈtɪəriə] Cafeteria, Selbstbedienungsrestaurant II
cage [keɪdʒ] Käfig I
°**Cajun** [ˈkeɪdʒən] Cajun
cake [keɪk] Kuchen, Torte I
calendar [ˈkælɪndə] Kalender I
call [kɔːl] rufen; anrufen; nennen I
be called heißen, genannt werden II • **call sb. names** jn. mit Schimpfwörtern hänseln, jm. Schimpfwörter nachrufen III
call [kɔːl] Ruf, Schrei; Anruf II
make a call ein Telefongespräch führen, telefonieren II
calm down [ˌkɑːm ˈdaʊn] sich beruhigen II • **calm sb. down** jn. beruhigen II
came [keɪm] *siehe* **come**
camel [ˈkæml] Kamel II
camera [ˈkæmərə] Kamera, Fotoapparat I
camp [kæmp] zelten III
camp [kæmp] Camp, Lager IV 2 (53)
campground [ˈkæmpˌgraʊnd] *(AE)* Zeltplatz III
camping gear [ˈkæmpɪŋ ˌgɪə] Campingausrüstung IV Intro (9)
campsite [ˈkæmpsaɪt] Zeltplatz III
can [kən, kæn]
1. können I
2. dürfen I
Can I help you? Kann ich Ihnen helfen? / Was kann ich für Sie tun? *(im Geschäft)* I
canal [kəˈnæl] Kanal III
candle [ˈkændl] Kerze IV 2 (36)
cannot [ˈkænɒt] kann nicht IV 2 (51)
canoe [kəˈnuː] Kanu III
canoe [kəˈnuː] paddeln, Kanu fahren III
canyon [ˈkænjən] Cañon IV Intro (8)
cap [kæp] Mütze, Kappe II
capital [ˈkæpɪtl] Hauptstadt III
capital letter [ˌkæpɪtl ˈletə] Großbuchstabe III
°**Capitol** [ˈkæpɪtəl] Kapitol
captain [ˈkæptɪn] Kapitän/in III
caption [ˈkæpʃn] Bildunterschrift IV 3 (56)
car [kɑː] Auto I
car park [ˈkɑː pɑːk] Parkplatz III
caravan [ˈkærəvæn] Wohnwagen II
card [kɑːd] (Spiel-, Post-)Karte I
care (about) [keə] sich interessieren (für); sich kümmern (um);

wichtig nehmen III • °**feel cared about** sich behütet/beschützt fühlen • **I care about the environment.** Die Umwelt liegt mir am Herzen. III • **I don't care about money.** Geld ist mir egal. III • **Who cares?** Ist doch egal! / Na und? III
care [keə]: **take care of sth.** sich um etwas kümmern III
career [kəˈrɪə] Karriere III
careful [ˈkeəfl] vorsichtig I
caretaker [ˈkeəteɪkə] Hausmeister/in II
°**carne con chile** mexikanische Bezeichnung für Chili con Carne
carrot [ˈkærət] Möhre, Karotte I
cart [kɑːt] Wagen, Karren IV 2 (54)
cartoon [kɑːˈtuːn] Cartoon (Zeichentrickfilm; Bilderwitz) II
case [keɪs] Fall II
casino [kəˈsiːnəʊ] (Spiel)kasino IV Intro (13)
castle [ˈkɑːsl] Burg, Schloss II
cat [kæt] Katze I
catch [kætʃ], **caught, caught** fangen; erwischen II
cathedral [kəˈθiːdrəl] Kathedrale, Dom III
cattle (pl) [ˈkætl] Vieh, Rinder IV Intro (12)
caught [kɔːt] siehe **catch**
cause [kɔːz] verursachen IV 2 (38)
cause [kɔːz] Ursache IV 2 (38)
°**'cause** [kəz] (infml) weil (= **because**)
CD [ˌsiːˈdiː] CD I • **CD player** CD-Spieler I
ceilidh [ˈkeɪli] Musik- und Tanzveranstaltung, vor allem in Schottland und Irland III
celebrate [ˈselɪbreɪt] feiern IV 2 (38)
celebration [ˌseləˈbreɪʃn] Feier IV 2 (38)
celebrity [səˈlebrəti]
1. berühmte Persönlichkeit, Prominente(r) III
°**2** Berühmheit (Promi)
cello [ˈtʃeləʊ] Cello III
cellphone [ˈselfəʊn] (AE) Mobiltelefon, Handy II
cent (c) [sent] Cent I
cent: per cent [pəˈsent] Prozent III
centimetre (cm) [ˈsentɪmiːtə] Zentimeter III
central [ˈsentrəl] Zentral-, Mittel- III
centre [ˈsentə] Zentrum, Mitte I
century [ˈsentʃəri] Jahrhundert II
chair [tʃeə] Stuhl I
champion [ˈtʃæmpiən] Meister/in, Champion I
championship [ˈtʃæmpiənʃɪp] Meisterschaft III

chance [tʃɑːns] Chance II
change [tʃeɪndʒ]
1. Wechselgeld I
2. (Ver-)Änderung, Wechsel IV 4 (78)
change [tʃeɪndʒ]
1. umsteigen III
2. (sich) (ver-)ändern IV 1 (29/200)
3. wechseln IV 1 (29/200)
4. umtauschen IV 1 (29/200)
5. umwandeln IV 1 (29/200)
6. **change stations** (Radio) umschalten IV 1 (29/200)
7. sich umziehen IV 1 (29/200)
▶ S.200 (to) change
character [ˈkærəktə] Charakter, Persönlichkeit IV 5 (102)
characteristic [ˌkærəktəˈrɪstɪk] (charakteristisches) Merkmal IV 5 (107)
charge (at sb.) [tʃɑːdʒ] stürmen; (jn.) angreifen IV 2 (53)
charity [ˈtʃærəti] Wohlfahrtsorganisation I
°**chart** [tʃɑːt] Tabelle, Diagramm, Schaubild
chase sb. [tʃeɪs] jn. jagen; jm. hinterherjagen IV 2 (52)
chat (-tt-) [tʃæt] chatten, plaudern II
chat [tʃæt] Chat, Unterhaltung II
chat room [ˈtʃæt ruːm] Chatroom III
chat show Talkshow II
cheap [tʃiːp] billig, preiswert II
check [tʃek] (über)prüfen, kontrollieren I • °**check sth. out** (infml) (sich) etwas anschauen
checklist [ˈtʃeklɪst] Checkliste III
checkpoint [ˈtʃekpɔɪnt] Kontrollpunkt (zur Selbstüberprüfung) I
cheer [tʃɪə] jubeln II
cheerleader [ˈtʃɪəliːdə] Cheerleader (Stimmungsanheizer/in bei Sportereignissen) IV 4 (79)
cheese [tʃiːz] Käse I
chemist [ˈkemɪst] Drogerie, Apotheke II • **at the chemist's** beim Apotheker III
chicken [ˈtʃɪkɪn] Huhn; (Brat-) Hähnchen I
chief [tʃiːf] Häuptling IV 2 (40)
child [tʃaɪld], pl **children** [ˈtʃɪldrən] Kind I
°**chili con carne** [ˌtʃɪli ˌkɒn ˈkɑːneɪ] scharfes Gericht aus Fleisch, Chilischoten und anderen Zutaten
chill out [ˌtʃɪl ˈaʊt] (infml) sich entspannen, relaxen III
Chinese [tʃaɪˈniːz] chinesisch IV 1 (23)
chips (pl) [tʃɪps]
1. (BE) Pommes frites I
2. (AE) Chips IV 1 (24/198)

chocolate [ˈtʃɒklət] Schokolade I
choir [ˈkwaɪə] Chor I
°**choked** [tʃəʊkt] hier: bewegt
choose [tʃuːz], **chose, chosen** (sich) aussuchen, (aus)wählen I
chose [tʃəʊz] siehe **choose**
chosen [ˈtʃəʊzn] siehe **choose**
Christ [kraɪst] Christus IV 2 (38)
°**Christmas** [ˈkrɪsməs] Weihnachten
°**Chupacabra** [ˌtʃuːpəˈkæbrə] Chupacabra (lateinamerikanisches Fabelwesen)
church [tʃɜːtʃ] Kirche I • **go to church** in die Kirche gehen III
cinema [ˈsɪnəmə] Kino II • **go to the cinema** ins Kino gehen II
circle [ˈsɜːkl] Kreis III
°**circuit** [ˈsɜːkɪt] Kreislauf
circus [ˈsɜːkəs] (runder) Platz III
city [ˈsɪti] Stadt, Großstadt I **city centre** [ˌsɪti ˈsentə] Stadtzentrum, Innenstadt I
civil rights (pl) [ˌsɪvl ˈraɪts] Bürgerrechte IV 5 (99)
civil war [ˌsɪvl ˈwɔː] Bürgerkrieg IV 5 (98)
clap (-pp-) [klæp] (Beifall) klatschen IV 4 (92)
clarinet [ˌklærɪˈnet] Klarinette III
class [klɑːs]
1. (Schul-)Klasse I • **class teacher** Klassenlehrer/in I
2. Unterricht; Kurs IV 2 (39)
classic [ˈklæsɪk] klassisch III
classical [ˈklæsɪkl] klassisch III
classmate [ˈklɑːsmeɪt] Klassenkamerad/in, Mitschüler/in I
classroom [ˈklɑːsruːm; ˈklɑːsrʊm] Klassenzimmer I
clause [klɔːz] (Teil-, Glied-)Satz III
clean [kliːn] sauber II
clean [kliːn] sauber machen, putzen I • **clean one's teeth** sich die Zähne putzen III
cleaner [ˈkliːnə] Putzfrau, -mann II
clear [klɪə] klar, deutlich I
clever [ˈklevə] klug, schlau I
cleverness [ˈklevənəs] Klugheit, Schlauheit IV 4 (86)
click on sth. [klɪk] etwas anklicken II
cliff [klɪf] Klippe III
°**climate change** [ˈklaɪmət ˌtʃeɪndʒ] Klimawandel
climb [klaɪm] klettern; hinaufklettern (auf) I • **Climb a tree.** Klettere auf einen Baum. I
clinic [ˈklɪnɪk] Klinik II
clock [klɒk] (Wand-, Stand-, Turm-) Uhr I
close (to) [kləʊs] nahe (bei, an) III **That was close.** Das war knapp. II

close [kləʊz] schließen, zumachen I
closely [ˈkləʊsli]: look closely at sth. etw. genau anschauen III
closed [kləʊzd] geschlossen II
clothes (pl) [kləʊðz, kləʊz] Kleider, Kleidungsstücke I
clothing [ˈkləʊðɪŋ] Kleidung IV 4 (78)
piece of clothing Kleidungsstück IV 4 (78)
cloud [klaʊd] Wolke II
cloudy [ˈklaʊdi] bewölkt II
clown [klaʊn] Clown/in I
club [klʌb] Klub; Verein I
coach [kəʊtʃ] Trainer/in III
coast [kəʊst] Küste II
°code [kəʊd] Kodex, Regeln
coffee [ˈkɒfi] Kaffee IV 1 (19)
coffee to go Kaffee zum Mitnehmen IV 1 (19)
cola [ˈkəʊlə] Cola I
cold [kəʊld] kalt I • be cold frieren I
cold [kəʊld] Erkältung II • have a cold erkältet sein, eine Erkältung haben II
collapse [kəˈlæps] zusammenbrechen; einstürzen IV 1 (17)
collect [kəˈlekt] sammeln I
collection [kəˈlekʃn] Sammlung IV Intro (12)
collector [kəˈlektə] Sammler/in II
college [ˈkɒlɪdʒ] Hochschule, Fachschule III
collocation [ˌkɒləˈkeɪʃn] Kollokation (Wörter, die oft zusammen vorkommen) IV 3 (64)
colonist [ˈkɒlənɪst] Kolonist/in; Siedler/in IV 2 (37)
colony [ˈkɒləni] Kolonie IV 2 (37)
colour [ˈkʌlə] Farbe I • What colour is …? Welche Farbe hat …? I
colourful [ˈkʌləfl] bunt IV Intro (8)
column [ˈkɒləm] Säule III
come [kʌm], came, come kommen I • come from stammen von/aus IV 1 (19) • come home nach Hause kommen I • come in hereinkommen I • Come on. 1. Na los, komm. II; 2. Ach komm! / Na hör mal! II • come together zusammenkommen IV 2 (38) • come true wahr werden II • °come up heller werden (Licht) • come up with sth. sich etwas ausdenken, sich etwas einfallen lassen IV 1 (29)
comedy [ˈkɒmədi] Comedyshow, Komödie II
comfort [ˈkʌmfət] trösten IV 1 (29)
comfortable [ˈkʌmftəbl] bequem I
comic [ˈkɒmɪk] Comic-Heft I
comment [ˈkɒment] Kommentar IV 3 (58)

commit (-tt-) [kəˈmɪt]: commit a crime ein Verbrechen begehen IV 2 (53)
Commonwealth [ˈkɒmənwelθ]: the Commonwealth Gemeinschaft der Länder des ehemaligen Britischen Weltreichs III
community hall [kəˈmjuːnəti] Gemeinschaftshalle, -saal / Gemeindehalle, -saal III
company [ˈkʌmpəni] Firma, Gesellschaft III • °ladder company Zug (Einheit der Feuerwache)
compare [kəmˈpeə] vergleichen II
°compare [kəmˈpeə]: beyond compare ohne Vergleich
comparison [kəmˈpærɪsn] Steigerung; Vergleich II
competition [ˌkɒmpəˈtɪʃn] Wettbewerb III
°complete [kəmˈpliːt] vervollständigen
°complicated [ˈkɒmplɪkeɪtɪd] kompliziert
°composer [kəmˈpəʊzə] Komponist/in
computer [kəmˈpjuːtə] Computer I
computer science [kəmˌpjuːtə ˈsaɪəns] Computerwissenschaft, Informatik III
°con [kɒn]: pros and cons Vor- und Nachteile
concern [kənˈsɜːn]: To whom it may concern (bes. AE) Sehr geehrte Damen und Herren IV 4 (85/215)
▶ S.215 Beginning and ending letters
concert [ˈkɒnsət] Konzert II
°condolences (pl) [kənˈdəʊlənsɪs]: give your condolences sein Beileid ausdrücken
°condor [ˈkɒndɔː] Kondor
°Confederate States [kənˈfedərət] Konföderierte Staaten (die "Südstaaten", die sich 1861 von den USA abspalteten)
confuse [kənˈfjuːz] verwirren IV 2 (53/206)
confusion [kənˈfjuːʒn] Verwirrung IV 2 (53)
Congratulations! [kənˌgrætʃuˈleɪʃnz] Herzlichen Glückwunsch! III
conjunction [kənˈdʒʌŋkʃn] Konjunktion
°connect [kəˈnekt] verbinden
consequence [ˈkɒnsɪkwəns] Folge, Konsequenz IV 2 (38)
°construction [kənˈstrʌkʃn] Konstruktion
contact sb. [ˈkɒntækt] sich mit jm. in Verbindung setzen; mit jm. Kontakt aufnehmen III
contact [ˈkɒntækt] Kontakt IV 5 (112)

°contain [kənˈteɪn] beinhalten
°content [ˈkɒntent] Gehalt, Inhalt
context [ˈkɒntekst] Zusammenhang, Kontext IV 1 (27)
continent [ˈkɒntɪnənt] Kontinent IV 2 (47)
continue [kənˈtɪnjuː] weitermachen (mit); weiterreden; weitergehen II
control [kənˈtrəʊl]: under control unter Kontrolle IV 5 (103)
conversation [ˌkɒnvəˈseɪʃn] Gespräch, Unterhaltung II
cook [kʊk] kochen, zubereiten II
cook [kʊk] Koch, Köchin II
cooker [ˈkʊkə] Herd I
cookie [ˈkʊki] (AE) Keks IV 1 (24/198)
cool [kuːl]
1. kühl I
2. cool I
copy [ˈkɒpi] kopieren II
copy [ˈkɒpi] Kopie, Abschrift IV 4 (78)
corner [ˈkɔːnə] Ecke I • on the corner of Sand Street and London Road Sand Street, Ecke London Road II
corn [kɔːn] (AE, no pl) Mais IV 2 (37)
cornflakes [ˈkɔːnfleɪks] Cornflakes I
correct [kəˈrekt] korrigieren, verbessern II
correct [kəˈrekt] richtig, korrekt II
correction [kəˈrekʃn] Korrektur, Berichtigung IV 4 (86)
cost [kɒst], cost, cost kosten III
cost [kɒst] Preis, Kosten IV 5 (108/219)
▶ S.219 Verbs & nouns with the same form
costume [ˈkɒstjuːm] Kostüm, Verkleidung I
cotton [ˈkɒtn] Baumwolle IV 3 (72)
could [kəd, kʊd]: he could … er konnte … II
could [kəd, kʊd]: we could … wir könnten … II
count [kaʊnt] zählen II
countdown [ˈkaʊntdaʊn] Countdown III
counter [ˈkaʊntə]
1. Spielstein II
2. Theke, Ladentisch IV 1 (19)
country [ˈkʌntri] Land (auch als Gegensatz zur Stadt) II • in the country auf dem Land II
°county [ˈkaʊnti] Landkreis, Bezirk
°county fair [ˈkaʊnti feə] etwa: Landwirtschaftsschau, -ausstellung
couple [ˈkʌpl]: a couple of ein paar/ Paar III
°courage [ˈkʌrɪdʒ] Mut
course [kɔːs] Kurs, Lehrgang III
course: of course [əv ˈkɔːs] natürlich, selbstverständlich I
court [kɔːt]
1. Platz, Court III

2. Gericht(shof) IV 5 (111)
°**Supreme Court** oberster Gerichtshof
cousin ['kʌzn] Cousin, Cousine I
cover ['kʌvə] zudecken, bedecken IV 3 (59)
cover ['kʌvə]
1. (CD-)Hülle I
°**2.** Umschlag *(von Buch)*
cow [kaʊ] Kuh II
°**crap** [kræp] *(infml, rude)* Mist
crash [kræʃ] abstürzen III
crazy ['kreɪzi] verrückt III
cream [kri:m] Sahne; Creme IV 1 (19)
cream cheese [ˌkri:m 'tʃi:z] Frischkäse IV 1 (19)
creative [kri'eɪtɪv] kreativ, einfallsreich IV 3 (56)
crew [kru:] Crew, (Schiffs-)Mannschaft III
cricket ['krɪkɪt] Kricket III
crime [kraɪm] Verbrechen; Kriminalität IV 2 (53) • **commit a crime** ein Verbrechen begehen IV 2 (53)
crime film Krimi IV 2 (53/205)
crime story Krimi IV 2 (53/205)
crisis ['kraɪsɪs] Krise IV 5 (114)
crisps *(pl)* [krɪsps] Kartoffelchips I
critic ['krɪtɪk] Kritiker/in IV 1 (29)
°**criticize** ['krɪtɪsaɪz] kritisieren
crocodile ['krɒkədaɪl] Krokodil II
cross [krɒs] überqueren; (sich) kreuzen II
°**cross sth. out** [ˌkrɒs_'aʊt] etwas durchstreichen
crosswalk ['krɒswɔ:k] *(AE)* Fußgängerüberweg IV 1 (16)
crowd [kraʊd] (Menschen-)Menge III
crowded ['kraʊdɪd] voller Menschen, überfüllt III
°**crown sb.** [kraʊn] jn. krönen
cruel ['kru:əl] grausam IV 5 (113)
°**crunch** [krʌntʃ]: **go crunch** Knirsch machen
cry [kraɪ]
1. schreien I • **cry in pain** vor Schmerzen schreien I
2. weinen III
cup [kʌp]
1. Tasse II • **a cup of tea** eine Tasse Tee II
2. Pokal II
cupboard ['kʌbəd] Schrank I
°**curious** ['kjʊəriəs] neugierig
°**curtain** ['kɜ:tən] Vorhang
cut (-tt-) [kʌt], **cut, cut** schneiden II • **cut sth. off** etwas abschneiden, abtrennen III • **cut sth. out** ausschneiden III • **cut the grass** Rasen mähen IV Intro (11)

cut [kʌt] Schnitt IV 5 (108/219)
▶ S.219 Verbs & nouns with the same form
cycle ['saɪkl] (mit dem) Rad fahren II
cycle path ['saɪkl pɑ:θ] Radweg II

D

dad [dæd] Papa, Vati; Vater I
°**daddy** ['dædi] Papa
daily ['deɪli] täglich IV Intro (9)
°**dairy** ['deəri] Milchgeschäft
°**damage** ['dæmɪdʒ] Schaden
damn [dæm] verdammt IV 2 (52)
dance [dɑ:ns] tanzen I
dance [dɑ:ns] Tanz I • **dance floor** Tanzfläche III
dancer ['dɑ:nsə] Tänzer/in II
dancing ['dɑ:nsɪŋ] Tanzen I
dancing lessons Tanzstunden, Tanzunterricht I
danger (to) ['deɪndʒə] Gefahr (für) I
dangerous ['deɪndʒərəs] gefährlich II
dark [dɑ:k] dunkel I
dark [dɑ:k]: **after dark** nach Einbruch der Dunkelheit IV 1 (19)
date [deɪt] Datum I • **date of birth** Geburtsdatum IV 2 (38)
date [deɪt] *(bes. AE)* mit jm. (aus)gehen; sich (regelmäßig) mit jm. treffen III
daughter ['dɔ:tə] Tochter I
day [deɪ] Tag I • **one day** eines Tages I • **days of the week** Wochentage I • **the day before yesterday** vorgestern II • **that day** an jenem Tag III
°**daylight** ['deɪlaɪt] Tageslicht
dead [ded] tot I
deaf [def] taub, gehörlos III
deal with sb./sth. [di:l], **dealt, dealt** sich mit jm./etwas beschäftigen; handeln von etwas IV 5 (107)
deal [di:l] Angebot IV 3 (70) • **make a deal** ein Abkommen/eine Abmachung treffen III • **It's a deal!** Abgemacht! III
dealt [delt] *siehe* **deal**
dear [dɪə] Schatz, Liebling I • **Oh dear!** Oje! II
dear [dɪə]: **Dear Jay ...** Lieber Jay, ... I **Dear Sir or Madam ...** Sehr geehrte Damen und Herren IV 4 (85/215)
▶ S.215 Beginning and ending letters
death [deθ] Tod IV 1 (18) • **death sentence** Todesstrafe IV 2 (53/205) **fall to your death** zu Tode stürzen IV 1 (18)
debts *(pl)* [dets] Schulden IV 2 (54)
December [dɪ'sembə] Dezember I

decide (on sth.) [dɪ'saɪd] sich entscheiden (für etwas), (etwas) beschließen II
°**decision** [dɪ'sɪʒn] Entscheidung
°**Declaration of Independence** [ˌdekləˈreɪʃn ˌɪndɪˈpendəns] Unabhängigkeitserklärung
°**declare** [dɪ'kleə] erklären
deep [di:p] tief IV Intro (8)
deer, *pl* **deer** [dɪə] Reh, Hirsch II
°**defeat sb.** [dɪ'fi:t] jn. besiegen
defence [dɪ'fens] Verteidigung III
°**defense** [dɪ'fens] *(AE)* Verteidigung
°**define** [dɪ'faɪn] definieren
°**definition** [ˌdefɪ'nɪʃn] Definition
degree [dɪ'gri:] Grad II
delay [dɪ'leɪ] aufhalten IV 5 (103)
delay [dɪ'leɪ] Verspätung IV 5 (103)
▶ S.219 Verbs & nouns with the same form
deli ['deli] Deli *(Lebensmittelgeschäft mit Fastfoodrestaurant)* IV 1 (19)
delicious [dɪ'lɪʃəs] köstlich, lecker II
deliver [dɪ'lɪvə] (aus)liefern, austragen IV 3 (61)
°**delta** ['deltə] Delta
dentist ['dentɪst] Zahnarzt, -ärztin IV 4 (90)
department store [dɪ'pɑ:tmənt stɔ:] Kaufhaus II
departure [dɪ'pɑ:tʃə] Abfahrt; Abflug IV 5 (106)
depend on sth./sb. [dɪ'pend] sich auf etwas/jn verlassen IV 1 (29)
dependable [dɪ'pendəbl] zuverlässig IV 1 (29/199)
describe sth. (to sb.) [dɪ'skraɪb] (jm.) etwas beschreiben II
description [dɪ'skrɪpʃn] Beschreibung II
desert ['dezət] Wüste IV 3 (60)
design [dɪ'zaɪn] entwickeln, entwerfen I
°**designer** [dɪ'zaɪnə] Designer/in
desk [desk] Schreibtisch I
destroy [dɪ'strɔɪ] zerstören III
detail ['di:teɪl] Detail, Einzelheit III
°**detailed** ['di:teɪld] detailliert
detective [dɪ'tektɪv] Detektiv/in I
diagonal [daɪ'ægənəl] diagonal, schräg IV 2 (51)
°**diagram** ['daɪəgræm] Diagramm
dial (-ll-) ['daɪəl] wählen *(Telefonnummer)* II
°**dialogue** ['daɪəlɒg] Dialog
diary ['daɪəri] Tagebuch; Terminkalender I
dice, *pl* **dice** [daɪs] Würfel II **throw the dice** würfeln II
dictionary ['dɪkʃənri] Wörterbuch, *(alphabetisches)* Wörterverzeichnis I

did [dɪd] siehe **do** • **Did you go?** Bist du gegangen? / Gingst du? I **we didn't go** ['dɪdnt] wir sind nicht gegangen/wir gingen nicht I
die (of) (-ing form: **dying**) [daɪ] sterben (an) II
difference ['dɪfrəns] Unterschied III
different (from) ['dɪfrənt] verschieden, unterschiedlich; anders (als) I
difficult ['dɪfɪkəlt] schwierig, schwer I
dining room ['daɪnɪŋ ruːm; 'daɪnɪŋ rʊm] Esszimmer I
dinner ['dɪnə] Abendessen, Abendbrot I • **have dinner** Abendbrot essen I
dinosaur ['daɪnəsɔː] Dinosaurier IV Intro (12)
direct [də'rekt] Regie führen III
°**direct** [daɪ'rekt] direkt
direct speech [də'rekt] direkte Rede III
directions (pl) [də'rekʃnz] Wegbeschreibung(en) II
director [də'rektə] Regisseur/in III
°**dirt floor** [ˌdɜːt 'flɔː] Erdfußboden
dirty ['dɜːti] schmutzig II
disabled [dɪs'eɪbld] (körper)behindert III
disadvantage [ˌdɪsəd'vɑːntɪdʒ] Nachteil IV 3 (58)
disagree (with) [ˌdɪsə'griː] anderer Meinung sein (als), nicht übereinstimmen (mit) II
disappear [ˌdɪsə'pɪə] verschwinden II
disappoint sb. [ˌdɪsə'pɔɪnt] jn. enttäuschen IV 5 (113/220)
disappointed (with sb., with/about sth.) [ˌdɪsə'pɔɪntɪd] enttäuscht (von jm./etwas) IV 5 (113)
°**disaster** [dɪ'zɑːstə] Katastrophe
disc jockey ['dɪsk dʒɒki] Diskjockey III
disco ['dɪskəʊ] Disko I
discover [dɪ'skʌvə] entdecken; herausfinden II
°**discovery** [dɪ'skʌvəri] Entdeckung • °**discovery pack** Entdeckungsset, Kennenlernset
discriminate against sb. [dɪ'skrɪmɪneɪt] jn. diskriminieren, jn. benachteiligen IV 3 (58)
discrimination (against) [dɪˌskrɪmɪ'neɪʃn] Diskriminierung (von), Benachteiligung (von) IV 3 (58/208)
°**discuss** [dɪs'kʌs] besprechen
discussion [dɪ'skʌʃn] Diskussion II
disease [dɪ'ziːz] (ansteckende) Krankheit IV 2 (45)

dish [dɪʃ] Gericht (Speise) III **dishes** (pl) ['dɪʃɪz] Geschirr I • **do the dishes** das Geschirr abwaschen I
dishwasher ['dɪʃwɒʃə] Geschirrspülmaschine I
°**dislike** [dɪs'laɪk] nicht mögen
display [dɪ'spleɪ] Display IV 5 (102) • **be on display** ausgestellt sein IV 5 (102)
°**display sth.** [dɪ'spleɪ] etwas ausstellen
distance ['dɪstəns] Entfernung IV 1 (16)
°**district** ['dɪstrɪkt] Gegend
divide (into) [dɪ'vaɪd] (sich) teilen (in), (sich) aufteilen (in) II
divorced [dɪ'vɔːst] geschieden I
DJ ['diːdʒeɪ] Diskjockey III
DJ ['diːdʒeɪ] (Musik/CDs/Platten) auflegen (in der Disko) III
do [duː], **did, done** tun, machen I **do a gig** einen Auftritt haben, ein Konzert geben III • **do a good job** gute Arbeit leisten II • **do an exercise** eine Übung machen II **do a project** ein Projekt machen, durchführen II • **do sb. a favour** jm. einen Gefallen tun IV 4 (91) **do sport** Sport treiben I • **do the dishes** das Geschirr abwaschen I **How am I doing?** Wie komme ich voran? (Wie sind meine Fortschritte?) III
doctor ['dɒktə] Arzt/Ärztin, Doktor I • **at/to the doctor's** beim/zum Arzt III
documentary [ˌdɒkju'mentri] Dokumentarfilm II
dog [dɒg] Hund I
doll [dɒl] Puppe IV 2 (36)
dollar ($) ['dɒlə] Dollar IV 1 (16)
°**dolphin** ['dɒlfɪn] Delfin
°**dominate** ['dɒmɪneɪt] dominieren, beherrschen
done [dʌn] siehe **do**
don't [dəʊnt]: **Don't listen to Dan.** Hör/Hört nicht auf Dan. I • **I don't like ...** Ich mag ... nicht. / Ich mag kein(e) ... I
door [dɔː] Tür I
doorbell ['dɔːbel] Türklingel I
dossier ['dɒsieɪ] Mappe, Dossier (des Sprachenportfolios) I
double ['dʌbl] zweimal, doppelt, Doppel- I
double bass [ˌdʌbl 'beɪs] Kontrabass III
dough [dəʊ] Teig IV 1 (19)
down [daʊn] hinunter, herunter, nach unten I • **down there** (nach) dort unten II

download [ˌdaʊn'ləʊd] runterladen, downloaden II
downstairs [ˌdaʊn'steəz] unten; nach unten I
downtown ['daʊntaʊn] Stadtzentrum IV 1 (16/194) • **downtown bus** (AE) Bus in Richtung Stadtzentrum IV 1 (16)
Dr., Dr ['dɒktə] Dr. IV 5 (99)
draft [drɑːft] Entwurf IV 1 (25)
dragon ['drægən] Drache III
°**drain** [dreɪn]: **storm drain** Regenwasserkanalisation
drama ['drɑːmə] 1. Schauspiel, darstellende Kunst I 2. Fernsehspiel; Drama IV 5 (100)
drank [dræŋk] siehe **drink**
draw [drɔː], **drew, drawn** 1. zeichnen III °**2** anziehen, anlocken
draw [drɔː] Unentschieden III
drawing ['drɔːɪŋ] Zeichnung III
drawn [drɔːn] siehe **draw**
dream [driːm] Traum I • **dream house** Traumhaus I • °**never in my wildest dreams** nicht einmal in meinen kühnsten Träumen
dream (of, about) [driːm] träumen (von) II • **dream on** weiterträumen III
°**dreamy** ['driːmi] träumerisch
dress [dres] sich kleiden, anziehen IV 2 (40)
dress [dres] Kleid I
°**dress code** ['dres ˌkəʊd] Kleiderordnung, Bekleidungsregeln
dressed [drest]: **get dressed** sich anziehen I
drew [druː] siehe **draw**
drink [drɪŋk] Getränk I
drink [drɪŋk], **drank, drunk** trinken I
°**drinking fountain** ['drɪŋkɪŋ ˌfaʊntɪn] Trinkbrunnen
drive [draɪv], **drove, driven** (ein Auto / mit dem Auto) fahren II
drive [draɪv] (Auto)fahrt IV Intro (10)
driven ['drɪvn] siehe **drive**
driver ['draɪvə] Fahrer/in II
drop (-pp-) [drɒp] 1. fallen lassen I 2. fallen I °**3** sich fallen lassen °**drop down** sich ducken • **drop sb. off** jn. absetzen (aussteigen lassen) IV 5 (101)
drove [drəʊv] siehe **drive**
drown [draʊn] ertrinken IV 3 (60)
drum [drʌm] Trommel; Schlagzeug III • **drumstick** Trommelstock III **play the drums** Schlagzeug spielen III

drunk *siehe* **drink**
drunk [drʌŋk] betrunken IV 4 (91)
dry [draɪ] trocken III
°**dumpster** ['dʌmpstə] *(AE)* Müllcontainer
during *(prep)* ['djʊərɪŋ] während III
dust [dʌst] Staub IV 3 (73)
dustbin ['dʌstbɪn] Mülltonne II
DVD [ˌdiː viː 'diː] DVD I
°**dynamo** ['daɪnəməʊ] *hier:* Antriebskraft, Motor

E

each [iːtʃ] jeder, jede, jedes (einzelne) I • **each other** einander, sich (gegenseitig) III
ear [ɪə] Ohr I
earache ['ɪəreɪk] Ohrenschmerzen II
early ['ɜːli] früh I
earring ['ɪərɪŋ] Ohrring I
earthquake ['ɜːθkweɪk] Erdbeben IV 4 (92)
earthworm ['ɜːθwɜːm] Regenwurm IV 3 (72)
east [iːst] Osten; nach Osten; östlich II • **eastbound** ['iːstbaʊnd] Richtung Osten III • **eastern** ['iːstən] östlich, Ost- III
easy ['iːzi] leicht, einfach I
eat [iːt]**, ate, eaten** essen I
eaten ['iːtn] *siehe* **eat**
°**economic** [ˌiːkəˈnɒmɪk] wirtschaftliche(r, s)
°**economy** [ɪˈkɒnəmi] (Volks)Wirtschaft
edit ['edɪt] redigieren III
editor ['edɪtə] Redakteur/in III
education [ˌedʒuˈkeɪʃn] (Schul-, Aus-)Bildung; Erziehung IV 3 (58)
°**higher education** Hochschulwesen; Hochschulbildung
effect (on) [ɪˈfekt] Wirkung, Auswirkung (auf) IV 2 (38)
e-friend ['iːfrend] Brieffreund/in *(im Internet)* I
°**e.g.** [ˌiː ˈdʒiː] z. B. (zum Beispiel)
egg [eg] Ei I
eightish ['eɪtɪʃ] ungefähr acht (Jahre/Uhr) IV 1 (29/199)
either ['aɪðə, 'iːðə]**: not (…) either** auch nicht II
elect sb. sth. [ɪˈlekt] jn. zu etwas wählen IV 4 (90)
election [ɪˈlekʃn] Wahl *(von Kandidaten bei einer Abstimmung)* IV 4 (90/216)
electric [ɪˈlektrɪk] elektrisch, Elektro- III

electricity [ɪˌlekˈtrɪsəti] Strom, Elektrizität III • **static electricity** elektrische Aufladung IV 1 (18)
electronic [ɪˌlekˈtrɒnɪk] elektronisch III
°**electronics** [ɪˌlekˈtrɒnɪks] Elektronik
elementary school [ˌelɪˈmentri skuːl] *(USA)* Grundschule *(für 6- bis 11-Jährige)* IV 4 (78)
°**elements** ['eləmənts]**: the elements** schlechtes Wetter
elephant ['elɪfənt] Elefant I
elevator ['elɪveɪtə] *(AE)* Fahrstuhl, Aufzug II
else [els]**: anybody/anything else** sonst (noch) jemand/etwas **anywhere else** sonst (noch) irgendwo(hin) • **somebody else** jemand anders • **something else** etwas anderes • **somewhere else** woanders(hin) • **who/what/where/why/… else?** wer/was/wo/warum/… (sonst) noch? III
°**'em** [əm] *(infml) siehe* **them**
e-mail ['iːmeɪl] E-Mail I
embarrassed [ɪmˈbærəst] verlegen IV 4 (91)
embarrassing [ɪmˈbærəsɪŋ] peinlich IV 4 (91/216)
emergency [ɪˈmɜːdʒənsi] Notfall, Not- IV 1 (28)
°**empanadas** *(pl)* [ˌempəˈnɑːdəz] gefüllte Teigtaschen
empty ['empti] leer I
encyclopedia [ɪnˌsaɪkləˈpiːdiə] Enzyklopädie, Lexikon II
end [end] Ende; Schluss I • **at the end (of)** am Ende (von) I **achieve an end** ein Ziel erreichen IV 2 (54)
end [end] zu Ende gehen IV 5 (101)
°**end up in** landen in
ending ['endɪŋ] Ende, (Ab-)Schluss *(einer Geschichte, eines Films usw.)* III • **happy ending** Happyend II
enemy ['enəmi] Feind/in II
engineer [ˌendʒɪˈnɪə] Ingenieur/in II
English ['ɪŋglɪʃ] Englisch; englisch I
enjoy [ɪnˈdʒɔɪ] genießen I
enough [ɪˈnʌf] genug I
enroll for/in/on sth. [ɪnˈrəʊl] sich (für etwas) anmelden IV 3 (73)
enter ['entə]
1. betreten IV 1 (18) • **enter a country** in ein Land einreisen IV 4 (18)
2. eingeben, eintragen II
°**3.** *(Theater)* auftreten; „Auftritt"
entertain sb. [ˌentəˈteɪn] jn. unterhalten IV 5 (107)
entertainment [ˌentəˈteɪnmənt] Unterhaltung (Vergnügen) IV 2 (42)

°**enthusiastic** [ɪnˌθjuːziˈæstɪk] enthusiastisch
entry ['entri]
1. Eintrag, Eintragung *(im Wörterbuch/Tagebuch)* III
2. Einsendung, Beitrag *(zu einem Wettbewerb)* III
environment [ɪnˈvaɪrənmənt] Umwelt IV 3 (61/210)
environmental [ɪnˌvaɪrənˈmentl] Umwelt- IV 3 (61)
equal ['iːkwəl] gleich IV 5 (102)
equalize ['iːkwəlaɪz] ausgleichen; das Ausgleichstor erzielen III
equipment [ɪˈkwɪpmənt] Ausrüstung III
eraser [ɪˈreɪzə(r), ɪˈreɪsə(r)] *(AE)* Radiergummi IV 1 (24/198)
°**erupt** [ɪˈrʌpt] ausbrechen, umschlagen
escape from sb./sth. [ɪˈskeɪp] vor jm./aus etwas fliehen; entkommen IV 1 (18)
°**especially** [ɪˈspeʃəli] besonders, vor allem IV Intro (10)
essay (about, on) ['eseɪ] Aufsatz (über) I
etc. (et cetera) [etˈsetərə] usw. (und so weiter) IV 5 (103)
ethnic ['eθnɪk] ethnisch, Volks- IV 3 (64)
°**eulogy** ['juːlədʒi] Trauerrede • **give a eulogy** eine Trauerrede halten
euro (€) ['jʊərəʊ] Euro I
even ['iːvn]
1. sogar II
2. (sogar) schon III
evening ['iːvnɪŋ] Abend I • **in the evening** abends, am Abend I **on Friday evening** freitagabends, am Freitagabend I
event [ɪˈvent] Ereignis II
ever ['evə] je, jemals III • **ever?** je? / jemals? / schon mal? II
°**ever since** [ˌevə ˈsɪns] seitdem
every ['evri] jeder, jede, jedes I
everybody ['evribɒdi] jeder, alle II
everyday *(adj)* ['evrideɪ] Alltags-; alltäglich III
everyone ['evriwʌn] jeder; alle III
everything ['evriθɪŋ] alles I
°**everything bagel** ein Bagel mit verschiedenen Gewürzen im Teig IV 1 (19)
everywhere ['evriweə] überall I
exact [ɪgˈzækt] genau III
example [ɪgˈzɑːmpl] Beispiel I
for example zum Beispiel I
excellent ['eksələnt] ausgezeichnet, hervorragend IV 4 (78)
▶ S.213 US school grades

except [ɪkˈsept] außer, bis auf IV 3 (72)
exchange [ɪksˈtʃeɪndʒ] (Schüler-)Austausch III
exchange [ɪksˈtʃeɪndʒ] aus-, umtauschen III; (Geld) wechseln III
excited [ɪkˈsaɪtɪd] (positiv) aufgeregt, begeistert II
exciting [ɪkˈsaɪtɪŋ] aufregend, spannend II
Excuse me, ... [ɪkˈskjuːz miː] Entschuldigung, ... / Entschuldigen Sie, ... I
execution [ˌeksɪˈkjuːʃn] Hinrichtung IV 2 (53)
exercise [ˈeksəsaɪz] Übung, Aufgabe I • **do an exercise** eine Übung machen II • **exercise book** [ˈeksəsaɪz bʊk] Schulheft, Übungsheft I • **prewriting exercise** Übung vor dem Schreiben III
exhibition (on) [ˌeksɪˈbɪʃn] Ausstellung (über) IV 2 (40)
°**exit** [ˈeksɪt, ˈegzɪt] (Theater) abgehen; „ab"
°**expand** [ɪkˈspænd] (Notizen) weiter ausführen
expect [ɪkˈspekt] erwarten, annehmen, vermuten IV 4 (79)
expensive [ɪkˈspensɪv] teuer I
experience [ɪkˈspɪəriəns] Erfahrung; Erlebnis IV 4 (79)
experienced [ɪkˈspɪəriənst] erfahren IV 4 (79/214)
explain sth. to sb. [ɪkˈspleɪn] jm. etwas erklären, erläutern II
explanation [ˌekspləˈneɪʃn] Erklärung II
°**explode** [ɪkˈspləʊd] explodieren
explore [ɪkˈsplɔː] erkunden, erforschen I
explorer [ɪkˈsplɔːrə] Entdecker/in, Forscher/in II
explosion [ɪkˈspləʊʒn] Explosion IV 5 (103)
°**express** [ɪkˈspres] ausdrücken
expression [ɪkˈspreʃn] Ausdruck III
extra [ˈekstrə] zusätzlich I
extracurricular activities (kurz: **extracurriculars**) [ˌekstrəkəˈrɪkjələz] schulische Angebote außerhalb des regulären Unterrichts, oft als Arbeitsgemeinschaften IV 4 (78)
extraordinary [ɪkˈstrɔːdnri] außergewöhnlich IV 1 (29)
eye [aɪ] Auge I • **keep an eye on sth./ sb.** nach jm./etwas Ausschau halten IV 2 (40) • **She couldn't believe her eyes.** Sie traute ihren Augen kaum. III • °**They had their eyes on him.** Sie ließen ihn nicht aus den Augen.

F

face [feɪs] Gesicht I
fact [fækt] Tatsache, Fakt III
factory [ˈfæktri] Fabrik II
factual text [ˈfæktʃuːl] Sachtext IV 3 (68)
failure [ˈfeɪljə] ungenügend IV 4 (78)
▶ S.213 US school grades
fair [feə] fair, gerecht II
faithfully [ˈfeɪθfəli]: **Yours faithfully** (BE) mit freundlichen Grüßen IV 4 (85/215)
fall [fɔːl], **fell, fallen** fallen, stürzen; hinfallen II • **fall down** runterfallen; hinfallen II • **fall in love (with sb.)** sich verlieben (in jn.) IV 4 (90) • **fall off** herunterfallen (von) II • **fall to your death** zu Tode stürzen IV 1 (18)
fallen [ˈfɔːlən] siehe fall
°**false** [fɔːls] falsch
family [ˈfæməli] Familie I • **family man** Familienmensch IV 1 (29) • **family tree** (Familien-)Stammbaum I
famous (for) [ˈfeɪməs] berühmt (für, wegen) II
fan [fæn] Fan, Anhänger/in III
fantastic [fænˈtæstɪk] fantastisch, toll I
far [fɑː] weit (entfernt) I • **far and wide** weit und breit IV 4 (80) • **so far** bis jetzt, bis hierher III
faraway [ˈfɑːrəweɪ] abgelegen III
farm [fɑːm] Bauernhof, Farm II
farmer [ˈfɑːmə] Bauer/Bäuerin, Landwirt/in; (Fisch-)Züchter/in III
farmhouse [ˈfɑːmhaʊs] Bauernhaus III
fashion [ˈfæʃn] Mode II
fast [fɑːst] schnell II
fat [fæt] dick IV 4 (90)
°**fatty** [ˈfæti] (beleidigend) Fettsack
father [ˈfɑːðə] Vater I
fault [fɔːlt] Schuld, Fehler IV 2 (39) • **it's your fault** du hast Schuld IV 2 (39/203)
favour [ˈfeɪvə]: **do sb. a favour** jm. einen Gefallen tun IV (91)
favourite [ˈfeɪvərɪt] Lieblings- • **my favourite colour** meine Lieblingsfarbe I
favourite [ˈfeɪvərɪt] Favorit/in; Liebling III
fear (of) [fɪə] Furcht, Angst (vor) III
February [ˈfebruəri] Februar I
fed [fed] siehe feed
feed [fiːd], **fed, fed** füttern I
feel [fiːl], **felt, felt** fühlen; sich fühlen II; sich anfühlen II • °**make sb.**

feel small jm. das Gefühl geben, klein zu sein • °**feel cared about** sich behütet/beschützt fühlen
feeling [ˈfiːlɪŋ] Gefühl III
feet [fiːt] Plural von „foot" I
fell [fel] siehe fall
felt [felt] siehe feel
felt tip [ˈfelt tɪp] Filzstift I
female [ˈfiːmeɪl] Weibchen II
fence [fens] Zaun IV 1 (18)
ferry [ˈferi] Fähre III
festival [ˈfestɪvl] Fest, Festival II
fetch [fetʃ] holen, abholen IV 2 (45)
few [fjuː] wenige IV 4 (79) • **a few** ein paar, einige II
▶ S.214 little („wenig") – few („wenige")
fewer [ˈfjuːə] weniger IV 3 (58)
fiction [ˈfɪkʃn] Belletristik; Prosaliteratur IV 5 (107)
°**fictional** [ˈfɪkʃənəl]: **fictional story** Erzähltext
fiddle [ˈfɪdl] (infml) Fiedel, Geige III • **play the fiddle** Geige spielen III
field [fiːld] Feld, Acker, Weide II • **in the field** auf dem Feld II
°**fierce heat** [fɪəs] glühende Hitze
fight (for) [faɪt], **fought, fought** kämpfen (für, um) III
fight [faɪt] Kampf IV 5 (108/219)
▶ S.219 Verbs & nouns with the same form
°**figure** [ˈfɪgə] Zahl
file [faɪl]: **background file** etwa: Hintergrundinformation II • **grammar file** Grammatikanhang I • **skills file** Anhang mit Lern- und Arbeitstechniken I
fill sth. (with sth.) [fɪl] etwas (mit etwas) (aus)füllen IV 1 (19/197)
°**fill in 1.** einsetzen; **2** ausfüllen
filling [ˈfɪlɪŋ] (Brot-)Belag IV 1 (19)
film [fɪlm] Film I • **crime film** Krimi IV 5 (53/205) • **film star** Filmstar I
film [fɪlm] filmen III
final [ˈfaɪnl] Finale, Endspiel III
final [ˈfaɪnl] letzte(r, s); End- III
finally [ˈfaɪnəli] endlich, schließlich IV Intro (12)
°**finance** [ˈfaɪnæns] Finanz(wesen)
find [faɪnd], **found, found** finden I
find out (about) herausfinden (über) I
fine [faɪn]
1. gut, ausgezeichnet; in Ordnung II
2. (gesundheitlich) gut II
I'm/He's fine. Es geht mir/ihm gut. II
fine [faɪn] Geldstrafe IV 1 (16)
finger [ˈfɪŋgə] Finger I

finish ['fɪnɪʃ] beenden, zu Ende machen; enden I • °**finish with sb.** mit jm. Schluss machen
°**fire** [faɪə] schießen
fire ['faɪə] Feuer, Brand II • **There's no smoke without fire.** Wo Rauch ist, ist auch Feuer. IV 2 (36/201)
°**fire captain** ['faɪə ˌkæptɪn] Zugführer/in (Feuerwehr)
firefighter ['faɪəfaɪtə] Feuerwehrmann, -frau IV 1 (17)
°**firehouse** ['faɪəhaʊs] (AE) (kleinere) Feuerwache
fireman ['faɪəmən] Feuerwehrmann II
firewoman ['faɪəˌwʊmən] Feuerwehrfrau II
fire station ['faɪə ˌsteɪʃn] Feuerwache IV 1 (17)
first [fɜːst]
1. erste(r, s) I
2. zuerst, als Erstes I • **be first** der/die Erste sein I • **for the first time** zum ersten Mal II • **First Nations** die Ersten Nationen (indianische Ureinwohner/innen Kanadas) III
first floor [ˌfɜːst flɔː] erster Stock (BE) / Erdgeschoss (AE) IV 1 (18/196)
▶ S.196 floor
fish, pl **fish/fishes** [fɪʃ] Fisch I
fish [fɪʃ] fischen, angeln III
fisherman ['fɪʃəmən], pl **fishermen** ['fɪʃəmən] Angler, Fischer III
fist [fɪst] Faust IV 4 (92)
fit (-tt-) [fɪt] passen I
flash [flæʃ] aufblitzen; leuchten IV 2 (53)
flash [flæʃ] Lichtblitz III
flat [flæt] Wohnung I
flat [flæt] flach, eben II
flavour ['fleɪvə] Geschmack, Geschmacksrichtung II
flea market ['fliː ˌmɑːkɪt] Flohmarkt III
flew [fluː] siehe **fly**
flight [flaɪt] Flug II
°**float** [fləʊt] treiben
°**flood** [flʌd] überfluten
floor [flɔː]
1. Fußboden I • **dance floor** Tanzfläche III
2. Stock(werk) IV 1 (18) • **first floor** erster Stock (BE) / Erdgeschoss (AE) IV 1 (18/196) • **ground floor** (BE) Erdgeschoss IV 1 (18/196) • **on the second floor** im zweiten Stock (BE) / im ersten Stock (AE) IV 1 (18/196)
▶ S.196 floor
flow [fləʊ] fließen IV 3 (61)
flow chart ['fləʊ tʃɑːt] Flussdiagramm I

flower ['flaʊə] Blume; Blüte II
flown [fləʊn] siehe **fly**
flu [fluː] Grippe II
flute [fluːt] Querflöte III
fly [flaɪ], **flew, flown** fliegen II
flyer ['flaɪə] Flugblatt, Flyer IV 3 (61)
fog [fɒg] Nebel II
foggy ['fɒgi] neblig II
°**folder** ['fəʊldə] Mappe
folk (music) ['fəʊk ˌmjuːzɪk] Folk (meist englischsprachige, volkstümliche Musik mit Elementen der Rockmusik) III
folks [fəʊks] (infml, bes. AE) Leute III
follow ['fɒləʊ] folgen; verfolgen I • **the following ...** die folgenden ... III
food [fuːd] Essen; Lebensmittel; Futter I
foot [fʊt], pl **feet** [fiːt]
1. Fuß I • **on foot** zu Fuß III
2. Fuß (Längenmaß; ca. 30 cm) IV Intro (12)
football ['fʊtbɔːl] Fußball I • **football boots** Fußballschuhe, -stiefel I • °**football field** Footballfeld **football pitch** Fußballplatz, -feld II
footballer ['fʊtbɔːlə] Fußballspieler/in III
footnote ['fʊtnəʊt] Fußnote, Anmerkung IV 5 (103)
°**footwear** ['fʊtweə] Schuhe, Schuhwerk
for [fə, fɔː] für I • **for a moment** einen Moment lang II • **for a while** eine Weile, einige Zeit IV 1 (18) • **for breakfast/lunch/dinner** zum Frühstück/Mittagessen/Abendbrot I • **for example** zum Beispiel I • **for his birthday** zu seinem Geburtstag III • **for lots of reasons** aus vielen Gründen I • **for miles** meilenweit II • **(in prison) for murder** (im Gefängnis) wegen Mordes IV 2 (53) • **for sale** (auf Schild) zu verkaufen IV Intro (11/192) • **for the first time** zum ersten Mal II • °**for the price of** zum Preis von • **for three days** drei Tage (lang) I • **for years** seit Jahren III • **just for fun** nur zum Spaß I • **What for?** [ˌwɒt 'fɔː] Wofür? II • **What's for homework?** Was haben wir als Hausaufgabe auf? I
force sb. to do sth. [fɔːs] jn. dazu bringen/jn. zwingen, etwas zu tun IV 5 (113)
foreground ['fɔːgraʊnd] Vordergrund II

forehead ['fɔːhed, 'fɒrɪd] Stirn IV 3 (72)
°**foreman** ['fɔːmən] Vorarbeiter
forest ['fɒrɪst] Wald II
forgave [fə'geɪv] siehe **forgive**
forget (-tt-) [fə'get], **forgot, forgotten** vergessen III
forgive sb. for sth. [fə'gɪv], **forgave, forgiven** jm. etwas vergeben, verzeihen IV Intro (12)
forgiven [fə'gɪvn] siehe **forgive**
forgot [fə'gɒt] siehe **forget**
forgotten [fə'gɒtn] siehe **forget**
fork [fɔːk] Gabel III
form [fɔːm] bilden IV Intro (8)
form [fɔːm]
1. (Schul-)Klasse I • **form teacher** Klassenlehrer/in I
°**2.** Form
°**formal** ['fɔːml] formell, förmlich
°**former** ['fɔːmə] ehemalige(r, s)
fort [fɔːt] Fort III
°**fortunately** ['fɔːtʃnətli] glücklicherweise
forum ['fɔːrəm] Forum IV 3 (58)
forward ['fɔːwəd]: **look forward to sb./sth.** sich auf jn./etwas freuen IV Intro (9)
fought [fɔːt] siehe **fight**
foul [faʊl] foulen III
found [faʊnd] siehe **find**
found [faʊnd] gründen IV 2 (38)
°**fountain** ['faʊntɪn]: **drinking fountain** Trinkbrunnen
fox [fɒks] Fuchs II
free [friː]
1. frei I • **free time** Freizeit, freie Zeit I • **free-time activities** Freizeitaktivitäten II
2. kostenlos I
freeway ['friːweɪ] (AE) Autobahn IV 5 (98)
French [frentʃ] Französisch I
French fries [ˌfrentʃ 'fraɪz] (bes. AE) Pommes frites IV 1 (24)
°**fresh** [freʃ] frisch
Friday ['fraɪdeɪ, 'fraɪdi] Freitag I
fridge [frɪdʒ] Kühlschrank I
friend [frend] Freund/in I • **make friends (with)** Freunde finden; sich anfreunden (mit) II
friendliness ['frendlinəs] Freundlichkeit IV 4 (86)
friendly ['frendli] freundlich II
fries ['fraɪz]: **(French) fries** (bes. AE) Pommes frites IV 1 (24)
frisbee ['frɪzbi] Frisbee IV 1 (127)
frog [frɒg] Frosch II
from [frəm, frɒm]
1. aus I
2. von I
dresses from the 60s Kleider aus

den 60ern / aus den 60er Jahren II • **from all over the UK / England** aus dem gesamten Vereinigten Königreich / aus ganz England III • **from all over the world** aus der ganzen Welt II • **from Monday to Friday** von Montag bis Freitag III • **from my point of view** aus meiner Sicht; von meinem Standpunkt aus gesehen II • **I'm from ...** Ich komme/bin aus ... I • **Where are you from?** Wo kommst du her? I
front [frʌnt]: **at the front** vorne, im vorderen Teil III • **in front of** vor (räumlich) I • **to the front** nach vorn I • **front door** [ˌfrʌnt 'dɔː] Wohnungstür, Haustür I • **front page** Titelseite III
fruit [fruːt] Obst, Früchte; Frucht I • **fruit salad** Obstsalat I • **pick fruit** Obst pflücken IV 3 (59)
fry [fraɪ] braten III
full [fʊl] voll I
fun [fʌn] Spaß I • **have fun** Spaß haben, sich amüsieren I • **Have fun!** Viel Spaß! I • **just for fun** nur zum Spaß I • **Riding is fun.** Reiten macht Spaß. I
°**fund-raising** [ˈfʌnd reɪzɪŋ] Geldbeschaffung
funeral [ˈfjuːnərəl] Trauerfeier IV 5 (110)
funny [ˈfʌni] witzig, komisch I
furniture (no pl) [ˈfɜːnɪtʃə] Möbel III
future [ˈfjuːtʃə] Zukunft I

G

°**gal** [gæl] (infml) = **girl**
gallery [ˈgæləri] Galerie III
game [geɪm] Spiel I • **a game of football** ein Fußballspiel II • °**board game** Brettspiel
°**gang-related** [ˈgæŋrɪˌleɪtɪd] in Verbindung mit (kriminellen) Banden
garage [ˈgærɑːʒ] Garage II • °**underground garage** Tiefgarage
garbage [ˈgɑːbɪdʒ] (AE) Müll, Abfall IV 1 (24)
garden [ˈgɑːdn] Garten I
gas [gæs]
1. Gas IV 5 (103)
2. (AE) Benzin IV Intro (12) • **gas station** (AE) Tankstelle IV Intro (12)
gate [geɪt] Flugsteig III
°**gateway** [ˈgeɪtweɪ] Tor
gave [geɪv] siehe **give**
gear (no pl) [gɪə] Ausrüstung IV 1 (29) • **camping gear** Campingausrüstung IV Intro (9) • **sports**

gear Sportausrüstung, Sportsachen II
general [ˈdʒenrəl] allgemeine(r, s) III • °**in general** im Allgemeinen
generally [ˈdʒenrəl] im Allgemeinen III
geography [dʒiˈɒgrəfi] Geografie, Erdkunde I
German [ˈdʒɜːmən] Deutsch; deutsch; Deutsche(r) I
Germany [ˈdʒɜːməni] Deutschland I
get (-tt-) [get], got, got
1. bekommen, kriegen II
2. holen, besorgen II
3. gelangen, (hin)kommen I
4. **get angry/hot/...** wütend/ heiß/... werden II • °**Get real!** (AE, infml) etwa: Sei realistisch
5. **get off (the train/bus)** (aus dem Zug/Bus) aussteigen I • **get on (the train/bus)** (in den Zug/Bus) einsteigen I
6. **get up** aufstehen I
I don't get it. Das versteh ich nicht. / Das kapier ich nicht. II
get along zurechtkommen IV 3 (58)
get away from sth./sb. von etwas/jm. weggehen, sich entfernen III
get bored sich langweilen, gelangweilt sein IV 5 (102) • **get dressed** sich anziehen I • **get involved (in)** sich engagieren (für, bei); sich beteiligen (an) IV 4 (79) • **get lost** sich verlaufen III • **Get out of my sight.** Geh mir aus den Augen. IV 2 (52) • **get ready (for)** sich fertig machen (für), sich vorbereiten (auf) I • **get sth. right** etwas richtig machen III • **get sth. wrong** etwas falsch machen III • **get things ready** Dinge fertig machen, vorbereiten I • **get used to sth./sb.** sich gewöhnen an jn./etwas IV 3 (73) • **What can I get you?** Was kann/darf ich euch/Ihnen bringen? II

getting by in English [ˌgetɪŋ ˈbaɪ] etwa: auf Englisch zurechtkommen I
giant [ˈdʒaɪənt] riesige(r,s), Riesen- IV 3 (61)
gig [gɪg] (infml) Gig, Auftritt III • **do a gig** einen Auftritt haben, ein Konzert geben III
giraffe [dʒəˈrɑːf] Giraffe II
girl [gɜːl] Mädchen I
girlfriend [ˈgɜːlfrend] Freundin III
gist [dʒɪst] das Wesentliche III
give [gɪv], gave, given geben I • **give sth. back** etwas zurückgeben I • **give sb. a hug** jn. umarmen IV 2 (39) • **give a smile** lächeln

IV 1 (19) • **give sb. a smile** jn. anlächeln IV 1 (19) • **give a source** eine Quelle angeben IV 2 (42) • **give a speech** eine Rede halten IV 1 (28/199) • °**give up your seat to sb.** jm. seinen Platz überlassen °**give your condolences** (pl) sein Beileid ausdrücken
given [ˈgɪvn] siehe **give**
glad [glæd] froh, dankbar IV Intro (10)
°**gladly** [ˈglædli] gerne
glass [glɑːs] Glas I • **a glass of water** ein Glas Wasser I
glasses (pl) [ˈglɑːsɪz] (eine) Brille I
gloves (pl) [glʌvz] Handschuhe II
glue [gluː] (auf-, ein)kleben II
glue [gluː] Klebstoff I • **glue stick** [ˈgluː stɪk] Klebestift I
go [gəʊ], went, gone
1. gehen I; fahren II
2. **go hard/bad/deaf/blind/crazy/...** hart/schlecht/taub/blind/verrückt/... werden III
go abroad ins Ausland gehen/fahren II • **go ahead** in Führung gehen III • **go by car/bike/...** mit dem Auto/Rad/... fahren II • °**go crunch** Knirsch machen • **go for a run** laufen gehen IV 2 (45) • **go for a walk** spazieren gehen, einen Spaziergang machen II • **go home** nach Hause gehen I • °**go into a line of work** einen Beruf anfangen
go off 1. losfahren, -gehen IV 1 (28); 2. (Waffe) losgehen; (Bombe) explodieren IV 2 (53) • **go on** 1. weitergehen; weiterreden III; 2. angehen (Licht) III • **go on a hike** eine Wanderung machen IV Intro (9)
go on a trip einen Ausflug machen II • **go on a walk** eine Wanderung/einen Spaziergang machen IV Intro (10) • **go on holiday** in Urlaub fahren II • **go out** weg-, raus-, ausgehen I • **go riding/shopping/swimming** reiten/einkaufen/schwimmen gehen I • **go skiing** Ski laufen/fahren III • **go surfing** wellenreiten gehen, surfen gehen II • **go to** führen nach (Straße, Weg) II • **go to bed** ins Bett gehen I • **go to mass** die Messe besuchen IV 1 (29) • **go to the cinema** ins Kino gehen II • **go well** gut (ver)laufen, gutgehen II • **go with** gehören zu, passen zu III • °**go wrong** schiefgehen • **Let's go.** Auf geht's! (wörtlich: Lass uns gehen.) I • **coffee to go** Kaffee zum Mitnehmen IV 1 (19) • **What are you going to do?** Was wirst du tun? / Was hast du vor zu tun? I

goal [gəʊl] Tor *(im Sport)* III • **score a goal** ein Tor schießen, einen Treffer erzielen III
goalkeeper [ˈgəʊlkiːpə] Torwart, Torfrau III
goat [gəʊt] Ziege IV 2 (36)
God [gɒd] Gott IV 5 (113)
gold [gəʊld] Gold III
°**golf** [gɒlf] Golf
gone [gɒn] *siehe* **go** • **be gone** weg sein, nicht da sein II
°**gonna** [ˈgɒnə] *(infml)* = **going to**
good [gʊd]
1. gut I • **Good afternoon.** Guten Tag. *(nachmittags)* I • **Good luck (with ...)!** Viel Glück (bei/mit ...)! I • **Good morning.** Guten Morgen. I
2. brav II
°3. *(infml AE)* = **well**
▶ S.213 US school grades
Goodbye. [ˌgʊdˈbaɪ] Auf Wiedersehen. I • **say goodbye** sich verabschieden I
°**goods** *(pl)* [gʊdz] Waren
goose bumps *(pl)* [ˈguːs ˌbʌmps] *(AE)* Gänsehaut IV 3 (74)
goose pimples *(pl)* [ˈguːs ˌpɪmpəlz] *(BE)* Gänsehaut IV 3 (73/212)
gorge [gɔːdʒ] Schlucht IV Intro (8)
gorilla [gəˈrɪlə] Gorilla IV 1 (18)
gossip [ˈgɒsɪp] schwatzen, klatschen, tratschen III
got [gɒt] *siehe* **get**
got [gɒt]: **I've got ...** Ich habe ... I • **I haven't got a chair.** Ich habe keinen Stuhl. I
°**govern** [ˈgʌvən] verwalten
government [ˈgʌvənmənt] Regierung *(als Schulfach etwa:* Staatskunde*)* IV 4 (78)
governor [ˈgʌvənə] Gouverneur/in IV 3 (56)
grab (-bb-) [græb] schnappen, packen III
grade [greɪd]
1. *(AE)* Jahrgangsstufe, Klasse IV Intro (11)
1. (Schul-)Note, Zensur IV 3 (58)
graduate [ˈgrædʒueɪt] *(AE)* den Schulabschluss machen IV 5 (113) *(BE)* den Hochschulabschluss machen IV 5 (113)
grammar [ˈgræmə] Grammatik I • **grammar file** Grammatikanhang I • **grammar school** Gymnasium III
grand [grænd] eindrucksvoll, beeindruckend IV Intro (12)
grandchild [ˈgræntʃaɪld], *pl* **grandchildren** [-ˌtʃɪldrən] Enkel/in I
granddaughter [ˈgrændɔːtə] Enkelin II
grandfather [ˈgrænfɑːðə] Großvater I

grandma [ˈgrænmɑː] Oma I
grandmother [ˈgrænmʌðə] Großmutter I
grandpa [ˈgrænpɑː] Opa I
grandparents [ˈgrænpeərənts] Großeltern I
grandson [ˈgrænsʌn] Enkel II
granny [ˈgræni] Oma II
grape [greɪp] Weintraube IV 3 (72)
grass [grɑːs] Gras, Rasen IV Intro (11) • **cut the grass** Rasen mähen IV Intro (11)
great [greɪt] großartig, toll I
great-grandmother/-father [ˌgreɪt ˈgrænmʌðə], [ˌgreɪt ˈgrænfɑːðə] Urgroßmutter/-vater III
green [griːn] grün I
greet [griːt] begrüßen IV 3 (72)
grew [gruː] *siehe* **grow**
grey [greɪ] grau II
grid [grɪd] Gitter; Rechteckschema IV 5 (98)
ground [graʊnd] (Erd-)Boden III
ground floor [ˌgraʊnd ˈflɔː] *(BE)* Erdgeschoss IV 1 (18/171)
▶ S.196 floor
Ground Zero [ˌgraʊnd ˈzɪərəʊ] Bodennullpunkt *(Bezeichnung für das zerstörte World Trade Center in New York)* IV 1 (15)
group [gruːp] Gruppe I • **group word** Oberbegriff II
grow [grəʊ], **grew, grown**
1. wachsen II • **grow up** erwachsen werden; aufwachsen III
2. *(Getreide usw.)* anbauen, anpflanzen IV 2 (38)
grown [grəʊn] *siehe* **grow**
°**grown-up** [ˌgrəʊn ˈʌp] Erwachsene(r)
grumble [ˈgrʌmbl] murren, nörgeln II
guard [gɑːd] Wachposten IV 2 (53) °**National Guard** Nationalgarde
guess [ges] raten, erraten, schätzen II • **Guess what!** [ˌges ˈwɒt] Stell dir vor! / Stellt euch vor! II
°**guess** [ges] Vermutung
guest [gest] Gast I
guide [gaɪd] Fremdenführer/in, Reiseleiter/in IV 2 (41)
guided tour [ˌgaɪdɪd ˈtʊə] Führung IV 2 (50)
guinea pig [ˈgɪni pɪg] Meerschweinchen I
guitar [gɪˈtɑː] Gitarre I • **play the guitar** Gitarre spielen I
gun [gʌn] Schusswaffe IV 2 (53)
guy [gaɪ] Typ, Kerl II • **guys** *(pl)* Leute II
gym [dʒɪm] Sporthalle, Turnhalle; Fitnessstudio IV 4 (90)

H

had [hæd] *siehe* **have**
hair *(no pl)* [heə] Haar, Haare I
hairdresser [ˈheədresə] Friseur/in III • **at the hairdresser's** beim Friseur III
half [hɑːf], *pl* **halves** [hɑːvz]
1. Hälfte III
2. Halbzeit III
half [hɑːf] halbe(r, s) II • **half an hour** eine halbe Stunde II • **half past 11** halb zwölf (11.30 / 23.30) I • **half-time** Halbzeit(pause) II • **three and a half days/weeks** dreieinhalb Tage/Wochen IV Intro (8)
half-pipe [ˈhɑːfpaɪp] Halfpipe *(halbierte Röhre für Inlineskater)* III
hall [hɔːl]
1. Flur, Diele I
2. Halle, Saal III • **community hall** Gemeinschaftshalle, -saal III • **sports hall** Sporthalle III
hallway [ˈhɔːlweɪ] *(AE)* Korridor, Gang IV 4 (79)
hamburger [ˈhæmbɜːgə] Hamburger I
hamster [ˈhæmstə] Hamster I
hand sb. sth. [hænd] jm. etwas reichen IV 3 (74)
hand [hænd] Hand I • **second-hand** gebraucht; aus zweiter Hand III
handkerchief [ˈhæŋkətʃiːf] Taschentuch IV 3 (72)
handout [ˈhændaʊt] Arbeitsblatt, Informationsblatt, Handout IV 2 (42)
hang sb. [hæŋ] jn. hängen IV 5 (112)
hang sth. (up) [hæŋ], **hung, hung** etwas aufhängen IV 5 (112/220)
hang out [ˌhæŋ ˈaʊt], **hung, hung** *(infml)* rumhängen, abhängen III
happen (to) [ˈhæpən] geschehen, passieren (mit) I
happiness [ˈhæpinəs] Glück IV 4 (86)
happy [ˈhæpi] glücklich, froh I • **Happy birthday.** Herzlichen Glückwunsch zum Geburtstag. I • **happy ending** Happyend II
harbour [ˈhɑːbə] Hafen III
hard [hɑːd] hart; schwer, schwierig II • **work hard** hart arbeiten II
harvest [ˈhɑːvɪst] Ernte IV 2 (38)
hat [hæt] Hut I
hate [heɪt] hassen, gar nicht mögen I
have [həv, hæv], **had, had** haben, besitzen II • **have an argument** eine Auseinandersetzung haben, sich streiten II • **have a baby** ein Baby/Kind bekommen II • **have**

a bath baden, ein Bad nehmen II
have a cold erkältet sein, eine Erkältung haben II • **have a massage** sich massieren lassen II
have a sauna in die Sauna gehen II • **have a shower** (sich) duschen I • **have a sore throat** Halsschmerzen haben II • **have a temperature** Fieber haben II
have breakfast frühstücken I
have dinner Abendbrot essen I
have ... for breakfast ... zum Frühstück essen/trinken I • **have fun** Spaß haben, sich amüsieren I
Have fun! Viel Spaß! I • **have a good time** sich gut amüsieren III
have to do tun müssen I • °**have your eyes on sb.** ein Auge auf etwas/jn. haben
have got: I've got ... [aɪv ˈɡɒt] Ich habe ... I • **I haven't got a chair.** [ˈhævnt ɡɒt] Ich habe keinen Stuhl. I
he [hiː] er I
head [hed] Kopf I • **nod (your head)** (mit dem Kopf) nicken III **shake your head** den Kopf schütteln III
°**head office** [ˌhed ˈɒfɪs] Zentrale
headache [ˈhedeɪk] Kopfschmerzen II
heading [ˈhedɪŋ] Überschrift IV 1 (27)
headline [ˈhedˌlaɪn] Schlagzeile III
headphones (pl) [ˈhedfəʊnz] Kopfhörer III
head teacher [ˌhed ˈtiːtʃə] Schulleiter/in III
health [helθ] Gesundheit; Gesundheitslehre IV 4 (78)
°**health care** [ˈhelθ ˌkeə] Gesundheitswesen
healthy [ˈhelθi] gesund II
hear [hɪə], **heard, heard** hören I
heard [hɜːd] siehe **hear**
heart [hɑːt] Herz I • **heart attack** Herzinfarkt IV 1 (28)
°**heat** [hiːt] Hitze
heaven [ˈhevn] Himmel (im religiösen Sinn) IV 4 (91)
heavy metal [ˌhevi ˈmetl] Heavymetal III
hedgehog [ˈhedʒhɒɡ] Igel II
held [held] siehe **hold**
helicopter [ˈhelɪkɒptə] Hubschrauber, Helikopter II
Hello. [həˈləʊ] Hallo. / Guten Tag. I
helmet [ˈhelmɪt] Helm III
help [help] helfen I • **Can I help you?** Kann ich Ihnen helfen? / Was kann ich für Sie tun? (im Geschäft) I
help [help] Hilfe I

helpful [ˈhelpfl] hilfreich, nützlich IV 2 (41)
helpless [ˈhelpləs] hilflos IV 3 (64)
her [hə, hɜː]
1. ihr, ihre I
2. sie; ihr I
herb [hɜːb] (Gewürz-)Kraut III
here [hɪə]
1. hier I • **round here** hier (in der Gegend) IV 3 (58)
2. hierher I
Here you are. Bitte sehr. / Hier bitte. I
heritage [ˈherɪtɪdʒ] Erbe IV 4 (80)
°**Hermannite** [ˈhɜːmənaɪt] Bewohner/in von Hermann
hero [ˈhɪərəʊ], pl **heroes** [ˈhɪərəʊz] Held/in II
hers [hɜːz] ihrer, ihre, ihrs II
herself [hɜːˈself]
1. sich III
2. selbst IV 1 (18/196)
▶ S.196 German „selbst"
Hey! [heɪ] Hallo! III
Hi! [haɪ] Hallo! I • **Say hi to your parents for me.** Grüß deine Eltern von mir. I
hid [hɪd] siehe **hide**
hidden [ˈhɪdn] siehe **hide**
hide [haɪd], **hid, hidden** sich verstecken; (etwas) verstecken I
high [haɪ] hoch III • °**higher education** Hochschulwesen; Hochschulbildung
°**highlight** [ˈhaɪlaɪt] hervorheben
highlight [ˈhaɪˌlaɪt] Höhepunkt III
high school [ˈhaɪ skuːl] (USA) Schule für 14- bis 18-Jährige IV Intro (12)
°**high-speed** [ˌhaɪ ˈspiːd] Hochgeschwindigkeits-
°**high-tech** [ˌhaɪ ˈtek] Hightech-
highway [ˈhaɪweɪ] (USA) Fernstraße (oft mit vier oder mehr Spuren) IV Intro (12)
hijacker [ˈhaɪdʒækə] (Flugzeug-)Entführer/in IV 1 (17)
hike [haɪk] wandern IV Intro (9)
hike [haɪk] Wanderung, Marsch IV Intro (9)
hill [hɪl] Hügel II
hilly [ˈhɪli] hügelig III
him [hɪm] ihn; ihm I
himself [hɪmˈself]
1. sich III
2. selbst IV 1 (18/196)
▶ S.196 German „selbst"
hip hop [ˈhɪp ˌhɒp] Hiphop IV 1 (25)
hippo [ˈhɪpəʊ] Flusspferd II
°**hippie** [ˈhɪpi] Hippie
his [hɪz]
1. sein, seine I
2. seiner, seine, seins II

°**historical** [hɪsˈtɒrɪkəl] historisch
history [ˈhɪstri] Geschichte I
hit (-tt-) [hɪt], **hit, hit**
1. schlagen III
2. treffen IV 1 (29)
hobby [ˈhɒbi] Hobby I
hockey [ˈhɒki] Hockey I • **hockey pitch** Hockeyplatz, -feld II
hockey shoes Hockeyschuhe I
°**hog** [hɒɡ] Schwein
hold [həʊld], **held, held** halten II
°**hold on(to sth.)** sich (an etwas) festhalten • **hold a competition** einen Wettbewerb veranstalten III
°**hold things together** die Dinge zusammenhalten
hole [həʊl] Loch I
holiday(s) [ˈhɒlədeɪ] Ferien I • **be on holiday** in Urlaub sein II • **go on holiday** in Urlaub fahren II **holiday home** Ferienhaus, -wohnung III
home [həʊm] Heim, Zuhause I
at home daheim, zu Hause I
come home nach Hause kommen I • **get home** nach Hause kommen I • **go home** nach Hause gehen II
homeland [ˈhəʊmlænd] Heimat(land) IV 4 (80)
homeless [ˈhəʊmləs] obdachlos IV 3 (56)
homeowner [ˈhəʊmˌəʊnə] Eigenheimbesitzer/in IV 3 (61)
hometown [ˈhaʊmˌtaʊn] Heimat(stadt) IV Intro (9)
homework (no pl) [ˈhəʊmwɜːk] Hausaufgabe(n) I • **do homework** die Hausaufgabe(n) machen I **What's for homework?** Was haben wir als Hausaufgabe auf? I
Hooray! [huˈreɪ] Hurra! II
hope [həʊp] hoffen I • **I hope so.** Ich hoffe es. II
hope (of) [həʊp] Hoffnung (auf) III
hopeful [ˈhəʊpfl] hoffnungsvoll IV 2 (40)
hopeless [ˈhəʊpləs] hoffnungslos IV 2 (39) • **You're hopeless.** Dir ist nicht zu helfen. IV 2 (39)
horrible [ˈhɒrəbl] scheußlich, grauenhaft II
horror [ˈhɒrə] Entsetzen, Grauen, Horror III
horse [hɔːs] Pferd I
hose [həʊz] Schlauch IV 3 (73)
hospital [ˈhɒspɪtl] Krankenhaus II
He's gone to hospital. Er ist ins Krankenhaus gegangen. III • **He's in hospital.** Er ist im Krankenhaus. III
host [həʊst] Gastgeber IV 1 (16/194)

hostess ['həʊstes] Gastgeberin *(in USA auch: Frau, die in einem Restaurant die Gäste in Empfang nimmt)* IV 1 (16)
hostel ['hɒstl] Herberge, Wohnheim III • **youth hostel** Jugendherberge III
hot [hɒt] heiß I • **hot chocolate** heiße Schokolade I • **hot-water bottle** Wärmflasche II
hotel [həʊ'tel] Hotel II
hotline ['hɒtlaɪn] Hotline II
hour ['aʊə] Stunde I • **half an hour** eine halbe Stunde I • **a 24-hour supermarket** ein Supermarkt, der 24 Stunden geöffnet ist III • **a two-hour operation** eine zweistündige Operation III
house [haʊs] Haus I • **at the Shaws' house** im Haus der Shaws / bei den Shaws zu Hause I
how [haʊ] wie I • **How about you grabbing that table?** Wie wär's, wenn ihr den Tisch dort schnappt? IV 1 (19) • **How are you?** Wie geht es dir/Ihnen/euch? II • **How do you know …?** Woher weißt/kennst du …? I • **how many?** wie viele? I • **how much?** wie viel? I • **How much is/are …?** Was kostet/kosten …? / Wie viel kostet/kosten …? I • **How old are you?** Wie alt bist du? I • **How was …?** Wie war …? I • **How shall I put it?** Wie soll ich es formulieren/ausdrücken? IV 1 (30/200) • **how to do sth.** wie man etwas tut / tun kann / tun soll IV Intro (11)
▶ S.192 Question words + to-infinitive
however [haʊ'evə] trotzdem IV 3 (60)
°**hub** [hʌb] Mittelpunkt
hug (-gg-) [hʌg] umarmen IV 5 (108/219)
hug [hʌg] Umarmung IV 2 (39) **give sb. a hug** jn. umarmen IV 2 (39)
▶ S.219 Verbs & nouns with the same form
huge [hju:dʒ] riesig, sehr groß III
human ['hju:mən] Mensch, menschliches Wesen IV 2 (38)
hundred ['hʌndrəd] hundert I
hung [hʌŋ] siehe **hang**
hungry ['hʌŋgri] hungrig I • **be hungry** Hunger haben, hungrig sein I
hunt [hʌnt] Jagd III
hunt [hʌnt] jagen III
°**hurricane** ['hʌrɪkən, 'hʌrɪkeɪn] Hurrikan, Orkan
hurry ['hʌri] eilen; sich beeilen II **hurry up** sich beeilen I

hurry ['hʌri]**: be in a hurry** in Eile sein, es eilig haben I
hurt [hɜ:t]**, hurt, hurt** wehtun; verletzen I
hurt [hɜ:t] verletzt II • °**badly hurt** schwer verletzt
husband ['hʌzbənd] Ehemann II
°**hush** [hʌʃ] sei still
hut [hʌt] Hütte IV 2 (53)
hutch [hʌtʃ] (Kaninchen-)Stall I

I

I [aɪ] ich I • **I'm** [aɪm] ich bin I • **I'm from …** Ich komme aus … / Ich bin aus … I • **I'm … years old.** Ich bin … Jahre alt. I • **I'm sorry.** Entschuldigung. / Tut mir leid. I
ice [aɪs] Eis II
ice cream [ˌaɪs'kri:m] (Speise-)Eis I
ice hockey ['aɪsˌhɒki] Eishockey III
ice rink ['aɪs rɪŋk] Schlittschuhbahn II
idea [aɪ'dɪə] Idee, Einfall I
identification, ID [aɪˌdentɪfɪ'keɪʃn , aɪ 'di:] Ausweis IV Intro (10)
identity [aɪ'dentɪti] Identität IV 5 (110)
if [ɪf]
1. wenn, falls II
2. ob II
ill [ɪl] krank II
illegal [ɪ'li:gl] illegal, ungesetzlich IV 3 (58)
illness ['ɪlnəs] Krankheit IV 4 (45/204)
illustrate ['ɪləstreɪt] veranschaulichen, illustrieren IV 43 (68)
°**illustration** [ɪləˈstreɪʃn] Bild
°**image** ['ɪmɪdʒ] Bild
imagination [ɪˌmædʒɪ'neɪʃn] Fantasie, Vorstellung(skraft) IV 4 (86)
imagine sth. [ɪ'mædʒɪn] sich etwas vorstellen III
imitate ['ɪmɪteɪt] nachmachen III
immediately [ɪ'mi:dɪətli] sofort IV 5 (112)
immigrant ['ɪmɪgrənt] Einwanderer/Einwanderin IV 1 (15)
immigrate ['ɪmɪgreɪt] einwandern IV 1 (15)
immigration [ˌɪmɪ'greɪʃn] Einwanderung IV 1 (15) • °**immigration station** Einwanderungsstelle
important [ɪm'pɔ:tnt] wichtig II
impossible [ɪm'pɒsəbl] unmöglich II
impressed [ɪm'prest] beeindruckt IV 5 (102)
impressive [ɪm'presɪv] beeindruckend, eindrucksvoll III

improve [ɪm'pru:v] verbessern III
in [ɪn] II • **the best view in the world** die beste Aussicht der Welt IV 1 (18) • **in 2050** im Jahr 2050 II • **in … Street** in der …straße I • **in English** auf Englisch I • **in front of** vor *(räumlich)* I • °**in general** im Allgemeinen • **in here** hier drinnen I • **in next to no time** im Nu III • **in other places** an anderen Orten, anderswo III • °**in particular** insbesondere • **in school** *(AE)* in der Schule IV 3 (58) • **in the afternoon** nachmittags, am Nachmittag I • **in the country** auf dem Land II • **in the evening** abends, am Abend I • **in the field** auf dem Feld II • **in the morning** am Morgen, morgens I • **in the photo/picture** auf dem Foto/Bild I • **in there** dort drinnen I • **in the sky** am Himmel II • **in the world** auf der Welt II • **in the yard** auf dem Hof II • **in time** [ɪn 'taɪm] rechtzeitig II
include [ɪn'klu:d] einschließen IV Intro (8)
°**including** [ɪn'ŋklu:dɪŋ] einschließlich
incredible [ɪn'kredɪbl] unglaublich IV 4 (90)
°**indeed** [ˌɪn'di:d] *(altmodisch)* in der Tat
infinitive [ɪn'fɪnətɪv] Infinitiv *(Grundform des Verbs)* I
°**independent** [ˌɪndɪ'pendənt] unabhängig
Indian ['ɪndɪən]
1. Inder/in I
2. Indianer/in IV 2 (36)
indirect speech [ˌɪndə'rekt] indirekte Rede III
industrial [ɪn'dʌstrɪəl] industriell III
industry ['ɪndəstri] Industrie III °**manufacturing industry** Fertigungsindustrie
inform sb. (about/of sth.) [ɪn'fɔ:m] jn. (über etwas) informieren IV 5 (107)
information (about/on) *(no pl)* [ˌɪnfə'meɪʃn] Information(en) (über) I
injury ['ɪndʒəri] Verletzung II
innovation [ˌɪnə'veɪʃn] Innovation, Neuerung IV 3 (56)
insect ['ɪnsekt] Insekt IV 3 (59)
°**insecticide** [ɪn'sektɪsaɪd] Insektenvernichtungsmittel
inside [ˌɪn'saɪd]
1. innen (drin), drinnen I; Innen- IV 1 (18)
2. nach drinnen II

3. inside the car ins Auto (hinein), ins Innere des Autos II
install [ɪnˈstɔːl] installieren, einrichten II
installation [ˌɪnstəˈleɪʃn] Installation, Einrichtung II
instant message [ˌɪnstənt ˈmesɪdʒ] Nachricht, die man im Internet austauscht (in Echtzeit) III
instead of [ɪnˈsted_əv] anstelle von, statt IV 2 (39)
instructions (pl) [ɪnˈstrʌkʃnz] (Gebrauchs-)Anweisung(en), Anleitung(en) II
instrument [ˈɪnstrəmənt] Instrument III
°**integration** [ˌɪntɪˈɡreɪʃn]
interest sb. [ˈɪntrəst] jn. interessieren IV 5 (108)
°**interest** [ˈɪntrest] Interesse
interested [ɪntrəstɪd]: **be interested (in)** interessiert sein (an), sich interessieren (für) III
interesting [ˈɪntrəstɪŋ] interessant I
international [ˌɪntəˈnæʃnəl] international II
internet [ˈɪntənet] Internet I • **surf the internet** im Internet surfen II
interrupt [ˌɪntəˈrʌpt] unterbrechen IV 2 (39)
°**Interstate** [ˌɪntəˈsteɪt] Autobahn
interview [ˈɪntəvjuː] befragen, interviewen IV 3 (66)
into [ˈɪntə, ˈɪntʊ]
1. in ... (hinein) I
2. be into sth. (infml) etwas mögen III
introduce sb. (to sb.) [ˌɪntrəˈdjuːs] jn. (jm.) vorstellen IV 3 (74)
introduce sb. to sth. [ˌɪntrəˈdjuːs] jn. in etwas einführen IV 5 (101)
introduction (to) [ˌɪntrəˈdʌkʃn] Einführung (in) III
invent [ɪnˈvent] erfinden III
inventor [ɪnˈventə] Erfinder/in III
invitation (to) [ˌɪnvɪˈteɪʃn] Einladung (zu) I
invite (to) [ɪnˈvaɪt] einladen (zu) I
involved [ɪnˈvɒlvd]: **get involved (in)** sich engagieren (für, bei); sich beteiligen (an) IV 4 (35)
irregular [ɪˈreɡjələ] unregelmäßig I
is [ɪz] ist I
island [ˈaɪlənd] Insel II
°**issue** [ˈɪsjuː, ˈɪʃuː]: **address an issue** sich mit einer Frage/Aufgabe befassen
it [ɪt] er/sie/es I • **It's £1.** Er/Sie/Es kostet 1 Pfund. I
IT [ˌaɪ ˈtiː], **information technology** [tekˈnɒlədʒi] IT (Informationstechnologie) II

itself [ɪtˈself]
1. sich III
2. selbst IV 1 (18/196)
▶ S.196 German „selbst"
its [ɪts] sein/seine; ihr/ihre I

J

jacket [ˈdʒækɪt] Jacke, Jackett II
°**jam** [dʒæm]: **traffic jam** Verkehrsstau
January [ˈdʒænjuəri] Januar I
jazz [dʒæz] Jazz III
jeans (pl) [dʒiːnz] Jeans I
°**jerk** [dʒɜːk] (beleidigend) Trottel, Blödmann
jet lag [ˈdʒet ˌlæɡ] Jetlag IV 1 (17)
°**jewellery** [ˈdʒuːəlri] Schmuck
°**jewelry** [ˈdʒuːəlri] (AE) Schmuck
Jewish [ˈdʒuːɪʃ] jüdisch IV 1 (19)
job [dʒɒb] Aufgabe, Job I • **do a good job** gute Arbeit leisten II
join sb./sth. [dʒɔɪn] sich jm. anschließen; bei jm./etwas mitmachen II
join in [ˌdʒɔɪn_ˈɪn] mitmachen III
joke [dʒəʊk] Witz I
joke [dʒəʊk] scherzen, Witze machen II
journalist [ˈdʒɜːnəlɪst] Journalist/in IV 1 (24)
journey [ˈdʒɜːni] Reise, Fahrt III
°**Jr.** siehe **Junior**
judge sb. (by) [dʒʌdʒ] jn. beurteilen, einschätzen (nach) IV 5 (102)
judo [ˈdʒuːdəʊ] Judo I • **do judo** Judo machen I
jug [dʒʌɡ] Krug I • **a jug of milk** ein Krug Milch I
juice [dʒuːs] Saft I
July [dʒuˈlaɪ] Juli I
jumble sale [ˈdʒʌmbl seɪl] Wohltätigkeitsbasar I
jump [dʒʌmp] springen II
June [dʒuːn] Juni I
jungle [ˈdʒʌŋɡl] Dschungel IV 1 (18)
junior [ˈdʒuːniə]
1. Junioren-, Jugend- I
2. junior (to sb.) jm. untergeordnet IV 1 (29)
°**Junior (Jr.)** [ˈdʒuːniə] (bes. in den USA, unterscheidet den Sohn vom gleichnamigen Vater) der Jüngere
just [dʒʌst]
1. (einfach) nur, bloß I
2. gerade (eben), soeben II
just then genau in dem Moment; gerade dann II
3. just like you genau wie du II
just as ... as ebenso ... wie IV 4 (79)
4. einfach III

K

kangaroo [ˌkæŋɡəˈruː] Känguru II
°**kayaking** [ˈkaɪækɪŋ] Kajakfahren
keep [kiːp], **kept, kept** (be)halten; aufbewahren III • **keep an eye on sth./sb.** nach jm./etwas Ausschau halten IV 2 (40) • **keep (on) doing sth.** etwas weiter tun; etwas ständig tun IV 2 (54) • **keep in touch** in Verbindung bleiben, Kontakt halten III • **keep quiet** still sein, leise sein IV 2 (39) • **keep sth. alive** etwas am Leben halten IV 4 (80) **keep sth. warm/cool/open/...** etwas warm/kühl/offen/... halten III
keeper [ˈkiːpə] Torwart, Torfrau III
kept [kept] siehe **keep**
ketchup [ˈketʃəp] Ketchup IV 4 (86)
key [kiː] Schlüssel I • **key word** Stichwort, Schlüsselwort I • **key ring** Schlüsselring IV Intro (12)
keyboard [ˈkiːbɔːd] Keyboard (elektronisches Tasteninstrument) III
kick [kɪk] (mit dem Fuß) treten (gegen) IV 5 (113) • °**alive and kicking** gesund und munter
°**kick** [kɪk] Kitzel
kid [kɪd] Kind, Jugendliche(r) I
kill [kɪl] töten I
°**killer bee** [ˈkɪlə ˈbiː] „Killerbiene", Afrikanisierte Honigbiene
°**killer whale** [ˈkɪlə ˌweɪl] Großer Schwertwal, Killerwal
kilogram (kg) [ˈkɪləɡræm], **kilo** [ˈkiːləʊ] Kilogramm, Kilo III • **a kilogram of oranges** ein Kilogramm Orangen III • **a 150-kilogram bear** ein 150 Kilogramm schwerer Bär III
kilometre (km) [ˈkɪləmiːtə] Kilometer III • **a ten-kilometre walk** eine Zehn-Kilometer-Wanderung III • **square kilometre** Quadratkilometer III
kind (of) [kaɪnd] Art (von) III **kind of scary** (infml) irgendwie unheimlich III
kindergarten [ˈkɪndəɡɑːtn] Kindergarten; (USA) Vorschule (für 5- bis 6-Jährige) IV 4 (78)
king [kɪŋ] König I
kiss [kɪs] (sich) küssen IV 1 (18)
kiss [kɪs] Kuss I
kitchen [ˈkɪtʃɪn] Küche I
kite [kaɪt] Drachen I
knee [niː] Knie I
knew [njuː] siehe **know**
knife [naɪf], pl **knives** [naɪvz] Messer III
knock (on) [nɒk] (an)klopfen (an) I
°**knock** [nɒk] Klopfen, Klopfgeräusch

know [nəʊ], **knew, known**
1. wissen I
2. kennen I
How do you know ...? Woher weißt du ...?/Woher kennst du ...? I • **know about sth.** von etwas wissen; über etwas Bescheid wissen II • **..., you know.** ..., wissen Sie. / ..., weißt du. I • **You know what, Sophie?** Weißt du was, Sophie? I
known [nəʊn] bekannt IV Intro (8) siehe **know**

L

ladder [ˈlædə] (die) Leiter IV 1 (30)
°**ladder company** Zug (Einheit der Feuerwache)
laid [leɪd] siehe **lay**
lain [leɪn] siehe **lie**
lake [leɪk] (Binnen-)See II
lamp [læmp] Lampe I
land [lænd] landen II
land [lænd] Land III • **on land** auf dem Land III
lane [leɪn] Gasse, Weg III
language [ˈlæŋgwɪdʒ] Sprache I
large [lɑːdʒ] groß I
lasagne [ləˈzænjə] Lasagne I
last [lɑːst] letzte(r, s) I • **the last day** der letzte Tag I • **at last** endlich, schließlich I
last-minute [ˌlɑːst ˈmɪnɪt]: **a last-minute shot** ein Schuss in der letzten Minute III
late [leɪt] spät; zu spät I • **be late** zu spät sein/kommen I • **Sorry, I'm late.** Entschuldigung, dass ich zu spät bin/komme. I
later [ˈleɪtə] später II
latest [ˈleɪtɪst] neueste(r, s) III
°**Latino** [ləˈtiːnəʊ] Amerikaner/in lateinamerikanischer Herkunft
laugh [lɑːf] lachen I • **laugh out loud** laut lachen II
laughter [ˈlɑːftə] Gelächter II
law [lɔː] Gesetz IV 2 (52)
lay [leɪ] siehe **lie**
lay the table [leɪ], **laid, laid** den Tisch decken I
layer [ˈleɪə] Schicht IV Intro (12)
lead (to sth.) [led], **led, led** (zu etwas) führen IV 2 (38)
leader [ˈliːdə] (An-)Führer/in, Leiter/in IV 2 (52)
°**lean on sth.** [liːn] sich auf etwas stützen
learn [lɜːn] lernen I • **learn about sth.** etwas über etwas erfahren, etwas über etwas herausfinden II

least [liːst] am wenigsten IV 4 (79/214) • **at least** zumindest, wenigstens I
leather [ˈleðə] Leder III
leave [liːv], **left, left**
1. (weg)gehen; abfahren II
2. verlassen II
3. **leave (behind)** zurücklassen IV 1 (30) • °**leave sb./sth. alone** jn. in Ruhe lassen; jn. allein lassen °**leave out** auslassen • °**those they have left behind** die Hinterbliebenen
led [led] siehe **lead**
left [left] siehe **leave** • **be left** übrig sein II
left [left] linke(r, s) I • **look left** nach links schauen I • **on the left** links, auf der linken Seite I • **take a left** (AE) nach links/rechts abbiegen IV 1 (16) • **to the left** nach links III • **turn left** (nach) links abbiegen II
leg [leg] Bein I
legal [ˈliːgl] legal 3 (58/208)
leisure centre [ˈleʒə sentə] Freizeitzentrum, -park II
lemonade [ˌleməˈneɪd] Limonade I
lend sb. sth. [lend], **lent, lent** jm. etwas leihen II
lent [lent] siehe **lend**
lentil [ˈlentəl] Linse (Hülsenfrucht) III
leotard [ˈliːətɑːd] Gymnastikanzug; Turnanzug III
less [les] weniger IV 3 (59) • **more or less** mehr oder weniger IV 1 (29)
lesson [ˈlesn] (Unterrichts-)Stunde I • **lessons** (pl) Unterricht I
let [let], **let, let** lassen II • **Let's ...** Lass uns ... / Lasst uns ... I • **Let's go.** Auf geht's! (wörtlich: Lass uns gehen.) I • **Let's look at the list.** Sehen wir uns die Liste an. / Lasst uns die Liste ansehen. I • **let sb. do sth.** jm. erlauben, etwas zu tun; zulassen, dass jd. etwas tut III
letter [ˈletə]
1. Buchstabe I • **capital letter** Großbuchstabe III • **small letter** Kleinbuchstabe III
2. **letter (to)** [ˈletə] Brief (an) II
lettuce [ˈletɪs] (Kopf-)Salat II
liberty [ˈlɪbəti] Freiheit IV 1 (15)
library [ˈlaɪbrəri] Bibliothek, Bücherei I
license plate [ˈlaɪsns pleɪt] (AE) Nummernschild IV Intro (12)
lie [laɪ], **lay, lain** liegen IV 3 (73)
life [laɪf], pl **lives** [laɪvz] Leben II • **life sentence** lebenslängliche Haftstrafe IV 2 (53/205) • **way of life** Lebensart III

lift [lɪft] (an-, hoch)heben IV 2 (53)
lift [lɪft] Fahrstuhl, Aufzug II
light [laɪt] Licht III
°**lighting** [ˈlaɪtɪŋ] Beleuchtung
like [laɪk]
1. wie I • **just like you** genau wie du II • **language like that** solche Sprache IV 2 (39) • **like what?** wie zum Beispiel? IV 2 (41) • **What was the weather like?** Wie war das Wetter? II
2. (infml) als ob III
like [laɪk] mögen, gernhaben I • **like sth. better** etwas lieber mögen II • **like sth. very much** etwas sehr mögen II • **I like dancing/swimming...** Ich tanze/schwimme... gern. I • **I'd like ...** (= I would like ...) Ich hätte gern ... / Ich möchte gern ... I • **I'd like to go** (= I would like to go) Ich würde gern gehen / Ich möchte gehen I • **I wouldn't like to go** Ich würde nicht gern gehen / Ich möchte nicht gehen I • **Would you like ...?** Möchtest du ...? / Möchten Sie ...? I
limit [ˈlɪmɪt] Begrenzung, Beschränkung II • **speed limit** Geschwindigkeitsbegrenzung, -beschränkung III
line [laɪn]
1. Zeile II
2. (U-Bahn-)Linie III
3. Schlange, Reihe (wartender Menschen) IV 1 (16) • **Line starts here.** Hier anstellen. IV 1 (16) • **line of work** Beruf, berufliche Richtung IV 1 (30) • **be in a line of work** einen Beruf ausüben IV 1 (30)
link [lɪŋk] verbinden, verknüpfen I
link [lɪŋk] Verbindung III
linking word [ˈlɪŋkɪŋ wɜːd] Bindewort II
lion [ˈlaɪən] Löwe II
lip [lɪp] Lippe IV 1 (18)
list [lɪst] auflisten, aufzählen II
list [lɪst] Liste I • **put your name on a list** sich eintragen IV 4 (89)
listen (to) [ˈlɪsn] zuhören; sich etwas anhören I • **listen for sth.** auf etwas horchen, achten III
listener [ˈlɪsnə] Zuhörer/in II
litter [ˈlɪtə] Abfälle zurücklassen IV 1 (16)
litter [ˈlɪtə] Abfall IV 1 (16/194)
little [ˈlɪtl]
1. klein I
2. wenig IV 4 (79) • **a little** ein bisschen, ein wenig IV 1 (29)
°**little-known** wenig bekannt
▶ S.214 little („wenig") – few („wenige")
live [lɪv] leben, wohnen I

live [laɪv]: **live concert** Livekonzert III • **live music** Livemusik II
lives [laɪvz] *Plural von „life"* I
living-history museum Freilichtmuseum *(mit kostümierten Fremdenführer/innen, historischen Aufführungen usw.)* IV 2 (40)
living room ['lɪvɪŋ ruːm; rʊm] Wohnzimmer I
load [ləʊd] beladen III
lobby ['lɒbi] Eingangshalle IV 1 (18)
°**Lobsterback** ['lɒbstəˌbæk] *etwa:* Hummerrücken *(die britischen Soldaten trugen eine knallrote Uniform)*
local ['ləʊkl] örtlich, Lokal-; am/vom Ort III
location [ləʊ'keɪʃn] (Einsatz-)Ort, Platz III
loch [lɒx] (Binnen-)See in Schottland III
lock [lɒk] Schleuse III
lock [lɒk] abschließen, zuschließen I • **lock up** abschließen II
logo ['ləʊɡəʊ] Logo, Markenzeichen III
°**lonely** ['ləʊnli] einsam
long [lɒŋ] lang I • **a long way (from)** weit entfernt (von) I • **a long time** lange III
look [lʊk]
1. schauen, gucken I
2. **look different/great/old** anders/toll/alt aussehen I • **look after sth./sb.** sich um etwas/jn. kümmern; auf etwas/jn. aufpassen II • **look at** ansehen, anschauen I **look at sth. closely** etwas genau anschauen III • **look for** suchen II • **look forward to sb./sth.** sich auf jn./etwas freuen IV Intro (9) **look left and right** nach links und rechts schauen I • **look around/round** sich umsehen I • °**look out for sb.** auf jn. achten • **look up (from)** hochsehen, aufschauen (von) II • **look up to sb.** zu jm. aufsehen IV 1 (30) • **look up words** Wörter nachschlagen III
°**look** [lʊk] (Über-)Blick
Lord [lɔːd] Herr(gott) IV 2 (38)
lose [luːz], **lost, lost** verlieren II
lost [lɒst] *siehe* **lose** • **get lost** sich verlaufen II
lot [lɒt]: **a lot (of), lots of** eine Menge, viel, viele I / II • **He likes her a lot.** Er mag sie sehr. I • **lots more** viel mehr I • **Thanks a lot!** Vielen Dank! I
loud [laʊd] laut I • °**read sth. out loud** etwas vorlesen

love [lʌv] lieben, sehr mögen I **love sth. very much** etwas sehr lieben II
love [lʌv]
1. Liebe II
2. „Liebes", „Liebling" III
fall in love (with sb.) sich verlieben (in jn.) IV 4 (90) • **Love ...** Liebe Grüße, ... *(Grußformel am Ende eines Briefes)* I
▶ S.215 Beginning and ending letters
lovely ['lʌvli] schön, hübsch, wunderbar II
°**lox** [lɒks] *Yiddish:* (gepökelter) Lachs
luck [lʌk]: **Good luck (with ...)!** Viel Glück (bei/mit ...)! I
luckily ['lʌkɪli] zum Glück, glücklicherweise II
lucky ['lʌki]: **be lucky** Glück haben III
°**lump (in your throat)** [lʌmp] Kloß (im Hals)
lunch [lʌntʃ] Mittagessen I • **for lunch** zum Mittagessen III **lunch break** Mittagspause I **lunchtime** ['lʌntʃtaɪm] Mittagszeit III
lyrics *(pl)* ['lɪrɪks] Liedtext(e) III

M

machine [mə'ʃiːn] Maschine, Gerät II
mad [mæd] verrückt I • **mad about** verrückt nach III
madam ['mædəm]: **Dear Sir or Madam ...** Sehr geehrte Damen und Herren IV 4 (85/215)
▶ S.215 Beginning and ending letters
made [meɪd] *siehe* **make**
made [meɪd]: **to be made of sth.** aus etwas (gemacht) sein III
°**madman** ['mædmən] Verrückter
magazine [ˌmæɡə'ziːn] Zeitschrift, Magazin I
°**magnitude** ['mæɡnɪˌtjuːd] Stärke *(eines Erdbebens)*
mail sb. [meɪl] jn. anmailen I **mail sb. sth.** jm. etwas schicken, senden *(vor allem per E-Mail)* III
main [meɪn] Haupt- III
maize *(no pl)* [meɪz] *(BE)* Mais IV 2 (37)
°**majestic** [mə'dʒestɪk] majestätisch
majority [mə'dʒɒrəti] Mehrheit IV 3 (58)
make [meɪk], **made, made** machen; bauen I • **make a call** ein Telefongespräch führen, telefonieren II
make a deal ein Abkommen/eine Abmachung treffen III • **make a mess** alles durcheinanderbringen, alles in Unordnung bringen • **make a speech** eine Rede halten IV 1 (28/199) • **make friends (with)** Freunde finden; sich anfreunden (mit) II • **make sb. sth.** jn. zu etwas machen III • °**make sb. feel small** jm. das Gefühl geben, klein zu sein • °**make sense** Sinn ergeben • **make sure** sich vergewissern IV 4 (87)
make-up ['meɪkʌp] Make-up II **make-up artist** Maskenbildner/in
male [meɪl] Männchen II
mall [mɔːl, *BE auch* mæl] (großes) Einkaufszentrum III
°**mamma** ['mæmə] Mama
man [mæn], *pl* **men** [men] Mann I
manager ['mænədʒə] Manager/in III
°**manufacturing industry** [ˌmænjə'fæktʃərɪŋ] Fertigungsindustrie
many ['meni] viele I • **how many? wie viele?** I
map [mæp] Landkarte, Stadtplan II
March [mɑːtʃ] März I
°**march** [mɑːtʃ] marschieren
march [mɑːtʃ] Marsch, Demonstration IV 5 (102)
mark [mɑːk] (Schul-)Note, Zensur IV 3 (58)
mark [mɑːk]: **quotation marks** Anführungszeichen, -striche III
mark sth. (up) [ˌmɑːk _ 'ʌp] etwas markieren, kennzeichnen II
market ['mɑːkɪt] Markt II
marmalade ['mɑːməleɪd] Orangenmarmelade I
married (to) ['mærɪd] verheiratet (mit) I
marry ['mæri] heiraten III
mass [mæs] Messe (Gottesdienst) IV 1 (29)
°**massacre** ['mæsəkə] Massaker
massage ['mæsɑːʒ] Massage II **have a massage** sich massieren lassen II
°**masseuse** [mæ'sɜːz, *AE* mə'suːs] Masseurin
°**match sth (to sth.)** [mætʃ] etwas (zu etwas) zuordnen
match [mætʃ] Spiel, Wettkampf I
material [mə'tɪəriəl] Material, Stoff II
maths [mæθs] Mathematik I
matter ['mætə]: **What's the matter?** Was ist los? / Was ist denn? II
may [meɪ] dürfen I
May [meɪ] Mai I
maybe ['meɪbi] vielleicht I

Dictionary (English – German) 241

mayor ['meə] Bürgermeister/in IV 5 (99)
me [miː] mir; mich I • **Me too.** Ich auch. I • **more than me** mehr als ich II • **That's me.** Das bin ich. I **Why me?** Warum ich? I
meal [miːl] Mahlzeit, Essen III **set meal** Menü III
mean [miːn], **meant, meant**
1. bedeuten II
2. meinen, sagen wollen I
mean [miːn] gemein IV 1 (29)
meaning ['miːnɪŋ] Bedeutung I
meant [ment] siehe **mean**
meat [miːt] Fleisch I
°**mecca** ['mekə] Mekka
medal ['medl] Medaille III
media (pl) ['miːdiə] Medien III
mediate ['miːdieɪt] vermitteln IV 1 (26)
mediation [ˌmiːdi'eɪʃn] Vermittlung, Sprachmittlung, Mediation II
medium ['miːdiəm] mittel-, mittlere(r,s); mittelgroß III
meet [miːt], **met, met**
1. treffen; kennenlernen I
2. sich treffen I
meeting ['miːtɪŋ] Versammlung, Besprechung IV 4 (79)
member ['membə]: **member of staff** (BE), **staff member** (AE) Mitarbeiter/in IV 2 (40)
men [men] Plural von „man" I
°**mention** ['menʃn] erwähnen
menu ['menjuː] Speisekarte; Menü (Computer) III
merry-go-round [ˈmerɪɡəʊˌraʊnd] Karussell IV 5 (112)
mess [mes]: **make a mess** alles durcheinanderbringen, alles in Unordnung bringen I
message: **instant message** [ˌɪnstənt 'mesɪdʒ] Nachricht, die man im Internet austauscht (in Echtzeit) III
met [met] siehe **meet**
method ['meθəd] Methode IV 3 (59)
metre ['miːtə] Meter II
mice [maɪs] Plural von „mouse" I
microphone ['maɪkrəfəʊn] Mikrofon III
middle (of) ['mɪdl] Mitte; Mittelteil I
middle school ['mɪdl ˌskuːl] (USA) Schule für 11- bis 14-Jährige IV Intro (11)
°**mid-forties** [mɪd'fɔːtiz] Mitte vierzig
might [maɪt]: **you might need help** du könntest (vielleicht) Hilfe brauchen III
°**mighty** ['maɪti] mächtig
migrant worker [ˌmaɪɡrənt 'wɜːkə] Wanderarbeiter/in IV 3 (56)

mild [maɪld] mild III
mile [maɪl] Meile (= ca. 1,6 km) II **for miles** meilenweit II
milk [mɪlk] melken IV 2 (45)
milk [mɪlk] Milch I
milkshake ['mɪlkʃeɪk] Milchshake I
million ['mɪljən] Million III
millionaire [ˌmɪljə'neə] Millionär/in IV Intro (12/193)
mime [maɪm] vorspielen, pantomimisch darstellen II
mind [maɪnd]: **Mind your own business.** Das geht dich nichts an! / Kümmere dich um deine eigenen Angelegenheiten! II **Never mind.** [ˌnevə 'maɪnd] Kümmere dich nicht drum. / Macht nichts. II
mind map ['maɪnd mæp] Mindmap („Gedankenkarte", „Wissensnetz") I
mine [maɪn] meiner, meine, meins II
minister ['mɪnɪstə]
1. Minister/in IV 2 (54/207) • **prime minister** Premierminister/in IV 2 (54/207)
2. Pfarrer/in, Pastor/in IV 2 (54)
minority [maɪ'nɒrəti] Minderheit IV 3 (58)
mints (pl) [mɪnts] Pfefferminzbonbons I
minute ['mɪnɪt] Minute I • **Wait a minute.** Warte mal! / Moment mal! II • **a 30-minute ride** eine 30-minütige Fahrt III
Minuteman ['mɪnɪtˌmən] Angehöriger der amerikanischen Miliz IV 2 (52)
°**miraculous** [mɪ'rkjuːləs] Wunder-, wunderhaft
mirror ['mɪrə] Spiegel II
Miss White [mɪs] Frau White (unverheiratet) I
miss [mɪs]
1. vermissen II
2. verpassen II
Miss a turn. Einmal aussetzen. II
missing ['mɪsɪŋ]: **be missing** fehlen II
mistake [mɪ'steɪk] Fehler I • **by mistake** aus Versehen IV 2 (53/206)
mix [mɪks] mischen, mixen III
°**mixed-up** [ˌmɪkst_'ʌp] durcheinander
mixture ['mɪkstʃə] Mischung III
mobile (phone) ['məʊbaɪl] Mobiltelefon, Handy I
model ['mɒdl] Modell(-flugzeug, -schiff usw.) I; (Foto-)Modell II
°**modern** ['mɒdn] modern
mole [məʊl] Maulwurf II

mom [mɑːm] (AE) Mutti, Mama; Mutter III
moment ['məʊmənt] Augenblick, Moment I • **at the moment** im Moment, gerade, zurzeit I • **for a moment** einen Moment lang II
Monday ['mʌndeɪ, 'mʌndi] Montag I • **Monday morning** Montagmorgen I
money ['mʌni] Geld I • **Money doesn't grow on trees.** Redensart: Geld wächst nicht auf Bäumen; Geld liegt nicht auf der Straße. III **raise money (for)** Geld sammeln (für) IV Intro (11)
monitor ['mɒnɪtə] Bildschirm, Monitor III
monkey ['mʌŋki] Affe II
monster ['mɒnstə] Monster, Ungeheuer III
month [mʌnθ] Monat I
°**monument** ['mɒnjumənt] Denkmal, Monument
moon [muːn] Mond II
°**moonlight** ['muːnlaɪt] Mondlicht
more [mɔː] mehr I • **lots more** viel mehr I • **more boring (than)** langweiliger (als) II • **more or less** mehr oder weniger IV 1 (29) • **more quickly (than)** schneller (als) II **more than me** mehr als ich II **no more music** keine Musik mehr I • **not (...) any more** nicht mehr II • **one more** noch ein(e), ein(e) weitere(r, s) I
morning ['mɔːnɪŋ] Morgen, Vormittag I • **in the morning** morgens, am Morgen I • **Monday morning** Montagmorgen I • **on Friday morning** freitagmorgens, am Freitagmorgen I
mosque [mɒsk] Moschee III
most [məʊst] (der/die/das) meiste ...; am meisten II • **most people** die meisten Leute I • **(the) most boring ...** der/die/das langweiligste ...; am langweiligsten II
motel [məʊ'tel] Motel III
mother ['mʌðə] Mutter I
°**motor** ['məʊtə] mit dem Auto fahren
motorway ['məʊtəweɪ] (BE) Autobahn IV 5 (98)
mountain ['maʊntən] Berg II
°**mountaintop** ['maʊntntɒp] Berggipfel
mouse [maʊs], pl **mice** [maɪs] Maus I
mouth [maʊθ] Mund I
move [muːv]
1. bewegen; sich bewegen II
Move back one space. Geh ein

Feld zurück. II • °**move on** weitergehen, weitermachen • **Move on one space.** Geh ein Feld vor. II
2. **move (to)** umziehen (nach, in) II • **move in** einziehen II • **move out** ausziehen II
move [muːv] Umzug IV 4 (81)
movement [ˈmuːvmənt] Bewegung II
movie [ˈmuːvi] Film IV 1 (18)
MP3 player [ˌempiːˈθriː ˌpleɪə] MP3-Spieler I
Mr, Mr. ... [ˈmɪstə] Herr ... I
Mrs, Mrs. ... [ˈmɪsɪz] Frau ... I
Ms, Ms. ... [mɪz, məz] Frau ... II
much [mʌtʃ] viel I • **how much?** wie viel? I • **How much is/are ...?** Was kostet/kosten ...? / Wie viel kostet/kosten ...? I • **like/love sth. very much** etwas sehr mögen/sehr lieben II • **Thanks very much!** Danke sehr! / Vielen Dank! II
°**mud pot** [ˈmʌd ˌpɒt] Schlammtopf I
muesli [ˈmjuːzli] Müsli I
mule [mjuːl] Maultier IV Intro (8)
mule train Maultierkarawane IV Intro (13)
multi- [ˈmʌlti] viel-, mehr-; multi-, Multi- IV Intro (12) • **multi-coloured** mehrfarbig IV Intro (12/193) • **multi-millionaire** Multimillionär(in) IV Intro (12/193)
mum [mʌm] Mama, Mutti; Mutter I
murderer [ˈmɜːdərə] Mörder/in III
murder [ˈmɜːdə] (er)morden III
murder [ˈmɜːdə] Mord III
museum [mjuˈziːəm] Museum I
music [ˈmjuːzɪk]
1. Musik I • **Music is for dancing.** etwa: Musik ist zum Tanzen da. III
2. Noten III • **I can read music.** Ich kann Noten lesen. III
musical [ˈmjuːzɪkl] Musical I
musician [mjuːˈzɪʃn] Musiker/in III
must [mʌst] müssen I
mustard [ˈmʌstəd] Senf IV 4 (86)
mustn't do [ˈmʌsnt] nicht tun dürfen II
my [maɪ] mein/e I • **My name is ...** Ich heiße ... / Mein Name ist ... I
It's my turn. Ich bin dran / an der Reihe. I
myself [maɪˈself]
1. mir/mich III
2. selbst IV 1 (18/196)
▶ S.196 German „selbst"
mystery [ˈmɪstri] Rätsel, Geheimnis II

N

name [neɪm] Name I • **My name is ...** Ich heiße ... / Mein Name ist ... I • **What's your name?** Wie heißt du? I • **call sb. names** jn. mit Schimpfwörtern hänseln, jm. Schimpfwörter nachrufen III • **put your name on a list** sich eintragen IV 4 (89)
name [neɪm] nennen; benennen II
narrator [nəˈreɪtə] Erzähler/in IV 3 (74)
nation [ˈneɪʃn] Nation, Volk III
the First Nations die Ersten Nationen (indianische Ureinwohner/innen Kanadas) III
national [ˈnæʃnəl] national III
°**National Guard** Nationalgarde
national park Nationalpark IV Intro (8)
Native American [ˌneɪtɪv_əˈmerɪkən] amerikanische(r) Ureinwohner/in, Indianer/in IV Intro (10)
natural [ˈnætʃrəl] natürlich, Natur- II
near [nɪə] in der Nähe von, nahe (bei) I
nearly [ˈnɪəli] fast, beinahe IV 3 (64)
neat [niːt]
1. gepflegt II • **neat and tidy** schön ordentlich II
2. (AE, infml) großartig, toll, klasse III
°**necessary** [ˈnesəseri] notwendig, nötig
neck [nek] Hals IV 2 (54)
need [niːd] brauchen, benötigen I • °**We don't need no more.** (infml) = **We don't need any more.**
needn't do [ˈniːdnt] nicht tun müssen, nicht zu tun brauchen II
neighbour [ˈneɪbə] Nachbar/in I
°**neighbourhood** [ˈneɪbəhʊd] Gegend
nervous [ˈnɜːvəs] nervös, aufgeregt I
network [ˈnetwɜːk] (Fernseh-/Radio-) Sendernetz IV 5 (99)
never [ˈnevə] nie, niemals I
°**never in my wildest dreams** nicht einmal in meinen kühnsten Träumen • **Never mind.** Kümmere dich nicht drum. / Macht nichts. II
new [njuː] neu I
news (no pl) [njuːz] Nachrichten I
°**breaking news** Eilmeldung, aktuelle Nachricht
news agency [ˈnjuːz_ˌeɪdʒənsi] Nachrichtenagentur IV 5 (100)
newspaper [ˈnjuːspeɪpə] Zeitung I
next [nekst]: **be next** der/die Nächste sein I • **the next day** am nächsten Tag I • **the next photo** das nächste Foto I • **What have we got next?** Was haben wir als Nächstes? I
next to [nekst] neben I
nice [naɪs] schön, nett I • **nice and cool/clean/...** schön kühl/sauber/... I • **Nice to meet you.** Nett, dich/euch/Sie kennenzulernen. III
°**nigger** [ˈnɪɡə] (abwertend, beleidigend) Nigger
night [naɪt] Nacht, später Abend I • **at night** nachts, in der Nacht I • **on Friday night** freitagnachts, Freitagnacht I
nightclub [ˈnaɪtklʌb] Nachtklub III
nil [nɪl] null III
no [nəʊ] nein I
no [nəʊ] kein, keine I • **no more music** keine Musik mehr I • °**We don't need no more.** (infml) = **We don't need any more.** • **no people at all** überhaupt keine Menschen IV 2 (53/206) • **No way!** [ˌnəʊ ˈweɪ] Auf keinen Fall! / Kommt nicht in Frage! II; Was du nicht sagst! / Das kann nicht dein Ernst sein! III
▶ S.206 not at all, no ... at all
no., pl nos. [ˈnʌmbə] Nr. III
noble [ˈnəʊbl] ehrenhaft; adlig IV 1 (30)
nobody [ˈnəʊbədi] niemand II
nod (-dd-) [nɒd] nicken (mit) II
nod (your head) (mit dem Kopf) nicken III
noise [nɔɪz] Geräusch; Lärm I
noisy [ˈnɔɪzi] laut, lärmend II
°**noon** [nuːn] Mittag
no one [ˈnəʊ wʌn] niemand III
non-fiction [ˈnɒnˌfɪkʃn] Sachliteratur IV 5 (107)
non-violent [ˌnɒn ˈvaɪələnt] gewaltlos, gewaltfrei IV 5 (102)
north [nɔːθ] Norden; nach Norden; nördlich II • **northbound** [ˈnɔːθbaʊnd] Richtung Norden III
north-east [ˌnɔːθˈiːst] Nordosten; nach Nordosten; nordöstlich II
northern [ˈnɔːðən] nördlich, Nord- III • **north-west** [ˌnɔːθˈwest] Nordwesten; nach Nordwesten; nordwestlich II
nose [nəʊz] Nase I
not [nɒt] nicht I • **not (...) any** kein, keine I • **not (...) any more** nicht mehr II • **not (...) anybody** niemand II • **not (...) anything** nichts II • **not (...) anywhere** nirgendwo(hin) II • **not at all** gar nicht, überhaupt nicht, überhaupt kein(e) IV 2 (53/206) • **not (...) either** auch nicht II • **not only ... but also ...** nicht nur ... sondern auch ...

Dictionary (English – German)

IV 5 (102/218) • **not (…) yet** noch nicht II
▶ S.206 not at all, no … at all
note [nəʊt]
1. Mitteilung, Notiz I • **take notes (on)** sich Notizen machen (über, zu) I
2. Ton III
nothing [ˈnʌθɪŋ] nichts II
nothing at all gar nichts, überhaupt nichts IV 2 (53/206)
▶ S.206 not at all, no … at all
notice [ˈnəʊtɪs] (be)merken IV 1 (29)
°**notice** [ˈnəʊtɪs] Notiz, Mitteilung
notice board [ˈnəʊtɪs bɔːd] schwarzes Brett, Anschlagtafel IV 4 (78)
novel [ˈnɒvl] Roman IV 5 (107)
November [nəʊˈvembə] November I
now [naʊ] nun, jetzt I • **(and) now for …** und jetzt … (kündigt ein neues Thema an) III • **now and again** ab und zu, von Zeit zu Zeit III
nowadays [ˈnaʊədeɪz] heutzutage IV 1 (29)
°**number** [ˈnʌmbə] nummerieren
number [ˈnʌmbə] Zahl, Ziffer, Nummer I
number plate [ˈnʌmbə ˌpleɪt] Nummernschild IV Intro (12)
nut [nʌt] Nuss III

O

o [əʊ] null I
obey [əˈbeɪ] gehorchen; sich halten an IV 4 (78/213)
observatory [əbˈzɜːvətri] Aussichtsplattform IV 1 (18)
°**occupation** [ˌɒkjuˈpeɪʃn] Besetzung
ocean [ˈəʊʃn] Ozean IV 3 (61)
o'clock [əˈklɒk]: **eleven o'clock** elf Uhr I
October [ɒkˈtəʊbə] Oktober I
of [əv, ɒv] von I • **of the summer holidays** der Sommerferien I • **a kilogram of oranges** ein Kilogramm Orangen II
of course [əv ˈkɔːs] natürlich, selbstverständlich I
off [ɒf]: **take 10 c off** 10 Cent abziehen I
offer [ˈɒfə] (an)bieten IV 1 (18)
°**officer** [ˈɒfɪsə] Beamte(r)/Beamtin
°**official** [əˈfɪʃl] offiziell
often [ˈɒfn] oft, häufig I
Oh dear! Oje! II
°**Oh my!** [əʊ ˈmaɪ] Oje!
Oh well … [əʊ ˈwel] Na ja … / Na gut … I

°**oil** [ɔɪl] Öl
OK [əʊˈkeɪ] okay, gut, in Ordnung I
°**okay** [əʊˈkeɪ] okay
old [əʊld] alt I • **How old are you?** Wie alt bist du? I • **I'm … years old.** Ich bin … Jahre alt. I
old-fashioned [ˌəʊldˈfæʃnd] altmodisch IV 5 (106)
oldie [ˈəʊldi] (infml) Oldie III
Olympic Games [əˌlɪmpɪk ˈgeɪmz] Olympische Spiele IV 5 (99)
on [ɒn]
1. auf I
2. weiter III
3. (Radio, Licht usw.) an, eingeschaltet II
go on angehen III • **on a/my shift** in einer/meiner Schicht IV 1 (17)
on 13th June am 13. Juni I • **on foot** zu Fuß III • **on Friday** am Freitag I • **on Friday afternoon** freitagnachmittags, am Freitagnachmittag I • **on Friday evening** freitagabends, am Freitagabend I • **on Friday morning** freitagmorgens, am Freitagmorgen I • **on Friday night** freitagnachts, Freitagnacht I • **on his street** in seiner Straße III • **on the beach** am Strand II • **on the board** an die Tafel I • **on the left** links, auf der linken Seite I • **on the Missouri River** am Missourifluss IV 4 (80)
on the phone am Telefon I • **on the plane** im Flugzeug II • **on the radio** im Radio I • **on the right** rechts, auf der rechten Seite I
on the scene vor Ort, zur Stelle IV 5 (103) • **on the second floor** im zweiten Stock (BE) / im ersten Stock (AE) IV 1 (18/196) • **on the train** im Zug I • **on their/your/the way (to)** unterwegs (nach) IV 1 (19) • **on the weekend** (AE) am Wochenende IV 2 (39) • **on top of** oben auf IV 1 (18) • **on TV** im Fernsehen I • **What page are we on?** Auf welcher Seite sind wir? I • **be on holiday** in Urlaub sein II • **go on holiday** in Urlaub fahren II • **straight on** geradeaus weiter II
once [wʌns] einmal III • **once/twice a week** (einmal/zweimal) pro Woche III
one [wʌn] eins, ein, eine I • **one day** eines Tages I • **one more** noch ein/e, ein/e weitere(r, s) I • **a new one** ein neuer / eine neue / ein neues II • **my old ones** meine alten II • **one tough girl** (AE, infml) etwa: ein wirklich toughes Mädchen III

onion [ˈʌnjən] Zwiebel III
online [ˌɒnˈlaɪn] online, Online- III
only [ˈəʊnli]
1. nur, bloß I • **not only … but also …** nicht nur … sondern auch … IV 5 (102/218)
2. erst II
3. **the only guest** der einzige Gast I
onto [ˈɒntə, ˈɒntʊ] auf (… hinauf) III
open [ˈəʊpən]
1. öffnen, aufmachen I
2. sich öffnen I
open [ˈəʊpən] geöffnet, offen I
open-air concert [ˌəʊpən ˈeə ˌkɒnsət] Open-Air-Konzert, Konzert im Freien • **opening times** Öffnungszeiten IV 3 (69)
opera [ˈɒprə] Oper III
opera house [ˈɒprə haʊs] Oper, Opernhaus III
operation (on) [ˌɒpəˈreɪʃn] Operation (an) III
opinion (on/of) [əˈpɪnjən] Meinung (zu/von) IV 2 (39) • **in my opinion** meiner Meinung nach IV 2 (39/203)
opponent [əˈpəʊnənt] Gegner/in IV 4 (92)
opposite [ˈɒpəzɪt] gegenüber (von) II
opposite [ˈɒpəzɪt] Gegenteil IV 3 (64)
or [ɔː] oder I
orange [ˈɒrɪndʒ] orange(farben) I
orange [ˈɒrɪndʒ] Orange, Apfelsine I • **orange juice** [ˈɒrɪndʒ dʒuːs] Orangensaft I
°**orca** [ˈɔːkə] Großer Schwertwal, Killerwal
order [ˈɔːdə] bestellen II
°**ordinary** [ˈɔːdnri] gewöhnlich
organization [ˌɔːgənaɪˈzeɪʃn] Organisation IV 3 (70)
organize [ˈɔːgənaɪz] organisieren, veranstalten III
original (n; adj) [əˈrɪdʒənl] Original; Original-, ursprünglich IV 3 (89)
original version Originalfassung IV 4 (89/216)
other [ˈʌðə] andere(r, s) I • **the others** die anderen I • **the other way round** anders herum II
otherwise [ˈʌðəwaɪz] sonst IV 1 (17)
Ouch! [aʊtʃ] Autsch! I
our [aʊə] unser, unsere I
ours [aʊəz] unsere(r, s) III
ourselves [aʊəˈselvz]
1. uns III
2. selbst IV 1 (18/196)
▶ S.196 German „selbst"
out [aʊt] heraus, hinaus; draußen II
be out weg sein, nicht da sein I

out of ... aus ... (heraus/hinaus) I
°**out of Naples** nach dem Auslaufen in Neapel
outfit ['aʊtfɪt] Outfit *(Kleidung; Ausrüstung)* II
outdoor ['aʊtdɔ:] im Freien, Außen- III
outline ['aʊtlaɪn] Gliederung IV 3 (71)
outside [ˌaʊt'saɪd]
1. draußen I; Außen- IV 1 (18)
2. nach draußen II
3. **outside the room** vor dem Zimmer; außerhalb des Zimmers I
°**outsider** [aʊt'saɪdə] Außensteher/in
oven ['ʌvn] Ofen, Backofen IV 1 (19)
over ['əʊvə]
1. über, oberhalb von I • **all over the world** auf der ganzen Welt III • **from all over the world** aus der ganzen Welt II • **over there** da drüben, dort drüben I • **over to ...** hinüber zu/nach ... II • **over time** [ˌəʊvə 'taɪm] im Laufe der Zeit IV 1 (30)
2. **be over** vorbei sein, zu Ende sein I
own [əʊn] besitzen IV 3 (61)
own [əʊn]: **our own pool** unser eigenes Schwimmbecken II • **on our/my/... own** allein, selbstständig *(ohne Hilfe)* IV Intro (11)
owner ['əʊnə] Besitzer/in, Eigentümer/in IV 3 (61/210)

P

pack [pæk] packen, einpacken II
packet ['pækɪt] Päckchen, Packung, Schachtel I • **a packet of mints** ein Päckchen/eine Packung Pfefferminzbonbons I
paddle ['pædl] paddeln III
paddle ['pædl] Paddel III
°**paddle steamer** ['pædl ˌsti:mə] Raddampfer
pads [pædz] Knieschützer; Schulterpolster III
page [peɪdʒ] (Buch-, Heft-)Seite I • **What page are we on?** Auf welcher Seite sind wir? I
paid [peɪd] siehe pay
pain [peɪn] Schmerz(en) I • **cry in pain** vor Schmerzen schreien I
paint [peɪnt] (an)malen I; anstreichen II
paint [peɪnt] Farbe, Lack IV 5 (108/219)
▶ S.219 Verbs & nouns with the same form
painter ['peɪntə] Maler/in II
painting ['peɪntɪŋ] Gemälde, Bild; Malerei III

pair [peə]: **a pair (of)** ein Paar II
palace ['pæləs] Palast, Schloss III
panic ['pænɪk] in Panik geraten III
pants (pl) [pænts] (AE) Hose IV 1 (24/198)
paper ['peɪpə] Papier I
parade [pə'reɪd] Parade, Umzug IV 2 (38)
paradise ['pærədaɪs] Paradies III
paragraph ['pærəgrɑ:f] Absatz *(in einem Text)* II
Paralympics [ˌpærə'lɪmpɪks] Paralympische Spiele *(Olympische Spiele für Sportler/innen mit körperlicher Behinderung)* III
paramedic [ˌpærə'medɪk] Sanitäter/in II
paraphrase ['pærəfreɪz] umschreiben, anders ausdrücken III
parcel ['pɑ:sl] Paket I
pardon ['pɑ:dn] begnadigen IV 2 (53)
parent ['peərənt]: **a single parent** ein(e) Alleinerziehende(r) II
parents ['peərənts] Eltern I
park [pɑ:k] Park I • **car park** Parkplatz III • **national park** Nationalpark IV Intro (8)
parking lot ['pɑ:kɪŋ lɒt] (AE) Parkplatz IV 5 (103)
parliament ['pɑ:ləmənt] Parlament III
parrot ['pærət] Papagei I
part [pɑ:t] Teil I • **take part in sth.** teilnehmen an etwas III
participate (in) [pɑ:'tɪsɪpeɪt] teilnehmen (an) IV 5 (101)
°**particular** [pə'tɪkjulə]: **in particular** insbesondere
partner ['pɑ:tnə] Partner/in I
party ['pɑ:ti] Party I
pass [pɑ:s] (herüber)reichen, weitergeben I • **pass sth. on** etwas weiterleiten, -geben IV 4 (81) • **pass round** herumgeben I
passenger ['pæsɪndʒə] Passagier/in, Fahrgast III
passive ['pæsɪv] Passiv III
past [pɑ:st] Vergangenheit II
past [pɑ:st] vorbei (an), vorüber (an) II • **half past 11** halb zwölf (11.30 / 23.30) I • **quarter past 11** Viertel nach 11 (11.15 / 23.15) II
°**pastrami** [pæ'strɑ:mi] *gewürztes geräuchertes Rindfleisch*
°**patch** [pætʃ] Aufnäher, Abzeichen *(aus Stoff)*
path [pɑ:θ] Pfad, Weg II • **bridle path** ['braɪdl ˌpɑ:θ] Reitweg III
patrol [pə'trəʊl] Streife, Patrouille IV 3 (60)
°**pause** [pɔ:z] eine Pause machen
°**pause** [pɔ:z] Pause

pavement ['peɪvmənt] Gehweg, Bürgersteig IV 1 (16)
pay (for) [peɪ], **paid, paid** bezahlen II
PE [ˌpi:_'i:], **Physical Education** [ˌfɪzɪkəl_edʒu'keɪʃn] Sportunterricht, Turnen I
pedestrian [pə'destrɪən] Fußgänger/in IV 1 (16)
pedestrian crossing [pəˌdestrɪən 'krɒsɪŋ] Fußgängerüberweg IV 1 (16)
pen [pen] Kugelschreiber, Füller I
penalty ['penəlti] Strafstoß; Elfmeter *(Fußball)* III
pence (p) (pl) [pens] Pence *(Plural von „penny")* I
pencil ['pensl] Bleistift I • **pencil case** ['pensl keɪs] Federmäppchen I • **pencil sharpener** ['pensl ˌʃɑ:pnə] Bleistiftspitzer I
penny ['peni] *kleinste britische Münze* I
people ['pi:pl] Menschen, Leute I
per [pɜ:, pə] pro III
per cent (%) [pə'sent] Prozent III
perfect ['pɜ:fɪkt] perfekt; ideal; vollkommen IV 1 (18)
°**performance** [pə'fɔ:məns] Auftritt
performer: **(street) performer** [pə'fɔ:mə] Straßenkünstler/in III
period ['pɪərɪəd] (Unterrichts-/Schul-)Stunde IV 2 (39)
person ['pɜ:sn] Person I
personal ['pɜ:sənl] persönlich III
°**persuade** [pə'sweɪd] überzeugen, -reden
pet [pet] Haustier I • **pet shop** Tierhandlung I
petrol ['petrəl] Benzin IV Intro (12)
petrol station ['petrəl ˌsteɪʃn] Tankstelle IV Intro (12)
phone [fəʊn] anrufen I
phone [fəʊn] Telefon I • **on the phone** am Telefon I • **phone number** Telefonnummer I • **pick up the phone** den Hörer abnehmen II
photo ['fəʊtəʊ] Foto I • **in the photo** auf dem Foto I • **take photos** Fotos machen, fotografieren I
photographer [fə'tɒgrəfə] Fotograf/in II
phrase [freɪz] Ausdruck, (Rede-)Wendung II
piano [pi'ænəʊ] Klavier, Piano I
play the piano Klavier spielen I
pick [pɪk]: **pick fruit/flowers** Obst/Blumen pflücken IV 3 (59) • **pick sb. up** jn. abholen III • **pick sth. up** etwas hochheben, aufheben III

pick up the phone den Hörer abnehmen II
picnic ['pɪknɪk] Picknick II
picture ['pɪktʃə] Bild I • **in the picture** auf dem Bild I
pie [paɪ] Obstkuchen; Pastete II
piece [piːs]: **a piece of** ein Stück I **a piece of paper** ein Stück Papier I **a piece of clothing** Kleidungsstück IV 4 (78)
pilgrim ['pɪlgrɪm] Pilger/in IV 2 (38)
pilot ['paɪlət] Pilot/in IV 1 (28)
pink [pɪŋk] pink(farben), rosa I
°**pioneer** [ˌpaɪə'nɪə] Pionier/in
pipe [paɪp] Pfeife III
pirate ['paɪrət] Pirat, Piratin I
pitch [pɪtʃ]: **football/hockey pitch** Fußball-/Hockeyplatz, -feld II
pity ['pɪti]: **It's a pity (that …)** Es ist schade, dass … II
pizza ['piːtsə] Pizza I
°**place a tax on sth.** ['tæks] etwas versteuern
place [pleɪs] Ort, Platz I • **place of birth** Geburtsort IV 2 (38) • **take place** stattfinden II • **in other places** an anderen Orten, anderswo III
plain [pleɪn] einfach, schlicht; hier: „natur"; ohne alles IV 1 (19)
°**the Plains (pl)** [pleɪnz] die Prärie
plan [plæn] Plan I
plan (-nn-) [plæn] planen II
plane [pleɪn] Flugzeug II • **on the plane** im Flugzeug II
planet ['plænɪt] Planet II
plant [plɑːnt] (ein-, aus-, be-)pflanzen IV 3 (59/209)
plant [plɑːnt] Pflanze IV 3 (59)
°**plantation** [ˌplæn'teɪʃn] Plantage
plastic ['plæstɪk] Plastik, Kunststoff IV 3 (59)
plate [pleɪt] Teller I • **a plate of chips** ein Teller Pommes frites I **license plate** (AE) Nummernschild IV Intro (12) • **number plate** Nummernschild IV Intro (12)
platform ['plætfɔːm] Bahnsteig, Gleis III
play [pleɪ] spielen I • **play a trick on sb.** jm. einen Streich spielen II **play football** Fußball spielen I **play the drums** Schlagzeug spielen III • **play the fiddle** Geige spielen III • **play the guitar** Gitarre spielen I • **play the piano** Klavier spielen I • **play the violin** Geige spielen III
play [pleɪ] Theaterstück I
°**play date** ['pleɪ ˌdeɪt] Verabredung zum Spielen
player ['pleɪə] Spieler/in I

please [pliːz] bitte (in Fragen und Aufforderungen) I
pleased [pliːzd]: **be pleased** sich freuen IV 5 (114)
plenty of ['plenti_əv] reichlich, viel(e) IV 1 (19)
°**plot** [plɒt] Handlung
plug [plʌg] Stecker III
pm [ˌpiː'em]: **7 pm** 7 Uhr abends/ 19 Uhr I
pocket ['pɒkɪt] Tasche (an Kleidungsstück) II • **pocket money** ['pɒkɪt ˌmʌni] Taschengeld II
poem ['pəʊɪm] Gedicht I
point [pɔɪnt] Punkt II • **11.4 (eleven point four)** 11,4 (elf Komma vier) II • **point of view** Standpunkt II **from my point of view** aus meiner Sicht; von meinem Standpunkt aus gesehen II • **There was no point.** Es hatte keinen Sinn. III • **What's the point?** Was soll das? III
point (at/to sth.) [pɔɪnt] zeigen, deuten (auf etwas) II
°**polar bear** [ˌpəʊlə 'beə] Eisbär
police (pl) [pə'liːs] Polizei I • **police station** Polizeiwache, Polizeirevier II
polite [pə'laɪt] höflich IV 3 (74)
politician [ˌpɒlə'tɪʃn] Politiker/in IV 1 (29)
politics ['pɒlətɪks] (die) Politik IV 2 (42)
°**pollute** [pə'luːt] verschmutzen
pollution [pə'luːʃn] Verschmutzung IV 3 (61) • °**storm drain pollution** Verschmutzung aus der Regenwasserkanalisation
poltergeist ['pəʊltəgaɪst] Poltergeist I
ponytail ['pəʊniteɪl] Pferdeschwanz (Frisur) III
pool [puːl] Schwimmbad, Schwimmbecken II
poor [pɔː, pʊə] arm I • **poor Sophie** (die) arme Sophie I
pop (music) [pɒp] Pop(musik) III
popcorn ['pɒpkɔːn] Popcorn II
popular ['pɒpjələ] populär, beliebt III
population [ˌpɒpju'leɪʃn] Bevölkerung, Einwohner(zahl) III
°**port** [pɔːt] Hafen(stadt)
°**positive** ['pɒzətɪv] positiv
possibility [ˌpɒsə'bɪlɪti] Möglichkeit IV 4 (86)
possible ['pɒsəbl] möglich II
post [pəʊst] Post (Briefe, Päckchen, …) III
post office ['pəʊst ˌɒfɪs] Postamt II
postcard ['pəʊstkɑːd] Postkarte II
poster ['pəʊstə] Poster I

postscript ['pəʊstskrɪpt] Postskript III
potato [pə'teɪtəʊ], pl **potatoes** Kartoffel I • **potato chips** (AE) Kartoffelchips IV 1 (24/198)
°**pound** [paʊnd] (wild) pochen
pound (£) [paʊnd] Pfund (britische Währung) I
pound [paʊnd] Pfund (Gewichtseinheit): **a three-pound ball** ein drei Pfund schwerer Ball III
practice ['præktɪs] hier: Übungsteil I
practice ['præktɪs] (AE) üben; trainieren IV 3 (92)
practise ['præktɪs]
1. üben; trainieren I
°2. ausüben (Religion)
pray [preɪ] beten IV 2 (45/204)
prayer [preə] Gebet IV 2 (45)
precinct ['priːsɪŋkt]: **shopping precinct** Einkaufsviertel, Einkaufsstraße III
°**precious Lord** ['preʃəs] hier: lieber Herr
prefer sth. (to sth.) (-rr-) [prɪ'fɜː] etwas (einer anderen Sache) vorziehen; etwas lieber tun (als etwas) IV Intro (11)
prefix ['priːfɪks] Präfix III
prejudice (against) ['predʒudɪs] Voreingenommenheit (gegen), Vorurteil (gegenüber) IV 3 (58/208)
prejudiced: ['predʒudɪst]: **be prejudiced (against)** voreingenommen sein (gegen), Vorurteile haben (gegenüber) IV 3 (58)
prepare [prɪ'peə] vorbereiten; sich vorbereiten II • **prepare for** sich vorbereiten auf II
°**prescribe** [prɪ'skraɪb] verschreiben
present ['preznt]
1. Gegenwart I
2. Geschenk I
present sth. (to sb.) [prɪ'zent] (jm.) etwas präsentieren, vorstellen I; überreichen III
presentation [ˌpreznˈteɪʃn] Präsentation, Vorstellung I
present-day [ˌpreznt 'deɪ] heutige(r, s) IV 2 (38)
presenter [prɪ'zentə] Moderator/in II
president ['prezɪdənt] Präsident/in IV 1 (128)
pretty ['prɪti]
1. hübsch I
2. **pretty cool/good/…** ziemlich cool/gut/… II
prevent sth. [prɪ'vent] etwas verhindern IV 3 (61) • **prevent sb./sth. from doing sth.** jn./etwas daran hindern, etwas zu tun IV 3 (61)

prewriting exercise [ˌpriːˈraɪtɪŋ] Übung vor dem Schreiben III
price [praɪs] (Kauf-)Preis I • °**for the price of** zum Preis von
prime minister [ˌpraɪm ˈmɪnɪstə] Premierminister/in IV 2 (54/207)
principal [ˈprɪnsəpl] (bes. AE) Schulleiter/in IV 3 (73)
print sth. out [ˌprɪnt ˈaʊt] etwas ausdrucken II
prison [ˈprɪzn] Gefängnis IV 2 (53) **in prison for murder** im Gefängnis wegen Mordes IV 2 (53)
prisoner [ˈprɪznə] Gefangene(r) IV 2 (53/205)
prize [praɪz] Preis, Gewinn I
°**pro** [prəʊ]: **pros and cons** Vor- und Nachteile
probably [ˈprɒbəbli] wahrscheinlich II
problem [ˈprɒbləm] Problem II
produce [prəˈdjuːs] produzieren, erzeugen, herstellen II
professional [prəˈfeʃənl] professionell IV (30)
program [ˈprəʊɡræm] (AE) Programm IV Intro (8)
programme [ˈprəʊɡræm] programmieren; planen IV 5 (108/219)
programme [ˈprəʊɡræm]
1. Programm I
2. (Fernseh-/Radio-)Sendung IV 5 (100)
▶ S.219 Verbs & nouns with the same form
project (about, on) [ˈprɒdʒekt] Projekt (über, zu) I • **do a project** ein Projekt machen, durchführen II
promise [ˈprɒmɪs] versprechen II
°**promise** [ˈprɒmɪs] Versprechen
pronunciation [prəˌnʌnsiˈeɪʃn] Aussprache I
proof (no pl) [pruːf] Beweis(e) II
°**proofread** [ˈpruːfriːd] Korrektur lesen
°**props** (pl) [prɒps] Requisiten
protect sb./sth. (from sb./sth.) [prəˈtekt] jn./etwas (be)schützen (vor jm./etwas) IV 3 (59)
protest (against/about) [prəˈtest] protestieren (gegen) IV 4 (92)
protest [ˈprəʊtest] Protest IV 2 (51)
▶ S.219 Verbs & nouns with the same form
proud (of sb./sth.) [praʊd] stolz (auf jn./etwas) II
°**prove** [pruːv] beweisen
°**province** [ˈprɒvɪns] Provinz
PS [ˌpiːˈes] **(postscript** [ˈpəʊstskrɪpt]) PS, Postskript (Nachschrift unter Briefen) III
pub [pʌb] Kneipe, Lokal II

public [ˈpʌblɪk] öffentlich IV Intro (8) **public transport** öffentlicher Verkehr IV 2 (50)
public [ˈpʌblɪk]: **the public** die Öffentlichkeit IV Intro (8)
publish [ˈpʌblɪʃ] veröffentlichen III
pull [pʊl] ziehen I
pullover [ˈpʊləʊvə] Pullover II
°**punctuation** [ˌpʌŋktʃuˈeɪʃn] Interpunktion, Zeichensetzung
punk [pʌŋk] Punker/in II
°**Puritan** [ˈpjuːrɪtən] Puritaner/in
purple [ˈpɜːpl] violett; lila I
purse [pɜːs] Geldbörse II
push [pʊʃ] drücken, schieben, stoßen I
put (-tt-) [pʊt], put, put legen, stellen, (etwas wohin) tun I • **put sth. away** wegräumen IV 5 (102) • **put sth. in order** etwas in Ordnung bringen IV 1 (30) • **put sb. to bed** jn. ins Bett bringen III • **put sth. on** etwas anziehen (Kleidung); etwas aufsetzen (Hut, Helm) II **put out a fire** ein Feuer löschen IV 1 (17) • **put your name on a list** sich eintragen IV 4 (89) • **You know how to put it.** Sie wissen, wie man es formuliert/ausdrückt. IV 1 (30)
°**puzzle** [ˈpʌzl] Rätsel
puzzled [ˈpʌzld] verwirrt II
pyjamas (pl) [pəˈdʒɑːməz] Schlafanzug II

Q

quality [ˈkwɒləti] Eigenschaft; Qualität IV 1 (30)
quarter [ˈkwɔːtə]: **quarter past 11** Viertel nach 11 (11.15 / 23.15) I **quarter to 12** Viertel vor 12 (11.45 / 23.45) I • °**French Quarter** Französisches Stadtviertel
quay [kiː] Kai III
queen [kwiːn] Königin III
question [ˈkwestʃn] Frage I • **ask questions** Fragen stellen II
queue [kjuː] Schlange, Reihe (wartender Menschen) IV (16)
quick [kwɪk] schnell I
quiet [ˈkwaɪət] leise, still, ruhig I **keep quiet** still sein, leise sein IV 2 (39)
quite [kwaɪt] ziemlich; ganz III
quiz [kwɪz], pl **quizzes** [ˈkwɪzɪz] Quiz, Ratespiel I
quotation marks [kwəʊˈteɪʃn ˌmɑːks] Anführungszeichen, -striche III

R

rabbit [ˈræbɪt] Kaninchen I
°**racism** [ˈreɪsɪzm] Rassismus
racket [ˈrækɪt] Schläger (Badminton, Tennis, Squash) III
radio [ˈreɪdiəʊ] Radio I • **on the radio** im Radio I
raft [rɑːft] Schlauchboot, Floß IV Intro (8)
raft [rɑːft] mit einem Schlauchboot/Floß fahren IV Intro (8)
railway [ˈreɪlweɪ] Eisenbahn II
rain [reɪn] Regen II
rain [reɪn] regnen II
rainy [ˈreɪni] regnerisch II • **rainy season** Regenzeit II
raise money (for) [reɪz] Geld sammeln (für) IV Intro (11)
ran [ræn] siehe run
rang [ræŋ] siehe ring
ranger [ˈreɪndʒə] Ranger/in, Aufseher/in III
rap [ræp] Rap(musik) (rhythmischer Sprechgesang) I
rapids (pl) [ˈræpɪdz] Stromschnellen III
rapper [ˈræpə] Rapper/in IV 1 (25)
rat [ræt] Ratte III
RE [ˌɑːrˈiː], **Religious Education** [rɪˌlɪdʒəs ˌedʒuˈkeɪʃn] Religion, Religionsunterricht I
reach [riːtʃ] erreichen III
°**react** [riˈækt] reagieren
reaction (to) [riˈækʃn] Reaktion (auf) IV 5 (114)
read [riːd], read, read lesen I °**read sth. out loud** etwas vorlesen
reader [ˈriːdə] Leser/in II
ready [ˈredi] bereit, fertig I • **get ready (for)** sich fertig machen (für), sich vorbereiten (auf) I • **get things ready** Dinge fertig machen, vorbereiten I
real [rɪəl] echt, wirklich I • °**Get real!** (AE, infml) etwa: Sei realistisch • **real late** (AE, infml) wirklich spät, echt spät III
realistic [ˌriːəˈlɪstɪk] realistisch, wirklichkeitsnah III
reality [riˈæləti] Wirklichkeit, Realität IV 4 (86) • **reality show** Reality-Show IV 5 (100)
realize [ˈrɪəlaɪz] erkennen, merken I
really [ˈrɪəli] wirklich I
reason [ˈriːzn] Grund, Begründung I • **the reason why** der Grund, warum IV 2 (38) • **for lots of reasons** aus vielen Gründen I
▶ S.200–201 Giving reasons
receive [rɪˈsiːv] erhalten III

Dictionary (English – German)

recess ['riːses] (AE) Pause (zwischen Schulstunden) IV 3 (74) • **during recess** in der Pause IV 3 (74)
recognize ['rekəgnaɪz] erkennen IV 1 (29)
record [rɪ'kɔːd] aufnehmen III
recorder [rɪ'kɔːdə] Blockflöte III
recording [rɪ'kɔːdɪŋ] Aufnahme, Aufzeichnung III
recover (from) [rɪ'kʌvə] sich erholen (von) II
recycled [ˌriː'saɪkld] wiederverwertet, wiederverwendet, recycelt II
recycling [ˌriː'saɪklɪŋ] Wiederverwertung, Recycling II
red [red] rot I
reddish ['redɪʃ] rötlich IV 3 (29)
reduce sth. (by) [rɪ'dʒuːs] etwas reduzieren (um) IV 3 (61)
referee [ˌrefə'riː] Schiedsrichter/in III
reflex ['riːfleks] Reflex IV 4 (90)
°**reform** [rɪ'fɔːm] Reform
regular ['regjələ] regelmäßig III
rehearsal [rɪ'hɜːsl] Probe (am Theater) I
rehearse [rɪ'hɜːs] proben (am Theater) I
relations (pl) [rɪ'leɪʃnz] Beziehungen IV 3 (58)
relative ['relətɪv] Verwandte(r) II
relax [rɪ'læks] (sich) entspannen, sich ausruhen II
release [rɪ'liːs] (CD, Film usw.) herausbringen, auf den Markt bringen III
reliable [rɪ'laɪəbl] zuverlässig IV 5 (103)
religion [rɪ'lɪdʒən] Religion IV 1 (29/199)
religious [rɪ'lɪdʒəs] gläubig, religiös IV 1 (29)
remember sth. [rɪ'membə]
 1. sich an etwas erinnern I
 2. sich etwas merken I
repair [rɪ'peə] reparieren, ausbessern III
repeat [rɪ'piːt] wiederholen II
replace sth. (with) [rɪ'pleɪs] etwas ersetzen (durch) III
reply (to) [rɪ'plaɪ] antworten (auf), beantworten; erwidern III
report (on) [rɪ'pɔːt] Bericht, Reportage (über) I
report (to sb.) [rɪ'pɔːt] jm. berichten II
reporter [rɪ'pɔːtə] Reporter/in II
represent [ˌreprɪ'zent] repräsentieren, vertreten II
°**representation** [ˌreprɪzen'teɪʃn] Vertretung

°**representative** [ˌreprɪ'zentətɪv] Vertreter/in
rescue ['reskjuː] Rettung, Rettungsdienst IV 1 (28)
research (no pl) [rɪ'sɜːtʃ, 'riːsɜːtʃ] Recherche, Forschung(en) III
researcher [rɪ'sɜːtʃə, 'riːsɜːtʃə] Rechercheur/in III
reservation [ˌrezə'veɪʃn] Reservat IV Intro (10)
resources (pl) [rɪ'zɔːsɪs, rɪ'sɔːsɪz] Mittel, Ressourcen IV 5 (114)
rest [rest] Rest II
restart [ˌriː'stɑːt] neu starten (Computer) II
restaurant ['restrɒnt] Restaurant II
restroom ['restˌruːm] (AE) (öffentliche) Toilette IV 3 (74)
result [rɪ'zʌlt] Ergebnis, Resultat I
°**resurrect** [ˌrezə'rekt] wieder beleben
°**return** [rɪ'tɜːn] zurückkehren
revise [rɪ'vaɪz] überarbeiten IV 1 (25)
revision [rɪ'vɪʒn] Wiederholung (des Lernstoffs) I
revolution [ˌrevə'luːʃn] Revolution IV 2 (39)
°**revolutionary** [ˌrevə'luːʃənri] revolutionär
rhino ['raɪnəʊ] Nashorn II
rhythm ['rɪðəm] Rhythmus II
rich [rɪtʃ] reich II
ridden ['rɪdn] siehe ride
riddle ['rɪdl] Rätsel, Scherzfrage III
ride [raɪd], **rode, ridden** reiten I
 ride a bike Rad fahren I
ride [raɪd]: **(bike) ride** (Rad-)Fahrt, (Rad-)Tour II • **(bus) ride** (Bus-)Fahrt II • **take a ride** eine Spritztour/Fahrt machen III
riding ['raɪdɪŋ] Reiten, Reitsport I
 go riding ['raɪdɪŋ] reiten gehen I
 riding boots (pl) Reitstiefel III
 riding hat Reitkappe, Reiterhelm III
right [raɪt] richtig I • **all right** [ɔːl 'raɪt] gut, in Ordnung II • **be right** Recht haben I • **get sth. right** etwas richtig machen III • **That's right.** Das ist richtig. / Das stimmt. I • **You need a school bag, right?** Du brauchst eine Schultasche, stimmt's? / nicht wahr? I
right [raɪt] Recht IV 5 (99/217) • **civil rights** (pl) Bürgerrechte IV 5 (99)
right [raɪt] rechte(r, s) I • **look right** nach rechts schauen I • **on the right** rechts, auf der rechten Seite I • **to the right** nach rechts III • **turn right** (nach) rechts abbiegen II • **take a right** (AE) nach links/rechts abbiegen IV 1 (16)

right [raɪt]: **right behind you** direkt/genau hinter dir II • **right now** jetzt sofort; jetzt gerade I
rim [rɪm] Rand, Kante IV Intro (8)
ring [rɪŋ] Ring II
ring [rɪŋ], **rang, rung** klingeln, läuten II
ringtone ['rɪŋtəʊn] Klingelton III
riot ['raɪət] Aufruhr, Krawall IV 5 (110)
ripe [raɪp] reif IV 3 (66)
rise [raɪz], **rose, risen** (auf)steigen IV 3 (72)
risen ['rɪzn] siehe **rise**
°**risk** [rɪsk] riskieren • **risk your life** sein Leben aufs Spiel setzen
river ['rɪvə] Fluss II
°**Rm.** siehe **room**
road [rəʊd] Straße I • **Park Road** [ˌpɑːk 'rəʊd] Parkstraße I
°**roar** [rɔː] (von Waffe) Donnern
rock [rɒk] Fels, Felsen III
rock (music) [rɒk] Rock(musik) III
°**rock and roll** [ˌrɒkənd'rəʊl] Rock and Roll
rode [rəʊd] siehe **ride**
role [rəʊl] Rolle III
°**roll along** [ˌrəʊl_ə'lɒŋ] ruhig dahinfließen
roll [rəʊl] Brötchen II
°**roller skates** ['rəʊlə skeɪts] Rollschuhe
°**roller-coaster** ['rəʊləˌkəʊstə] Achterbahn
Roman ['rəʊmən] römisch; Römer, Römerin II
roof ['ruːf] Dach II
room [ruːm, rʊm] Raum, Zimmer I
°**root** [ruːt] Wurzel
rope [rəʊp] Seil IV 2 (54) • °**show sb. the ropes** jn anlernen, einarbeiten
rose [rəʊz] siehe **rise**
round [raʊnd] rund II • **round brackets** runde Klammern IV 5 (103)
round [raʊnd] um ... (herum); in ... umher II • **round here** hier (in der Gegend) IV 3 (58) • **the other way round** anders herum II
route [ruːt] Strecke, Route IV Intro (12)
routine [ruː'tiːn] Routine IV 2 (45)
row [rəʊ] Reihe IV 3 (72)
royal ['rɔɪəl] königlich, Königs II
rubber ['rʌbə] Radiergummi I
rubbish ['rʌbɪʃ] (Haus-)Müll, Abfall II • **rubbish collection** Müllabfuhr II
rucksack ['rʌksæk] Rucksack III
rude [ruːd] unhöflich, unverschämt II
rugby ['rʌgbi] Rugby III
ruin ['ruːɪn] Ruine IV Intro (10)

rule [ruː] Regel, Vorschrift III • **break a rule** gegen eine Regel verstoßen IV 4 (78)
ruler [ˈruːlə] Lineal I
run [rʌn] (Wett-)Lauf II • **go for a run** laufen gehen IV 2 (45)
run (-nn-) [rʌn], **ran, run**
1. laufen, rennen I
2. verlaufen *(Straße; Grenze)* IV 3 (60)
°**runaway** [ˈrʌnəweɪ] flüchtige(r, s)
rung [rʌŋ] *siehe* **ring**
runner [ˈrʌnə] Läufer/in II
running shoes [ˈrʌnɪŋ ʃuːz] Laufschuhe III
running track [ˈrʌnɪŋ træk] Laufbahn *(Sport)* III
°**rush** [rʌʃ] Ansturm

S

sad [sæd] traurig II
saddle [ˈsædl] Sattel III
sadness [ˈsædnəs] Traurigkeit IV 4 (86)
safe [seɪf] Tresor, Safe IV 3 (66)
safe (from) [seɪf] sicher, in Sicherheit (vor) II
safety [ˈseɪfti] Sicherheit IV 1 (27)
said [sed] *siehe* **say**
sail [seɪl] (mit dem Schiff) fahren; segeln IV 2 (38)
saint [seɪnt] Heilige(r) IV 1 (29)
salad [ˈsæləd] Salat *(als Gericht oder Beilage)* I
sale [seɪl] (Aus-, Schluss-)Verkauf IV Intro (11)
salmon [ˈsæmən], *pl* **salmon** Lachs III
same [seɪm]: **the same ...** der-/die-/dasselbe ...; dieselben ... I • **be/look the same** gleich sein/aussehen I
°**sand** [sænd] Sand
sandwich [ˈsænwɪtʃ, ˈsænwɪdʒ] Sandwich, *(zusammengeklapptes)* belegtes Brot I
sandy [ˈsændi] sandig IV 3 (72)
sang [sæŋ] *siehe* **sing**
°**sarcastic** [sɑːˈkæstɪk] sarkastisch
sat [sæt] *siehe* **sit**
Saturday [ˈsætədeɪ, ˈsætədi] Samstag, Sonnabend I
sauce [sɔːs] Soße III
sauna [ˈsɔːnə] Sauna II • **have a sauna** in die Sauna gehen II
sausage [ˈsɒsɪdʒ] (Brat-, Bock-)Würstchen, Wurst I
save [seɪv]
1. retten II
2. sparen II

saw [sɔː] *siehe* **see**
saxophone [ˈsæksəfəʊn] Saxophon III
say [seɪ], **said, said** sagen I • **It says here: ...** Hier steht: ... / Es heißt hier: ... II • **say goodbye** sich verabschieden I • **Say hi to your parents for me.** Grüß deine Eltern von mir. I • **say sorry** sich entschuldigen II • **They say ...** Man sagt, ...
scan (-nn-) [skæn]: **scan a text** einen Text schnell nach bestimmten Wörtern/Informationen absuchen II
scared [skeəd] verängstigt I • **be scared (of)** Angst haben (vor) I
scary [ˈskeəri] unheimlich; gruselig I • **kind of scary** *(infml)* irgendwie unheimlich III
scene [siːn] Szene I • **on the scene** vor Ort, zur Stelle IV 5 (103)
scenery [ˈsiːnəri]
1. Landschaft I
°2. Bühnenbild
schedule [*AE*: ˈskedʒuːl, *BE*: ˈʃedjuːl] *(bes. AE)* Stundenplan IV 1 (24/198)
school [skuːl] Schule I • **at school** in der Schule I • **from school** aus der Schule III • **in school** *(AE)* in der Schule IV 3 (58) • **school bag** Schultasche I • **school office** Sekretariat IV 4 (78) • **school subject** Schulfach I
science [ˈsaɪəns] Naturwissenschaft I
score [skɔː] Spielstand; Punktestand III • **final score** Endstand *(beim Sport)* III • **What's the score?** Wie steht es? *(beim Sport)* III
score (a goal) [skɔː], [ɡəʊl] ein Tor schießen, einen Treffer erzielen III
Scottish [ˈskɒtɪʃ] schottisch III
scrapbook [ˈskræpbʊk] Sammelalbum IV 4 (81)
scream [skriːm] schreien IV 2 (54)
scream [skriːm] Schrei IV 5 (108/219)
▶ S.219 Verbs & nouns with the same form
sea [siː] Meer, (die) See I • **at sea** auf See I
°**seal** [siːl] Robbe
°**sea lion** [ˈsiː ˌlaɪən] Seelöwe
season [ˈsiːzn] Jahreszeit II • **rainy season** Regenzeit II
seat [siːt] Sitz, Platz IV 3 (72)
°**seat sb.** [siːt] jm. einen (Sitz-)Platz zuweisen, jn. an seinen Platz führen
second [ˈsekənd] Sekunde I
second [ˈsekənd] zweite(r, s) I
second-hand [ˌsekənd ˈhænd] gebraucht; aus zweiter Hand III • **a second-half goal** ein Tor in der zweiten Hälfte/Halbzeit III
secret (n) [ˈsiːkrət] Geheimnis IV 2 (45)
secret (adj) [ˈsiːkrət] geheim IV 2 (45/204)
section [ˈsekʃn] Abschnitt, Teil II; (Themen-)Bereich III
see [siː], **saw, seen**
1. sehen I
2. **see sb.** jn. besuchen, jn. aufsuchen II
See? Siehst du? I • **See you.** Bis bald. / Tschüs. I
seem (to be/to do) [siːm] (zu sein/tun) scheinen III
seen [siːn] *siehe* **see**
see-through [ˈsiːθruː] durchsichtig IV 4 (78)
segregate [ˈseɡrɪɡeɪt] trennen *(nach Rasse, Religion, Geschlecht)* IV 5 (102/218)
segregation [ˌseɡrɪˈɡeɪʃn] Trennung *(nach Rasse, Religion, Geschlecht)* IV 5 (102)
selection (of) [sɪˈlekʃn] Auswahl (an) II
sell [sel], **sold, sold** verkaufen I
semester [sɪˈmestə] Semester *(Schulhalbjahr in den USA)* IV 2 (39)
semi-final [ˌsemiˈfaɪnl] Halbfinale III
send [send], **sent, sent** senden, schicken II
▶ S.195 Verbs with two objects
senior [ˈsiːniə]
1. **senior (to sb.)** (rang)höher (als jd.) IV 1 (29)
2. leitende(r, s) IV 1 (29)
senior [ˈsiːniə] Rentner/in, Senior/in IV 1 (127)
°**sense** [sens]: **make sense** Sinn ergeben
sent [sent] *siehe* **send**
sentence sb. (to sth.) [ˈsentəns] jn. verurteilen (zu etwas) IV 2 (53)
sentence [ˈsentəns]
1. Satz I • **sentence for sentence** Satz um Satz II
2. Urteil, Strafe IV 2 (53) • **death sentence** Todesstrafe IV 2 (53) **life sentence** lebenslängliche Haftstrafe IV 2 (53)
separate [ˈseprət] getrennt, separat, extra IV 5 (111)
September [sepˈtembə] September I
°**sequoia** [sɪˈkwɔɪə] Sequoia, Mammutbaum
series, *pl* **series** [ˈsɪəriːz] (Sende-)Reihe, Serie II

Dictionary (English – German) 249

°serve [sɜːv]: **he served two terms as president** er hatte zwei Amtszeiten als Präsident
service ['sɜːvɪs]
  1. Dienst (am Kunden), Service II
  2. Gottesdienst; *hier:* Trauerfeier IV 1 (28)
session ['seʃn]: **training session** Trainingsstunde, -einheit III
set a trap (for sb.) (-tt-) [set], **set, set** (jm.) eine Falle stellen II
set meal [ˌset 'miːl] Menü III
set up (-tt-) [set], **set, set** aufstellen, aufbauen III
°setting ['setɪŋ] Schauplatz
settler ['setlə] Siedler/in IV 2 (38)
several ['sevrəl] mehrere, verschiedene IV 2 (53)
sew (on) [səʊ], **sewed, sewn** (an)nähen IV Intro (11)
sewn [səʊn] *siehe* sew
°shack [ʃæk] Hütte
°shade [ʃeɪd] Schatten *(von der Sonne geschützt)*
shadow ['ʃædəʊ] Schatten *(Umriss)* III
shake [ʃeɪk], **shook, shaken** zittern; schütteln IV 2 (53) • °**shake sb. up** jn. erschüttern • **shake your head** den Kopf schütteln III • °**shake (hands)** sich die Hand geben
Shall we ...? [ʃæl] Wollen wir ...? / Sollen wir ...? III
shape [ʃeɪp] Form, Gestalt II
share sth. (with sb.) [ʃeə]
  1. sich etwas teilen (mit jm.) I; etwas gemeinsam (mit jm.) haben/nutzen IV 2 (39)
  2. jm. etwas mitteilen IV 2 (39)
she [ʃiː] sie I
sheep, *pl* sheep [ʃiːp] Schaf II
°sheet [ʃiːt] Blatt *(Papier)*
shelf [ʃelf], *pl* shelves [ʃelvz] Regal(brett) I
shift [ʃɪft] Schicht *(bei der Arbeit)* IV 1 (17)
shine [ʃaɪn], **shone, shone**
  1. scheinen *(Sonne)* II
  2. glänzen IV 2 (54)
°shiny ['ʃaɪni] glänzend
ship [ʃɪp] Schiff I
shirt [ʃɜːt] Hemd I • **football shirt** (Fußball-)Trikot III
shiver ['ʃɪvə] zittern II
shoe [ʃuː] Schuh I
shocked [ʃɒkt] schockiert III
°shocking ['ʃɒkɪŋ] schockierend
shone [ʃɒn, *AE* ʃəʊn] *siehe* shine
shoot [ʃuːt] **shot, shot**
  1. (er)schießen IV 2 (45)
  2. *(Film)* drehen; fotografieren IV 5 (101)

shop [ʃɒp] Laden, Geschäft I
  shop assistant [ˈʃɒp_əˌsɪstənt] Verkäufer/in I
shop (-pp-) [ʃɒp] einkaufen (gehen) I
shopping ['ʃɒpɪŋ] (das) Einkaufen I
  go shopping einkaufen gehen I
  shopping list Einkaufsliste I
  shopping mall (großes) Einkaufszentrum III • **shopping precinct** Einkaufsviertel, -straße *(autofrei)* III
short [ʃɔːt] kurz I • **a short time** kurz IV 1 (28)
shorts (pl) [ʃɔːts] Shorts, kurze Hose I • °**boxer shorts** Boxershorts
shot [ʃɒt] *siehe* shoot
shot [ʃɒt] Schuss III
should [ʃəd, ʃʊd]: **you should ...** du solltest ... / ihr solltet ... I • **you should have asked** du hättest fragen sollen IV 5 (101)
shoulder ['ʃəʊldə] Schulter I
shout [ʃaʊt] schreien, rufen I
  shout at sb. jn. anschreien II
show [ʃəʊ] Show, Vorstellung I
show [ʃəʊ], **showed, shown** zeigen I • **show sb. around** jn. (in der Stadt/im Museum/... herumführen) III • °**show sb. the ropes** jn anlernen, einarbeiten • °**show an animal** ein Tier vorführen, ausstellen
  ▶ S.195 Verbs with two objects
show off [ˌʃəʊ_'ɒf], **showed off, shown off** angeben, prahlen IV 1 (30)
shower ['ʃaʊə] Dusche I • **have a shower** (sich) duschen I
shown [ʃəʊn] *siehe* show
shut up [ˌʃʌt_'ʌp], **shut, shut** den Mund halten II
shy [ʃaɪ] schüchtern, scheu II
sick [sɪk] krank IV 3 (73) • **I feel sick** Mir ist schlecht IV 3 (73/212)
side [saɪd] Seite II • **side door** Seitentür IV 4 (91)
sidewalk ['saɪdwɔːk] *(AE)* Gehweg, Bürgersteig IV 1 (16)
°sigh [saɪ] seufzen
sight [saɪt]: **Get out of my sight.** Geh mir aus den Augen. IV 2 (52) • °**within sight of** in Sicht von
sights (pl) [saɪts] Sehenswürdigkeiten II
sightseeing ['saɪtˌsiːɪŋ] Sightseeing; das Anschauen von Sehenswürdigkeiten IV 1 (18)
sign [saɪn] unterschreiben III
sign [saɪn] Schild; Zeichen III

silent letter [ˌsaɪlənt 'letə] „stummer" Buchstabe *(nicht gesprochener Buchstabe)* II
°silicon chip [ˌsɪlɪkən 'tʃɪp] Siliziumchip, integrierter Schaltkreis
silly ['sɪli] albern, dumm II
°similar ['sɪmɪlə] ähnlich
since September [sɪns] seit September III
Sincerely (yours) [sɪn'sɪəli] *(AE)* mit freundlichen Grüßen IV 4 (85/215)
  ▶ S.215 Beginning and ending letters
sing [sɪŋ], **sang, sung** singen I
singer ['sɪŋə] Sänger/in II
single ['sɪŋgl]
  1. ledig, alleinstehend I • **a single parent** ein(e) Alleinerziehende(r) II
  °2. **every single day** jeden einzelnen Tag
sink [sɪŋk] Spüle, Spülbecken I
sir [sɜː] Sir *(höfliche Anrede, z. B. für Kunden, Vorgesetzte oder Lehrer)* IV 5 (112) • **Dear Sir or Madam ...** Sehr geehrte Damen und Herren IV 4 (85/215)
  ▶ S.215 Beginning and ending letters
sister ['sɪstə] Schwester I
sister city ['sɪstə ˌsɪti] *(AE)* Partnerstadt IV 4 (81)
sit (-tt-) [sɪt], **sat, sat** sitzen; sich setzen I • **sit down** sich hinsetzen II • **sit up** sich aufsetzen II
Sit with me. Setz dich zu mir. / Setzt euch zu mir. I
situation [ˌsɪtjuˈeɪʃn] Situation IV 1 (29)
size [saɪz] Größe I
skate [skeɪt] Inliner/Skateboard fahren I
skateboard ['skeɪtbɔːd] Skateboard I
skates (pl) [skeɪts] Inliner I
sketch [sketʃ] Sketch I
ski [skiː] Ski III
ski [skiː] Ski laufen/fahren III
skiing ['skiːɪŋ]: **go skiing** Ski laufen/fahren III
ski slope ['skiː sləʊp] Skipiste III
skill [skɪl] Fähigkeit, Fertigkeit IV 1 (30)
skills file ['skɪlz faɪl] Anhang mit Lern- und Arbeitstechniken I
skim a text (-mm-) [skɪm] einen Text überfliegen *(um den Inhalt grob zu erfassen)* III
skin [skɪn] Haut IV 5 (102)
skirt [skɜːt] Rock II
sky [skaɪ] Himmel II • **in the sky** am Himmel II
skyline ['skaɪˌlaɪn] Horizont, Skyline IV 1 (19)

skyscraper [ˈskaɪskreɪpə] Wolkenkratzer IV 1 (17)
°**slam** [slæm]: **slam against the windows** gegen die Fenster klatschen
slave [sleɪv] Sklave, Sklavin II
slavery [ˈsleɪvəri] Sklaverei IV 5 (111)
sledge [sledʒ] Schlitten III
sleep [sliːp], **slept, slept** schlafen I
sleep [sliːp] Schlaf III
sleepover [ˈsliːpəʊvə] Schlafparty III
slept [slept] *siehe* **sleep**
°**slipper** [ˈslɪpə]: **bedroom slipper** Hausschuh
slogan [ˈsləʊɡən] Slogan, Losung IV 5 (110)
slope: ski slope Skipiste III
slow [sləʊ] langsam II
°**slur (-rr-)** [slɜː] lallen
small [smɔːl] klein II • **small letters** Kleinbuchstaben III
smart [smɑːt] schlau IV 4 (90)
smell [smel] riechen II
smell [smel] Geruch II
smile [smaɪl] lächeln I • **smile at sb.** jn. anlächeln II
smile [smaɪl] Lächeln II • **give (sb.) a smile** lächeln, jn. anlächeln IV 1 (19)
smoke [sməʊk] rauchen IV 5 (108/219)
smoke [sməʊk] Rauch IV 2 (36) **There's no smoke without fire.** Wo Rauch ist, ist auch Feuer. IV 2 (36/201)
▶ S.219 Verbs & nouns with the same form
smoothie [ˈsmuːði] *dickflüssiger Fruchtshake mit Milch, Joghurt oder Eiscreme* II
smuggle [ˈsmʌɡl] schmuggeln IV 5 (113)
snack [snæk] Snack, Imbiss II
snake [sneɪk] Schlange I
snow [snəʊ] Schnee II
snowball [ˈsnəʊbɔːl] Schneeball IV 4 (91)
so [səʊ]
1. also; deshalb, daher I • **So? Und? / Na und?** II • **So what?** [səʊ ˈwɒt] Und? / Na und? II
▶ S.200–201 Giving reasons
2. **so sweet** so süß I • **so far** bis jetzt, bis hierher III • **so (that)** sodass, damit III
3. **I hope so.** Ich hoffe es. II **I think so.** Ich glaube (ja). II **I don't think so.** Das finde/glaube ich nicht. I • **Do you really think so?** Meinst du wirklich? / Glaubst du das wirklich? II
soap [səʊp] Seife I

soap (opera) [ˈsəʊp ˌɒprə] Seifenoper IV 5 (100)
°**social networking website** [ˌsəʊʃl ˈnetwɜːkɪŋ] *eine Website zur Bildung und Unterhaltung sozialer Netzwerke*
Social Studies [ˌsəʊʃl ˈstʌdiz] Gemeinschaftskunde, Politische Bildung, Sozialkunde IV 2 (39)
sock [sɒk] Socke, Strumpf I
soda [ˈsəʊdə] *(AE)* Limonade IV 3 (59)
sofa [ˈsəʊfə] Sofa I
soft [sɒft] weich, sanft III • **soft drink** alkoholfreies Getränk IV 3 (68)
software [ˈsɒftweə] Software II
soil [sɔɪl] (Erdreich) Erde IV 2 (40)
sold [səʊld] *siehe* **sell**
sold out [ˌsəʊld ˈaʊt]: **be sold out** ausverkauft/vergriffen sein III
soldier [ˈsəʊldʒə] Soldat/in IV 2 (52)
solve [sɒlv] lösen IV 5 (114)
some [səm, sʌm] einige, ein paar I **some cheese/juice/money** etwas Käse/Saft/Geld I
somebody [ˈsʌmbədi] jemand I **Find/Ask somebody who ...** Finde/Frage jemanden, der ... II
somehow [ˈsʌmhaʊ] irgendwie IV 4 (90)
someone [ˈsʌmwʌn] jemand III
something [ˈsʌmθɪŋ] etwas I
sometimes [ˈsʌmtaɪmz] manchmal II
somewhere [ˈsʌmweə] irgendwo(hin) II
son [sʌn] Sohn I
song [sɒŋ] Lied, Song I
soon [suːn] bald I • **as soon as** sobald, sowie II
sore [sɔː]: **be sore** wund sein, wehtun II • **have a sore throat** Halsschmerzen haben II
sorry [ˈsɒri]: **(I'm) sorry.** Entschuldigung. / Tut mir leid. I • **Sorry, I'm late.** Entschuldigung, dass ich zu spät bin/komme. I • **Sorry? Wie bitte?** I • **say sorry** sich entschuldigen II
sort [sɔːt] einteilen; sortieren IV 5 (103)
sort (of) [sɔːt] Art, Sorte II
▶ S.219 Verbs & nouns with the same form
soul [səʊl]
1. Soul(musik) III
°2. Seele
sound [saʊnd] klingen, sich (gut usw.) anhören I
sound [saʊnd] Laut; Klang I
sound file [ˈsaʊnd faɪl] Tondatei, Soundfile III
soup [suːp] Suppe II
sour [ˈsaʊə] sauer III

source [sɔːs] Quelle (Informationsquelle, Textquelle) IV 2 (42)
south [saʊθ] Süden; nach Süden; südlich II • **southbound** [ˈsaʊθbaʊnd] Richtung Süden III **south-east** [ˌsaʊθˈiːst] Südosten; nach Südosten; südöstlich II • **southern** [ˈsʌðən] südlich, Süd- III • **south-west** [ˌsaʊθˈwest] Südwesten; nach Südwesten; südwestlich II
souvenir [ˌsuːvəˈnɪə] Andenken, Souvenir II
space [speɪs]
1. Weltraum II
2. **Move back one space.** Geh ein Feld zurück. II • **Move on one space.** Geh ein Feld vor. II
spaghetti [spəˈɡeti] Spaghetti II
spark [spɑːk] Funke IV 1 (18)
speak (to) [spiːk], **spoke, spoken** sprechen (mit), reden (mit) II
special [ˈspeʃl] besondere(r, s) II **Did you do anything special?** Habt ihr irgendetwas Besonderes gemacht? II
specific [spəˈsɪfɪk] bestimmte(r, s), spezifische(r, s) IV 2 (51)
spectacular [spekˈtækjələ] spektakulär IV (18)
speech [spiːtʃ] Rede IV 1 (28) **make/give a speech** eine Rede halten IV 1 (28/199)
speed [spiːd] rasen, schnell fliegen III
speed [spiːd] Geschwindigkeit III **speed limit** Geschwindigkeitsbegrenzung, -beschränkung III
spell [spel] buchstabieren I
spend [spend], **spent, spent: spend money (on)** Geld ausgeben (für) II • **spend time (on)** Zeit verbringen (mit) II
spent [spent] *siehe* **spend**
spice [spaɪs] Gewürz III
spicy [ˈspaɪsi] würzig, scharf gewürzt III
°**spider** [ˈspaɪdə]: **black widow spider** Schwarze oder Echte Witwe (*giftige Spinne*)
spill [spɪl] verschütten IV 3 (72)
°**spirit** [ˈspɪrɪt] Geist
spit (at sb.) (-tt-) [spɪt], **spat, spat** (jn. an)spucken IV 5 (113)
splash [splæʃ] spritzen IV 5 (113)
°**splash-resistant** [ˌsplæʃ rɪˈzɪstənt] spritzwassergeschützt
spoke [spəʊk] *siehe* **speak**
spoken [ˈspəʊkən] *siehe* **speak**
spoon [spuːn] Löffel III
sport [spɔːt] Sport; Sportart I **do sport** Sport treiben I

sports gear *(no pl)* ['spɔːts gɪə] Sportausrüstung, Sportsachen II
sports hall ['spɔːts hɔːl] Sporthalle III
spot (-tt-) [spɒt] entdecken III
spray [spreɪ] spritzen, (be)sprühen, sprayen IV 3 (59)
spread [spred], **spread, spread** (sich) ausbreiten, (sich) verbreiten IV 2 (38)
spring [sprɪŋ]
1. Frühling I
2. Quelle *(Wasser)* IV 2 (36)
spy [spaɪ] Spion/in I
square [skweə] Platz *(in der Stadt)* II
square km (sq km) [skweə] Quadratkilometer III
square brackets [ˌskweə 'brækɪts] eckige Klammern IV 5 (103)
squash [skwɒʃ], *pl* **squash** Kürbis IV 2 (37)
squeeze [skwiːz] drücken; (aus)pressen III
squirrel ['skwɪrəl] Eichhörnchen II
stadium ['steɪdɪəm] Stadion III
staff [stɑːf] Personal, Belegschaft; Lehrerkollegium IV 2 (40) • **member of staff** *(BE)* Mitarbeiter/in IV 2 (40) • **staff member** *(AE)* Mitarbeiter/in IV 2 (40)
stage [steɪdʒ] Bühne I • °**stage right** Bühne rechts • °**stage direction** Regieanweisung
stairs *(pl)* [steəz] Treppe; Treppenstufen I
stamp [stæmp] Briefmarke I
stand [stænd], **stood, stood**
1. stehen; sich (hin)stellen II
2. ertragen, aushalten, ausstehen II • **I can't stand it.** Ich kann es nicht ertragen/aushalten/ausstehen. II
°**stand up for sth./sb.** [ˌstænd_'ʌp] sich für etwas/jn. einsetzen
star [stɑː]
1. Stern II
2. (Film-, Pop-)Star I
°**stare** [steə] starren
start [stɑːt] starten, anfangen, beginnen (mit) I • °**to start us off** erstens, zuerst mal
state [steɪt] Staat III
°**statement** ['steɪtmənt] Aussage
static (electricity) ['stætɪk, ˌstætɪk_ɪˌlek'trɪsəti] elektrische Aufladung IV 1 (18)
station ['steɪʃn]
1. Bahnhof I • **at the station** am Bahnhof I
2. **(radio/pop) station** (Radio-/Pop-)Sender III

statue ['stætʃuː] Statue II
stay [steɪ] bleiben; wohnen, übernachten II • **stay out** nicht nach Hause kommen, draußenbleiben III
steak [steɪk] (Rinder-)Steak IV Intro (8)
steal [stiːl], **stole, stolen** stehlen II
°**steamer** ['stiːmə] Dampfschiff
steel [stiːl] Stahl III
steel drum [ˌstiːl 'drʌm] Steeldrum III
steer [stɪə] lenken, steuern III
°**St. Elmo's Fire** [sənt ˌelməʊz 'faɪə] Elmsfeuer
step [step]
1. Schritt I • **take steps** Schritte machen/unternehmen III • **take sth. a step at a time** etwas eins nach dem anderen tun; etwas Schritt für Schritt tun IV 1 (28)
2. Stufe IV 5 (112)
°**step** [step] sich aufstellen
stereo ['sterɪəʊ] Stereoanlage III
stew [stjuː] Eintopf(gericht) III
stick (on) [ˌstɪk_'ɒn], **stuck, stuck** (auf)kleben I
stick: (drum-)stick [stɪk] Trommelstock III
stick out of sth. [stɪk], **stuck, stuck** aus etwas herausragen, herausstehen III
still [stɪl]
1. (immer) noch I
2. trotzdem, dennoch II
still [stɪl] still *(bewegungslos)* IV 3 (73)
stole [stəʊl] *siehe* **steal**
stolen ['stəʊlən] *siehe* **steal**
stomach ['stʌmək] Magen II **stomach ache** Magenschmerzen, Bauchweh II
stone [stəʊn] Stein II
stood [stʊd] *siehe* **stand**
stop (-pp-) [stɒp]
1. aufhören I
2. anhalten I
Stop that! Hör auf damit! / Lass das! I
stop [stɒp] Halt, Anhalten IV Intro (12)
storm [stɔːm] Sturm; Gewitter II • °**storm drain** ['stɔːm ˌdreɪn] Regenwasserkanalisation
stormy ['stɔːmi] stürmisch II
story ['stɔːri] Geschichte, Erzählung I • **crime story** Krimi IV 2 (53/205)
straight [streɪt] direkt IV Intro (12)
straight on [ˌstreɪt_'ɒn] geradeaus weiter II
straightaway [ˌstreɪtə'weɪ] sofort, gleich III

strange [streɪndʒ] seltsam, sonderbar I
°**stranger** ['streɪndʒə] Fremde(r)
strawberry ['strɔːbəri] Erdbeere II
street [striːt] Straße I • **at 7 Park Street** in der Parkstraße 7 I
street performer [pə'fɔːmə] Straßenkünstler/in III
stress ['stres] Betonung III
stretch [stretʃ] sich (er)strecken IV Intro (12)
strict [strɪkt] streng III
strike [straɪk] Streik III • **be on strike** streiken, sich im Streik befinden III • **go on strike** streiken, in den Streik treten III
string [strɪŋ] Saite III
°**stroll** [strəʊl] Spaziergang, Bummel
strong [strɒŋ] stark II
structure ['strʌktʃə] strukturieren, aufbauen II
structure ['strʌktʃə] Struktur; Gliederung III
°**struggle** ['strʌgl] Kampf
stuck [stʌk] *siehe* **stick**
student ['stjuːdənt] Schüler/in; Student/in I • **exchange student** Austauschschüler/in III
studio ['stjuːdɪəʊ] Studio I
study ['stʌdi] lernen; studieren III
study hall ['stʌdi hɔːl] *Zeit zum selbstständigen Lernen in der Schule* IV 4 (78)
study skills *(pl)* ['stʌdi skɪlz] Lern- und Arbeitstechniken I
stuff [stʌf] Zeug, Kram I
style [staɪl] Stil III
sub-heading ['sʌbˌhedɪŋ] Zwischenüberschrift IV 2 (51)
subject ['sʌbdʒɪkt]
1. Subjekt I
2. Schulfach I
3. Thema IV 2 (39)
4. Untertan/in; Staatsangehörige/r *(in einer Monarchie)* IV 2 (52)
subway ['sʌbweɪ]: **the subway** *(AE)* die U-Bahn II
succeed (in sth.) [sək'siːd] Erfolg haben, erfolgreich sein (mit etwas, bei etwas) IV 3 (58)
success [sək'ses] Erfolg III
such [sʌtʃ]: **such a nice person** so ein netter Mensch III • **such good books** so gute Bücher III • **such as** wie zum Beispiel III
sudden ['sʌdn] plötzlich IV 5 (113)
suddenly ['sʌdnli] plötzlich, auf einmal I
suffer (from) ['sʌfə] leiden (an) IV 4 (87)
suffix ['sʌfɪks] Suffix, Nachsilbe IV 1 (27)

sugar [ˈʃʊgə] Zucker II
°**suggestion** [səˈdʒestʃn] Vorschlag
summary [ˈsʌməri] Zusammenfassung IV 4 (89)
summer [ˈsʌmə] Sommer I
°**summertime** [ˈsʌmətaɪm] Sommer I
sun [sʌn] Sonne II
Sunday [ˈsʌndeɪ, ˈsʌndi] Sonntag I
sung [sʌŋ] *siehe* **sing**
sunglasses *(pl)* [ˈsʌnɡlɑːsɪz] (eine) Sonnenbrille I
°**sunlight** [ˈsʌnˌlaɪt] Sonnenlicht
sunny [ˈsʌni] sonnig II
sunrise [ˈsʌnraɪz] Sonnenaufgang IV 3 (72)
sunset [ˈsʌnset] Sonnenuntergang IV 3 (72)
sunshine [ˈsʌnʃaɪn] Sonnenschein IV 4 (89)
suntan [ˈsʌnˌtæn]: **have a suntan** sonnengebräunt sein III
supermarket [ˈsuːpəmɑːkɪt] Supermarkt I
supper [ˈsʌpə] Abendessen, Abendbrot IV 3 (60)
support [səˈpɔːt]: **support a team** eine Mannschaft unterstützen; Fan einer Mannschaft sein III
support [səˈpɔːt] Unterstützung IV 5 (108/219)
▶ S.219 Verbs & nouns with the same form
supporter [səˈpɔːtə] Anhänger/in, Fan III
suppose [səˈpəʊz] annehmen, vermuten I
°**supreme: the Supreme Court** [suːˌpriːm ˈkɔːt] der Oberste Gerichtshof
sure [ʃʊə, ʃɔː] sicher I • **make sure** sich vergewissern IV 4 (87)
surf the internet [sɜːf] im Internet surfen II
surfboard [ˈsɜːfbɔːd] Surfbrett II
surfing [ˈsɜːfɪŋ]: **go surfing** wellenreiten gehen, surfen gehen II
surprise (for/to) [səˈpraɪz] Überraschung (für) III
surprise sb. [səˈpraɪz] jn. überraschen III
surprised (at sth.) [səˈpraɪzd] überrascht (über etwas) III
surround [səˈraʊnd]: **be surrounded** umgeben sein IV 2 (53)
survey (on) [ˈsɜːveɪ] Umfrage, Untersuchung (über) II
survival [səˈvaɪvl] Überleben II
survive [səˈvaɪv] überleben II
swam [swæm] *siehe* **swim**
swap (-pp-) [swɒp] tauschen I
swap sth. (for sth.) etwas (ein)tauschen (für/gegen etwas) IV 4 (90)
sweat [swet] schwitzen IV 1 (18)

sweat [swet] Schweiß IV 3 (72)
sweatshirt [ˈswetʃɜːt] Sweatshirt I
sweep [swiːp], **swept, swept** fegen, kehren IV 3 (72)
sweet [swiːt] süß I
sweetheart [ˈswiːthɑːt] Liebling, Schatz II
sweets *(pl)* Süßigkeiten I
swept [swept] *siehe* **sweep**
swim (-mm-) [swɪm], **swam, swum** schwimmen I
swimmer [ˈswɪmə] Schwimmer/in II
swimming [ˈswɪmɪŋ] Schwimmen I • **go swimming** schwimmen gehen I
swimming pool [ˈswɪmɪŋ puːl] Schwimmbad, -becken II
swimming trunks [trʌŋks] Badehose III
swimsuit [ˈswɪmsuːt] Badeanzug III
swum [swʌm] *siehe* **swim**
syllable [ˈsɪləbl] Silbe I
°**symbol** [ˈsɪmbəl] Symbol
synagogue [ˈsɪnəɡɒɡ] Synagoge III
synonym [ˈsɪnənɪm] Synonym *(Wort mit gleicher oder sehr ähnlicher Bedeutung)* IV 3 (64)
system [ˈsɪstəm] System IV 3 (61)

T

table [ˈteɪbl]
1. Tisch I • **table tennis** [ˈteɪbl tenɪs] Tischtennis I • **table tennis bat** Tischtennisschläger III
°2. Tabelle
tablecloth [ˈteɪblklɒθ] Tischdecke IV 2 (36)
take [teɪk], **took, taken**
1. nehmen I • °**take sb./sth. seriously** jn./etwas ernst nehmen
2. (weg-, hin)bringen I
3. dauern, *(Zeit)* brauchen III
I can take it. Ich halt's aus. / Ich kann's aushalten. IV 4 (91) • **take a break** eine Pause machen IV 1 (25)
°**take a breath** Luft holen • **take a left/right** *(AE)* nach links/rechts abbiegen IV Intro (16) • **take a trip** *(AE)* einen Ausflug/eine Reise machen IV Intro (9) • **Take another turn.** hier: Würfel noch einmal. II • **take care of sth./sb.** sich um etwas/jn. kümmern III • **take notes** sich Notizen machen I
take sth. off etwas ausziehen *(Kleidung)*; etwas absetzen *(Hut, Helm)* II • **take 10 c off** 10 Cent abziehen I • **take sth. out** etwas herausnehmen I • **take sth. over** etwas übernehmen; etwas in seine Macht bringen IV 1 (17) • **take part in sth.** teilnehmen an etwas III
take photos Fotos machen, fotografieren I • **take place** stattfinden II • **take a ride** eine Spritztour/Fahrt machen III • **take sth. a step at a time** etwas eins nach dem anderen tun; etwas Schritt für Schritt tun IV 1 (28) • **take steps** Schritte machen/unternehmen III • **take turns to do sth.** sich abwechseln, etwas zu tun IV 1 (29)
I'll take it. *(beim Einkaufen)* Ich werde es (ihn, sie) nehmen. / Ich nehme es (ihn, sie). I
takeaway [ˈteɪkəweɪ] Restaurant, das auch Essen zum Mitnehmen verkauft; Essen zum Mitnehmen III
taken [ˈteɪkən] *siehe* **take**
talent [ˈtælənt] Talent, Begabung III
talk [tɔːk]: **talk (about)** reden (über), sich unterhalten (über) I
talk (to) reden (mit), sich unterhalten (mit) I
talk Rede, Gespräch; Vortrag, Referat IV 5 (108/219)
▶ S.219 Verbs & nouns with the same form
tall [tɔːl]
1. groß *(Person)* III
2. hoch *(Gebäude, Baum)* IV 1 (18)
°**task** [tɑːsk] Aufgabe
taste [teɪst] schmecken; kosten, probieren IV 1 (19)
taste [teɪst] Geschmack IV 1 (19) • **be in good/bad taste** geschmackvoll/-los sein IV 4 (78)
▶ S.219 Verbs & nouns with the same form
°**tattoo** [təˈtuː] Tätowierung
taught [tɔːt] *siehe* **teach**
tavern [ˈtævən] Schenke, Gastwirtschaft IV 2 (52)
°**tax** [tæks] Steuer • **place a tax on sth.** etwas versteuern
°**taxation** [tækˈseɪʃn] Besteuerung
°**tax collector** [ˈtæks kəˌlektə] Steuerbeamte(r)/-beamtin
taxi [ˈtæksi] Taxi III
tea [tiː] Tee; *(auch:)* leichte Nachmittags- oder Abendmahlzeit I
tea bag Teebeutel IV 3 (65)
teach [tiːtʃ], **taught, taught** unterrichten, lehren I
teacher [ˈtiːtʃə] Lehrer/in I • **head teacher** Schulleiter/in III
team [tiːm] Team, Mannschaft I
tear [teə], **tore, torn** (zer)reißen IV 4 (78) • °**tear sth. off** etwas abreißen
tear [tɪə] Träne II
tease [tiːz] necken, auf den Arm nehmen III

Dictionary (English – German)

teaspoon ['tiːspuːn] Teelöffel III
technique [tek'niːk] (Arbeits-)Verfahren, Technik, Methode IV 1 (27)
teddy bear ['tedi beə] Teddybär III
teen (bes. AE) [tiːn] Teenager- III
°**teenage** ['tiːneɪdʒ] Teenager-
teenager ['tiːneɪdʒə] Teenager, Jugendliche(r) II
teeth [tiːθ] Plural von „tooth" I
telephone ['telɪfəʊn] Telefon I
telephone number Telefonnummer I
television (TV) ['telɪvɪʒn] Fernsehen I
tell (about) [tel], **told, told** erzählen (von), berichten (über) I • **Tell me your names.** Sagt mir eure Namen. I • **tell sb. the way** jm. den Weg beschreiben II
temperature ['temprətʃə] Temperatur II • **have a temperature** Fieber haben II
°**tenement** ['tenəmənt] Mietshaus
tennis ['tenɪs] Tennis I
tense [tens] (grammatische) Zeit, Tempus II
tent [tent] Zelt IV Intro (11)
term [tɜːm]
  1. Trimester II
  °2. **he served two terms as president** er hatte zwei Amtszeiten als Präsident
terrible ['terəbl] schrecklich, furchtbar I
°**terrific** [təˈrɪfɪk] gewaltig
terrified ['terɪfaɪd]: **be terrified (of)** schreckliche Angst haben (vor) IV 5 (112)
terrorism ['terərɪzm] Terrorismus IV 1 (28)
test [test] Klassenarbeit, Test, Prüfung II
text [tekst] Text I
text (message) ['tekst ˌmesɪdʒ] SMS II
text sb. [tekst] jm. eine SMS schicken II
than [ðæn, ðən] als II • **more than me** mehr als ich II
thank [θæŋk]: **Thank God.** Gott sei Dank. IV 2 (18) • **Thank you.** Danke (schön). I • **Thanks.** Danke. I • **Thanks a lot!** Vielen Dank! I • **Thanks very much!** Danke sehr! / Vielen Dank! II • **give thanks** danken, feierlich danksagen IV 2 (38)
°**Thanksgiving** [ˌθæŋksˈgɪvɪŋ] Danksagung
that [ðət, ðæt]
  1. das (dort) I
  2. jene(r, s) I • **that day** an jenem Tag III • **That's me.** Das bin ich. I **That's right.** Das ist richtig. / Das stimmt. I • **That's up to you.** Das liegt bei dir. / Das kannst/musst du (selbst) entscheiden. III • **that's why** deshalb, darum I
  ▶ S.200–201 Giving reasons
that [ðət, ðæt] dass I
that [ðət, ðæt] der, die, das; die (Relativpronomen) III
the [ðə, ði] der, die, das; die I
theatre ['θɪətə] Theater II
their [ðeə]
  1. ihr, ihre (Plural) I
  2. sein oder ihr (= **his or her**) IV 4 (58/208)
  ▶ S.208 they
theirs [ðeəz] ihrer, ihre, ihrs II
them [ðəm, ðem]
  1. sie; ihnen I • **the two of them** die beiden; alle beide II
  2. ihn oder sie (= **him or her**) IV 4 (58/208)
  ▶ S.208 they
theme park ['θiːm pɑːk] Themenpark II
themselves [ðəmˈselvz]
  1. sich III
  2. selbst IV 1 (18/196)
  ▶ S.196 German „selbst"
then [ðen]
  1. dann, danach I
  2. damals II
  Then what? Was dann? II • **just then** genau in dem Moment; gerade dann II
°**therapy** ['θerəpi] Therapie
there [ðeə]
  1. da, dort I
  2. dahin, dorthin I
  down there (nach) dort unten II **in there** dort drinnen I • **over there** da drüben, dort drüben I **up there** dort oben III • **there are** es sind (vorhanden); es gibt I **there's** es ist (vorhanden); es gibt I • **there isn't a …** es ist kein/e …; es gibt kein/e … I
thermometer [θəˈmɒmɪtə] Thermometer II
these [ðiːz] diese, die (hier) I
they [ðeɪ]
  1. sie (Plural) I • **They say …** Man sagt, … III
  2. er oder sie (= **he or she**) IV 4 (58/208)
  ▶ S.208 they
°**thick** [θɪk]: **It's thick in the Irish blood.** etwa: Es liegt den Iren im Blut.
thief [θiːf], pl **thieves** [θiːvz] Dieb/in II
thing [θɪŋ] Ding, Sache I • **What was the best thing about …?** Was war das Beste an …? II
think [θɪŋk], **thought, thought** glauben, meinen, denken I • **Do you really think so?** Meinst du wirklich? / Glaubst du das wirklich? II • **I think so.** Ich glaube (ja). I • **I don't think so.** Das finde/glaube ich nicht. I • **think about 1.** nachdenken über II; **2.** denken über, halten von II **think of 1.** denken über, halten von II **2.** denken an; sich ausdenken II
third [θɜːd] dritte(r, s) I
thirsty ['θɜːsti] durstig I • **be thirsty** Durst haben, durstig sein I
this [ðɪs]
  1. dies (hier) I
  2. diese(r, s) I
  This is Isabel. Hier spricht Isabel. / Hier ist Isabel. (am Telefon) II • **this morning/afternoon/evening** heute Morgen/Nachmittag/Abend I • **this way** hier entlang, in diese Richtung II
those [ðəʊz] die (da), jene (dort) I
thought [θɔːt] siehe **think**
thought [θɔːt] Gedanke IV 3 (59)
°**thought bubble** Denkblase
thousand ['θaʊznd] tausend I
threw [θruː] siehe **throw**
throat [θrəʊt] Hals, Kehle II • **have a sore throat** [sɔː ˈθrəʊt] Halsschmerzen haben II
through [θruː] durch II
throughout October [θruːˈaʊt] den ganzen Oktober hindurch IV 4 (80)
throw [θrəʊ], **threw, thrown** werfen II • **throw the dice** würfeln II **throw up** sich übergeben IV 4 (91)
thrown [θrəʊn] siehe **throw**
Thursday ['θɜːzdeɪ, 'θɜːzdi] Donnerstag I
ticket ['tɪkɪt]
  1. Eintrittskarte I
  2. Fahrkarte III
ticket machine ['tɪkɪt məˌʃiːn] Fahrkartenautomat III
ticket office ['tɪkɪt ˌɒfɪs] Kasse (für den Verkauf von Eintrittskarten); Fahrkartenschalter IV 1 (18)
tide [taɪd] Gezeiten, Ebbe und Flut II • **the tide is in** es ist Flut II **the tide is out** es ist Ebbe II
tidy ['taɪdi] aufräumen I
tidy ['taɪdi] ordentlich, aufgeräumt II
tie (-ing form: **tying**) [taɪ] (fest)binden IV 2 (54)

tiger ['taɪgə] Tiger II
tight [taɪt] eng; fest IV 4 (78)
tights (pl) [taɪts] Strumpfhose III
till [tɪl] bis (zeitlich) I
time [taɪm] Zeit; Uhrzeit I • **in time** rechtzeitig II • **What's the time?** Wie spät ist es? I • **a long time** lange III • **a short time** kurz IV 1 (28) • **time zone** Zeitzone IV Intro (9)
time(s) [taɪmz] Mal(e); -mal II • **for the first time** zum ersten Mal II
timeline ['taɪmlaɪn] Zeitstrahl, Zeitleiste IV 2 (38)
timetable ['taɪmteɪbl] Stundenplan I
timing ['taɪmɪŋ]: **bad timing** schlechtes Timing, schlechte Wahl des Zeitpunkts III
tip [tɪp]
1. Tipp III
2. Spitze IV Intro (12)
tired ['taɪəd] müde I • **be tired of sth.** genug von etwas haben, etwas satt haben IV 1 (18) • **get tired of sth.** einer Sache überdrüssig werden, die Lust an etwas verlieren IV 4 (91)
title ['taɪtl] Titel, Überschrift I
to [tə, tu]
1. zu, nach I • **an e-mail to** eine E-Mail an I • **to Jenny's** zu Jenny I • **to the doctor's** zum Arzt III • **to the front** nach vorn I • **I've never been to Bath.** Ich bin noch nie in Bath gewesen. II • **write to** schreiben an I
2. **quarter to 12** Viertel vor 12 (11.45 / 23.45) I • **from Monday to Friday** von Montag bis Freitag III
3. **try to do** versuchen, zu tun I
4. um zu I
▶ S.200–201 Giving reasons
toast [təʊst] Toast(brot) I
today [tə'deɪ] heute I
toe [təʊ] Zeh I
together [tə'geðə] zusammen I
toilet ['tɔɪlət] Toilette I
told [təʊld] siehe **tell**
tomato [tə'mɑːtəʊ], pl **tomatoes** Tomate II
tomorrow [tə'mɒrəʊ] morgen I
°**ton** [tʌn] (Gewichtseinheit, in den USA 907 kg) etwa: Tonne I
tonight [tə'naɪt] heute Nacht, heute Abend I
too [tuː]: **from Bristol too** auch aus Bristol I • **Me too.** Ich auch. I
too much/big/… [tuː] zu viel/groß/… I
took [tʊk] siehe **take**
tool [tuːl] Werkzeug IV Intro (11)

tooth [tuːθ], pl **teeth** [tiːθ] Zahn I
toothache ['tuːθeɪk] Zahnschmerzen II
top [tɒp]
1. Spitze, oberes Ende I • **at the top (of)** oben, am oberen Ende, an der Spitze (von) I
2. Top, Oberteil I
top [tɒp] (adj) Spitzen-, oberste(r, s) III
topic ['tɒpɪk] Thema, Themenbereich I • **topic sentence** Satz, der in das Thema eines Absatzes einführt II
tore [tɔː] siehe **tear**
torn [tɔːn] siehe **tear**
°**tortilla** [tɔː'tiːə] Maiskuchen I
tortoise ['tɔːtəs] Schildkröte I
°**totally** ['təʊtəli] völlig, total I
touch [tʌtʃ] berühren, anfassen I
touch [tʌtʃ]: **keep in touch** in Verbindung bleiben, Kontakt halten III
tough [tʌf] tough, selbstsicher, zäh III; schwierig, hart IV 4 (81)
tour (of the house) [tʊə] Rundgang, Tour (durch das Haus) I
°**tourism** ['tʊərɪzm] Tourismus I
tourist ['tʊərɪst] Tourist/in II • **tourist information** Fremdenverkehrsamt II
toward [tə'wɔːd] (AE) siehe **towards**
towards Mr Green [tə'wɔːdz] auf Mr Green zu, in Mr Greens Richtung I
towel ['taʊəl] Handtuch II
tower ['taʊə] Turm I
town [taʊn] Stadt I • **the centre of town** die Mitte der Stadt III • **in town** in der Stadt III • **into town** in die Stadt II
°**trace sb.** [treɪs] jm. nachgehen, Informationen über jn. einholen I
track [træk] Stück, Titel, Track (auf einer CD) III
trade [treɪd] Handel II
tradition [trə'dɪʃn] Tradition IV 2 (42)
traditional [trə'dɪʃənl] traditionell III
traffic ['træfɪk] Verkehr II • °**traffic jam** Verkehrsstau I
trail [treɪl] (Lehr-)Pfad IV Intro (12)
train [treɪn] Zug I • **on the train** im Zug I • **mule train** Maultierkarawane IV Intro (13) • °**wagon train** Planwagenkolonne, -zug I
train [treɪn] trainieren III
trainers (pl) ['treɪnəz] Turnschuhe II
training session ['seʃn] Trainingsstunde, -einheit II
tram [træm] Straßenbahn III
translate (from … into) [træns'leɪt] übersetzen (aus … in) III

translation [træns'leɪʃn] Übersetzung II
°**transparency** [træns'pærənsi] Folie (für Overheadprojektor) I
transport (no pl) ['trænspɔːt] Transport(wesen) III • **public transport** öffentlicher Verkehr IV 2 (50)
trap [træp] Falle II
trap (-pp-) [træp] (mit einer Falle) fangen III
travel (-ll-) ['trævl] reisen II
Travelcard ['trævlkɑːd] Tages-/Wochen-/Monatsfahrkarte (der Londoner Verkehrsbetriebe) III
treason ['triːzn] Hochverrat IV 2 (52)
tree [triː] Baum I
trendy ['trendi] modisch, schick III
tribal ['traɪbl] Stammes- IV Intro (10)
tribe [traɪb] (Volks-)Stamm IV Intro (10/191)
°**tribute** ['trɪbjuːt] Würdigung I
trick [trɪk]
1. (Zauber-)Kunststück, Trick I • **do tricks** (Zauber-)Kunststücke machen I
2. Streich II • **play a trick on sb.** jm. einen Streich spielen II
trip [trɪp] Reise; Ausflug I • **go on a trip** einen Ausflug/eine Reise machen II • **take a trip** (AE) einen Ausflug/eine Reise machen IV Intro (9) •
trombone [trɒm'bəʊn] Posaune III
trouble ['trʌbl] Schwierigkeiten, Ärger II • **be in trouble** in Schwierigkeiten sein; Ärger kriegen II
trousers (pl) ['traʊzəz] Hose II
true [truː] wahr II • **come true** wahr werden II
truly ['truːli]: **Yours truly** (AE) mit freundlichen Grüßen IV 4 (85/215)
▶ S.215 Beginning and ending letters
trumpet ['trʌmpɪt] Trompete III
try [traɪ]
1. versuchen I
2. probieren, kosten I
try and do sth. / try to do sth. versuchen, etwas zu tun I • **try sth. on** etwas anprobieren (Kleidung) I
tsunami [tsuː'nɑːmi] Tsunami III
T-shirt ['tiːʃɜːt] T-Shirt I
tube [tjuːb]: **the Tube** (no pl) (BE) die Londoner U-Bahn III
Tuesday ['tjuːzdeɪ, -di] Dienstag I
tune [tjuːn]: **tune a radio to a station** ein Radio auf einen Sender einstellen IV 5 (100) • **You're tuned to Radio Bristol** Sie hören gerade Radio Bristol IV 5 (100/217)
tune [tjuːn] Melodie III

tunnel ['tʌnl] Tunnel II
turkey ['tɜːki] Pute, Truthahn IV 2 (36)
turn [tɜːn]
1. sich umdrehen II • **turn around** sich umdrehen IV 2 (52) • **turn left/right** (nach) links/rechts abbiegen II • **turn to sb.** sich jm. zuwenden; sich an jn. wenden II
2. **turn sth. off/on** etwas aus-/einschalten I • **turn sth. down/up** etwas leiser/lauter stellen III
turn [tɜːn]: **(It's) my turn.** Ich bin dran / an der Reihe. I • **Miss a turn.** Einmal aussetzen. II • **Take another turn.** hier: Würfel noch einmal. II • **take turns to do sth.** sich abwechseln IV 1 (29)
TV [tiːˈviː] Fernsehen I • **on TV** im Fernsehen I • **watch TV** fernsehen I
twice [twaɪs] zweimal III
twin [twɪn]: **twin brother** Zwillingsbruder I • **twins** (pl) Zwillinge I **twin town** Partnerstadt I
°**type** [taɪp] Typ
°**type** [taɪp]: **bold type** Fettdruck I

U

ultimate ['ʌltɪmət] ultimativ, perfekt IV Intro (8)
unanswered [ˌʌnˈɑːnsəd] unbeantwortet IV 2 (51)
uncle ['ʌŋkl] Onkel I
unclear [ˌʌnˈklɪə] unklar, undeutlich II
uncomfortable [ʌnˈkʌmftəbl] unbequem II
unconscious [ʌnˈkɒnʃəs] bewusstlos II
°**uncool** [ˌʌnˈkuːl] (infml) uncool III
under ['ʌndə] unter I
under control [kənˈtrəʊl] unter Kontrolle IV 5 (103)
underground ['ʌndəɡraʊnd]: **the underground** die U-Bahn II
underground [ˌʌndəˈɡraʊnd] unterirdisch IV 1 (29) • °**underground garage** Tiefgarage
°**underline** [ˌʌndəˈlaɪn] unterstreichen
understand [ˌʌndəˈstænd], **understood, understood** verstehen, begreifen I
understanding [ˌʌndəˈstændɪŋ] verständnisvoll IV 3 (74)
understood [ˌʌndəˈstʊd] siehe **understand**
°**underwear** ['ʌndəweə] Unterwäsche

unfair [ʌnˈfeə] unfair, ungerecht II
unfriendly [ʌnˈfrendli] unfreundlich II
unhappy [ʌnˈhæpi] unglücklich II
unhealthy [ʌnˈhelθi] ungesund III
uniform [ˈjuːnɪfɔːm] Uniform I
unimportant [ˌʌnɪmˈpɔːtnt] unwichtig III
uninteresting [ʌnˈɪntrəstɪŋ] uninteressant II
unit ['juːnɪt] Kapitel, Lektion I
united: **the United Kingdom (UK)** [juːˌnaɪtɪd ˈkɪŋdəm], [juːˈkeɪ] das Vereinigte Königreich (Großbritannien und Nordirland) III • **the United States (US)** [juːˌnaɪtɪd ˈsteɪts], [ˌjuːˈes] die Vereinigten Staaten (von Amerika) III
unknown [ʌnˈnəʊn] unbekannt IV 5 (109)
unlike [ʌnˈlaɪk] im Gegensatz zu III
unload [ʌnˈləʊd] entladen III
unsafe [ʌnˈseɪf] nicht sicher, gefährlich III
unsure [ˌʌnˈʃʊə, ˌʌnˈʃɔː] unsicher II
untidy [ʌnˈtaɪdi] unordentlich III
until [ənˈtɪl] bis II
up [ʌp] hinauf, herauf, nach oben I • **up the hill** den Hügel hinauf II • **up there** dort oben III • **That's up to you.** Das liegt bei dir. / Das kannst/musst du (selbst) entscheiden. III • **What's up?** Was ist los? IV 5 (101)
upset (about) [ʌpˈset] aufgebracht, gekränkt, mitgenommen (wegen) III
upset sb. (-tt-) [ʌpˈset], **upset, upset** jn. ärgern, kränken, aus der Fassung bringen III
°**upside down** [ˌʌpsaɪd ˈdaʊn] umgedreht, auf dem Kopf
upstairs [ˌʌpˈsteəz] oben; nach oben I
us [əs, ʌs] uns I
US [ˌjuːˈes] US-amerikanische(r, s) IV 1 (17)
use [juːz] benutzen, verwenden I
use [juːs] Gebrauch III
used [juːst] **get used to sth./sb.** sich gewöhnen an jn./etwas IV 3 (73)
°**useful** [ˈjuːsfəl] nützlich
useless ['juːsləs] nutzlos, unnütz IV 3 (58)
usual [ˈjuːʒuəl] gewöhnlich, üblich IV 2 (42)
usually [ˈjuːʒuəli] meistens, gewöhnlich, normalerweise I

V

vacation [vəˈkeɪʃn, AE: veɪˈkeɪʃn] (AE) Urlaub, Ferien III
valley [ˈvæli] Tal II • **valley floor** Talboden II
value [ˈvæljuː] Wert IV 3 (58)
vegetable [ˈvedʒtəbl] (ein) Gemüse III
verse [vɜːs] Vers (von der Bibel); Strophe IV 2 (45)
version [ˈvɜːʃn] Fassung IV 4 (89/216) **original version** Originalfassung IV 4 (89/216)
very [ˈveri] sehr I • **like/love sth. very much** etwas sehr mögen/lieben II • **Thanks very much!** Danke sehr! / Vielen Dank! II
victim [ˈvɪktɪm] Opfer III
victory [ˈvɪktəri] Sieg IV 2 (52)
video [ˈvɪdiəʊ] Video III
°**video sharing website** [ˈvɪdiəʊ ˌʃeərɪŋ] Videoportal
view (of) [vjuː]
1. Aussicht, Blick (auf) II
2. Ansicht, Meinung III • **in my view** meiner Ansicht nach III • **point of view** [ˌpɔɪnt əv ˈvjuː] Standpunkt II • **from my point of view** aus meiner Sicht; von meinem Standpunkt aus gesehen II
villa [ˈvɪlə] Ferienhaus; Villa II
village [ˈvɪlɪdʒ] Dorf I
vineyard [ˈvɪnjəd] Weinberg IV 3 (72)
violence [ˈvaɪələns] Gewalt, Gewalttätigkeit IV 5 (102/218)
violent [ˈvaɪələnt] gewalttätig, gewaltsam IV 5 (102/218)
violin [ˌvaɪəˈlɪn] Violine, Geige III **play the violin** Geige spielen III
°**Virgin** [ˈvɜːdʒɪn] Jungfrau
°**Virginian** [vəˈdʒɪniən] Virginianer/in
visibility [ˌvɪzəˈbɪləti] Sicht(weite) IV 1 (18)
visit [ˈvɪzɪt] besuchen, aufsuchen II
visit [ˈvɪzɪt] Besuch II
visitor [ˈvɪzɪtə] Besucher/in, Gast I
vocabulary [vəˈkæbjələri] Vokabelverzeichnis, Wörterverzeichnis I
voice [vɔɪs] Stimme I
volleyball [ˈvɒlibɔːl] Volleyball I
volunteer [ˌvɒlənˈtɪə] sich freiwillig melden, sich bereit erklären IV 5 (112)
volunteer work [ˌvɒlənˈtɪə] Arbeit als Freiwillige(r) III
vote for/against sb./sth. [vəʊt] für/gegen jn./etwas stimmen IV 4 (90)
vote [vəʊt] Stimme; Stimmrecht III
vowel sound [ˈvaʊəl saʊnd] Vokallaut II

W

°**wagon train** [ˈwægən treɪn] Planwagenkolonne, -zug
wait (for) [ˈweɪt fɔː] warten (auf) I • **I can't wait to see …** ich kann es kaum erwarten, … zu sehen I • **Wait a minute.** Warte mal! / Moment mal! II • **Wait and see!** Wart's ab! III
°**waiting room** [ˈweɪtɪŋ ruːm, rʊm] Wartezimmer
wake [weɪk], **woke, woken**:
1. **wake sb. (up)** jn. (auf)wecken III
2. **wake up** aufwachen III
walk [wɔːk] (zu Fuß) gehen, laufen I; spazieren gehen III • **walk on** weiterlaufen III • **walk around** herumlaufen III
walk [wɔːk] Spaziergang II • **go for a walk** spazieren gehen, einen Spaziergang machen II
wall [wɔːl] Wand; Mauer II
°**walrus** [ˈwɔːlrəs] Walross
wander [ˈwɒndə] schlendern, herumirren IV 1 (19)
want [wɒnt] (haben) wollen I • **want to do** tun wollen I • **They want me to say something.** Sie möchten, dass ich etwas sage IV 1 (28)
war [wɔː] Krieg III
wardrobe [ˈwɔːdrəʊb] Kleiderschrank I
warm [wɔːm] warm II
warn sb. (about/of sth.) [wɔːn] jn. vor etwas warnen IV 3 (60)
warning [ˈwɔːnɪŋ] Warnung IV 3 (60)
°**warrior** [ˈwɒrɪə] Krieger/in
was [wəz, wɒz]: **(I/he/she/it) was** siehe **be**
wash [wɒʃ] waschen I • **I wash my hands.** Ich wasche mir die Hände. I
washing machine [ˈwɒʃɪŋ məʃiːn] Waschmaschine II
waste sth. (on) [weɪst] etwas verschwenden, vergeuden (für) III
waste [weɪst] Verschwendung IV 2 (54)
watch [wɒtʃ] beobachten, sich etwas ansehen; zusehen I • **watch TV** fernsehen I
watch [wɒtʃ] Armbanduhr I
water [ˈwɔːtə] Wasser I
waterfall [ˈwɔːtəfɔːl] Wasserfall III
wave [weɪv] winken II
wave [weɪv] Welle IV 3 (56)
way [weɪ]
1. Weg; Strecke II • **a long way (from)** weit entfernt (von) I • **ask sb. the way** jn. nach dem Weg fra-

gen II • **on the way (to)** auf dem Weg (zu/nach) II • **tell sb. the way** jm. den Weg beschreiben II • **What's the best way to get there?** Wie komme ich am besten dahin? III • **I'm on my way.** Ich bin (schon) unterwegs. IV 5 (101)
2. Richtung II • **the other way round** anders herum II • **the wrong way** in die falsche Richtung II • **this way** hier entlang, in diese Richtung II • **which way?** in welche Richtung? / wohin? II
3. **No way!** [ˌnəʊ ˈweɪ] Auf keinen Fall! / Kommt nicht in Frage! II; Was du nicht sagst! / Das kann nicht dein Ernst sein! III
4. **by the way** übrigens, nebenbei (bemerkt) III
5. Art und Weise • **way of life** Lebensart III • **the way you …** so wie du …, auf dieselbe Weise wie du … IV 4 (92)
we [wiː] wir I
weak [wiːk] schwach II
wealth [welθ] Reichtum IV 3 (60/209)
wealthy [ˈwelθi] reich IV 3 (60)
wear [weə], **wore, worn** tragen, anhaben (Kleidung) I
weather [ˈweðə] Wetter II
webcam [ˈwebkæm] Webcam, Internetkamera II
website [ˈwebsaɪt] Website II
Wednesday [ˈwenzdeɪ, ˈwenzdi] Mittwoch I
week [wiːk] Woche I • **days of the week** Wochentage I • **a three-week holiday** ein dreiwöchiger Urlaub III • **once a week** einmal pro Woche III
weekend [ˌwiːkˈend] Wochenende I • **at the weekend** am Wochenende I • **on the weekend** (AE) am Wochenende IV 2 (39)
weigh [weɪ] wiegen III
weight [weɪt] Gewicht IV 3 (72)
weird [wɪəd] seltsam III
welcome [ˈwelkəm]
1. **Welcome (to Bristol).** Willkommen (in Bristol). I
2. **You're welcome.** Gern geschehen. / Nichts zu danken. I
welcome sb. (to) [ˈwelkəm] jn. begrüßen, willkommen heißen (in) I • **They welcome you to …** Sie heißen dich in … willkommen I
well [wel] (gesundheitlich) gut; gesund, wohlauf II
well [wel] gut II • **go well** gut (ver)laufen, gutgehen II • **You looked after them well.** Du hast

dich gut um sie gekümmert. II
Oh well … Na ja … / Na gut … I
Well, … Nun, … / Also, … I
Welsh [welʃ] walisisch; Walisisch II
went [went] siehe **go**
were [wə, wɜː]: **(we/you/they) were** siehe **be**
west [west] Westen; nach Westen; westlich II • **westbound** [ˈwestbaʊnd] Richtung Westen III
western [ˈwestən] westlich, West- III
wet [wet] feucht, nass II
°**whale** [weɪl] Wal • **whale-watching** Walbeobachtung
what [wɒt]
1. was I
2. welche(r, s) I
like what? wie zum Beispiel? IV 2 (41) • **So what?** [ˌsəʊ ˈwɒt] Und? / Na und? II • **Then what?** Was dann? II • **they didn't know what to do** sie wussten nicht, was sie tun sollten; sie wussten nicht, was zu tun war III
▶ S.192 Question words + to-infinitive
What a bummer! (infml) So ein Mist! / Wie schade! III • **What about …?** 1. Was ist mit …? / Und …? I; 2. Wie wär's mit …? I • **What are you talking about?** Wovon redest du? I • **What can I get you?** Was kann/darf ich euch/Ihnen bringen? II • **What colour is …?** Welche Farbe hat …? I • **What for?** [ˌwɒt ˈfɔː] Wofür? II • **What have we got next?** Was haben wir als Nächstes? I • **What kind of car …?** Was für ein Auto …? III • **What page are we on?** Auf welcher Seite sind wir? I • **What's for homework?** Was haben wir als Hausaufgabe auf? I • **What's the best way to get there?** Wie komme ich am besten dahin? III • **What's the point?** Was soll das? III • **What's the time?** Wie spät ist es? I • **What's the matter?** Was ist los? / Was ist denn? II • **What's up?** Was ist los? IV 5 (101) • **What's wrong with you?** Was fehlt dir? I • **What's your name?** Wie heißt du? I • **What was the weather like?** Wie war das Wetter? II
whatever [ˌwɒtˈevə] egal; wie dem auch sei; was (auch) immer IV 1 (18) • **whatever the movie** egal, in welchem Film IV 1 (18)
▶ S.196 whatever, etc.
wheel [wiːl] Rad III • **big wheel** Riesenrad III
wheelchair [ˈwiːltʃeə] Rollstuhl I

when [wen] wann I • **When's your birthday?** Wann hast du Geburtstag? I
when [wen]
1. wenn I • °**when things don't go your way** wenn die Dinge nicht so laufen, wie du möchtest
2. als I
whenever [ˌwen'evə] wann (auch) immer; egal, wann IV 1 (18)
▶ S.196 whatever, etc.
where [weə]
1. wo I
2. wohin I
Where are you from? Wo kommst du her? I • **He had no idea where to go.** Er hatte keine Ahnung, wo er gehen sollte. IV Intro (11/192)
▶ S.192 Question words + to-infinitive
wherever [ˌwer'evə] wo(hin) (auch) immer; egal, wo(hin) IV 1 (18)
▶ S.196 whatever, etc.
whether ['weðə] ob IV 2 (41)
which [wɪtʃ] welche(r, s) I • **Which picture ...?** Welches Bild ...? I • **which way?** in welche Richtung? / wohin? I
which [wɪtʃ] der, die, das; die (Relativpronomen) III
while [waɪl]
1. (conj) während III
2. (n) **(for) a while** eine Weile, einige Zeit IV 1 (18)
whisper ['wɪspə] flüstern I
whistle ['wɪsl] pfeifen II
whistle ['wɪsl] Pfiff; (Triller-)Pfeife II
white [waɪt] weiß I
who [huː]
1. wer I
2. wen / wem II
Who did she talk to? Mit wem hat sie geredet? II • **He had no idea who to ask.** Er hatte keine Ahnung, wen er fragen sollte. IV Intro (11/192)
▶ S.192 Question words + to-infinitive
who [huː] der, die, das; die (Relativpronomen) III
whoever [ˌhuː'evə] wer/wen/wem (auch) immer; egal, wer/wen/wem IV 1 (18)
▶ S.196 whatever, etc.
whole [həʊl] ganze(r, s), gesamte(r, s) II • **the whole of 2006** das ganze Jahr 2006 II
whom [huːm]: **To whom it may concern** (bes. AE) Sehr geehrte Damen und Herren IV 4 (85/215)
▶ S.215 Beginning and ending letters
whose [huːz] wessen II • **Whose are these?** Wem gehören diese? II

whose [huːz]: **the man whose statue ...** der Mann, dessen Statue ... II
why [waɪ] warum I • **Why me?** Warum ich? I • **that's why** deshalb, darum I
wide [waɪd] weit, breit III • **far and wide** weit und breit IV 4 (80)
°**widow** ['wɪdəʊ]: **black widow spider** Schwarze oder Echte Witwe (giftige Spinne)
wife [waɪf], pl **wives** [waɪvz] Ehefrau II
wild [waɪld] wild II • °**never in my wildest dreams** nicht einmal in meinen kühnsten Träumen
wildfire ['waɪldfaɪə] Waldbrand, Buschbrand IV 3 (56)
wildlife ['waɪldlaɪf] Tierwelt, frei lebende Tiere IV 3 (56)
will [wɪl]: **you'll be cold (= you will be cold)** du wirst frieren; ihr werdet frieren II • **you'll have travelled** du wirst gereist sein III
win (-nn-) [wɪn], **won, won** gewinnen I
win [wɪn] Sieg III
wind [wɪnd] Wind I
°**wind** [waɪnd], **wound, wound** sich winden, sich schlängeln
window ['wɪndəʊ] Fenster I
windy ['wɪndi] windig I
wine [waɪn] Wein IV 4 (76/213)
winemaker ['waɪnmeɪkə] Winzer/in IV 4 (81)
winemaking ['waɪnmeɪkɪŋ] Weinherstellung IV 4 (76)
°**winery** ['waɪnəri] Weingut
wing [wɪŋ] Flügel IV Intro (12)
winner ['wɪnə] Gewinner/in, Sieger/in II
winter ['wɪntə] Winter I
wipe [waɪp] (ab)wischen IV 3 (72)
wish [wɪʃ] sich etwas wünschen III • **You wish!** etwa: Das hättest du wohl gerne! III
wish [wɪʃ]: **Best wishes** Viele Grüße IV 4 (85/215)
▶ S.215 Beginning and ending letters
with [wɪð]
1. mit I
2. bei I
Sit with me. Setz dich zu mir. / Setzt euch zu mir. I • **be with sb.** mit jm. zusammen sein IV 4 (91)
°**within sight of** [saɪt] in Sicht von
without [wɪ'ðaʊt] ohne I
wives [waɪvz] pl von „**wife**" II
woke [wəʊk] siehe **wake**
woken [wəʊkn] siehe **wake**
wolf [wʊlf], pl **wolves** [wʊlvz] Wolf II

woman ['wʊmən], pl **women** ['wɪmɪn] Frau I
won [wʌn] siehe **win**
wonder ['wʌndə] sich fragen, gern wissen wollen II
°**wonder** ['wʌndə] Staunen, Wunder
wonderful ['wʌndəfəl] wunderbar II
won't [wəʊnt]: **you won't be cold (= you will not be cold)** du wirst nicht frieren; ihr werdet nicht frieren II
wood [wʊd] Holz II • **woods** (pl) Wald, Wälder II
°**wooden** ['wʊdn] hölzern, Holz-
woodpecker ['wʊdpekə] Specht II
woods (pl) [wʊdz] Wald, Wälder II
word [wɜːd] Wort I • **word building** Wortbildung II • **word field** Wortfeld III
wore [wɔː] siehe **wear**
work [wɜːk]
1. arbeiten I • **work hard** hart arbeiten II • **work on sb./sth.** an jn./etwas arbeiten I • **work out** klappen, gutgehen IV 4 (81) • **work sth. out** etwas herausfinden, etwas herausarbeiten IV 1 (27)
2. funktionieren III
work [wɜːk] Arbeit I • **at work** bei der Arbeit / am Arbeitsplatz I • **volunteer work** Arbeit als Freiwillige(r) III • **be in a line of work** einen Beruf ausüben IV 1 (30) • °**world of work** Berufswelt
worker ['wɜːkə] Arbeiter/in II
workplace ['wɜːkpleɪs] Arbeitsplatz (Ort) IV 5 (101)
worksheet ['wɜːkʃiːt] Arbeitsblatt I
workshop ['wɜːkʃɒp] Workshop, Lehrgang III
world [wɜːld] Welt I • **all over the world** auf der ganzen Welt III • **from all over the world** aus der ganzen Welt II • **in the world** auf der Welt II • **world music** Weltmusik III • °**world of work** Berufswelt
world-famous [ˌwɜːld 'feɪməs] weltberühmt IV 3 (71)
worldwide [ˌwɜːld'waɪd] weltweit IV 5 (99)
worn [wɔːn] siehe **wear**
worried ['wʌrid]: **be worried (about)** beunruhigt sein, besorgt sein (wegen) I
worry ['wʌri] Sorge, Kummer II
worry (about) ['wʌri] sich Sorgen machen (wegen, um) I • **Don't worry.** Mach dir keine Sorgen. I

worse (than) [wɜːs] schlechter, schlimmer (als) II
worst [wɜːst]: **(the) worst** am schlechtesten, schlimmsten; der/die/das schlechteste, schlimmste … II
worth [wɜːθ]: **it is worth doing sth.** es lohnt sich, etwas zu tun IV 2 (52) **It's worth it.** Es lohnt sich. IV 2 (52/205) • **It isn't worth it.** Es lohnt sich nicht. IV 2 (52/205)
would [wəd, wʊd] würde, würdest, würden II • **I'd like … (= I would like …)** Ich hätte gern … / Ich möchte gern … I • **Would you like …?** Möchtest du …? / Möchten Sie …? I • **I'd like to go (= I would like to go)** Ich würde gern gehen / Ich möchte gehen I • **I wouldn't like to go** ich würde nicht gern gehen / ich möchte nicht gehen I
°**wound** [waʊnd] *siehe* **wind**
wrist [rɪst] Handgelenk IV 5 (113)
write [raɪt]**, wrote, written** schreiben I • **write down** aufschreiben I • **write to** schreiben an I
writer [ˈraɪtə] Schreiber/in; Schriftsteller/in II
written [ˈrɪtn] *siehe* **write**
wrong [rɒŋ] falsch, verkehrt I **get sth. wrong** etwas falsch machen III • °**go wrong** schiefgehen • **the wrong way** in die falsche Richtung II • **What's wrong with you?** Was fehlt dir? II
wrote [rəʊt] *siehe* **write**

X

°**xoxo** *(AE)* Küsse
°**xxx** *(BE)* Küsse

Y

°**ya** [jə] *(infml)* = **you**
yard [jɑːd]
 1. Hof II • **in the yard** auf dem Hof II
 2. Yard (Längenmaß, 0,91 m) IV 2 (53)
yawn [jɔːn] gähnen II
°**yeah** [jeə] *(infml)* ja
year [jɪə]
 1. Jahr I • **a 70-year-old teacher** ein 70-jähriger Lehrer III
 2. Jahrgangsstufe I
yellow [ˈjeləʊ] gelb I
yes [jes] ja I
yesterday [ˈjestədeɪ, ˈjestədi] gestern I • **the day before yesterday** vorgestern II • **yesterday morning/afternoon/evening** gestern Morgen/Nachmittag/Abend I
yet [jet]**: not (…) yet** noch nicht II **yet?** schon? II
°**Yiddish** [ˈjɪdɪʃ] jiddisch; Jiddisch
yoga [ˈjəʊgə] Yoga I
yogurt [ˈjɒgət] Jogurt III
you [juː]
 1. du; Sie I
 2. ihr I
 3. dir; dich; euch I
 4. man III
 How are you? Wie geht es dir/Ihnen/euch? II • **You're welcome.** Gern geschehen. / Nichts zu danken. I • **you two** ihr zwei I • **You wish!** *etwa:* Das hättest du wohl gerne! III
young [jʌŋ] jung I
your [jɔː]
 1. dein/e I
 2. Ihr I
 3. euer/eure I
yours [jɔːz]
 1. deiner, deine, deins II
 2. eurer, eure, eures II
 Yours faithfully mit freundlichen Grüßen IV 4 (85/215) • **Yours sincerely** *(BE)* mit freundlichen Grüßen IV 4 (85/215) • **Yours truly** *(AE)* mit freundlichen Grüßen IV 4 (85/215)
 ▶ S.215 Beginning and ending letters
yourself [jəˈself, jɔːˈself]
 1. dir/dich III • **about yourself** über dich selbst III
 2. selbst IV 1 (18/196)
 ▶ S.196 German „selbst"
yourselves [jəˈselvz, jɔːˈselvz]
 1. euch/sich III
 2. selbst IV 1 (18/196)
 ▶ S.196 German „selbst"
youth [juːθ] Jugend III
youth group [ˈjuːθ ˌgruːp] Jugendgruppe IV Intro (11)
youth hostel [ˈjuːθ ˌhɒstəl] Jugendherberge III
yummy [ˈjʌmi] *(infml)* lecker III

Z

°**zap** [zæp] *(infml)* jn. mit einer knappen, bissigen Bemerkung kritisieren
zebra [ˈzebrə] Zebra II
zero [ˈzɪərəʊ] null I
zone [zəʊn] Zone, Bereich III **time zone** Zeitzone IV Intro (9)
zoo [zuː] Zoo, Tierpark I

Dictionary (German – English)

Das **German – English Dictionary** enthält den **Lernwortschatz** der Bände 1 bis 4 von *English G 21*. Es kann dir eine erste Hilfe sein, wenn du vergessen hast, wie etwas auf Englisch heißt.

Wenn du wissen möchtest, wo das englische Wort zum ersten Mal in *English G 21* vorkommt, dann kannst du im **English – German Dictionary** (S. 222–258) nachschlagen.

Im **German – English Dictionary** werden folgende **Abkürzungen** und **Symbole** verwendet:

jm.	= jemandem	sb.	= somebody	pl	= plural (Mehrzahl)	BE	= British English
jn.	= jemanden	sth.	= something	no pl	= no plural	AE	= American English

▶ Der Pfeil verweist auf Kästchen im Vocabulary (S. 190–221), in denen du weitere Informationen findest.

A

ab und zu now and again
abbiegen: (nach) links/rechts abbiegen turn left/right *(BE)*; take a left/right *(AE)* [tɜːn]
Abend evening [ˈiːvnɪŋ]; *(später Abend)* night [naɪt] • **am Abend, abends** in the evening
Abendbrot, -essen dinner [ˈdɪnə]; supper [ˈsʌpə] • **Abendbrot essen** have dinner/supper **zum Abendbrot** for dinner/supper
Abenteuer adventure [ədˈventʃə]
aber but [bət, bʌt] • **Aber klar!** You bet!
abfahren *(wegfahren)* leave [liːv]
Abfahrt departure [dɪˈpɑːtʃə]
Abfall litter [ˈlɪtə]; rubbish *(BE)* [ˈrʌbɪʃ]; garbage [ˈgɑːbɪdʒ] *(AE)*
 Abfälle zurücklassen litter [ˈlɪtə]
Abflug departure [dɪˈpɑːtʃə]
abgelegen faraway [ˈfɑːrəweɪ]
Abgemacht! It's a deal! [diːl]
abhängen hang out [ˌhæŋ_ˈaʊt] *(infml)*
abholen fetch [fetʃ] • **jn. abholen** pick sb. up [ˌpɪk_ˈʌp]
Abkommen: ein Abkommen treffen make a deal [diːl]
Abkürzung abbreviation [əˌbriːviˈeɪʃn]
Abmachung: eine Abmachung treffen make a deal [diːl]
abnehmen: den Hörer abnehmen pick up the phone [ˌpɪk_ˈʌp]
Absatz *(in einem Text)* paragraph [ˈpærəgrɑːf]
abschließen *(Zimmer)* lock up [ˌlɒk_ˈʌp]
Abschluss *(einer Geschichte, eines Films usw.)* ending [ˈendɪŋ]
abschneiden cut off [ˌkʌt_ˈɒf]
Abschnitt section [ˈsekʃn]
Abschrift copy [ˈkɒpi]
absetzen: etwas absetzen *(Hut)* take sth. off [ˌteɪk_ˈɒf] • **jn. absetzen** *(aussteigen lassen)* drop sb. off [ˌdrɒp_ˈɒf]

absolut absolutely [ˌæbsəˈluːt]
abstürzen crash [kræʃ]
Abtei abbey [ˈæbi]
abtrennen cut off [ˌkʌt_ˈɒf]
abwarten: Wart's ab! Wait and see!
abwaschen: das Geschirr abwaschen do the dishes [ˈdɪʃɪz]
abwechseln: sich abwechseln, etwas zu tun take turns to do sth. [tɜːnz]
abwischen wipe [waɪp]
abziehen: 10 Cent abziehen take 10 c off [ˌteɪk_ˈɒf]
achten (auf) *(beim Zuhören)* listen (for) [ˈlɪsn]
Acker field [fiːld]
addieren (zu) add (to) [æd]
adlig noble [ˈnəʊbl]
Adresse address [əˈdres]
Affe monkey [ˈmʌŋki]
akkurat accurate [ˈækjərət]
Akrobat/in acrobat [ˈækrəbæt]
aktiv active [ˈæktɪv]
Aktivität activity [ækˈtɪvəti]
Aktivist/in activist [ˈæktəvɪst]
Akzent accent [ˈæksənt]
albern silly [ˈsɪli]
Album album [ˈælbəm]
Alkohol alcohol [ˈælkəhɒl]
alkoholfreies Getränk soft drink
alle *(die ganze Gruppe)* all [ɔːl]
 alle beide the two of them
Allee avenue [ˈævənjuː]
allein alone [əˈləʊn]; *(ohne Hilfe)* on our/my/... own
Alleinerziehende(r) single parent [ˌsɪŋgl ˈpeərənt]
alleinstehend single [ˈsɪŋgl]
allergisch (gegen etwas) allergic (to sth.) [əˈlɜːdʒɪk]
alles everything [ˈevriθɪŋ]; all [ɔːl]
 alles, was wir jetzt (noch) tun müssen, ... all we have to do now ...
allgemeine(r, s) general [ˈdʒenrəl]
Alltags-; alltäglich everyday *(adj)* [ˈevrideɪ]
Alphabet alphabet [ˈælfəbet]
als 1. *(zeitlich)* when [wen]; *(während)* as [əz, æz]

2. **größer/teurer als** bigger/more expensive than [ðæn, ðən] • **mehr als** more than • **mehr als ich** more than me
3. **als ob** like [laɪk] *(infml)*
also *(daher, deshalb)* so [səʊ]
 Also, ... Well, ... [wel]
 ▶ S. 200–201 Giving reasons
als ob as if [əzˈɪf]
alt old [əʊld]
Alter age [eɪdʒ] • **im Alter von 16** at (the age of) 16
altmodisch old-fashioned [ˌəʊldˈfæʃənd]
am 1. **am Bahnhof** at the station **am Himmel** in the sky • **am Missourifluss** on the Missouri River **am oberen Ende (von)** at the top (of) • **am Strand** on the beach **am Telefon** on the phone • **am unteren Ende (von)** at the bottom (of) [ˈbɒtəm]
2. *(nahe bei)* **am Meer** by the sea
3. *(zeitlich)* **am 13. Juni** on 13th June • **am Morgen/Nachmittag/Abend** in the morning/afternoon/evening • **am Ende (von)** at the end (of) • **am Freitag** on Friday **am Freitagmorgen** on Friday morning • **am nächsten Morgen/Tag** the next morning/day • **am Wochenende** at the weekend
amen amen [ɑːˈmen]
amerikanische(r) Ureinwohner/in Native American [ˌneɪtɪv_əˈmerɪkən]
amüsieren: sich (gut) amüsieren have fun [hæv ˈfʌn]; have a good time
an 1. **an dem/den Tisch (dort)** at that table • **an der Spitze (von)** at the top (of) • **an der/die Tafel** on the board • **schreiben an** write to **an jenem Tag** that day
2. *(nahe bei)* **an der See** by the sea
3. **Was war das Beste an ...?** What was the best thing about ...?
4. **an sein** *(Radio, Licht usw.)* be on
anbauen *(Getreide usw.)* grow [grəʊ]

anbieten offer [ˈɒfə]
Andenken souvenir [ˌsuːvəˈnɪə]
andere(r, s) other [ˈʌðə] • **die anderen** the others • **ein(e) andere(r, s) ...** another ... [əˈnʌðə]
anderer Meinung sein (als) disagree (with) [ˌdɪsəˈgriː]
ändern: (sich) ändern change [tʃeɪndʒ]
▶ S.200 (to) change
anders (als) different (from) [ˈdɪfrənt]
anders herum the other way round • **etwas anders ausdrücken** paraphrase sth. [ˈpærəfreɪz]
anders: jemand anders somebody else [els] • **etwas anders** something else
anderswo in other places
Änderung change [tʃeɪndʒ]
Anfang beginning [bɪˈgɪnɪŋ]
anfangen (mit) start [stɑːt]
anfassen touch [tʌtʃ]
anfreunden: sich anfreunden (mit) make friends (with)
anfühlen: sich gut anfühlen feel good [fiː]
Anführer/in leader [ˈliːdə]
Anführungsstriche, -zeichen quotation marks [kwəʊˈteɪʃn ˌmɑːks]
angeben (prahlen) show off [ˌʃəʊ ˈɒf]
Angebot deal [diːl]
angehen (Licht) go on
Angler fisherman [ˈfɪʃəmən], pl fishermen [ˈfɪʃəmən]
angreifen attack [əˈtæk] • **(jn.) angreifen** charge (at sb.) [tʃɑːdʒ]
Angriff attack [əˈtæk]
Angst (vor) fear (of) [fɪə] • **Angst haben (vor)** be afraid (of) [əˈfreɪd]; be scared (of) [skeəd] • **schreckliche Angst haben (vor)** be terrified (of) [ˈterɪfaɪd]
anhaben (Kleidung) wear [weə]
anhalten stop [stɒp]
Anhalten stop [stɒp]
Anhänger/in fan [fæn]; supporter [səˈpɔːtə]
anheben (hochheben) lift [lɪft]
anhören 1. **sich etwas anhören** listen to sth. [ˈlɪsn]
2. **sich gut anhören** sound good [saʊnd]
anklicken: etwas anklicken click on sth. [klɪk]
anklopfen (an) knock (on) [nɒk]
ankommen arrive [əˈraɪv]
Ankündigung announcement [əˈnaʊnsmənt]
Ankunft arrival [əˈraɪvl]
anlächeln: jn. anlächeln smile at sb. [smaɪl]; give sb. a smile

Anleitung(en) (Gebrauchsanweisung(en)) instructions (pl) [ɪnˈstrʌkʃnz]
anmailen: jn. anmailen mail sb. [meɪl]
anmalen paint [peɪnt]
anmelden: sich (für etwas) anmelden enroll for/in/on sth. [ɪnˈrəʊl]
annähen sew on [səʊ]
annehmen (vermuten) suppose [səˈpəʊz]; expect [ɪkˈspekt]
Anorak anorak [ˈænəræk]
anpflanzen (Getreide usw.) grow [grəʊ]
anprobieren (Kleidung) try on [ˌtraɪ ˈɒn]
Anruf call [kɔːl]; phone call [ˈfəʊn kɔːl]
anrufen call [kɔːl]; phone [fəʊn]
Ansage announcement [əˈnaʊnsmənt]
anschauen look at [lʊk] • **etwas genau anschauen** look closely at sth. [ˈkləʊsli]
Anschlagtafel bulletin board [ˈbʊlətɪn bɔːd] (AE), notice board [ˈnəʊtɪs bɔːd] (BE)
anschließen: sich jm. anschließen join sb. [dʒɔɪn]
anschreien: jn. anschreien shout at sb. [ʃaʊt]
Anschrift (Adresse) address [əˈdres]
ansehen: sich etwas ansehen look at sth. [lʊk]; watch sth. [wɒtʃ]
Ansicht view [vjuː] • **meiner Ansicht nach** in my view
anspucken: jn. anspucken spit at sb. [spɪt]
anstelle von instead of [ɪnˈsted əv]
anstreichen paint [peɪnt]
Antonym antonym [ˈæntənɪm]
Antwort (auf) answer (to) [ˈɑːnsə]
antworten (auf) answer (to) [ˈɑːnsə]; reply (to) [rɪˈplaɪ]
Anweisung(en) (Gebrauchsanweisung(en)) instructions (pl) [ɪnˈstrʌkʃnz]
Anzeige (Inserat) advert [ˈædvɜːt]; ad [æd]
anziehen: etwas anziehen (Kleidung) put sth. on [ˌpʊt ˈɒn] • **sich anziehen** get dressed [get ˈdrest], dress [dres]
Apfel apple [ˈæpl]
Apfelsine orange [ˈɒrɪndʒ]
Apotheke chemist [ˈkemɪst]
Apotheker: beim Apotheker at the chemist's
Appetit appetite [ˈæpɪtaɪt]
April April [ˈeɪprəl]
Arbeit work [wɜːk] • **bei der Arbeit/am Arbeitsplatz** at work • **gute Arbeit leisten** do a good job

Arbeit als Freiwillige(r) volunteer work [ˌvɒlənˈtɪə ˌwɜːk]
arbeiten (an) work (on) [wɜːk]
Arbeiter/in worker [ˈwɜːkə]
Arbeitsblatt worksheet [ˈwɜːkʃiːt], handout [ˈhændˌaʊt]
Arbeitsplatz (Ort) workplace [ˈwɜːkpleɪs]
Arbeits- und Lerntechniken study skills [ˈstʌdi skɪlz]
Arbeitsverfahren technique [tekˈniːk]
Architekt/in architect [ˈɑːkɪtekt]
Archiv archive [ˈɑːkaɪv]
Ärger (Schwierigkeiten) trouble [ˈtrʌbl] • **Ärger kriegen** be in trouble
ärgern: jn. ärgern (kränken) upset sb. [ʌpˈset]
arm poor [pɔː, pʊə]
Arm arm [ɑːm] • **jn. auf den Arm nehmen** (necken) tease sb. [tiːz]
Armbanduhr watch [wɒtʃ]
Armee army [ˈɑːmi]
Art (Sorte) sort (of) [sɔːt]; kind (of) [kaɪnd]
Artikel article [ˈɑːtɪkl]
Arzt/Ärztin doctor [ˈdɒktə] • **beim/zum Arzt** at/to the doctor's
atmen breathe [briːð]
Attraktion attraction [əˈtrækʃn]
auch: auch aus Bristol from Bristol too [tuː]; also from Bristol [ˈɔːlsəʊ] • **Ich auch.** Me too. • **auch nicht** not (...) either [ˈaɪðə, ˈiːðə] • **nicht nur ... sondern auch ...** not only ... but also ...
auf on [ɒn]; **auf (... hinauf)** onto [ˈɒntə, ˈɒntʊ] • **auf dem Bild/Foto** in the picture/photo • **auf dem Feld** in the field • **auf der ganzen Welt** all over the world • **auf dem Hof** in the yard • **auf dem Land** in the country/land • **auf dem Weg (zu/nach)** on the way (to) • **auf der Welt** in the world • **auf einmal** suddenly [ˈsʌdnli] • **auf Englisch** in English • **Auf geht's!** Let's go. **auf jn. zu** towards sb. [təˈwɔːdz] **Auf keinen Fall!** No way! • **auf See** at sea • **Auf welcher Seite sind wir?** What page are we on? **Auf Wiedersehen.** Goodbye. [ˌgʊdˈbaɪ]
aufbauen (Ausrüstung) set up [set]
aufbewahren keep [kiːp]
aufblitzen flash [flæʃ]
aufbrechen break open [ˌbreɪk ˈəʊpn]
aufführen (Szene, Dialog) act [ækt]
Aufgabe (im Schulbuch) exercise [ˈeksəsaɪz]; (Job) job [dʒɒb]
aufgebracht (wegen) upset (about) [ˌʌpˈset]

aufgeräumt *(ordentlich)* tidy [ˈtaɪdi]
aufgeregt *(nervös)* nervous [ˈnɜːvəs]; *(begeistert)* excited [ɪkˈsaɪtɪd]
aufhalten *(verzögern)* delay [dɪˈleɪ]
aufhängen: etwas aufhängen hang sth. (up) [hæŋ]
aufheben *(vom Boden)* pick up
aufhören stop [stɒp]
aufkleben stick on [ˌstɪk ˈɒn]
Aufladung: elektrische Aufladung static (electricity) [ˌstætɪk ɪˌlekˈtrɪsəti]
auflegen: *(Musik in der Disko)* **auflegen** DJ [ˈdiːdʒeɪ]
auflisten list [lɪst]
aufmachen open [ˈəʊpən]
Aufnahme *(Ton, Video)* recording [rɪˈkɔːdɪŋ]
aufnehmen 1. *(Ton, Video)* record [rɪˈkɔːd]
2. mit jm. Kontakt aufnehmen contact sb. [ˈkɒntækt]
aufpassen: auf etwas/jn. aufpassen look after sth./sb. [ˌlʊk ˈɑːftə]
aufräumen tidy [ˈtaɪdi]
aufregend exciting [ɪkˈsaɪtɪŋ]
Aufruhr riot [ˈraɪət]
Aufsatz essay [ˈeseɪ]
aufschauen (von) look up (from) [ˌlʊk ˈʌp]
aufschreiben write down [ˌraɪt ˈdaʊn]
aufsehen: zu jm. aufsehen look up to sb.
Aufseher/in *(im Park)* ranger [ˈreɪndʒə]
aufsetzen: etwas aufsetzen *(Hut)* put sth. on [ˌpʊt ˈɒn] • **sich aufsetzen** sit up [ˌsɪt ˈʌp]
aufstehen get up [ˌget ˈʌp]
aufsteigen rise [raɪz]
aufstellen *(Ausrüstung)* set up [set]
aufsuchen: jn. aufsuchen see sb. [siː]
auftauchen *(erscheinen)* appear [əˈpɪə]
aufteilen (in); sich aufteilen (in) divide (into) [dɪˈvaɪd]
Auftritt *(Konzert)* gig [gɪg] *(infml)* **einen Auftritt haben** do a gig
aufwachen wake up [weɪk]
aufwachsen grow up [grəʊ]
aufwecken: jn. aufwecken wake sb. (up) [weɪk]
aufzählen *(auflisten)* list [lɪst]
Aufzeichnung *(Aufnahme)* recording [rɪˈkɔːdɪŋ]
Aufzug lift [lɪft] *(BE)*; elevator [ˈelɪveɪtə] *(AE)*
Auge eye [aɪ] • **Geh mir aus den Augen.** Get out of my sight. [saɪt] **Sie glaubte ihren Augen kaum.** She couldn't believe her eyes.
Augenblick moment [ˈməʊmənt]
August August [ˈɔːgəst]

aus: Ich komme/bin aus ... I'm from ... [frəm, frɒm] • **aus ... (heraus/hinaus)** out of ... [ˈaʊt ˌəv] • **aus dem gesamten Vereinigten Königreich** from all over the UK • **aus dem Zug/Bus aussteigen** get off the train/bus • **aus der ganzen Welt** from all over the world **aus der Schule** from school • **aus etwas (gemacht) sein** to be made of sth. • **aus ganz England** from all over England • **aus meiner Sicht** from my point of view • **aus Versehen** by mistake • **aus vielen Gründen** for lots of reasons **Kleider aus den 60ern / aus den 60er Jahren** dresses from the 60s [ˈsɪkstiz] • **aus zweiter Hand** (gebraucht) second-hand
ausbessern repair [rɪˈpeə]
Ausbildung education [ˌedʒuˈkeɪʃn]
ausbreiten: (sich) ausbreiten spread [spred]
ausdenken: sich etwas ausdenken think of sth. [θɪŋk]; come up with sth. [ˌkʌm ˈʌp]
Ausdruck *((Rede-)Wendung)* phrase [freɪz]; expression [ɪkˈspreʃn]
ausdrucken: etwas ausdrucken print sth. out [ˌprɪnt ˈaʊt]
ausdrücken: Sie wissen, wie man es ausdrückt. You know how to put it. [pʊt]
auseinander apart [əˈpɑːt]
Auseinandersetzung argument [ˈɑːgjumənt] • **eine Auseinandersetzung haben** *(sich streiten)* have an argument
ausfüllen: etwas (mit etwas) ausfüllen fill sth. (with sth.) [fɪl]
Ausflug trip [trɪp] • **einen Ausflug machen** go on a trip; take a trip *(bes. AE)*
ausgeben: Geld ausgeben (für) spend money (on) [spend]
ausgehen *(weg-, rausgehen)* go out [ˌgəʊ ˈaʊt] • **mit jm. ausgehen** *(regelmäßig)* date *(besonders AE)* [deɪt]
ausgestellt sein *(z. B. im Museum)* be on display
ausgezeichnet fine [faɪn]; excellent [ˈeksələnt]
▶ S.213 US school grades
ausgleichen *(das Ausgleichstor erzielen)* equalize [ˈiːkwəlaɪz]
aushalten *(ertragen)* stand [stænd] **Ich halt's aus. / Ich kann's aushalten.** I can take it. • **Ich kann es nicht aushalten.** I can't stand it.
Ausland: im Ausland abroad [əˈbrɔːd] **ins Ausland gehen/fahren** go abroad

ausleihen: sich etwas ausleihen borrow sth. [ˈbɒrəʊ]
ausliefern deliver [dɪˈlɪvə]
auspflanzen plant [plɑːnt]
auspressen squeeze [skwiːz]
ausruhen: sich ausruhen relax [rɪˈlæks]
Ausrüstung equipment [ɪˈkwɪpmənt]; gear [gɪə]
ausschalten: den Computer ausschalten turn off the computer [ˌtɜːn ˈɒf]
Ausschau: nach jm./etwas Ausschau halten keep an eye on sth./sb. [aɪ]
ausschneiden cut out [ˌkʌt ˈaʊt]
aussehen: anders/toll/alt aussehen look different/great/old [lʊk] **gleich aussehen** look the same
Außen- outdoor [ˈaʊtdɔː]; outside [ˌaʊtˈsaɪd]
außer except [ɪkˈsept]
außerdem besides [bɪˈsaɪdz]
außergewöhnlich extraordinary [ɪkˈstrɔːdnri]
außerhalb seines Zimmers outside his room [ˌaʊtˈsaɪd]
aussetzen: Einmal aussetzen. Miss a turn. [tɜːn]
Aussicht *(Blick)* view [vjuː] • **die beste Aussicht der Welt** the best view in the world
Aussichtsplattform observatory [əbˈzɜːvətri]
Aussprache pronunciation [prəˌnʌnsiˈeɪʃn]
ausstehen *(ertragen)* stand [stænd] **Ich kann es nicht ausstehen.** I can't stand it.
aussteigen (aus dem Zug/Bus) get off (the train/bus) [ˌget ˈɒf]
ausstellen: ausgestellt sein be on display
Ausstellung über exhibition on [ˌeksɪˈbɪʃn]
ausstrahlen: *(eine Sendung)* **ausstrahlen** broadcast [ˈbrɔːdkɑːst]
aussuchen: (sich) etwas aussuchen choose sth. [tʃuːz]
Austausch exchange [ɪksˈtʃeɪndʒ]
austauschen exchange [ɪksˈtʃeɪndʒ]
Austauschschüler/in exchange student
austragen deliver [dɪˈlɪvə]
ausüben: einen Beruf ausüben be in a line of work
Ausverkauf sale [seɪl]
ausverkauft sein be sold out [səʊld]
Auswahl (an) selection (of) [sɪˈlekʃn]
auswählen choose [tʃuːz]
Ausweis identification [aɪˌdentɪfɪˈkeɪʃn ˌkɑːd]
Auswirkung (auf) effect (on) [ɪˈfekt]

ausziehen 1. *(aus Wohnung)* move out [ˌmuːv_'aʊt]
2. **etwas ausziehen** *(Kleidung)* take sth. off [ˌteɪk_'ɒf]
Auto car [kɑː]; auto ['ɔːtəʊ] *(AE)*
Autobahn freeway ['friːweɪ] *(AE)*, motorway ['məʊtəweɪ] *(BE)*
Autobiografie autobiography [ˌɔːtəʊbaɪ'ɒɡrəfi]
Autofahrt drive [draɪv]
Autsch! Ouch! [aʊtʃ]

B

Baby baby ['beɪbi] • **ein Baby bekommen** have a baby
Backofen oven ['ʌvn]
Badeanzug swimsuit ['swɪmsuːt]
Badehose swimming trunks *(pl)* [trʌŋks]
baden *(ein Bad nehmen)* have a bath [bɑːθ]
Badewanne bath [bɑːθ]
Badezimmer bathroom ['bɑːθruːm]
Badminton badminton ['bædmɪntən]
Bagel *(ringförmiges Brötchen)* bagel ['beɪɡl]
Bahnhof station ['steɪʃn] • **am Bahnhof** at the station
Bahnsteig platform ['plætfɔːm]
Bakterien bacteria *(pl)* [bæk'tɪəriə]
bald soon [suːn] • **Bis bald.** See you. ['siː juː]
Ball *(im Sport; Tanz)* ball [bɔːl]
Banane banana [bə'nɑːnə]
Band *(Musikgruppe)* band [bænd]
Banjo banjo ['bændʒəʊ]
Bank *(Sparkasse)* bank [bæŋk]
Bankräuber/in bank robber ['rɒbə]
Bar bar [bɑː]
Bär bear [beə]
Baseball baseball ['beɪsbɔːl]
Baseballmütze baseball cap [kæp]
Basketball basketball ['bɑːskɪtbɔːl]
Bassgitarre bass; bass guitar [beɪs]
Bauchweh stomach ache ['stʌmək_eɪk]
bauen build [bɪld]
Bauer/Bäuerin farmer ['fɑːmə]
Bauernhaus farmhouse ['fɑːmhaʊs]
Bauernhof farm [fɑːm]
Baum tree [triː]
Baumwolle cotton ['kɒtn]
beantragen: etwas beantragen apply for [ə'plaɪ]
beantworten answer ['ɑːnsə]; reply to [rɪ'plaɪ]
bedecken cover ['kʌvə]
bedeuten mean [miːn]
Bedeutung meaning ['miːnɪŋ]

beeilen: sich beeilen hurry ['hʌri]; hurry up [ˌhʌri_'ʌp]
beeindruckend impressive [ɪm'presɪv]; grand [ɡrænd]
beeindruckt impressed [ɪm'prest]
beenden finish ['fɪnɪʃ]
beerdigen bury ['beri]
befragen interview ['ɪntəvjuː]
Begabung talent ['tælənt]
begehen: ein Verbrechen begehen commit a crime [kə'mɪt]
begeistert excited [ɪk'saɪtɪd]
Beginn beginning [bɪ'ɡɪnɪŋ]
beginnen (mit) start [stɑːt]; begin [bɪ'ɡɪn]
begnadigen pardon ['pɑːdn]
begraben bury ['beri]
begreifen understand [ˌʌndə'stænd]
Begrenzung limit ['lɪmɪt]
Begründung reason ['riːzn]
begrüßen greet [ɡriːt]
behalten keep [kiːp]
behindert disabled [dɪs'eɪbld]
bei: bei den Shaws zu Hause at the Shaws' house • **bei der Arbeit** at work • **Englisch bei Mr Kingsley** English with Mr Kingsley • **beim Apotheker/Arzt/Friseur** at the chemist's/doctor's/hairdresser's
beide both [bəʊθ] • **die beiden / alle beide** the two of them
Beifall klatschen clap [klæp]
Bein leg [leɡ]
beinahe almost ['ɔːlməʊst]; nearly ['nɪəli]
Beispiel example [ɪɡ'zɑːmpl] • **zum Beispiel** for example • **wie (zum Beispiel)** such as • **wie zum Beispiel? / wie was?** like what?
Beitrag *(Wettbewerbseinsendung)* entry ['entri]
bekannt known [nəʊn]
Bekanntgabe announcement [ə'naʊnsmənt]
bekanntgeben announce [ə'naʊns]
bekommen get [ɡet] • **ein Baby bekommen** have a baby
beladen load [ləʊd]
Belag *(auf oder in Brot)* filling ['fɪlɪŋ]
belebt *(Straße; Ort)* busy ['bɪzi]
Belegschaft staff [stɑːf]
beliebt popular ['pɒpjələ]
bellen bark [bɑːk]
Belletristik fiction ['fɪkʃn]
bemerken notice ['nəʊtɪs]
benachteiligen: jn. benachteiligen discriminate against sb. [ˌdɪ'skrɪmɪneɪt]
Benachteiligung (von) discrimination (against) [dɪˌskrɪmɪ'neɪʃn]
benennen name [neɪm]
benötigen need [niːd]

benutzen use [juːz]
Benzin gas [ɡæs] *(AE)*; petrol ['petrəl] *(BE)*
beobachten watch [wɒtʃ]
bepflanzen plant [plɑːnt]
bequem comfortable ['kʌmftəbl]
Bereich area ['eəriə]; section ['sekʃn]; zone [zəʊn]
bereit ready ['redi] • **sich bereit erklären** volunteer [ˌvɒlən'tɪə]
bereits already [ɔːl'redi]
Berg mountain ['maʊntən]
Bericht (über) report (on) [rɪ'pɔːt]
berichten: jm. etwas berichten tell sb. about sth. [tel]; report sth. to sb. [rɪ'pɔːt]
berichtigen correct [kə'rekt]
Berichtigung correction [kə'rekʃn]
Beruf, berufliche Richtung line of work [ˌlaɪn_əv_'wɜːk] • **einen Beruf ausüben** be in a line of work
beruhigen: jn. beruhigen calm sb. down [ˌkɑːm_'daʊn] • **sich beruhigen** calm down
berühmt (für, wegen) famous (for) ['feɪməs] • **berühmte Persönlichkeit** celebrity [sə'lebrəti]
berühren touch [tʌtʃ]
beschäftigen: sich mit jm./etwas beschäftigen deal with sb./sth. [diːl]
beschäftigt busy ['bɪzi]
Bescheid: über etwas Bescheid wissen know about sth. [nəʊ]
beschließen: (etwas) beschließen decide (on sth.) [dɪ'saɪd]
Beschränkung limit ['lɪmɪt]
beschreiben: (jm.) etwas beschreiben describe sth. (to sb.) [dɪ'skraɪb] • **jm. den Weg beschreiben** tell sb. the way
Beschreibung description [dɪ'skrɪpʃn]
beschützen: jn./etwas beschützen (vor jm./etwas) protect sb./sth. (from sb./sth.) [prə'tekt]
besiegen beat [biːt]
besitzen own [əʊn]
Besitzer/in owner ['əʊnə]
besondere(r, s) special ['speʃl]
besorgen *(holen)* get [ɡet]
besorgt sein (wegen) be worried (about) ['wʌrid]
Besprechung meeting ['miːtɪŋ]
besprühen spray [spreɪ]
besser better ['betə]
beste: am besten (the) best [best] • **der/die/das beste ...; die besten ...** the best ... • **die beste Aussicht der Welt** the best view in the world • **Was war das Beste an ...?** What was the best thing about ...? • **Wie komme ich am besten dahin?** What's the best way to get there?

bestellen order [ˈɔːdə]
bestimmte(r, s) specific [spəˈsɪfɪk]
Besuch visit [ˈvɪzɪt]
besuchen: jn. besuchen visit sb. [ˈvɪzɪt]; see sb. [siː] • **die Messe besuchen** go to mass [mæs]
Besucher/in visitor [ˈvɪzɪtə]
beten pray [preɪ]
beteiligen: sich beteiligen (an) get involved (in) [ɪnˈvɒlvd]
Betonung stress [ˈstres]
betreten enter [ˈentə]
betrunken drunk [drʌŋk]
Bett bed [bed] • **jn. ins Bett bringen** put sb. to bed
beunruhigt sein (wegen) be worried (about) [ˈwʌrid]
beurteilen: jn. beurteilen (nach) judge sb. (by) [dʒʌdʒ]
Beutel bag [bæɡ]
Bevölkerung population [ˌpɒpjuˈleɪʃn]
bevor before [bɪˈfɔː]
bewegen; sich bewegen move [muːv]
Bewegung movement [ˈmuːvmənt]
Beweis(e) proof (no pl) [pruːf]
bewerben: sich bewerben (um/für etwas) apply for [əˈplaɪ]
bewölkt cloudy [ˈklaʊdi]
bewundern admire [ədˈmaɪə]
bewusstlos unconscious [ʌnˈkɒnʃəs]
bezahlen: etwas bezahlen pay for sth. [peɪ]
Beziehungen relations (pl) [rɪˈleɪʃnz]
Bezirk (Stadtteil) borough [ˈbʌrə]
Bibliothek library [ˈlaɪbrəri]
Bibel Bible [ˈbaɪbl]
bieten offer [ˈɒfə]
Bild picture [ˈpɪktʃə]; (Gemälde) painting [ˈpeɪntɪŋ] • **auf dem Bild** in the picture
bilden form [fɔːm]
Bildschirm monitor [ˈmɒnɪtə]
Bildung education [ˌedʒuˈkeɪʃn] • **Politische Bildung** Social Studies [ˌsəʊʃl ˈstʌdiz]
Bildunterschrift caption [ˈkæpʃn]
billig cheap [tʃiːp]
binden tie [taɪ]
Bindewort linking word [ˈlɪŋkɪŋ wɜːd]
Biografie biography [baɪˈɒɡrəfi]
Biologie biology [baɪˈɒlədʒi]
biologisch biological [ˌbaɪəˈlɒdʒɪkl]
bis (zeitlich) till [tɪl]; until [ənˈtɪl] • **bis auf** except [ɪkˈsept] • **Bis bald.** See you. [siː juː] • **bis jetzt/hierher** so far • **(spätestens) bis zum Ende des Lieds** by the end of the song • **von Montag bis Freitag** from Monday to Friday
bisschen: ein bisschen a bit [bɪt]; a little [ˈlɪtl]
▶ S.211 little („wenig") – few („wenige")

bitte 1. (in Fragen und Aufforderungen) please [pliːz]
2. Bitte sehr. / Hier bitte. Here you are.
3. Bitte, gern geschehen. You're welcome. [ˈwelkəm]
4. Wie bitte? Sorry? [ˈsɒri]
bitten: jn. um etwas bitten ask sb. for sth. [ɑːsk]
blasen (wehen) blow [bləʊ]
blau blue [bluː]
bleiben stay [steɪ] • **in Verbindung bleiben** keep in touch
Bleistift pencil [ˈpensl]
Bleistiftanspitzer pencil sharpener [ˈpensl ʃɑːpnə]
Blick (Aussicht) view [vjuː]
blind blind [blaɪnd] • **blind werden** go blind
Block (Häuser-, Wohnblock) block [blɒk]
Blockflöte recorder [rɪˈkɔːdə]
blockieren block [blɒk]
blond blond, (bei Frauen oft:) blonde [blɒnd]
bloß just [dʒʌst]; only [ˈəʊnli]
Blues blues [bluːz]
Blume flower [ˈflaʊə] • **Blumen pflücken** pick flowers
Bluse blouse [blaʊz]
Blut blood [blʌd]
bluten bleed [bliːd]
Blüte flower [ˈflaʊə]
Boden (Erdboden) ground [ɡraʊnd]; (Fußboden) floor [flɔː]
Bogen (Waffe, zum Musizieren) bow [bəʊ]
Bohne bean [biːn]
Bombe bomb [bɒm]
Boot boat [bəʊt]
Boss boss [bɒs]
Boulevard avenue [ˈævənjuː]
Boykott boycott [ˈbɔɪkɒt]
brainstormen (so viele Ideen wie möglich sammeln) brainstorm [ˈbreɪnstɔːm]
Brand fire [ˈfaɪə]
braten fry [fraɪ]
brauchen need [niːd]; (Zeit) take [teɪk] • **nicht zu tun brauchen** needn't do [ˈniːdnt]
braun brown [braʊn]
brav good [ɡʊd]
brechen break [breɪk]
breit wide [waɪd] • **weit und breit** far and wide [fɑː]
brennen burn [bɜːn]
Brett: schwarzes Brett bulletin board [ˈbʊlətɪn bɔːd] (AE), notice board [ˈnəʊtɪs bɔːd] (BE)
Brief (an) letter (to) [ˈletə]

Brieffreund/in (im Internet) e-friend [ˈiːfrend]
Briefmarke stamp [stæmp]
Brille: (eine) Brille glasses (pl) [ˈɡlɑːsɪz]
bringen: (mit-, her)bringen bring [brɪŋ] • **(weg-, hin)bringen** take [teɪk] • **etwas in Ordnung bringen** put sth. in order [ˈɔːdə] • **etwas in seine Macht bringen** take sth. over • **jn. aus der Fassung bringen** upset sb. [ʌpˈset] • **jn. dazu bringen, etwas zu tun** force sb. to do sth. [fɔːs] • **jn. ins Bett bringen** put sb. to bed • **Was kann/darf ich euch/Ihnen bringen?** (im Restaurant) What can I get you? • **zustande bringen** achieve [əˈtʃiːv]
Brite, Britin; britisch British [ˈbrɪtɪʃ]
Broschüre booklet [ˈbʊklət]
Brot bread (no pl) [bred]
Brotbelag filling [ˈfɪlɪŋ]
Brötchen roll [rəʊl]
Brücke bridge [brɪdʒ]
Bruder brother [ˈbrʌðə]
Buch book [bʊk]
Bücherei library [ˈlaɪbrəri]
Buchstabe letter [ˈletə]
buchstabieren spell [spel]
Bucht bay [beɪ]
Bühne stage [steɪdʒ]
bunt colourful [ˈkʌləfl]
Burg castle [ˈkɑːsl]
Bürgerkrieg civil war [ˌsɪvl ˈwɔː]
Bürgermeister/in mayor [ˈmeə]
Bürgerrechte civil rights (pl) [ˌsɪvl ˈraɪts]
Bürgersteig pavement [ˈpeɪvmənt] (BE), sidewalk [ˈsaɪdwɔːk] (AE)
Bus bus [bʌs] • **Bus in Richtung Stadtzentrum** downtown bus (AE)
Buschbrand wildfire [ˈwaɪldfaɪə]
Busfahrt bus ride [ˈbʌs raɪd]
Bushaltestelle bus stop [ˈbʌs stɒp]
Bus-Monatskarte bus pass [ˈbʌs pɑːs]
Butter butter [ˈbʌtə]

C

Café café [ˈkæfeɪ]
Cafeteria cafeteria [ˌkæfəˈtɪəriə]
Camp camp [kæmp]
Campingausrüstung camping gear [ˈkæmpɪŋ ɡɪə]
Cañon canyon [ˈkænjən]
Cartoon cartoon [kɑːˈtuːn]
CD CD [ˌsiːˈdiː] • **CD-Spieler** CD player [ˌsiːˈdiː ˌpleɪə]
Cello cello [ˈtʃeləʊ]
Cent cent (c) [sent]
Champion champion [ˈtʃæmpiən]

Dictionary (German – English)

Chance chance [tʃɑːns]
Charakter character ['kærəktə]
charakteristisches Merkmal characteristic [ˌkærəktə'rɪstɪk]
Chat *(Unterhaltung)* chat [tʃæt]
Chatroom chat room ['tʃæt ruːm]
chatten chat [tʃæt]
Checkliste checklist ['tʃeklɪst]
Cheerleader *(Stimmungsanheizer/in bei Sportereignissen)* cheerleader ['tʃɪəliːdə]
Chef/in boss [bɒs]
chinesisch Chinese [tʃaɪ'niːz]
Chor choir ['kwaɪə]
Christus Christ [kraɪst]
Clown/in clown [klaʊn]
Cola cola ['kəʊlə]
Comedyshow comedy ['kɒmədi]
Comic-Heft comic ['kɒmɪk]
Computer computer [kəm'pjuːtə]
Computerwissenschaft computer science [kəmˌpjuːtə 'saɪəns]
cool cool [kuːl]
Cornflakes cornflakes ['kɔːnfleɪks]
Countdown countdown ['kaʊntdaʊn]
Court court [kɔːt]
Cousin, Cousine cousin ['kʌzn]
Creme cream [kriːm]
Crew crew [kruː]

D

da, dahin *(dort, dorthin)* there [ðeə]
 da drüben over there [ˌəʊvə 'ðeə]
Dach roof ['ruːf]
daheim at home [ət 'həʊm]
daher *(deshalb)* so [səʊ]; that's why ['ðæts ˌwaɪ]
 ▶ S.200–201 Giving reasons
damals then [ðen]
Dame: Sehr geehrte Damen und Herren Dear Sir [sɜː] or Madam ... ['mædm] *(BE)*, To whom it may concern [kən'sɜːn] *(bes. AE)*
 ▶ S.215 Beginning and ending letters
damit *(sodass)* so that
 ▶ S.200–201 Giving reasons
danach *(zeitlich)* after that [ˌɑːftə 'ðæt]
dankbar glad [glæd]
danken *(feierlich danksagen)* give thanks [θæŋks]
Danke. Thank you. ['θæŋk juː]; Thanks. • **Danke sehr!** Thanks very much! • **Vielen Dank!** Thanks a lot!
dann then [ðen] • **Was dann?** Then what?
darstellende Kunst drama ['drɑːmə]
darum so [səʊ]; that's why ['ðæts ˌwaɪ]
das *(Artikel)* the [ðə, ði]

das *(Relativpronomen)* **1.** *(für Dinge)* which; that
 2. *(für Personen)* who; that
das *(dort)* *(Singular)* that [ðət, ðæt]; *(Plural)* those [ðəʊz] • **Das bin ich.** That's me. • **Das liegt bei dir. / Das kannst/musst du (selbst) entscheiden.** That's up to you.
dass that [ðət, ðæt]
dasselbe the same [seɪm]
Datum date [deɪt]
dauern *(Zeit brauchen)* take [teɪk]
decken: den Tisch decken lay the table [ˌleɪ ðə 'teɪbl]
dein(e) ... your ... [jɔː]
deiner, deine, deins yours [jɔːz]
Demonstration march [mɑːtʃ]
denken think [θɪŋk] • **denken an** think of • **Was denkst du über ...?** What do you think about/of ...?
dennoch still [stɪl]
der *(Artikel)* the [ðə, ði]
der *(Relativpronomen)* **1.** *(für Personen)* who; that
 2. *(für Dinge)* which; that
deren *(Relativpronomen)*: **die Frau, deren Statue ...** the woman whose statue ... [hjuːz]
derselbe the same [seɪm]
deshalb so [səʊ]; that's why ['ðæts ˌwaɪ]
 ▶ S.200–201 Giving reasons
dessen *(Relativpronomen)*: **der Mann, dessen Statue ...** the man whose statue ... [huːz]
Detail detail ['diːteɪl]
Detektiv/in detective [dɪ'tektɪv]
deuten (auf etwas) *(zeigen)* point (at/to sth.) [pɔɪnt]
deutlich clear [klɪə]
Deutsch; deutsch; Deutsche(r) German ['dʒɜːmən]
Deutschland Germany ['dʒɜːməni]
Dezember December [dɪ'sembə]
diagonal diagonal [daɪ'ægənəl]
dich you [juː]; *(Reflexivpronomen)* yourself [jə'self, jɔː'self]
dick fat [fæt]
die *(Artikel)* the [ðə, ði]
die *(Relativpronomen)* **1.** *(für Personen)* who; that
 2. *(für Dinge)* which, that
die *(dort)* *(Singular)* that [ðət, ðæt]; *(Plural)* those [ðəʊz] • **die (hier)** *(Singular)* this [ðɪs]; *(Plural)* these [ðiːz]
Dieb/in thief [θiːf], *pl* thieves [θiːvz]
Diele hall [hɔːl]
Dienst (am Kunden) *(Service)* service ['sɜːvɪs]
Dienstag Tuesday ['tjuːzdeɪ, 'tjuːzdi] *(siehe auch unter „Freitag")*

dies (hier); diese(r, s) *(Singular)* this [ðɪs]; *(Plural)* these [ðiːz]
dieselbe(n) the same [seɪm]
Ding thing [θɪŋ]
Dinosaurier dinosaur ['daɪnəsɔː]
dir you [juː]; *(Reflexivpronomen)* yourself [jə'self, jɔː'self] • **Dir ist nicht zu helfen.** You're hopeless. ['həʊpləs]
direkt straight [streɪt] • **direkte Rede** direct speech [də'rekt]
direkt hinter dir right behind you
Diskjockey disc jockey ['dɪsk dʒɒki]; DJ ['diːdʒeɪ]
Disko disco ['dɪskəʊ]
diskriminieren: jn. diskriminieren discriminate against sb. [dɪ'skrɪmɪneɪt]
Diskriminierung (von) discrimination (against) [dɪˌskrɪmɪ'neɪʃn]
Diskussion discussion [dɪ'skʌʃn]
Display display [dɪs'pleɪ]
Doktor doctor ['dɒktə]
Dokumentarfilm documentary [ˌdɒkju'mentri]
Dollar dollar ($) ['dɒlə]
Dom cathedral [kə'θiːdrəl]
Donnerstag Thursday ['θɜːzdeɪ, 'θɜːzdi] *(siehe auch unter „Freitag")*
Doppel-, doppelt double ['dʌbl]
Dorf village ['vɪlɪdʒ]
dort, dorthin there [ðeə] • **dort drinnen** in there • **dort drüben** over there • **dort oben** up there
 dort unten down there
Dossier dossier ['dɒsieɪ]
downloaden download [ˌdaʊn'ləʊd]
Dr. Dr., Dr ['dɒktə]
Drache dragon ['drægən]
Drachen kite [kaɪt]
Drama drama ['drɑːmə]
dran: Ich bin dran. It's my turn. [tɜːn]
draußen outside [ˌaʊt'saɪd]; out [aʊt]
 nach draußen outside
draußenbleiben stay out [steɪ ˌaʊt]
drehen *(Film)* shoot [ʃuːt]
drei: ein dreiwöchiger Urlaub a three-week holiday
dreieinhalb Tage/Wochen three and a half days/weeks
drinnen inside [ˌɪn'saɪd] • **dort drinnen** in there [ˌɪn 'ðeə] • **hier drinnen** in here [ˌɪn 'hɪə] • **nach drinnen** inside
dritte(r, s) third [θɜːd]
Drogerie chemist ['kemɪst]
drüben: da/dort drüben over there [ˌəʊvə 'ðeə]
drücken push [pʊʃ]; squeeze [skwiːz]
Dschungel jungle ['dʒʌŋgl]
du you [juː]

dumm (albern) silly ['sɪli]
dunkel dark [dɑːk]
Dunkelheit: nach Einbruch der Dunkelheit after dark [dɑːk]
durch through [θruː]; (in ... umher) around [əˈraʊnd] • **durch die Stadt** around the town
durcheinander: alles durcheinanderbringen make a mess [ˌmeɪk‿ə ˈmes]
durchführen: ein Projekt durchführen do a project
Durchsage announcement [əˈnaʊnsmənt]
Durchschnitt average [ˈævərɪdʒ]
durchschnittlich average [ˈævərɪdʒ]
▶ S.213 US school grades
durchsichtig see-through [ˈsiːθruː]
dürfen can [kən, kæn]; may [meɪ]; be allowed to [əˈlaʊd] • **nicht dürfen** mustn't [ˈmʌsnt]
Durst haben, durstig sein be thirsty [ˈθɜːsti]
Dusche shower [ˈʃaʊə]
duschen; sich duschen have a shower [ˈʃaʊə]
DVD DVD [ˌdiː viːˈdiː]

E

Ebbe und Flut (Gezeiten) tide [taɪd] • **es ist Ebbe** the tide is out
eben (flach) flat [flæt]
ebenso ... wie just as ... as [əz, æz]
echt real [rɪəl] • **echt spät** real late (AE, infml)
Ecke corner [ˈkɔːnə] • **Sand Street, Ecke London Road** on the corner of Sand Street and London Road
eckige Klammern square brackets [ˌskweə ˈbrækɪts]
egal whatever [ˌwɒtˈevə] • **egal, in welchem Film** whatever the movie • **egal, wann** whenever [ˌwenˈevə] • **egal, wer/wen/wem** whoever [ˌhuːˈevə] • **egal, wo(hin)** wherever [ˌwerˈevə] • **Geld ist mir egal.** I don't care about money. **Ist doch egal!** Who cares? [ˌhuːˈkeəz])
▶ S.196 whatever, etc.
Ehefrau wife [waɪf], pl wives [waɪvz]
Ehemann husband [ˈhʌzbənd]
ehrenhaft noble [ˈnəʊbl]
Ei egg [eg]
Eichhörnchen squirrel [ˈskwɪrəl]
eigene(r, s): unser eigenes Schwimmbad our own pool [əʊn]
Eigenheimbesitzer/in homeowner [ˈhəʊmˌəʊnə]
Eigenschaft quality [ˈkwɒləti]

eigentlich actually [ˈæktʃuəli]
▶ S.215 actually
Eigentümer/in owner [ˈəʊnə]
Eile: in Eile sein be in a hurry [ˈhʌri]
eilen (sich beeilen) hurry [ˈhʌri]
eilig: es eilig haben be in a hurry [ˈhʌri]
ein(e) a, an [ə, ən]; one [wʌn]
ein(e) andere(r, s) ... another ... [əˈnʌðə] • **eine Menge** a lot (of) [lɒt]; lots (of) [lɒts] • **ein neuer / eine neue / ein neues** a new one [wʌn] • **ein paar** some [səm, sʌm]; (einige wenige) a few [fjuː] • **ein Paar** a pair (of) [peə] • **eines Tages** one day
einander (sich gegenseitig) each other
Einbruch: nach Einbruch der Dunkelheit after dark [dɑːk]
eindrucksvoll impressive [ɪmˈpresɪv]; grand [grænd]
einfach (nicht schwierig) easy [ˈiːzi]
einfach (nur) just [dʒʌst]
einfach (schlicht) plain [pleɪn]
Einfall (Idee) idea [aɪˈdɪə]
einfallen: sich etwas einfallen lassen come up with sth. [ˌkʌmˈʌp]
einfallsreich creative [kriˈeɪtɪv]
einführen: jn. in etwas einführen introduce sb. to sth. [ˌɪntrəˈdjuːs]
Einführung (in) introduction (to) [ˌɪntrəˈdʌkʃn]
Eingangshalle lobby [ˈlɒbi]
eingeben: etwas eingeben (in den Computer) enter sth. [ˈentə]
eingeschaltet sein (Radio, Licht usw.) be on
einige some [səm, sʌm]; (einige wenige) a few [fjuː]
einigen: sich einigen (auf) agree (on) [əˈgriː]
einkaufen: einkaufen gehen go shopping [ˌgəʊ ˈʃɒpɪŋ]
Einkaufen shopping [ˈʃɒpɪŋ]
Einkaufsliste shopping list
Einkaufsstraße, -viertel shopping precinct [ˈpriːsɪŋkt]
Einkaufszentrum (shopping) mall [mɔːl]; BE auch [mæl]
einladen (zu) invite (to) [ɪnˈvaɪt]
Einladung (zu) invitation (to) [ˌɪnvɪˈteɪʃn]
einmal once [wʌns] • **Einmal aussetzen.** Miss a turn. [tɜːn] • **auf einmal** suddenly [ˈsʌdnli]
einpacken pack [pæk]
einpflanzen plant [plɑːnt]
einreisen: in ein Land einreisen enter a country [ˈentə]

eins, ein, eine one [wʌn] • **etwas eins nach dem anderen tun** take sth. a step at a time
Einsatzort location [ləˈkeɪʃn]
einschalten: den Computer einschalten turn on the computer [ˌtɜːn ˈɒn]
einschätzen: jn. einschätzen (nach) judge sb. (by) [dʒʌdʒ]
einschließen include [ɪnˈkluːd]
einschüchtern bully [ˈbʊli]
Einsendung (zu einem Wettbewerb) entry [ˈentri]
einsteigen (in den Zug/Bus) get on (the train/bus) [ˌgetˈɒn]
einstellen: ein Radio auf einen Sender einstellen tune a radio to a station [tjuːn] • **sich (auf etwas) einstellen** adjust (to sth.) [əˈdʒʌst]
Einstellung zu attitude to/towards [ˈætɪtjuːd]
einstürzen collapse [kəˈlæps]
eintauschen: etwas eintauschen (für/gegen etwas) swap sth. (for sth.) [swɒp]
einteilen sort [sɔːt]
Eintopf(gericht) stew [stjuː]
Eintrag, Eintragung (im Wörterbuch/Tagebuch) entry [ˈentri]
eintragen: etwas eintragen (in Formular) enter sth. [ˈentə] • **sich eintragen** put your name on a list
eintreffen (ankommen) arrive [əˈraɪv]
Eintrittskarte ticket [ˈtɪkɪt]
Einwanderer/Einwanderin immigrant [ˈɪmɪgrənt]
einwandern immigrate [ˈɪmɪgreɪt]
Einwanderung immigration [ˌɪmɪˈgreɪʃn]
Einwohner(zahl) population [ˌpɒpjuˈleɪʃn]
Einzelheit detail [ˈdiːteɪl]
einziehen (in Wohnung) move in [ˌmuːvˈɪn]
einzig: der einzige Gast the only guest [ˈəʊnli]
Eis ice [aɪs]; (Speiseeis) ice cream [ˌaɪs ˈkriːm]
Eisenbahn railway [ˈreɪlweɪ]
Eishockey ice hockey [ˈaɪs hɒki]
Elefant elephant [ˈelɪfənt]
elektrisch electric [ɪˈlektrɪk]
elektrische Aufladung static (electricity) [ˈstætɪk, ˌstætɪk‿ɪˌlekˈtrɪsəti]
Elektrizität electricity [ɪˌlekˈtrɪsəti]
Elektro- electric [ɪˈlektrɪk]
elektronisch electronic [ˌɪlekˈtrɒnɪk]
Elfmeter (Fußball) penalty [ˈpenəlti]
Eltern parents [ˈpeərənts]
E-Mail (an) e-mail (to) [ˈiːmeɪl]
End- final [ˈfaɪnl]

Ende 1. end [end]; *(einer Geschichte, eines Films usw.)* ending ['endɪŋ] **am Ende (von)** at the end (of) **zu Ende gehen** end [end] • **zu Ende machen** finish ['fɪnɪʃ] • **zu Ende sein** be over ['əʊvə] **2. oberes Ende** *(Spitze)* top [tɒp] **am oberen Ende (von)** at the top (of) **3. unteres Ende** bottom ['bɒtəm] **am unteren Ende (von)** at the bottom (of) ['bɒtəm]
enden finish ['fɪnɪʃ]
endlich at last [ət 'lɑːst]; finally ['faɪnəli]
Endspiel final ['faɪnl]
Endstand *(beim Sport)* final score [,faɪnl 'skɔː]
eng tight [taɪt]
engagieren: sich engagieren (für, bei) get involved (in) [ɪn'vɒlvd]
Engel angel ['eɪndʒl]
Englisch; englisch English ['ɪŋglɪʃ]
Enkel grandson ['grænsʌn]; grandchild ['græntʃaɪld], *pl* grandchildren ['græntʃɪldrən]
Enkelin granddaughter ['grændɔːtə]; grandchild ['græntʃaɪld], *pl* grandchildren ['græntʃɪldrən]
entdecken discover [dɪ'skʌvə]; spot [spɒt]
Entdecker/in *(Forscher/in)* explorer [ɪk'splɔːrə]
entfernen: sich von etwas/jm. entfernen get away from sth./sb.
Entfernung distance ['dɪstəns]
Entführer/in *(Flugzeug)* hijacker ['haɪdʒækə]
entkommen escape [ɪ'skeɪp]
entladen unload [,ʌn'ləʊd]
entlang der Straße / die Straße entlang along the street [ə'lɒŋ]
entleihen: etwas entleihen *(sich etwas ausleihen)* borrow sth. ['bɒrəʊ]
entscheiden: sich entscheiden (für etwas) decide (on sth.) [dɪ'saɪd] **Das kannst/musst du (selbst) entscheiden.** That's up to you.
entschuldigen: sich entschuldigen say sorry ['sɒri]
Entschuldigung 1. *(Tut mir leid)* I'm sorry. ['sɒri] • **Entschuldigung, dass ich zu spät komme.** Sorry, I'm late. **2. Entschuldigung, ... / Entschuldigen Sie, ...** *(Darf ich mal stören?)* Excuse me, ... [ɪk'skjuːz miː]
Entsetzen horror ['hɒrə]
entspannen; sich entspannen relax [rɪ'læks]; chill out [,tʃɪl 'aʊt] *(infml)*
enttäuschen disappoint [,dɪsə'pɔɪnt]

enttäuscht (von jm./etwas) disappointed (with sb., with/about sth.) [,dɪsə'pɔɪntɪd]
entwerfen design [dɪ'zaɪn]
entwickeln *(entwerfen)* design [dɪ'zaɪn]
Entwurf draft [drɑːft]
Enzyklopädie encyclopedia [ɪn,saɪklə'piːdiə]
er 1. *(männliche Person)* he [hiː] **2.** *(Ding, Tier)* it [ɪt]
Erbe *(das Erbe)* heritage ['herɪtɪdʒ]
Erdbeben earthquake ['ɜːθkweɪk]
Erdbeere strawberry ['strɔːbəri]
Erdboden ground [graʊnd]
Erde *(Erdreich)* soil [sɔɪl]
Erdgeschoss first floor [,fɜːst flɔː] *(AE)*; ground floor [,graʊnd 'flɔː] *(BE)*
▶ S.196 floor
Erdkunde geography [dʒi'ɒgrəfi]
Ereignis event [ɪ'vent]
erfahren: etwas über etwas erfahren learn sth. about sth. [lɜːn]
erfahren *(adj)* experienced [ɪk'spɪəriənst]
Erfahrung experience [ɪk'spɪəriəns]
erfinden invent [ɪn'vent]
Erfinder/in inventor [ɪn'ventə]
Erfolg success [sək'ses] • **Erfolg (mit/bei etwas) haben** succeed (in sth.) [sək'siːd]
erfolgreich sein (mit etwas, bei etwas) succeed (in sth.) [sək'siːd]
erforschen explore [ɪk'splɔː]
ergänzen add (to) [æd]
Ergebnis result [rɪ'zʌlt]
erhalten receive [rɪ'siːv]
erhältlich available [ə'veɪləbl]
erholen: sich erholen (von) recover (from) [rɪ'kʌvə]
erinnern: sich erinnern (an) remember [rɪ'membə]
erkältet sein have a cold [kəʊld]
Erkältung cold [kəʊld] • **eine Erkältung haben** have a cold
erkennen *(merken)* realize ['rɪəlaɪz]; *(wiedererkennen)* recognize ['rekəgnaɪz]
erklären: jm. etwas erklären explain sth. to sb. [ɪk'spleɪn] **sich bereit erklären** volunteer [,vɒlən'tɪə]
Erklärung explanation [,eksplə'neɪʃn]
erkunden explore [ɪk'splɔː]
erlauben allow [ə'laʊ] • **jm. erlauben, etwas zu tun** let sb. do sth.
erläutern: jm. etwas erläutern explain sth. to sb. [ɪk'spleɪn]
Erlebnis experience [ɪk'spɪəriəns]
ermorden murder ['mɜːdə]
Ernst: Das kann nicht dein Ernst sein! No way! [,nəʊ 'weɪ]

Ernte harvest ['hɑːvɪst]
erraten guess [ges]
erreichen reach [riːtʃ]; achieve [ə'tʃiːv] • **ein Ziel erreichen** achieve an end
erscheinen appear [ə'pɪə]
erschießen shoot [ʃuːt]
ersetzen (durch) replace (with) [rɪ'pleɪs]
erst only ['əʊnli]
erstaunlich amazing [ə'meɪzɪŋ]
erste(r, s) first [fɜːst] • **als Erstes** first • **erster Stock** first floor [,fɜːst flɔː] *(BE)*; second floor *(AE)* • **der erste Tag** the first day • **der/die Erste sein** be first • **die Ersten Nationen** *(indianische Ureinwohner/innen Kanadas)* the First Nations
▶ S.196 floor
erstrecken: sich erstrecken stretch [stretʃ]
ertragen *(aushalten)* stand [stænd] **Ich kann es nicht ertragen.** I can't stand it.
ertrinken drown [draʊn]
erwachsen werden grow up [grəʊ_'ʌp]
Erwachsene(r) adult ['ædʌlt] • **das Leben als Erwachsene/r** adult life
erwarten expect [ɪk'spekt] • **ich kann es kaum erwarten, ... zu sehen** I can't wait to see ... [weɪt]
erwidern (auf) reply (to) [rɪ'plaɪ]
erwischen *(fangen)* catch [kætʃ]
erzählen (von) tell (about) [tel]
Erzähler/in narrator [nə'reɪtə]
Erzählung story ['stɔːri]
erzeugen *(produzieren)* produce [prə'djuːs]
Erziehung education [,edʒu'keɪʃn]
erzielen achieve [ə'tʃiːv] • **einen Treffer erzielen** score a goal [skɔː], [gəʊl]
es it [ɪt] • **es gibt** *(es ist vorhanden)* there's; *(es sind vorhanden)* there are
essen eat [iːt] • **Abendbrot essen** have dinner • **Toast zum Frühstück essen** have toast for breakfast
Essen food [fuːd]; *(Mahlzeit)* meal [miːl]
Esszimmer dining room ['daɪnɪŋ ruːm]
Etagenbett bunk (bed) [bʌŋk]
ethnisch ethnic ['eθnɪk]
etwas something ['sʌmθɪŋ]; *(irgendetwas)* anything ['eniθɪŋ]; *(ein bisschen)* a bit [bɪt] • **etwas Käse/Saft** some cheese/juice [səm, sʌm]
etwas anderes something else [els]
sonst (noch) etwas anything else

euch you [juː]; *(Reflexivpronomen)* yourselves [jɔːˈselvz]
euer, eure ... your ... [jɔː]
eurer, eure, eures yours [jɔːz]
Euro euro [ˈjʊərəʊ]
explodieren *(Bombe)* go off
Explosion explosion [ɪkˈspləʊʒn]
extra separate [ˈseprət]

F

Fabrik factory [ˈfæktri]
Fachschule college [ˈkɒlɪdʒ]
fähig sein, etwas zu tun be able to do sth. [ˈeɪbl]
Fähigkeit skill [skɪl]
Fähre ferry [ˈferi]
fahren go [gəʊ]; *(ein Auto / mit dem Auto)* drive [draɪv] • **in Urlaub fahren** go on holiday • **mit dem Auto/Zug/Rad/... fahren** go by car/train/bike/... • **mit dem Schiff fahren** sail [seɪl] • **mit einem Schlauchboot/Floß fahren** raft [rɑːft] • **Inliner/Skateboard fahren** skate [skeɪt] • **Rad fahren** cycle [ˈsaɪkl]; ride a bike [ˌraɪd ə ˈbaɪk]
Fahrer/in driver [ˈdraɪvə]
Fahrgast passenger [ˈpæsɪndʒə]
Fahrkarte ticket [ˈtɪkɪt]
Fahrkartenautomat ticket machine [ˈtɪkɪt məˌʃiːn]
Fahrkartenschalter ticket office [ˈtɪkɪt ˌɒfɪs]
Fahrrad bike [baɪk]
Fahrstuhl lift [lɪft] *(BE)*; elevator [ˈelɪveɪtə] *(AE)*
Fahrt: (Rad-/Bus-)Fahrt (bike/bus) ride [raɪd]; journey [ˈdʒɜːni]
fair fair [feə]
Fakt fact [fækt]
Fall 1. *(Kriminalfall)* case [keɪs] 2. **Auf keinen Fall!** No way! [ˌnəʊ ˈweɪ]
Falle trap [træp] • **(jm.) eine Falle stellen** set a trap (for sb.) [set]
fallen fall [fɔːl]; drop [drɒp]
fallen lassen drop [drɒp]
falls if [ɪf]
falsch wrong [rɒŋ] • **etwas falsch machen** get sth. wrong • **in die falsche Richtung** the wrong way
Familie family [ˈfæməli] • **Familienmensch** family man
Fan fan [fæn]; supporter [səˈpɔːtə] • **Fan einer Mannschaft sein** support a team [səˈpɔːt]
fangen catch [kætʃ]
Fantasie *(Vorstellungskraft)* imagination [ɪˌmædʒɪˈneɪʃn]
fantastisch fantastic [fænˈtæstɪk]

Farbe 1. colour [ˈkʌlə] • **Welche Farbe hat ...?** What colour is ...? 2. *(zum Anstreichen)* paint [peɪnt]
Farm farm [fɑːm]
Fassung 1. version [ˈvɜːʃn] 2. **jn. aus der Fassung bringen** upset sb. [ʌpˈset]
fast almost [ˈɔːlməʊst]; nearly [ˈnɪəli]
Faust fist [fɪst]
Favorit/in favourite [ˈfeɪvərɪt]
Februar February [ˈfebruəri]
Federball badminton [ˈbædmɪntən]
Federballschläger badminton racket [ˈrækɪt]
Federmäppchen pencil case [ˈpensl keɪs]
fegen sweep [swiːp]
fehlen *(nicht da sein)* be missing [ˈmɪsɪŋ] • **Was fehlt dir?** *(bei Krankheit)* What's wrong with you?
Fehler mistake [mɪˈsteɪk], fault [fɔːlt]
Feier celebration [ˌseləˈbreɪʃn]
feierlich danksagen give thanks
feiern celebrate [ˈselɪbreɪt]
Feind/in enemy [ˈenəmi]
Feld 1. field [fiːld] • **auf dem Feld** in the field 2. *(bei Brettspielen)* **Geh ein Feld vor.** Move on one space. [speɪs] **Geh ein Feld zurück.** Move back one space.
Fenster window [ˈwɪndəʊ]
Ferien holidays [ˈhɒlədeɪz]; vacation *(AE)* [vəˈkeɪʃn, veɪˈkeɪʃn] • **Ferien haben/machen** be on holiday
Ferienhaus holiday home; villa
Ferienwohnung holiday home
fern faraway [ˈfɑːr əˈweɪ]
Fernglas binoculars *(pl)* [bɪˈnɒkjuləz]
fernsehen watch TV [ˌwɒtʃ tiːˈviː]
Fernsehen television [ˈtelɪvɪʒn]; TV [tiːˈviː] • **im Fernsehen** on TV
Fernstraße *(in den USA, oft mit vier oder mehr Spuren)* highway [ˈhaɪweɪ]
Fernsehspiel drama [ˈdrɑːmə]
fertig *(bereit)* ready [ˈredi] • **sich fertig machen (für)** *(sich vorbereiten)* get ready (for) • **Dinge fertig machen (für)** *(vorbereiten)* get things ready (for)
Fertigkeit skill [skɪl]
Fest, Festival festival [ˈfestɪvl]
fest *(eng)* tight [taɪt]
festbinden tie [taɪ]
feucht wet [wet]
Feuer fire [ˈfaɪə] • **ein Feuer löschen** put out a fire • **Wo Rauch ist, ist auch Feuer.** There's no smoke without fire.
Feuerwache fire station [ˈfaɪə ˌsteɪʃn]
Feuerwehrfrau firefighter [ˈfaɪəfaɪtə]; firewoman [ˈfaɪəˌwʊmən]

Feuerwehrmann firefighter [ˈfaɪəfaɪtə]; fireman [ˈfaɪəmən]
Fieber haben have a temperature [ˈtemprətʃə]
Fiedel *(Geige)* fiddle [ˈfɪdl] *(infml)*
Film film [fɪlm]; movie [ˈmuːvi]
filmen film [fɪlm]
Filmstar film star [ˈfɪlm stɑː]
Filzstift felt tip [ˈfelt tɪp]
Finale final [ˈfaɪnl]
finden *(entdecken)* find [faɪnd] • **Freunde finden** make friends
Finger finger [ˈfɪŋgə]
Firma company [ˈkʌmpəni]
Fisch fish, *pl* fish [fɪʃ]
Fischer fisherman, *pl* fishermen [ˈfɪʃəmən, ˈfɪʃəmen]
Fitnessstudio gym [dʒɪm]
flach *(eben)* flat [flæt]
Flasche bottle [ˈbɒtl] • **eine Flasche Milch** a bottle of milk
Fleisch meat [miːt]
fliegen fly [flaɪ] • *(schnell)* **fliegen** speed [spiːd]
fliehen: vor jm./aus etwas fliehen escape from sb./sth. [ɪˈskeɪp]
fließen flow [fləʊ]
Flohmarkt flea market [ˈfliː ˌmɑːkɪt]
Floß raft [rɑːft] • **mit einem Floß fahren** raft
Flug flight [flaɪt]
Flugblatt flyer [ˈflaɪə]
Flügel wing [wɪŋ]
Flughafen airport [ˈeəpɔːt]
Flugsteig gate [geɪt]
Flugzeug plane [pleɪn] • **im Flugzeug** on the plane
Flugzeugentführer/in hijacker [ˈhaɪdʒækə]
Flur hall [hɔːl]
Fluss river [ˈrɪvə]
Flussdiagramm flow chart [ˈfləʊ tʃɑːt]
Flusspferd hippo [ˈhɪpəʊ]
flüstern whisper [ˈwɪspə]
Flyer flyer [ˈflaɪə]
Flut: Ebbe und Flut *(Gezeiten)* tide [taɪd] • **es ist Flut** the tide is in
Folge *(Ergebnis)* consequence [ˈkɒnsɪkwəns]
folgen follow [ˈfɒləʊ] • **die folgenden ...** the following ...
Football American football [əˌmerɪkən ˈfʊtbɔːl]
Form *(Gestalt)* shape [ʃeɪp]
formulieren: Sie wissen, wie man es formuliert. You know how to put it. [pʊt]
Forscher/in *(Entdecker/in)* explorer [ɪkˈsplɔːrə]
Forschung(en) research *(no pl)* [rɪˈsɜːtʃ, ˈriːsɜːtʃ]
Fort fort [fɔːt]

fort away [ə'weɪ]
Forum forum ['fɔ:rəm]
Foto photo ['fəʊtəʊ] • **auf dem Foto** in the photo • **Fotos machen** take photos
Fotoapparat camera ['kæmərə]
Fotograf/in photographer [fə'tɒgrəfə]
fotografieren take photos [teɪk 'fəʊtəʊz] • **jn. fotografieren** take a photo of sb.; shoot sb. [ʃu:t]
foulen (Sport) foul [faʊl]
Frage question ['kwestʃn] • **Fragen stellen** ask questions • **Kommt nicht in Frage!** No way!
fragen ask [ɑ:sk] • **nach etwas fragen** ask about sth. • **jn. nach dem Weg fragen** ask sb. the way • **sich fragen** wonder ['wʌndə]
Französisch French [frentʃ]
Frau woman ['wʊmən], pl women ['wɪmɪn] • **Frau Brown** Mrs Brown ['mɪsɪz]; Ms Brown [mɪz, məz]; (unverheiratet) Miss Brown [mɪs]
frei free [fri:] • **freie Zeit** free time • **im Freien** outdoor ['aʊtdɔ:]
Freiheit liberty ['lɪbəti]
Freilichtmuseum (mit kostümierten Fremdenführer/innen, historischen Aufführungen usw.) living-history museum
Freitag Friday ['fraɪdeɪ, 'fraɪdi] **freitagabends, am Freitagabend** on Friday evening • **freitagnachts, Freitagnacht** on Friday night
freiwillig: Arbeit als Freiwillige(r) volunteer work [ˌvɒlən'tɪə ˌwɜ:k] • **sich freiwillig melden** volunteer [ˌvɒlən'tɪə]
Freizeit free time [ˌfri: 'taɪm]
Freizeitaktivitäten free-time activities [ˌfri: taɪm æk'tɪvətiz]
Freizeitzentrum, -park leisure centre ['leʒə sentə]
Fremdenführer/in guide [gaɪd]
Fremdenverkehrsamt tourist information ['tʊərɪst ˌɪnfə,meɪʃn]
freuen: sich freuen be pleased [pli:zd] • **sich auf jn./etwas freuen** look forward to sb./sth. ['fɔ:wəd]
Freund friend [frend]; (Partner) boyfriend ['bɔɪfrend] • **Freunde finden** make friends
Freundin friend [frend]; (Partner) girlfriend ['gɜ:lfrend]
freundlich friendly ['frendli] • **mit freundlichen Grüßen** Sincerely (yours) [sɪn'sɪəli] (AE); Yours faithfully ['feɪθfəli] (BE); Yours sincerely (BE); Yours truly ['tru:li] (AE)
▶ S.215 Beginning and ending letters
Freundlichkeit friendliness ['frendlinəs]

frieren be cold [kəʊld]
Frisbee frisbee ['frɪzbi]
Frischkäse cream cheese [ˌkri:m 'tʃi:z]
Friseur/in hairdresser ['heədresə] **beim Friseur** at the hairdresser's
froh happy ['hæpi]; glad [glæd]
Frosch frog [frɒg]
Frucht, Früchte fruit [fru:t]
früh early ['ɜ:li]
Frühling spring [sprɪŋ]
Frühstück breakfast ['brekfəst] • **zum Frühstück** for breakfast
frühstücken have breakfast
Frühstückspension Bed and Breakfast (B&B) [ˌbed ən 'brekfəst]
Fuchs fox [fɒks]
fühlen; sich fühlen feel [fi:l]
führen (zu, nach) (Straße) lead (to) [li:d] go (to); (zur Folge haben) lead (to) • **ein Telefongespräch führen** make a call [kɔ:l]
Führer/in leader ['li:də]
Führung 1. guided tour [ˌgaɪdɪd 'tʊə] 2. **in Führung gehen** (Sport) go ahead
füllen: etwas (mit etwas) füllen fill sth. (with sth.) [fɪl]
Füller pen [pen]
Funke spark [spɑ:k]
funktionieren work [wɜ:k]
für for [fə, fɔ:] • **Was für ein Auto ...?** What kind of car ...?
Furcht (vor) fear (of) ['fɪə]
furchtbar terrible ['terəbl]; awful ['ɔ:fl]
Fuß (auch Längenmaß, ca. 30 cm) foot [fʊt], pl feet [fi:t] • **zu Fuß** on foot
Fußball football ['fʊtbɔ:l]
Fußballplatz, -feld football pitch [pɪtʃ]
Fußballschuhe, -stiefel football boots ['fʊtbɔ:l bu:ts]
Fußballspieler/in footballer ['fʊtbɔ:lə]
Fußballtrikot football shirt [ʃɜ:t]
Fußboden floor [flɔ:]
Fußgänger/in pedestrian [pə'destrɪən]
Fußgängerüberweg crosswalk ['krɒswɔ:k] (AE); pedestrian crossing [pə,destrɪən 'krɒsɪŋ] (BE)
Fußnote footnote ['fʊtnəʊt]
Futter food [fu:d]
füttern feed [fi:d]

G

Gabel fork [fɔ:k]
gähnen yawn [jɔ:n]
Galerie gallery ['gæləri]
Gang (Flur) hallway ['hɔ:lweɪ] (AE)

Gänsehaut goose bumps (pl) ['gu:s ˌbʌmps] (AE); goose pimples (pl) ['gu:s 'pɪmplz] (BE)
ganz quite [kwaɪt] • **Das ist ganz falsch.** This is all wrong.
ganze(r, s) whole [həʊl] • **auf der ganzen Welt** all over the world **aus der ganzen Welt** from all over the world • **das ganze Jahr 2006** the whole of 2006 • **das ganze Jahr hindurch** all year round **den ganzen Oktober hindurch** throughout October [θru:'aʊt] • **den ganzen Tag (lang)** all day **die ganze Zeit** all the time
gar nicht not at all
gar nichts nothing at all
▶ S.206 not at all, no ... at all
Garage garage ['gærɑ:ʒ]
Garten garden ['gɑ:dn]
Gas gas [gæs]
Gasse lane [leɪn]
Gast guest [gest]; (Besucher/in) visitor ['vɪzɪtə]
Gastgeber host [həʊst]
Gastgeberin hostess ['həʊstes]
Gebäude building ['bɪldɪŋ]
geben give [gɪv] • **es gibt** (es ist vorhanden) there's; (es sind vorhanden) there are • **jm. das Gefühl geben, klein zu sein** make sb. feel small • **jm. die Schuld geben (an)** blame sb. (for) [bleɪm]
Gebet prayer [preə]
Gebiet area ['eərɪə]
geboren sein/werden be born [bɔ:n]
Gebrauch use [ju:s]
gebraucht (aus zweiter Hand) second-hand [ˌsekənd 'hænd]
gebrochen (Arm, Bein) broken ['brəʊkən]
Geburt birth [bɜ:θ]
Geburtsdatum date of birth [deɪt]
Geburtsort place of birth [pleɪs]
Geburtstag birthday ['bɜ:θdeɪ] **Herzlichen Glückwunsch zum Geburtstag.** Happy birthday. • **Ich habe im Mai / am 13. Juni Geburtstag.** My birthday is in May / on 13th June. • **Wann hast du Geburtstag?** When's your birthday? • **zu seinem Geburtstag** for his birthday
Gedanke thought [θɔ:t]
Gedicht poem ['pəʊɪm]
geehrt: Sehr geehrte Damen und Herren Dear Sir [sɜ:] or Madam ... ['mædm] (BE), To whom it may concern [kən'sɜ:n] (bes. AE)
▶ S.215 Beginning and ending letters
Gefahr danger ['deɪndʒə]
gefährlich dangerous ['deɪndʒərəs]; (nicht sicher) unsafe [ʌn'seɪf]

Gefallen: jm. einen Gefallen tun do sb. a favour ['feɪvə]
Gefangene(r) prisoner ['prɪznə]
Gefängnis prison ['prɪzn] • **im Gefängnis wegen Mordes** in prison for murder
Gefühl feeling ['fi:lɪŋ] • **jm. das Gefühl geben, klein zu sein** make sb. feel small
gegen against [ə'genst] • **gegen sechs Uhr** around six
Gegend area ['eərɪə]
Gegensatz: im Gegensatz zu unlike [ˌʌn'laɪk]
Gegenteil opposite ['ɒpəzɪt]
gegenüber (von) opposite ['ɒpəzɪt]
Gegenwart present ['preznt]
Gegner/in opponent [ə'pəʊnənt]
geheim secret ['si:krət]
Geheimnis secret ['si:krət]; (Rätsel) mystery ['mɪstri]
gehen 1. go [gəʊ]; (zu Fuß gehen) walk [wɔːk]; (weggehen) leave [liːv] **Auf geht's!** Let's go. • **einkaufen gehen** go shopping • **Geh ein Feld vor.** Move on one space. [speɪs] • **Geh ein Feld zurück.** Move back one space. • **Geh mir aus den Augen.** Get out of my sight. [saɪt] **in die Sauna gehen** have a sauna ['sɔːnə] • **ins Ausland gehen** go abroad [ə'brɔːd] • **ins Bett gehen** go to bed • **in Führung gehen** (Sport) go ahead • **ins Kino gehen** go to the cinema ['sɪnəmə] • **nach Hause gehen** go home • **reiten/schwimmen gehen** go riding/swimming • **spazieren gehen** walk; go for a walk [wɔːk]
2. **Es geht mir/ihm gut.** I'm/He's fine. [faɪn] • **Wie geht es dir/Ihnen/euch?** How are you?
3. **Es geht um Mr Green.** This is about Mr Green. • **Das geht dich nichts an!** Mind your own business. [ˌmaɪnd jərˌəʊn 'bɪznəs]
gehorchen obey [ə'beɪ]
gehören (zu) 1. belong (to) [bɪ'lɒŋ] • **Wem gehören diese?** Whose are these? [huːz]
2. (passen zu) go with
gehörlos deaf [def]
Gehweg pavement ['peɪvmənt] (BE), sidewalk ['saɪdwɔːk] (AE)
Geige violin [ˌvaɪə'lɪn]; fiddle ['fɪdl] (infml) • **Geige spielen** play the violin/fiddle
gekränkt (wegen) upset (about) [ˌʌp'set]
Gelächter laughter ['lɑːftə]
gelangen (hinkommen) get [get]

gelangweilt sein get bored with sb./sth. [bɔːd]
gelb yellow ['jeləʊ]
Geld money ['mʌni] • **Geld ausgeben (für)** spend money (on) [spend] • **Geld sammeln (für)** raise money (for) [reɪz]
Geldbörse purse [pɜːs]
Geldstrafe fine [faɪn]
Gemälde painting ['peɪntɪŋ]
gemein mean [miːn]
Gemeindehalle, -saal community hall [kəˌmjuːnəti 'hɔːl]
gemeinsam: etwas gemeinsam mit jm. haben/nutzen share sth. (with sb.) [ʃeə]
Gemeinschaftshalle community hall [kəˌmjuːnəti 'hɔːl]
Gemeinschaftskunde Social Studies [ˌsəʊʃl 'stʌdiz]
Gemeinschaftssaal community hall [kəˌmjuːnəti 'hɔːl]
Gemüse: (ein) **Gemüse** vegetable ['vedʒtəbl]
genannt werden be called [kɔːld]
genau 1. (Adjektiv) accurate ['ækjərət]; exact [ɪg'zækt]
2. (Adverb) **etwas genau anschauen** look closely at sth. ['kləʊsli] • **genau hinter dir** right behind you • **genau in dem Moment** just then • **genau wie du** just like you
genießen enjoy [ɪn'dʒɔɪ]
genug enough [ɪ'nʌf] • **genug von etwas haben** be tired of sth. [taɪəd]
geöffnet open ['əʊpən]
Geografie geography [dʒi'ɒgrəfi]
gepflegt neat [niːt]
gerade at the moment; (soeben) just [dʒʌst] • **gerade dann** (genau in dem Moment) just then • **jetzt gerade** (in diesem Moment) right now [raɪt 'naʊ]
geradeaus weiter straight on [streɪt 'ɒn]
Gerät (Maschine) machine [mə'ʃiːn]
geraten: in Panik geraten panic ['pænɪk]
Geräusch noise [nɔɪz]
gerecht fair [feə]
Gericht 1. (Gerichtshof) court [kɔːt]
2. (Speise) dish [dɪʃ]
gern: Ich hätte gern ... / Ich möchte gern ... I'd like ... (= I would like ...) [laɪk] • **Ich schwimme/tanze/... gern.** I like swimming/dancing/... • **Ich würde gern gehen** I'd like to go • **Ich würde nicht gern gehen** I wouldn't like to go • **Das hättest du wohl gerne!** You wish! [wɪʃ]

Gern geschehen. You're welcome. ['welkəm]
gernhaben like [laɪk]
Geruch smell
gesamte(r, s) whole [həʊl] • **aus dem gesamten Vereinigten Königreich** from all over the UK
Geschäft shop [ʃɒp]
geschehen (mit) happen (to) ['hæpən]
Geschenk present ['preznt]
Geschichte 1. story ['stɔːri]
2. (vergangene Zeiten) history ['hɪstri]
geschieden divorced [dɪ'vɔːst]
Geschirr dishes (pl) ['dɪʃɪz] • **das Geschirr abwaschen** do the dishes
Geschirrspülmaschine dishwasher ['dɪʃwɒʃə]
geschlossen closed [kləʊzd]
Geschmack taste [teɪst]; (Geschmacksrichtung) flavour
geschmacklos sein be in bad taste
Geschmack(srichtung) flavour ['fleɪvə]
geschmackvoll sein be in good taste
Geschwindigkeit speed [spiːd]
Geschwindigkeitsbegrenzung, -beschränkung speed limit ['lɪmɪt]
Gesellschaft company ['kʌmpəni]
Gesetz law [lɔː]
Gesicht face [feɪs]
Gespräch conversation [ˌkɒnvə'seɪʃn]; talk [tɔːk]
Gestalt (Form) shape [ʃeɪp]
gestern yesterday ['jestədeɪ, 'jestədi] • **gestern Morgen/Nachmittag/Abend** yesterday morning/afternoon/evening
gesund healthy ['helθi]
Gesundheit health [helθ]
Gesundheitslehre health [helθ]
Getränk drink [drɪŋk] • **alkoholfreies Getränk** soft drink
getrennt separate ['seprət] • **voneinander getrennt** apart [ə'pɑːt]
Gewalt violence ['vaɪələns]
gewaltfrei, -los non-violent [ˌnɒn 'vaɪələnt]
gewaltsam, -tätig violent ['vaɪələnt]
Gewalttätigkeit violence ['vaɪələns]
Gewicht weight [weɪt]
Gewinn prize [praɪz]
gewinnen win [wɪn]
Gewinner/in winner ['wɪnə]
Gewitter storm [stɔːm]
gewöhnen: sich (an etwas) gewöhnen adjust (to sth.) [ə'dʒʌst] • **sich gewöhnen an jn./etwas** get used to sth./sb. [juːst]

gewöhnlich usual(ly) [ˈjuːʒuəl, ˈjuːʒuəli]
Gewürz spice [spaɪs]
Gewürzkraut herb [hɜːb]
gewürzt: scharf gewürzt spicy [ˈspaɪsi]
Gezeiten *(Ebbe und Flut)* tide [taɪd]
Gig gig [ɡɪɡ] *(infml)*
Giraffe giraffe [dʒəˈrɑːf]
Gitarre guitar [ɡɪˈtɑː] • **Gitarre spielen** play the guitar
Gitter(netz) grid [ɡrɪd]
glänzen shine [ʃaɪn]
Glas glass [ɡlɑːs] • **ein Glas Wasser** a glass of water
glauben think [θɪŋk]; believe [bɪˈliːv] • **an etwas glauben** believe in sth. • **Das glaube ich nicht. / Ich glaube nicht.** I don't think so. • **Ich glaube (ja).** I think so. • **Glaubst du das wirklich?** Do you really think so? • **Sie glaubte ihren Augen kaum.** She couldn't believe her eyes.
gläubig religious [rɪˈlɪdʒəs]
gleich 1. *(sofort)* straightaway [ˌstreɪtəˈweɪ]
2. **gleich sein/aussehen** be/look the same [seɪm] • **gleiche Rechte** equal rights [ˈiːkwəl]
Gleis *(Bahnsteig)* platform [ˈplætfɔːm]
Gliederung structure [ˈstrʌktʃə]; outline [ˈaʊtlaɪn]
Gliedsatz clause [klɔːz]
Glocke bell [bel]
Glück happiness [ˈhæpɪnəs] • **Glück haben** be lucky [lʌki] • **Viel Glück (bei/mit …)!** Good luck (with …)! [ɡʊd ˈlʌk] • **zum Glück** *(glücklicherweise)* luckily [ˈlʌkɪli]
glücklich happy [ˈhæpi]
glücklicherweise luckily [ˈlʌkɪli]
Glückwunsch: Herzlichen Glückwunsch! Congratulations! [kənˌɡrætʃʊˈleɪʃnz]; *(zum Geburtstag)* Happy birthday!
Gold gold [ɡəʊld]
Gorilla gorilla [ɡəˈrɪlə]
Gott God [ɡɒd] • **Gott sei Dank.** Thank God.
Gottesdienst service [ˈsɜːvɪs]
Gouverneur/in governor [ˈɡʌvənə]
Grad degree [dɪˈɡriː]
Grammatik grammar [ˈɡræmə]
Gras grass [ɡrɑːs]
grau grey [ɡreɪ]
Grauen horror [ˈhɒrə]
grauenhaft horrible [ˈhɒrəbl]
grausam cruel [ˈkruːəl]
Grenze border [ˈbɔːdə]
Grippe flu [fluː]
groß big [bɪɡ]; large [lɑːdʒ]; *(Person)* tall [tɔːl]; *(riesig)* huge [hjuːdʒ]

großartig great [ɡreɪt]; neat *(AE, infml)* [niːt]; awesome [ˈɔːsəm] *(AE, infml)*
Großbuchstabe capital letter [ˌkæpɪtl ˈletə]
Größe *(Schuhgröße usw.)* size [saɪz]
Großeltern grandparents [ˈɡrænpeərənts]
Großmutter grandmother [ˈɡrænmʌðə]
Großstadt city [ˈsɪti]
Großvater grandfather [ˈɡrænfɑːðə]
grün green [ɡriːn]
Grund reason [ˈriːzn] • **aus vielen Gründen** for lots of reasons • **der Grund, warum** the reason why
▶ S.200–201 Giving reasons
gründen found [faʊnd]
Grundschule *(für 6- bis 11-Jährige in den USA)* elementary school [ˌelɪˈmentri skuːl]
Gruppe group [ɡruːp]; *(Musikgruppe)* band [bænd]
gruselig scary [ˈskeəri]
Gruß: Liebe Grüße, … *(Briefschluss)* Love … [lʌv] • **mit freundlichen Grüßen** Sincerely (yours) [sɪnˈsɪəli] *(AE)*; Yours faithfully [ˈfeɪθfəli] *(BE)*; Yours sincerely *(BE)*; Yours truly [ˈtruːli] *(AE)*
▶ S.215 Beginning and ending letters
Grüß deine Eltern von mir. Say hi to your parents for me.
gucken look [lʊk]
gut good [ɡʊd]; *(okay)* OK [əʊˈkeɪ]; *(in Ordnung)* all right [ɔːl ˈraɪt]; *(gesundheitlich gut, wohlauf)* well [wel]; fine [faɪn] • **gut (ver)laufen** go well • **Du hast dich gut um sie gekümmert.** You looked after them well. [wel] • **Es geht mir/ihm gut.** I'm/He's fine. • **gute Arbeit leisten** do a good job • **Guten Morgen.** Good morning. • **Guten Tag.** Hello.; *(nachmittags)* Good afternoon.
gutgehen *(gut verlaufen)* go well [wel]; work out [ˌwɜːk ˈaʊt]
Gymnasium grammar school [ˈɡræmə ˌskuːl]
Gymnastikanzug *(für Frauen und Mädchen)* leotard [ˈliːətɑːd]

H

Haar, Haare hair *(no pl)* [heə]
haben have got [ˈhæv ɡɒt]; have [həv, hæv] • **Ich habe keinen Stuhl.** I haven't got a chair. • **Ich habe am 13. Juni/im Mai Geburtstag.** My birthday is on 13th June/in May. • **Wann hast du Geburtstag?** When's your birthday? • **haben wollen** want [wɒnt] • **Was haben wir als Hausaufgabe auf?** What's for homework?
Hafen harbour [ˈhɑːbə]
Haftstrafe: lebenslängliche Haftstrafe life sentence [ˈlaɪf ˌsentəns]
Hähnchen chicken [ˈtʃɪkɪn]
halbe(r, s) half [hɑːf] • **eine halbe Stunde** half an hour • **halb zwölf** half past 11
Halbfinale semi-final [ˌsemiˈfaɪnl]
Halbzeit *(Sport)* half, *pl* halves [hɑːf, hɑːvz] • **ein Tor in der zweiten Halbzeit** a second-half goal
Halbzeit(pause) half-time
Halfpipe *(halbierte Röhre für Inlineskater)* half-pipe [ˈhɑːfpaɪp]
Hälfte half, *pl* halves [hɑːf, hɑːvz] • **ein Tor in der zweiten Hälfte** a second-half goal
Halle hall [hɔːl]
Hallo! Hi! [haɪ]; Hello. [həˈləʊ]; Hey! [heɪ]
Hals *(innen)* throat [θrəʊt]; *(außen)* neck [nek]
Halsschmerzen haben have a sore throat [sɔː ˈθrəʊt]
Halt stop [stɒp]
halten 1. hold [həʊld]
2. *(aufbewahren; behalten)* keep [kiːp] • **etwas am Leben halten** keep sth. alive [əˈlaɪv] • **etwas warm/kühl/offen/… halten** keep sth. warm/cool/open/… • **Kontakt halten** keep in touch [tʌtʃ] • **nach jm./etwas Ausschau halten** keep an eye on sth./sb. [aɪ]
3. **den Mund halten** shut up [ˌʃʌt ˈʌp]
4. **Was hältst du von …?** What do you think about/of …?
5. **sich halten an** *(Regeln, Gesetze)* obey [əˈbeɪ]
Haltung gegenüber attitude to/towards [ˈætɪtjuːd]
Hamburger hamburger [ˈhæmbɜːɡə]
Hamster hamster [ˈhæmstə]
Hand hand [hænd] • **aus zweiter Hand** *(gebraucht)* second-hand [ˌsekənd ˈhænd]
Handel trade [treɪd]
handeln von etwas deal with sth. [diːl]
Handgelenk wrist [rɪst]
Handlung action [ˈækʃn]
Handout handout [ˈhændaʊt]
Handschuhe gloves *(pl)* [ɡlʌvz]
Handtasche bag [bæɡ]
Handtuch towel [ˈtaʊəl]

Handy mobile (phone) ['məʊbaɪl] (BE); cellphone ['selfəʊn] (AE)
hängen: jn. hängen hang sb. [hæŋ]
hänseln: jn. mit Schimpfwörtern hänseln call sb. names
Happyend happy ending [ˌhæpi-'endɪŋ]
hart hard [hɑːd]; tough [tʌf] • **hart arbeiten** work hard • **hart werden** go hard
hassen hate [heɪt]
häufig often ['ɒfn]
Haupt- main [meɪn]
Häuptling chief [tʃiːf]
Hauptstadt capital ['kæpɪtl]
Haus house [haʊs] • **im Haus der Shaws / bei den Shaws zu Hause** at the Shaws' house • **nach Hause gehen** go home [həʊm] • **nach Hause kommen** come home; get home • **zu Hause** at home • **zurück zu Hause** back home [ˌbæk 'həʊm]
Hausaufgabe(n) homework (no pl) ['həʊmwɜːk]; assignment [ə'saɪnmənt] (AE) • **die Hausaufgabe(n) machen** do homework • **Was haben wir als Hausaufgabe auf?** What's for homework?
Häuserblock block [blɒk]
Hausmeister/in caretaker ['keəteɪkə]
Haustier pet [pet]
Haustür front door [ˌfrʌnt 'dɔː]
Haut skin [skɪn]
heben (hochheben) lift [lɪft]
Heer army ['ɑːmi]
Heilige(r) saint [seɪnt]
Heim home [həʊm]
Heimat(land) homeland ['həʊmlænd]
Heimat(stadt) hometown ['həʊmˌtaʊn]
heiraten marry ['mæri]
heiß hot [hɒt]
heißen 1. (genannt werden) be called [kɔːld] • **Ich heiße ...** My name is ... • **Wie heißt du?** What's your name?
2. **Sie heißen dich in ... willkommen** They welcome you to ... ['welkəm]
Heißluftballon balloon [bə'luːn]
hektisch busy ['bɪzi]
Held/in hero ['hɪərəʊ], pl heroes ['hɪərəʊz]
helfen help [help] • **Dir ist nicht zu helfen.** You're hopeless. ['həʊplɪs]
Helikopter helicopter ['helɪkɒptə]
hell (leuchtend) bright [braɪt]
Helm helmet ['helmɪt]
Hemd shirt [ʃɜːt]
herauf up [ʌp]

heraus out [aʊt] • **aus ... heraus** out of ... ['aʊt_əv]
herausarbeiten: etwas herausarbeiten work sth. out
herausbringen (CD, Film usw.) release [rɪ'liːs]
herausfinden find out [ˌfaɪnd_'aʊt]; (entdecken) discover [dɪ'skʌvə] • **etwas über etwas herausfinden** learn sth. about sth. [lɜːn], work sth. out about sth.
herausnehmen take out [ˌteɪk_'aʊt]
herausragen, -stehen (aus) stick out (of) [stɪk]
Herberge hostel ['hɒstl]
herbringen bring [brɪŋ]
Herbst autumn ['ɔːtəm]
Herd cooker ['kʊkə]
hereinkommen come in [ˌkʌm_'ɪn]
Herr: Herr Brown Mr Brown ['mɪstə] • **Sehr geehrte Damen und Herren** Dear Sir [sɜː] or Madam ... ['mædm] (BE), To whom it may concern [kən'sɜːn] (bes. AE)
▶ S.215 Beginning and ending letters
Herr(gott) Lord [lɔːd]
herstellen (produzieren) produce [prə'djuːs]
herüber across [ə'krɒs]
herum: anders herum the other way round [raʊnd] • **um ... herum** round, around
herum-: jn. herumführen (in der Stadt/im Museum/...) show sb. around • **etwas herumgeben** pass sth. round [raʊnd] • **herumgehen** walk around • **herumirren** wander ['wɒndə] • **herumlaufen** walk around • **herumrennen** run around • **herumspringen** jump around
herunter down [daʊn]
herunterfallen (von) fall off [ˌfɔːl_'ɒf]
hervorragend excellent ['eksələnt]
▶ S.213 US school grades
Herz heart [hɑːt] • **Recycling liegt mir am Herzen.** I care about recycling.
Herzinfarkt heart attack [ə'tæk]
Herzlichen Glückwunsch! Congratulations! [kənˌgrætʃu'leɪʃnz]; (zum Geburtstag) Happy birthday!
Herzlichen Glückwunsch zum Geburtstag. Happy birthday. [ˌhæpi 'bɜːθdeɪ]
heute today [tə'deɪ] • **heute Morgen/Nachmittag/Abend** this morning/afternoon/evening
heute Nacht tonight [tə'naɪt]
heutige(r, s) present-day [ˌpreznt 'deɪ]
heutzutage nowadays ['naʊədeɪz]

hier here [hɪə] • **hier (in der Gegend)** round here • **Hier anstellen.** Line starts here. • **Hier bitte. (Bitte sehr.)** Here you are. • **hier drinnen** in here [ˌɪn 'hɪə] • **hier entlang** this way ['ðɪs weɪ] • **Hier spricht/ist Isabel.** (am Telefon) This is Isabel. **Hier steht: ... / Es heißt hier: ...** (im Text) It says here: ...
hierher here [hɪə] • **bis hierher** so far
Hilfe help [help]
hilflos helpless ['helpləs]
hilfreich helpful ['helpfl]
Himmel 1. sky [skaɪ] • **am Himmel** in the sky
2. (im religiösen Sinn) heaven ['hevn]
hinauf up [ʌp] • **den Hügel hinauf** up the hill
hinaufklettern (auf) climb [klaɪm] • **Klettere auf einen Baum.** Climb a tree.
hinaus out [aʊt] • **aus ... hinaus** out of ... ['aʊt_əv]
hindern: jn./etwas daran hindern, etwas zu tun prevent sb./sth. from doing sth. [prɪ'vent]
hindurch: das ganze Jahr hindurch all year round • **den ganzen Oktober hindurch** throughout October [θruː'aʊt]
hinein: in ... hinein into ... [ˈɪntə, ˈɪntʊ]
hinfallen fall [fɔːl]; fall down
hinkommen (gelangen) get [get]
Hinrichtung execution [ˌeksɪ'kjuːʃn]
hinsetzen: sich hinsetzen sit down [ˌsɪt 'daʊn]
hinstellen: sich hinstellen stand (up) [ˌstænd_'ʌp]
hinten (im Zimmer) at the back (of the room) [bæk]
hinter behind [bɪ'haɪnd] • **im hinteren Teil (des Zimmers)** at the back (of the room) [bæk]
Hintergrund background ['bækgraʊnd]
hinterherjagen: jm. hinterherjagen chase sb. [tʃeɪs]
Hintertür back door
hinüber across [ə'krɒs] • **hinüber zu/nach ...** over to ... ['əʊvə]
hinunter down [daʊn]
hinzufügen (zu) add (to) [æd]
Hiphop hip hop ['hɪp ˌhɒp]
Hirsch deer, pl deer [dɪə]
Hobby hobby ['hɒbi], pl hobbies
hoch high [haɪ], (Gebäude, Baum) tall [tɔːl]
hochheben pick up [ˌpɪk_'ʌp]; lift [lɪft]

Hochschulabschluss: den Hochschulabschluss machen graduate ['grædʒueɪt] (BE)
Hochschule college ['kɒlɪdʒ]
hochsehen (von) look up (from) [ˌlʊk_'ʌp]
Hochverrat treason ['triːzn]
Hockey hockey ['hɒki]
Hockeyplatz, -feld hockey pitch [pɪtʃ]
Hockeyschuhe hockey shoes ['hɒki ʃuːz]
Hof yard [jɑːd] • **auf dem Hof** in the yard
hoffen hope [həʊp] • **Ich hoffe es.** I hope so.
Hoffnung hope [həʊp]
hoffnungslos hopeless ['həʊpləs]
hoffnungsvoll hopeful ['həʊpfʊl]
höflich polite [pə'laɪt]
Höhepunkt highlight ['haɪlaɪt]
höher (als jd.) (ranghöher) senior (to sb.) ['siːnɪə]
holen (besorgen) get [get]; fetch [fetʃ]
Holz wood [wʊd]
horchen (auf) listen (for)
hören hear [hɪə] • **Na hör mal! Come on.** [ˌkʌm_'ɒn] • **Sie hören gerade Radio Bristol** You're tuned to Radio Bristol [tjuːnd]
Horizont skyline ['skaɪˌlaɪn]
Horror horror ['hɒrə]
Hose trousers (pl) ['traʊzəz] (BE); pants (pl) [pænts] (AE)
Hotel hotel [həʊ'tel]
Hotline hotline ['hɒtlaɪn]
hübsch pretty ['prɪti]; (schön; wunderbar) lovely ['lʌvli]
Hubschrauber helicopter ['helɪkɒptə]
Hügel hill [hɪl]
hügelig hilly ['hɪli]
Huhn chicken ['tʃɪkɪn]
Hülle cover ['kʌvə]
Hund dog [dɒg]
hundert hundred ['hʌndrəd]
Hunger haben, hungrig sein be hungry ['hʌŋgri]
Hurra! Hooray! [hu'reɪ]
Hut hat [hæt]
Hütte cabin ['kæbɪn]; hut [hʌt]

I

ich I [aɪ] • **Ich auch.** Me too. [ˌmiː'tuː] • **Das bin ich.** That's me. **Warum ich?** Why me?
ideal perfect ['pɜːfɪkt]
Idee idea [aɪ'dɪə]
Identität identity [aɪ'dentɪti]
Igel hedgehog ['hedʒhɒg]
ihm him; (bei Dingen, Tieren) it

ihn him; (bei Dingen, Tieren) it
ihnen them [ðəm, ðem]
Ihnen (höfliche Anrede) you [juː]
ihr (Plural von „du") you [juː]
ihr: Hilf ihr. Help her. [hə, hɜː]
ihr(e) ... (besitzanzeigend) (zu „she") her ... [hə, hɜː]; (zu „they") their ... [ðeə]
Ihr(e) ... (höfliche Anrede) your ... [jɔː]
ihrer, ihre, ihrs (zu „she") hers [hɜːz]; (zu „they") theirs [ðeəz]
Ihrer, Ihre, Ihrs (höfliche Anrede) yours [jɔːz]
illegal illegal [ɪ'liːgl]
illustrieren illustrate ['ɪləstreɪt]
im: im Allgemeinen generally ['dʒenrəli] • **im Ausland** abroad [ə'brɔːd] • **im Fernsehen** on TV • **im Flugzeug** on the plane • **im Haus der Shaws** at the Shaws' house • **im hinteren Teil (des Zimmers)** at the back (of the room) [bæk] • **im Internet surfen** surf the internet • **im Jahr 2050** in 2050 • **im Mai** in May • **im Radio** on the radio • **im Zug** on the train
immer always ['ɔːlweɪz] • **immer noch** still [stɪl]
in in • **in ... (hinein)** into ... ['ɪntə, 'ɪntʊ] • **in der ...straße** in ... Street • **in der Hamiltonstraße 7** at 7 Hamilton Street • **in der Nacht** at night • **in der Nähe von** near • **in der Pause** (zwischen Schulstunden) at break • **in der Schule** at school • **in der Stadt umher** around the town • **in die falsche Richtung** the wrong way • **in die Sauna gehen** have a sauna • **in die Stadt** into town • **in Eile sein** be in a hurry • **in den Zug/Bus einsteigen** get on the train/bus • **ins Bett gehen** go to bed • **ins Kino gehen** go to the cinema • **in Schwierigkeiten sein** be in trouble ['trʌbl] • **in seiner Straße** in/on his street • **in Urlaub fahren** go on holiday • **in Urlaub sein** be on holiday • **in welche Richtung?** which way? • **Ich bin noch nie in Bath gewesen.** I've never been to Bath.
Indianer/in Native American [ˌneɪtɪv_ə'merɪkən]; Indian ['ɪndɪən]
indirekt: indirekte Rede indirect speech [ˌɪndə'rekt]
Industrie industry ['ɪndəstri]
industriell industrial [ɪn'dʌstrɪəl]
Infinitiv infinitive [ɪn'fɪnətɪv]
Informatik computer science [kəmˌpjuːtə'saɪəns]

Information(en) (über) information (about/on) (no pl) [ˌɪnfə'meɪʃn]
Informationsblatt handout [ˌhænd_ˌaʊt]
Informationstechnologie (IT) information technology (IT) [tek'nɒlədʒi], [ˌaɪ'tiː]
informieren: jn. (über etwas) informieren inform sb. (about/of sth.) [ɪn'fɔːm]
Ingenieur/in engineer [ˌendʒɪ'nɪə]
Inliner skates [skeɪts] • **Inliner fahren** skate
innen (drin) inside [ˌɪn'saɪd]
Innen- inside [ˌɪn'saɪd]
Innenstadt city centre [ˌsɪti 'sentə]
Innovation innovation [ˌɪnə'veɪʃn]
Insekt insect ['ɪnsekt]
Insel island ['aɪlənd]
Inserat advert ['ædvɜːt]; ad [æd]
Installation installation [ˌɪnstə'leɪʃn]
installieren install [ɪn'stɔːl]
Instrument instrument ['ɪnstrəmənt]
interessant interesting ['ɪntrəstɪŋ]
interessieren: jn. interessieren interest sb. ['ɪntrəst] • **sich interessieren (für)** be interested (in); care (about) [keə]
interessiert (an) interested (in) ['ɪntrəstɪd]
international international [ˌɪntə'næʃnəl]
Internet internet ['ɪntənet] • **im Internet surfen** surf the internet
interviewen interview ['ɪntəvjuː]
irgendetwas anything ['eniθɪŋ] **Habt ihr irgendetwas Besonderes gemacht?** Did you do anything special?
irgendjemand anybody ['enibɒdi]; anyone ['eniwʌn]
irgendwelche any ['eni]
irgendwie somehow ['sʌmhaʊ] **irgendwie unheimlich** kind of scary [kaɪnd] (infml)
irgendwo(hin) somewhere ['sʌmweə]; anywhere ['eniweə]
IT (Informationstechnologie) IT (information technology) [ˌaɪ 'tiː], [tek'nɒlədʒi]

J

ja yes [jes]
Jacke, Jackett jacket ['dʒækɪt]
Jagd hunt [hʌnt]
jagen (Tiere) hunt [hʌnt]; (verfolgen) chase [tʃeɪs]
Jahr year [jɪə] • **im Jahr 2050** in 2050 • **Kleider aus den 60er Jahren** dresses from the 60s

Dictionary (German – English)

['sɪkstɪz] • **ein 70-jähriger Lehrer** a 70-year-old teacher
Jahrestag anniversary [,ænɪ'vɜːsəri]
Jahreszeit season ['siːzn]
Jahrgangsstufe year [jɪə] (BE); grade [greɪd] (AE)
Jahrhundert century ['sentʃəri]
Januar January ['dʒænjuəri]
Jazz jazz [dʒæz]
je (jemals) ever ['evə]
Jeans jeans (pl) [dʒiːnz]
jede(r, s) ... (Begleiter) 1. every ... ['evri] 2. (jeder einzelne) each ... [iːtʃ]
jeder (alle) everybody ['evribɒdi]; everyone ['evriwʌn]
jemals ever ['evə]
jemand somebody ['sʌmbədi]; someone ['sʌmwʌn]; (irgendjemand) anybody ['enibɒdi]; anyone ['eniwʌn]
jemand anders somebody else [els]
sonst jemand anybody else
jene(r, s) (Singular) that [ðæt, ðæt]; (Plural) those [ðəʊz] • **an jenem Tag** that day
jetzt now [naʊ] • **jetzt gerade, jetzt sofort** right now • **bis jetzt** so far
Job job [dʒɒb]
Jogurt yogurt ['jɒɡət]
Journalist/in journalist ['dʒɜːnəlɪst]
jubeln cheer [tʃɪə]
jüdisch Jewish ['dʒuːɪʃ]
Judo judo ['dʒuːdəʊ] • **Judo machen** do judo
Jugend youth [juːθ]
Jugend- junior ['dʒuːniə]
Jugendgruppe youth group ['juːθ ˌɡruːp]
Jugendherberge youth hostel ['juːθ ˌhɒstəl]
Jugendliche(r) kid [kɪd]; teenager ['tiːneɪdʒə]
Juli July [dʒu'laɪ]
jung young [jʌŋ]
Junge boy [bɔɪ]
Juni June [dʒuːn]
Junioren- junior ['dʒuːniə]

K

Kaffee coffee ['kɒfi] • **Kaffee zum Mitnehmen** coffee to go
Käfig cage [keɪdʒ]
Kai quay [kiː]
Kalender calendar ['kælɪndə]
kalt cold [kəʊld]
Kamel camel ['kæml]
Kamera camera ['kæmərə]
Kampf fight [faɪt]
kämpfen (für, um) fight (for) [faɪt]
Kanal canal [kə'næl]
Känguru kangaroo [,kæŋɡə'ruː]

Kaninchen rabbit ['ræbɪt]
Kante rim [rɪm]
Kanu canoe [kə'nuː] • **Kanu fahren** canoe
kapieren: Das kapier ich nicht. I don't get it.
Kapitän/in captain ['kæptɪn]
Kappe cap [kæp]
kaputt broken ['brəʊkən] • **kaputt gehen** break [breɪk] • **kaputt machen** break [breɪk]
Karotte carrot ['kærət]
Karren cart [kɑːt]
Karriere career [kə'rɪə]
Karte (Post-, Spielkarte) card [kɑːd]
Kartoffel potato [pə'teɪtəʊ], pl potatoes
Kartoffelchips crisps (pl) [krɪsps] (BE); potato chips (pl) [pə'teɪtəʊ ˌtʃɪps] (AE)
Karussel merry-go-round ['meriɡəʊˌraʊnd]
Käse cheese [tʃiːz]
Kasino (Spielkasino) casino [kə'siːnəʊ]
Kasse (für den Verkauf von Eintrittskarten) ticket office ['tɪkɪt ˌɒfɪs] (Theater-, Kinokasse) box office ['bɒks ˌɒfɪs]
Kästchen, Kasten box [bɒks]
Kathedrale cathedral [kə'θiːdrəl]
Katze cat [kæt]
kaufen buy [baɪ]
Kaufhaus department store [dɪ'pɑːtmənt stɔː]
kaum: Sie glaubte ihren Augen kaum. She couldn't believe her eyes.
Kehle throat [θrəʊt]
kehren sweep [swiːp]
kein(e) no; not a; not (...) any • **Ich habe keinen Stuhl.** I haven't got a chair. • **Ich mag kein(e) ...** I don't like ... • **keine Musik mehr** no more music
Keks biscuit ['bɪskɪt] (BE); cookie ['kʊki] (AE)
kennen know [nəʊ]
kennenlernen meet [miːt] • **Nett, dich/euch/Sie kennenzulernen.** Nice to meet you.
kennzeichnen mark up [,mɑːk ˈʌp]
Kerl guy [ɡaɪ]
Kerze candle ['kændl]
Ketchup ketchup ['ketʃəp]
Keyboard (elektronisches Tasteninstrument) keyboard ['kiːbɔːd]
Kilogramm, Kilo (kg) kilogram, kilo (kg) ['kɪləɡræm] • **ein Kilogramm Orangen** a kilogram of oranges **ein 150 Kilogramm schwerer Bär** a 150-kilogram bear

Kilometer kilometre (km) ['kɪləmiːtə] • **eine Zehn-Kilometer-Wanderung** a ten-kilometre walk
Kind child [tʃaɪld], pl children ['tʃɪldrən]; kid [kɪd]
Kindergarten kindergarten ['kɪndəɡɑːtn]
Kino cinema ['sɪnəmə] • **ins Kino gehen** go to the cinema
Kinokasse box office ['bɒks ˌɒfɪs]
Kirche church [tʃɜːtʃ] • **in die Kirche gehen** go to church
Kiste box [bɒks]
Klammer (in Texten) bracket ['brækɪt] **eckige Klammern** square brackets [skweə] • **runde Klammern** round brackets [raʊnd]
Klang sound [saʊnd]
klappen (funktionieren) work out [ˌwɜːk ˈaʊt]
klar clear [klɪə] • **Aber klar!** You bet!
Klarinette clarinet [ˌklærɪ'net]
Klasse class [klɑːs]; form [fɔːm]
klasse great [ɡreɪt]; neat (AE, infml) [niːt]; awesome ['ɔːsəm] (AE, infml)
Klassenarbeit test [test]
Klassenkamerad/in classmate ['klɑːsmeɪt]
Klassenlehrer/in class teacher; form teacher
Klassenzimmer classroom ['klɑːsruːm]
klassisch (typisch, zeitlos) classic [klæsɪk]; (Musik) classical ['klæsɪkl]
klatschen 1. Beifall klatschen clap [klæp]
2. (tratschen) gossip ['ɡɒsɪp]
Klavier piano [pi'ænəʊ] • **Klavier spielen** play the piano
kleben: (auf-, ein)kleben glue [ɡluː]
Klebestift glue stick ['ɡluː stɪk]
Klebstoff glue [ɡluː]
Kleid dress [dres]
kleiden: sich kleiden dress [dres]
Kleiderschrank wardrobe ['wɔːdrəʊb]
Kleidung, Kleidungsstücke clothes (pl) [kləʊðz, kləʊz], clothing ['kləʊðɪŋ]
Kleidungsstück piece of clothing
klein little ['lɪtl]; small [smɔːl]
Kleinbuchstabe small letter
Kleinstadt town [taʊn]
klettern climb [klaɪm] • **Klettere auf einen Baum.** Climb a tree.
Klingel bell [bel]
klingeln ring [rɪŋ]
Klingelton ringtone ['rɪŋtəʊn]
klingen sound [saʊnd]
Klinik clinic ['klɪnɪk]
klopfen (an) knock (on) [nɒk]
Klub club [klʌb]
klug clever ['klevə]
Klugheit cleverness ['klevənəs]

Dictionary (German – English)

knapp: Das war knapp. That was close. [kləʊs]
Kneipe pub [pʌb]
Knie knee [niː]
Knochen bone [bəʊn]
Knopf button [ˈbʌtn]
Koch cook [kʊk]
kochen 1. *(Essen zubereiten)* cook [kʊk]
2. *(zum Kochen bringen)* boil [bɔɪl]
Köchin cook [kʊk]
Koje *(Etagenbett)* bunk (bed) [bʌŋk]
Kollokation collocation [ˌkɒləˈkeɪʃn]
Kolonie colony [ˈkɒləni]
Kolonist/in colonist [ˈkɒlənɪst]
komisch *(witzig)* funny [ˈfʌni]
Komma: elf Komma vier (11,4) eleven point four (11.4)
kommen come [kʌm]; *(hinkommen)* get [get] • **Ich komme aus …** I'm from … • **Wo kommst du her?** Where are you from? • **nach Hause kommen** come home; get home • **nicht nach Hause kommen** stay out • **zu spät kommen** be late • **Kommt nicht in Frage!** No way! • **Ach komm!** Come on. [ˌkʌmˈɒn] • **Na los, komm.** Come on. • **Wie komme ich am besten dahin?** What's the best way to get there?
Kommentar comment [ˈkɒment]
Komödie comedy [ˈkɒmədi]
König king [kɪŋ]
Königin queen [kwiːn]
königlich, Königs- royal [ˈrɔɪəl]
können can [kən, kæn]; be able to [ˈeɪbl]
konnte(n): ich/er konnte … I/he could … [kəd, kʊd]
könnte(n): ich/er könnte … I/he could … [kəd, kʊd] • **du könntest (vielleicht) Hilfe brauchen** you might need help [maɪt]
Konsequenz consequence [ˈkɒnsɪkwəns]
Kontakt contact [ˈkɒntækt] • **Kontakt halten** keep in touch [tʌtʃ] • **mit jm. Kontakt aufnehmen** contact sb.
Kontext context [ˈkɒntekst]
Kontinent continent [ˈkɒntɪnənt]
Kontrabass bass, double bass [ˌdʌbl ˈbeɪs]
Kontrolle: unter Kontrolle under control [kənˈtrəʊl]
kontrollieren *(prüfen)* check [tʃek]
Konzert concert [ˈkɒnsət] • **ein Konzert geben** do a gig *(infml)* **Open-Air-Konzert, Konzert im Freien** open-air concert [ˌəʊpən ˈeə ˌkɒnsət]

Kopf head [hed] • **(mit dem Kopf) nicken** nod (your head) [nɒd] **den Kopf schütteln** shake your head [ʃeɪk]
Kopfhörer headphones *(pl)* [ˈhedfəʊnz]
Kopfschmerzen headache [ˈhedeɪk]
Kopie copy [ˈkɒpi]
kopieren copy [ˈkɒpi]
Korb basket [ˈbɑːskɪt] • **ein Korb Äpfel** a basket of apples
Körper body [ˈbɒdi]
körperbehindert disabled [dɪsˈeɪbld]
korrekt correct [kəˈrekt]
Korrektur correction [kəˈrekʃn]
Korridor hallway [ˈhɔːlweɪ] *(AE)*
korrigieren correct [kəˈrekt]
kosten *(Essen probieren)* try [traɪ]; taste [teɪst]
kosten cost [kɒst] • **Er/Sie/Es kostet 1 Pfund.** It's £1. • **Sie kosten 35 Pence.** They are 35 p. • **Wie viel kostet/kosten …?** How much is/are …?
Kosten cost [kɒst]
kostenlos free [friː]
köstlich delicious [dɪˈlɪʃəs]
Kostüm *(Verkleidung)* costume [ˈkɒstjuːm]
Kram stuff [stʌf]
krank ill [ɪl]; sick [sɪk]
kränken: jn. kränken *(aus der Fassung bringen)* upset sb. [ʌpˈset]
Krankenhaus hospital [ˈhɒspɪtl] • **Er ist im Krankenhaus.** He's in hospital. • **Er ist ins Krankenhaus gegangen.** He's gone to hospital.
Krankenwagen ambulance [ˈæmbjələns]
Krankheit *(allgemein)* illness [ˈɪlnəs]; *(ansteckend)* disease [dɪˈziːz]
Kraut herb [hɜːb]
Krawall *(Aufruhr)* riot [ˈraɪət]
kreativ creative [kriˈeɪtɪv]
Kreis circle [ˈsɜːkl]
kreuzen; sich kreuzen cross [krɒs]
Kricket cricket [ˈkrɪkɪt]
Krieg war [wɔː]
kriegen get [get]
Krimi crime film [ˈkraɪm ˌfɪlm]; crime story [ˈkraɪm ˌstɔːri]
Kriminalität crime [kraɪm]
Krise crisis [ˈkraɪsɪs]
Kritiker/in critic [ˈkrɪtɪk]
Krokodil crocodile [ˈkrɒkədaɪl]
Krug jug [dʒʌg] • **ein Krug Orangensaft** a jug of orange juice
Küche kitchen [ˈkɪtʃn]
Kuchen cake [keɪk]
Kugelschreiber pen [pen]
Kuh cow [kaʊ]
kühl cool [kuːl]

Kühlschrank fridge [frɪdʒ]
Kummer worry [ˈwʌri]
kümmern: sich um etwas/jn. kümmern look after sth./sb. [ˌlʊk ˈɑːftə]; care about sth./sb. [keə]; take care of sth./sb. • **Kümmer dich nicht drum.** Never mind. [ˌnevə ˈmaɪnd] **Kümmere dich um deine eigenen Angelegenheiten!** Mind your own business. [ˌmaɪnd jər ˌəʊn ˈbɪznəs]
Kunst art [ɑːt]
Kunst-, künstlich artificial [ˌɑːtɪˈfɪʃl]
Kunststoff plastic [ˈplæstɪk]
Kürbis squash, *pl* squash [skwɒʃ]
Kurs course [kɔːs]; class [klɑːs]
kurz short [ʃɔːt]; a short time **kurze Hose** shorts *(pl)* [ʃɔːts]
Kuss kiss [kɪs]
küssen: (sich) küssen kiss [kɪs]
Küste coast [kəʊst]

L

lächeln smile [smaɪl]; give a smile
Lächeln smile [smaɪl]
lachen laugh [lɑːf] • **laut lachen** laugh out loud
Lachs salmon *pl* salmon [ˈsæmən]
Lack paint [peɪnt]
Laden *(Geschäft)* shop [ʃɒp]
Ladentisch counter [ˈkaʊntə]
Lage: in der Lage sein, etwas zu tun be able to do sth. [ˈeɪbl]
Lager camp [kæmp]
Lampe lamp [læmp]
Land *(auch als Gegensatz zur Stadt)* country [ˈkʌntri]; *(Grund und Boden)* land [lænd] • **auf dem Land** *(im Gegensatz zur Stadt)* in the country; *(nicht auf dem Wasser)* on land
landen land [lænd]
Landkarte map [mæp]
Landschaft scenery [ˈsiːnəri]
Landwirt/in farmer [ˈfɑːmə]
Landwirtschaft agriculture [ˈægrɪkʌltʃə]
lang long [lɒŋ] • **drei Tage lang** for three days • **einen Moment lang** for a moment • **lange** a long time
langsam slow [sləʊ]
langweilen: sich langweilen get bored [bɔːd]
langweilig boring [ˈbɔːrɪŋ]
Lärm noise [nɔɪz]
lärmend noisy [ˈnɔɪzi]
Lasagne lasagne [ləˈzænjə]
lassen let [let] • **Lass uns … / Lasst uns …** Let's … • **Lass das!** Stop that!
Lauf run [rʌn] • **im Laufe der Zeit** over time

Laufbahn *(Sport)* running track [træk]
laufen run [rʌn]; go for a run • **gut laufen** *(gutgehen)* go well
Läufer/in runner [ˈrʌnə]
Laufschuhe running shoes
laut loud [laʊd]; *(lärmend)* noisy [ˈnɔɪzi] • **laut lachen** laugh out loud
Laut sound [saʊnd]
läuten ring [rɪŋ]
leben live [lɪv]; be alive [əˈlaɪv]
Leben life [laɪf], *pl* lives [laɪvz] • **am Leben sein** be alive [əˈlaɪv] • **das Leben als Erwachsene/r** adult life • **etwas am Leben halten** keep sth. alive [əˈlaɪv]
Lebensart way of life
lebenslängliche Haftstrafe life sentence [ˈlaɪf ˌsentəns]
Lebensmittel food [fuːd]
lecker delicious [dɪˈlɪʃəs]; yummy [ˈjʌmi] *(infml)*
Leder leather [ˈleðə]
ledig single [ˈsɪŋgl]
leer empty [ˈempti]
legen *(hin-, ablegen)* put [pʊt]
lehren teach [tiːtʃ]
Lehrer/in teacher [ˈtiːtʃə]
Lehrerkollegium staff [stɑːf]
Lehrgang course [kɔːs]; workshop [ˈwɜːkʃɒp]
Lehrpfad trail [treɪl]
Leibwächter/in, Leibwache bodyguard [ˈbɒdigɑːd]
leicht *(nicht schwierig)* easy [ˈiːzi]
Leichtathletik athletics [æθˈletɪks]
leid: Tut mir leid. I'm sorry. [ˈsɒri]
leiden (an) suffer (from) [ˈsʌfə]
leider I'm afraid [əˈfreɪd]
leihen: jm. etwas leihen lend sb. sth. [lend] • **sich etwas leihen** borrow sth. [ˈbɒrəʊ]
leise quiet [ˈkwaɪət] • **leise sein** keep quiet [kiːp]
Leiter *(die)* ladder [ˈlædə]
Leiter/in *(Anführer/in)* leader [ˈliːdə]
Lektion *(im Schulbuch)* unit [ˈjuːnɪt]
lenken steer [stɪə]
lernen learn [lɜːn]; study [ˈstʌdi]
Lern- und Arbeitstechniken study skills [ˈstʌdi skɪlz]
lesen read [riːd]
Leser/in reader [ˈriːdə]
letzte(r, s) last [lɑːst]; final [ˈfaɪnl] • **ein Schuss in der letzten Minute** a last-minute shot [ˌlɑːst ˈmɪnɪt]
leuchten flash [flæʃ]
leuchtend bright [braɪt]
Leute people [ˈpiːpl]; guys [gaɪz]; folks [fəʊks] *(infml, besonders AE)*
Lexikon encyclopedia [ɪnˌsaɪkləˈpiːdiə]

Licht light [laɪt]
Lichtblitz flash [flæʃ]
Liebe love [lʌv]
Liebe Grüße, ... *(Briefschluss)* Love ... [lʌv]
lieben love [lʌv] • **etwas sehr lieben** love sth. very much
lieber: etwas lieber mögen like sth. better • **etwas lieber tun (als etwas)** prefer to do sth. (to sth.) [prɪˈfɜː]
Lieber Jay, ... Dear Jay ... [dɪə]
Liebling dear [dɪə]; love [lʌv]; sweetheart [ˈswiːthɑːt]; *(Favorit/in)* favourite [ˈfeɪvərɪt]
Lieblings-: meine Lieblingsfarbe my favourite colour [ˈfeɪvərɪt]
Lied song [sɒŋ]
Liedtext(e) lyrics *(pl)* [ˈlɪrɪks]
liefern deliver [dɪˈlɪvə]
liegen lie [laɪ] • **Das liegt bei dir.** That's up to you. • **Recycling liegt mir am Herzen.** I care about recycling.
lila purple [ˈpɜːpl]
Limonade lemonade [ˌleməˈneɪd]; soda [ˈsəʊdə] *(AE)*
Lineal ruler [ˈruːlə]
Linie *(U-Bahn)* line [laɪn]
linke(r, s) left [left] • **links, auf der linken Seite** on the left • **(nach) links abbiegen** turn left *(BE)*; take a left *(AE)* • **nach links** to the left • **nach links schauen** look left
Linse *(Hülsenfrucht)* lentil [ˈlentəl]
Lippe lip [lɪp]
Liste list [lɪst]
Livekonzert live concert [laɪv]
Livemusik live music [laɪv]
Loch hole [həʊl]
Löffel spoon [spuːn]
Logo logo [ˈləʊgəʊ]
lohnen: Es lohnt sich. It's worth it. [wɜːθ] • **Es lohnt sich nicht.** It isn't worth it. • **es lohnt sich, etwas zu tun** it is worth doing sth.
Lokal *(Kneipe)* pub [pʌb]
lokal local [ˈləʊkl]
löschen: ein Feuer löschen put out a fire
lösen *(Problem usw.)* solve [sɒlv]
losfahren go off
losgehen *(auch Waffe)* go off
Losung slogan [ˈsləʊgən]
Löwe lion [ˈlaɪən]
Luft air [eə]
Luftballon balloon [bəˈluːn]
Lust: die Lust an etwas verlieren get tired of sth. [ˈtaɪəd]

M

machen do [duː]; make [meɪk] • **die Hausaufgabe(n) machen** do homework • **einen Ausflug machen** go on a trip • **eine Pause machen** take a break • **einen Spaziergang machen** go for a walk; go on a walk • **eine Spritzfahrt/-tour machen** take a ride • **eine Übung machen** do an exercise • **etwas falsch/richtig machen** get sth. wrong/right • **Ferien machen** be on holiday • **Fotos machen** take photos • **jm. Vorwürfe machen (wegen)** blame sb. (for) [bleɪm] • **jn. zu etwas machen** make sb. sth. • **Judo machen** do judo **Macht nichts.** Never mind. [ˌnevə ˈmaɪnd] • **sich Notizen machen** take notes • **Schritte machen** take steps • **sich Sorgen machen (wegen, um)** worry (about) [ˈwʌri] • **(Zauber-) Kunststücke machen** do tricks **Reiten macht Spaß.** Riding is fun.
Macht: etwas in seine Macht bringen take sth. over
Mädchen girl [gɜːl]
Magazin *(Zeitschrift)* magazine [ˌmægəˈziːn]
Magen stomach [ˈstʌmək]
Magenschmerzen stomach ache [ˈstʌmək ˌeɪk]
mähen: Rasen mähen cut the grass [grɑːs]
Mahlzeit meal [miːl]
Mai May [meɪ]
Mais corn *(no pl)* [kɔːn] *(AE)*; maize *(no pl)* [meɪz] *(BE)*
Make-up make-up [ˈmeɪkʌp]
Mal(e); -mal time(s) [taɪm(z)] • **zum ersten Mal** for the first time
malen paint [peɪnt]
Maler/in painter [ˈpeɪntə]
Malerei painting [ˈpeɪntɪŋ]
Mama mum [mʌm]; mom *(AE)* [mɑːm]
man you [juː] • **Man sagt, ...** They say ...
Manager/in manager [ˈmænədʒə]
manchmal sometimes [ˈsʌmtaɪmz]
Mann man [mæn], *pl* men [men]
Mann! boy! *(AE, infml)*
Männchen male [meɪl]
Mannschaft team [tiːm]; crew [kruː]
Mappe *(des Sprachenportfolios)* dossier [ˈdɒsieɪ]
Markenzeichen logo [ˈləʊgəʊ]
markieren mark up [ˌmɑːk ˈʌp]
Markt market [ˈmɑːkɪt] • **auf den Markt bringen** *(CD, Film usw.)* release [rɪˈliːs]

Marmelade (*Orangenmarmelade*) marmalade ['mɑːməleɪd]
Marsch march [mɑːtʃ]; (*Wanderung*) hike; walk
März March [mɑːtʃ]
Maschine machine [məˈʃiːn]
Massage massage [ˈmæsɑːʒ]
massieren: sich massieren lassen have a massage [ˈmæsɑːʒ]
Material material [məˈtɪərɪəl]
Mathematik maths [mæθs]
Mauer wall [wɔːl]
Maultier mule [mjuːl]
Maultierkarawane mule train [treɪn]
Maulwurf mole [məʊl]
Maus mouse [maʊs], *pl* mice [maɪs]
Medaille medal [ˈmedl]
Mediation (*Sprachmittlung*) mediation [ˌmiːdiˈeɪʃn]
Medien media (*pl*) [ˈmiːdiə]
Meer sea [siː]
Meerschweinchen guinea pig [ˈɡɪni pɪɡ]
mehr more [mɔː] • **mehr als** more than • **mehr als ich** more than me • **mehr oder weniger** more or less • **nicht mehr** not (...) any more • **viel mehr** lots more • **keine Musik mehr** no more music
mehr- multi- [ˈmʌlti] • **mehrfarbig** multi-coloured [ˌmʌltiˈkʌləd]
mehrere several [ˈsevrəl]
Mehrheit majority [məˈdʒɒrəti]
Meile (= *ca. 1,6 km*) mile [maɪl]
meilenweit for miles [maɪlz]
mein(e) ... my ... [maɪ] • **meine neuen** my new ones [wʌnz]
meinen (*glauben, denken*) think [θɪŋk]; (*sagen wollen*) mean [miːn] **Meinst du wirklich?** Do you really think so?
meiner, meine, meins mine [maɪn]
Meinung (zu/von) view (on/of) [vjuː]; opinion [əˈpɪnjən] (on/of) **anderer Meinung sein (als)** disagree (with) [ˌdɪsəˈɡriː] • **meiner Meinung nach** in my opinion
meist: (der/die/das) meiste ...; am meisten most [məʊst] • **die meisten Leute** most people
meistens usually [ˈjuːʒuəli]
Meister/in (*Champion*) champion [ˈtʃæmpiən]
Meisterschaft championship [ˈtʃæmpiənʃɪp]
melden: sich freiwillig melden volunteer [ˌvɒlənˈtɪə]
melken milk [mɪlk]
Melodie tune [tjuːn]
Menge 1. (*Menschenmenge*) crowd [kraʊd]

2. **eine Menge** (*viel, viele*) a lot (of) [lɒt]; lots (of)
Mensch human [ˈhjuːmən]
Mensch! boy! (*AE, infml*)
Menschen people [ˈpiːpl] • **voller Menschen** crowded [ˈkraʊdɪd]
Menschenmenge crowd [kraʊd]
menschliches Wesen human [ˈhjuːmən]
Menü 1. (*Restaurant*) set meal [ˌset ˈmiːl]
2. (*Computer*) menu [ˈmenjuː]
merken 1. notice [ˈnəʊtɪs]; (*erkennen*) realize [ˈrɪəlaɪz]
2. **sich etwas merken** remember sth. [rɪˈmembə]
Merkmal characteristic [ˌkærəktəˈrɪstɪk]
Messe (*Gottesdienst*) mass [mæs] **die Messe besuchen** go to mass
Messer knife, *pl* knives [naɪf]
Meter metre [ˈmiːtə]
Methode technique [tekˈniːk]; method [ˈmeθəd]
mich me [miː]; (*Reflexivpronomen*) myself [maɪˈself]
Mikrofon microphone [ˈmaɪkrəfəʊn]
Milch milk [mɪlk]
Milchshake milkshake [ˈmɪlkʃeɪk]
mild mild [maɪld]
Million million [ˈmɪljən]
Millionär/in millionaire [ˌmɪljəˈneə]
Minderheit minority [maɪˈnɒrəti]
Mindmap mind map [ˈmaɪnd mæp]
Minister/in minister [ˈmɪnɪstə]
Minute minute [ˈmɪnɪt] • **ein Schuss in der letzten Minute** a last-minute shot • **eine 30-minütige Fahrt** a 30-minute ride
mir me [miː]; (*Reflexivpronomen*) myself [maɪˈself]
mischen mix [mɪks]
Mischung mixture [ˈmɪkstʃə]
Mist: So ein Mist! What a bummer! [ˈbʌmə] (*infml*)
mit with [wɪð] • **mit dem Auto/Zug/Rad/... fahren** go by car/train/bike/... • **mit 16** at (the age of) 16 • **Mit wem hat sie geredet?** Who did she talk to?
Mitarbeiter/in member of staff [stɑːf] (*BE*); staff member (*AE*)
mitbringen bring [brɪŋ]
mitgenommen (wegen) upset (about) [ˌʌpˈset]
mitmachen join in [dʒɔɪn] • **bei etwas/jm. mitmachen** join sth./sb. [dʒɔɪn]; take part in sth.
Mitschüler/in classmate [ˈklɑːsmeɪt]
Mittagessen lunch [lʌntʃ] • **zum Mittagessen** for lunch

Mittagspause lunch break [ˈlʌntʃ breɪk]
Mittagszeit lunchtime [ˈlʌntʃtaɪm]
Mitte centre [ˈsentə]; middle [ˈmɪdl] **die Mitte der Stadt** the centre of town
mitteilen: jm. etwas mitteilen share sth. (with sb.) [ʃeə]
Mitteilung (*Notiz*) note [nəʊt]
Mittel (*Ressourcen*) resources (*pl*) [rɪˈzɔːsɪs, rɪˈsɔːsɪz]
Mittel- central [ˈsentrəl]
mittel-, mittlere(r,s); mittelgroß medium [ˈmiːdiəm]
Mittwoch Wednesday [ˈwenzdeɪ, ˈwenzdi] (*siehe auch unter „Freitag"*)
mixen mix [mɪks]
Möbel furniture (*no pl*) [ˈfɜːnɪtʃə]
Möbelstück piece of furniture [ˌpiːs əv ˈfɜːnɪtʃə]
Mobiltelefon mobile phone [ˌməʊbaɪl ˈfəʊn]; mobile [ˈməʊbaɪl] (*BE*); cellphone [ˈselfəʊn] (*AE*)
möchte: Ich möchte gern ... (haben) I'd like ... (= I would like ...) [laɪk] **Ich möchte gehen** I'd like to go **Ich möchte nicht gehen** I wouldn't like to go • **Möchtest du / Möchten Sie ...?** Would you like ...?
Mode fashion [ˈfæʃn]
Modell (*-auto, -schiff; Fotomodell*) model [ˈmɒdl]
Moderator/in presenter [prɪˈzentə]
modisch trendy [ˈtrendi]
mögen like [laɪk]; (*sehr mögen*) love [lʌv]; be into sth. (*infml*) • **etwas lieber mögen** like sth. better **etwas sehr mögen** like sth. very much
möglich possible [ˈpɒsəbl]
Möglichkeit possibility [ˌpɒsəˈbɪləti]
Möhre carrot [ˈkærət]
Moment moment [ˈməʊmənt] **einen Moment lang** for a moment • **im Moment** at the moment • **genau in dem Moment** just then **Moment mal!** Wait a minute. [ˈmɪnɪt]
Monat month [mʌnθ]
Monatsfahrkarte (*der Londoner Verkehrsbetriebe*) Travelcard [ˈtrævlkɑːd]
Mond moon [muːn]
Monitor monitor [ˈmɒnɪtə]
Monster monster [ˈmɒnstə]
Montag Monday [ˈmʌndeɪ, ˈmʌndi] (*siehe auch unter „Freitag"*)
Mord murder [ˈmɜːdə] • **im Gefängnis wegen Mordes** in prison for murder
morden murder [ˈmɜːdə]
Mörder/in murderer [ˈmɜːdərə]
morgen tomorrow [təˈmɒrəʊ]

Dictionary (German – English)

Morgen morning [ˈmɔːnɪŋ] • **am Morgen, morgens** in the morning
Moschee mosque [mɒsk]
Motel motel [məʊˈtel]
MP3-Spieler MP3 player [ˌempiːˈθriː ˌpleɪə]
müde tired [taɪəd]
Müll rubbish [ˈrʌbɪʃ] (BE); garbage [ˈɡɑːbɪdʒ] (AE)
Müllabfuhr rubbish collection [ˈrʌbɪʃ kəˌlekʃn]
Mülltonne bin [bɪn]; dustbin [ˈdʌstbɪn]
multi-, Multi- multi- [ˈmʌlti] **Multimillionär/in** multi-millionaire [ˌmʌltiˌmɪljəˈneə]
Mund mouth [maʊθ] • **den Mund halten** shut up [ˌʃʌtˈʌp]
murren grumble [ˈɡrʌmbl]
Museum museum [mjuːˈziːəm]
Musical musical [ˈmjuːzɪkl]
Musik music [ˈmjuːzɪk]
Musiker/in musician [mjuːˈzɪʃn]
Müsli muesli [ˈmjuːzli]
müssen have to; must [mʌst] **nicht müssen** needn't [ˈniːdnt]
mutig brave [breɪv]
Mutter mother [ˈmʌðə]
Mutti mum [mʌm]; mom (AE) [mɑːm]
Mütze cap [kæp]

N

Na ja … / Na gut … Oh well … [əʊ ˈwel]
Na und? So? [səʊ]; So what? [səʊ ˈwɒt]; Who cares? [ˌhuː ˈkeəz]
nach 1. (örtlich) to [tə, tu] • **nach draußen** outside • **nach drinnen** inside • **nach Hause gehen** go home • **nach Hause kommen** come home; get home • **nach oben** up; (im Haus) upstairs [ˌʌpˈsteəz] • **nach unten** down; (im Haus) downstairs [ˌdaʊnˈsteəz] • **nach vorn** to the front [frʌnt]
2. (zeitlich) after • **Viertel nach 11** quarter past 11 [pɑːst]
3. nach etwas fragen ask about sth. [əˈbaʊt] • **jn. nach dem Weg fragen** ask sb. the way
Nachbar/in neighbour [ˈneɪbə]
nachdem after [ˈɑːftə]
nachdenken über think about [θɪŋk]
nachmachen imitate [ˈɪmɪteɪt]
Nachmittag afternoon [ˌɑːftəˈnuːn] • **am Nachmittag, nachmittags** in the afternoon
Nachrichten news (no pl) [njuːz]
Nachrichtenagentur news agency [ˈnjuːz ˌeɪdʒənsi]

nachrufen: jm. Schimpfwörter nachrufen call sb. names
Nachsilbe suffix [ˈsʌfɪks]
nächste(r, s): am nächsten Tag the next day [nekst] • **der Nächste sein** be next • **Was haben wir als Nächstes?** What have we got next?
Nacht night [naɪt] • **heute Nacht** tonight [təˈnaɪt] • **in der Nacht, nachts** at night
Nachteil disadvantage [ˌdɪsədˈvɑːntɪdʒ]
Nachtklub nightclub [ˈnaɪtklʌb]
nahe (bei, an) near [nɪə]; close (to) [kləʊs]
Nähe: in der Nähe von near [nɪə]
nähen sew [səʊ]
Name name [neɪm]
Nase nose [nəʊz]
Nashorn rhino [ˈraɪnəʊ]
nass wet [wet]
Nation nation [ˈneɪʃn] • **die Ersten Nationen** (indianische Ureinwohner/innen Kanadas) the First Nations
national national [ˈnæʃnəl]
Nationalpark national park
natürlich (selbstverständlich) of course [əv ˈkɔːs]
natürlich, Natur- natural [ˈnætʃrəl]
Naturwissenschaft science [ˈsaɪəns]
Nebel fog [fɒɡ]
neben next to [nekst]
nebenbei (bemerkt) by the way
neblig foggy [ˈfɒɡi]
necken tease [tiːz]
nehmen take [teɪk] • **Ich nehme es.** (beim Einkaufen) I'll take it. • **auf den Arm nehmen** (necken) tease [tiːz] • **wichtig nehmen** care (about) [keə]
nein no [nəʊ]
nennen (rufen, bezeichnen) call [kɔːl]; (benennen) name [neɪm]
nervös nervous [ˈnɜːvəs]
nett nice [naɪs] • **Nett, dich/euch/Sie kennenzulernen.** Nice to meet you.
neu new [njuː] • **neu starten** (Computer) restart [ˌriːˈstɑːt]
Neuerung innovation [ˌɪnəˈveɪʃn]
neueste(r, s) latest [ˈleɪtɪst]
nicht not [nɒt] • **auch nicht** not (…) either [ˈaɪðə, ˈiːðə] • **gar nicht** not at all • **nicht mehr** not (…) any more • **nicht nur … sondern auch …** not only … but also … • **Das glaube ich nicht. / Ich glaube nicht.** I don't think so. • **Du brauchst ein …, nicht wahr?** You need a …, right?
noch nicht not (…) yet [jet] • **über-**

haupt nicht not at all
▶ S.206 not at all, no … at all
nichts nothing [ˈnʌθɪŋ]; not (…) anything [ˈeniθɪŋ] • **gar nichts** nothing at all • **Macht nichts.** Never mind. [ˌnevə ˈmaɪnd] • **Nichts zu danken.** You're welcome. [ˈwelkəm] • **überhaupt nichts** nothing at all
▶ S.206 not at all, no … at all
nicken: (mit dem Kopf) nicken nod your head [nɒd]
nie, niemals never [ˈnevə]
niemand nobody [ˈnəʊbədi]; no one [ˈnəʊ wʌn]; not (…) anybody [ˈenibɒdi]; not (…) anyone
nirgendwo(hin) not (…) anywhere [ˈeniweə]
noch: noch ein(e) … another … [əˈnʌðə]; one more … [mɔː] • **noch einmal** again [əˈɡen] • **noch nicht** not (…) yet [jet] • **noch 70 Meter** another 70 metres • **(immer) noch** still [stɪl] • **wer/was/wo/… noch** who/what/where/… else [els]
Nord- northern [ˈnɔːðən]
Norden north [nɔːθ] • **nach Norden** north • **Richtung Norden** northbound [ˈnɔːθbaʊnd]
nördlich north [nɔːθ]; northern [ˈnɔːðən]
Nordosten north-east [ˌnɔːθˈiːst]
nach Nordosten north-east
nordöstlich north-east [ˌnɔːθˈiːst]
Nordwest north-west [ˌnɔːθˈwest]
nach Nordwesten north-west
nordwestlich north-west [ˌnɔːθˈwest]
nörgeln grumble [ˈɡrʌmbl]
normalerweise usually [ˈjuːʒuəli]
Not- emergency [ɪˈmɜːdʒənsi]
Note (Zensur) grade [ɡreɪd] (BE auch: mark [mɑːk])
Noten music [ˈmjuːzɪk] • **Noten lesen** read music
Notfall emergency [ɪˈmɜːdʒənsi]
Notiz note [nəʊt] • **sich Notizen machen** take notes
November November [nəʊˈvembə]
Nr. No. [ˈnʌmbə], pl Nos.
Nu: im Nu in next to no time
null o [əʊ]; zero [ˈzɪərəʊ]; (beim Sport) nil [nɪl]
Nummer number [ˈnʌmbə]
Nummernschild number plate [ˈnʌmbə pleɪt] (BE); license plate [ˈlaɪsns pleɪt] (AE)
nun now [naʊ] • **Nun, …** Well, … [wel]
nur only [ˈəʊnli]; just [dʒʌst] • **nur zum Spaß** just for fun • **nicht nur … sondern auch …** not only … but also …
Nuss nut [nʌt]

nutzen: etwas gemeinsam mit jm. nutzen share sth. (with sb.) [ʃeə]
nützlich helpful [ˈhelpfl]
nutzlos useless [ˈjuːsləs]

O

ob if [ɪf]; whether [ˈweðə] • **Und ob!** You bet!
obdachlos homeless [ˈhəʊmləs]
oben *(an der Spitze)* at the top (of) [tɒp]; *(im Haus)* upstairs [ˌʌpˈsteəz] • **dort oben** up there • **nach oben** up; *(im Haus)* upstairs • **oben auf** on top of
Oberbegriff group word [ˈɡruːp wɜːd]
oberhalb von over [ˈəʊvə]; above [əˈbʌv]
oberste(r, s) top [tɒp]
Oberteil top [tɒp]
Obst fruit [fruːt] • **Obst pflücken** pick fruit [pɪk]
Obstkuchen pie [paɪ]
Obstsalat fruit salad [ˈfruːt ˌsæləd]
obwohl although [ɔːlˈðəʊ]
oder or [ɔː]
Ofen oven [ˈʌvn]
öffentlich public [ˈpʌblɪk] • **öffentlicher Verkehr** public transport [ˈtrænspɔːt]
Öffentlichkeit: die Öffentlichkeit the public [ˈpʌblɪk]
öffnen open [ˈəʊpən]
Öffnungszeiten opening times [ˈəʊpənɪŋ taɪmz]
oft often [ˈɒfn]
ohne without [wɪˈðaʊt]
Ohr ear [ɪə]
Ohrenschmerzen earache [ˈɪəreɪk]
Ohrring earring [ˈɪərɪŋ]
Oje! Oh dear! [əʊ ˈdɪə]
okay OK [əʊˈkeɪ]
Oktober October [ɒkˈtəʊbə]
Oldie oldie [ˈəʊldi] *(infml)*
Olympische Spiele Olympic Games [əˌlɪmpɪk ˈɡeɪmz]
Oma grandma [ˈɡrænmɑː]; granny [ˈɡræni]
Onkel uncle [ˈʌŋkl]
online, Online- online [ˌɒnˈlaɪn]
Opa grandpa [ˈɡrænpɑː]
Open-Air-Konzert open-air concert [ˌəʊpən ˈeə ˌkɒnsət]
Oper, Opernhaus opera (house) [ˈɒprə haʊs]
Operation (an) operation (on) [ˌɒpəˈreɪʃn]
Opfer victim [ˈvɪktɪm]
Orange orange [ˈɒrɪndʒ]
orange(farben) orange [ˈɒrɪndʒ]

Orangenmarmelade marmalade [ˈmɑːməleɪd]
Orangensaft orange juice [ˈɒrɪndʒ dʒuːs]
ordentlich tidy [ˈtaɪdi]
Ordnung: in Ordnung all right [ɔːl ˈraɪt]; fine [faɪn] • **etwas in Ordnung bringen** put sth. in order [ˈɔːdə]
Organisation organization [ˌɔːɡənaɪˈzeɪʃn]
organisieren organize [ˈɔːɡənaɪz]
Original original [əˈrɪdʒənl]
Original- original [əˈrɪdʒənl] • **Originalfassung** original version [ˈvɜːʃn]
Ort place [pleɪs]; location [ləˈkeɪʃn] • **am/vom Ort** local [ˈləʊkl] • **an anderen Orten** in other places • **vor Ort** on the scene [siːn]
örtlich local [ˈləʊkl]
Ost- eastern [ˈiːstən]
Osten east [iːst] • **nach Osten** east **Richtung Osten** eastbound [ˈiːstbaʊnd]
östlich east [iːst]; eastern [ˈiːstən]
Outfit *(Kleidung; Ausrüstung)* outfit [ˈaʊtfɪt]
Ozean ocean [ˈəʊʃn]

P

paar: ein paar some [səm, sʌm]; a couple (of) [ˈkʌpl]; *(einige wenige)* a few [fjuː]
Paar: ein Paar a pair (of) [peə]; a couple (of) [ˈkʌpl]
Päckchen packet [ˈpækɪt] • **ein Päckchen Pfefferminzbonbons** a packet of mints
packen 1. *(Koffer, Auto)* pack [pæk] 2. *(greifen, schnappen)* grab [ɡræb]
Packung packet [ˈpækɪt] • **eine Packung Pfefferminzbonbons** a packet of mints
Paddel paddle [ˈpædl]
paddeln canoe [kəˈnuː]; paddle [ˈpædl]
Paket parcel [ˈpɑːsl]
Palast palace [ˈpæləs]
Panik: in Panik geraten panic [ˈpænɪk]
pantomimisch darstellen mime [maɪm]
Papa dad [dæd]
Papagei parrot [ˈpærət]
Papier paper [ˈpeɪpə]
Parade parade [pəˈreɪd]
Paradies paradise [ˈpærədaɪs]
Paralympische Spiele Paralympics [ˌæpærəˈlɪmpɪks]
Park park [pɑːk]

Parkplatz *(für viele Autos)* car park (BE); parking lot [ˈpɑːkɪŋ lɒt] (AE)
Parlament parliament [ˈpɑːləmənt]
Partner/in partner [ˈpɑːtnə]
Partnerstadt twin town [ˌtwɪn ˈtaʊn] (BE); sister city [ˈsɪstə ˌsɪti] (AE)
Party party [ˈpɑːti]
Passagier/in passenger [ˈpæsɪndʒə]
passen fit [fɪt] • **passen zu** go with
passieren (mit) happen (to) [ˈhæpən]
Passiv passive [ˈpæsɪv]
Pastete pie [paɪ]
Pastor/in *(freikirchlich)* minister [ˈmɪnɪstə]
Patrouille patrol [pəˈtrəʊl]
Pause break [breɪk] • **eine Pause machen** take a break • **in der Pause** *(zwischen Schulstunden)* at break (BE); during recess [ˈriːses] (AE)
peinlich embarrassing [ɪmˈbærəsɪŋ]
Pence pence (p) [pens]
perfekt perfect [ˈpɜːfɪkt]; ultimate [ˈʌltɪmət]
Person person [ˈpɜːsn]
Personal staff [stɑːf]
persönlich personal [ˈpɜːsənl]
Persönlichkeit character [ˈkærəktə] • **berühmte Persönlichkeit** celebrity [səˈlebrəti]
Pfad path [pɑːθ]; *(Lehrpfad)* trail [treɪl]
Pfarrer/in *(freikirchlich)* minister [ˈmɪnɪstə]
Pfefferminzbonbons mints [mɪnts]
Pfeife 1. *(zum Rauchen; Orgelpfeife)* pipe [paɪp] 2. *(Trillerpfeife)* whistle [ˈwɪsl]
pfeifen whistle [ˈwɪsl]
Pfeil arrow [ˈærəʊ]
Pferd horse [hɔːs]
Pferdeschwanz *(Frisur)* ponytail [ˈpəʊniteɪl]
Pfiff whistle [ˈwɪsl]
Pflanze plant [plɑːnt]
pflanzen plant [plɑːnt]
pflücken: Obst/Blumen pflücken pick fruit/flowers [pɪk]
Pfund 1. *(britische Währung)* pound (£) [paʊnd] • **Es kostet 1 Pfund.** It's £1. 2. *(Gewichtseinheit)* pound [paʊnd] • **ein drei Pfund schwerer Ball** a three-pound ball
Piano piano [piˈænəʊ]
Picknick picnic [ˈpɪknɪk]
piepsen bleep [bliːp]
Piepton bleep [bliːp]
Pilger/in pilgrim [ˈpɪlɡrɪm]
Pilot/in pilot [ˈpaɪlət]
pink(farben) pink [pɪŋk]
Pirat/in pirate [ˈpaɪrət]
Pizza pizza [ˈpiːtsə]
Plan plan [plæn]

planen plan [plæn]; programme ['prəʊgræm]
Planet planet ['plænɪt]
Plastik plastic ['plæstɪk]
Platz *(Ort, Stelle)* place [pleɪs]; *(in der Stadt, quadratisch)* square [skweə]; *(in der Stadt, rund)* circus ['sɜːkəs]; *(im Sport)* court [kɔːt]; *(Einsatzort)* location [ləʊ'keɪʃn]; *(Sitz)* seat [siːt]
Plätzchen biscuit ['bɪskɪt]
plaudern chat [tʃæt]
plötzlich sudden ['sʌdn]; suddenly ['sʌdnli]
Pokal cup [kʌp]
Politiker/in politician [ˌpɒlə'tɪʃn]
Politische Bildung Social Studies [ˌsəʊʃl 'stʌdiz]
Politik politics ['pɒlətɪks]
Polizei police *(pl)* [pə'liːs]
Polizeiwache, Polizeirevier police station [pə'liːs steɪʃn]
Poltergeist poltergeist ['pəʊltəgaɪst]
Pommes frites chips *(pl)* [tʃɪps]; (French) fries [ˌfrentʃ 'fraɪz] *(bes. AE)*
Popcorn popcorn ['pɒpkɔːn]
Pop(musik) pop (music) [pɒp]
Popsender pop station ['steɪʃn]
populär popular ['pɒpjələ]
Posaune trombone [trɒm'bəʊn]
Post *(Briefe, Päckchen, …)* post [pəʊst]
Postamt post office ['pəʊst ˌɒfɪs]
Poster poster ['pəʊstə]
Postkarte postcard ['pəʊstkɑːd]
Postskript *(Nachschrift unter Briefen)* postscript ['pəʊstskrɪpt]
Präfix prefix ['priːfɪks]
prahlen show off [ˌʃəʊ 'ɒf]
Präsentation presentation [ˌpreznˈteɪʃn]
präsentieren: (jm.) etwas präsentieren present sth. (to sb.) [prɪ'zent]
Präsident/in president ['prezɪdənt]
Preis 1. *(Kaufpreis)* price [praɪs]; cost [kɒst]
▶ S.222 Verbs & nouns with the same form
2. *(Gewinn)* prize [praɪz]
Premierminister/in prime minister [ˌpraɪm 'mɪnɪstə]
pressen squeeze [skwiːz]
pro per [pɜː, pə] • **einmal/zweimal pro Woche** once/twice a week
Probe *(am Theater)* rehearsal [rɪ'hɜːsl]
proben *(am Theater)* rehearse [rɪ'hɜːs]
probieren try [traɪ]; *(Essen auch:)* taste [teɪst]
Problem problem ['prɒbləm]
produzieren produce [prə'djuːs]
professionell professional [prə'feʃənl]
Programm programme ['prəʊgræm] *(BE)*, program ['prəʊgræm] *(AE)*

programmieren programme ['prəʊgræm]
Projekt (über, zu) project (on, about) ['prɒdʒekt] • **ein Projekt machen, durchführen** do a project
Prominente(r) celebrity [sə'lebrəti]
Prosaliteratur fiction ['fɪkʃn]
Protest protest ['prəʊtest]
protestieren (gegen) protest (against/about) [prə'test]
Prozent per cent (%) [pə'sent]
prüfen *(überprüfen)* check [tʃek]
Prüfung *(Test, Klassenarbeit)* test [test]
PS *(Nachschrift unter Briefen)* PS ['piːˌ'es]
Pullover pullover ['pʊləʊvə]
Punker/in punk [pʌŋk]
Punkt *(bei Test, Quiz)* point [pɔɪnt]
Punktestand score [skɔː]
Puppe doll [dɒl]
pusten blow [bləʊ]
Pute turkey ['tɜːki]
putzen clean [kliːn] • **sich die Zähne putzen** clean your teeth
Putzfrau, -mann cleaner ['kliːnə]

Q

Quadratkilometer square kilometre (sq km) [skweə]
Qualität quality ['kwɒləti]
Quelle 1. *(Informations-, Textquelle)* source [sɔːs] • **eine Quelle angeben** give a source
2. *(Wasser)* spring [sprɪŋ]
Querflöte flute [fluːt]
Quiz quiz [kwɪz], *pl* quizzes ['kwɪzɪz]

R

Rad 1. wheel ['wiːl]
2. *(Fahrrad)* bike [baɪk] • **Rad fahren** cycle ['saɪkl]; ride a bike [ˌraɪd ə 'baɪk]
Radfahrt bike ride ['baɪk raɪd]
Radiergummi rubber ['rʌbə] *(BE)*; eraser [ɪ'reɪzə(r), ɪ'reɪsə(r)] *(bes. AE)*
Radio radio ['reɪdiəʊ] • **im Radio** on the radio • **ein Radio auf einen Sender einstellen** tune a radio to a station [tjuːn] • **ein Radio umschalten** change stations
▶ S.200 (to) change
Radiosender radio station ['steɪʃn]
Radtour bike tour ['baɪk tʊə]
Radweg cycle path ['saɪkl pɑːθ]
Rand rim [rɪm]

rangehen *(Telefon)* answer (the phone) ['ɑːnsə]
ranghöher (als jd.) senior (to sb.) ['siːniə]
Ranger/in ranger ['reɪndʒə]
Rap rap [ræp]
Rapper/in rapper ['ræpə]
Rasen grass [grɑːs] • **Rasen mähen** cut the grass [kʌt]
rasen speed [spiːd]
raten guess [ges]
Ratespiel quiz [kwɪz], *pl* quizzes ['kwɪzɪz]
Rätsel *(Geheimnis)* mystery ['mɪstri]; *(Spiel)* riddle ['rɪdl]
Ratte rat [ræt]
Rauch smoke [sməʊk] • **Wo Rauch ist, ist auch Feuer.** There's no smoke without fire.
rauchen smoke [sməʊk]
Raum room [ruːm]
Reaktion (auf) reaction (to) [ri'ækʃn]
realistisch realistic [ˌriːə'lɪstɪk]
Realität reality [ri'æləti]
Reality-Show reality show [ʃəʊ]
Rechercheur/in researcher [rɪ'sɜːtʃə, 'riːsɜːtʃə]
Recht *(moralisch)* right [raɪt]
Recht haben be right [raɪt]
rechte(r, s) right [raɪt] • **rechts, auf der rechten Seite** on the right • **(nach) rechts abbiegen** turn right *(BE)*; take a right *(AE)* • **nach rechts** to the right • **nach rechts schauen** look right
Rechteckschema grid [grɪd]
rechtzeitig in time [ɪn 'taɪm]
recycelt recycled [ˌriː'saɪkld]
Recycling recycling [ˌriː'saɪklɪŋ]
Redakteur/in editor ['edɪtə]
Rede talk [tɔːk] • **eine Rede halten** make/give a speech [spiːtʃ]
direkte Rede direct speech [də'rekt]
indirekte Rede indirect speech [ˌɪndə'rekt]
reden (mit, über) talk (to, about) [tɔːk]; speak (to, about) [spiːk]
Wovon redest du? What are you talking about?
redigieren edit ['edɪt]
reduzieren: etwas reduzieren (um) reduce sth. (by) [rɪ'djuːs]
Referat talk [tɔːk]
Reflex reflex ['riːfleks]
Regal(brett) shelf [ʃelf], *pl* shelves [ʃelvz]
Regel *(Vorschrift)* rule [ruːl]
regelmäßig regular ['regjələ]
Regen rain [reɪn]
Regenwurm earthworm ['ɜːθwɜːm]
Regenzeit rainy season ['reɪni ˌsiːzn]
Regierung government ['gʌvənmənt]

Dictionary (German – English)

Regisseur/in director [dəˈrektə]
regnen rain [reɪn]
regnerisch rainy [ˈreɪni]
Reh deer, pl deer [dɪə]
reich rich [rɪtʃ]; wealthy [ˈwelθi]
reichen (weitergeben) pass [pɑːs]; hand [hænd]
reichlich plenty of [ˈplenti_əv]
Reichtum wealth [welθ]
reif ripe [raɪp]
Reihe 1. row [rəʊ] • **Du bist an der Reihe.** It's your turn. [tɜːn]
2. (Sendereihe, Serie) series, pl series [ˈsɪəriːz]
3. (wartender Menschen) line [laɪn] (AE); queue [kjuː] (BE)
Reise trip [trɪp]; journey [ˈdʒɜːni] • **eine Reise machen** go on a trip; take a trip (AE)
Reiseleiter/in guide [gaɪd]
reisen travel [ˈtrævl]
reißen tear [teə]
reiten ride [raɪd] • **reiten gehen** go riding
Reiterhelm, -kappe riding hat [hæt]
Reitstiefel riding boots (pl) [buːts]
Reitweg bridle path [ˈbraɪdl pɑːθ]
relaxen chill out [ˌtʃɪl_ˈaʊt] (infml)
Religion religion [rɪˈlɪdʒən] • (Religionsunterricht) RE [ˌɑːr_ˈiː], Religious Education [rɪˌlɪdʒəs_edʒuˈkeɪʃn]
religiös religious [rɪˈlɪdʒəs]
rennen run [rʌn]
Rentner/in senior [ˈsiːniə]
reparieren repair [rɪˈpeə]
Reportage (über) report (on) [rɪˈpɔːt]
Reporter/in reporter [rɪˈpɔːtə]
repräsentieren represent [ˌreprɪˈzent]
Reservat reservation [ˌrezəˈveɪʃn]
Ressourcen resources (pl) [rɪˈzɔːsɪs, rɪˈsɔːsɪz]
Rest rest [rest]
Restaurant restaurant [ˈrestrɒnt]; (Imbissstube, Café) café [ˈkæfeɪ]
Resultat result [rɪˈzʌlt]
retten save [seɪv]
Rettung, Rettungsdienst rescue [ˈreskjuː]
Revolution revolution [ˌrevəˈluːʃn]
Rhythmus rhythm [ˈrɪðəm]
richtig right [raɪt]; (korrekt) correct [kəˈrekt] • **etwas richtig machen** get sth. right
Richtung way [weɪ] • **berufliche Richtung** line of work [ˌlaɪn_əv ˈwɜːk] • **in diese Richtung** this way **in die falsche Richtung** the wrong way • **in welche Richtung?** which way? • **Richtung Norden** northbound [ˈnɔːθbaʊnd] • **Richtung Osten** eastbound [ˈiːstbaʊnd] • **Richtung Süden** southbound

[ˈsaʊθbaʊnd] • **Richtung Westen** westbound [ˈwestbaʊnd]
riechen smell [smel]
Riesen- giant [ˈdʒaɪənt] • **Riesenrad** big wheel [ˌbɪg ˈwiːl]
riesig huge [hjuːdʒ]
riesige(r,s) giant [ˈdʒaɪənt]
Rinder cattle (pl) [ˈkætl]
Rindersteak steak [steɪk]
Ring ring [rɪŋ]
Rock skirt [skɜːt]
Rock(musik) rock (music) [rɒk]
Rolle role [rəʊl]
Rollstuhl wheelchair [ˈwiːltʃeə]
Roman novel [ˈnɒvl]
Römer, Römerin; römisch Roman [ˈrəʊmən]
rosa pink [pɪŋk]
rot red [red]
rötlich reddish [ˈredɪʃ]
Route route [ruːt]
Routine routine [ruːˈtiːn]
Rucksack rucksack [ˈrʌksæk]
Ruf call [kɔːl]
rufen call [kɔːl]; shout [ʃaʊt] • **die Polizei rufen** call the police
Rugby rugby [ˈrʌgbi]
ruhig quiet [ˈkwaɪət]
Ruine ruin [ˈruːɪn]
rumhängen hang out [ˌhæŋ_ˈaʊt] (infml)
rund round [raʊnd] • **runde Klammern** round brackets [raʊnd]
Rundgang (durch das Haus) tour (of the house) [tʊə]
runterladen download [ˌdaʊnˈləʊd]

S

Saal hall [hɔːl]
Sache thing [θɪŋ]
Sachliteratur non-fiction [ˈnɒnˌfɪkʃn]
Sachtext factual text [ˈfæktʃuːl]
Saft juice [dʒuːs]
sagen say [seɪ] • **Man sagt, ... They say ...** • **Sagt mir eure Namen.** Tell me your names. [tel] • **Was du nicht sagst!** No way! [ˌnəʊ ˈweɪ]
Sahne cream [kriːm]
Saite string [strɪŋ]
Salat 1. (Kopfsalat) lettuce [ˈletɪs]
2. (Gericht, Beilage) salad [ˈsæləd]
Sammelalbum scrapbook [ˈskræpbʊk]
sammeln collect [kəˈlekt] • **Geld sammeln (für)** raise money (for) [reɪz]
Sammler/in collector [kəˈlektə]
Sammlung collection [kəˈlekʃn]

Samstag Saturday [ˈsætədeɪ, ˈsætədi] (siehe auch unter „Freitag")
sandig sandy [ˈsændi]
Sandwich sandwich [ˈsænwɪtʃ]
sanft soft [sɒft]
Sänger/in singer [ˈsɪŋə]
Sanitäter/in paramedic [ˌpærəˈmedɪk]
satt: etwas satt haben be tired of sth. [taɪəd]
Sattel saddle [ˈsædl]
Satz sentence [ˈsentəns]; (Teil-, Gliedsatz) clause [klɔːz] • **Satz um Satz** sentence for sentence
sauber clean [kliːn] • **sauber machen** clean
sauer sour [saʊə]
Säule column [ˈkɒləm]
Sauna sauna [ˈsɔːnə] • **in die Sauna gehen** have a sauna
Säure acid [ˈæsɪd]
Saxophon saxophone [ˈsæksəfəʊn]
Schachtel packet [ˈpækɪt]
schade: Es ist schade, dass ... It's a pity (that ...) [ˈpɪti] • **Wie schade!** What a bummer! [ˈbʌmə] (infml)
Schaf sheep, pl sheep [ʃiːp]
Schale bowl [bəʊl] • **eine Schale Cornflakes** a bowl of cornflakes
scharf: scharf gewürzt spicy [ˈspaɪsi]
Schatten (einer Person, eines Gegenstands) shadow [ˈʃædəʊ]
Schatz dear [dɪə]; sweetheart [ˈswiːthɑːt]
schätzen (erraten) guess [ges]
schauen look [lʊk]
Schauspiel drama [ˈdrɑːmə]
Schauspieler/in actor [ˈæktə]
scheinen (Sonne) shine [ʃaɪn]
scheinen: zu sein/tun scheinen seem to be/to do [siːm]
Schenke tavern [ˈtævən]
scherzen joke [dʒəʊk]
Scherzfrage riddle [ˈrɪdl]
scheu shy [ʃaɪ]
scheußlich horrible [ˈhɒrəbl]
Schicht 1. (Fels-, Erdschicht usw.) layer [ˈleɪə]
2. (bei der Arbeit) shift [ʃɪft] • **in einer/meiner Schicht** on a/my shift
schick trendy [ˈtrendi]
schicken (an) send (to) [send]; (vor allem per E-Mail) mail (to) • **jm. eine SMS schicken** text sb. [tekst]
schieben push [pʊʃ]
Schiedsrichter/in referee [ˌrefəˈriː]
schießen shoot [ʃuːt] • **ein Tor schießen** score a goal [skɔː]
Schiff boat [bəʊt]; ship [ʃɪp]
Schiffsmannschaft crew [kruː]
Schild sign [saɪn]
Schildkröte tortoise [ˈtɔːtəs]

Dictionary (German – English)   **281**

Schimpfwort: jn. mit Schimpfwörtern hänseln, jm. Schimpfwörter nachrufen call sb. names
Schinkenspeck bacon ['beɪkən]
Schlaf sleep [sli:p]
Schlafanzug pyjamas (pl) [pə'dʒɑːməz]
schlafen sleep [sli:p]; (nicht wach sein) be asleep [ə'sli:p]
Schlafparty sleepover ['sli:pəʊvə]
Schlafzimmer bedroom ['bedru:m]
schlagen beat [bi:t]; hit [hɪt]
Schläger (Badminton, Tennis, Squash) racket ['rækɪt]
Schlagzeile headline ['hed,laɪn]
Schlagzeug drums [drʌmz] • **Schlagzeug spielen** play the drums
Schlange 1. (Tier) snake [sneɪk] 2. (wartender Menschen) line [laɪn] (AE); queue [kju:] (BE)
schlau clever ['klevə]; smart [smɑːt]
Schlauch hose [həʊz]
Schlauchboot raft [rɑːft] • **mit einem Schlauchboot fahren** raft
Schlauheit cleverness ['klevənəs]
schlecht bad [bæd] • **schlechter** worse [wɜːs] • **am schlechtesten; der/die/das schlechteste** (the) worst [wɜːst] • **Mir ist schlecht.** I feel sick. • **schlecht werden** go bad • **schlechtes Timing** bad timing ['taɪmɪŋ]
schlendern wander ['wɒndə]
Schleuse lock [lɒk]
schlicht plain [pleɪn]
schließen (zumachen) close [kləʊz]
schließlich at last [ət 'lɑːst]; finally ['faɪnəli]
schlimm bad [bæd] • **schlimmer** worse [wɜːs] • **am schlimmsten; der/die/das schlimmste** (the) worst [wɜːst]
Schlitten sledge [sledʒ]
Schlittschuhbahn ice rink ['aɪs rɪŋk]
Schloss castle ['kɑːsl]; palace ['pæləs]
Schlucht gorge [gɔːdʒ]
Schluss (einer Geschichte, eines Films usw.) ending ['endɪŋ]
Schlüssel key [ki:]
Schlüsselring key ring ['ki: rɪŋ]
Schlüsselwort key word ['ki: wɜːd]
Schlussverkauf sale [seɪl]
schmecken taste [teɪst]
Schmerz(en) pain [peɪn] • **schreien vor Schmerzen** cry in pain [kraɪ]
schmuggeln smuggle ['smʌgl]
schmutzig dirty ['dɜːti]
schnappen (greifen) grab [græb]
Schnee snow [snəʊ]
Schneeball snowball ['snəʊbɔːl]

schneiden cut [kʌt]
schnell quick [kwɪk]; fast [fɑːst]
Schnitt cut [kʌt]
schockiert shocked [ʃɒkt]
Schokolade chocolate ['tʃɒklət]
schon already [ɔːl'redi] • **schon?** yet? [jet] • **schon mal?** ever? ['evə] • **(vorher) schon mal** before [bɪ'fɔː] • **sogar schon** even ['iːvn]
schön beautiful ['bjuːtɪfl]; (nett) nice [naɪs]; (hübsch; wunderbar) lovely ['lʌvli] • **schön kühl/sauber/…** nice and cool/clean/… • **schön ordentlich** neat and tidy
Schönheit beauty ['bjuːti]
schottisch Scottish ['skɒtɪʃ]
schräg diagonal [daɪ'ægənəl]
Schrank cupboard ['kʌbəd]; (Kleiderschrank) wardrobe ['wɔːdrəʊb]
schrecklich terrible ['terəbl]; awful ['ɔːfl] • **schreckliche Angst haben (vor)** be terrified (of) ['terɪfaɪd]
Schrei scream [skri:m]
schreiben (an) write (to) [raɪt]
Schreiber/in writer ['raɪtə]
Schreibtisch desk [desk]
schreien shout [ʃaʊt]; scream [skri:m]; cry [kraɪ] • **schreien vor Schmerzen** cry in pain
Schriftsteller/in writer ['raɪtə]
Schritt step [step] • **etwas Schritt für Schritt tun** take sth. a step at a time • **Schritte machen/unternehmen** take steps
schüchtern shy [ʃaɪ]
Schuh shoe [ʃuː]
Schulabschluss: den Schulabschluss machen graduate ['grædʒueɪt] (AE)
Schulbildung education [,edʒu'keɪʃn]
Schuld fault [fɔːlt] • **du hast Schuld** it's your fault • **jm. die Schuld geben (an)** blame sb. (for) [bleɪm]
Schulden debts (pl) [dets]
Schule school [skuːl] • **aus der Schule** from school • **in der Schule** at school (BE); in school (AE)
Schüler/in student ['stjuːdənt]
Schüleraustausch exchange [ɪks'tʃeɪndʒ]
Schulfach (school) subject ['sʌbdʒɪkt]
Schulheft exercise book ['eksəsaɪz bʊk]
Schulklasse class [klɑːs]; form [fɔːm]
Schulleiter/in head teacher [,hed 'tiːtʃə]; principal ['prɪnsəpl] (bes. AE)
Schulnote (Zensur) grade [greɪd] (BE auch: mark [mɑːk])
Schulstunde period ['pɪəriəd]
Schultasche school bag ['skuːl bæg]
Schulter shoulder ['ʃəʊldə]

Schulterpolster (beim American Football) pad [pæd]
Schultyrann bully ['bʊli]
Schuss shot [ʃɒt]
Schüssel bowl [bəʊl]
Schusswaffe gun [gʌn]
schütteln shake [ʃeɪk] • **den Kopf schütteln** shake your head
schützen: jn./etwas schützen (vor jm./etwas) protect sb./sth. from sb./sth. [prə'tekt]
Schützer (Knieschützer usw. für Inlineskater) pad [pæd]
schwach weak [wiːk]
schwarz black [blæk]
schwarzes Brett bulletin board ['bʊlətɪn bɔːd] (AE), notice board ['nəʊtɪs bɔːd] (BE)
schwatzen (klatschen, tratschen) gossip ['gɒsɪp]
Schweiß sweat [swet]
schwer (schwierig) difficult ['dɪfɪkəlt]; hard [hɑːd]
Schwester sister ['sɪstə]
schwierig difficult ['dɪfɪkəlt]; hard [hɑːd]; tough [tʌf]
Schwierigkeiten trouble ['trʌbl] • **in Schwierigkeiten sein** be in trouble
Schwimmbad, -becken swimming pool ['swɪmɪŋ puːl]
schwimmen swim [swɪm] • **schwimmen gehen** go swimming
Schwimmer/in swimmer ['swɪmə]
schwitzen sweat [swet]
See 1. lake [leɪk]; (in Schottland) loch [lɒx] 2. (die See, das Meer) sea [siː] • **auf See** at sea
segeln sail [seɪl]
Segen blessing ['blesɪŋ]
sehen see [siː] • **Siehst du?** See?
Sehenswürdigkeiten sights (pl) [saɪts] • **das Anschauen von Sehenswürdigkeiten** sightseeing ['saɪt,siːɪŋ]
sehr very ['veri] • **Danke sehr!** Thanks very much! • **Er mag sie sehr.** He likes her a lot. [ə 'lɒt] **etwas sehr mögen/sehr lieben** like/love sth. very much
Seife soap [səʊp]
Seifenoper soap (opera) ['səʊp ,ɒprə]
Seil rope [rəʊp]
sein (Verb) be [biː]
sein(e) … (besitzanzeigend) (zu „he") his …; (zu „it") its …
seiner, seine, seins … his [hɪz]
seit 1. (mit Zeitpunkt) since [sɪns] • **since September** seit September 2. (mit Zeitraum) for [fɔː] • **seit Jahren** for years

Dictionary (German – English)

Seite 1. side [saɪd] • **auf der linken Seite** on the left • **auf der rechten Seite** on the right
2. *(Buch-, Heftseite)* page [peɪdʒ] **Auf welcher Seite sind wir?** What page are we on?
Seitentür side door [ˌsaɪd 'dɔː]
Sekretariat school office [ˌskuːl 'ɒfɪs]
Sekunde second [ˈsekənd]
selbst my-, your-, him-, her-, itself; our-, your-, themselves
▶ S.196 German „selbst"
Selbstbedienungsrestaurant *(Cafeteria)* cafeteria [ˌkæfəˈtɪəriə]
selbstsicher tough [tʌf]
selbstständig *(ohne Hilfe)* on our/ my/... own
selbstverständlich of course [əv 'kɔːs]
seltsam strange [streɪndʒ]; weird [wɪəd]
Semester *(Schulhalbjahr in den USA)* semester [sɪˈmestə]
senden 1. **senden (an)** *(schicken)* send (to) [send]; *(vor allem per E-Mail)* mail (to) [meɪl]
2. *(ausstrahlen)* broadcast [ˈbrɔːdkɑːst]
Sender *(Radio)* station • **ein Radio auf einen Sender einstellen** tune a radio to a station [tjuːn]
Sendernetz *(Fernsehen/Radio)* network [ˈnetwɜːk]
Sendereihe series, *pl* series [ˈsɪəriːz]
Sendung *(Fernsehen/Radio)* programme [ˈprəʊɡræm]
Senf mustard [ˈmʌstəd]
Senior/in *(Rentner/in)* senior [ˈsiːniə]
separat separate [ˈseprət]
September September [sepˈtembə]
Serie *(Sendereihe)* series, *pl* series [ˈsɪəriːz]
Service *(Dienst am Kunden)* service [ˈsɜːvɪs]
Sessel armchair [ˈɑːmtʃeə]
setzen: sich setzen sit [sɪt] • **Setz dich / Setzt euch zu mir.** Sit with me. • **sich mit jm. in Verbindung setzen** contact sb. [ˈkɒntækt]
Shorts shorts *(pl)* [ʃɔːts]
Show show [ʃəʊ]
sich 1. *(Reflexivpronomen)* herself [hɜːˈself]; himself [hɪmˈself]; itself [ɪtˈself]; themselves [ðəmˈselvz]
2. **sich (gegenseitig)** *(einander)* each other [ˌiːtʃ ˈʌðə]
sicher 1. *(in Sicherheit)* safe (from) [seɪf] • **nicht sicher** unsafe [ʌnˈseɪf]
2. **sicher sein** *(nicht zweifeln)* be sure [ʃʊə, ʃɔː]
Sicherheit safety [ˈseɪfti] • **in Sicherheit (vor)** safe (from) [seɪf]

Sicht: aus meiner Sicht from my point of view [ˌpɔɪnt əv ˈvjuː]
Sicht(weite) visibility [ˌvɪzəˈbɪləti]
sie 1. *(weibliche Person)* she [ʃiː] • **Frag sie.** Ask her. [hə, hɜː]
2. *(Ding, Tier)* it [ɪt]
3. *(Plural)* they [ðeɪ] • **Frag sie.** Ask them. [ðəm, ðem]
4. **Sie** *(höfliche Anrede)* you [juː]
Siedler/in settler [ˈsetlə]; colonist [ˈkɒlənɪst]
Sieg win [wɪn]; victory [ˈvɪktəri]
Sieger/in winner [ˈwɪnə]
Silbe syllable [ˈsɪləbl]
singen sing [sɪŋ]
Sinn: Es hatte keinen Sinn. There was no point. [pɔɪnt]
Situation situation [ˌsɪtjuˈeɪʃn]
Sitz seat [siːt]
sitzen sit [sɪt]
Skateboard skateboard [ˈskeɪtbɔːd] • **Skateboard fahren** skate [skeɪt]
Sketch sketch [sketʃ]
Ski ski [skiː] • **Ski laufen/fahren** ski; go skiing
Skipiste ski slope [ˈskiː sləʊp]
Sklave, Sklavin slave [sleɪv]
Sklaverei slavery [ˈsleɪvəri]
Slogan slogan [ˈsləʊɡən]
SMS text message [ˈtekst ˌmesɪdʒ] • **jm. eine SMS schicken** text sb. [tekst]
Snack snack [snæk]
so 1. **so groß/aufregend wie** as big/exciting as
2. **so süß** so sweet [səʊ] • **so ein netter Mensch** such a nice person [sʌtʃ] • **so gute Bücher** such good books
sobald as soon as [əz ˈsuːn əz]
Socke sock [sɒk]
sodass so that
▶ S.200–201 Giving reasons
soeben just [dʒʌst]
Sofa sofa [ˈsəʊfə]
sofort straightaway [ˌstreɪtəˈweɪ]; immediately [ɪˈmiːdiətli]
Software software [ˈsɒftweə]
sogar even [ˈiːvn]
Sohn son [sʌn]
solche Sprache language like that
Soldat/in soldier [ˈsəʊldʒə]
sollen: du hättest fragen sollen you should have asked [ʃʊd] • **Sollen wir ...?** Shall we ...? [ʃæl] • **Was soll das?** What's the point? [pɔɪnt]
sollte(n): ich/er sollte ... I/he should [ʃəd, ʃʊd] • **sie wussten nicht, was sie tun sollten** they didn't know what to do
▶ S.192 Question words + to-infinitive

Sommer summer [ˈsʌmə]
sonderbar strange [streɪndʒ]
sondern but [bət, bʌt] • **nicht nur ... sondern auch ...** not only ... but also ... [ˈɔːlsəʊ]
Song song [sɒŋ]
Sonnabend Saturday [ˈsætədeɪ, ˈsætədi] *(siehe auch unter „Freitag")*
Sonne sun [sʌn]
Sonnenaufgang sunrise [ˈsʌnraɪz]
Sonnenbrille: (eine) Sonnenbrille sunglasses *(pl)* [ˈsʌnɡlɑːsɪz]
sonnengebräunt sein have a suntan [ˈsʌnˌtæn]
Sonnenschein sunshine [ˈsʌnʃaɪn]
Sonnenuntergang sunset [ˈsʌnset]
sonnig sunny [ˈsʌni]
Sonntag Sunday [ˈsʌndeɪ, ˈsʌndi] *(siehe auch unter „Freitag")*
sonst *(andernfalls)* otherwise [ˈʌðəwaɪz] • **sonst (noch) jemand/etwas/irgendwo** anybody/anything/anywhere else [els]
Sorge worry [ˈwʌri] • **sich Sorgen machen (wegen, um)** worry (about) • **Mach dir keine Sorgen.** Don't worry.
Sorte sort (of) [sɔːt]
sortieren sort [sɔːt]
Soße sauce [sɔːs]
Soul(musik) soul [səʊl]
Souvenir souvenir [ˌsuːvəˈnɪə]
sowie *(sobald)* as soon as [əz ˈsuːn əz]
sowieso anyway [ˈeniweɪ]
Sozialkunde Social Studies [ˌsəʊʃl ˈstʌdiz]
Spaghetti spaghetti [spəˈɡeti]
spannend exciting [ɪkˈsaɪtɪŋ]
sparen save [seɪv]
Spaß fun [fʌn] • **Spaß haben** have fun • **nur zum Spaß** just for fun • **Reiten macht Spaß.** Riding is fun. • **Viel Spaß!** Have fun!
spät late [leɪt] • **Wie spät ist es?** What's the time? • **zu spät sein/kommen** be late
später later [ˈleɪtə]
spazieren gehen go for a walk [wɔːk]; walk [wɔːk]
Spaziergang walk [wɔːk] • **einen Spaziergang machen** go for a walk
Specht woodpecker [ˈwʊdpekə]
Speisekarte menu [ˈmenjuː]
spektakulär spectacular [spekˈtækjələ]
sperren block [blɒk]
spezifische(r, s) specific [spəˈsɪfɪk]
Spiegel mirror [ˈmɪrə]
Spiel game [ɡeɪm]; *(Wettkampf)* match [mætʃ] • **Olympische Spiele** Olympic Games [əˌlɪmpɪk ˈɡeɪmz]

spielen play [pleɪ]; *(Szene, Dialog)* act [ækt] • **Fußball spielen** play football • **Gitarre/Klavier/Geige/Schlagzeug spielen** play the guitar/the piano/the violin/the drums • **jm. einen Streich spielen** play a trick on sb.
Spieler/in player ['pleɪə]
Spielkasino casino [kə'siːnəʊ]
Spielstand *(Punktestand)* score [skɔː]
Spielstein *(für Brettspiele)* counter ['kaʊntə]
Spion/in spy [spaɪ]
Spitze tip [tɪp]
Spitze *(oberes Ende)* top [tɒp] *(Flügel-, Schuhspitze)* tip [tɪp] • **an der Spitze (von)** at the top (of)
Spitzen- top [tɒp]
Sport; Sportart sport [spɔːt] • **Sport treiben** do sport
Sportausrüstung, Sportsachen sports gear *(no pl)* ['spɔːts gɪə]
Sporthalle sports hall ['spɔːts hɔːl]; gym [dʒɪm]
Sportunterricht PE [ˌpiːˈiː], Physical Education [ˌfɪzɪkəl ˌedʒuˈkeɪʃn]
Sprache language ['læŋgwɪdʒ]
Sprachmittlung *(Mediation)* mediation [ˌmiːdiˈeɪʃn]
sprayen spray [spreɪ]
sprechen (mit) speak (to) [spiːk] • **Hier spricht Isabel.** *(am Telefon)* This is Isabel.
springen jump [dʒʌmp]
spritzen splash [splæʃ]
Spritztour: eine Spritztour machen take a ride [raɪd]
sprühen spray [spreɪ]
spucken spit [spɪt]
Spülbecken, Spüle sink [sɪŋk]
Staat state [steɪt]
Staatsangehörige/r *(in einer Monarchie)* subject ['sʌbdʒɪkt]
Stadion stadium ['steɪdiəm]
Stadt *(Großstadt)* city ['sɪti]; *(Kleinstadt)* town [taʊn] • **die Mitte der Stadt** the centre of town • **in der Stadt** in town
Stadtplan map [mæp]
Stadtzentrum city centre [ˌsɪti ˈsentə] *(BE)*; downtown ['daʊntaʊn] *(AE)*
Stahl steel [stiːl]
Stall *(für Kaninchen)* hutch [hʌtʃ]
Stamm *(Volksstamm)* tribe [traɪb]
Stammbaum family tree [ˈfæməli triː]
stammen von/aus come from [kʌm]
Stammes- tribal ['traɪbl]
ständig: etwas ständig tun keep (on) doing sth.
Standpunkt point of view [ˌpɔɪnt_əv ˈvjuː] • **von meinem Standpunkt aus gesehen** from my point of view
Star *(Film-, Popstar)* star [stɑː]
stark strong [strɒŋ]
starten start [stɑːt] • **neu starten** *(Computer)* restart [ˌriːˈstɑːt]
statt instead of [ɪnˈsted_əv]
stattfinden take place [ˌteɪk ˈpleɪs]
Statue statue ['stætʃuː]
Staub dust [dʌst]
Steak steak [steɪk]
Stecker plug [plʌg]
Steeldrum steel drum [ˌstiːl ˈdrʌm]
stehen stand [stænd] • **Hier steht: ...** *(im Text)* It says here: ... • **Wie steht es?** *(beim Sport)* What's the score?
stehlen steal [stiːl]
steigen rise [raɪz]
Steigerung comparison [kəmˈpærɪsn]
Stein stone [stəʊn]
Stelle: zur Stelle on the scene [siːn]
stellen *(hin-, abstellen)* put [pʊt] **etwas leiser/lauter stellen** turn sth. down/up • **Fragen stellen** ask questions • **(jm.) eine Falle stellen** set a trap (for sb.) [set] • **sich (hin)stellen** stand [stænd] **Stell dir vor! / Stellt euch vor!** Guess what! [ˌges ˈwɒt]
sterben (an) die (of) [daɪ]
Stereoanlage stereo ['steriəʊ]
Stern star [stɑː]
steuern steer [stɪə]
Stichwort *(Schlüsselwort)* key word [ˈkiː wɜːd]
Stiefel boot [buːt]
Stil style [staɪl]
still 1. *(leise)* quiet ['kwaɪət] • **still sein** keep quiet [kiːp] **2.** *(bewegungslos)* still [stɪl]
Stimme voice [vɔɪs]; *(bei Abstimmungen)* vote [vəʊt]
stimmen: für/gegen jn./etwas stimmen vote for/against sb./sth. [vəʊt] • **Das stimmt.** That's right. [raɪt] • **Du brauchst ein Lineal, stimmt's?** You need a ruler, right?
Stimmrecht vote [vəʊt]
Stirn forehead ['fɒhed, 'fɒrɪd]
Stock *(Stockwerk)* floor [flɔː] • **erster Stock** first floor *(BE)*; second floor *(AE)* • **im ersten Stock** on the first floor *(BE)*; on the second floor *(AE)* ▶ S.196 floor
Stoff *(Material)* material [məˈtɪəriəl]
stolz (auf jn./etwas) proud (of sb./sth.) [praʊd]
stoßen push [pʊʃ]
Strafe *(Haftstrafe)* sentence ['sentəns]
Strafstoß penalty ['penəlti]
Strand beach [biːtʃ] • **am Strand** on the beach
Straße road [rəʊd]; street [striːt] • **in seiner Straße** in/on his street
Straßenbahn tram [træm]
Straßenkünstler/in (street) performer [pəˈfɔːmə]
Strecke way [weɪ]; route [ruːt]
strecken: sich strecken stretch [stretʃ]
Streich trick [trɪk] • **jm. einen Streich spielen** play a trick on sb.
Streife patrol [pəˈtrəʊl]
Streik strike [straɪk]
streiken 1. *(sich im Streik befinden)* be on strike [straɪk] **2.** *(in den Streik treten)* go on strike
Streit argument ['ɑːgjumənt]
streiten: sich streiten argue ['ɑːgjuː]; have an argument ['ɑːgjumənt]
streng strict [strɪkt]
Strom electricity [ɪˌlekˈtrɪsəti]
Stromschnellen rapids *(pl)* ['ræpɪdz]
Strophe verse [vɜːs]
Struktur structure ['strʌktʃə]
strukturieren structure ['strʌktʃə]
Strumpf sock [sɒk]
Strumpfhose tights *(pl)* [taɪts]
Stück piece [piːs]; *(auf einer CD)* track [træk] • **ein Stück Papier** a piece of paper
Student/in student ['stjuːdənt]
studieren study ['stʌdi]
Studio studio ['stjuːdiəʊ]
Stufe *(Treppen-)* step [step]
Stuhl chair [tʃeə]
stumm: „stummer" Buchstabe *(nicht gesprochener Buchstabe)* silent letter [ˌsaɪlənt ˈletə]
Stunde hour [aʊə]; *(Schulstunde)* lesson ['lesn]; period ['pɪəriəd] • **eine halbe Stunde** half an hour [hɑːf] **ein Supermarkt, der 24 Stunden geöffnet ist** a 24-hour supermarket • **eine zweistündige Operation** a two-hour operation [ˌɒpəˈreɪʃn]
Stundenplan timetable ['taɪmteɪbl] *(BE)*; schedule *(bes. AE)* [AE: ˈskedʒuːl, BE: ˈʃedjuːl]
Sturm storm [stɔːm]
stürmen *(rennen)* charge [tʃɑːdʒ]
stürmisch stormy ['stɔːmi]
stürzen *(hinfallen)* fall [fɔːl] • **zu Tode stürzen** fall to your death
Subjekt subject ['sʌbdʒɪkt]
suchen look for ['lʊk fɔː]
Süd- southern ['sʌðən]
Süden south [saʊθ] • **nach Süden** south • **Richtung Süden** southbound ['saʊθbaʊnd]
südlich south [saʊθ]; southern ['sʌðən]

Dictionary (German – English)

Südosten south-east [ˌsaʊθˈiːst]
  nach Südosten south-east
südöstlich south-east [ˌsaʊθˈiːst]
Südwesten south-west [ˌsaʊθˈwest]
  nach Südwesten south-west
südwestlich south-west [ˌsaʊθˈwest]
Suffix suffix [ˈsʌfɪks]
Supermarkt supermarket [ˈsuːpəməkɪt]
Suppe soup [suːp]
Surfbrett surfboard [ˈsɜːfbɔːd]
surfen gehen go surfing [ˈsɜːfɪŋ]
  im Internet surfen surf the internet [sɜːf]
süß sweet [swiːt]
Süßigkeiten sweets (pl) [swiːts]
Sweatshirt sweatshirt [ˈswetʃɜːt]
Synagoge synagogue [ˈsɪnəɡɒɡ]
Synonym synonym [ˈsɪnənɪm]
System system [ˈsɪstəm]
Szene scene [siːn]

T

Tafel (Wandtafel) board [bɔːd] • **an der/die Tafel** on the board
Tag day [deɪ] • **an jenem Tag** that day • **drei Tage (lang)** for three days • **eines Tages** one day
  Guten Tag. Hello.; (nachmittags) Good afternoon. [ɡʊdˌɑːftəˈnuːn]
Tagebuch diary [ˈdaɪəri]
Tagesfahrkarte (der Londoner Verkehrsbetriebe) Travelcard [ˈtrævlkɑːd]
täglich daily [ˈdeɪli]
Tal valley [ˈvæli]
Talboden valley floor [ˌvæli ˈflɔː]
Talent talent [ˈtælənt]
Talkshow chat show [ˈtʃæt ʃəʊ]
Tante aunt [ɑːnt]; auntie [ˈɑːnti]
Tankstelle gas station [ˈɡæs ˌsteɪʃn] (AE); petrol station [ˈpetrəl ˌsteɪʃn] (BE)
Tanz dance [dɑːns]
tanzen dance [dɑːns]
Tänzer/in dancer [ˈdɑːnsə]
Tanzfläche dance floor [ˈdɑːns flɔː]
Tanzstunden, Tanzunterricht dancing lessons [ˈdɑːnsɪŋ ˌlesnz]
tapfer brave [breɪv]
Tasche (Tragetasche, Beutel) bag [bæɡ]; (Hosentasche, Jackentasche) pocket [ˈpɒkɪt]
Taschengeld pocket money [ˈpɒkɪt ˌmʌni]
Taschentuch handkerchief [ˈhæŋkətʃɪf]
Tasse cup [kʌp] • **eine Tasse Tee** a cup of tea
Tat action [ˈækʃn]
Tätigkeit activity [ækˈtɪvəti]
Tatsache fact [fækt]

tatsächlich actually [ˈæktʃuəli]
  ▶ S.215 actually
taub deaf [def] • **taub werden** go deaf
tauschen: etwas tauschen (für/gegen etwas) swap sth. (for sth.) [swɒp]
tausend thousand [ˈθaʊznd]
Taxi taxi [ˈtæksi]
Team team [tiːm]
Technik technique [tekˈniːk]
Teddybär teddy bear [ˈtedi beə]
Tee tea [tiː]
Teebeutel tea bag [ˈtiː ˌbæɡ]
Teelöffel teaspoon [ˈtiːspuːn]
Teenager teenager [ˈtiːneɪdʒə]
Teenager- teen [tiːn] (besonders AE)
Teig dough [dəʊ]
Teil part [pɑːt]; (eines Textes) section [ˈsekʃn]
teilen: (sich) teilen (in) divide (into) [dɪˈvaɪd] • **sich etwas teilen (mit jm.)** share sth. (with sb.) [ʃeə]
teilnehmen an etwas take part in sth.; participate in something [pɑːˈtɪsɪpeɪt]
Teilsatz clause [klɔːz]
Telefon (tele)phone [ˈtelɪfəʊn] • **am Telefon** on the phone
Telefongespräch: ein Telefongespräch führen make a call [kɔːl]
Telefonnummer (tele)phone number [ˈtelɪfəʊn ˌnʌmbə]
Teller plate [pleɪt] • **ein Teller Pommes frites** a plate of chips
Temperatur temperature [ˈtemprətʃə]
Tempus (grammatische Zeit) tense [tens]
Tennis tennis [ˈtenɪs]
Termin appointment [əˈpɔɪntmənt]
Terminkalender diary [ˈdaɪəri]
Terrorismus terrorism [ˈterərɪzm]
Test test [test]
teuer expensive [ɪkˈspensɪv]
Text text [tekst]
Theater theatre [ˈθɪətə]
Theaterkasse box office [ˈbɒks ˌɒfɪs]
Theaterstück play [pleɪ]
Theke counter [ˈkaʊntə]
Thema, Themenbereich topic [ˈtɒpɪk]; section [ˈsekʃn]; subject [ˈsʌbdʒɪkt]
Themenpark theme park [ˈθiːm pɑːk]
Thermometer thermometer [θəˈmɒmɪtə]
tief deep [diːp]
Tier animal [ˈænɪml]; (Haustier) pet [pet] • **frei lebende Tiere** wildlife [ˈwaɪldlaɪf]
Tierhandlung pet shop [ˈpet ʃɒp]
Tierpark zoo [zuː]
Tierwelt wildlife [ˈwaɪldlaɪf]

Tiger tiger [ˈtaɪɡə]
Timing: schlechtes Timing bad timing [ˈtaɪmɪŋ]
Tipp tip [tɪp]
Tisch table [ˈteɪbl]
Tischdecke tablecloth [ˈteɪblklɒθ]
Tischtennis table tennis [ˈteɪbl ˌtenɪs]
Tischtennisschläger table tennis bat [bæt]
Titel title [ˈtaɪtl]; (auf einer CD) track [træk]
Titelseite front page [ˌfrʌnt ˈpeɪdʒ]
Toast(brot) toast [təʊst]
Tochter daughter [ˈdɔːtə]
Tod death [deθ] • **zu Tode stürzen** fall to your death
Todesstrafe death sentence [ˈdeθ ˌsentəns]
Todestag anniversary of sb.'s death [ˌænɪˈvɜːsəri]
Toilette toilet [ˈtɔɪlət]; (öffentlich) restroom [ˈrestruːm] (AE)
toll fantastic [fænˈtæstɪk]; great [ɡreɪt]; neat (AE, infml) [niːt]; awesome [ˈɔːsəm] (AE, infml)
Tomate tomato [təˈmɑːtəʊ], pl tomatoes
Ton note [nəʊt]
Tondatei sound file [ˈsaʊnd faɪl]
Top (Oberteil) top [tɒp]
Tor (im Sport) goal [ɡəʊl] • **ein Tor schießen** score a goal
Torte cake [keɪk]
Torwart, Torfrau (goal)keeper [ˈkiːpə]
tot dead [ded]
töten kill [kɪl]
tough tough [tʌf]
Tour: (Rad-)Tour (bike) tour [tʊə] **Tour durch das Haus** (Rundgang) tour of the house
Tourist/in tourist [ˈtʊərɪst]
Track (auf einer CD) track [træk]
Tradition tradition [trəˈdɪʃn]
traditionell traditional [trəˈdɪʃənl]
tragen (Kleidung) wear [weə]
Trainer/in coach [kəʊtʃ]
trainieren practise [ˈpræktɪs] (BE); practice [ˈpræktɪs] (AE); train [treɪn]
Trainingseinheit, -stunde training session [ˈseʃn]
Träne tear [tɪə]
Transport(wesen) transport (no pl) [ˈtrænspɔːt]
tratschen gossip [ˈɡɒsɪp]
Trauerfeier funeral (service) [ˈfjuːnərəl]
Traum dream [driːm]
träumen (von) dream (of, about) [driːm]
Traumhaus dream house
traurig sad [sæd]
Traurigkeit sadness [ˈsædnəs]

treffen 1. *(Ziel)* hit [hɪt]
2. **treffen; sich treffen** *(sich begegnen)* meet [miːt] • **ein Abkommen / eine Abmachung treffen** make a deal [diːl] • **sich (regelmäßig) mit jm. treffen** date sb. [deɪt] *(bes. AE)*
Treffer: einen Treffer erzielen score a goal [skɔː], [ɡəʊl]
trennen *(nach Rasse, Religion, Geschlecht)* segregate ['seɡrɪɡeɪt]
Trennung *(nach Rasse, Religion, Geschlecht)* segregation [ˌseɡrɪ'ɡeɪʃn]
Treppe(nstufen) stairs *(pl)* [steəz]
Tresor safe [seɪf]
treten (gegen) kick [kɪk]
Trick *(Zauberkunststück)* trick [trɪk]
Trikot shirt [ʃɜːt]
Trimester term [tɜːm]
trinken drink [drɪŋk] • **Milch zum Frühstück trinken** have milk for breakfast
trocken dry [draɪ]
Trommel drum [drʌm]
Trommelstock drumstick ['drʌmstɪk]
Trompete trumpet ['trʌmpɪt]
trösten comfort ['kʌmfət]
trotzdem anyway ['eniweɪ]; still [stɪl]; however [haʊ'evə]
Truthahn turkey ['tɜːki]
Tschüs. Bye. [baɪ]; See you. ['siː juː]
T-Shirt T-shirt ['tiː ʃɜːt]
Tsunami tsunami [tsuːˈnɑːmi]
tun do [duː] • **Tue, was ich tue.** Do what I do. • **tun müssen** have to do • **tun wollen** want to do [wɒnt] • **Tut mir leid.** I'm sorry. ['sɒri]
Tunnel tunnel ['tʌnl]
Tür door [dɔː]
Türklingel doorbell ['dɔːbel]
Turm tower ['taʊə]
Turnanzug *(für Frauen und Mädchen)* leotard ['liːətɑːd]
Turnen *(Sportunterricht)* PE [ˌpiː ˈiː], Physical Education [ˌfɪzɪkəl ˌedʒu'keɪʃn]
Turnhalle gym [dʒɪm]
Turnschuhe trainers *(pl)* ['treɪnəz]
Tut mir leid. I'm sorry. ['sɒri]
Tüte bag [bæɡ]
Typ *(Kerl)* guy [ɡaɪ]
Tyrann bully ['bʊli]
tyrannisieren bully ['bʊli]

U

U-Bahn: die U-Bahn the underground ['ʌndəɡraʊnd] *(BE)*; the subway ['sʌbweɪ] *(AE)*; *(in London)* the Tube *(no pl)* [tjuːb]
U-Bahn-Linie line [laɪn]

üben practise ['præktɪs] *(BE)*; practice ['præktɪs] *(AE)*
über 1. about [ə'baʊt] • **über dich selbst** about yourself
2. *(räumlich)* over ['əʊvə]; *(quer über)* across [ə'krɒs]; *(oberhalb von)* above [ə'bʌv]
3. *(mehr als)* over
überall everywhere ['evriweə]
überarbeiten revise [rɪ'vaɪz]
überdrüssig: einer Sache überdrüssig werden get tired of sth. ['taɪəd]
übereinstimmen: nicht übereinstimmen (mit) disagree (with) [ˌdɪsə'ɡriː]
überfliegen: einen Text überfliegen *(um den Inhalt grob zu erfassen)* skim a text [skɪm]
überfüllt crowded ['kraʊdɪd]
übergeben: sich übergeben throw up [θrəʊ]
überhaupt: überhaupt keine Menschen no people at all • **überhaupt nicht** not at all • **überhaupt nichts** nothing at all
▶ S.206 not at all, no ... at all
überleben survive [sə'vaɪv]
Überleben survival [sə'vaɪvl]
übernachten *(über Nacht bleiben)* stay [steɪ]
übernehmen: etwas übernehmen take sth. over
überprüfen check [tʃek]
überqueren cross [krɒs]
überraschen surprise [sə'praɪz]
überrascht (über etwas) surprised (at sth.) [sə'praɪzd]
Überraschung (für) surprise (for/to) [sə'praɪz]
Überschrift title ['taɪtl]; heading ['hedɪŋ]
überreichen present [prɪ'zent]
übersetzen (aus ... in) translate (from ... into) [træns'leɪt]
Übersetzung translation [træns'leɪʃn]
übrig sein be left [left]
übrigens by the way; actually ['æktʃuəli]
▶ S.215 actually
Übung *(Schulbuch)* exercise ['eksəsaɪz] • **eine Übung machen** do an exercise
Übungsheft exercise book ['eksəsaɪz bʊk]
Uhr 1. *(Armbanduhr)* watch [wɒtʃ]; *(Wand-, Stand-, Turmuhr)* clock [klɒk]
2. **elf Uhr** eleven o'clock • **7 Uhr morgens/vormittags** 7 am [ˌeɪ ˈem] • **7 Uhr nachmittags/abends** 7 pm [ˌpiː ˈem] • **um 8 Uhr 45** at 8.45
Uhrzeit time [taɪm]

ultimativ ultimate ['ʌltɪmət]
um 1. *(örtlich)* um ... (herum) round [raʊnd]; around [ə'raʊnd] • **um den See (herum)** around the lake
2. *(zeitlich)* **um 8.45** at 8.45 **um sechs Uhr herum** around six
3. **Es geht um Mr Green.** This is about Mr Green.
4. **um zu** to
▶ S.200–201 Giving reasons
umarmen hug [hʌɡ] • **jn. umarmen** hug sb.; give sb. a hug [hʌɡ]
Umarmung hug [hʌɡ]
umdrehen: sich umdrehen turn [tɜːn]; turn around [ə'raʊnd]
Umfrage (über) survey (on) ['sɜːveɪ]
umgeben sein be surrounded [sə'raʊndɪd]
umher: in ... umher round [raʊnd]; around [ə'raʊnd] • **in der Stadt umher** around the town
umher-: umhergehen walk around **umherrennen** run around **umherspringen** jump around
umschalten *(Radio)* change stations
▶ S.200 (to) change
umschreiben *(anders ausdrücken)* paraphrase ['pærəfreɪz]
umsehen: sich umsehen look round/around [ˌlʊk 'raʊnd]
umsteigen change [tʃeɪndʒ]
umtauschen exchange [ɪks'tʃeɪndʒ]; change [tʃeɪndʒ]
▶ S.203 (to) change
umwandeln change [tʃeɪndʒ]
▶ S.200 (to) change
Umwelt environment [ɪn'vaɪrənmənt]
Umwelt- environmental [ɪnˌvaɪrən'mentl]
umziehen 1. *(nach, in)* *(die Wohnung wechseln)* move (to) [muːv]
2. **sich umziehen** change [tʃeɪndʒ]
▶ S.200 (to) change
Umzug 1. *(Parade)* parade [pə'reɪd]
2. *(Wohnungswechsel)* move [muːv]
unbeantwortet unanswered [ˌʌn'ɑːnsəd]
unbekannt unknown [ˌʌn'nəʊn]
unbequem uncomfortable [ʌn'kʌmftəbl]
uncool uncool [ˌʌn'kuːl] *(infml)*
und and [ənd, ænd] • **Und? / Na und?** So? [səʊ]; So what? [səʊ 'wɒt]; Who cares? [ˌhuː 'keəz] • **Und ob!** You bet!
undeutlich *(unklar)* unclear [ʌn'klɪə]
Unentschieden draw [drɔː] • **2:2 unentschieden** 2 all
unfähig useless ['juːsləs]
unfair unfair [ˌʌn'feə]
Unfall accident ['æksɪdənt]
unfreundlich unfriendly [ʌn'frendli]

ungefähr about [əˈbaʊt] • **ungefähr acht (Jahre/Uhr)** eightish [ˈeɪtɪʃ]
Ungeheuer monster [ˈmɒnstə]
ungerecht unfair [ˌʌnˈfeə]
ungenügend failure [ˈfeɪljə]
▶ S.213 US school grades
ungesetzlich illegal [ɪˈliːgl]
ungesund unhealthy [ʌnˈhelθi]
unglaublich amazing [əˈmeɪzɪŋ]; incredible [ɪnˈkredɪbl]
unglücklich unhappy [ʌnˈhæpi]
unheimlich scary [ˈskeəri]
unhöflich rude [ruːd]
Uniform uniform [ˈjuːnɪfɔːm]
uninteressant uninteresting [ʌnˈɪntrəstɪŋ]
unklar unclear [ˌʌnˈklɪə]
unmöglich impossible [ɪmˈpɒsəbl]
unordentlich untidy [ʌnˈtaɪdi]
Unordnung: alles in Unordnung bringen make a mess [ˌmeɪk ə ˈmes]
unregelmäßig irregular [ɪˈregjələ]
uns us [əs, ʌs]; *(Reflexivpronomen)* ourselves [aʊəˈselvz]
unser(e) ... our ... [ˈaʊə] • **unser eigenes Schwimmbad** our own pool [əʊn]
unserer, unsere, unseres ours [ˈaʊəz]
unsicher unsure [ˌʌnˈʃʊə, ˌʌnˈʃɔː]
unten *(im Haus)* downstairs [ˌdaʊnˈsteəz] • **am unteren Ende (von)** at the bottom (of) [ˈbɒtəm] • **dort unten** down there • **nach unten** down [daʊn]; *(im Haus)* downstairs
unter 1. under [ˈʌndə]; below [bɪˈləʊ] • **unter Kontrolle** under control [kənˈtrəʊl]
2. *(zwischen mehreren Personen oder Dingen)* among [əˈmʌŋ]
unterbrechen interrupt [ˌɪntəˈrʌpt]
untere(r, s): am unteren Ende (von) at the bottom (of) [ˈbɒtəm]
untergeordnet: (jm.) untergeordnet junior (to sb.) [ˈdʒuːniə]
unterhalb (von) below [bɪˈləʊ]
unterhalten: jn. unterhalten entertain sb. [ˌentəˈteɪn] • **sich unterhalten (mit, über)** talk (to, about) [tɔːk]
Unterhaltung 1. *(Gespräch)* conversation [ˌkɒnvəˈseɪʃn]
2. *(Vergnügen)* entertainment [ˌentəˈteɪnmənt]
unterirdisch underground [ˌʌndəˈgraʊnd]
Unterkunft accommodation [əˌkɒməˈdeɪʃn]
Unterricht lessons *(pl)* [ˈlesnz]; class [klɑːs]
unterrichten teach [tiːtʃ]
Unterrichtsstunde period [ˈpɪəriəd]
Unterschied difference [ˈdɪfrəns]

unterschiedlich different [ˈdɪfrənt]
unterschreiben sign [saɪn]
unterstützen: eine Mannschaft unterstützen support a team [səˈpɔːt]
Unterstützung support [səˈpɔːt]
Untersuchung (über) *(Umfrage)* survey (on) [ˈsɜːveɪ]
Untertan/in subject [ˈsʌbdʒɪkt]
unterwegs: ich bin (schon) unterwegs (nach) I'm on my way (to)
unverschämt rude [ruːd]
unwichtig unimportant [ˌʌnɪmˈpɔːtnt]
Ureinwohner/in: amerikanische(r) Ureinwohner/in Native American [ˌneɪtɪv əˈmerɪkən]
Urgroßmutter great-grandmother [ˌgreɪt ˈgrænmʌðə]
Urgroßvater great-grandfather [ˌgreɪt ˈgrænfɑːðə]
Urlaub holiday [ˈhɒlədeɪ]; vacation [vəˈkeɪʃn, veɪˈkeɪʃn] *(AE)* • **in Urlaub fahren** go on holiday • **in Urlaub sein** be on holiday
Ursache cause [kɔːz]
ursprünglich original [əˈrɪdʒənl]
Urteil sentence [ˈsentəns]
US-amerikanische(r, s) US [juːˈes]
usw. etc. [etˈsetərə]

V

Vater father [ˈfɑːðə]
Vati dad [dæd]
v. Chr. BC [ˌbiːˈsiː]
Verabredung appointment [əˈpɔɪntmənt]
verabschieden: sich verabschieden say goodbye [ˌseɪ gʊdˈbaɪ]
verändern: (sich) verändern change [tʃeɪndʒ]
▶ S.200 (to) change
Veränderung change [tʃeɪndʒ]
verängstigt scared [skeəd]
veranschaulichen illustrate [ˈɪləstreɪt]
veranstalten organize [ˈɔːgənaɪz] • **einen Wettbewerb veranstalten** hold a competition [ˌkɒmpəˈtɪʃn]
verbessern 1. *(besser machen)* improve [ɪmˈpruːv]
2. *(korrigieren)* correct [kəˈrekt]
verbinden *(einander zuordnen)* link [lɪŋk]
Verbindung link [lɪŋk] • **in Verbindung bleiben** keep in touch [tʌtʃ] • **sich mit jm. in Verbindung setzen** contact sb. [ˈkɒntækt]
Verbrechen crime [kraɪm] • **ein Verbrechen begehen** commit a crime [kəˈmɪt]
verbreiten: (sich) verbreiten spread [spred]

verbrennen burn [bɜːn]
verbringen: Zeit verbringen (mit etwas) spend time (on sth.) [spend]
verdammt damn [dæm]
Verein club [klʌb]
vereinigt: das Vereinigte Königreich (Großbritannien und Nordirland) the United Kingdom [juːˌnaɪtɪd ˈkɪŋdəm], the UK [juːˈkeɪ] • **die Vereinigten Staaten (von Amerika)** the United States (of America) [juːˌnaɪtɪd ˈsteɪts], the US [juːˈes]
Verfahren technique [tekˈniːk]
verfolgen follow [ˈfɒləʊ]
Vergangenheit past [pɑːst]
vergeben: jm. etwas vergeben forgive sb. for sth. [fəˈgɪv]
vergessen forget [fəˈget]
vergeuden (für) waste (on) [weɪst]
vergewissern: sich vergewissern make sure [ʃʊə, ʃɔː]
Vergleich comparison [kəmˈpærɪsn]
vergleichen compare [kəmˈpeə]
vergraben bury [ˈberi]
vergriffen sein be sold out [ˌsəʊld ˈaʊt]
verheiratet (mit) married (to) [ˈmærɪd]
verhindern: etwas verhindern prevent sth. [prɪˈvent]
Verkauf sale [seɪl]
verkaufen sell [sel] • **zu verkaufen** *(auf Schild)* for sale [fəˈseɪl]
Verkäufer/in shop assistant [ˈʃɒp əˌsɪstənt]
Verkehr traffic [ˈtræfɪk] • **öffentlicher Verkehr** public transport [ˈtrænspɔːt]
verkehrsreich busy [ˈbɪzi]
verkehrt *(falsch)* wrong [rɒŋ]
Verkleidung *(Kostüm)* costume [ˈkɒstjuːm]
verknüpfen *(einander zuordnen)* link [lɪŋk]
verlassen 1. leave [liːv]
2. sich auf etwas/jn verlassen depend on sth./sb. [dɪˈpend]
verlaufen *(Straße; Grenze)* run • **sich verlaufen** get lost [lɒst]
verlegen embarrassed [ɪmˈbærəst]
verletzen hurt [hɜːt]
verletzt hurt [hɜːt]
Verletzung injury [ˈɪndʒəri]
verlieben: sich verlieben (in jn.) fall in love (with sb.) [lʌv]
verlieren lose [luːz] • **die Lust an etwas verlieren** get tired of sth. [ˈtaɪəd]
vermissen miss [mɪs]
vermitteln mediate [ˈmiːdieɪt]
Vermittlung *(Sprachmittlung, Mediation)* mediation [ˌmiːdiˈeɪʃn]

vermuten suppose [sə'pəʊz]; expect [ɪk'spekt]
veröffentlichen publish ['pʌblɪʃ]
verpassen miss [mɪs]
verrückt mad [mæd]; crazy ['kreɪzi]
 verrückt nach mad about [mæd]
 verrückt werden go crazy
Vers *(von der Bibel)* verse [vɜːs]
Versammlung meeting ['miːtɪŋ]
verschieden different ['dɪfrənt]
verschiedene *(mehrere, einige)* several ['sevrəl]
Verschmutzung pollution [pə'luːʃn]
verschütten spill [spɪl]
verschwenden (für) waste (on) [weɪst]
Verschwendung waste [weɪst]
verschwinden disappear [ˌdɪsə'pɪə]
Versehen: aus Versehen by mistake [mɪ'steɪk]
Verspätung delay [dɪ'leɪ]
versperren block [blɒk]
versprechen promise ['prɒmɪs]
verständnisvoll understanding [ˌʌndə'stændɪŋ]
verstecken; sich verstecken hide [haɪd]
verstehen understand [ˌʌndə'stænd] • **Das versteh ich nicht.** I don't get it.
verstoßen: gegen eine Regel verstoßen break a rule [breɪk]
versuchen try [traɪ] • **versuchen zu tun** try and do / try to do
Verteidigung defence [dɪ'fens]
vertreten *(repräsentieren)* represent [ˌreprɪ'zent]
verursachen cause [kɔːz]
verurteilen: jn. verurteilen (zu etwas) sentence sb. (to sth.) ['sentəns]
Verwandte(r) relative ['relətɪv]
verwenden use [juːz]
verwirren confuse [kən'fjuːz]
verwirrt puzzled ['pʌzld]
Verwirrung confusion [kən'fjuːʒn]
verzeihen: jm. etwas verzeihen forgive sb. for sth. [fə'gɪv]
Video video ['vɪdiəʊ]
Vieh cattle *(pl)* ['kætl]
viel a lot (of) [lɒt]; lots (of) [lɒts]; much [mʌtʃ], plenty of ['plenti_əv]
viele a lot (of); lots (of); many ['meni], plenty of • **Viel Glück (bei/mit …)!** Good luck (with …)! • **viel mehr** lots more • **Viele Grüße** all the best; best wishes [wɪʃɪz] • **Viel Spaß!** Have fun! • **wie viel?** how much? • **wie viele?** how many? • **Vielen Dank!** Thanks a lot!
▶ S.215 Beginning and ending letters
viel- multi- ['mʌlti]

vielleicht maybe ['meɪbi] • **du könntest vielleicht Hilfe brauchen** you might need help [maɪt]
Viertel: Viertel nach 11 quarter past 11 ['kwɔːtə] • **Viertel vor 12** quarter to 12
Villa villa ['vɪlə]
violett purple ['pɜːpl]
Violine violin [ˌvaɪə'lɪn]; fiddle ['fɪdl] *(infml)*
Vogel bird [bɜːd]
Vokabelverzeichnis vocabulary [və'kæbjələri]
Vokallaut vowel sound ['vaʊəl saʊnd]
Volksstamm tribe [traɪb]
voll full [fʊl] • **voller Menschen** crowded ['kraʊdɪd]
Volleyball volleyball ['vɒlibɔːl]
völlig absolutely [ˌæbsə'luːt]
vollkommen perfect ['pɜːfɪkt]
von of [əv, ɒv]; from [frəm, frɒm] • **ein Aufsatz von …** an essay by … [baɪ] • **von Montag bis Freitag** from Monday to Friday
voneinander getrennt apart [ə'pɑːt]
vor 1. *(räumlich)* in front of [ɪn 'frʌnt_əv]
 2. *(zeitlich)* **vor dem Abendessen** before dinner [bɪ'fɔː] • **vor einer Minute** a minute ago [ə'gəʊ] • **vor Ort** on the scene [siːn] • **Viertel vor 12** quarter to 12
vorankommen: Wie komme ich voran? How am I doing?
vorbei (an) *(vorüber)* past [pɑːst]
vorbei sein be over ['əʊvə]
vorbereiten prepare [prɪ'peə] • **sich vorbereiten (auf)** prepare (for); get ready (for) ['redi] • **Dinge vorbereiten** get things ready
vordere(r, s): im vorderen Teil at the front [frʌnt]
Vordergrund foreground ['fɔːgraʊnd]
voreingenommen sein (gegen) be prejudiced (against) ['predʒudɪst]
Voreingenommenheit (gegen) prejudice (against) ['predʒudɪs]
Vorfahr/in ancestor ['ænsestə]
vorgestern the day before yesterday
Vormittag morning ['mɔːnɪŋ]
vorne at the front [frʌnt]
vorrätig available [ə'veɪləbl]
Vorschrift rule [ruːl]
Vorschule *(für 5- bis 6-Jährige in den USA)* kindergarten ['kɪndəgɑːtn]
vorsichtig careful ['keəfl]
vorspielen *(pantomimisch darstellen)* mime [maɪm]
vorstellen 1. **(jm.) etwas vorstellen** *(präsentieren)* present sth. (to sb.) [prɪ'zent]

2. **jn. (jm.) vorstellen** introduce sb. (to sb.) [ˌɪntrə'djuːs]
3. **sich etwas vorstellen** imagine sth. [ɪ'mædʒɪn] • **Stell dir vor! / Stellt euch vor!** Guess what! [ˌges 'wɒt]
Vorstellung *(Präsentation)* presentation [ˌprezn'teɪʃn]; *(Show)* show [ʃəʊ]
Vorstellung(skraft) imagination [ɪˌmædʒɪ'neɪʃn]
Vorteil (gegenüber jm./etwas) advantage (over sb./sth.) [əd'vɑːntɪdʒ]
Vortrag talk [tɔːk]
vorüber (an) *(vorbei)* past [pɑːst]
Vorurteil (gegenüber) prejudice (against) ['predʒudɪs] • **Vorurteile haben (gegenüber)** be prejudiced (against) ['predʒudɪst]
Vorwurf: jm. Vorwürfe machen (wegen) blame sb. (for) [bleɪm]
vorziehen: etwas (einer anderen Sache) vorziehen prefer sth. (to sth.) [prɪ'fɜː]

W

Wachposten guard [gɑːd]
wachsen grow [grəʊ]
Wagen *(schwerer Pferdewagen)* cart [kɑːt]
Wahl *(von Kandidaten bei einer Abstimmung)* election [ɪ'lekʃn]
wählen 1. *(auswählen)* choose [tʃuːz]
 2. *(durch eine Wahl)* **jn. zu etwas wählen** elect sb. sth. [ɪ'lekt]
 3. *(Telefonnummer)* dial ['daɪəl]
wahr true [truː] • **wahr werden** come true
während 1. **während des Spiels** during the game ['djʊərɪŋ]
 2. **während wir spielten** while we were playing [waɪl]
wahrscheinlich probably ['prɒbəbli]
Wald forest ['fɒrɪst]; woods *(pl)* [wʊdz]
Waldbrand wildfire ['waɪldfaɪə]
walisisch; Walisisch Welsh [welʃ]
Wand wall [wɔːl]
Wanderarbeiter/in migrant worker [ˌmaɪgrənt 'wɜːkə]
wandern hike; walk [haɪk]
Wanderung hike; walk [haɪk] • **eine Wanderung machen** go on a hike/walk
wann when [wen] • **wann (auch) immer** whenever [ˌwen'evə]
 ▶ S.196 whatever, etc.
warm warm [wɔːm]
Wärmflasche hot-water bottle [ˌhɒt 'wɔːtə bɒtl]

warnen: jn. vor etwas warnen warn sb. (about/of sth.) [wɔ:n]
Warnung warning [ˈwɔ:nɪŋ]
warten (auf) wait (for) [weɪt] • **Warte mal!** Wait a minute. [ˈmɪnɪt]
warum why [waɪ] • **Warum ich?** Why me?
was what [wɒt] • **Was dann?** Then what? • **Was fehlt dir?** (bei Krankheit) What's wrong with you? • **Was für ein Auto ...?** What kind of car ...? • **Was haben wir als Hausaufgabe auf?** What's for homework? • **Was haben wir als Nächstes?** What have we got next? • **Was ist los? / Was ist denn?** What's the matter? [ˈmætə], What's up? • **Was ist mit ...?** What about ...? • **Was kann/darf ich euch/Ihnen bringen?** What can I get you? • **Was kostet/kosten ...?** How much is/are ...? **Was war das Beste an ...?** What was the best thing about ...? • **alles, was wir jetzt (noch) tun müssen, ...** all we have to do now ... **sie wussten nicht, was sie tun sollten** they didn't know what to do
▶ S.192 Question words + to-infinitive
was (auch) immer whatever [ˌwɒtˈevə]
▶ S.196 whatever, etc.
waschen wash [wɒʃ] • **Ich wasche mir das Gesicht.** I wash my face.
Waschmaschine washing machine [ˈwɒʃɪŋ məˌʃi:n]
Wasser water [ˈwɔ:tə]
Wasserfall waterfall [ˈwɔ:təfɔ:l]
Webcam webcam [ˈwebkæm]
Website website [ˈwebsaɪt]
Wechsel change [tʃeɪndʒ]
Wechselgeld change [tʃeɪndʒ]
wechseln change [tʃeɪndʒ]; (Geld) exchange [ɪksˈtʃeɪndʒ]
▶ S.200 (to) change
wecken: jn. wecken wake sb. (up) [weɪk]
Wecker alarm clock [əˈlɑ:m klɒk]
weg away [əˈweɪ] • **weg sein** (nicht da sein) be gone [gɒn]; (aus dem Haus sein) be out [aʊt]
Weg way [weɪ]; (Pfad) path [pɑ:θ]; (Gasse) lane • **auf dem Weg (zu/nach)** on the way (to) • **jm. den Weg beschreiben** tell sb. the way **jn. nach dem Weg fragen** ask sb. the way
Wegbeschreibung(en) directions (pl) [dəˈrekʃnz]
wegen because of [bɪˈkɒz_əv] (im Gefängnis) **wegen Mordes**

(in prison) for murder
▶ S.200–201 Giving reasons
weggehen leave [li:v]; (raus-, ausgehen) go out; get away
wegräumen put sth. away [əˈweɪ]
wehen blow [bləʊ]
wehtun hurt [hɜ:t]; be sore [sɔ:]
Weibchen female [ˈfi:meɪl]
weich soft [sɒft]
Weide field [fi:ld]
weil because [bɪˈkɒz]
▶ S.200–201 Giving reasons
Weile: eine Weile (for) a while [waɪl]
Wein wine [waɪn]
Weinberg vineyard [ˈvɪnjəd]
weinen cry [kraɪ]
Weinherstellung winemaking [ˈwaɪnmeɪkɪŋ]
Weintraube grape [greɪp]
weiß white [waɪt]
weit 1. (breit) wide [waɪd] • **weit und breit** far and wide [fɑ:]
2. weit (entfernt) far [fɑ:]; a long way
weiter: geradeaus weiter straight on [streɪt_ˈɒn] • **etwas weiter tun** keep (on) doing sth.
weitere(r, s): ein(e) weitere(r, s) one more [mɔ:] • **weitere 70 Meter** another 70 metres [əˈnʌðə]
weiter-: etwas weitergeben pass sth. (on) • **weitergehen** continue [kənˈtɪnju:]; go on [ˌgəʊ_ˈɒn] • **weiterlaufen** walk on [ˌwɔ:k_ˈɒn] • **etwas weiterleiten** pass sth. on • **weitermachen** continue; go on • **weiterreden** continue; go on • **weiterträumen** dream on [ˌdri:m_ˈɒn]
welche(r, s) which [wɪtʃ] • **Auf welcher Seite sind wir?** What page are we on? [wɒt] • **Welche Farbe hat ...?** What colour is ...?
Welle wave [weɪv]
wellenreiten gehen go surfing [ˈsɜ:fɪŋ]
Wellensittich budgie [ˈbʌdʒi]
Welt world [wɜ:ld] • **auf der Welt** in the world • **auf der ganzen Welt** all over the world • **aus der ganzen Welt** from all over the world **die beste Aussicht der Welt** the best view in the world
weltberühmt world-famous [ˌwɜ:ld
ˈfeɪməs]
Weltmusik world music
Weltraum space [speɪs]
weltweit worldwide [ˌwɜ:ldˈwaɪd]
wem? who? [hu:] • **Mit wem hat sie geredet?** Who did she talk to? **Wem gehören diese?** Whose are these? [hu:z]
wen? who? [hu:]

wenden: sich an jn. wenden turn to sb. [tɜ:n]
wenig 1. (mit nicht zählbarem Nomen) **wenig Zeit/Wasser** little time/water [ˈlɪtl] • **ein wenig** (ein bisschen) a little • **weniger** less [les] • **mehr oder weniger** more or less • **am wenigsten** least [li:st]
2. (mit Nomen im Plural) **wenige Stunden/Flaschen** few hours/bottles [fju:]; (ein paar) a few hours/bottles • **weniger** fewer [ˈfju:ə] • **am wenigsten** fewest [ˈfju:ɪst]
▶ S.211 little („wenig") – few („wenige")
wenigstens at least [ət ˈli:st]
wenn 1. (zeitlich) when [wen]
2. (falls) if [ɪf]
wer who [hu:] • **wer/wen/wem (auch) immer** whoever [ˌhu:ˈevə]
▶ S.196 whatever, etc.
Werbespot advert [ˈædvɜ:t]; ad [æd]
werden become [bɪˈkʌm] • **Bauer/Bäuerin, Lehrer/in, ... werden** be a farmer, a teacher, ... • **geboren werden** be born [bɔ:n] • **wütend/heiß/... werden** get angry/hot/... • **wahr werden** come true • **hart/schlecht/taub/blind/verrückt/... werden** go hard/bad/deaf/blind/crazy/... • **du wirst frieren; ihr werdet frieren** you'll be cold (= you will be cold) [wɪl] • **du wirst nicht frieren; ihr werdet nicht frieren** you won't be cold (= you will not be cold) [wəʊnt] • **du wirst gereist sein** you'll have travelled
werfen throw [θrəʊ]
Werkzeug tool [tu:l]
Wert value [ˈvælju:]
wesentlich: das Wesentliche gist [dʒɪst]
wessen? whose? [hu:z]
West- western [ˈwestən]
Westen west [west] • **nach Westen** west • **Richtung Westen** westbound [ˈwestbaʊnd]
westlich west [west]; western [ˈwestən]
Wettbewerb competition [ˌkɒmpəˈtɪʃn] • **einen Wettbewerb veranstalten** hold a competition
wetten bet [bet]
Wetter weather [ˈweðə]
wichtig important [ɪmˈpɔ:tnt]
wichtig nehmen care about [keə]
wie 1. (Fragewort) how [haʊ] • **Wie bitte?** Sorry? [ˈsɒri] • **Wie geht es dir/Ihnen/euch?** How are you? [ˌhaʊ_ˈɑ: ju] • **Wie heißt du?** What's your name? • **wie man etwas tut / tun kann / tun soll** how to do sth. **Wie spät ist es?** What's the time?

Dictionary (German – English)

wie viel? how much? • **wie viele?** how many? • **Wie war ...?** How was ...? • **Wie war das Wetter?** What was the weather like? • **Wie wär's mit ...?** What about ...? • **Wie wär's, wenn ihr den Tisch dort schnappt?** How about you grabbing that table?
▶ S.195 Question words + to-infinitive
2. as • **so groß/aufregend wie** as big/exciting as
3. **wie ein Filmstar** like a film star [laɪk] • **genau wie du** just like you • **wie (zum Beispiel)** such as [sʌtʃ_'æz] • **wie zum Beispiel?** like what?
wie dem auch sei whatever [ˌwɔt'evə]
wieder again [ə'gen]
wiederholen repeat [rɪ'piːt]
Wiederholung (des Lernstoffs) revision [rɪ'vɪʒn]
Wiedersehen: Auf Wiedersehen. Goodbye. [ˌgʊd'baɪ]
wiederverwendet/-verwertet recycled [ˌriː'saɪkld]
Wiederverwertung recycling [ˌriː'saɪklɪŋ]
wiegen weigh [weɪ]
wild wild [waɪld]
willkommen: Willkommen (in ...). Welcome (to ...). ['welkəm] • **Sie heißen dich in ... willkommen** They welcome you to ...
Wind wind [wɪnd]
windig windy ['wɪndi]
Windjacke anorak ['ænəræk]
winken wave [weɪv]
Winter winter ['wɪntə]
Winzer/in winemaker ['waɪnmeɪkə]
wir we [wiː]
wirklich 1. (Adverb: tatsächlich) really ['rɪəli]; real [rɪəl] (AE, infml) **Meinst du wirklich?/Glaubst du das wirklich?** Do you really think so?
2. (Adjektiv: echt) real [rɪəl]
Wirklichkeit reality [rɪ'æləti]
wirklichkeitsnah realistic [ˌriː'lɪstɪk]
Wirkung (auf) effect (on) [ɪ'fekt]
wischen wipe [waɪp]
wissen know [nəʊ] • **sie wussten nicht, was sie tun sollten** they didn't know what to do • **von etwas wissen; über etwas Bescheid wissen** know about sth. • **..., wissen Sie. / ..., weißt du.** ..., you know. • **Weißt du was, Sophie?** You know what, Sophie? • **Woher weißt du ...?** How do you know ...?
▶ S.192 Question words + to-infinitive
wissen wollen wonder ['wʌndə]

Witz joke [dʒəʊk] • **Witze machen** joke
witzig funny ['fʌni]
wo where [weə] • **Wo kommst du her?** Where are you from?
wo(hin) (auch) immer wherever [ˌwer'evə]
▶ S.196 whatever, etc.
woanders somewhere else [els]
Woche week [wiːk] • **ein dreiwöchiger Urlaub** a three-week holiday • **einmal/zweimal pro Woche** once/twice a week
Wochenende weekend [ˌwiːk'end] • **am Wochenende** at the weekend (BE); on the weekend (AE)
Wochenfahrkarte (der Londoner Verkehrsbetriebe) Travelcard ['trævlkɑːd]
Wochentage days of the week
Wofür? What for? [ˌwɒt 'fɔː]
Woher weißt du ...? How do you know ...? [nəʊ]
wohin where [weə]; (in welche Richtung) which way
Wohlfahrtsorganisation charity ['tʃærəti]
Wohltätigkeitsbasar jumble sale ['dʒʌmbl seɪl]
Wohnblock block [blɒk]
wohnen live [lɪv]
Wohnheim hostel ['hɒstl]
Wohnung flat [flæt] (BE); apartment [ə'pɑːtmənt] (bes. AE)
Wohnungstür front door [ˌfrʌnt 'dɔː]
Wohnwagen caravan ['kærəvæn]
Wohnzimmer living room ['lɪvɪŋ ruːm]
Wolf wolf, pl wolves [wʊlf, wʊlvz]
Wolke cloud [klaʊd]
Wolkenkratzer skyscraper ['skaɪskreɪpə]
wollen (haben wollen) want [wɒnt] • **tun wollen** want to do • **Wollen wir ...?** Shall we ...? [ʃæl]
Workshop workshop ['wɜːkʃɒp]
Wort word [wɜːd]
Wortbildung word building ['wɜːd ˌbɪldɪŋ]
Wörterbuch dictionary ['dɪkʃənri]
Wörterverzeichnis vocabulary [və'kæbjələri]; (alphabetisches) dictionary ['dɪkʃənri]
Wortfeld word field
Wovon redest du? What are you talking about?
wund sein be sore [sɔː]
wunderbar wonderful ['wʌndəfəl]; (schön, hübsch) lovely ['lʌvli]
wünschen: sich etwas wünschen wish sth. [wɪʃ]
würde(n): ich/er würde ... I/he would ... [wəd, wʊd]

Würfel dice, pl dice [daɪs]
würfeln throw the dice [ˌθrəʊ ðə 'daɪs] • **Würfel noch einmal.** Take another turn. [tɜːn]
Wurst, Würstchen sausage ['sɒsɪdʒ]
würzig spicy ['spaɪsi]
Wüste desert ['dezət]
wütend sein (über etwas/auf jn.) be angry (about sth./with sb.) ['æŋgri]

Y

Yard (Längenmaß, 0,91 m) yard [jɑːd]
Yoga yoga ['jəʊgə]

Z

zäh tough [tʌf]
Zahl number ['nʌmbə]
zählen count [kaʊnt]
Zahn tooth [tuːθ], pl teeth [tiːθ] • **sich die Zähne putzen** clean one's teeth
Zahnarzt, -ärztin dentist ['dentɪst]
Zahnschmerzen toothache ['tuːθeɪk]
zanken: sich zanken argue ['ɑːgjuː]
Zauberkunststück trick [trɪk] • **Zauberkunststücke machen** do tricks
Zaun fence [fens]
Zebra zebra ['zebrə]
Zeh toe [təʊ]
Zeichen sign [saɪn]
zeichnen draw [drɔː]
Zeichnung drawing ['drɔːɪŋ]
zeigen show [ʃəʊ] • **auf etwas zeigen** point at/to sth. [pɔɪnt]
Zeile line [laɪn]
Zeit time [taɪm]; (grammatische Zeit) tense [tens] • **einige Zeit** (for) a while [waɪl] • **im Laufe der Zeit** over time • **von Zeit zu Zeit** now and again • **Zeit verbringen (mit)** spend time (on) [spend]
Zeitleiste timeline ['taɪmlaɪn]
Zeitschrift magazine [ˌmægə'ziːn]
Zeitstrahl timeline ['taɪmlaɪn]
Zeitung newspaper ['njuːspeɪpə]
Zeitzone time zone [zəʊn]
Zelt tent [tent]
zelten camp [kæmp]
Zeltplatz campground ['kæmpgraʊnd] (AE); campsite ['kæmpsaɪt] (BE)
Zensur (Schulnote) grade [greɪd] (BE auch: mark [mɑːk])
Zentimeter centimetre (cm) ['sentɪmiːtə]
Zentral- central ['sentrəl]
Zentrum centre ['sentə]

zerbrechen break [breɪk]
zerbrochen broken [ˈbrəʊkən]
zerreißen tear [teə]
zerstören destroy [dɪˈstrɔɪ]
Zeug (Kram) stuff [stʌf]
Ziege goat [gəʊt]
ziehen pull [pʊl]
Ziel aim [eɪm] • **ein Ziel erreichen** achieve an end [end]
ziemlich gut quite good [kwaɪt]; pretty good [ˈprɪti]
Ziffer number [ˈnʌmbə]
Zimmer room [ruːm]
zittern shiver [ˈʃɪvə]; shake [ʃeɪk]
Zone zone [zəʊn]
Zoo zoo [zuː]
zu 1. (örtlich) to [tə, tu] • **zum Arzt** to the doctor's • **zu Jenny** to Jenny's • **zu Hause** at home **Setz dich zu mir.** Sit with me.
2. **zum Beispiel** for example [ɪgˈzɑːmpl] • **zum Frühstück/ Mittagessen/Abendbrot** for breakfast/lunch/dinner • **zu seinem Geburtstag** for his birthday
3. **zu viel** too much [tuː] • **zu spät sein/kommen** be late
4. **versuchen zu tun** try and do / try to do
5. **um zu** to
zubereiten (kochen) cook [kʊk]
Zucker sugar [ˈʃʊgə]
zudecken cover [ˈkʌvə]
zuerst first [fɜːst]
Zug train [treɪn] • **im Zug** on the train
Zuhause home [həʊm]
zuhören listen (to) [ˈlɪsn]
Zuhörer/in listener [ˈlɪsnə]
zulassen (erlauben) allow [əˈlaʊ] **zulassen, dass jd. etwas tut** let sb. do sth.
zumachen close [kləʊz]
zumindest at least [ət ˈliːst]
zurechtkommen get along [əˈlɒŋ]
zurück (nach) back (to) [bæk] **zurück zu Hause** back home [ˌbæk ˈhəʊm]
zurückgeben give back [ˌgɪv ˈbæk]
zurücklassen leave (behind) [liː] **Abfälle zurücklassen** litter [ˈlɪtə]
zurzeit at the moment [ˈməʊmənt]
zusammen together [təˈgeðə] • **mit jm. zusammen sein** be with sb.
zusammenbrechen collapse [kəˈlæps]
Zusammenfassung summary [ˈsʌməri]
Zusammenhang context [ˈkɒntekst]
zusammenkommen come together [təˈgeðə]
zusätzlich extra [ˈekstrə]
zusehen watch [wɒtʃ]
zustande bringen achieve [əˈtʃiːv]
zustimmen: jm. zustimmen agree with sb. [əˈgriː]
zuverlässig dependable [dɪˈpendəbl]; reliable [rɪˈlaɪəbl]
zuwenden: sich jm. zuwenden turn to sb. [tɜːn]
zwar actually [ˈæktʃuəli]
▶ S.215 actually
zweimal twice [twaɪs]
zweisprachig bilingual [ˌbaɪˈlɪŋgwəl]
zweite(r, s) second [ˈsekənd] • **aus zweiter Hand** second-hand
Zwiebel onion [ˈʌnjən]
Zwillinge twins (pl) [twɪnz]
Zwillingsbruder twin brother [ˈtwɪn ˌbrʌðə]
zwingen: jn. zwingen, etwas zu tun force sb. to do sth. [fɔːs]
zwischen (zwei Personen oder Dingen) between [bɪˈtwiːn]; (mehreren Personen oder Dingen) among [əˈmʌŋ]
Zwischenüberschrift sub-heading [ˈsʌbˌhedɪŋ]

English sounds (Englische Laute)

Die Lautschrift in den eckigen Klammern zeigt dir, wie ein Wort ausgesprochen wird. In der folgenden Übersicht findest du alle Lautzeichen.

Vokale (Selbstlaute)

[iː]	green	[ʊ]	book	[ɪə]	here	
[i]	happy	[ʌ]	mum	[eə]	where	
[ɪ]	in	[ɜː]	T-shirt	[ʊə]	tour	
[e]	yes	[ə]	a partner			
[æ]	black	[eɪ]	skate			
[ɑː]	park	[aɪ]	time			
[ɒ]	song	[ɔɪ]	boy			
[ɔː]	morning	[əʊ]	old			
[uː]	blue	[aʊ]	now			

Konsonanten (Mitlaute)

[b]	box	[l]	hello	[ʒ]	television
[p]	play	[r]	red	[tʃ]	teacher
[d]	dad	[w]	we	[dʒ]	Germany
[t]	ten	[j]	you	[θ]	thanks
[g]	good	[f]	full	[ð]	this
[k]	cat	[v]	very	[h]	he
[m]	mum	[s]	sister	[x]	loch
[n]	no	[z]	please		
[ŋ]	sing	[ʃ]	shop		

The English alphabet (Das englische Alphabet)

a	[eɪ]	h	[eɪtʃ]	o	[əʊ]	v	[viː]	
b	[biː]	i	[aɪ]	p	[piː]	w	[ˈdʌbljuː]	
c	[siː]	j	[dʒeɪ]	q	[kjuː]	x	[eks]	
d	[diː]	k	[keɪ]	r	[ɑː]	y	[waɪ]	
e	[iː]	l	[el]	s	[es]	z	[zed]	
f	[ef]	m	[em]	t	[tiː]			
g	[dʒiː]	n	[en]	u	[juː]			

Classroom English

Was *du* im Klassenzimmer sagen kannst	What *you* can say in the classroom
Du brauchst Hilfe	**You need help**
Können Sie mir bitte helfen?	Can you help me, please?
Auf welcher Seite sind wir, bitte?	What page are we on, please?
Was heißt … auf Englisch/Deutsch?	What's … in English/German?
Wie spricht man das erste Wort in Zeile 2 aus?	How do you say the first word in line 2?
Können Sie bitte … buchstabieren?	Can you spell …, please?
Können Sie es bitte an die Tafel schreiben?	Can you write it on the board, please?
Kann ich es auf Deutsch sagen?	Can I say it in German?
Können Sie/Kannst du bitte lauter sprechen?	Can you speak louder, please?
Können Sie/Kannst du das bitte noch mal sagen?	Can you say that again, please?
Über Texte und Themen sprechen	**Talking about texts and topics**
Ich finde die Geschichte …	I think the story is …
schön/interessant/langweilig/schrecklich/….	nice/interesting/boring/terrible/…
Es war lustig/gruselig/langweilig/…, als …	It was funny/scary/boring/… when …
Ich fand es gut/nicht gut, als …	I liked it/didn't like it when …
Ich finde Tom hat recht/nicht recht, weil …	I think Tom is right/wrong because …
Ich bin mir nicht sicher. Vielleicht …	I'm not sure. Maybe …
Was meinst du?	What do you think?
Ich stimme … zu/nicht zu, weil …	I agree/disagree (with …) because …
Hausaufgaben und Übungen	**Homework and exercises**
Tut mir leid, ich habe mein Schulheft nicht dabei, Herr …	Sorry, I haven't got my exercise book, Mr …
Ich habe meine Hausaufgaben vergessen, Frau …	I've forgotten my homework, Mrs/Ms/Miss …
Ich kann Nummer 3 nicht lösen.	I can't do number 3.
Entschuldigung, ich bin noch nicht fertig.	Sorry, I haven't finished yet.
Ich habe … Ist das auch richtig?	I've got … Is that right too?
Tut mir leid, das weiß ich nicht.	Sorry, I don't know.
Was haben wir (als Hausaufgabe) auf?	What's for homework?
Bei der Partnerarbeit	**Work with a partner**
Kann ich mit Julian arbeiten?	Can I work with Julian?
Wer ist dran? - Du bist dran.	Whose turn is it? - It's your turn.
Ich finde, wir sollten/könnten …	I think we should/could …
Was machen wir zuerst?	What are we going to do first?
What your teacher says	**Was dein/e Lehrer/in sagt**
Open your books at page 24, please.	Schlagt bitte Seite 24 auf.
Look at the picture/line 8/… on page 24.	Seht euch das Bild/Zeile 8/… auf Seite 24 an.
Copy/Complete the chart/network/…	Übertragt/Vervollständigt die Tabelle/das Wörternetz/…
Correct the mistakes.	Verbessert die Fehler.
Take notes.	Macht euch Notizen.
Do exercise 3 for homework, please.	Macht bitte Übung 3 als Hausaufgabe.
Have you finished?	Seid ihr fertig? / Bist du fertig?
Switch off your mobile phones.	Schaltet eure Handys aus.
Walk around the class and ask other students.	Geht durch die Klasse und fragt andere Schüler/innen.
Discuss … with …	Diskutiere/Diskutiert … mit …
Give a presentation about …	Halte/Haltet einen Vortrag über …
Report to the class.	Berichte/Berichtet der Klasse.

Irregular verbs

Infinitive	Simple past form	Past participle	
(to) be	was/were	been	sein
(to) beat	beat	beaten	schlagen; besiegen
(to) become	became	become	werden
(to) begin	began	begun	beginnen, anfangen (mit)
(to) bleed [iː]	bled [e]	bled [e]	bluten
(to) blow	blew	blown	wehen, blasen, pusten
(to) break	broke	broken	zerbrechen, kaputt machen
(to) bring	brought	brought	(mit-, her)bringen
(to) broadcast	broadcast	broadcast	ausstrahlen; senden
(to) build	built	built	bauen
(to) buy	bought	bought	kaufen
(to) catch	caught	caught	fangen; erwischen
(to) choose [uː]	chose [əʊ]	chosen [əʊ]	(aus)wählen; (sich) aussuchen
(to) come	came	come	kommen
(to) cut	cut	cut	schneiden
(to) deal with [iː]	dealt [e]	dealt [e]	sich beschäftigen mit
(to) do	did	done [ʌ]	tun, machen
(to) draw	drew	drawn	zeichnen
(to) drink	drank	drunk	trinken
(to) drive [aɪ]	drove	driven [ɪ]	(ein Auto) fahren
(to) eat	ate [et, eɪt]	eaten	essen
(to) fall	fell	fallen	(hin)fallen, stürzen
(to) feed	fed	fed	füttern
(to) feel	felt	felt	(sich) fühlen; sich anfühlen
(to) fight	fought	fought	kämpfen
(to) find	found	found	finden
(to) fly	flew	flown	fliegen
(to) forget	forgot	forgotten	vergessen
(to) forgive	forgave	forgiven	vergeben, verzeihen
(to) get	got	got	bekommen; holen; werden; (hin)kommen
(to) give	gave	given	geben
(to) go	went	gone [ɒ]	gehen, fahren
(to) grow	grew	grown	wachsen; anbauen, anpflanzen
(to) hang	hung	hung	(etwas) aufhängen
(to) have (have got)	had	had	haben, besitzen
(to) hear [ɪə]	heard [ɜː]	heard [ɜː]	hören
(to) hide [aɪ]	hid [ɪ]	hidden [ɪ]	(sich) verstecken
(to) hit	hit	hit	treffen; schlagen
(to) hold	held	held	halten
(to) hurt	hurt	hurt	wehtun; verletzen
(to) keep	kept	kept	(be)halten; aufbewahren
(to) know [nəʊ]	knew [njuː]	known [nəʊn]	wissen; kennen
(to) lay the table	laid	laid	den Tisch decken
(to) lead [iː]	led [e]	led [e]	führen
(to) leave	left	left	(weg)gehen; abfahren; verlassen; zurücklassen
(to) lend	lent	lent	leihen
(to) let	let	let	lassen

Irregular verbs

Infinitive	Simple past form	Past participle	
(to) lie	lay	lain	liegen
(to) lose [uː]	lost [ɒ]	lost [ɒ]	verlieren
(to) make	made	made	machen; bauen; bilden
(to) mean [iː]	meant [e]	meant [e]	bedeuten; meinen
(to) meet	met	met	(sich) treffen
(to) pay	paid	paid	bezahlen
(to) put	put	put	legen, stellen, *(wohin)* tun
(to) read [iː]	read [e]	read [e]	lesen
(to) ride [aɪ]	rode	ridden [ɪ]	reiten; *(Rad)* fahren
(to) ring	rang	rung	klingeln, läuten
(to) rise [aɪ]	rose	risen [ɪ]	(auf)steigen
(to) run	ran	run	rennen, (ver)laufen
(to) say [eɪ]	said [e]	said [e]	sagen
(to) see	saw	seen	sehen; besuchen, aufsuchen
(to) sell	sold	sold	verkaufen
(to) send	sent	sent	schicken, senden
(to) set a trap	set	set	eine Falle stellen
(to) sew	sewed	sewn	(an)nähen
(to) shake	shook	shaken	schütteln
(to) shine	shone [ɒ, *AE* əʊ]	shone [ɒ]	scheinen *(Sonne)*
(to) shoot [uː]	shot [ɒ]	shot [ɒ]	(er)schießen
(to) show	showed	shown	zeigen
(to) shut up	shut	shut	den Mund halten
(to) sing	sang	sung	singen
(to) sit	sat	sat	sitzen; sich setzen
(to) sleep	slept	slept	schlafen
(to) speak	spoke	spoken	sprechen
(to) spend	spent	spent	*(Zeit)* verbringen; *(Geld)* ausgeben
(to) spit	spat	spat	spucken
(to) spread [e]	spread [e]	spread [e]	(sich) ausbreiten, (sich) verbreiten
(to) stand	stood	stood	stehen; sich (hin)stellen
(to) steal	stole	stolen	stehlen
(to) stick	stuck	stuck	herausragen, herausstehen; (auf)kleben
(to) sweep [iː]	swept [e]	swept [e]	fegen, kehren
(to) swim	swam	swum	schwimmen
(to) take	took	taken	nehmen; (weg-, hin)bringen; dauern, *(Zeit)* brauchen
(to) teach	taught	taught	unterrichten, lehren
(to) tear [eə]	tore [ɔː]	torn [ɔː]	(zer)reißen
(to) tell	told	told	erzählen, berichten
(to) think	thought	thought	denken, glauben, meinen
(to) throw	threw	thrown	werfen
(to) understand	understood	understood	verstehen
(to) upset	upset	upset	ärgern, kränken, aus der Fassung bringen
(to) wake up	woke	woken	aufwachen; wecken
(to) wear [eə]	wore [ɔː]	worn [ɔː]	tragen *(Kleidung)*
(to) win	won [ʌ]	won [ʌ]	gewinnen
(to) write	wrote	written	schreiben

List of names

First names
(Vornamen)

Abel [ˈeɪbl]
Adonis [əˈdəʊnɪs]
Angus [ˈæŋɡəs]
Anne [æn]
Arnold [ˈɑːnəld]
Barack [bəˈrɑːk, bəˈræk]
Ben [ben]
Benny [ˈbeni]
Bess [bes]
Bill [bɪl]
Brad [bræd]
Caitlin [ˈkeɪtlɪn, ˈkætlɪn]
Carrie [ˈkæri]
Celia [ˈsiːljə]
Chris [krɪs]
Christopher [ˈkrɪstəfə]
Chuck [tʃʌk]
Cindy [ˈsɪndi]
Dan [dæn]
Danny [ˈdæni]
David [ˈdeɪvɪd]
Dennis [ˈdenɪs]
Diana [daɪˈænə]
Diego [diˈeɪɡəʊ]
Don [dɒn]
Donna [ˈdɒnə]
Edward [ˈedwəd]
Elizabeth [ɪˈlɪzəbəθ]
Ella [ˈelə]
Elvis [ˈelvɪs]
Eric [ˈerɪk]
Framji [ˈfræmdʒi]
Frank [fræŋk]
Frederick [ˈfredərɪk]
George [dʒɔːdʒ]
Golda [ˈɡəʊldə]
Grace [ɡreɪs]
Gracie [ˈɡreɪsi]
Graham [ˈɡreɪəm]
Hannah [ˈhænə]
Harry [ˈhæri]
Heidi [ˈhaɪdi]
Huckleberry [ˈhʌklberi]
Indu [ˈɪnduː]
Ito [ˈiːtəʊ]
Jake [dʒeɪk]
James [dʒeɪmz]
Janet [ˈdʒænət]
Javier [xæviˈeə]
Jesse [ˈjesi]
Jim [dʒɪm]
Joan [dʒəʊn]
John [dʒɒn]
Josephine [ˈdʒəʊzəfiːn, ˈdʒəʊsəfiːn]
Junior [ˈdʒuːniə]
Katrina [kəˈtriːnə]
Kim [kɪm]
Kitty [ˈkɪti]
Langston [ˈlæŋstən]
Larry [ˈlæri]
Lauryn [ˈlɒrən]
Lazarus [ˈlæzərəs]

Lee [liː]
Leonard [ˈlenəd]
Letitia [ləˈtɪʃə]
Lil' Kim [ˌlɪl ˈkɪm]
Louie [ˈluːi]
Luis [luːˈiːs, ˈluːɪs]
Luther [ˈluːθə]
Madison [ˈmædɪsən]
Marge [mɑːdʒ]
Maria [məˈriə]
Mark [mɑːk]
Martin [ˈmɑːtɪn]
Marvin [ˈmɑːvɪn]
Massasoit [mæsəˈsɔɪt]
Melba [ˈmelbə]
Melinda [məˈlɪndə]
Melissa [məˈlɪsə]
Metacom [ˈmetəkɒm]
Michael [ˈmaɪkl]
Mike [maɪk]
Missy [ˈmɪsi]
Nate [neɪt]
Nathan [ˈneɪθən]
Neil [niəl]
Nick [nɪk]
Nikki [ˈnɪki]
Norman [ˈnɔːmən]
Panchito [pænˈtʃiːtəʊ]
Paul [pɔːl]
Penelope [pəˈneləpi]
Pink [pɪŋk]
Porgy [ˈpɔːɡi]
Rachel [ˈreɪtʃəl]
Rafe [reɪf]
Ralph [rælf]
Ricardo [rɪˈkɑːdəʊ]
Rick [rɪk]
Robert [ˈrɒbət]
Roberto [rəˈbeətəʊ, rəˈbɜːtəʊ]
Rochelle [rɒˈʃel]
Rosa [ˈrəʊzə]
Rowdy [ˈraʊdi]
Rubin [ˈruːbɪn]
Ryan [ˈraɪən]
Sally [ˈsæli]
Sam [sæm]
Samuel [ˈsæmjuəl]
Sarah [ˈseərə]
Sherman [ˈʃɜːmən]
Shirley [ˈʃɜːli]
Sinita [sɪˈniːtə]
Stevie [ˈstiːvi]
Sullivan [ˈsʌlɪvən]
Tapenum [ˈtæpənəm]
Ted [ted]
Theodore [ˈθiədɔː]
Theresa [təˈriːzə, təˈriːsə]
Thomas [ˈtɒməs]
Tyson [ˈtaɪsn]
Victor [ˈvɪktə]
Wamsutta [wæmsʌtə]
Wayne [weɪn]

Family names
(Familiennamen)

Alexie [əˈleksi]
Aranda [əˈrændə]
Adams [ˈædəmz]
Ballou [bəˈluː]
Barrera [bəˈreərə]
Berry [ˈberi]
Bertanelli [ˌbɜːtəˈneli]
Bethune [bəˈθuːn]
Branch [brɑːntʃ]
Brown [braʊn]
Cabot [ˈkæbət]
Campbell [ˈkæmbəl]
Clapton [ˈklæptən]
Clinton [ˈklɪntən]
Collier [ˈkɒljə]
Columbus [kəˈlʌmbəs]
Crutcher [ˈkrʌtʃə]
D'Agostino [ˌdæɡəˈstiːnəʊ]
Dickens [ˈdɪkɪnz]
Dougherty [ˈdɒxəti, ˈdɔːrəti]
Ebb [eb]
Elliot [ˈeliət]
Erl [ɜːl]
Esquith [ˈeskwɪθ]
Finn [fɪn]
Fitzgerald [ˌfɪtsˈdʒerəld]
Franklin [ˈfræŋklɪn]
Gallagher [ˈɡæləɡə, ˈɡæləhə]
Gaye [ɡeɪ]
Gershwin [ˈɡɜːʃwɪn]
Giovanni [dʒəˈvɑːni]
Grant [ɡrɑnt]
Hawley [ˈhɔːli]
Hill [hɪl]
Hoefler [ˈhəʊflə]
Hughes [hjuːz]
Jackson [ˈdʒæksən]
James [dʒeɪmz]
Jefferson [ˈdʒefəsən]
Johnson [ˈdʒɒnsən]
Josephine [ˈdʒəʊzəfiːn]
Kay [keɪ]
Kennedy [ˈkenədi]
Kilbane [kɪlˈbeɪn]
King [kɪŋ]
Kornblum [ˈkɔːnbluːm]
Kruger [ˈkruːɡə]
Langer [ˈlæŋə]
Lee [liː]
Lefevre [ləˈfiːvə]
Lema [ˈleɪmə]
Lorraine [ləˈreɪn]
Lowe [ləʊ]
Lyle [laɪl]
Madison [ˈmædɪsən]
McCabe [məˈkeɪb]
McCourt [məˈkɔːt]
Meeker [ˈmiːkə]
Morales [məˈrɑːlez, məˈræləs]
Morton [ˈmɔːtn]
Muir [mjʊə]
Nelson [ˈnelsn]
Nielson [ˈniːlsn]

Obama [əʊˈbɑːmə]
O'Malley [əʊˈmæli]
Parks [pɑːks]
Pattillo [pəˈtɪləʊ]
Pitt [pɪt]
Potter [ˈpɒtə]
Presley [ˈpresli]
Putnam [ˈpʌtnəm]
Ravenhill [ˈreɪvnhɪl]
Revere [rɪˈvɪə]
Robeson [ˈrəʊbsən]
Rockwell [ˈrɒkwel]
Roebling [ˈrəʊblɪŋ]
Roosevelt [ˈrəʊzəvelt]
Ross [rɒs]
Salgado [sælˈɡɑːdəʊ]
Salinger [ˈsælɪndʒə]
Sanford [ˈsænfəd]
Schwarzenegger [ˈʃwɔːtsənegə]
Shakespeare [ˈʃeɪkspɪə]
Simpson [ˈsɪmpsən]
Spirit [ˈspɪrɪt]
Steinbeck [ˈstaɪnbek]
Sullivan [ˈsʌlɪvən]
Tripp [trɪp]
Turner [ˈtɜːnə]
Twain [tweɪn]
Vaerst [veəst]
Washington [ˈwɒʃɪŋtən]
Wonder [ˈwʌndə]
Young [jʌŋ]

List of names

Place names
(Ortsnamen)

Alcatraz [ˈælkətræz]
Amarillo [ˌæməˈrɪləʊ]
the Apollo Theater [əˈpɒləʊ]
the Atlantic Ocean
  [ətˌlæntɪk ˈəʊʃn]
Atlanta [ətˈlæntə]
Avenida Pico [ˌɑːvəˈniːdə
  ˈpiːkəʊ, ˌævəˈniːdə ˈpiːkəʊ]
Baltimore [ˈbɒltɪmɔː]
Battery Park [ˈbætəri]
Bayou Country [ˈbaɪu:]
Bonita Park [bəˈniːtə]
Boston [ˈbɒstən]
Bristol [ˈbrɪstl]
Broadway [ˈbrɔːdweɪ]
the Bronx [ˈbrɒnks]
Brooklyn [ˈbrʊklɪn]
Brownsville [ˈbraʊnzvɪl]
Bull Run [ˈbʊlˌrʌn]
Calle Campo [ˌkaɪjəˈkæmpəʊ]
Cambridge [ˈkeɪmbrɪdʒ]
Cape Cod [ˌkeɪpˈkɒd]
the Castor River [ˈkɑːstə]
Central Park [ˌsentrəlˈpɑːk]
Chambers Street
  [ˌtʃeɪmbəz striːt]
Chicago [ʃɪˈkɑːgəʊ]
Chinatown [ˈtʃaɪnətaʊn]
Cole's Hill [ˌkəʊlzˈhɪl]
Cologne [kəˈləʊn] *(Köln)*
the Colorado River
  [ˌkɒləˈrɑːdəʊ]
Concord [ˈkɒnkɔːd]
Coney Island [ˌkəʊniˈaɪlənd]
Cupertino [ˌkuːpəˈtiːnəʊ]
Death Valley [ˌdeθˈvæli]
Ellis Island [ˌelɪsˈaɪlənd]
the Empire State Building
  [ˌempaɪəˈsteɪtˌbɪldɪŋ]
Excalibur [ekˈskælɪbə]
Festhalle [ˈfesthɔːl]
Fifth Avenue [ˌfɪθˈævənjuː]
Fisherman's Wharf
  [ˌfɪʃəmənzˈwɔːf]
Fresno [ˈfreznəʊ]
the Gateway Arch
  [ˌgeɪtweɪˈɑːtʃ]
the General Sherman
  [ˌdʒenrəlˈʃɜːmən]
the Globe Theatre
  [ˌgləʊbˈθɪətə]
Graceland [ˈgreɪslænd]
the Grand Canyon
  [ˌgrændˈkænjən]
the Great Smoky Mountains
  [ˌgreɪtˌsməʊkiˈmaʊntɪnz]
Haight-Ashbury [ˌheɪtˈæʃbəri]
Harlem [ˈhɑːləm]
Harvard [ˈhɑːvəd]
Havasupai [ˌhævəˈsuːpaɪ]
Herald Square [ˌherəldˈskweə]
Hermann [ˈhɜːmən]
Hermannthal [ˈhɜːməntɑːl]
Hobart [ˈhəʊbɑːt]
Holbrook [ˈhəʊlbrʊk]
Hollywood Boulevard
  [ˌhɒliwʊdˈbuːləvɑːd]
the Hudson River [ˈhʌdsən]
Independence [ˌɪndɪˈpendəns]
Institute of Technology
  [ˌɪnstɪtjuːtˌəv tekˈnɒlədʒi]
Jamestown [ˈdʒeɪmztaʊn]
Japantown [dʒəˈpænˌtaʊn]
**Jefferson National Expansion
  Memorial** [ˌjefəsənˌnæʃnəl
  ɪkˈspænʃən mɪˌmɔːrɪəl]
Kaibab Trail [ˈkaɪbæb treɪl]
Kennedy Airport
  [ˌkenədiˈeəpɔːt]
Kettle Hill [ˌketlˈhɪl]
Lake Michigan [ˌleɪkˈmɪʃɪgən]
Las Vegas [ˌlæsˈveɪgəs]
Lassen Volcanic National Park
  [ˌlæsnˌvɒlˈkænɪk]
Lexington [ˈleksɪŋtən]
Lincoln Memorial
  [ˌlɪnkənmɪˈmɔːrɪəl]
Little Rock [ˌlɪtlˈrɒk]
Los Angeles [lɒsˈændʒəliːz]
Louisbourg [ˈluːɪsbɜːg]
Madison [ˈmædɪsən]
Manhattan [mænˈhætn]
Marin County [məˌrɪnˈkaʊnti]
Martha's Vineyard
  [ˌmɑːθəzˈvɪnjəd]
Mashpee [ˈmæʃpi]
Memphis [ˈmemfɪs]
the Missouri River [mɪˈzʊəri]
Montgomery [məntˈgʌməri]
Mount Greylock
  [ˌmaʊntˈgreɪlɒk]
Mount Rushmore
  [ˌmaʊntˈrʌʃmɔː]
Mountain View
  [ˌmaʊntɪnˈvjuː]
**Museum of Westward
  Expansion**
  [ˌwestwədɪkˈspænʃn]
Naples [ˈneɪpəlz]
Nashville [ˈnæʃvɪl]
National Seashore
  [ˌnæʃnəlˈsiːˌʃɔː]
New England [ˌnjuːˈɪŋglənd]
New Orleans [ˌnjuːˈɔːliənz,
  ˌnjuː ɔːˈliːnz]
the Pacific Ocean
  [pəˌsɪfɪkˈəʊʃn]
Palo Alto [ˌpæləʊˈæltəʊ]
Patuxet [pəˈtʌksɪt]
Phantom Ranch
  [ˌfæntəmˈrɑːntʃ]
Plimoth Plantation
  [ˌplɪməθˌplænˈteɪʃn]
Plymouth [ˈplɪməθ]
Poche [ˈpəʊtʃeɪ]
Point Reyes [ˌpɔɪntˈreɪjez]
Purdue [ˈpɜːdjuː]
Queens [kwiːnz]
Raleigh [ˈrɔːli]
Reardon [ˈrɪədən]
Red Sox [ˈredˌsɒks]
Redding [ˈredɪŋ]
the Rhine [raɪn] *(Rhein)*
Richmond [ˈrɪtʃmənd]
Rome [rəʊm]
San Clemente [ˌsænkləˈmenti]
San Diego [ˌsændiˈeɪgəʊ]
San Francisco
  [ˌsænfrənˈsɪskəʊ]
San José [ˌsænhəʊˈzeɪ]
Santa Clara [ˌsæntəˈkleərə]
Santa Rosa [ˌsæntəˈrəʊzə]
Sausalito [ˌsɔːsəˈliːtəʊ]
Shorecliffs [ˈʃɔːklɪfs]
Sicily [ˈsɪsəli]
Silicon Valley [ˌsɪlɪkənˈvæli]
South Rim [ˌsaʊθˈrɪm]
Spokane [spəʊˈkæn]
the Statue of Liberty
  [ˌstætjuːˌəvˈlɪbəti]
St Paul's Cathedral
  [ˌsəntˌpɔːlzkəˈθiːdrəl]
St. Louis [səntˈluːɪs]
Staten Island [ˌstætənˈaɪlənd]
the Strip [strɪp]
Sunnyvale [ˈsʌnɪveɪl]
Talega [təˈleɪgə]
the Mission [ˈmɪʃn]
Times Square [ˌtaɪmzˈskweə]
Tucumcari [ˌtuːkəmˈkeəri]
Tusayan [tuːˈseɪən]
the Twin Towers [ˌtwɪnˈtaʊəz]
Union Square [ˌjuːniənˈskweə]
Uranus [ˈjʊərənəs]
Washington Square
  [ˌwɒʃɪŋtənˈskweə]
Washington, D.C. [ˈwɒʃɪŋtən]
Watsonville [ˈwɒtsənvɪl]
Wellpinit [ˈwelpɪnɪt]
Wilkes-Barre [ˈwɪlksˌbæri]
the World Trade Center
  [ˌwɜːldˈtreɪdˌsentə]
Yale [jeɪl]
the Yankee Stadium [ˈjæŋki]
Yorktown [ˈjɔːkˌtaʊn]
Yosemite [jəʊˈsemətɪ]

Other names
(Andere Namen)

the B-52s [ˌbiːfɪftiˈtuːz]
the Bearcats [ˈbeəkæts]
Bigfoot [ˈbɪgfʊt]
Brandtson [ˈbræntsən]
the Bruins [ˈbruːnz]
the Celtics [ˈseltɪks]
Journal-Constitution
  [ˌdʒɜːnəlˌkɒnstɪˈtjuːʃn]
King Kong [ˌkɪŋˈkɒŋ]
Lynyrd Skynyrd
  [ˌlenədˈskɪnəd]
Macy's [ˈmeɪsiːz]
Maifest [ˈmeɪfest]
the Mayflower [ˈmeɪflaʊə]
Medal of Honor
  [ˌmedlˌəvˈɒnə]
National Forest Service
  [ˌnæʃnəlˈfɒrɪstˌsɜːvɪs]
National Park Service
  [ˌnæʃnəlˈpɑːkˌsɜːvɪs]
Oktoberfest [ɒkˈtəʊbəfest]
Patriots [ˈpeɪtriəts]
Pawnee [pɔːˈniː]
R.E.M. [ˌɑːrˌiːˈem]
Republican Party [rɪˈpʌblɪkən]
Sierra Club [siˈerə]
Sioux [suː]
Skywalk [ˈskaɪwɔːk]
Supremes [suːˈpriːmz]
the Confederate States
  [kənˈfedərətˌsteɪts]
the Union [ˈjuːniən]
UNICEF [ˈjuːnɪsef]
Wampanoag [ˈwɒmpənɒg,
  ˈwɒmpənəʊəg]
Wurstfest [ˈwɜːstfest]
the Yankees [ˈjæŋkiz]

Countries and continents

Country/Continent	Adjective	Person	People
Africa ['æfrɪkə] *Afrika*	African ['æfrɪkən]	an African	the Africans
America [ə'merɪkə] *Amerika*	American [ə'merɪkən]	an American	the Americans
Asia ['eɪʃə, 'eɪʒə] *Asien*	Asian ['eɪʃn, 'eɪʒn]	an Asian	the Asians
Australia [ɒ'streɪliə] *Australien*	Australian [ɒ'streɪliən]	an Australian	the Australians
Austria ['ɒstriə] *Österreich*	Austrian ['ɒstriən]	an Austrian	the Austrians
Belgium ['beldʒəm] *Belgien*	Belgian ['beldʒən]	a Belgian	the Belgians
Canada ['kænədə] *Kanada*	Canadian [kə'neɪdiən]	a Canadian	the Canadians
China ['tʃaɪnə] *China*	Chinese [ˌtʃaɪ'niːz]	a Chinese	the Chinese
Croatia [krəʊ'eɪʃə] *Kroatien*	Croatian [krəʊ'eɪʃn]	a Croatian	the Croatians
Cuba ['kjuːbə] *Kuba*	Cuban ['kjuːbən]	a Cuban	the Cubans
the Czech Republic [ˌtʃek rɪ'pʌblɪk] *Tschechien, die Tschechische Republik*	Czech [tʃek]	a Czech	the Czechs
Denmark ['denmɑːk] *Dänemark*	Danish ['deɪnɪʃ]	a Dane [deɪn]	the Danes
England ['ɪŋglənd] *England*	English ['ɪŋglɪʃ]	an Englishman/-woman	the English
Europe ['jʊərəp] *Europa*	European [ˌjʊərə'piːən]	a European	the Europeans
Finland ['fɪnlənd] *Finnland*	Finnish ['fɪnɪʃ]	a Finn [fɪn]	the Finns
France [frɑːns] *Frankreich*	French [frentʃ]	a Frenchman/-woman	the French
Georgia ['dʒɔːdʒə] *Georgien*	Georgian ['dʒɔːdʒən]	a Georgian	the Georgians
Germany ['dʒɜːməni] *Deutschland*	German ['dʒɜːmən]	a German	the Germans
(Great) Britain ['brɪtn] *Großbritannien*	British ['brɪtɪʃ]	a Briton ['brɪtn]	the British
Greece [griːs] *Griechenland*	Greek [griːk]	a Greek	the Greeks
Holland ['hɒlənd] *Holland, die Niederlande*	Dutch [dʌtʃ]	a Dutchman/-woman	the Dutch
Hungary ['hʌŋgəri] *Ungarn*	Hungarian [hʌŋ'geəriən]	a Hungarian	the Hungarians
India ['ɪndiə] *Indien*	Indian ['ɪndiən]	an Indian	the Indians
Ireland ['aɪələnd] *Irland*	Irish ['aɪrɪʃ]	an Irishman/-woman	the Irish
Italy ['ɪtəli] *Italien*	Italian [ɪ'tæliən]	an Italian	the Italians
Japan [dʒə'pæn] *Japan*	Japanese [ˌdʒæpə'niːz]	a Japanese	the Japanese
Korea [kə'riə] *Korea*	Korean [kə'riən]	a Korean	the Koreans
Mexico ['meksɪkəʊ] *Mexiko*	Mexican ['meksɪkən]	a Mexican	the Mexicans
the Netherlands ['neðələndz] *die Niederlande, Holland*	Dutch [dʌtʃ]	a Dutchman/-woman	the Dutch
New Zealand [ˌnjuː 'ziːlənd] *Neuseeland*	New Zealand [ˌnjuː 'ziːlənd]	a New Zealander	the New Zealanders
Norway ['nɔːweɪ] *Norwegen*	Norwegian [nɔː'wiːdʒən]	a Norwegian	the Norwegians
Pakistan [ˌpækɪ'stæn, ˌpɑːkɪ'stɑːn] *Pakistan*	Pakistani [ˌpækɪ'stæni, ˌpɑːkɪ'stɑːni]	a Pakistani	the Pakistanis
the Philippines ['fɪlɪpiːnz] *die Philippinen*	Philippine ['fɪlɪpiːn]	a Filipino [ˌfɪlɪ'piːnəʊ]/ Filipina [ˌfɪlɪ'piːnə]	the Filipinos/ Filipinas
Poland ['pəʊlənd] *Polen*	Polish ['pəʊlɪʃ]	a Pole [pəʊl]	the Poles
Portugal ['pɔːtʃʊgl] *Portugal*	Portuguese [ˌpɔːtʃu'giːz]	a Portuguese	the Portuguese
Russia ['rʌʃə] *Russland*	Russian ['rʌʃn]	a Russian	the Russians
Scotland ['skɒtlənd] *Schottland*	Scottish ['skɒtɪʃ]	a Scotsman/-woman, a Scot [skɒt]	the Scots, the Scottish
Slovakia [sləʊ'vɑːkiə, sləʊ'vækiə] *die Slowakei*	Slovak ['sləʊvæk]	a Slovak	the Slovaks
Slovenia [sləʊ'viːniə] *Slowenien*	Slovenian [sləʊ'viːniən], Slovene ['sləʊviːn]	a Slovene, a Slovenian	the Slovenes, the Slovenians
Spain [speɪn] *Spanien*	Spanish ['spænɪʃ]	a Spaniard ['spænɪəd]	the Spaniards
Sweden ['swiːdn] *Schweden*	Swedish ['swiːdɪʃ]	a Swede [swiːd]	the Swedes
Switzerland ['swɪtsələnd] *die Schweiz*	Swiss [swɪs]	a Swiss	the Swiss
Turkey ['tɜːki] *die Türkei*	Turkish ['tɜːkɪʃ]	a Turk [tɜːk]	the Turks
the United Kingdom (the UK) [juˌnaɪtɪd 'kɪŋdəm, juː'keɪ] *das Vereinigte Königreich (Großbritannien und Nordirland)*	British ['brɪtɪʃ]	a Briton ['brɪtn]	the British
the United States of America (the USA) [juˌnaɪtɪd ˌsteɪts əv ə'merɪkə, juː_es_'eɪ] *die Vereinigten Staaten von Amerika*	American [ə'merɪkən]	an American	the Americans
Wales [weɪlz] *Wales*	Welsh [welʃ]	a Welshman/-woman	the Welsh

Acknowledgments

Illustrationen

Silke Bachmann, Hamburg (S. 32; 90–91; 101; 103); **Roland Beier**, Berlin (S. 46 oben; 47–49; 62; 66; 69; 71 strawberries logo; 86; 88; 126–127; 139; 147 unten; 155–221); **Dr. Volkhard Binder**, Berlin (S. 36; 43 British colonies; 44; 57 Bild 9 map (M); 104; 147 oben; 150); **Carlos Borrell**, Berlin (vordere und hintere Umschlaginnenseite; 22 (u. 128); 83 oben); **Stéphane Gamain/ NB Illustration**, London (S. 24; 60); **Michael Teßmer**, Hamburg (S. 37; 46 unten; S. 53); **Korinna Wilkes**, Berlin (S. 80 Mitte)

Bildquellen

Michelle Abesamis, New York (S. 26 zoo); **Adobe Systems Incorporated**, San Jose (S. 57 logo); **Agentur Focus**, Hamburg (S. 111 unten: Magnum Photos/ Elliott Erwitt); **Alamy**, Abingdon (Inhaltsverz. Caitlin (u. 9 oben li.): Geoff du Feu (RF), Luis (u. 11 oben): David R. Frazier Photolibrary, Inc.; S. 11 school bus: Directphoto.org, pool: Radius Images; S. 12 cowboy: Robert Harding Picture Library Ltd./Tony Gervis; S. 13 casino: D. Hurst, Excalibur: James Nesterwitz; S. 14 subway: Frances Roberts; S. 16 oben girls (M): Andrew Rubtsov, Bild 2 (M): Jack Sullivan, Bild 4: John Taylor, Bild 5: David R. Frazier Photolibrary, Inc., Bild 6: Dieter Melhorn; S. 17 oben: Picture Partners, li.: eStock Photo/Gg; S. 18 li.: Sandra Baker; S. 19 oben: dbimages/Derek Brown; S. 22 oben li.: Janine Wiedel Photolibrary, unten li.: WorldFoto; S. 26 oben li.: Alex Segre, unten li.: Ambient Images Inc./Tony Perrottet; S. 43 unten: Lebrecht Music and Arts Photo Library; S. 44 re.: David Lyons; S. 56 Bild 2: David R. Frazier Photolibrary, Inc.; S. 65 Bild 4 li.: History Archive; S. 73: Bon Appetit; S. 77 Bild C: Danita Delimont; S. 79 Mitte: GPI Stock; S. 84 li.: Juergen Hasenkopf; S. 85: JUPITERIMAGES/ Comstock Images (RF); S. 87: VStock (RF); S. 108 cockpit (M): imagebroker/Thomas Sbampato, boy (M): Jupiterimages/Goodshoot (RF); S. 129 oben: Geraint Lewis; S. 130 Bild 5 li., 7 re.: Mary Evans Picture Library; S. 131: Authors Image/Mickael David (RF); S. 136 oben re.: wendy connett; S. 137 Mitte: Gavin Gough; S. 138 unten: Gail Mooney-Kelly; S. 148 observation room: Andre Jenny, park: Rich Iwasaki; **Animal Planet**, München (S. 100 Animal Planet logo); **Arteaga Photos LTD.**, St. Louis (S. 149 Bild 1 u. 3); **Associated Press**, Frankfurt/Main (S. 59 re.: PAUL SAKUMA; S. 110 oben; S. 111 oben re.; S. 112 oben; S. 114 oben: Danny Johnston; S. 146: Amy Sancetta); **Bridgeman Art Library**, Berlin (S. 42 li.: Jean Leon Jerome Ferris/Private Collection; S. 43 Boston Massacre: Paul Revere © Massachusetts Historical Society, Boston, MA, USA; S. 83 unten: Private Collection); **Richard Broadwell**, La Quinta (S. 56 Bild 6); **Cable News Network. A Time Warner Company**, Atlanta (S. 100 CNN logo); **CartoonStock**, Bath (S. 101: Mike Baldwin); **CBS Broadcasting Inc.**, Los Angeles (S. 100 CBS logo: Use of logo from CBS Eye Logos - Courtesy of CBS Broadcasting Inc., Los Angeles); **Cinetext**, Frankfurt/Main (S. 56 Bild 1 re.; S. 70 Bild 1: Cinetext Bildarchiv); **Cisco Systems Inc.**, San Jose (S. 57 logo); **The Coca-Cola Company**, Atlanta (S. 99 Bild B); **copy-us Verlags GmbH**, Kleve (S. 153/154 notes background: © 2007 by copy-us Verlags GmbH, Kleve, arrangiert für Männerchor von Manni Bernhard/www.copy-us. com); **Corbis**, Düsseldorf (S. 7 (u. 157): Reuters/Jeff Topping; S. 8 oben: Tom Bean; S. 14/15 Central Park: David Ball; S. 36 doll: Andrew Unangst (RF); S. 38: Blend Images/Ariel Skelley; S. 43 oben: Burstein Collection/Barney Burstein; S. 57 Bild 10: David Puu; S. 79 unten: Charles Gupton; S. 99 Bild G: Franz-Marc Frei; S. 103: Bettmann; S. 104 unten li.: Franz-Marc Frei; S. 105 oben: Sygma/Jeffrey Markowitz; S. 111 Mitte li.: Bettmann; S. 113 li. u. re.: Bettmann; S. 130 Bild 5 re.: Adam Woolfitt, Bild 8 li.: Bettmann; S. 143 oben: Chris Hellier; S. 149 Bild 2, Bild 4: Bettmann; S. 152 oben: Ralf-Finn Hestoft, unten: Reuters/Mark Blinch; S. 154 unten re.: Laura Levine); **Corel Library** (S. 80 US & German flag); **Creative Solutions**, San Clemente, CA (S. 61 (u. 71 logo): © 2008 IMAGES); **Denver Public Library**, Denver (S. 82 unten: Colorado Historical Society & Denver Art Museum); **FDNY/ NYC & Company**, New York (S. 27 FDNY logos: All New York City logos and marks depicted herein are the property of the City of New York and may not be used without prior written consent); **Emily L. Ferguson**, North Falmouth (S. 40 li. (u. 49 unten)); **First National Bank of Atlanta**, Atlanta (S. 99 Bild E: Atlanta burning photo: Taken from "Atlanta Rusurgens". Written and published by the First National Bank of Atlanta. November 1971, Atlanta. Photo: Metro-Goldwyn-Mayer); **Ellen Forney** (S. 141: Illustrations taken from The Absolutely True Diary of a Part-Time Indian by Sherman Alexie. Copyright © 2007 by Sherman Alexie. Illustrations coyright © by Ellen Forney. By permission of Little, Brown & Company); **FOX Broadcasting Company**, Los Angeles (S. 100 FOX logo: FOX is the trademark of FOX Broadcasting Company and is used with permission of FOX Broadcasting Company); **Fricke Studio**, Hermann (Inhaltsverz. Jake (u. 12 oben), Gracie; S. 10 oben, S. 39; S. 41; S. 49 oben; S. 76/77 Bild A; S. 77 Bild D, E, F; S. 79 oben; S. 80 unten 1. u. 2.v.li.; S. 81; S. 84 Mitte); **Getty Images**, München (S. 6: David McNew; S. 8 unten: Rainer Grosskopf; S. 12 unten li.: Louie Psihoyos; S. 13 oben li.: David McNew; S. 17 unten: Aurora/Ian Shive; S. 21 re.: Stone/Archive Holdings Inc.; S. 22 oben re.: Getty Images News/Gilles Mingasson, S. 23: Rich LaSalle; S. 34: AFP/Stan Honda; S. 40 re.: Joe Raedle; S. 44 Mitte oben: David Sandford, Mitte unten: Drew Hallowell; S. 56 Bild 3: David McNew; S. 60: Getty Images News/Chip Somodevilla; S. 62 oben: NICHOLAS KAMM; S. 63 oben re.: Photographer's Choice/Grant Faint; S. 68: Justin Sullivan; S. 83 Mitte: The Bridgeman Art Library/Charles Marion Russell; S. 95: Image Source (RF); S. 99 Bild D: Hulton Archive

Acknowledgments

Agence France Presse, Bild F (u. 110): WireImage; S. 102 unten: Popperfoto/Rolls Press; S. 111 oben li.: Hulton Archive/William Lovelace; S. 112 Mitte: Hulton Archive/Moore, unten re.: Popperfoto; S. 136 li.: Mitchell Funk, unten re.: Mario Tama; S. 153 Mitte: FPG; S. 154 oben: Michael Ochs Archives); **www.Gleis4.de** (S. 84 re.); **Google** (S. 57 logo: © Google Inc., Reprinted with Permission); **Grand Canyon NP Museum Collection**, Grand Canyon (S. 11 unten; S. 22 unten re.); **Heather Harris** (S. 143 unten li.; S. 145 oben li.); **Howard Architectural Models**, Inc., Toldedo (S. 137 oben li.); **Kurt Ingham**, Van Nuys (S. 143 unten re.; S. 144; S. 145 unten li. u. re.); **Intel GmbH**, München (S. 57 logo); **iStockphoto**, Calgary (S. 36 tablecloth: Claudiad; S. 70 Bild 3: Greg Nicholas; S. 97 Bild 4: dwphotos, Bild 7: Sergia Kishan, Bild 8: Lisa Fletcher; S. 105 Mitte: imaginewithme; S. 164 unten: james steidl); **Chris Junker**, Portland (S. 149 Arch skin); **jupiterimages**, Ottobrunn/München (Inhaltsverz. Madison (u. 13): Polka Dot Images (RF); **Russ Kendall Photography**, Bellingham (S. 36 oben li. u. re.); **Adam Kuban**, New York (S. 137 oben re.); **Major League Baseball Properties, Inc.** (S. 138 oben: Major League Baseball trademarks and copyrights are used with permission of Major League Baseball Properties, Inc.); **Massachusetts Commandery Military Order of the Loyal Legion and the U.S. Army Military History Institute** (S. 151); **mauritius images**, Mittenwald (S. 15 Times Square: age; S. 16 oben street (M): age); **John Miranda/www.johnmirandaphoto.com** (S. 13 unten li.); **Most Wanted Pictures**, Los Angeles (S. 56 Bild 5); **MTV Networks Germany GmbH**, Berlin (S. 100 MTV logo); **NASA**, Washington, DC (S. 57 logo); **National Park Service**, Washington, DC (S. 9 unten re.); **Peter Newcomb Photography**, St. Louis (S. 77 Bild B); **The New York Public Library**, New York (S. 20 unten re., S. 21 li.: Lewis Wickes Hine); **Thomas Parker**, Vienna, MO (S. 80 unten re.); **PARS International Corp.**, New York: (S. 100 newspaper: The Atlanta Journal-Constitution. Reprinted with permission from The Atlanta Journal-Constitution, Copyright © 2006); **Photolibrary**, London (S. 9 oben re.: Nonstock/Joseph De Sciose; S. 56 Bild 4: Gunnar Kullenberg; S. 57 Bild 7: Glow Images (RF); S. 98/99: Index Stock Imagery/Henryk T. Kaiser); **PhotoStock-Israel** (S. 148 tram: www.photographersdirect.com/Ohad Shahar); **Picture-Alliance**, Frankfurt/Main (S. 8 ranger: dpa/Jörg Schmitt; S. 27 Mitte: dpa-Report/PA Magdalena Mayo; S. 56 Bild 1 li.: dpa-Report/Ken James; S. 67: dpa-Bildarchiv/Christoph Dernbach; S. 99 Bild A: akg-images; S. 102 oben: dpaweb, dpa-Report/Thomas S. England; S. 104 unten re.: dpa/Abaca Rabbo 83583; S. 154 Mitte li.: Newscom/Andre Jenny; S. 162: HB-Verlag/Martin Sasse); **The Picture Desk**, London (S. 18 re.: The Kobal Collection/RKO); **Redferns**, London (S. 153 unten: Deltahaze Corporation; S. 154 unten li: Martin Philebey); **Karen Rinaldo**, Falmouth (S. 42 re. (u. 158): The First Thanksgiving, 1621 © 1995 Karen Rinaldo); **The Norman Rockwell Museum**, Stockbridge, MA (S. 114 unten: From the Collection of the Norman Rockwell Museum. Reproduced by courtesy of the Norman Rockwell Family Agency, Inc.); **Shutterstock**, New York (S. 8 rafting: Anton Foltin; S. 9 unten li.: Bruce Grubbs; S. 12 condor: Condor 36, book: Martina I. Meyer; S. 14 li.: gary718, unten re.: Zina Seletskaya; S. 16 Bild 1: Stephen Finn; S. 19 unten li.: Hannamariah, unten re: Scott Rothstein; S. 25: Vladimir Korostyshevskiy; S. 26 tiger: Bill Kennedy; S. 35 Bild 1: Ali Mazraie Shadi, Bild 2: Jason Kasumovic, Bild 3: cardiae, Bild 4: Jostein Hauge, Bild 5: Christa DeRidder, Bild 6: Miguel Angel Salinas Salinas, Bild 7: sonya etchison, Bild 8: Max Blain, Bild 9: erikdegraaf fotografie; S. 36 bow & arrow (M): keellla, turkey: Chepko Danil Vitalevich, smoke: Rafal Olkis, spring: jirijura, bible: Donald P Oehman, candle: ivvv1975, goat: Daniel Goodchild; S. 44 unten li.: Stanislav Khrapov; S. 49 Mitte: absolut; S. 57 Bild 11: Chee-Onn Leong; S. 59 li.: Norman Chan; S. 62/63 Golden Gate Bridge: Brandon Holmes; S. 62 Mitte: Albo; S. 63 oben li.: Rena Schild, Hollywood (u. 130 Bild 6 li.): Byron W. Moore, Oscar: Oliver Johannes Uhrig, unten li.: David Alexander Liu; S. 65 Bild 1 li.: Guus van Raaphorst, Bild 3 re.: Deborah Reny; S. 69: Peter Brett Charlton; S. 70 Bild 2: stocksnapp, Bild 4: Ivan Stevanovic; S. 71: Michal G. Smith; S. 76/77 (u. 80) vine: Lezh; S. 80 grapes: Gordan; S. 89: Ron Hilton; S. 97 Bild 1: Maxim Petrichuk, Bild 2: Palto, Bild 3: Jose Marines, Bild 5: B. Speckart, Bild 6: Olga Chernetskaya, Bild 9: Glenda M. Powers; S. 104 oben re.: Mayskyphoto; S. 105 unten: Matej Krajcovic; S. 128: Johnny Kuo; S. 129 re.: Ilja Mašik, unten: Olga Lyubkina; S. 135 oben: Chee-Onn Leong; S. 164 oben: Tatiana Popova); **Spectrum Photofile Inc.**, Toronto (S. 57 Bild 8); **SRI** (S. 57 logo: Reprinted with Permission); **Stone Hill Winery**, Hermann (S. 82 oben); **Topeka Room, Topeka & Shawnee County Public Library**, Topeka (S. 111 Mitte re.); **ullstein bild**, Berlin (S. 20/21 Ellis Island: histopics; S. 62 unten: Peter Arnold Inc.; S. 65 Bild 1 re, Bild 2 re., Bild 3 li.: Granger Collection, Bild 2 li.: AISA, Bild 4 re.: TopFoto; S. 99 Bild C: dpa; S. 104 oben li.: Röhnert, S. 130 Bild 6 re.: Granger Collection, Bild 7 li.: Imagebroker.net, Bild 8 re.: Jung; S. 134 li. u. re.: Granger Collection; S. 135 unten re.: Granger Collection; S. 137 unten: CARO/Muhs; S. 154 Mitte: Probst); **U.S. Department of the Interior, National Park Service** (S. 148/149 Gateway Arch (Artist: David Leech); S. 148 Gateway Arch triangle detail (Artist David Leech); S. 149 construction progress (Artist: David Leech)); **David Weigert**, Newton (S. 16 Bild 3); **Yahoo** (S. 57 logo: Reproduced with permission of Yahoo! Inc.® 2008 by Yahoo! Inc. YAHOO! and the YAHOO! logo are trademarks of Yahoo! Inc.); **Yen-Wen Lu**, Los Altos (S. 10 unten)

Acknowledgments

Titelbild
Corbis, Düsseldorf (yellow cab (M): image100 (RF), Times Square (M): Jose Fuste Raga); **Corel Library** (US flag Hintergrund (M))

Textquellen
S. 28–30: *The Writer and the firefighter.* Abridged and adapted from "The Guys" by Anne Nelson. Reprinted by permission of International Creative Management, Inc. Copyright © 2002 by Anne Nelson; S. 20: Statements by Celia Adler, Lazarus Salamon, Edward Corsi, Golda Meir taken from "I was dreaming to come to America" by Veronica Lawlor, © 1995 by Veronica Lawlor. Used by permission of Viking Penguin, A Division of Penguin Young Readers Group, A Member of Penguin Group (USA) Inc., 345 Hudson Street, New York, NY 10014. All rights reserved, Statement by Leonard Covello taken from "Immigrant Kids" by Russel Freedman. Used by permission of Dutton Children's Books, A Division of Penguin Young Readers Group, A Member of Penguin Group (USA), Inc., 345 Hudson Street, New York, NY 10014. All rights reserved; S. 52–54: *I am going to save my brother.* Adapted with the permission of Simon & Schuster Books for Young Readers, an imprint of Simon & Schuster Children's Publishing Division from "My brother Sam is dead" by James Lincoln Collier and Christopher Collier. Copyright © 1974 James Lincoln Collier and Christopher Collier; S. 61: *The San Clemente Clean Ocean Program.* Adapted from "San Clemente Clean Ocean Program" flyer issued by City of San Clemente. Used by permission; S. 72–74: *The Circuit* by Francisco Jiménez. Abridged and adapted. Taken from "The Circuit, Stories from the Life of a Migrant Child". University of New Mexico Press, Albuquerque. © 1997 Francisco Jiménez; S. 90–92: *Angus Bethune's moment.* Adapted from "Telephone Man" from "Athletic Shorts" © 1989, 1991 by Chris Crutcher. Printed with permission from Greenwillow Books, an imprint of HarperCollins Publishers; S. 107: *Fire Kills Woman, 2 Young daughters.* Adapted. Copyright 2008 The Associated Press. All rights reserved; S. 112–114: *Melba's story.* Excerpts taken from "Warriors don't Cry. The Searing Memoir of the Battle to Integrate Little Rock's Central High" by Melba Pattillo Beals. Abridged edition. Simon Pulse, 1995; S. 116–124: *Famous* abridged and adapted from "Totally over you" by Mark Ravenhill. Copyright © Mark Ravenhill, 2003. This is a condensed version of the original play for students of English. A full length version of the play is published by Samuel French Ltd. All rights whatsoever in this play are strictly reserved and application for performance etc., must be made before rehearsal to Casarotto Ramsay & Associates Ltd., 7-12 Noel Street, London W1F 8GQ. No performance may be given unless a license has been obtained; S. 136: *Skyscraper* by Dennis Lee. From "Alligator Pie" (Macmillan of Canada, 1974; Key Porter Books, 2001). Copyright © 1974 Dennis Lee. With permission of the author; S. 136: Excerpt from *The New Yorkers* by Nikki Giovanni. Taken from "Poems of New York", selected and edited by Elizabeth Schmidt, Everyman's Library Pocket Poets. New York, 2002. Reprinted by permission of the author, *Subway rush hour* © 1994 by the Estate of Langston Hughes; S. 137: *To the visitor.* © 2003 Frank McCourt; S. 140: *That's why you talk so funny.* From "The absolutely true diary of a part-time Indian" by Sherman Alexie. Copyright © 2007 by Sherman Alexie. By permission of Little, Brown & Company; S. 146: *Child labour on the US-Mexican border.* Abridged and adapted from "Illegal child labor in Mexico puts food on tables of Americans" by Chris Hawley. The Arizona Republic, May 9, 2008; S. 156: Auszug von S. 582 aus „English G 2000 Wörterbuch - Das Wörterbuch zum Lehrwerk". Herausgegeben von der Langenscheidt-Redaktion Wörterbücher und der Cornelsen-Redaktion Englisch. © 2002 Cornelsen Verlag GmbH & Co. OHG, Berlin und Langenscheidt KG, Berlin und München

Liedquellen
S. 12: *Route 66.* M+T: Troup, Bobby. 1946 by Burke & Van Heusen Inc. Chappell & Co. GmbH & Co. KG, Hamburg; S. 19: *A heart in New York.* K+T: Gallagher, Benny/Lyle, Graham. © Good Single Ltd./Imagem Songs Ltd. Tj musicservice GmbH, Hamburg. Imagem Music GmbH, Hamburg; S. 57: *Gone to California.* K+T: Moore, Alecia/Perry, Linda. EMI April Music Inc./ Famous Music Corp. EMI Music Publishing Germany GmbH & Co. KG, Hamburg. Famous Music Publishing Germany GmbH & Co. KG, Berlin, *Earthquakes and sharks.* K+T: Brandtson; S. 104: *Summertime.* K+T: Gershwin, George/Gershwin, Ira/ Heyward, Dorothy & DuBose. © 1935 by George Gershwin (™) Music, DuBose and Dorothy Heyward Memorial Fund Pub. And Ira Gershwin Music. All rights administered by WB Music Corp. "Gershwin is a trademark of Gershwin Enterprises". Für Deutschland, GUS und osteuropäische Länder: Chappell & Co. GmbH & Co. KG.; S. 137: *New York, New York.* K+T: Ebb, Fred. By EMI Unart Catalog Inc. D/A/CH/Osteuropäische Länder. EMI Partnership Musikverlag GmbH, Hamburg; S. 154: *Johnny B. Goode.* T: Berry, Chuck. ARC Music Corp. Good Tunes AG, Geneva

The United States of America

State		Entered Union	Also known as	Population (2007)	Capital
Alabama (AL)	[ˌæləˈbæmə]	1819	The Yellowhammer State	4,627,851	Montgomery
Alaska (AK)	[əˈlæskə]	1959	The Last Frontier	683,478	Juneau
Arizona (AZ)	[ˌærɪˈzəʊnə]	1912	The Grand Canyon State	6,338,755	Phoenix
Arkansas (AR)	[ˈɑːkənsɔː]	1836	The Natural State	2,834,797	Little Rock
California (CA)	[ˌkæləˈfɔːniə]	1850	The Golden State	36,553,215	Sacramento
Colorado (CO)	[ˌkɒləˈrɑːdəʊ]	1876	The Centennial State	4,861,515	Denver
Connecticut (CT)	[kəˈnetɪkət]	1788	The Constitution State	3,502,309	Hartford
Delaware (DE)	[ˈdeləweə]	1787	The First State	864,764	Dover
Florida (FL)	[ˈflɒrɪdə]	1845	The Sunshine State	18,251,243	Tallahassee
Georgia (GA)	[ˈdʒɔːdʒə]	1788	The Peach State	9,544,750	Atlanta
Hawaii (HI)	[həˈwaɪi]	1959	The Aloha State	1,283,388	Honolulu
Idaho (ID)	[ˈaɪdəhəʊ]	1890	The Gem State	1,499,402	Boise
Illinois (IL)	[ˌɪləˈnɔɪ]	1818	The Prairie State	12,852,548	Springfield
Indiana (IN)	[ˌɪndiˈænə]	1816	The Hoosier State	6,345,289	Indianapolis
Iowa (IA)	[ˈaɪəwə]	1846	The Hawkeye State	2,988,046	Des Moines
Kansas (KS)	[ˈkænzəs]	1861	The Sunflower State	2,775,997	Topeka
Kentucky (KY)	[kenˈtʌki]	1792	The Bluegrass State	4,241,474	Frankfort
Louisiana (LA)	[luˌiːziˈænə]	1812	The Pelican State	4,293,204	Baton Rouge
Maine (ME)	[meɪn]	1820	The Pine Tree State	1,317,207	Augusta
Maryland (MD)	[ˈmeərɪlənd]	1788	The Old Line State	5,618,344	Annapolis
Massachusetts (MA)	[ˌmæsəˈtʃuːsɪts]	1788	The Bay State	6,449,755	Boston
Michigan (MI)	[ˈmɪʃɪɡən]	1837	The Great Lakes State	10,071,822	Lansing
Minnesota (MN)	[ˌmɪnɪˈsəʊtə]	1858	The North Star State	5,197,621	Saint Paul
Mississippi (MS)	[ˌmɪsɪˈsɪpi]	1817	The Magnolia State	2,918,785	Jackson
Missouri (MO)	[mɪˈzʊəri]	1821	The Show Me State	5,878,415	Jefferson City
Montana (MT)	[mɒnˈtænə]	1889	The Treasure State	957,861	Helena
Nebraska (NE)	[nəˈbræskə]	1867	The Cornhusker State	1,774,571	Lincoln
Nevada (NV)	[nəˈvɑːdə]	1864	The Silver State	2,565,382	Carson City
New Hampshire (NH)	[ˌnjuːˈhæmpʃə]	1788	The Granite State	1,315,828	Concord
New Jersey (NJ)	[ˌnjuːˈdʒɜːzi]	1787	The Garden State	8,685,920	Trenton
New Mexico (NM)	[ˌnjuːˈmeksɪkəʊ]	1912	The Land of Enchantment	1,969,915	Santa Fe
New York (NY)	[ˌnjuːˈjɔːk]	1788	The Empire State	19,297,729	Albany
North Carolina (NC)	[ˌnɔːθ kærəˈlaɪnə]	1789	The Tar Heel State	9,061,032	Raleigh
North Dakota (ND)	[ˌnɔːθ dəˈkəʊtə]	1889	The Peace Garden State	639,715	Bismarck
Ohio (OH)	[əʊˈhaɪəʊ]	1803	The Buckeye State	11,466,917	Columbus
Oklahoma (OK)	[ˌəʊkləˈhəʊmə]	1907	The Sooner State	3,617,316	Oklahoma City
Oregon (OR)	[ˈɒrɪɡən]	1859	The Beaver State	3,747,455	Salem
Pennsylvania (PA)	[ˌpenslˈveɪniə]	1787	The Keystone State	12,432,792	Harrisburg
Rhode Island (RI)	[ˌrəʊdˈaɪlənd]	1790	The Ocean State	1,057,832	Providence
South Carolina (SC)	[ˌsaʊθ kærəˈlaɪnə]	1788	The Palmetto State	4,407,709	Columbia
South Dakota (SD)	[ˌsaʊθ dəˈkəʊtə]	1889	The Mount Rushmore State	796,214	Pierre
Tennessee (TN)	[ˌtenəˈsiː]	1796	The Volunteer State	6,156,719	Nashville
Texas (TX)	[ˈteksəs]	1845	The Lone Star State	23,904,380	Austin
Utah (UT)	[ˈjuːtɑː]	1896	The Beehive State	2,645,330	Salt Lake City
Vermont (VT)	[vəˈmɒnt]	1791	The Green Mountain State	621,254	Montpelier
Virginia (VA)	[vəˈdʒɪniə]	1788	The Old Dominion State	7,712,091	Richmond
Washington (WA)	[ˈwɒʃɪŋtən]	1889	The Evergreen State	6,468,424	Olympia
West Virginia (WV)	[ˌwest vəˈdʒɪniə]	1863	The Mountain State	1,812,035	Charleston
Wisconsin (WI)	[wɪsˈkɒnsɪn]	1848	The Badger State	5,601,640	Madison
Wyoming (WY)	[waɪˈəʊmɪŋ]	1890	The Equality or Cowboy State	522,830	Cheyenne